DIMENSIONS OF
HUMAN
BEHAVIOR

FIFTH EDITION

DIMENSIONS OF
HUMAN
BEHAVIOR

The Changing Life Course

FIFTH EDITION

Elizabeth D. Hutchison

Virginia Commonwealth University, Emerita

and Contributors

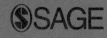

Los Angeles | London | New Delhi
Singapore | Washington DC

SAGE

Los Angeles | London | New Delhi
Singapore | Washington DC

FOR INFORMATION:

SAGE Publications, Inc.
2455 Teller Road
Thousand Oaks, California 91320
E-mail: order@sagepub.com

SAGE Publications Ltd.
1 Oliver's Yard
55 City Road
London, EC1Y 1SP
United Kingdom

SAGE Publications India Pvt. Ltd.
B 1/I 1 Mohan Cooperative Industrial Area
Mathura Road, New Delhi 110 044
India

SAGE Publications Asia-Pacific Pte. Ltd.
3 Church Street
#10-04 Samsung Hub
Singapore 048763

Acquisitions Editor: Kassie Graves
Digital Content Editor: Lauren Habib
Editorial Assistant: Carrie Baarns
Production Editor: Jane Haenel
Copy Editor: Mark Bast
Typesetter: C&M Digitals (P) Ltd.
Proofreader: Scott Oney
Indexer: Terri Corry
Cover Designer: Michael Dubowe
Marketing Manager: Shari Countryman

Printed in the United States of America

Library of Congress Cataloging-in-Publication Data

Dimensions of human behavior. The changing life course/[authored by] Elizabeth D. Hutchison, Virginia Commonwealth University, and contributors. — Fifth edition.

pages cm
Includes bibliographical references and index.

ISBN 978-1-4833-0390-1 (pbk. : alk. paper)

1. Social psychology. 2. Human behavior. 3. Life cycle, Human. 4. Social service. I. Hutchison, Elizabeth D. II. Title: Changing life course.

HM1033.D553 2015
302—dc23   2014019011

This book is printed on acid-free paper.

14 15 16 17 18 10 9 8 7 6 5 4 3 2 1

BRIEF CONTENTS

DETAILED CONTENTS

CASE STUDIES

(Continued)

PREFACE

Like many people, my life has been full of change since the first edition of this book was published in 1999. After a merger/acquisition, my husband took a new position in Washington, DC, and we moved to the nation's capital from Richmond, Virginia, where we had lived for 13 years. I changed my teaching affiliation from the Richmond campus of the Virginia Commonwealth University School of Social Work to the satellite program in northern Virginia. While I worked on the second edition of the book in 2002, my mother-in-law, for whom my husband and I had served as primary caregivers, began a fast decline and died rather quickly. A year later, my mother had a stroke, and my father died a month after that. Shortly after, my son relocated from Pennsylvania to North Carolina, and my daughter entered graduate school. In 2005, we celebrated the marriage of my daughter. After the third edition was published, we welcomed a first grandchild, my husband started an encore career in California, and my son was married. In the year I worked on the fourth edition, I retired from teaching and joined my husband in California, we welcomed a second grandchild, and my mother's health went into steep decline and she died. That was a year of great change in our family. Since the publication of the fourth edition, my son has moved back to Massachusetts and now lives in the neighborhood where we lived when he was a toddler. He and his wife are raising their own toddler there, and when we visit them, I am reminded that sometimes the life course takes us in circles. These events have all had an impact on my life course as well as the life journeys of my extended family.

But change has not been confined to my multigenerational family. Since the first edition of the book was published, we had a presidential election for which the outcome stayed in limbo for weeks. The economy has peaked, declined, revitalized, and then gone into the deepest recession since the Great Depression in the 1930s. Terrorists hijacked airplanes and forced them to be flown into the twin towers of the World Trade Center in New York City and into the Pentagon near my school. The United States entered military conflicts in Afghanistan and Iraq, and the one in Afghanistan continues to be waged at this writing, the longest war in U.S. history. Thirty-three students at Virginia Tech died in a mass murder/suicide rampage that shook the campus on a beautiful spring day, and a number of school shootings have broken our collective hearts. Natural disasters have killed and traumatized millions around the world, and the climate is becoming increasingly unstable. New communication technologies have continued to be developed at a fast clip, increasing our global interdependence and changing our behavior in ways both good and bad. The United States elected, and then reelected, its first African American president, but our government has been locked in an increasingly polarized philosophical division.

Since I was a child listening to my grandmother's stories about the challenges, joys, and dramatic as well as mundane events in her life, I have been captivated by people's stories. I have learned that a specific event can be understood only in the context of an ongoing life story. As social workers you will hear many life stories, and I encourage you to remember that each person you meet is on a journey that is much more than your encounters might suggest. I also encourage you to think about your own life story and how it helps and hinders your ability to really see and hear the stories of others.

Organized around life course time, this book tries to help you understand, among other things, the relationship between time and human behavior. The companion volume to this book, *Person and Environment*, analyzes relevant dimensions of person and environment and presents up-to-date reports on theory and research about each of these dimensions. The purpose of this volume is to show how these multiple dimensions of person and environment work together with dimensions of time to produce patterns in unique life course journeys.

LIFE COURSE PERSPECTIVE

As in the second, third, and fourth editions, my colleagues and I have chosen a life course perspective to capture the dynamic, changing nature of person-environment transactions. In the life course perspective, human behavior is not a linear march through time, nor is it simply played out in recurring cycles. Rather, the life course journey is a moving spiral, with both continuity and change, marked by both predictable and unpredictable twists and turns. It is influenced by changes in the physical and social environment as well as by changes in the personal biological, psychological, and spiritual dimensions.

The life course perspective recognizes *patterns* in human behavior related to biological age, psychological age, and social age norms. In the first edition, we discussed theory and research about six age-graded periods of the life course, presenting both the continuity and the change in these patterns. Because mass longevity is leading to finer distinctions among life phases, nine age-graded periods were discussed in the second through fourth editions and are again covered in this fifth edition. The life course perspective also recognizes *diversity* in the life course related to historical time, gender, race, ethnicity, social class, and so forth, and we emphasize group-based diversity in our discussion of age-graded periods. Finally, the life course perspective recognizes the *unique life stories* of individuals—the unique configuration of specific life events and person-environment transactions over time.

GENERAL KNOWLEDGE AND UNIQUE SITUATIONS

The purpose of the social and behavioral sciences is to help us to understand *general patterns* in person-environment transactions over time. The purpose of social work assessment is to understand *unique configurations* of person and environment dimensions at a given time. Those who practice social work must weave what they know about unique situations with general knowledge. To assist you in this process, as we did in the first four editions, we begin each chapter with stories, which we then intertwine with contemporary theory and research. Most of the stories are composite cases and do not correspond to actual people known to the authors. We also call attention to the successes and failures of theory and research to accommodate human diversity related to gender, race, ethnicity, culture, sexual orientation, disability, and so on.

In this fifth edition, we continue to use some special features that we hope will aid your learning process. As in the first four editions, key terms are presented in bold type in the chapters and defined in the Glossary. As in the second, third, and fourth editions, we present orienting questions at the beginning of each chapter to help the reader to begin to think about why the content of the chapter is important for social workers. Key ideas are summarized at the beginning of each chapter to give readers an overview of what is to come. As in the fourth edition, critical thinking questions are used throughout the chapters to help you ask questions about the material you are reading. Active learning exercises and web resources are presented at the end of each chapter.

The bulk of this fifth edition will be familiar to instructors who used the fourth edition of *Dimensions of Human Behavior: The Changing Life Course*. Many of the changes that do occur came at the suggestion of instructors and students who have been using the fourth edition. To respond to the rapidity of changes in complex societies, all chapters have been comprehensively updated. As the contributing authors and I worked to revise the book, we were surprised to learn how much the knowledge base had changed since we worked on the fourth edition. We had not experienced such major change between editions in the past, and this led us to agree with the futurists who say that we are at a point where the rate of cultural change will continue to accelerate rapidly. You will want to use the many wonders of the World Wide Web to update information that you suspect is outdated.

ALSO NEW IN THIS EDITION

The more substantial revisions for this edition include the following:

- Content on the impact of information, communication, and medical technologies on human behavior in every phase of life is greatly expanded.
- Coverage of the global context of human behavior continues to expand.
- Coverage of advances in neuroscience continues to expand.
- More content has been added on the effects of gender, race, ethnicity, social class, sexual orientation, and disability on life course trajectories.
- New content on gender identity was added to several chapters.
- New exhibits have been added and others updated.
- Some new case studies have been added to reflect contemporary issues.

- The number of critical thinking questions is increased in every chapter.
- Web resources have been updated.
- SAGE edge offers a robust online environment featuring an impressive array of tools and resources for review, study, and further exploration, keeping both instructors and students on the cutting edge of teaching and learning. Explore more at edge.sagepub.com/hutchisonclc5e

ONE LAST WORD

I hope that reading this book helps you to understand how people change from conception to death and why different people react to the same situations in different ways. I also hope that you will gain a greater appreciation for the ongoing life stories in which specific events are embedded. In addition, when you finish reading this book, I hope that you will have new ideas about how to reduce risk and increase protective factors during different age-graded periods and how to help clients find meaning and purpose in their own life stories.

You can help me in my learning process by letting me know what you liked or didn't like about the book.

—*Elizabeth D. Hutchison*
Rancho Mirage, California
ehutch@vcu.edu

ACKNOWLEDGMENTS

A project like this book is never completed without the support and assistance of many people. A fifth edition stands on the back of the first, second, third, and fourth editions, and over the years, a large number of people have helped me keep this project going. I am grateful to all of them, some of them known to me and others working behind the scenes in a way not visible to me.

Steve Rutter, former publisher and president of Pine Forge Press, shepherded every step of the first edition and provided ideas for many of the best features of the second edition that are carried forward in this book. Along with Paul O'Connell, Becky Smith, and Maria Zuniga, he helped to refine the outline for the second edition, and that outline continues to be used, in large part, in this fifth edition. I am especially grateful to Becky Smith, who worked with me as developmental editor for the first two editions. She taught me so much about writing, and I often find myself thinking *How would Becky present this?*

The contributing authors and I are grateful for the assistance Dr. Maria E. Zuniga offered during the drafting of the second edition. She contributed the David Sanchez case study in Chapter 1 and provided many valuable suggestions on how to improve the coverage of cultural diversity in each chapter. Her suggestions improved the second edition immensely and have stayed with us as lasting lessons about human behavior in a multicultural society.

I am grateful once again to work with a fine group of contributing authors. They were gracious about timelines and incorporating feedback from reviewers. Most important, they were committed to providing a state-of-the-art knowledge base for understanding human behavior across the life course.

We were lucky to be working again with the folks at Sage. It has been wonderful to have the disciplined and creative editorial assistance of Kassie Graves again. Kassie came on board at Sage while I was working on the third edition, and she has been a delight to work with over the last three editions. She is dependable, thoughtful, collegial, and a lot of fun. She has been supportive when life events have complicated my deadlines. Maggie Stanley and Liz Luizzi assisted me in numerous ways to get work on the fifth edition up and running. Carrie Baarns came on board in time to shepherd me through the various stages of editing and putting the book into production. She is a jewel. Once the drafting was done, Mark Bast came into my life as copy editor extraordinaire. He caught our mistakes and offered improved language, and he did it with such a delightful sense of humor. Jane Haenel came on board as production editor for this fifth edition and has contributed reader-friendly design features while helping us manage tight deadlines. She and her assistants have turned words and ideas into a book.

I am grateful to my former faculty colleagues at Virginia Commonwealth University (VCU) who set a high standard for scientific inquiry and teaching excellence. They also provided love and encouragement through both good and hard times. My conversations about the human behavior curriculum with colleagues Rosemary Farmer, Marcia Harrigan, Holly Matto, and Mary Secret over many years have stimulated much thinking and resulted in many ideas found in this book.

My students over almost 30 years also deserve a special note of gratitude. They taught me all the time, and many things that I have learned in interaction with them show up in the pages of this book. They also provided a great deal of joy to my life journey. Those moments when I learn of former students doing informed, creative, and humane social work are special moments, indeed, and I am happy to say there are many such moments. I have also enjoyed receiving e-mails from students from other universities who are using the book and have found their insights to be very helpful.

My deepest gratitude goes to my husband, Hutch. Since the first edition of this book was published, we have weathered several challenging years and experienced many celebratory moments. He is a kind, generous, patient man, and his technical assistance on my writing projects is a major reason I can meet writing deadlines. But, more important, he makes sure that I take time for fun and celebration. What a joy it has been to travel so much of my life journey with him.

Finally, I am enormously grateful to a host of reviewers who thoughtfully evaluated the fourth edition and provided very useful feedback about how to improve on it. Their ideas were very helpful in framing our work on this fifth edition:

Carol A. Heintzelman
Millersville University of Pennsylvania

Bernadette Jeffrey
California University of Pennsylvania

Jamie Mitchell
Wayne State University

Gwenelee S. O'Neal
West Chester University

Barbara Pierce
Northwestern State University of Louisiana

Lisa M. Shannon
Moorehead State University

David Skiba
Niagara University

To Kathy, Jim, and Carolyn, sweet siblings who have known me longer than anyone else alive.
Thanks for all the love and support through all of the phases of my life.

CHAPTER 1

A Life Course Perspective

Elizabeth D. Hutchison

Chapter Outline

Opening Questions

- Why do social workers need to understand how people change from conception to death?
- What do social workers need to know about biological, psychological, social, and spiritual changes over the life course?
- What are some sources of diversity in human life journeys?

Key Ideas

As you read this chapter, take note of these central ideas:

1. The life course perspective attempts to understand the continuities as well as the twists and turns in the paths of individual lives.

2. The life course perspective recognizes the influence of historical changes on human behavior.

3. The life course perspective recognizes the importance of timing not just in terms of chronological age, but also in terms of biological age, psychological age, social age, and spiritual age.

4. The life course perspective emphasizes the ways in which humans are interdependent and gives special attention to the family as the primary arena for experiencing and interpreting the wider social world.

5. The life course perspective sees humans as capable of making choices and constructing their own life journeys within systems of opportunities and constraints.

6. The life course perspective emphasizes diversity in life journeys and the many sources of that diversity.

7. The life course perspective recognizes the linkages between early life experiences and later experiences in adulthood.

CASE STUDY 1.1

David Sanchez's Search for Connections

David Sanchez has a Hispanic name, but he is a member of the Navajo tribe. He was raised by his maternal grandmother after his father was killed in a car accident when David was 7. His mother had been very ill since his birth and was too overwhelmed by her husband's death to take care of David. Just as David became attached to his grandmother, the Bureau of Indian Affairs (BIA) moved him to a boarding school. His hair was cut short with a tuft left at his forehead, which gave the teachers something to pull when he was being reprimanded.

Like most American Indian children, David suffered this harshness in silence. But, for some time, he has felt that it is important to break this silence. He has told his grandchildren about having his mouth washed out with soap for speaking Navajo. He jokes that he has been baptized in four different religions—Mormon, Catholic, Lutheran, and Episcopalian—because these were the religious groups running the boarding schools he attended. He also remembers the harsh beatings for not studying, or for committing other small infractions, before the BIA changed its policies for boarding homes and the harsh beatings diminished. David often spent holidays at the school, because his grandmother had no money for transportation. He remembers feeling so alone. When he did visit his grandmother, he realized he was forgetting his Navajo and saw that she was aging quickly.

David joined the Marines when he was 18, like many high school graduates of that era, and his grandmother could not understand why he wanted to join the "White man's war." David now recognizes why his grandmother questioned his decision to go to war. During his alcohol treatments, especially during the use of the Native sweat lodge, he often relived the horrible memories of the bombings and killings in Vietnam; these were the memories he spent his young adult life trying to silence with his alcohol abuse. Like many veterans, he ended up on the streets, homeless, seeking only the numbness his alcoholism provided. But the memories were always there. Sometimes his memories of the children in the Vietnam villages reminded him of the children from the boarding schools who had been so scared; some of the Vietnamese children even looked like his Native American friends. David receives a disability check for a partial disability from the war.

David has spent most of his life in New Mexico, but about a decade ago, he began to make trips to Los Angeles to visit his son, Marco, and his family. During these visits, David started to recognize how much his years of alcohol abuse hurt his son. After Mrs. Sanchez divorced David, he could never be relied on to visit Marco or to provide child support. Now that Marco has his own family, David hopes that by teaching his grandchildren the ways of the Navajo, he will pay Marco back a little for neglecting him. During visits, David began to talk about his own childhood, and Marco realized how much his father suffered as a child. After several visits, Marco asked David to teach him and his son how to speak Navajo. This gesture broke down some of the bad feelings between them.

During one of his trips to Los Angeles, David was taken to the emergency room and then hospitalized for what turned out to be a diabetic coma. He had been aware of losing weight during the past year, and felt ill at times, but thought these symptoms were just signs of getting older or perhaps the vestiges of his alcoholism from the ages of 20 to 43. Although he had been sober for 7 years, he was never surprised when his body reminded him how he had abused it. The social worker at the Los Angeles hospital helped David make plans to return to New Mexico and receive services at the local Veterans Administration (VA) hospital outpatient clinic. He had not been back to the VA since his rehabilitation from alcohol abuse, and he was happy to find that the social worker he had known during his rehabilitation was now working in the outpatient clinic.

It was through the Native American medicine retreats during David's rehabilitation that he began to touch a softer reality. He began to believe in a higher order again. Although his father's funeral had been painful, David experienced his grandmother's funeral in a more spiritual way. It was as if she was there guiding him to enter his new role. David now realizes this was a turning point in his life. At his grandmother's funeral, David's great-uncle, a medicine man, asked him to come and live with him because he was getting too old to cut or carry wood. He also wanted to teach David age-old cures that would enable him to help others struggling with alcohol dependency, from Navajo as well as other tribes. Although David is still learning, his work with other alcoholics has been inspirational, and he finds he can make special connections to Vietnam veterans.

David recently attended a conference where one of the American Indian speakers talked about the transgenerational trauma that families experienced because of the horrible beatings children encountered at the boarding schools. David is thankful that his son has broken the cycle of alcoholism and did not face the physical abuse to which he was subjected. But he is sad that his son was depressed for many years as a teen and young man. Now, both he and Marco are working to heal their relationship. They draw on the meaning and strength of their cultural and spiritual rituals. David's new role as spiritual and cultural teacher in his family has provided him with respect he never anticipated. Finally he is able to use his grandmother's wise teachings and his healing apprenticeship with his great-uncle to help his immediate family and his tribe.

A social worker like the one who helped Mr. Sanchez with his discharge plans from the L.A. hospital must be aware that discharge planning involves one life transition that is a part of a larger life trajectory.

—Maria E. Zuniga

Phoung Le, Serving Family and Community

Le Thi Phoung, or Phoung Le as she is officially known in the United States, grew up in Saigon, South Vietnam, in the midst of war and upheaval. She has some fond memories of her first few years when Saigon was beautiful and peaceful. She loves to remember riding on her father's shoulders down the streets of Saigon on a warm day and shopping with her grandmother in the herb shops. But she also has chilling memories of the military presence on the streets, the devastation caused by war, and the persistent fear that pervaded her home.

Phoung was married when she was 17 to a man chosen by her father. She smiles when she recounts the story of her future groom and his family coming to visit with the lacquered boxes full of betrothal gifts of nuts, teas, cake, and fruit. She admits that, at the time, she was not eager to marry and wondered why her father was doing this to her. But she is quick to add that her father made a wise choice, and her husband Hien is her best friend and is, as his name suggests, "nice, kind, and gentle." Their first child, a son, was born just before Phoung's 20th birthday, and Phoung reveled in being a mother.

Unfortunately, on Phoung's 20th birthday, April 30, 1975, life in Saigon turned horrific; that is the day that the North Vietnamese army overran Saigon. For Phoung and Hien, as well as for most people living in South Vietnam, just surviving became a daily struggle. Both Phoung's father and her father-in-law were in the South Vietnamese military and both were imprisoned by the Viet Cong for a few years. Both managed to escape and moved their families around until they were able to plan an escape from Vietnam by boat. Family members got separated during the escape, and others were lost when pirates attacked their boats. Phoung's father and one brother have never been heard from since the pirate attack.

Phoung and Hien and their son spent more than 2 years in a refugee camp in Thailand before being resettled in Southern California. Their second child, a daughter, was born in the camp, and a second daughter was born 1 year after they resettled in California. Over time, other family members were able to join them in the large Vietnamese community where they live. Phoung's and Hien's opportunities for education were limited during the war years, but both came from families who valued education, and both managed to receive several years of schooling. Luckily, because they were living in a large Vietnamese community, language did not serve as a major barrier to employment in the United States. Phoung found a job working evenings as a waitress at a restaurant in Little Saigon, and Hien worked two jobs, by day as a dishwasher in a restaurant and by night cleaning office buildings in Little Saigon. Phoung's mother lived with Phoung and Hien and watched after the children while Phoung and Hien worked. Hien's parents lived a few blocks away, and several siblings and cousins of both Phoung and Hien were in the neighborhood. The Vietnamese community provided much social support and cultural connection. Phoung loved taking the children to visit the shops in Little Saigon and found special pleasure in visiting the herb shops where the old men sat around and spoke animatedly in Vietnamese.

Phoung grieved the loss of her beloved father and brother, but she wanted to create a positive life for her children. She was happy that she was able to stay connected to her cultural roots and happy that her children lived in a neighborhood where they did not feel like outsiders. But she also wanted her children to be able to be successful outside the Vietnamese community as well as a resource for the community. She was determined that her children would have the education that she and Hien had been denied. Although she could have gotten by well in her neighborhood without English, she studied English along with her children because she wanted to model for the children how to live a bilingual, bicultural life. She was pleased that the children did well in school and was not surprised at how quickly the older two adapted to life in their adopted country. Sometimes there was tension in the multigenerational family about how the children were acculturating, and Phoung often served as the mediator in these tensions. She understood the desire of the older generation to keep cultural traditions, and she herself loved traditions such as the celebration of the Chinese New Year, with the colorful dresses and the little red lai-see envelopes of good luck money that were given to the children. She wanted her children to have these traditional experiences. But she also was tuned in to the children's desire to be connected with some aspects of the dominant culture, such as the music and other popular media. She was also aware of how hard it was for the family elders to enforce the traditional family hierarchy when they were dependent on younger family members to help them navigate life in the English-speaking world outside their cultural enclave.

When her children reached adolescence, Phoung herself was uncomfortable with the Western cultural ideal for adolescent independence from the family, but she found ways to give her children some space while also holding them close and keeping them connected to their cultural roots. Other mothers in the neighborhood began to seek her advice about how to handle the challenging adolescent years. When her own adolescent children began to be impatient with the pervasive sadness they saw in their grandparents, Phoung suggested that they do some oral history with their grandparents. This turned out to be a therapeutic experience for all involved. The grandparents were able to sift through their lives in Vietnam and the years since, give voice to all that had been lost, but also begin to recognize the strength it took to survive and their good fortune to be able to live among family and a community where much was familiar. The grandchildren were able to hear a part of their family narrative that they did not know because the family had preferred not to talk about it. Phoung was so pleased with this outcome that she asked to start a program of intergenerational dialogue at the Vietnamese Community Service Center. She thought that this might be one way to begin to heal the trauma in her community while also giving the younger generation a strong cultural identity as they struggled to live in a multicultural world. She continues to be an active force in that program, even though her own children are grown.

Their 40s and early 50s brought both great sorrow and great joy to Phoung and Hien. Within a 2-year period, Phoung's mother and Hien's mother and father died. Phoung and Hien became the family elders. They provided both economic and emotional support during times of family crisis, such as a sibling's cancer, a niece's untimely pregnancy, and a nephew's involvement with a neighborhood gang. But there was also great joy. Phoung was very good at her job and became the supervisor of the wait staff at the best restaurant in Little Saigon. Hien was able to buy his own herb shop. After attending the local community college, the children were all able to go on to university and do well. Their son became an engineer, the older daughter became a physician, and the younger daughter recently finished law school. Their son is now father to two young children, and Phoung finds great joy in being a grandmother. She is playing an important role in keeping the grandchildren connected to some Vietnamese traditions. Phoung finds this phase of life to be a time of balance in all areas of her life, and she is surprised and pleased to find renewed interest in spiritual growth through her Buddhist practices.

Social workers working with refugee families must be aware of the conditions that led these families to flee their home countries as well as the adjustments they have made upon resettlement.

CASE STUDY 1.3

The Suarez Family After September 11, 2001

Maria is a busy, active 15-year-old whose life was changed by the events of September 11, 2001. Her mother, Emma Suarez, worked at the World Trade Center and did not survive the attack.

(Continued)

(Continued)

Emma was born in Puerto Rico and came to the mainland to live in the South Bronx when she was 5, along with her parents, a younger brother, two sisters, and an older brother. Emma's father, Carlos, worked hard to make a living for his family, sometimes working as many as three jobs at once. After the children were all in school, Emma's mother, Rosa, began to work as a domestic worker in the homes of a few wealthy families in Manhattan.

Emma was a strong student from her first days in public school and was often at the top of her class. Her younger brother, Juan, and the sister closest to her in age, Carmen, also were good students, but they were never the star pupils that Emma was. The elder brother, Jesus, and sister, Aida, struggled in school from the time they came to the South Bronx, and both dropped out before they finished high school. Jesus has returned to Puerto Rico to live on the farm with his grandparents.

During her summer vacations from high school, Emma often cared for the children of some of the families for whom her mother worked. One employer was particularly impressed with Emma's quickness and pleasant temperament and took a special interest in her. She encouraged Emma to apply to colleges during her senior year in high school. Emma was accepted at City College and was planning to begin as a full-time student after high school graduation.

A month before Emma was to start school, however, her father had a stroke and was unable to return to work. Rosa and Aida rearranged their work schedules so that they could share the care of Carlos. Carmen had a husband and two young children of her own. Emma realized that she was now needed as an income earner. She took a position doing data entry in an office in the World Trade Center and took evening courses on a part-time basis. She was studying to be a teacher, because she loved learning and wanted to pass on that love to other students.

And then Emma found herself pregnant. She knew that Alejandro Padilla, a young man in one of her classes at school, was the father. Alejandro said that he was not ready to marry, however. Emma returned to work a month after Maria was born, but she did not return to school. At first, Rosa and Aida were not happy that Emma was pregnant with no plans to marry, but once Maria was born, they fell hopelessly in love with her. They were happy to share the care of Maria, along with Carlos, while Emma worked. Emma cared for Maria and Carlos in the evenings so that Rosa and Aida could work.

Maria was, indeed, an engaging baby, and she was thriving with the adoration of Rosa, Carlos, Aida, Juan, and Emma. Emma missed school, but she held on to her dreams to be a teacher someday.

On the morning of September 11, 2001, Emma left early for work at her job on the 84th floor of the south tower of the World Trade Center, because she was nearing a deadline on a big project. Aida was bathing Carlos when Carmen called about a plane hitting the World Trade Center. Aida called Emma's number, but did not get through to her.

The next few days, even weeks, are a blur to the Suarez family. Juan, Carmen, and Aida took turns going to the Family Assistance Center, but there was no news about Emma. At one point, because Juan was worried about Rosa, he brought her to the Red Cross Disaster Counseling Center where they met with a social worker who was specially trained for working in disaster situations. Rosa seemed to be near collapse.

Juan, Rosa, and Aida all missed a lot of work for a number of weeks, and the cash flow sometimes became problematic. They were blessed with the generosity of their Catholic parish, employers, neighbors, and a large extended family, however, and financial worries were not their greatest concerns at that time. They struggled to understand the horrific thing that happened to Emma, and although she didn't understand what had happened, Maria was aware of a great sadness in the household for several years. Emma's remains were never identified, but the Catholic parish helped the family plan a memorial service.

Maria is lucky to have such a close, loving family, and they have tried to give her a good life. She continues to live with Aida and Rosa. Juan has married and has two young children now, living around the corner from Aida and Rosa. Carlos died in 2011, 10 days before the 10-year anniversary of the 9/11 attacks. Carmen and her family also live nearby, and Maria has become close friends with Carmen's two daughters. She also has a special relationship with Carmen, who reminds her of the pictures she has seen of her mother.

Maria is a good student and hopes to attend college and study to be a teacher. She loves to hear stories about the mother she can't remember, and one of Rosa's favorite stories is about how smart Emma was and what a great teacher she would have been. On Maria's 13th birthday, Rosa gave her the necklace that had been Emma's 13th birthday gift, and Maria wears it every day. Growing up in the Bronx, Maria has seen many television images of those airplane attacks at the World Trade Center. She was disturbed, however, by all of the media coverage at the time of the 10th anniversary of the attack. She began to think a lot about what her mother might have suffered before her death, and she had nightmares for several nights. She built a small memorial to her mother in the backyard and goes there to talk with her mother when she is feeling particularly sad or when good things happen.

A social worker doing disaster relief must be aware of the large impact that disasters have on the multigenerational family, both in the present and for years to come.

A DEFINITION OF THE LIFE COURSE PERSPECTIVE

One of the things that the stories of David Sanchez, Phoung Le, and the Suarez family have in common is that they unfolded over time, across multiple generations. We all have stories that unfold as we progress through life. A useful way to understand this relationship between time and human behavior is the **life course perspective**, which looks at how biological, psychological, and social factors act independently, cumulatively, and interactively to shape people's lives from conception to death, and across generations. Of course, time is only one dimension of human behavior; characteristics of the person and the environment in which the person lives also play a large part (see Exhibit 1.1). But it is common and sensible to try to understand a person by looking at the way that person has developed throughout different periods of life.

The purpose of this book and its companion volume *Dimensions of Human Behavior: Person and Environment* is to provide ways for you to think about the nature and complexities of the people and situations at the center of social work practice. To begin to do that, we must first clarify the purpose of social work and the approach it takes to individual and collective human behavior. This was laid out in the 2008 Educational Policy and Accreditation Standards of the Council on Social Work Education:

> The purpose of the social work profession is to promote human and community well-being. Guided by a person and environment construct, a global perspective, respect for human diversity, and knowledge based on scientific inquiry, social work's purpose is actualized through its quest for social and economic justice, the prevention of conditions that limit human rights, the elimination of poverty, and the enhancement of the quality of life for all persons. (Council on Social Work Education, 2008, p. 1)

Social workers also have a well-defined value base to guide their efforts to promote individual and community well-being. Six core values of the profession have been set out in a preamble to the Code of Ethics established by the National Association for Social Workers (NASW) in 1996 and revised in 2008 (NASW, 2008). These values are service, social justice, dignity and worth of the person, importance of human relationships, integrity, and competence. Throughout the chapters,

Exhibit 1.1 Person, Environment, and Time Dimensions

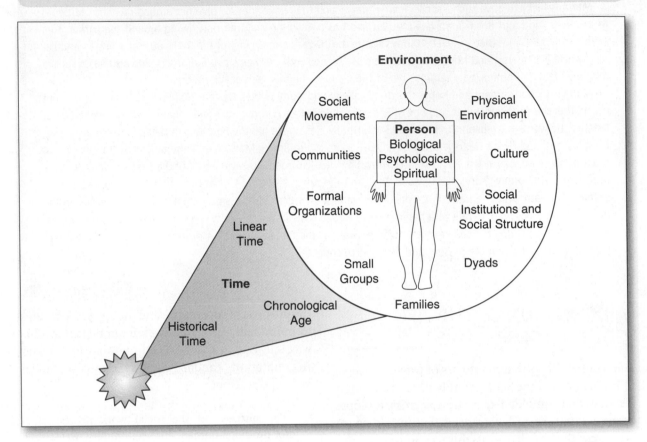

the contributing authors and I provide suggestions about needed social work services and how to provide those services in a trustworthy manner. We take social work's commitment to social justice seriously, and social justice issues are highlighted in every chapter. The life course perspective that forms the basis of this book puts equal value on individual agency and human connectedness; therefore, it serves as a good framework for social work's commitments to both the dignity and worth of the person as well as the importance of human relationships. The contributing authors and I draw on the best available evidence about the life course to assist you to develop and enhance expertise in serving people of all life stages.

You could think of the life course as a path. But note that it is not a straight path; it is a path with both continuities and twists and turns. Certainly,

we see twists and turns in the life stories of David Sanchez, Phoung Le, and Emma Suarez.

If you want to understand a person's life, you might begin with an **event history**, or the sequence of significant events, experiences, and transitions in a person's life from birth to death. An event history for David Sanchez might include suffering his father's death as a child, moving to live with his grandmother, being removed to a boarding school, fighting in the Vietnam War, getting married, becoming a father, divorcing, being treated for substance abuse, participating in medicine retreats, attending his grandmother's funeral, moving to live with his great-uncle, and reconnecting with Marco. Phoung Le's event history would most likely include military presence in the streets, getting married, becoming a mother, escaping from Saigon, time spent in a refugee camp, resettlement

Photo 1.1 The life course perspective emphasizes ways in which humans are interdependent and gives special emphasis to the family as the primary arena for experiencing the world.

© Kristy-Anne Glubish/Design Pics/Corbis

in California, family loss, and promotion at work. For young Maria Suarez, the events of September 11, 2001, will become a permanent part of her life story, even though she has no memory of that day. She looks forward to the time when she will realize her mother's dream of starting college.

You might also try to understand a person in terms of how that person's life has been synchronized with family members' lives across time. David Sanchez has begun to have a clearer understanding of his linkages to his great-uncle, father, son, and grandchildren. Phoung Le's and Maria Suarez's stories are thoroughly entwined with those of their multigenerational families.

Finally, you might view the life course in terms of how culture and social institutions shape the pattern of individual lives. David Sanchez's life

course was shaped by cultural and institutional preferences for placing Native American children in boarding schools during middle childhood and adolescence and for recommending the military for youth and young adults. Phoung Le lives biculturally and has taught her children to do that as well. Maria Suarez's life course was changed forever by culture-related geopolitical conflict.

THEORETICAL ROOTS OF THE LIFE COURSE PERSPECTIVE

The life course perspective (LCP) is a theoretical model that has been emerging over the last 50 years, across several disciplines. Sociologists, anthropologists, social historians, demographers, epidemiologists, and psychologists—working independently and, more recently, collaboratively—have all helped to give it shape.

Glen Elder Jr., a sociologist, was one of the early authors to write about a life course perspective, and his work is still foundational to the ongoing development of the perspective. In the early 1960s, he began to analyze data from three pioneering longitudinal studies of children that had been undertaken by the University of California, Berkeley. As he examined several decades of data, he was struck with the enormous impact of the Great Depression of the 1930s on individual and family pathways (Elder, 1974). He began to call for developmental theory and research that looked at the influence of historical forces on family, education, and work roles.

At about the same time, social history emerged as a serious field. Social historians were particularly interested in retrieving the experiences of ordinary people, from their own vantage point, rather than telling the historical story from the vantage point of wealthy and powerful persons. Tamara Hareven (1978, 1982a, 1996, 2000) played a key role in developing the subdiscipline of the history of the family.

As will become clearer later in the chapter, the life course perspective also draws on traditional theories of developmental psychology, which look at the events that typically occur in people's lives during different stages. The life course perspective differs from these psychological theories in one very important way, however. Developmental psychology looks for universal, predictable events and pathways, but the life course perspective calls attention to how historical time, social location, and culture affect the individual experience of each life stage.

The life course perspective is still relatively young, but its popularity has grown across a broad range of disciplines (Alwin, 2012). In recent years, it has begun to be used to understand the pathways of families (Min, Silverstein, & Lendon, 2012), organizations (King, 2009), and social movements (Della Porta & Diani, 2006). I suggest that it has potential for understanding patterns of stability and change in all types of social systems.

Gerontologists increasingly use the perspective to understand how old age is shaped by events experienced earlier in life (Seabrook & Avison, 2012), but it has also become an increasingly popular perspective for considering adolescent and young adult transitions, such as the transition to high school (Benner, 2011) and the transition to motherhood (Black, Holditch-Davis, & Miles, 2009). The life course perspective has become a major theoretical framework in criminology (Chen, 2009; Schroeder, Giordano, & Cernkovich, 2010) and the leading perspective driving longitudinal study of health behaviors and outcomes (Bauldry, Shanahan, Boardman, Miech, & Macmillan, 2012; Evans, Crogan, Belyea, & Coon, 2009). It has also been proposed as a useful perspective for understanding patterns of lifetime drug use (Hser, Longshore, & Anglin, 2007).

Critical Thinking Questions 1.1

Think of your own life path. How straight has your path been to date? What continuities can you identify? What, if any, twists and turns have been a part of your life journey to date?

BASIC CONCEPTS OF THE LIFE COURSE PERSPECTIVE

Scholars who write from a life course perspective and social workers who apply the life course perspective in their work rely on a handful of staple concepts: cohorts, transitions, trajectories, life events, and turning points (see Exhibit 1.2 for concise definitions). As you read about each concept, imagine how it applies to the lives of David Sanchez, Phoung Le, and Maria Suarez as well as to your own life.

Cohorts

As noted, Glen Elder Jr.'s observation that historical, sociocultural forces have an impact on individual and family pathways was a major inspiration for

Exhibit 1.2   Basic Concepts of the Life Course Perspective

Cohort: Group of persons who were born during the same time period and who experience particular social changes within a given culture in the same sequence and at the same age

Transition: Change in roles and statuses that represents a distinct departure from prior roles and statuses

Trajectory: Long-term pattern of stability and change, which usually involves multiple transitions

Life event: Significant occurrence involving a relatively abrupt change that may produce serious and long-lasting effects

Turning point: Life event or transition that produces a lasting shift in the life course trajectory

development of the life course perspective. With their attention to the historical context of developmental pathways, life course scholars have found the concept of cohort to be very useful. In the life course perspective, a **cohort** is a group of persons who were born during the same time period and who experience particular social changes within a given culture in the same sequence and at approximately the same age (Bjorklund, 2011; D. Newman, 2012). *Generation* is another term used to convey a similar meaning. Generation is usually used to refer to a period of about 20 years, but a cohort may be shorter than that, and life course scholars often make a distinction between the two terms, suggesting that a birth cohort becomes a generation only when it develops some shared sense of its social history and a shared identity (see Alwin, McCammon, & Hofer, 2006).

Cohorts differ in size, and these differences affect opportunities for education, work, and family life. For example, the baby boom that followed World War II (1946 to 1964) in the United States produced a large cohort. When this large cohort entered the labor force, surplus labor drove wages down and unemployment up (Pearlin & Skaff, 1996; Uhlenberg, 1996).

Some observers suggest that cohorts develop strategies for the special circumstances they face (Newman, 2008). They suggest that "boomers"—the large cohort born from 1946 to 1964—responded to the economic challenges of their demographic bubble by delaying or avoiding marriage, postponing childbearing, having fewer children, and increasing the presence of mothers in the labor force. However, one study found that large cohorts in affluent countries have higher rates of suicide than smaller cohorts, suggesting that not all members of large cohorts can find positive strategies for coping with competition for limited resources (Stockard & O'Brien, 2002). Other researchers have been interested in the adaptations of Generation X—born from 1965 to 1979—and the Millennial Generation—born from 1980 to the late 1990s. Gen Xers grew up with fewer siblings and experienced higher rates of parental divorce than the boomers. They have been less likely than earlier generations to marry (Carlson, 2009). The Millennial Generation is more ethnically diverse than previous cohorts and grew up in a time of great technological innovation. They have been found to be more tolerant of diversity and more media-connected than earlier cohorts (Pew Research Center, 2010).

One way to visualize the configuration of cohorts in a given society is through the use of a **population pyramid**, a chart that depicts the proportion of the population in each age group. As Exhibit 1.3 demonstrates, different regions of the world have significantly different population pyramids. The first pyramid shows that affluent countries in the Global North have both low birth rates and low death rates. The populations are getting older in these societies, with a declining youthful population. These countries are becoming increasingly dependent on immigration (typically more attractive to young adults) for a workforce and taxpayers to support the aging population. It is predicted that 82% of the projected U.S. population increase from 2005 to 2050 will be the result of immigration (Passel & Cohn, 2008). Despite the economic necessity of immigrants in societies with aging populations, in the United States, as in many other affluent countries, there are strong anti-immigrant sentiments and angry calls to close the borders.

The second pyramid in Exhibit 1.3 shows that less affluent countries in the Global South have high birth rates and shorter life expectancy, leading to a situation in which the majority of people are young. In these countries, young people tend to overwhelm labor markets and education systems,

and national standards of living decline. Some of these countries, such as the Philippines, have developed policies that encourage out-migration while other countries, such as China, have developed policies to limit fertility.

Exhibit 1.3 also shows the ratio of males to females in each population. A cohort's **sex ratio** is the number of males per 100 females. Sex ratios affect a cohort's marriage rates, childbearing practices, crime rates, and family stability. Although there are many challenges to getting reliable sex ratio data, it is estimated that there are 105 males born for every 100 females in the world (Central Intelligence Agency, 2013). However, several countries have a sex ratio at birth of more than 110 males per 100 females. It is thought that high sex ratios at birth represent a kind of sex discrimination in

Exhibit 1.3 Population Pyramids by Level of Affluence, 2010

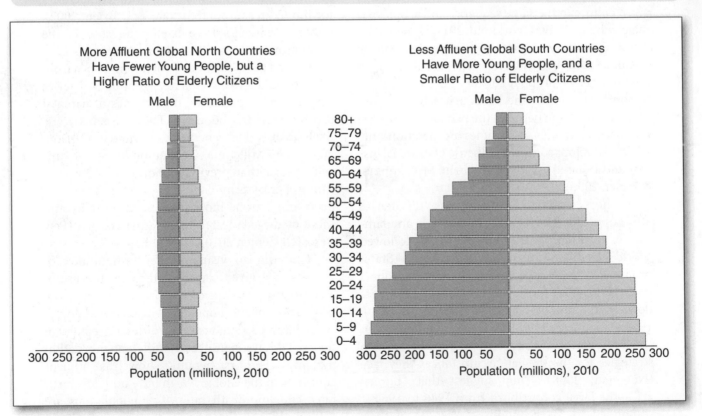

SOURCE: PRB Staff, "World Population Highlights: Key Findings From PRB's *2009 World Population Data Sheet*," *Population Bulletin* 64, no. 3 (2009).

some countries, where it might be attributed to sex-selected abortion and infanticide. As you can see in Exhibit 1.3, sex ratios decline across adulthood because males die at higher rates at every age. Sex ratios can be further unbalanced by war (which leads to greater male mortality) or death at childbirth (which leads to greater female mortality) or to high rates of either male or female out-migration or in-migration.

Transitions

A life course perspective is stagelike because it proposes that each person experiences a number of **transitions**, or changes in roles and statuses that represent a distinct departure from prior roles and statuses (Andrew & Ruel, 2010; Black et al., 2009). Life is full of such transitions: starting school, entering puberty, leaving school, getting a first job, leaving home, migrating, retiring, and so on. Leaving his grandmother's home for boarding school and enrolling in the military were important transitions for David Sanchez. Phoung Le has experienced a number of transitions, including the beginning of war, becoming a mother, escaping, moving to a refugee camp, and resettling in California. A transition is a process of gradual change that usually involves acquiring or relinquishing roles, but it can be any change in status, such as change in health status (Andrew & Ruel, 2010). A transition can produce both stress and opportunity (Benner, 2011).

Photo 1.2   The life course is full of transitions in roles and statuses; graduation from college or university is an important life transition that opens opportunities for future statuses and roles.

© ComStock/ThinkStock

Many transitions relate to family life: marriages, births, divorces, remarriages, deaths (McGoldrick, Carter, & Garcia-Preto, 2011a). Each transition changes family statuses and roles and generally is accompanied by family members' exits and entrances. We can see the dramatic effects of birth and death on the Suarez family as Maria entered and Emma exited the family circle. Health professionals have recently used the life course perspective, the concept of transitions in particular, to understand role changes that occur in family caregiving of older adults (Carpentier, Bernard, Grenier, & Guberman, 2010; Evans et al., 2009). The concept of transitions is also increasingly used to study the migration/immigration process (Gong, Xu, Fujishiro, & Takeuchi, 2011).

Transitions in collectivities other than the family, such as small groups, communities, and formal organizations, also involve exits and entrances of members as well as changes in statuses and roles. In college, for example, students pass through in a steady stream. Some of them make the transition from undergraduate to graduate student, and in that new status they may take on the new role of teaching or research assistant.

Trajectories

Each life course transition is embedded in a trajectory that gives form to the life course (Alwin, 2012). They are entry points to a new life phase. In contrast with transitions, **trajectories** involve a longer view of long-term patterns of stability and change in a person's life, involving multiple transitions. For example, you may look forward to graduating from your program of social work study. Graduation is a transition, but it is a transition that will be embedded in a career trajectory that will probably involve a number of other transitions along the way, such as a licensing exam, job changes, promotions, and perhaps periods of discontent or burnout. At some point, you may look back on your career path and see some patterns that at the moment you can't anticipate. Trajectories are best understood in the rearview mirror. We do not necessarily expect trajectories to be a straight line, but we do expect them to have some continuity of direction. For example, we assume that once David Sanchez became addicted to alcohol, he set forth on a path of increased use of alcohol and deteriorating ability to uphold his responsibilities, with multiple transitions involving family disruption and job instability. Indeed, Hser et al. (2007) recommend the life course perspective for understanding drug use trajectories (or careers) that may include onset of use, acceleration of use, regular use, cessation of use, and relapse. Treatment may or may not be included in this trajectory.

Because individuals and families live in multiple spheres, their lives are made up of multiple, intertwined trajectories—such as educational trajectories, family life trajectories, health trajectories, and work trajectories (Benner, 2011). These strands are woven together to form a life story. The interlocking trajectories of a life course can be presented visually on separate lifeline charts or as a single lifeline. See Exhibit 1.4 for instructions on completing a lifeline of interlocking trajectories.

Exhibit 1.4   My Lifeline (Interlocking Trajectories)

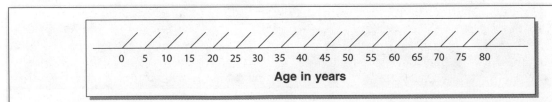

Assuming that you live until at least 80 years of age, chart how you think your life course trajectory will look. Write major events and transitions of your lifeline—you may want to write family events and transitions in one color, educational events and transitions in another, occupational events and transitions in another, and health events and transitions in another.

Life Events

Specific events predominate in the stories of David Sanchez, Phoung Le, and Maria Suarez: death of a parent, escape from the homeland, terrorist attack. A **life event** is a significant occurrence involving a relatively abrupt change that may produce serious and long-lasting effects (Settersten, 2003a). The term refers to the happening itself and not to the transitions that will occur because of the happening. For example, loss of a spouse is a relatively common life event in all societies. The death of the spouse is the life event, but it precipitates a transition that involves changes in roles and statuses. When we reflect on our own lives, most of us can quickly recall one or more major life events that had long-lasting impact.

One common method for evaluating the effect of life events is the use of a life events rating scale such as Thomas Holmes and Richard Rahe's Schedule of Recent Events, also called the Social Readjustment Rating Scale (Holmes, 1978; Holmes & Rahe, 1967). The Schedule of Recent Events, along with the rating of the stress associated with each event, appears in Exhibit 1.5. Holmes and Rahe constructed their schedule of events by asking respondents to rate the relative degree of adjustment required for different life events.

Inventories like the Schedule of Recent Events can remind us of some of the life events that affect human behavior and life course trajectories, but they also have limitations:

> Life events inventories are not finely tuned. One suggestion is to classify life events along several dimensions: major versus minor, anticipated versus unanticipated, controllable versus uncontrollable, typical versus atypical, desirable versus undesirable, acute versus chronic. (Settersten & Mayer, 1997, p. 246)

Most existing inventories are biased toward undesirable, rather than desirable, events. Not all life events prompt harmful life changes. Indeed, researchers have begun to distinguish between positive and negative life events and to measure their different impacts on human behavior. For example, one research team explored the impact of recalled positive and negative life events on the psychological well-being of adolescents and found that the impact of recalled life events varies by personality type (Garcia & Siddiqui, 2009). Another research team investigated how positive and negative life events trigger weight loss and weight gain, finding that weight loss is more associated with positive life events and weight gain with negative life events (Ogden, Stavrinaki, & Stubbs, 2009). And another research team examined the impact of positive and negative life events on oral health, finding that negative life events are associated with poor oral health but no association exists between oral health and positive life events (Brennan & Spencer, 2009). This latter research project reflects the way that the life course perspective is influencing research on predictors of health, including greater focus on the effects of life events.

However, the preponderance of research on the impact of life events on human behavior focuses on the negative impact of negative life events, and researchers still find life events scales to be useful tools. Some researchers are trying to understand the mechanisms that link stressful life events with immune system pathology (Herberth et al., 2008). Other often researched topics include the role of negative life events in depressive symptoms (Miklowitz & Johnson, 2009) and the impact of traumatic life events on mental health (Mongillo, Briggs-Gowan, Ford, & Carter, 2009). One research team recently found the Holmes-Rahe scale to be helpful in predicting suicide risk in a Madrid, Spain, sample (Blasco-Fontecilla et al., 2012). A Chinese research team used Zhang's life events scale and found death of a spouse and financial crisis to be associated with higher risk of cognitive impairment in older adults (Deng et al., 2012).

Specific life events have different meanings to various individuals and to various collectivities. Those distinctive meanings have not been measured in most research on life events (Hareven, 2000). One example of a study that has taken different meanings into account found that women report more vivid memories of life events in relationships than men report (Ross & Holmberg,

Exhibit 1.5 Life Change Events From the Holmes and Rahe Schedule of Recent Events

Life Event	Stress Rating
Death of a spouse	100
Divorce	73
Marital separation from mate	65
Detention in jail or other institutions	63
Death of a close family member	63
Major personal injury or illness	53
Marriage	50
Being fired at work	47
Marital reconciliation with mate	45
Retirement from work	45
Major change in the health or behavior of a family member	44
Pregnancy	40
Sexual difficulties	39
Gaining a new family member (e.g., through birth, adoption, elder moving in)	39
Major business readjustment (e.g., merger, reorganization, bankruptcy)	39
Major change in financial state (a lot worse off or a lot better off than usual)	38
Death of a close friend	37
Changing to a different line of work	36
Major change in the number of arguments with spouse (more or less)	35
Taking out a mortgage or loan for a major purchase	31
Foreclosure on a mortgage or loan	30
Major change in responsibilities at work (e.g., promotion, demotion, lateral transfer)	29
Son or daughter leaving home	29
Trouble with in-laws	29
Outstanding personal achievement	28
Wife beginning or ceasing work outside the home	26
Taking out a mortgage or loan for a lesser purchase (e.g., a car, TV, freezer)	26

Life Event	Stress Rating
Major change in sleeping habits (a lot more or a lot less sleep, or change in part of day when asleep)	25
Major change in number of family get-togethers (e.g., a lot more or a lot less than usual)	24
Major change in eating habits (a lot less food intake or very different meal hours or surroundings)	23
Vacation	20
Christmas	20
Minor violations of the law (e.g., traffic tickets, jaywalking, disturbing the peace)	20
Beginning or ceasing formal schooling	19
Major change in living conditions (e.g., building a new home, remodeling, deterioration of home or neighborhood)	19
Revision of personal habits (e.g., dress, manners, associations)	18
Trouble with the boss	17
Major change in working hours or conditions	16
Change in residence	15
Major change in usual type and/or amount of recreation	13
Major change in church activities (e.g., a lot more or a lot less than usual)	12
Major change in social activities (e.g., clubs, dancing, movies, visiting)	11
Change to a new school	5

SOURCE: Holmes, T. H., & Rahe, R. H. (1967). The social readjustment rating scale. *Journal of Psychosomatic Research, 11(2)*, 213–218.

1992). In an effort to capture the meanings that people make of life events, researchers have used the approach of asking respondents to recall life events rather than using existing life events inventories (Garcia & Siddiqui, 2009). For life events inventories to be useful, they must include events commonly experienced by the respondents.

Turning Points

David Sanchez describes becoming an apprentice medicine man as a turning point in his life. It would be interesting to ask Phoung Le whether she identifies any turning points in her life. Even though Maria Suarez was too young to think of September 11, 2001, as a turning point in her life, there is no doubt that the events of that day changed the course of her life. A **turning point** is a time when major change occurs in the life course trajectory. We sometimes call these "defining moments." The turning point may involve a transformation in how the person views the self in relation to the world and/or a transformation in how the person responds to risk and opportunity (Cappeliez, Beaupré, & Robitaille, 2008; Ferraro & Shippee, 2009). It serves as a lasting change and not just a temporary detour. As significant as they are to individuals' lives, turning points usually become obvious only as time passes (George, 2009). Yet in one Finnish study, 99% of respondents in their mid-30s reported that there had been at least one turning point in their lives; the average number of reported turning points was three (Rönkä, Oravala, & Pulkkinen, 2003).

The addition of the concept of turning point is an important way that the life course perspective departs from traditional developmental theory. According to traditional developmental theory, the developmental trajectory is more or less continuous, proceeding steadily from one phase to another. But life course trajectories are seldom so smooth and predictable. They involve many discontinuities, or sudden breaks, and some special life events become turning points that produce a lasting shift in the life course trajectory. Inertia tends to keep us on a particular trajectory, but turning points add twists and turns or even reversals to the life course. For example, we expect someone who is addicted to alcohol to continue to organize his or her life around that substance unless some event becomes a turning point for recovery (Hser et al., 2007).

Transitions and life events do not always produce the major change that would constitute a turning point. However, either a transition or life event may be perceived as a turning point as time passes. Longitudinal research indicates that three types of life events can serve as turning points (Rutter, 1996):

1. Life events that either close or open opportunities

2. Life events that make a lasting change on the person's environment

3. Life events that change a person's self-concept, beliefs, or expectations

Some events, such as migration to a new country, are momentous because they qualify as all three types of events (Gong et al., 2011). Migration, whether voluntary or involuntary, certainly makes a lasting change on the environment in which the person lives; it may also close and open opportunities and cause a change in self-concept and beliefs. Certainly, that seems to be the case for Phoung Le. Keep in mind, however, that individuals make subjective assessments of life events. The same type of life event may be a turning point for one individual, family, or other collectivity, but not for another. For example, one research team found that an HIV diagnosis was a turning point for 37% of their sample of HIV-positive people but was not reported as a turning point for 63% of the sample (Kremer, Ironson, & Kaplan, 2009). Another researcher found that myocardial infarction can be a turning point because it leads to reevaluation of attitudes about self, life, religion, and others (Baldacchino, 2011).

We have been talking about life events as turning points, but slower-moving transitions can also serve as turning points depending on the individual's assessment of their importance. For example, an Australian study of women found a change in the nature of turning points in midlife—before midlife, turning points were likely to be related to role transitions; but after midlife, they were more likely to be related to personal growth (Leonard, 2006). A transition can become a turning point under five conditions (Hareven, 2000):

1. When the transition occurs simultaneously with a crisis or is followed by a crisis

2. When the transition involves family conflict over the needs and wants of individuals and the greater good of the family unit

3. When the transition is "off-time," meaning that it does not occur at the typical stage in life

4. When the transition is followed by unforeseen negative consequences

5. When the transition requires exceptional social adjustments

One research team interviewed older adults aged 60 to 87 about perceived turning points in their lives and found that the most frequently reported turning points involved health and family. The perceived turning points occurred across the entire life course, but there was some clustering at midlife (ages 45–64), a period in which 32.2% of the reported turning points occurred (Cappeliez et al., 2008). Gender differences have been found in reported turning points in samples of young adults as well as samples of older adults, with women reporting more turning points in the family domain and men reporting more turning points in the work domain (Cappeliez et al., 2008; Rönkä et al., 2003). It is not clear whether this gender difference will be manifested in future cohorts if women's work trajectories continue to become more similar to men's. Researchers have studied the turning points that lead women to leave abusive relationships (Khaw & Hardesty, 2007) and the turning points in the caregiving careers of Mexican American women who care for older family members (Evans et al., 2009). This latter research identifies a "point of reckoning" turning point when the caregiver recognizes the need for extensive caregiving and reorganizes her life to accept responsibility for providing care.

Loss of a parent is not always a turning point, but when such a loss occurs off-time, as it did with David Sanchez and Maria Suarez, it is often a turning point. Emma Suarez may not have thought of her decision to take a job in the World Trade Center as a turning point, because she could not foresee the events of September 11, 2001.

Most life course pathways include multiple turning points, some that send life trajectories off track and others that bring life trajectories back on track. David Sanchez's Vietnam experience seems to have gotten him off track, and his grandmother's death seems to have gotten him back on track. In fact, we could say that the intent of many social work interventions is to get life course trajectories back on track. We do this when we plan interventions to precipitate a turning point toward recovery for a client with an addiction. Or we may plan an intervention to help a deteriorating community reclaim its lost sense of community and spirit of pride. It is interesting to note that many social service organizations have taken "Turning Point" for their name. Criminal justice researchers have been interested in learning what types of role transitions can become turning points in a criminal career, leading to desisting from criminal activities. They have found that for some offenders, marriage, military experience, employment, or becoming a parent can precipitate such a turning point (Michalsen, 2011; Schroeder et al., 2010). Researchers have also found that turning points can facilitate posttraumatic growth for men with histories of child sexual abuse although the exact nature of these turning points is not clear (Easton, Coohey, Rhodes, & Moorthy, 2013).

Critical Thinking Questions 1.2

Consider the life course story of either David Sanchez or Phoung Le. Based on the information you have, what do you think would be the chapter titles if David Sanchez wrote a book about his life? What would be the chapter titles if Phoung Le wrote about her life? How about a book about your own life to date: what would be the chapter titles of that book? Which show up more in the chapter titles, life transitions (changes in roles and statuses) or life events (significant happenings)?

MAJOR THEMES OF THE LIFE COURSE PERSPECTIVE_____

Two decades ago, Glen Elder Jr. (1994) identified four dominant, and interrelated, themes in the life course approach: interplay of human lives and historical time, timing of lives, linked or interdependent lives, and human agency in making choices. The meaning of these themes is discussed shortly, along with the meaning of two other related themes that Elder (1998) and Michael Shanahan (2000) have more recently identified as important: diversity in life course trajectories and developmental risk and protection. These six themes continue to be the framework for life course researchers across a number of disciplines, although different researchers emphasize different themes. The meaning of these themes is summarized in Exhibit 1.6.

Exhibit 1.6 Major Themes of the Life Course Perspective

Interplay of human lives and historical time: Individual and family development must be understood in historical context.

Timing of lives: Particular roles and behaviors are associated with particular age groups, based on biological age, psychological age, social age, and spiritual age.

Linked or interdependent lives: Human lives are interdependent, and the family is the primary arena for experiencing and interpreting wider historical, cultural, and social phenomena.

Human agency in making choices: The individual life course is constructed by the choices and actions individuals take within the opportunities and constraints of history and social circumstances.

Diversity in life course trajectories: There is much diversity in life course pathways as a result of, e.g., cohort variations, social class, culture, gender, and individual agency.

Developmental risk and protection: Experiences with one life transition or life event have an impact on subsequent transitions and events and may either protect the life course trajectory or put it at risk.

Interplay of Human Lives and Historical Time

As sociologists and social historians began to study individual and family life trajectories, they noted that persons born in different years face different historical worlds, with different options and constraints—especially in rapidly changing societies, such as the United States at the beginning of the 21st century. They suggested that historical time may produce **cohort effects** when distinctive formative experiences are shared at the same point in the life course and have a lasting impact on a birth cohort (Alwin & McCammon, 2003). The same historical events may affect different cohorts in different ways. For example, Elder's (1974) research on children and the Great Depression found that the life course trajectories of the cohort that were young children at the time of the economic downturn were more seriously affected by family hardship than the cohort that were in middle childhood and late adolescence at the time. He also notes, however, that these young children were adolescents when fathers were fighting in World War II and mothers were often in the workplace. More recently, Australian researchers (Page, Milner, Morrell, & Taylor, 2013) found that the cohort born after 1970–1974 was more prone to suicide across the young adult period than earlier cohorts. The researchers also found that this cohort faced higher rates of unemployment and underemployment as they entered young adulthood than earlier cohorts and propose a relationship between these two factors.

Analysis of large data sets by a number of researchers provides forceful evidence that changes in other social institutions impinge on family and individual life course trajectories (Vikat, Speder, Beets, Billari, & Buhler, 2007). Researchers have examined the impact of globalization, declining labor market opportunities, and rising housing costs on young adult transitions (see Newman, 2008; Scherger, 2009). These researchers are finding that transitions associated with young adulthood (leaving the parental home, marriage, first parenthood) are occurring later for the current cohort of young adults than for their parents in many countries, particularly in countries with weak welfare states. The popular media in the United States has described the relationship between some parents and their millennial young adults as helicopter parents and landing pad kids, suggesting that the intense support offered by many parents to their adult offspring violates earlier norms of the young adult transition. One research team found, however, that young adults who received such intense support reported better psychological adjustment and life satisfaction than young adults who did not receive such support. The parents were less satisfied with provision of intense support, however (Fingerman et al., 2013).

No doubt, researchers will be studying the impact of the global economic recession that began in late 2007 on life course trajectories of different cohorts. Other aspects of the current historical era that will most likely generate life course research are the wars in Afghanistan and Iraq and the election of the first African American president in the United States.

Tamara Hareven's (2000) historical analysis of family life documents the lag between social change and the development of public policy to respond to the new circumstances and the needs that arise with social change. One such lag today in the United States is between trends in employment among mothers and public policy regarding child care during infancy and early childhood. Social work planners and administrators confront the results of such a lag in their work. Thus, they have some responsibility to keep the public informed about the impact of changing social conditions on individuals, families, communities, and formal organizations.

Timing of Lives

"How old are you?" You have probably been asked that question many times, and no doubt you find yourself curious about the age of new acquaintances. Every society appears to use age as an important variable, and many social institutions in advanced industrial societies are organized, in part, around age—the age for starting school, the age of majority, retirement age, and so on (Settersten, 2003b). In the United States, our speech abounds with expressions related to age: "terrible 2s," "sweet 16," "20-something," "life begins at 40," "senior discounts," and lately "60 is the new 40."

Age is also a prominent attribute in efforts by social scientists to bring order and predictability to our understanding of human behavior. Life course scholars are interested in the age at which specific life events and transitions occur, which they refer to as the timing of lives. They may classify entrances and exits from particular statuses and roles as "off-time" or "on-time," based on social norms or shared expectations about the timing of such transitions (McFarland, Pudrovska, Schieman, Ellison, & Bierman, 2013). For example, child labor and childbearing in adolescence are considered off-time in late industrial and postindustrial countries, but in much of the world such timing of roles is seen as a part of the natural order (Dannefer, 2003a, 2003b). One research team found that people who were diagnosed with cancer at earlier ages had a greater increase in religiosity than people diagnosed at later ages, suggesting that off-time transitions are more stressful than on-time transitions (McFarland et al., 2013). Survivors' grief is probably deeper in cases of "premature loss" (Pearlin & Skaff, 1996), which is perhaps why Emma Suarez's family continues to say, "She was so young; she had so much life left." Certainly, David Sanchez reacted differently to his father's and his grandmother's deaths.

Dimensions of Age

Chronological age itself is not the only factor involved in timing of lives. Age-graded differences in roles and behaviors are the result of biological, psychological, social, and spiritual processes. Thus, age is often considered from each of the perspectives that make up the biopsychosocial framework (Solomon, Helvitz, & Zerach, 2009). Although life course scholars have not directly addressed the issue of spiritual age, it is an important perspective as well.

Biological age indicates a person's level of biological development and physical health, as measured by the functioning of the various organ systems. It is the present position of the biological person in relation to the potential life cycle. There is no simple, straightforward way to measure biological age. One method is to compare an individual's physical condition with the conditions of others; for example, bone density scans are compared with the scans of a healthy 20-year-old.

Psychological age has both behavioral and perceptual components. Behaviorally, psychological age refers to the capacities that people have and the skills they use to adapt to changing biological and environmental demands. Skills in memory, learning, intelligence, motivation, emotions, and so forth are all involved (Bjorklund, 2011). Perceptually, psychological age is based on how old people perceive themselves to be. Life course researchers have explored the perceptual aspect of psychological age since the 1960s; recent research has referred to this perceptual aspect of age as "subjective age" or "age identity." The preponderance of research on subjective age has focused on older adults and found that older adults in Western societies feel younger than their chronological age (Stephan, Chalabaev, Kotter-Grühn, & Jaconelli, 2013). This has not been found to be the case among Chinese oldest old, but recent research finds that the percentage of China's oldest old reporting not feeling old has increased in the past decade (Liang, 2014). It is important to remember that, traditionally, Chinese culture has accorded high status to old age, but the traditions are weakening. A French research team found that a sample of older adults performed significantly better on a physical test when they were told that their earlier performance on the same test was better than 80% of the people their age; the improvement did not happen in the control group who did not receive this feedback (Stephan et al., 2013). Researchers in Switzerland found that older adults identify more strongly with their generation than with their specific age group and feel more positive about their generation identity than their age-group identity (Weiss & Lang, 2012). Young adults have been found to feel their same age or slightly older. Middle-aged and older adults' subjective age is related to their self-reported health, but that is not the case for younger adults (Stephan, Demulier, & Terracciano, 2012).

Social age refers to the age-graded roles and behaviors expected by society—in other words, the socially constructed meaning of various ages. The concept of **age norm** is used to indicate the behaviors expected of people of a specific age in a given society at a particular point in time. Age norms may be informal expectations, or they may be encoded as formal rules and laws. For example, cultures have an informal age norm about the appropriate age to leave the parental home. Conversely, many countries have developed formal rules about the appropriate age for driving, drinking alcohol, and voting. Life course scholars suggest that age norms vary not only across historical time and across societies, but also by gender, race, ethnicity, and social class within a given time and society (Newman, 2008; Scherger, 2009). They have paid particular attention to recent changes in age norms for the transitions of young adulthood (Newman, 2008; Scherger, 2009).

Although biological age and psychological age are recognized in the life course perspective, social age receives special emphasis. For instance, life course scholars use life phases such as middle childhood and middle adulthood, which are based in large part on social age, to conceptualize human lives from birth to death. In this book, we talk about nine phases, from conception to very late adulthood. Keep in mind, however, that the number and nature of these life phases are socially constructed and have changed over time, with modernization and mass longevity leading to finer gradations in life phases and consequently a greater number of them. Such fine gradations do not exist in most nonindustrial and newly industrializing countries (Dannefer, 2003a, 2003b).

Spiritual age indicates the current position of a person in the ongoing search for meaning, purpose, and moral relationships. David Sanchez is certainly at a different position in his search for life's meaning than he was when he came home from Vietnam. Although life course scholars have not paid much attention to spiritual age, it has been the subject of study by some developmental psychologists and other social scientists. In an exploration of the meaning of adulthood edited by Erik Erikson in 1978, several authors explored the markers of adulthood from the viewpoint of a number of spiritual and religious traditions, including Christianity, Hinduism, Islam, Buddhism, and Confucianism. Several themes emerged across the various traditions: contemplation, moral action, reason, self-discipline, character improvement, loving actions, and close community with others. All the authors noted that spirituality is typically seen as a process of growth, a process with no end.

James Fowler (1981) has presented a theory of faith development, based on 359 in-depth interviews, that strongly links it with chronological age. Ken Wilber's (2000, 2001) integral theory of consciousness also proposes an association between age and spiritual development, but Wilber does not suggest that spiritual development is strictly linear. He notes, as do the contributors to the Erikson book, that there can be regressions, temporary leaps, and turning points in a person's spiritual development.

Standardization in the Timing of Lives

Life course scholars debate whether the trend is toward greater standardization in age-graded social roles and statuses or toward greater diversification (Brückner & Mayer, 2005; Scherger, 2009). Simone Scherger (2009) examined the timing of young adult transitions (moving out of parental home, marriage, becoming a parent) among 12 cohorts in West Germany. Cohorts of a 5-year range (e.g., born 1920–1924) were used for the analysis, beginning with the cohort born in 1920–1924 and ending with the cohort born in 1975–1979. This research indicated a trend toward destandardization. There was greater variability in the timing of transitions (moving out of the parental home, marriage, and becoming a parent) among the younger cohorts than among the older cohorts. Scherger also found the transitions were influenced by gender (men made the transitions later than women) and education level (higher education was associated with delay in the transitions). It is important to note, however, that another research team found that young adult transitions have remained stable in the Nordic countries where strong welfare institutions provide generous supports for the young adult transitions (Newman, 2008). The implication for social workers is that we must pay attention to the uniqueness of each person's life course trajectory, but we can use research about regularities in the timing of lives to inform social policy.

Many societies engage in **age structuring**, or standardizing of the ages at which social role transitions occur, by developing policies and laws that regulate the timing of these transitions. For example, in the United States there are laws and regulations about the ages for compulsory education, working (child labor), driving, drinking alcohol, being tried as an adult, marrying, holding public office, and receiving pensions and social insurance. However, countries vary considerably in the degree to which age norms are formalized (Newman, 2008). It is often noted that formal age structuring becomes more prevalent as nations modernize. European life course scholars suggest that U.S.-based life course scholars have underplayed the role of government in age structuring, suggesting that, in Europe, strong centralized governments play a larger role than in the United States in structuring the life course (Leisering, 2003; Marshall & Mueller, 2003). Indeed, there is evidence that life course pathways in Germany and Switzerland are more standardized than in the United States and Britain (Perrig-Chiello & Perren, 2005). There is also evidence that events and transitions in childhood and adolescence are much more age-normed and structured than in adulthood (Perrig-Chiello & Perren, 2005).

Formalized age structuring has created a couple of difficulties that affect social workers. One is that cultural lags often lead to a mismatch between changing circumstances and the age structuring in society. Consider the trend for corporations to offer early retirement, before the age of 65, in a time when people are living longer and with better health. This mismatch has implications both for public budgets and for individual lives, and since the 2008–2009 economic recession, more U.S. workers have been delaying retirement (Levanon, Cheng, & Goldman, 2011). Another problem with the institutionalization of age norms is increasing age segregation; people are spending more of their time in groups consisting entirely of people their own age. Social work services are increasingly organized around the settings of these age-segregated groups: schools, the workplace, long-term care, and so forth.

In spite of formal age structuring, as suggested earlier, there is much diversity in the sequencing and timing of adult life course markers, such as completing an education, beginning work, leaving home, marrying, and becoming a parent (Newman, 2008). An increasing number of students are delaying the entry into higher education (Roksa & Valez, 2012). The landscape of work is also changing, with less opportunity for continuous and stable employment, and this is creating greater diversity in work trajectories (Sweet & Meiksins, 2013). Research in the future will, no doubt, capture the diverse work trajectories that were influenced by the 2008–2009 economic recession. Life course trajectories also vary in significant ways by gender, race, ethnicity, and social class (Scherger, 2009). For example, although educational trajectories remain standardized for the most well-off, who move smoothly from secondary to higher education, they are less structured for other members of society (Roksa & Velez, 2012). Sources of diversity in life course perspectives are discussed later.

Linked or Interdependent Lives

The life course perspective emphasizes the interdependence of human lives and the ways in which people are reciprocally connected on several levels. It calls attention to how relationships both support and control an individual's behavior. **Social support**, which is defined as help rendered by others that benefits an individual or collectivity, is an obvious element of interdependent lives. Relationships also control behavior through expectations, rewards, and punishments. Social and behavioral scientists have paid particular attention to the family as a source of support and control. In addition, the lives of family members are linked across generations, with both opportunity and misfortune having an intergenerational impact. The cases of David Sanchez, Phoung Le, and Maria Suarez are rich examples of lives linked across generations. But they are also rich examples of how people's lives are linked with those of people outside the family.

Links Between Family Members

Certainly, parents' and children's lives are linked. Elder's longitudinal research of children raised during the Great Depression found that as parents experienced greater economic pressures, they faced a greater risk of depressed feelings and marital discord. Consequently, their ability to nurture their children was compromised, and their children were more likely to exhibit emotional distress, academic trouble, and problem behavior (Elder, 1974). The connection between family hardship, family nurturance, and child behaviors and well-being is now well established (e.g., Barajas, Philipsen, & Brooks-Gunn, 2008; Conger & Conger, 2008). In addition to the economic connection between parents and children, parents provide social capital for their children, in terms of role models and networks of social support (Szydlik, 2012).

It should also be noted that parents' lives are influenced by the trajectories of their children's lives. For example, parents may need to alter their work trajectories to respond to the needs of a terminally ill child. Or parents may forgo early retirement to assist their young adult children with education expenses. Parents may be negatively affected by stressful situations that their children face. Emma Suarez's tragedy was a source of great stress for her mother and her siblings. One research team found a relationship between the problems of adult children and the emotional and relational well-being of their parents. Research participants who reported having adult children with a greater accumulation of personal and social problems (e.g., chronic disease, mental health problems, substance abuse problems, work-related problems, relationship problems) also reported poorer levels of well-being than reported by participants whose children were reported to have fewer problems (Greenfield & Marks, 2006). Without longitudinal research, it is impossible to know which came first, reduced parental well-being or adult child problems, but

Photo 1.3 Parents' and children's lives are linked—when parents experience stress or joy, so do children, and when children experience stress and joy, so do parents.

© iStockphoto.com

this research does lend strong support for the idea that lives are linked across generations.

The pattern of mutual support between older adults and their adult children is formed by life events and transitions across the life course. It is also fundamentally changed when families go through historical disruptions such as wars or major economic downturns. For example, the traditional pattern of intergenerational support—parents supporting children—is often disrupted when one generation migrates and another generation stays behind. It is also disrupted in immigrant families when the children pick up the new language and cultural norms faster than the adults in the family and take on the role of interpreter for their parents and grandparents (Clark, Glick, & Bures, 2009).

What complicates matters is that family roles must often be synchronized across three or more generations at once. Sometimes this synchronization does not go smoothly. Divorce, remarriage, and discontinuities in parents' work and educational trajectories may conflict with the needs of children. Similarly, the timing of adult children's educational, family, and work transitions often conflicts with the needs of aging parents (Huinink & Feldhaus, 2009). The "generation in the middle" may have to make uncomfortable choices when allocating scarce economic and emotional resources. When a significant life event in one generation (such as death of a grandparent) is juxtaposed with a significant life event in another generation (such as birth of a child), families and individual family members are especially vulnerable (McGoldrick et al., 2011a).

Links With the Wider World

Although the life course perspective has its origins in Elder's (1974) research on the ways that families and individuals are linked to situations in the economic institution, it seems that we know a lot more at this point about the ways that individuals and their multigenerational families are interdependent than about the interdependence between individuals and families and other groups and collectivities. However, in recent years life course researchers have been documenting the ways that individual and family life course trajectories are linked to situations in the labor market, the housing market, the education system, and the welfare system (Newman, 2008; Scherger, 2009; Szydlik, 2012). This line of research is well illustrated by one research project that examined young adult transitions in Western Europe and Japan (Newman, 2008). Katherine Newman (2008) reports two divergent trends in the timing of young adult transitions in postindustrial societies. On the one hand, young adults are staying in the parental home for a prolonged period in Japan and the southern European countries. For example, in Japan, the age of marriage has been rising, and more than 60% of unmarried men and 70% of unmarried women aged 30 to 34 live with their parents. On the other hand, youth typically leave home at the age of 18 in the Nordic countries of northern Europe (Denmark, Finland, Norway, and Sweden). This raises a question about the structural arrangements in these countries that are producing such divergent trends in life course trajectories.

First, changes in the labor market are driving the delayed departure of young adults from the parental home in southern Europe and Japan (Newman, 2008). In the 1980s, when globalization began to produce higher unemployment, governments in southern Europe and Japan began to loosen their commitment to lifetime employment. As a result, companies began to hire part-time and temporary workers; such tenuous connection to the labor market is associated with continued co-residence of young adults with their parents. Unemployment has always been higher in southern Europe than in northern Europe, but the divergence in young adult transitions in these two European regions is not fully explained by conditions in the labor market.

Second, timing of departure from the parental home is linked to situations in the housing market. In the United States, there are a number of housing options for marginally employed young adults, including pooling resources with a roommate or romantic partner or finding rental housing in a less desirable neighborhood. Such options are dependent on a strong rental housing market, however. In southern European countries, great emphasis is put on owner-occupied housing and relatively little rental housing is available. For example, more than 85% of the population in Spain lives in homes they own. In addition, European banks typically are willing to lend only 50% of the cost of a house. In contrast, in the Nordic countries, there is a large rental sector in the housing market, with only 60% to 65% of the population living in homes that they own. Katherine Newman (2008) builds the case that these conditions in the housing market influence the timing of departure from the parental home.

Third, it is often suggested that there is a linkage between the education system and timing of departure from the parental home. More specifically, it is argued that young adults who participate in higher education leave the parental home later than those who do not participate in higher education and that the trend toward greater participation in higher education is an important factor in the trend toward later departure from the parental home (see Scherger, 2009). This is not the whole story, however, because the Nordic countries have a higher proportion of emerging adults in higher education than countries in southern Europe, and yet young adults in the Nordic countries depart the parental home earlier than those in southern Europe (Newman, 2008).

And, finally, there is strong evidence of a linkage between the welfare system and the timing of departure from the parental home (Newman, 2008). More specifically, the early departure from the parental home in Nordic countries is subsidized by a generous welfare system that provides generous housing and educational benefits. The Nordic governments provide much of what families are expected to provide in the weaker welfare systems in southern Europe and Japan.

Katherine Newman (2008) argues convincingly that it is a confluence of situations in different societal systems that impact individual and family life trajectories. In terms of linked lives, she found some evidence that young adults feel more closely linked to their families in Japan and southern Europe than in Nordic countries—a situation that carried both positive and negative consequences. Nordic young adults, conversely, feel more closely linked to the government and the welfare institution than young adults in Japan and southern Europe.

Using data from 11 European countries, Marc Szydlik (2012) has taken a similar look at the influence of the social welfare system on family solidarity between older adults and their adult children. He found strong family solidarity across the 11 countries but some differences in how the state and family are linked across national lines. He found that adult children in countries with strong social welfare systems provided more practical household help (home repairs, gardening, transportation, shopping, household chores, and paperwork) to their aging parents than adult children in countries with weaker social welfare systems. On the other hand, adult children in countries with weak social welfare systems provided more personal care (dressing, bathing, eating, getting in and out of bed, using the toilet) to their aging parents than adult children in countries with stronger social welfare systems. Szydlik suggests that societies with an aging population need family-friendly policies to protect family members from excessive demands, noting that middle-aged adults may get overburdened from the need to care for aging adults while also supporting their young adult offspring who are struggling in a labor market that is becoming increasingly less secure.

It is important for social workers to remember that lives are also linked in systems of institutionalized privilege and oppression. The life trajectories of members of minority groups in the United States are marked by discrimination and lack of opportunity, which are experienced pervasively as daily insults and pressures. However, various cultural groups have devised unique systems of social support to cope with the oppressive environments in which they live. Examples include the extensive and intensive natural support systems of Hispanic families like the Suarez family (Falicov, 2005) and the special role of the church for African Americans (Billingsley, 1999). Others construct lives of desperation or resistance in response to limited opportunities.

Philip McMichael (2012) reminds us that, in the global economy, lives are linked around the world. The lifestyles of people in affluent countries depend on cheap labor and cheap raw products in Africa, South America, the Caribbean, parts of Asia, and other places. Children and women in impoverished countries labor long hours to make an increasing share of low-cost products consumed in affluent countries. Women migrate from impoverished countries to become the domestic laborers in affluent countries, allowing women in affluent countries to leave the home to take advantage of career opportunities and allowing the domestic workers to send the money they make back home to support their own families.

Critical Thinking Questions 1.3

What, if any, historical event or events have had a large impact on your cohort? In your family of origin, what were the norms about when young adults should leave the parental home, complete formal education, establish a committed romantic relationship, or become a parent? How consistent are your own ideas about these young adult transitions with the ideas of your family of origin? Cross-national research indicates that the social welfare system has an influence on intergenerational family relationships. Do you think that research supports a strong welfare system or a weak welfare system? Explain.

Human Agency in Making Choices

Phoung Le and her husband made a decision that they wanted to live a bilingual, bicultural life, and this decision had a momentous impact on their own life course as well as the life course trajectories of their children. In other words, they participated in constructing their life courses through the exercise of **human agency**, or the use of personal power to achieve one's goals. The emphasis on human agency may be one of the most positive contributions of the life course perspective. Steven Hitlin and Glen Elder Jr. (2007) note that the concept of human agency is used by different theorists in different ways, but when used by life course theorists it refers to "attempts to exert influence to shape one's life trajectory" (p. 182). It involves acting with an orientation toward the future, with an eye for "possible selves" (Markus & Nurius, cited in Hitlin & Elder, 2007, p. 183).

A look at the discipline of social history might help to explain why considering human agency is so important to social workers. Social historians have attempted to correct the traditional focus on lives of elites by studying the lives of common people (Hareven, 2000). By doing so, they discovered that many groups once considered passive victims—for example, working-class people and slaves—actually took independent action to cope with the difficulties imposed by the rich and powerful. Historical research now shows that couples tried to limit the size of their families even in preindustrial societies (Wrigley, 1966), that slaves were often ingenious in their struggles to hold their families together (Gutman, 1976), and that factory workers used informal networks and kinship ties to manage, and sometimes resist, pressures for efficiency (Hareven, 1982b). These findings are consistent with social work approaches that focus on individual, family, and community strengths (Saleebey, 2012).

Emphasis on human agency in the life course perspective has been greatly aided by the work of psychologist Albert Bandura. Bandura proposes that humans are agentic, meaning they are capable of intentionally influencing their own functioning and life circumstances (Bandura, 2002, 2006). In his early work, he introduced the two concepts of *self-efficacy*, or sense of personal competence, and *efficacy expectation*, or expectation that one can personally accomplish a goal. More recently (Bandura, 2006), he has presented a psychological theory of human agency. This theory proposes three modes of human agency:

1. *Personal agency* is exercised individually, using personal influence to shape environmental events or one's own behavior.

2. *Proxy agency* is exercised to influence others who have greater resources to act on one's behalf to meet needs and accomplish goals.

3. *Collective agency* is exercised on the group level when people act together to meet needs and accomplish goals.

Bandura argues that everyday life requires use of all three modes of agency. There are many circumstances, such as those just discussed, where individuals can exercise personal agency to shape situations. However, there are many situations over which individuals do not have direct control, and they must seek out others who have greater influence to act on their behalf. Other circumstances exist in which goals are only achievable or more easily and comprehensively achievable by working collectively with others.

Cultural psychology critics of the concept of human agency have argued that it is a culture-bound concept that does not apply as well in collectivist societies as in individualistic societies (see Markus & Kitayama, 2003). They argue that individualistic societies operate on a model of *disjoint agency*, where agency resides in the independent self. In contrast, collectivist societies operate on a model of *conjoint agency*, where agency resides in relationships between interdependent selves. Markus and Kitayama (2003) provide empirical support for their proposal that agency is experienced differently by members of individualistic and collectivist societies. They cite several studies providing evidence that European American children perform better and are more confident if they are allowed to make choices (of tasks, objects, and so on), but Asian American children perform no better if allowed to make such choices. They also note that in U.S. coverage of the Olympics, athletes are typically asked about how they personally feel about their efforts and their success. In contrast, in Japanese coverage, athletes are typically asked "Who helped you achieve?" Markus and Kitayama do not deny that individuals from collectivist cultures sometimes think in terms of personal agency and individuals from individualistic cultures sometimes think in terms of collective agency. They argue, however, that there is a difference in the emphasis placed on these approaches to agency in different cultures. Gretchen Sisson (2012) suggests that in the United States, working-class individuals are more likely than middle-class individuals to follow a conjoint model of agency concerned with obligations to others. She notes that pregnancy prevention programs typically are based on a disjoint model, which may be inappropriate for the intended audience.

Bandura (2002, 2006) argues that although people in all cultures must use all three modes of agency (personal, proxy, and collective), there are cultural variations in the relative emphasis put on the different modes. He also argues that there are individual variations of preferences within cultures and that globalization is producing some cultural sharing.

Clearly, however, human agency has limits. Individuals' choices are constrained by the structural and cultural arrangements of a given historical era. For example, Phoung Le and her family did not have the choice to continue to live peacefully in Saigon. David Sanchez may have assumed that his choices were to voluntarily enlist or be drafted. Unequal opportunities also give some members of society more options than others have (Stephens, Hamedani, Markus, Bergsieker, & Eloul, 2009). Hitlin and Elder (2007) suggest both biological and social structural limits to agency. They note

research indicating that greater perceptions of personal control contribute to better health among older adults but also propose that agency declines across the life course because of declining physical functioning.

The concepts of proxy agency and collective agency bring us back to linked and interdependent lives. These concepts add important dimensions to the discussion of human agency and can serve to counterbalance the extreme individualism of U.S. society. The modes of agency also raise important issues for social workers. When do we encourage clients to use personal individual agency, when do we use our own influence as proxy agents for clients, and when is collective agency called for?

Diversity in Life Course Trajectories

Life course researchers have long had strong evidence of diversity in individuals' life patterns. Early research emphasized differences between cohorts, but increasing attention is being paid to variability within cohort groups. However, the life course research has been based on samples from affluent societies and fails to account for global diversity, particularly for the life course trajectories of the great majority of the world's people who live in nonindustrial or early industrializing countries (Dannefer, 2003a, 2003b). Consequently, the life course perspective has the potential to accommodate global diversity but has not adequately done so yet.

We also want to interject a word here about terminology and human diversity. As we attempted to uncover what is known about human diversity in life course trajectories, we struggled with terminology to define identity groups. We searched for consistent language to describe different groups, and we were dedicated to using language that identity groups would use to describe themselves. However, we ran into challenges endemic to our time related to the language of diversity. First, it is not the case that all members of a given identity group at any given time embrace the same terminology for their group. Second, as we reviewed literature from different historical moments, we recognized the shifting nature of terminology. In addition, even within a given era, we found that different researchers used different terms and had different decision rules about who comprises the membership of identity groups. So, in the end, you will find that we have not settled on fixed terminology used consistently to describe identity groups. Rather, we use the language of individual researchers when reporting their studies, because we want to avoid distorting their work. We hope you will recognize that the ever-changing language of diversity has both constructive potential to find creative ways to affirm diversity and destructive potential to dichotomize diversity into *the norm* and *the other*.

As we strive to provide a global context, we encounter current controversies about appropriate language to describe different sectors of the world. Following World War II, a distinction was made between First World, Second World, and Third World nations, with *First World* referring to the Western capitalist nations, *Second World* referring to the countries belonging to the socialist bloc led by the Soviet Union, and *Third World* referring to a set of countries that were primarily former colonies of the First World. More recently, many scholars have used the language of First World, Second World, and Third World to define global sectors in a slightly different way. *First World* has been used to describe the nations that were the first to industrialize, urbanize, and modernize. *Second World* has been used to describe nations that have industrialized but have not yet become central to the world economy. *Third World* has been used to refer to nonindustrialized nations that have few resources and are considered expendable in the global economy. This approach has lost favor in recent years. Immanuel Wallerstein (1974, 1979) uses different language but makes a similar distinction; he refers to wealthy *core* countries, newly industrialized *semiperiphery* countries, and the poorest *periphery* countries. Other writers divide the world into *developed* and *developing* countries (McMichael, 2012), referring to the level of industrialization, urbanization, and modernization. Still

others divide the world into the *Global North* and the *Global South*, calling attention to a history in which the Global North colonized and exploited the resources of the Global South. And, finally, some writers talk about the *West* versus the *East*, where the distinctions are largely cultural. We recognize that such categories carry great symbolic meaning and can mask systems of power and exploitation. As with diversity, we attempted to find a respectful language that could be used consistently throughout the book. Again, we found that different researchers have used different language and different characteristics to describe categories of nations, and when reporting on their findings, we have used their own language to avoid misrepresenting their findings.

Life course researchers have recently begun to incorporate intersectionality theory to understand diversity in life course trajectories (see Warner & Brown, 2011). **Intersectionality theory** recognizes that all of us are jointly and simultaneously members of a number of socially constructed identity groups, such as gender, race, ethnicity, social class, sexual orientation, age, religion, geographical location, and disability/ability. The theory is rooted in the writings of U.S. Black feminists who challenged the idea of a universal gendered experience (see Collins, 2012). For any one of us, our *social location*, or place in society, is at the intersection of our multiple identity groups. Either advantage or disadvantage is associated with each identity group, and when considering the life journey of any one individual, it is important to consider the multiple identity groups of which he or she is a part (see Hankivsky, 2012; Seng, Lopez, Sperlich, Hamama, & Meldrum, 2012).

An important source of diversity in a country with considerable immigration is the individual experience leading to the decision to immigrate, the journey itself, and the resettlement period (Clark et al., 2009). The decision to immigrate may involve social, religious, or political persecution, and it increasingly involves a search for economic gain. Or, as in Phuong Le's case, it may involve war and a dangerous political environment. The transit experience is sometimes traumatic, as was the case for Phoung Le and her relatives, who were attacked by pirates and separated, never to see some family members again. The resettlement experience requires establishment of new social networks, may involve changes in socioeconomic status, and presents serious demands for acculturating to a new physical and social environment. Phoung Le and her family were lucky to be able to settle into a large community of Vietnamese immigrants, a situation which eased the process of acculturation. Gender, race, social class, and age all add layers of complexity to the migration experience. Family roles often have to be renegotiated as children outstrip older family members in learning the new language. Tensions can also develop over conflicting approaches to the acculturation process (Falicov, 2011). Just as they should investigate their clients' educational trajectories, work trajectories, and family trajectories, social workers should be interested in the migration trajectories of their immigrant clients.

It seems, in any case, that Elder's four themes of the life course perspective can be used to more completely recognize diversity in its many forms:

1. *Interplay of human lives and historical time.* Cohorts tend to have different life trajectories because of the unique historical events each cohort encounters. Phoung Le recognizes that life in the United States is very different for her children than for her older relatives. But the same birth cohort in different parts of the world face very different historical events. For example, the post–World War II era was very different for young adults in Japan than it was in the United States (Newman, 2008). And the children of Syria in 2014 face very different historical events from the children in Australia.

2. *Timing of lives.* Age norms change with time, place, and culture. The life course perspective, developed in late industrial affluent countries, has paid little attention to such age norms as childhood marriage in Bangladesh, but it can be extended to accommodate a more global perspective (Chowdhury, 2004). Age norms also vary by social location or place in the social structure of a given

society, most notably by gender, race, ethnicity, level of education, geographical location, and social class (Scherger, 2009). These variables create differences from one cohort to another as well as differences among the individuals within a cohort.

3. *Linked or independent lives.* The differing patterns of social networks in which persons are embedded produce differences in life course experiences. Likewise, the different locations in the global economy produce very different life course trajectories. The intersection of multiple trajectories—for example, the family lifeline, the educational lifeline, and the work lifeline—introduces new possibilities for diversity in life course patterns. With the help of extended family, Phoung Le and her husband were able to synchronize their family lifelines and work lifelines.

4. *Human agency in making choices.* Human agency, particularly personal agency, allows for extensive individual differences in life course trajectories as individuals plan and make choices between options. It is not surprising, given these possibilities for unique experience, that the stories of individuals vary so much. It is also important to remember that proxy agency and collective agency can produce both individual and group-based differences in life course trajectories.

Developmental Risk and Protection

As the life course perspective has continued to evolve, it has more clearly emphasized the links between the life events and transitions of childhood, adolescence, and adulthood (Gilman, 2012; O'Rand, 2009). Studies indicate that childhood events sometimes shape people's lives 40 or more years later (Ferraro & Shippee, 2009). Indeed, recent biomedical research has suggested we should look at factors that occur earlier than childhood, focusing on fetal undernutrition as a contributing factor in late-life cognition and late-life health conditions such as coronary heart disease, type 2 diabetes, and hypertension (see Rooij, Wouters, Yonker, Painter, & Roseboom, 2010; Joss-Moore & Lane, 2009).

It is quite an old idea that what happens at one point in the life journey influences what happens at later points. No doubt, you have heard some version of this idea for most of your life. However, the idea of earlier life experience affecting later development has taken on new energy since the explosion of longitudinal research a few decades ago (Elder & Giele, 2009). In longitudinal research, the researchers follow a group of people over a period of time, rather than comparing different groups at one point in time. This allows them to study individual lives over time, noting the factors that influence individual life trajectories.

Two different research traditions have examined how early life experiences affect later outcomes, one based in sociology and the other based in ecological developmental psychology. The sociological tradition is interested in cumulative advantage/cumulative disadvantage (see Dannefer, 2003c). The ecological developmental tradition is interested in risk, protection, and resilience. As you can see, we are borrowing language from the ecological developmental tradition. For a long time, there was little cross-flow of ideas between these two disciplinary traditions, but recently, there has been some attempt to integrate them.

Let's look first at research that focuses on **cumulative advantage/cumulative disadvantage**. Life course scholars have borrowed these concepts from sociologist Robert Merton to explain inequality within cohorts across the life course (Ferraro & Shippee, 2009). Merton (1968) found that in scientific careers, large inequalities in productivity and recognition had accumulated. Scholarly productivity brings recognition, and recognition brings resources for further productivity, which of course brings further recognition and so on. Merton proposed that, in this way, scientists who are productive early in their careers accumulate advantage over time whereas other scientists accumulate disadvantage. Sociologists propose that cumulative advantage and cumulative disadvantage are socially constructed; social institutions and societal structures develop mechanisms that ensure increasing advantage for those who succeed early in life and increasing disadvantage for those who

struggle (Ferraro & Shippee, 2009). Researchers have applied the concepts of cumulative advantage/cumulative disadvantage to study racial health disparities across the life trajectory (see Shuey & Willson, 2008).

Consider the effect of advantages in schooling. Young children with affluent parents attend enriched early childhood programs and well-resourced primary and secondary schools, which position them for successful college careers, which position them for occupations that pay well, which provide opportunities for good health maintenance, which position them for healthy, secure old age. This trajectory of unearned advantage is sometimes referred to as **privilege** (McIntosh, 1988). Children who do not come from affluent families are more likely to attend underequipped schools, experience school failure or dropout, begin work in low-paying sectors of the labor market, experience unemployment, and arrive at old age with compromised health and limited economic resources. **Oppression** is the intentional or unintentional act or process of placing restrictions on an individual, group, or institution; it may include observable actions but more typically refers to complex, covert, interconnected processes and practices (such as discriminating, devaluing, and exploiting a group of individuals) reflected in a perpetuating exclusion and inequalities over time.

Now let's look at the other research tradition. Longitudinal research has also led researchers across several disciplines to study human lives through the lens of ecological developmental risk protection. They have attempted, with much success, to identify multidimensional **risk factors**, or factors at one stage of development that increase the probability of developing and maintaining problem conditions at later stages. They have also been interested in individuals who have adapted successfully in the face of risk and have identified **protective factors**, or factors (resources) that decrease the probability of developing and maintaining problem conditions (Hutchison, Matto, Harrigan, Charlesworth, & Viggiani, 2007; Jenson & Fraser, 2011).

Recently, gerontologists in the life course tradition have tried to integrate the cumulative advantage/disadvantage and the ecological developmental risk and protection streams of inquiry. Kenneth Ferraro and Tetyana Shippee (2009) present a cumulative inequality (CI) theory. They propose that advantage and disadvantage are created across multiple levels of systems, an idea similar to the multidimensional aspect of the ecological risk and protection approach. They also propose that "disadvantage increases exposure to risk but advantage increases exposure to opportunity" (p. 335). They further submit that "life course trajectories are shaped by the accumulation of risk, available resources, and human agency" (p. 335).

It is important to note that neither cumulative advantage/disadvantage theory nor the ecological developmental risk and protection approach argue that early deprivations and traumas inevitably lead to a trajectory of failure. Research on cumulative advantage/disadvantage is finding that cumulative processes are reversible under some conditions, particularly when human agency is exercised, resources are mobilized, and environmental conditions open opportunities (Ferraro & Shippee, 2009; O'Rand, 2009). For example, it has been found that when resources are mobilized to create governmental safety nets for vulnerable families at key life transitions, the effects of deprivation and trauma on health are reduced (Gilman, 2012).

In the ecological developmental risk and protection stream of inquiry, protective factors provide the antidote to risk factors and minimize the inevitability of a trajectory of failure. Researchers in this tradition have begun to recognize the power of humans to use protective factors to assist in a self-righting process over the life course to fare well in the face of adversity, a process known as **resilience** (Jenson & Fraser, 2011). For example, researchers have found that disadvantaged children who participated in an enriched preschool program had higher levels of education, employment, and earnings and lower levels of crime in adulthood than a control group of similar children who did not participate in the program (Heckman, Moon, Pinto, Savelyev, & Yavitz, 2010). Werner and Smith (2001) found that a relationship with one supportive adult can be a strong protective factor across

the life course for children with an accumulation of risk factors.

The life course perspective and the concept of cumulative disadvantage are beginning to influence community epidemiology, which studies the prevalence of disease across communities (e.g., Dupre, 2008; Mishra, Cooper, & Kuh, 2010). Researchers in this tradition are interested in social and geographical inequalities in the distribution of chronic disease. They suggest that risk for chronic disease gradually accumulates over a life course through episodes of illness, exposure to unfavorable environments, and unsafe behaviors, which they refer to as a *chain-of-risk model*. They are also interested in how some experiences in the life course can break the chain of risk. Exhibit 1.7 shows how phases of life are interwoven with various risks and protective factors.

STRENGTHS AND LIMITATIONS OF THE LIFE COURSE PERSPECTIVE

As a framework for thinking about the aspect of time in human behavior, the life course perspective has several advantages over traditional theories of human development. It encourages greater attention to the impact of historical and sociocultural change on human behavior, which seems particularly important in rapidly changing

Exhibit 1.7 Risk and Protective Factors for Specific Life Course Phases

Life Course Phase	Risk Factors	Protective Factors
Infancy	Poverty	Active, alert, high vigor
	Child abuse/neglect	Sociability
	Parental mental illness	Small family size
	Teenage motherhood	
Infancy–childhood	Poverty	"Easy," engaging temperament
	Child abuse/neglect	
	Divorce	
	Parental substance abuse	
Infancy–adolescence	Poverty	Maternal competence
	Child abuse/neglect	Close bond with primary caregiver (not necessarily biological parent)
	Parental mental illness	Supportive grandparents
	Parental substance abuse	
	Teenage motherhood	
	Divorce	
Infancy–adulthood	Poverty	Low distress/low emotionality
	Child abuse/neglect	Mother's education
	Teenage motherhood	
Early childhood	Poverty	Advanced self-help skills
Preschool–adulthood	Poverty	Supportive teachers
	Parental mental illness	Successful school experiences
	Parental substance abuse	
	Divorce	
Childhood–adolescence	Poverty	Strong achievement motivation
	Child abuse/neglect	Special talents, hobbies
	Parental mental illness	Positive self-concept

Life Course Phase	Risk Factors	Protective Factors
	Parental substance abuse	For girls: emphasis on autonomy with emotional support from primary caregiver
	Divorce	For boys: structure and rules in household
	Teenage parenthood	For both boys and girls: assigned chores
		Close, competent peer friends who are confidants
Childhood–adulthood	Poverty	Average/above-average intelligence
	Child abuse/neglect	Ability to distance oneself
	Parental mental illness	Impulse control
	Parental substance abuse	Strong religious faith
	Divorce	Supportive siblings
	Teenage parenthood	Mentors
Adolescence–adulthood	Poverty	Planning, foresight

global societies. Its emphasis on linked lives shines a spotlight on intergenerational relationships and the interdependence of lives. At the same time, with its attention to human agency, the life course perspective is not as deterministic as some earlier theories and acknowledges people's strengths and capacity for change. Life course researchers are also finding strong evidence for the malleability of risk factors and the possibilities for preventive interventions. With attention to the diversity in life course trajectories, the life course perspective provides a good conceptual framework for culturally sensitive practice. And finally, the life course perspective lends itself well to research that looks at cumulative advantage and cumulative disadvantage, adding to our knowledge about the impact of power and privilege and subsequently suggesting strategies for social justice.

To answer questions about how people change and how they stay the same across a life course is no simple task, however. Take, for example, the question of whether there is an increased sense of generativity, or concern for others, in middle adulthood. Should the researcher study different groups of people at different ages (perhaps a group of 20-year-olds, a group of 30-year-olds, a group of 40-year-olds, a group of 50-year-olds, and a group of 60-year-olds) and compare their responses, in what is known as a cross-sectional design? Or should the researcher study the same people over time (perhaps at 10-year intervals from age 20 to age 60) and observe whether their responses stay the same or change over time, in what is known as a longitudinal design? I hope you are already raising this question: What happens to the cohort effect in a cross-sectional study? This question is, indeed, always a problem with studying change over time with a cross-sectional design. Suppose we find that 50-year-olds report a greater sense of generativity than those in younger age groups. Can we then say that generativity does, indeed, increase in middle adulthood? Or do we have to wonder if there was something in the social and historical contexts of this particular cohort of 50-year-olds that encouraged a greater sense of generativity? Because of the possibility of cohort effects, it is important to know whether research was based on a cross-sectional or longitudinal design.

Although attention to diversity may be the greatest strength of the life course perspective, heterogeneity may be its biggest challenge. I am using diversity to refer to group-based differences and heterogeneity to refer to individual differences. The life course perspective, like other behavioral science perspectives, searches for patterns of human behavior. But the current level of heterogeneity in countries such as the United States limits our capacity to discern patterns. Along with trying to understand patterns, social workers must try to understand the unique circumstances of every case situation. Another challenge related to diversity—perhaps a larger challenge—is that most of the research of the life course perspective has been done with samples from wealthy advanced industrial societies. This is true of all existing social and behavioral science research. I would suggest, however, that there is nothing inherent in either the basic conceptions or the major themes of the life course perspective that make it inappropriate for use to understand human behavior at a global level. This is particularly true if human agency is understood to include proxy agency and collective agency, conjoint as well as disjoint agency.

Another possible limitation of the life course perspective is a failure to adequately link the micro world of individual and family lives to the macro world of social institutions and formal organizations. Social and behavioral sciences have, historically, divided the social world up into micro and macro and studied them in isolation. The life course perspective was developed by scholars like Glen Elder Jr. and Tamara Hareven, who were trying to bring those worlds together. Sometimes, however, this effort is more successful than at other times, and this remains a challenge for the future.

INTEGRATION WITH A MULTIDIMENSIONAL, MULTITHEORETICAL APPROACH

A companion volume to this book, *Dimensions of Human Behavior: Person and Environment*, recommends a multidimensional, multitheoretical approach for understanding human behavior. This recommendation is completely compatible with the life course perspective presented in this volume. The life course perspective clearly recognizes the biological and psychological dimensions of the person and can accommodate the spiritual dimension. The life course emphasis on linked or interdependent lives is consistent with the idea of the unity of person and environment presented in *Dimensions of Human Behavior: Person and Environment*. It can also easily accommodate the multidimensional environment (physical environment, culture, social institutions and social structure, families, small groups, formal organizations, communities, and social movements) discussed in the companion volume.

Likewise, the life course perspective is consistent with the multitheoretical approach presented in *Person and Environment*. The life course perspective has been developed by scholars across several disciplines, and they have increasingly engaged in cross-fertilization of ideas from a variety of theoretical perspectives. Because the life course can be approached from the perspective of the individual or from the perspective of the family or other collectivities, or seen as a property of cultures and social institutions that shape the pattern of individual lives, it builds on both psychological and sociological theories. Exhibit 1.8 demonstrates the overlap between the life course perspective and the eight theoretical perspectives presented in Chapter 2 of *Dimensions of Human Behavior: Person and Environment*.

Critical Thinking Questions 1.5

Which concepts and themes of the life course perspective seem most useful to you? Explain. Which, if any, concepts and themes would you want to argue with? Explain.

Exhibit 1.8 Overlap of the Life Course Perspective and Eight Theoretical Perspectives on Human Behavior

Theoretical Perspective	Life Course Themes and Concepts
Systems perspective: Human behavior is the outcome of reciprocal interactions of persons operating within linked social systems.	*Themes:* Timing of lives; linked or interdependent lives *Concepts:* Biological age, psychological age, social age, spiritual age
Conflict perspective: Human behavior is driven by conflict, dominance, and oppression in social life.	*Theme:* Developmental risk and protection *Concepts:* Cumulative advantage; cumulative disadvantage
Exchange and choice perspective: Human behavior is based on individual and collective actors seeking and exchanging resources and the choices made in pursuit of those resources.	*Theme:* Human agency in making choices *Concepts:* Choices; opportunities; constraints
Social constructionist perspective: Social reality is created when actors, in social interaction, develop a common understanding of their world.	*Themes:* Timing of lives; diversity in life course trajectories; developmental risk and protection *Concepts:* Making meaning of life events; social age; age norms; age structuring; acculturation; cumulative advantage and disadvantage
Psychodynamic perspective: Internal processes such as needs, drives, and emotions motivate human behavior; early childhood experiences are central to problems of living throughout life.	*Themes:* Timing of lives; developmental risk and protection *Concepts:* Psychological age; capacities; skills
Developmental perspective: Human behavior both changes and stays the same across the life span.	*Themes:* Interplay of human lives and historical time; timing of lives; developmental risk and protection *Concepts:* Life transitions; biological age, psychological age, social age, spiritual age; sequencing
Social behavioral perspective: Human behavior is learned when individuals interact with the environment; human behavior is influenced by personal expectations and meanings.	*Themes:* Interplay of human lives and historical time; human agency in making choices; diversity in life course trajectories; developmental risk and protection *Concepts:* Life events; human agency
Humanistic perspective: Human behavior can be understood only from the internal frame of reference of the individual; human behavior is driven by a desire for growth and competence.	*Themes:* Timing of lives; human agency in making choices *Concepts:* Spiritual age; meaning of life events and turning points; individual, family, and community strengths

Implications for Social Work Practice

The life course perspective has many implications for social work practice, including the following:

- Help clients make sense of their unique life's journeys so they can use that understanding to improve their current situations. Where appropriate, help them to construct a lifeline of interlocking trajectories.
- Try to understand the historical contexts of clients' lives and the ways that important historical events have influenced their behavior.
- Where appropriate, use life event inventories to get a sense of the level of stress in a client's life.
- Be aware of the potential to develop social work interventions that can serve as turning points that help individuals, families, small groups, communities, and organizations get back on track.
- Work with the media to keep the public informed about the impact of changing social conditions on individuals, families, communities, and formal organizations.
- Recognize the ways that the lives of family members are linked across generations and the impact of circumstances in one generation on other generations.
- Recognize the ways lives are linked in the global economy.
- Use existing research on risk, protection, and resilience to develop prevention programs.
- When working with recent immigrant and refugee families, be aware of the age norms in their countries of origin.
- Be aware of the unique systems of support developed by members of various cultural groups and encourage the use of those supports in times of crisis.
- Support and help to develop clients' sense of personal competence for making life choices.

Key Terms

age norm	intersectionality theory	risk factors
age structuring	life course perspective	sex ratio
biological age	life event	social age
cohort	oppression	social support
cohort effects	population pyramid	spiritual age
cumulative advantage	privilege	trajectories
cumulative disadvantage	protective factors	transitions
event history	psychological age	turning point
human agency	resilience	

Active Learning

1. Prepare your own lifeline of interlocking trajectories (see Exhibit 1.4 for instructions). What patterns do you see? What shifts? How important are the different sectors of your life—for example, family, education, work, health?

2. One research team found that 99% of young adult respondents to a survey on turning points reported that there had been turning points in their lives. Interview five adults and ask whether there have been turning points in their lives. If they answer no, ask about whether they see their life as a straight path or a path with twists and

turns. If they answer yes, ask about the nature of the turning point(s). Compare the events of your interviewees as well as the events in the lives of David Sanchez, Phoung Le, and Emma Suarez, with Rutter's three types of life events that can serve as turning points and Hareven's five conditions under which a transition can become a turning point.

3. Think of someone whom you think of as resilient, someone who has been successful against the odds. This may be you, a friend, a coworker, a family member, or a character from a book or movie. If the person is someone you know and to whom you have access, ask them to what they owe their success. If it is you or someone to whom you do not have access, speculate about the reasons for the success. How do their life journeys compare with the common risk and protective factors summarized in Exhibit 1.7?

Web Resources

No doubt you use the Internet in many different ways and know your way around it. I hope that when you find something in this book that confuses you or intrigues you, you will use the incredibly rich resources of the Internet to do further exploration. To help you get started with this process, each chapter of this textbook contains a list of Internet resources and websites that may be useful in your search for further information. Each site listing includes the address and a brief description of the contents of the site. Readers should be aware that the information contained in websites may not be truthful or reliable and should be confirmed before being used as a reference. Readers should also be aware that Internet addresses, or URLs, are constantly changing; therefore, the addresses listed may no longer be active or accurate. Many of the Internet sites listed in each chapter contain links to other Internet sites containing more information on the topic. Readers may use these links for further investigation.

Information not included in the Web Resources sections of each chapter can be found by using one of the many Internet search engines provided free of charge on the Internet. These search engines enable you to search using keywords or phrases, or you can use the search engines' topical listings. You should use several search engines when researching a topic, as each will retrieve different Internet sites.

Aol Search: http://search.aol.com

Ask: www.ask.com

bing: www.bing.com

Google: www.google.com

YAHOO!: http://search.yahoo.com

A number of Internet sites provide information on theory, research, and statistics on the life course:

Bronfenbrenner Center for Translational Research (BCTR): www.bctr.cornell.edu

Site presented by the Bronfenbrenner Center for Translational Research at Cornell University contains information on the center, publications, and news and resources.

Lifecourse Institute: www.nuigalway.ie/lifecourse

Site presented by the Lifecourse Institute at the National University of Ireland, Galway, home of three research centers, including the Centre for Disability Law & Policy, UNESCO Child and Family Research Centre, and the Irish Centre for Social Gerontology contains information about the life course and critical and working papers.

Maternal and Child Health Life Course Resource Guide: http://mchb.hrsa.gov/lifecourse

Site maintained by Maternal and Child Health of the Health Resources and Services Administration contains information on the life course approach to conceptualizing health care needs and services and a bibliography.

Michigan Study of Adolescent and Adult Life Transitions (MSALT): www.rcgd.isr.umich.edu/msalt/home.htm

Site presented by the Michigan Study of Adolescent and Adult Life Transitions project contains information about the longitudinal study begun in 1983, publications on the project, and family-oriented web resources.

Project Resilience: www.projectresilience.com

Site presented by Project Resilience, a private organization based in Washington, DC, contains information on teaching materials, products, and

training for professionals working in education, treatment, and prevention.

Twin Study at University of Helsinki: www .twinstudy.helsinki.fi

Site presented by the Department of Public Health at the University of Helsinki contains information on an ongoing project begun in 1974 to study environmental and genetic factors in selected chronic diseases with links to other related resources.

U.S. Census Bureau: www.census.gov

Site presented by the U.S. Census Bureau provides current and historical population data related to diversity and the life course.

Student Study Site

ⓈSAGE edge™

Sharpen your skills with SAGE edge at **edge.sagepub.com/hutchisonclc5e**

SAGE edge for students provides a personalized approach to help you accomplish your coursework goals in an easy-to-use learning environment.

CHAPTER 2

Conception, Pregnancy, and Childbirth

Marcia P. Harrigan and Suzanne M. Baldwin

Chapter Outline

Opening Questions

- What biological, psychological, social, and spiritual factors influence the beginning of the life course?

- What recent technological advances related to conception, pregnancy, and childbirth are important to social work intervention?

- What unique knowledge do social workers bring to multidisciplinary teams working with issues of conception, pregnancy, and childbirth?

Key Ideas

As you read this chapter, take note of these central ideas:

1. Conception, pregnancy, and childbirth should be viewed as normative life transitions that require family or family-like supportive relationships to maximize favorable outcomes.

2. Conception, pregnancy, and childbirth are influenced by changing family structures, gender roles, technological developments, and cultural expectations.

3. Almost all physical traits and many behavioral traits are influenced by the combined genes from the ovum and sperm that are joined at the time of conception. Few, but some, physical traits are impacted by the environment.

4. Women and men around the world attempt to gain control over conception and pregnancy; contraception and abortion have been means to gain control across time and place, and effective solutions for infertility are more recent.

5. The gestation period, during which the fertilized ovum becomes a fully developed infant, is typically divided into three trimesters of about 3 months each.

6. Newborns born prematurely, of low birth weight, or with congenital anomalies carry developmental risks across the life course.

7. Social workers need to recognize the special challenges in relation to conception, pregnancy, and childbirth faced by some special parent populations, including gay and lesbian parents, substance-abusing pregnant women, pregnant women with eating disorders, pregnant women with disabilities, incarcerated pregnant women, and HIV-infected pregnant women.

CASE STUDY 2.1

Jennifer Bradshaw's Experience With Infertility

Jennifer Bradshaw always knew that she would be a mom. She remembers being a little girl and wrapping up her favorite doll in her baby blanket. She would rock the doll and dream about the day when she would have a real baby of her own. Now, at 36, the dream of having her own baby is still just a dream as she struggles with infertility.

Like many women in her age group, Jennifer spent her late teens and 20s trying not to get pregnant. She focused on education, finding the right relationship, finances, and a career. As an African American woman, and the first person in her family to earn an MSW, she wanted to prove that she could be a successful clinical social worker. She thought that when she wanted to get pregnant, it would just happen; that it would be as easy as scheduling anything else on her calendar. When the time finally was right and she and her husband, Allan, decided to get pregnant, they couldn't.

With every passing month and every negative pregnancy test, Jennifer's frustration grew. First, she was frustrated with herself and had thoughts like, "What is wrong with me?" "Why is this happening to us?" and "We don't deserve this." She would look around and see pregnant teens and think, "Why them and not me?" She also was frustrated with her husband for not understanding how devastating this was to her and wondered to herself, "Could it be him with the problem?" In addition, she was frustrated with her family and friends and started avoiding them to escape their comments and the next baby shower. Now, she is baby-less and lonely. It has also been hard for Allan. For many men, masculinity is connected to virility; Allan would not even consider that he might be the one with the fertility problem, even though it is a male-factor issue in about 50% of infertility cases.

After months of struggling to get pregnant, multiple visits to the obstetrician/gynecologist, a laparoscopic surgery, a semen analysis, and timed intercourse (which began to feel like a chore), and after taking Clomid, a fertility drug that made her feel horrible, she and Allan finally accepted that they might need to see a specialist. She will never forget the first visit with the reproductive endocrinologist (RE). She was expecting a "quick fix," thinking that the RE would give her some special pills and then she would get pregnant. But, instead, he casually said to her, "I think your only option is in vitro fertilization [IVF], which runs about $16,000 per cycle, including medications." The RE also told her that for someone in her age range the success rate would be about 35% to 40%.

From her clinical practice and her friendship circle, Jennifer knows that many women think of in vitro as being a backup plan when they delay pregnancy. But she is learning that in vitro is a big deal. First, it is expensive. The $16,000 per cycle does not include the preliminary diagnostic testing, and in Jennifer's age group, the majority of women pursuing IVF will need at least two IVF cycles, $32,000 for two tries; three tries brings the bill up to $48,000. Jennifer has heard of couples spending close to $100,000 for infertility treatments.

Although about 15 states mandate insurance companies to cover fertility treatments, in the state where Jennifer lives, there is no fertility coverage mandate; consequently, her insurance company does not cover any infertility treatments. So at the very least, Jennifer and Allan would need to come up with $16,000 to give one IVF cycle a try. It's heartbreaking for them because they don't have $16,000, and their parents can't help them out. So to give IVF even one try, they need to borrow the money. They are considering taking out a home equity loan to pay for the needed IVF cycles and know that they are lucky to be in a position to do that. They have heard of people packing up and moving to states with mandated fertility coverage and/or quitting their jobs and finding jobs that carry specific insurance that will cover fertility treatments. Some couples are even traveling abroad for fertility treatments that can be had for much less than in the United States.

Jennifer has heard that IVF is physically and emotionally exhausting. First the in vitro patient is forced into menopause, and then the ovaries are hyperstimulated to release numerous eggs (up to 15 to 17 instead of 1), which can be painful. The eggs are surgically extracted, and finally the fertilized embryos are introduced to the IVF patient's body. Throughout this process, various hormone treatments are given via daily injections, multiple blood tests are taken, and at any point during the procedure something could go wrong and the IVF cycle could be called off. If all goes well, the IVF patient is left to keep her fingers crossed for the next 2 weeks waiting for a positive pregnancy test. If the test is negative, the treatment starts over again. Jennifer has heard that most women are an emotional wreck during the entire process because of the high stakes and the artificial hormones.

(Continued)

(Continued)

Jennifer and Allan decided to go the IVF route 7 months after visiting the R.E. Before they made this decision, however, Jennifer carefully tracked her BBT (basal body temperature), purchased a high-tech electronic fertility monitor, used an ovulation microscope, took multiple fertility supplements, and used sperm-friendly lubricant during intercourse. Still nothing helped. When she heard that acupuncture has been found to increase the success rate of IVF, she started seeing a fertility acupuncturist on a weekly basis for both herbal formulas and acupuncture treatments. The acupuncture treatments and herbs are averaging about $100 per week, also not covered by insurance in her state.

Jennifer and Allan have decided to give IVF three tries, and after that they will move on to the next plan, adoption. They adore each other and want more than anything to have their own little one, but if they cannot have that, they will adopt, and Jennifer will realize her dream of being a mom.

—Nicole Footen Bromfield

CASE STUDY 2.2

The Thompsons' Premature Birth

Within days of discovering she was pregnant, Felicia Thompson's husband, Will, suddenly deployed to a combat zone. Through e-mails, occasional cellular phone calls, and Skype, Felicia told Will details about the changes she experienced with the pregnancy, but his world was filled with smoke, dirt, bombs, and danger, punctuated with periods of boredom. Six months into the pregnancy, Felicia's changing figure was eliciting comments from her co-workers in the office where she worked part time as an office administrator. With weeks of nausea and fatigue behind her, she was experiencing a general sense of well-being. She avoided all news media as well as "war talk" at the office to protect herself from worry and anxiety. Yet, even the sound of an unexpected car pulling up to the front of her home produced chills of panic. Was this the time when the officers would come to tell her that Will had been killed or wounded in combat? Her best friend only recently had experienced what every military wife fears may happen.

Then, with dawn hours away, Felicia woke to cramping and blood. With 14 more weeks before her delivery date, Felicia was seized with fear. Wishing that Will were there, Felicia fervently prayed for herself and her fetus. The ambulance ride to the hospital became a blur of pain mixed with feelings of unreality. When she arrived in the labor and delivery suite, masked individuals in scrubs took control of her body while demanding answers to a seemingly endless number of questions. Felicia knew everything would be fine if only she could feel her son kick. Why didn't he kick? The pediatrician spoke of the risks of early delivery, and suddenly the doctors were telling her to push her son into the world.

In the newborn intensive care unit (NICU), a flurry of activity revolved around baby boy Thompson. Born weighing only 1 pound 3 ounces, this tiny red baby's immature systems were unprepared for the demands of the extrauterine world. He was immediately connected to a ventilator, intravenous lines were placed in his umbilicus and arm, and monitor leads were placed on all available surfaces. Nameless to his caregivers, the baby, whom his parents had already named Paul, was now the recipient of some of the most advanced technological interventions available in modern medicine. About an hour after giving birth, Felicia saw Paul for the first time. Lying on a stretcher, she tried to find resemblance to Will, who is of Anglo heritage, or herself, a light-skinned Latina, in this tiny form. Felicia's breathing synchronized to Paul's as she willed him to keep fighting.

Later, alone in her room, she was flooded with fear, grief, and guilt. What had she done wrong? Could Paul's premature birth have been caused by paint fumes from decorating his room? From her anxiety and worry about Will?

The Red Cross sent the standard message to Will. Was he in the field? Was he at headquarters? It mattered because Paul may not even be alive by the time Will found out he was born. How would he receive the news? Who would be nearby to comfort him? Would the command allow him to come home on emergency leave? If he were granted permission for emergency leave, it could be days of arduous travel, waiting for space on any military plane, before he landed somewhere in the United States. Felicia knew that Will would be given priority on any plane available; even admirals and generals step aside for men and women returning home to meet a family crisis. But, then again, the command may consider his mission so essential that only official notification of Paul's death would allow him to return home.

Thirteen days after his arrival, Paul took his first breath by himself. His hoarse, faint cry provoked both ecstasy and terror in his mother. A few days earlier Felicia had been notified by the Red Cross that her husband was on his way home, but information was not available regarding his arrival date. Now that her baby was off the ventilator, she watched Paul periodically miss a breath, which would lead to a decreased heart rate followed by monitors flashing and beeping. She longed for Will's physical presence and support.

Will arrived home 2 days later. He walked into the NICU having spent the last 72 hours flying. He started the trip being delivered to the airport in an armed convoy and landed stateside to find the world seemingly unchanged from his departure months before. Although Paul would spend the next 10 weeks in the hospital, Will had 14 days before starting the journey back to his job.

Paul's struggle to survive was the most exhilarating yet terrifying roller-coaster ride of his parents' lives. Shattered hopes were mended, only to be reshattered with the next telephone call from the NICU. Now Felicia dreaded the phone as well as the sound of an unfamiliar car. For Felicia, each visit to Paul was followed by the long trip home to the empty nursery. For Will, stationed thousands of miles away, there was uncertainty, guilt, helplessness, and sometimes an overwhelming sense of inadequacy. Felicia feared the arrival of a car with officers in it, and Will dreaded a Red Cross message that his son had died.

Great joy and equally intense anxiety pervaded Paul's homecoming day. After spending 53 days in the NICU and still weighing only 4 pounds, 13 ounces, Paul was handed to his mother. She made sure that a video was made so that Will could share in this moment. With more questions than answers about her son's future and her ability to take care of him, Felicia took their baby to his new home.

For the NICU social worker at the military hospital, the major goal is to support the family as they face this challenging transition to parenthood. In the past 53 days, the social worker has helped Felicia answer her questions, understand the unfamiliar medical language of the health care providers, and understand and cope with the strong emotions she is experiencing. The social worker also helped during the transition of Will's arrival from war and his departure back to war. Understanding the dynamics of the NICU, families in crisis, and the needs of the military family separated by an international conflict is critical to providing this family the level of support they need to manage their multifaceted role transitions.

Hazel Gereke's and Cecelia Kin's Experiences With the Options

Forty years ago, at age 44, Hazel Gereke gave birth to her fifth child, Terry. At the time of his birth, Terry's siblings ranged in age from 2 to 25, and his father was 48. Terry's mother tells the following story.

I menstruated regularly when I carried Terry and had long, heavy bleeding at first. I went to the doctor who said I was four-and-a-half months pregnant! I was too far along to do anything. You see, back then you had to have three doctors go before the hospital board to say the pregnancy jeopardized the mother's health. Well, my doctor was Catholic, so I knew that would not happen. I cried. My husband said, "Hazel, we'll love it!" I did not have an easy pregnancy with poor sleep, pains everywhere, and extended family demands on top of my other four kids.

Terry was hard to bottle feed, but the doctor said he was only a "little slow." After his first birthday, he sat, began to walk, and said "Mama," "Daddy," "bye-bye," and "eat"—about seven to 10 words. He was beginning to dress and potty train. But when he was 15 to 18 months old, he had terrible seizures all summer long. When I enrolled him in school and saw on the record "Down child," I went right away to the doctor, who said the test would cost $75. Well, I said, "There's no need for a test—it won't change what he is." I worried because my son, Mike, was teased by the other kids when the county bus came for Terry—they called it "the dummy bus." I always knew who had compassion, because if they did, Terry stayed around. Otherwise, he went to his room.

When asked if she thinks anything should have happened differently over the years, Hazel reluctantly but honestly replies that "the pregnancy should have been stopped." Then asked "What has Terry contributed to your family?" she replies, "He has kept the family together and taught us not to take things for granted."

Hazel Gereke has reminded us about the ambivalences and ambiguities that social workers need to keep in mind when working with pregnancy issues or at various points of decision making across the life course. Let's hear from another woman, Cecelia Kin, who faces the same genetic challenge 40 years later. Here are selected notes from her journal written during her pregnancy.

June 9th: Maybe we just were not meant to have another baby!!! WHAT we have been through is all too amazing: three miscarriages before we had our darling 18-month-old Meridy, plus two more miscarriages since then. Well, at least I know I can get pregnant and we did have a healthy kid so why not again?

August 20th: YEH! This pregnancy is going soooo well: 10 weeks along ALREADY! I am tired, but I've thrown up only once and feel sooo much different from the pregnancies I lost!!! Looking back, I knew that each one was not right!!! I felt AWFUL ALL the time!!! But not this time!!! What a relief!!! Or is it a reward?

September 1st: It's been more than a week since I wrote!!! Today we went for the ultrasound, both of us thinking it would be so perfect. It wasn't. How could this happen to us? What have we done or not done? Haven't I done everything I could possibly do? I eat right, steered clear of drugs and hate any kind of alcohol!!! I exercise regularly!!! I am in perfect health!!! Wham! I can't believe what we were told. I can't cry like this any longer. Writing about it may help; it usually does. So, here's how it went. We just sat there staring at each other after hearing: "A 1:25 chance of a baby with Down Syndrome." And they told us, "Don't worry"! You have to be kidding! We both insisted that the next step be done right away!!! so in three (LONG) days, we go back again, this time for something called chorionic villus testing!!! never heard of it.

September 16th: I can't believe this is happening; I feel so angry, so out of control. Then I think of Meridy and that we should just be thankful we have her and believe that our lives can be full, totally complete with just one kid. But, this is not what we want! How can I hold it all together? I don't want to cry all the time, especially at work!!! I feel like such a wuss!!! and, I can't really tell anyone, just my husband!!! Worse yet, I don't think that we agree that we will terminate the pregnancy. I feel so guilty, so alone, so empty. How can HE say, "Oh, we can handle that"? I'M the one who arranges child care, I'M the one who stays home if Meridy is sick, takes her to the doctor, buys her clothes, her food. He comes home to dinner and a smiling kid racing to jump in his arms. What would a child with Down Syndrome be like? I can't bear to think of standing there holding this child while HE plays with Meridy. Bills!!! I haven't even thought about that! Our life is great now but I work to provide extras!!! I love my job. I love my kid. I love my husband. I HATE what is happening. If I don't work, our lives are drastically changed!!! Not an option: I carry the health insurance; he is self-employed. Perhaps this is all a mistake, !!! you know, one of those "false positives" where I will get a call that all is just fine or they reported someone else's test!!! Right! Wishful thinking !!! Who could begin to understand where I AM COMING FROM? I know my family!!! they would never "get it"; I would be SOOOO judged if the word "abort" passed my lips!!! even by my mom, and we are soooo close!!! but not on this!!! and, in this small, small town EVEERYONE would know what I DID!!! Who can possibly help me—help us—with this mess?

Over the last 40 years, many things have changed: new technologies as well as changes in family norms and the decisions faced by those becoming parents. With new technologies, parents are faced with new, but still very difficult, decisions.

SOCIOCULTURAL ORGANIZATION OF CHILDBEARING

These four stories tell us that conception, pregnancy, and childbirth are experienced in different ways by different people. The biological processes vary little for the vast majority of women and their families, but researchers continue to study the psychological, social, and spiritual dimensions of childbearing. This chapter presents a multidimensional overview of current knowledge about conception, pregnancy, and childbirth gleaned from the literatures of anthropology, genetics, medicine, nursing, psychology, social work, and sociology.

As you read, keep in mind that all elements of childbearing have deep meaning for a society. We can draw on the social constructionist perspective to think about this. This perspective proposes that social reality is created when people, in social interaction, develop shared meaning, a common understanding of their world (you can read more about this in the chapter "Theoretical Perspectives on Human Behavior" in *Dimensions of Human Behavior: Person and Environment*). Meanings about and expectations for human behavior vary across time, place, and culture. Cultural groups develop common understandings about all aspects of procreation: the conditions under which it should happen; whether, and if so how, to control it; proper behavior of the pregnant woman and her family system; and the where and how of childbirth. Pregnancy and childbearing practices are changing with advances in technology and increased diversity in the population of childbearing age. As this is being written, we are in the midst of a major shift in the U.S. health care delivery system through the federal Patient Protection and Affordable Care Act (PPACA), passed by the U.S. Congress in 2010. As the law is implemented,

> In what other ways might culture affect the childbearing experience?

social workers will need to monitor the impact of this shift on the health and well-being of women and their families during the childbearing years.

In the United States, the social meaning of childbearing has changed rather dramatically in several ways over the past several decades (McGoldrick, Carter, & Garcia-Preto, 2011b):

- Various options for controlling reproduction are more available and accessible but oftentimes only to the economically advantaged.
- Over one third of pregnancies worldwide are unplanned, and one fourth are unwanted (Guttmacher Institute, 2013a).
- Childbirth is more commonly delayed, and more people are seeking fertility treatment and remaining involuntarily childless.
- The marriage rate has declined, and more children are born to unmarried mothers.
- The birth rate has declined, resulting in smaller families.
- Teen pregnancy declined over the last decade.
- There are greater variations in family values and sexual mores than in previous generations.
- Parents are less subject to traditional gender-role stereotyping.
- It is becoming much more common for gay and lesbian individuals and couples to become parents.
- Medical advances and cultural globalization are raising new ethical issues (Kristof & WuDunn, 2009).

These trends have prompted considerable debate over how our society should define *family*. The family operates at the intersection of society and the individual. For most people it serves as a safe haven and a cradle of emotional relationships. It is both the stage and partial script for the unfolding of the individual life course.

Family Diversity

We continue to witness what family historians call **family pluralism**, or recognition of many viable types of family structures. Such pluralism is nothing new, but our tolerance for all types of families has grown over the past few decades. The definition of family must reflect this pluralism. Yet unresolved moral, political, and economic issues abound (McGoldrick et al., 2011b). These debates influence research funding as well as family policy in such areas as who can marry, who can adopt, contraception, abortion, infertility treatment, and prenatal care.

Consider your own family beliefs about favorable and unfavorable circumstances of conception, pregnancy, and childbirth. Perhaps these views vary across the generations, but the views, forged by experiences of past generations, can still create an expectation for certain circumstances and behaviors. Consider the decision made by the Gereke family and the long-term impact on everyone in that immediate family. Also, consider Cecelia Kin's dilemma about abortion in light of the views of her parents as well as those of her husband and his family, all of whom live in a rural community. Think about how Jennifer Bradshaw's quest to become pregnant impacts and is impacted by her multigenerational family and that of her husband.

For families separated by major cultural differences and great geographical distances, as is the situation for most immigrant families, the response to multigenerational family expectations, rituals, and themes related to conception, pregnancy, and childbirth may be difficult or problematic. Such experiences pressure families to adapt and change. Still, responses to conception, pregnancy, and childbirth continue to resonate with the themes, myths, legacies, and secrets that bind families across many generations.

Conception and Pregnancy in Context

The three case studies at the beginning of this chapter remind us that the emotional reaction to conception may vary widely. The Thompsons' conception brought joy, in contrast to Jennifer Bradshaw's frustration and lost dreams followed by her rising hopefulness; Mr. Gereke voiced confidence in contrast to his wife's apprehension; Cecelia Kin feels caught between her own values and wishes and those of important people in her life. The conception experience is influenced by expectations the parents learned growing up in their own families of birth as well as by many other factors, including the parents' ages, health, marital status, and social status; cultural expectations; and peer expectations; school or employment circumstances, the social-political-economic context; and prior experiences with conception and childbearing, as well as the interplay of these factors with those of other people significant to the mother and father.

The conception experience may also be influenced by organized religion. The policies of religious groups reflect different views about the purpose of human sexual expression, whether for pleasure, procreation, or perhaps both. Many mainstream religions, in their denominational policy statements, specify acceptable sexual behaviors (Kurtz, 2012). Unwanted conception may be seen as an act of carelessness, promiscuity, or merely God's will—perhaps even punishment for wrongdoing. These beliefs are usually strongly held and have become powerful fodder for numerous social, political, economic, and religious debates related to conception, such as the continued debates about abortion legislation in the United States and around the globe.

Just as the experience of conception has varied over time and across cultures, so has the experience of pregnancy. It too is influenced by religious orientations, social customs, changing values, economics, and even political ideologies. For example, societal expectations of pregnant women in the United States have changed, from simply waiting for birth to actively seeking to maintain the mother's—and hence the baby's—health, preparing for the birth process, and sometimes even trying to influence the baby's cognitive and emotional development while the baby is in the uterus.

Childbirth in Context

Throughout history, families—and particularly women—have passed on to young girls the traditions of childbirth practices. These traditions are increasingly shaped by cultural, institutional, and technological changes. The multiple influences

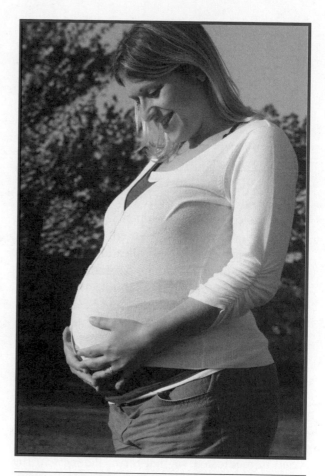

Photo 2.1 Societal views of pregnancy in the United States have changed from simply waiting to being actively involved in nurturing the mother's and baby's health.

© iStockphoto.com

on and changing nature of childbirth practices are exemplified in three related issues: childbirth education, place of childbirth, and who assists childbirth.

Childbirth Education

It is probably accurate to say that education to prepare women for childbirth has been evolving for a very long time, but a formal structure of childbirth education is a relatively new invention. In the United States, the early roots of formal childbirth education were established

> How does childbirth education support human agency in making choices?

during the Progressive Era when the Red Cross set up hygiene and health care classes for women as a public health initiative. In 1912, the U.S. Children's Bureau, created as a new federal agency to inform women about personal hygiene and birth, published a handbook titled *Prenatal Care*, emphasizing the need for medical supervision during pregnancy (Barker, 1998).

Childbirth education, as a formal structure, took hold in the United States and other wealthy countries in the 1960s, fueled by the women's and grassroots consumer movements. Pioneers in the childbirth education movement were reacting against the increasing medicalization of childbirth, and they encouraged women to regain control over the childbirth process. Early childbirth education classes were based on books by Grantly Dick-Read (1944), *Childbirth Without Fear*, and French obstetrician Dr. Fernand Lamaze (1958), *Painless Childbirth*. Lamaze proposed that women could use their intellect to control pain while giving birth if they were informed about their bodies and used relaxation and breathing techniques. Early classes involved small groups meeting outside the hospital during late pregnancy and emphasized unmedicated vaginal birth. Pioneers in the childbirth education movement believed that such childbirth classes would provide the knowledge and skills women needed to change maternity practices, and indeed, the movement had an impact on the development of family-centered maternity practices such as the presence of fathers in labor and delivery and babies rooming in with mothers after birth. Over time, childbirth education became institutionalized and was taught in large classes based in hospitals (Lothian, 2008).

There have been many societal changes in the 50 years since childbirth education was formalized, and in 2007, DeVries and DeVries suggested that childbirth education as it currently exists fits the ethos of the 1960s but is out of step with current societal trends. Here are some examples of how the experience of pregnancy and childbirth has

What historical trends are related to these changes in the view of childbirth?

changed since the early days of the childbirth education movement.

• Pregnant women had few sources of information about pregnancy and birth in the 1960s, but women today are overloaded with information from a number of sources. A 2013 U.S. survey of women's childbearing experiences found that besides maternity care providers and childbirth education classes, women reported getting information from online resources by using a number of different devices, including smartphone and tablet. Two out of three women received weekly educational e-mail messages, and one quarter received regular text messages about pregnancy and childbirth (Declercq, Sakala, Corry, Applebaum, & Herrlich, 2013). Other researchers have found that women rely heavily on the Internet (Lagan, Sinclair, & Kernohan, 2010) and reality television shows with a birth theme (Morris & McInerney, 2010) for this information. Women also make use of a plethora of books on pregnancy-based topics and learn from friends and family. Unfortunately, women may need help in sorting out inaccurate and out-of-date information from any of these sources. One study found that pregnant women sought information more often from commercial Internet sites than from not-for-profit organizational or professional sites, and misinformation may be a problem at some of these sites (Lima-Pereira, Bermudez-Tamayo, & Jasienska, 2012).

• The current generation of pregnant women is more likely than the earlier cohort of pregnant women to be involved in a variety of health promotion activities that will help them manage childbirth. For example, they may be involved in alternative modalities for relaxation and fitness, such as mindfulness meditation, yoga, Pilates, or massage (Fisher, Hauck, Bayes, & Byme, 2012; Morton & Hsu, 2007).

• Pregnant women are much more likely today to be employed today than in the 1960s and 70s. The multisession formats of most models of childbirth education often seem like an extra burden for contemporary pregnant women. One new trend in maternity care is to provide group appointments for prenatal care, incorporating education and group support along with maternity checkups. Research is showing that some women prefer group care and have better pregnancy and birth outcomes when participating in group care (Walker & Worrell, 2008).

- The current cohort of pregnant women are more likely to be unmarried than was true 50 years ago. The emphasis on husband involvement in traditional models of childbirth education may not resonate with many of these women.

- The current population of pregnant women is much more culturally diverse than the White, middle-class women for whom childbirth education was designed. Research indicates that childbirth education classes are still made up largely of White, middle-class women (Lothian, 2008).

- Many new technological and pharmaceutical childbirth interventions have been introduced in the past 15 years, and many contemporary pregnant women prefer high-tech, pain-free, and scheduled (if possible) birth. This is not a good fit with models of childbirth education from the earlier era that discourage medical intervention. There is some evidence, however, that today's women are given little choice in whether to use medical interventions (Declercq et al., 2013).

There have been a number of government initiatives that promote access to childbirth resources, initiated by the Maternity Care Access Act of 1989, which provided support for low-income women (Rabkin, Balassone, & Bell, 1995). Healthy People 2000, 2010 and 2020, an effort by the federal government to enhance the nation's health, supports prenatal education (Healthy People, 2014).

The research is inconclusive about whether childbirth education classes in the traditional model produce better pregnancy and childbirth outcomes (Koehn, 2008; Lothian, 2008), and there are mixed results as to whether the father's role is enhanced through childbirth education (Premberg, 2006; Premberg, Hellström, & Berg, 2008). As childbirth

education branches from the traditional classroom model to home-based services and interactive media presentations, it is important for social workers to help women negotiate the changing landscape to make the choice that fits them the best (Lothian, 2008) while ensuring that the educational needs of women of all racial and ethnic groups, disabilities, and localities are met.

Place of Childbirth

Large changes in the place of childbirth have occurred in many parts of the world in the past century. In 1900, almost all births in the United States as well as other countries occurred outside of hospitals, usually at home (MacDorman, Mathews, & Declercq, 2012). Today, in high- and moderate-income countries, labor wards in hospitals are the usual settings for childbirth (Hodnett, Downe, & Walsh, 2012). In the United States, the percentage of births occurring outside of the hospital dropped to 44% in 1940 and 1% in 1969 (MacDorman et al., 2012). Reflecting this trend, Hazel Gereke's first child was born at home, but her later children were born in a hospital. As formalized medical training developed, so did the medicalization of childbirth, and the current childbirth experience commonly includes such medical interventions as intravenous lines, electronic fetal monitors, and epidural anesthesiology (Lothian, 2008). Induced labor and cesarean delivery are becoming increasingly common.

In the early part of the 20th century, the feminist movement advocated for hospital childbirth because it was considered to be safer than home birth, but beginning in the 1960s, feminists began to advocate for less invasive deliveries in more friendly environments that give women more choices over their care (DeVries & DeVries, 2007). In the past few decades, in the United States and other wealthy countries, a variety of institutional care settings have been developed, ranging from freestanding birth centers located near a hospital to more home-like birthing rooms within hospital labor departments (Hodnett et al., 2012). The PPACA mandates payments for birthing centers.

In 2012, the Centers for Medicare and Medicaid Services (2012) included birthing center care as one of three options for enhanced prenatal care under the Strong Start Initiative. A very small minority of pregnant women, less than 1% in the United States, give birth at home (MacDorman et al., 2012; Wyckoff, 2013). The same is true for most European countries, with the exception of the Netherlands, where home birth has been seen as the first option for uncomplicated pregnancies; even so, the percentage of home births in the Netherlands decreased from 38.2% to 23.4% from 1990 to 2010 (Chervenak, McCullough, Brent, Leven, & Arabin, 2013). It is important to remember that in many low-income countries, high maternal mortality rates are due, in great part, to poor women in remote rural areas having no option but to give birth at home without access to emergency health care (Kristof & WuDunn, 2009). In some of these countries, birthing shelters are providing dormitory rooms near hospitals so that women can receive emergency care during childbirth if the need arises (First Ladies Community Initiative, 2013).

Although alternatives to conventional hospital settings, such as birthing centers and home-like birthing rooms, have been somewhat slow to develop in the United States, they are not considered controversial, and available research indicates some benefits and no drawbacks to them. Women giving birth in such settings have reduced likelihood of medical interventions, increased likelihood of spontaneous vaginal birth, and increased satisfaction (Hodnett et al., 2012; Stapleton, Osborne, & Illuzzi, 2013). Home birth has been very controversial, however. In 1975, the American College of Obstetricians and Gynecologists (ACOG) issued a policy statement that protested in-home births and asserted that acceptable levels of safety were only available in the hospital. This policy statement was reaffirmed in 2013; it was supported that same year by the American Academy of Pediatrics, who noted that babies born during a planned home birth have a two- to threefold increased risk of death (Wyckoff, 2013). In response, in 2012, three major midwifery groups (the American College of Nurse Midwives,

Midwives Alliance of North America, and National Association of Certified Professional Midwives) strongly endorsed the practice of home delivery and challenged the medical profession to consider the advantages of a woman delivering her **neonate** (newborn) in the sanctity of her home. The cross-national data on maternal and infant mortality suggests that place of birth is not the only, and probably not the most important, factor affecting birth outcomes. Sweden, where almost all births occur in the hospital, and the Netherlands, where a large minority of births occur at home, have two of the lowest maternal and infant mortality rates in the world, both substantially lower than the United States. The maternal mortality rate is 2.4 per 100,000 in Sweden, 6 per 100,000 in the Netherlands, and 21 per 100,000 in the United States, where less than 1% of births occur at home. The infant mortality rate is 2 per 100,000 in Sweden, 3 per 100,000 in the Netherlands, and 6 per 100,000 in the United States (World Bank, 2013a).

Childbirth is the most common reason for hospitalization in the United States, and maternity and newborn care is the most costly category of hospital expense for both public and private payers (DelliFraine et al., 2011; Kozhimannil, Hardeman, Attanasio, Blauer-Peterson, & O'Brien, 2013). Cesarean sections are the most commonly performed inpatient surgical operation in the United States, and the rate has increased from about 20% to 33% of births over the past 15 years (Podulka, Stranges, & Steiner, 2011). Moreover, there is a wide disparity in costs and the rates of cesarean sections among hospitals. With more than 50% of maternity hospital bills paid by Medicaid, the fifteenfold difference among hospitals in rates charged is a public policy issue (Kozhimannil, Law, & Virniq, 2013). In 2008, women covered by Medicaid had a significantly smaller chance of having a cesarean than women covered by private insurance, possibly due to fiscal oversight by governmental agencies (Misra, 2008). Forty years ago, women remained hospitalized for 7 to 10 days following birth, but today the average stay for a vaginal birth is 2.6 days (Podulka et al., 2011). Some research has shown, however, that early discharge of the mother and baby does

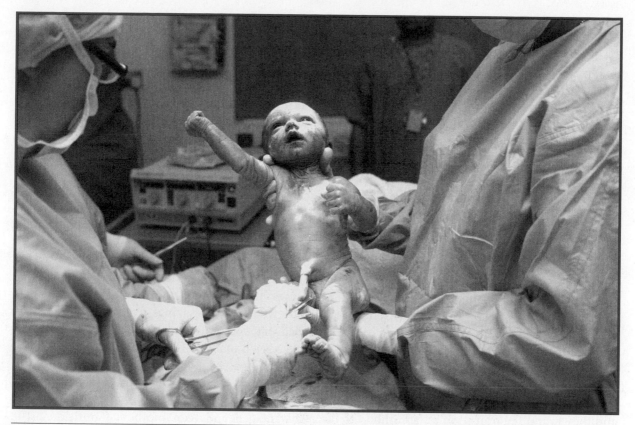

Photo 2.2 A typical delivery—here a newborn baby is delivered by medical professionals in a hospital delivery room.

© Vernon Wiley/iStockphoto.com

not increase negative outcomes, and many women prefer to leave the hospital shortly after giving birth. Yet many women appreciate continued assistance of health care workers and midwives after birth (Baker, 2006).

Who Assists Childbirth

In most countries of the world, childbirth was assisted exclusively by women until the middle of the 19th century when physicians, who were almost exclusively male, began delivering babies (Gardiner & Kosmitzki, 2011). Before childbirth became medicalized, midwives, trained birthing specialists, assisted most births. Midwifery went into decline in the United States for a few decades until two small programs based on the British model

of nurse-midwife—midwives with nursing training—were begun in the 1930s. Nurse-midwifery began to grow rapidly in the United States during the 1970s and 1980s (Parkland Memorial Hospital, 2000). Today 1 in 8 vaginal deliveries are attended by a nurse midwife, but most of these are in hospitals (Declercq, 2012). Most midwives work in a hospital setting (95.7%), 2% attend home deliveries, and 2.2% work in birthing centers (Martin et al., 2012). Most birthing centers have midwives as the primary care provider (Stapleton et al., 2013).

In most times and places, fathers have been excluded from participation in childbirth. This began to change in the United States and other countries in the 1970s, and worldwide there is an increasing trend for fathers to be present at the birth of their babies (Steen, Downe, Bamford, &

Edozien, 2012). In some cultures, however, there is still a taboo about fathers witnessing childbirth (Sengane, 2009). In the past 40 years of having fathers involved in the birthing process, research has indicated a number of benefits of this involvement, including improved maternal well-being, improved father-infant attachment, and paternal satisfaction (Alio, Lewis, Scarborough, Harris, & Fiscella, 2013; Premberg, Carlsson, Hellström, & Berg, 2011). In recent years, however, several pieces of qualitative research have reported that fathers are struggling with their role in the birthing process. One research team (Steen et al., 2012) examined the qualitative research on fathers' involvement with childbirth published from 1999 to 2009. They found that most fathers saw themselves as partner, had a strong desire to support their partner, and wanted to be fully engaged. They also found that fathers often felt uncertain, excluded, and fearful. They felt frustrated about their helplessness to relieve their partner's pain, they felt good when they could support their partner but bad when they did not feel supported by the childbirth team, and they found the transition to fatherhood to be profoundly life changing. Another research team (Bäckström & Hertfelt Wahn, 2011) found that fathers perceived themselves as receiving support when they were allowed to ask questions, when they had an opportunity to interact with the midwife and their partner, and when they could choose when to be involved and when to step back from involvement. They want to be recognized as part of the laboring couple. Recent attention has been given to the role of Black fathers in childbirth. In the United States, Black women are at a greater risk than White, non-Hispanic women to go through pregnancy and delivery without the support of the father due to the socioeconomic factors and discrimination that Black men face (Misra, Caldwell, Young, & Abelson, 2010).

In the past three decades, birth doulas have become a part of the childbirth experience for increasing numbers of women. *Doulas* are laywomen who are employed to stay with the woman through the entire labor, assisting with the nonmedical aspects of labor and delivery, encouraging her and providing comfort measures. A Cochrane systematic review of the research on the effects of continuous labor support found that women receiving such support had higher rates of spontaneous vaginal birth, lower rates of cesarean delivery, lower rates of epidural anesthesia, lower rates of instrument-assisted delivery, shorter labors, and higher levels of maternal satisfaction. They also found that labor support was most effective when provided by someone with special training, not on the hospital staff, and not a family member or close friend (Hodnett, Gates, Hofmeyr, Sakala, & Weston, 2012). Given this latter finding, it is important that the doula support the role of the father when he is present. Some policy analysts have pointed out that neither private nor public health insurance covers the cost of doulas but should consider doing so given the cost savings from reduced cesarean delivery, epidurals, and instrument-assisted delivery (Kozhimannil, Hardeman, et al., 2013). The PPACA, passed by Congress in 2010, allocated $1.5 million for community-based doula programs, following the success of a model program for disadvantaged and teen mothers (Sonfield, 2010). Think about the Thompsons' situation with Will in Afghanistan, unaware of the pending birth of his first child, and Felicia in premature labor without any family present. Perhaps a doula would have been a great benefit in that situation, as well as situations of other military wives.

Critical Thinking Questions 2.1

What were your reactions to the situations of the people in the three case studies at the beginning of this chapter? How would your reactions be helpful if you were to encounter each person in your social work practice? How would your reactions complicate your ability to be helpful to each one of them?

REPRODUCTIVE GENETICS _____

The life course perspective reminds us that we are linked back in time with our ancestry, as well as with our culture. Genetic factors are one important way that we are linked to our ancestry. Recognition of the need for genetics knowledge is not new to social work. In fact, Mary Richmond (1917) advocated that a social worker "get the facts of heredity" in the face of marriage between close relatives, miscarriage, tuberculosis, alcoholism, mental disorder, nervousness, epilepsy, cancer, deformities or abnormalities, or an exceptional ability. Very little was known about genetic mechanisms at the time, however.

Almost 40 years later, James Watson and Francis Crick (1953) first described the mechanisms of genetic inheritance. In 1990, the Human Genome Project (HGP) was funded by the U.S. Department of Energy and the National Institutes of Health as an international effort to map all the human genes, and that project was completed by 2003. As genetic knowledge continued to grow, the National Association of Social Workers established *Standards for Integrating Genetics Into Social Work Practice* in 2003. These standards cover ethics and values, genetics knowledge, practice skills, a client/practitioner collaborative practice model, interdisciplinary practice, self-awareness, genetics and cross-cultural knowledge, research, and advocacy (National Association of Social Workers, 2003). Genetic research continues around the world, with future findings that will impact social work practice.

Genetic Mechanisms

Chromosomes and genes are the essential components of the hereditary process. Genetic instructions are coded in **chromosomes** found in each cell; each chromosome carries **genes**, or segments of deoxyribonucleic acid (DNA), that contain the codes producing particular traits and dispositions. Each mature **germ cell**—ovum or sperm—contains 23 chromosomes, half of the set of 46 present in each parent's cells. As you can see in Exhibit 2.1, when the sperm penetrates the ovum (**fertilization**), the parents' chromosomes combine to make a total of 46 chromosomes arrayed in 23 pairs. The genes constitute a "map" that guides the protein and enzyme reactions for every subsequent cell in the developing person and across the life course. Thus, almost every physical trait and many behavioral traits are influenced by the combined genes from the ovum and sperm.

The Human Genome Project (1990–2003) researchers estimated that there are 20,000 to 25,000 genes in human DNA, with a broad range of total genes (449–2,400) across all chromosomes (Human Genome Project, 2010; National Center for Biotechnology Information, 2013). Research continues to articulate the complete sequencing of the 3 billion subunits of the human genome, an effort of global proportions involving both public and privately funded projects in more than 18 countries, including some developing countries (Human Genome Project, 2010).

Every person has a unique **genotype**, or array of genes, unless the person is an identical twin. Yet the environment may influence how each gene pilots the growth of cells. The result is a **phenotype** (observable trait) that differs somewhat from the genotype. Thus, even a person who is an identical twin has some unique characteristics. On initial observation, you may not be able to distinguish between identical twins, but if you look closely enough, you will probably find some variation, such as differences in the size of an ear, hair thickness, or temperament.

A chromosome and its pair have the same types of genes at the same location. The exception is the last pair of chromosomes, the **sex chromosomes**, which, among other things, determine sex. The ovum can contribute only an X chromosome to the 23rd pair, but the sperm can contribute either an X or a Y and therefore determines the sex of the developing person. A person with XX sex chromosomes is female; a person with XY sex chromosomes is male (refer to Exhibit 2.1).

A gene on one sex chromosome that does not have a counterpart on the other sex chromosome creates a **sex-linked trait**. A gene for red/green color blindness, for example, is carried only on the X chromosome. When an X chromosome that carries this gene is paired with a Y chromosome, which could not carry the gene, red/green color blindness

Exhibit 2.1   Germ Cell Division, Fertilization, and Chromosome Pairs

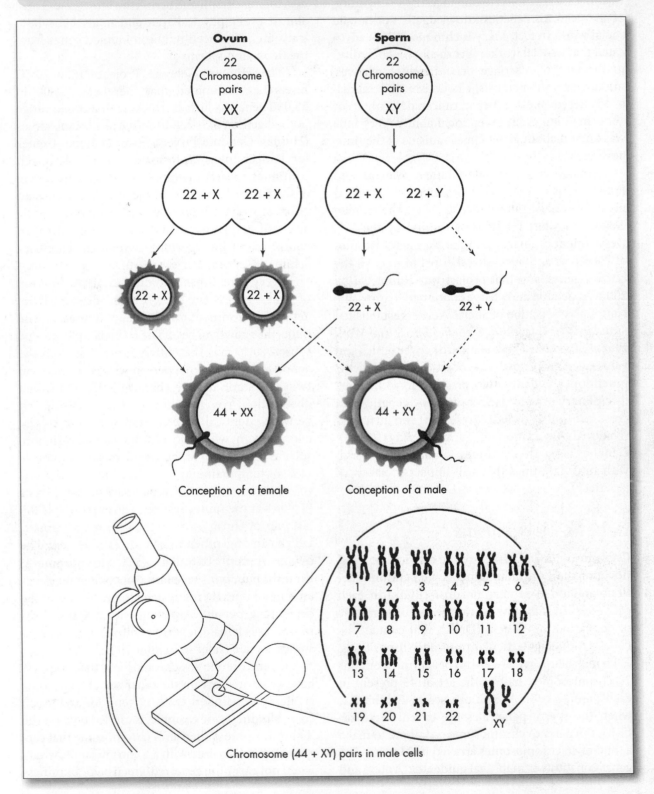

Conception of a female   Conception of a male

Chromosome (44 + XY) pairs in male cells

is manifested. So, almost all red/green color blindness is found in males. This gene for color blindness does not manifest if paired with an X chromosome unless the gene is inherited from both parents, which is rare. However, if a woman inherits the gene from either parent, she can unknowingly pass it on to her sons.

Whether genes express certain traits depends on their being either dominant or recessive. Traits governed by **recessive genes** (e.g., hemophilia, baldness, thin lips) will only be expressed if the responsible gene is present on each chromosome of the relevant pair. In contrast, traits governed by **dominant genes** (e.g., normal blood clotting, curly hair, thick lips) will be expressed if one or both paired chromosomes have the gene. When the genes on a chromosome pair give competing, yet controlling, messages, they are called **interactive genes**, meaning that both messages may be followed to varying degrees. Hair, eye, and skin color often depend on such interactivity. For example, a light-skinned person with red hair and hazel eyes may mate with a person having dark skin, brown hair, and blue eyes and produce a child with a dark complexion, red hair, and blue eyes.

Genetic Counseling

Recent research has identified many genes that govern some of the physical traits and mental/medical problems that Mary Richmond noted in 1917. Today the goal is to develop genetic interventions to prevent, ameliorate, or cure various diseases or disorders as well as inform decisions about conception, pregnancy, and childbirth. One example is the Preimplantation Genetic Diagnosis (PGD) test used for in vitro fertilization to ensure that the embryo has no mutations (Human Genome Project, 2010). More than 3,000 genetic tests are marketed, ranging in cost from hundreds to thousands of dollars; they are seldom covered by insurance, and there is limited scientific validity and reliability evidence for many tests (Centers for Disease Control and Prevention [CDC], 2013a). Noteworthy, however, are the 2008 Genetic Information and Nondiscrimination Act (GINA) that prohibits discrimination by U.S. insurance companies on the basis of genetic test results and the June 2013 unanimous Supreme Court decision to prohibit patenting of genes (National Human Genome Research Institute, 2013a).

Our rapidly increasing ability to read a person's genetic code and understand the impact it could have on the person's life oftentimes demands the expertise of a genetic counselor to provide information and advice to guide decisions for persons concerned about hereditary abnormalities. Social workers, with their biopsychosocial perspective, are well positioned to assess the need and in some circumstances provide such services, and the interdisciplinary field of genetic counseling acknowledges social work as one of its essential disciplines (Duke Eye Center, 2009; National Association of Social Workers, 2003; Price, 2008a, 2008b). Social workers need to understand the rising bioethical concerns that genetic research fosters and to use such knowledge to help clients faced with genetically related reproductive decisions. The U.S. government has the largest bioethics program in the world to address questions such as the following: Who should have access to genetic information? Do adoptive parents have the right to know the genetic background of an adoptee? Will genetic maps be used to make decisions about a pregnancy? Which genes should be selected for reproduction? Will persons who are poor be economically disadvantaged in the use of genetic information? Should all genetic information be shared with a client?

Recent advances in genetic research allow for earlier in utero diagnosis, which reduces or prevents the effects of some rare diseases and may provide more options for action. Today, for example, a late-life pregnancy such as Hazel Gereke's could be evaluated genetically using amniocentesis in the third trimester, or earlier in the first trimester using chorionic villus sampling, which allowed Cecelia Kin to know that her unborn child had Down syndrome. Such evaluation could lead to difficult decisions ranging from abortion to preparation for parenting a child with a disability. However, these options typically are laced with economic, political, legal, ethical, moral, and religious considerations.

Ethical issues related to genetic engineering have an impact not only at the individual and family levels but also at the societal level. For example, when we are able to manipulate genes at will, we must be on guard against genetic elitism. It is one thing to use genetic engineering to eliminate such inherited diseases as sickle-cell anemia but quite another to use it to select the sex, body type, or coloring of a child. We are living in a time of tremendous ethical complexity, involving the interplay of new reproductive technologies; changing family structures, values, and mores; political and religious debate; and economic considerations. As increasing numbers of persons gain the ability to control conception, plan pregnancy, and control pregnancy outcomes, social workers need to protect the interests of those who lack the knowledge and other resources to do so.

CONTROL OVER CONCEPTION AND PREGNANCY

How are decisions about timing of childbearing related to biological age, psychological age, social age, and spiritual age?

One way that humans exercise human agency is to attempt to get control over conception and pregnancy. The desire to plan the timing of childbearing is an ancient one, as is the desire to stimulate pregnancy in the event of infertility. Contraception and induced abortion have probably always existed in every culture but continue to generate much controversy. Effective solutions for infertility are more recent. It is important to remember that not all methods of controlling conception and pregnancy are equally acceptable to all people. Cultural and religious beliefs, as well as personal circumstances, make some people more accepting of certain methods than others. Social workers must be aware of this diversity of attitudes and preferences related to the control of conception and pregnancy. Cultural and religious beliefs also drive social policy in this area.

Although there is evidence that many women of the world want to control conception and pregnancy, unintended pregnancy is a global problem, estimated to be 30% of all pregnancies (Blumenthal, Voedisch, & Gemzell-Danielsson, 2011). About 49% of all pregnancies in the United States are unintended. The unintended pregnancy rate is significantly higher in the United States than in many other wealthy nations. In 31 states (clustered in the U.S. South and Southwest and states with large urban populations) and the District of Columbia, more than half of all pregnancies are unintended. These rates have remained somewhat flat since 1994 (Guttmacher Institute, 2013a). A greater percentage of unintended pregnancies are reported by teenagers, women aged 18 to 24, cohabiting women, low-income and less educated women, and minority women (Guttmacher Institute, 2013a; Mosher, Jones, & Abma, 2012). For those pregnancies resulting in birth, unintended births (vs. intended births) are associated with delayed or no prenatal care (19% of unintended vs. 8.2% intended births), smoking during pregnancy (16% vs. 10%), low birth weight (12% vs. 7.2%), and no breastfeeding (39% vs. 25%) (Mosher et al., 2012). Unintended pregnancy and birth are also associated with increased likelihood of pathological anger and rejection of the infant after birth (Brockington, Aucamp, & Fraser, 2006); increased stress; higher incidence of intimate partner violence both during the pregnancy and after delivery (Charles & Perreira, 2007); and more illicit drug use (Orr, James, & Reiter, 2008).

Contraception

The range of birth control options available today provides women and men in many parts of the world with the ability to plan pregnancy and childbirth more than ever before. Currently 62% of U.S. women of reproductive age use some form of contraception, and 99.1% of sexually active women use a contraceptive during their lifetime (Jones, Mosher, & Daniels, 2012). However, it is estimated that 222 million women in low-income countries who don't want to get pregnant have no access to contraceptives (World Health Organization [WHO], 2013a). Access to contraceptives is often driven by both medical and political considerations. Here are three examples. It was not until 1965 that the United States Supreme Court recognized that women had a constitutional right to use contraception in the historical case of *Griswold v. Connecticut* that involved a physician who was arrested for prescribing a contraceptive to a married couple (Termini & Lee, 2011). In 2000, the World Health Organization (WHO) increased medical restrictions on the use of oral and injected hormonal contraception, out of concern that they would not protect women from HIV, but they have since lifted those restrictions while advising women at risk of HIV that they should also use condoms or other preventive measures (World Health Organization, 2012a). The Patient Protection and Affordable Care Act mandates that insurance providers cover prescription contraception with no co-pay, but as this is being written, this provision of the law is hotly contested on a number of fronts.

As reported earlier, in spite of a wide range of birth control options, the rate of unplanned pregnancies around the world is high. The incorrect use of, or lack of access to, contraceptives is the primary cause for unplanned pregnancies. Worldwide, approximately one in three unplanned births is due to contraceptive failure. It is estimated that the abortion rate would decrease by one third to two thirds if effective contraception were available (Bradley, Croft, & Rutstein, 2011). With a projected world population of more than 9 billion people by 2050, and with birth rates highest in low-income countries, there is an urgent need to provide inexpensive, safe, convenient, and appropriate contraceptive devices to women and men worldwide (U.S. Census Bureau, 2011a). Because, globally, women who have access to longer-lasting contraceptives such as oral contraceptives and IUDs have lower failure rates, there is a push to make these contraceptives readily available at a low cost.

Forms of birth control are varied, in both effectiveness and costs. Complete sexual abstinence is the only form of contraception that has no financial cost and is completely effective. It is important for social workers to be familiar with the choices women have. Each birth control option needs to be considered in light of its cost, failure rate, potential health risks, and probability of use, given the user's sociocultural circumstances. Female and male contraception options include the following:

- *Breastfeeding.* Women who are exclusively breastfeeding and are amenorrhoeic (not menstruating) are less likely than other women to conceive during the first 6 months postpartum (Hale, 2007). Breastfeeding without the use of other contraceptives carries a pregnancy risk of less than 2% during the first year if a woman remains amenorrhoeic (Association of Reproductive Health Professionals, 2009). Breastfeeding does not protect against sexually transmitted infections (STIs).

- *Coitus interruptus.* Primarily seen as a male form of contraception, premature withdrawal of the penis from the vagina before ejaculation is probably the oldest form of birth control (Costantino et al., 2007). However, the failure rate is approximately 19% to 27% a year (4% if used perfectly) (Freundl, Sivin, & Batár, 2010). Coitus interruptus, often discounted as a contraceptive, offers no protection from STIs and HIV and may be unsatisfying for both partners (Dohetry & Stuart, 2011; Mahendru, Putran, & Khaled, 2009).

- *Periodic abstinence.* Natural family planning, or the rhythm method, is a term used for birth control that does not employ drugs or devices (Freundl et al., 2010) and involves either daily tracking of changes in the woman's body associated with the menstrual cycle or tracking changes in body temperature and mucous consistency with avoidance of intercourse during the fertile periods. The failure rate in 1 year is about 25%, but it is much lower if done perfectly (Jones et al., 2012). Natural family planning does not protect against STIs.

- *Barrier methods.* Barrier methods have been developed for use by both men and women. Condoms are a low-cost method of contraception with the highest use rate among adolescents, unmarried adults, and Black and Hispanic persons (Reece et al., 2010). The male condom (18% failure rate), the diaphragm (12% failure rate), and the cervical cap (12% failure rate) provide increased protection against STIs, with the male condom having the highest protection against HIV and hepatitis B (Centers for Disease Control and Prevention [CDC], 2013b; Jones et al., 2012). Dissatisfaction with male condom use is lower than for any other form of birth control, leading to a lower rate of discontinuance (12%) (Moreau, Cleland, & Trussell, 2007). The female condom, introduced in 1992, consists of either two flexible rings, a soft sponge, or a dissolvable capsule (Rowlands, 2009) and also provides some protection against STIs (Freundl et al., 2010). It has approximately a 5% failure rate when used correctly and an 18% to 25% failure rate when used incorrectly or inconsistently (MedlinePlus, 2012a) and is readily available at drug stores (Centers for Disease Control and Prevention, 2013b). It costs from $2.50 to $5.00 per use (Holtgrave et al., 2012). The female condom is visible after insertion (some women are requesting colored condoms) and may cause crackling or popping sounds. Approximately 52% of women discontinue use of the diaphragm and cervical cap because they are dissatisfied (Moreau et al., 2007). Both male and female condoms are used with a spermicide that provides a chemical barrier against pregnancy but not STIs (Freundl et al., 2010).

- *Oral contraceptives.* The introduction of birth control pills in the United States in 1960 precipitated major changes in reproductive rates. With a failure rate ranging from 0.3% to 9.0%, this method has revolutionized family planning (Freundl et al., 2010). Approximately 29% of women who start an oral contraceptive discontinue it because of dissatisfaction due to side effects (Moreau et al., 2007). Using a combined estrogen and progesterone pill continuously throughout the month (versus three out of four), most women will cease menstruation after several months. Using oral contraceptives that have estrogen can increase the risk of breast cancer, but the new regime that does not include the use of estrogen may actually reduce this risk (Rowlands, 2009). The combined (estrogen and progesterone) pill can increase blood pressure and the risk for heart attacks, blood clots, and strokes with higher rates for women who are over 35 and women who smoke (MedlinePlus, 2012b; Neto et al., 2012). The use of oral contraceptives also can lead to the development of inflammatory bowel disease (Cornish et al., 2008) and may be contraindicated in women who are obese (e.g., body mass index greater than 35) (Mahendru et al., 2009). The progesterone-only pill is safe for women who are breastfeeding (Mahendru et al., 2009).

- *Intramuscular injections.* Depomedroxy-progesterone acetate (Depo-Provera), a drug used for many years in Europe and introduced in the United States in 1992, protects women against pregnancy for up to 3 months. Women also may elect to self-inject on a monthly basis. There appear to be similar rates of satisfaction with the administration of this drug whether it is administered in the clinic every 3 months or self-injected on a monthly basis (Cameron, Glasier, & Johnstone, 2012). The failure rate is about 6% (Centers for Disease Control and Prevention, 2013b). There have been concerns that Depo-Provera leads to irregular bleeding, decreased bone density, headaches, delay in return to fertility, possible weight gain, and breast tenderness (Clark, Dillon, Sowers, & Nichols, 2005; Haider & Darney, 2007; National Women's Health Network, 2011). In addition, some research has shown that Depo-Provera increases the risk of invasive breast cancer more than twofold (Li et al., 2012).

- *Implants and patches.* Implants are tiny capsules inserted under the skin by a physician. Older systems consisted of six capsules that made insertion and removal difficult and increased the likelihood of complications (Rowlands, 2009). Implanon, a new single-rod implant, has been shown to be highly effective (i.e., a failure rate of less than 0.05%) and does not carry the risks of multiple rod implants (Freundl et al., 2010). A new implant, Nexplanon, may also be used for gynecological issues such as endometriosis (Palomba, Falbo, Dicelio, Materozzo, & Zullo, 2012). Women also have the option to select a transdermal patch, which is changed weekly for 3 weeks per monthly cycle (Rowlands, 2009). The patch has the same effectiveness as oral contraceptives in women who are not obese, about a 9% failure rate in the first year of use (Centers for Disease Control and Prevention, 2013b), but about 3% of women discontinue it because of skin irritation (Rowlands, 2009). In populations at high risk for unintended pregnancies and abortions, the patch has lower continuation and effectiveness rates than oral contraceptives, but in low-risk populations, women are more compliant using the patch than oral contraceptives (Bakhru & Stanwood, 2006; Miller & Holman, 2006).

• *Vaginal rings.* There are two forms of vaginal rings, one that is progestin only and provides continuous coverage and a second that is a combination estrogen and progestin ring that is in place for 3 weeks and then removed for 1 week. Both have the same failure rate as oral contraceptives and provide the convenience of ongoing birth control. With the combination ring, there is good cycle control. A new combination ring that will provide protection from STIs is currently under development (Brache, Payan, & Faundes, 2013). Additionally, in response to the worldwide need for effective, safe, and easily accessible birth control, a vaginal ring that can remain in place for 3 months is being researched (Jensen, 2013).

• *Intrauterine devices (IUDs).* The use of IUDs as routine contraception has been marked by controversy and legal disputes for a number of years. They were introduced in the early 1900s, but high rates of infection and tissue damage discouraged their use until the 1960s. Most manufacturers discontinued production in the 1980s following expensive legal settlements. However, there are two forms still available: one with copper (Cu-IUD), the other a levonorgestrel intrauterine system (LNG-IUS) that releases a hormone into the uterine cavity (Varma, Sinha, & Gupta, 2006). These newer IUDs are the most widely used contraceptive in the world and are considered safe and reliable (Human Reproduction Update, 2008). There is some evidence that the LNG-IUS can benefit women diagnosed with endometriosis or fibroids or who are in the early stages of endometrial cancer (Varma et al., 2006). The Cu-IUD has been shown to protect against endometrial cancer and can be used successfully by women who are at risk of or have HIV infection (Sivin & Batar, 2010). Approximately 15% of women discontinue use of the IUD within 1 year because of complications, but it has a contraceptive failure rate of less than 1% over a 1-year time (Blumenthal et al., 2011; Centers for Disease Control and Prevention, 2013b). The IUD has been found to be the optimal contraceptive for women approaching menopause (Bhathena & Guillebaud, 2006) and can be used by women who are breastfeeding (Hale, 2007). In addition to routine contraception, copper-bearing IUDs can provide emergency contraception. If inserted within 5 days postcoitus, there is a 99.86% pregnancy prevention rate (Cleland, Zhu, Goldstuck, Cheng, & Trussell, 2012).

• *Voluntary surgical sterilization.* Tubal ligation, surgical sterilization for women, is considered permanent and has an effectiveness rate of approximately 99.5% (Centers for Disease Control and Prevention, 2013b). Surgery to reverse tubal ligation can be performed either transvaginally or through laparoscopic surgery, usually with no complications (Chang et al., 2011). The overall success rate for successful pregnancies following reversal is from 60% to 70% (Caillet et al., 2010; Schepens, Moi, Wiegerinck, Houterman, & Koks, 2011). Hysterectomy, the removal of the uterus, is only done if there is a medical need and may involve the removal of the ovaries and fallopian tubes as well (Tan & Loth, 2010). Hysterectomy is irreversible. Vasectomy, or male sterilization, likewise is considered a most reliable method of contraception, with a failure rate of less than 0.2% in the first year (Centers for Disease Control and Prevention, 2013a). Vasectomy is not widely used as a contraceptive method (<7% of men in the United States have had a vasectomy), and approximately 20% of men who have had the surgery desire to have children in the future (Sharma et al., 2013). The reversal success rate is strongly influenced by the time elapsed since the vasectomy and the age of the female partner (van Dongen, Tekle, & Van Roijen, 2012), with a subsequent pregnancy rate of approximately 60% (Hinz et al., 2009).

• *Emergency contraception (EC).* Emergency contraception (EC) is the use of certain methods to prevent pregnancy after unprotected intercourse. The World Health Organization recognizes two types of EC: emergency contraception pills (ECP) and the copper IUD (World Health Organization, 2012b). There are several brands of ECP available in the United States, some taken in one dose and some in two doses. ECP prevents pregnancy by preventing ovulation, not by disrupting an established pregnancy or harming a developing embryo (Termini & Lee, 2011). In August 2006, the U.S. Food and Drug Administration (FDA) approved the nonprescription levonorgestrel, "the morning-after pill," otherwise known as "Plan B," to be available to women 18 years and older, but a prescription was required for younger women. Levonorgestrel can be taken in one dose or two. In the summer of 2013, a federal court decision lifted all restrictions for age of purchase for Plan B One Step, a one-dose pill (United States Federal Food and Drug Administration, 2013). ECP should be used as soon after intercourse as possible and is most effective if used in the first 72 hours (Termini & Lee, 2011). Ella, another emergency contraceptive, is available by prescription to women over the age of 17 and is effective for 5 days postintercourse. Plan B has been shown to be effective in preventing pregnancy up to 89% of the time but is not considered a substitute for ongoing contraception (Emergency Contraception Website, 2013). When inserted within 5 days of unprotected sex, the copper IUD is the most effective method of EC. It works by keeping the sperm from joining the egg or by keeping a fertilized egg from attaching to the uterus. It can be removed after the next period or kept in place for up to 10 years. Sometimes pregnancy can be prevented by taking a higher dose than usual of regular birth control pills, but this is not as effective as either ECP or the copper IUD. It is important for the social worker to be familiar with these forms of contraception, especially if he or she works with populations who have a high rate of undesired fertility and low rates of contraceptive use.

• *New contraceptive methods.* Numerous clinical trials are focused on providing contraceptives to those most in need, using easily delivered methods (Sitruk-Ware, Nath, & Mishell, 2013). Research is ongoing to develop an oral contraceptive that either avoids the use of estrogen or uses natural estrogen. A vaginal ring that can remain in place for up to 3 months and delivers only natural progesterone is being tested in other countries. Additionally, a vaginal ring that can be placed for up to a year is in clinical trials. New transdermal patches that deliver lower hormonal doses are being tested. Studies are under way to determine if vaginal gels are effective for intermittent use. Injectables that do not affect bone loss are being developed. Dual-purpose contraceptive methods, those that prevent both pregnancy and STIs, have gained support in the research and medical community. Several barrier methods, including dual-action vaginal rings, are in the developmental stage. Over the past 20 years, interest in male contraception has grown, and the search is on for male contraception that is simple, reversible, and effective. Oral contraceptives for men have been shown to have negative physiological effects and are not immediately effective. Focus on developing an oral contraceptive that does not have the adverse hormonal effects is under way, but progress is slow (Sitruk-Ware et al., 2013). Generally it takes 10 to 15 years for development of a new contraceptive (Aitken et al., 2008), but with new research techniques comes hope that the demands for affordable, accessible, effective, low-risk, and culturally acceptable contraceptive options will be met.

Medical Abortion

Abortion may be the most politicized, hotly debated social issue related to pregnancy today in the United States. Worldwide, some countries, like Ireland, are moving away from a total ban on abortion and others are broadening the grounds on which abortion may be legally performed (Guttmacher Institute, 2013b). It is difficult to get good estimates of global abortion rates, because countries where abortions are highly restricted do not document them, and abortions may be underreported in other places (Sedgh et al., 2012). The proportion of abortions worldwide that took place in developing countries increased from 78% in 1995 to 86% in 2008. In 2008, the lowest abortion rates were reported in western Europe (12 per 1,000 women, aged 15 to 44), southern Africa (15), and northern Europe (17). The highest rates were in Asia (26–36) and Latin America (32) (Sedgh et al., 2012). The global abortion rate declined substantially from 1995 to 2003 but stalled from 2003 to 2008 (Sedgh et al., 2012). A similar trend is seen in the United States (Guttmacher Institute, 2013b). The decline in the abortion rate is thought to be related to better education and an increase in availability of contraception options.

Highly restrictive abortion laws do not lead to fewer abortions. Global data indicate that the abortion rate is lowest in regions of the world that have liberal abortion laws (Sedgh et al., 2012). Abortion laws do make a difference, however, in whether abortion is safe or unsafe. It is estimated that 97% of abortions in Africa and 95% in Latin America were unsafe in 2008. These are regions where abortion is banned. In South Africa, the number of abortion-related deaths fell by 91% after the liberalization of abortion law (Guttmacher Institute, 2013b). Globally, the percentage of abortions that are unsafe increased from 44% in 1995 to 49% in 2008 (Sedgh et al., 2012).

In 1973, in *Roe v. Wade*, the U.S. Supreme Court legalized abortion in the first trimester and left it to the discretion of the woman and her physician. Four years later, in 1977, the Hyde Amendment limited federal funding for abortion, and the Supreme Court ruled in 1989, in *Webster v. Reproductive Health Services*, that Medicaid could no longer fund abortions, except in cases of rape, incest, or life endangerment (Guttmacher Institute, 2013b). Renewed annually, this ban on the use of federal funds for abortion has now extended to all federal employees and women in the military and the Indian Health Service. With much of the decision making related to abortion left to the states, there is wide variation in who has access to abortion, when, how, and at what cost. In some states, new rules are effectively decreasing access, particularly for poor and minority populations and others who are educationally disadvantaged. Seventeen states and the District of Columbia use state-only funds to cover abortions for women on Medicaid while four other states ban abortion coverage by private insurers. Eighty-seven percent of U.S. counties have no abortion provider, and 35% of women aged 15 to 44 live in these counties (Guttmacher Institute, 2013b), resulting in rural disparities in access to abortion.

During the first trimester and until **fetal viability** (the point at which the baby could survive outside the womb) in the second trimester, U.S. federal law allows for a pregnant woman to legally choose an abortion, although states can narrow this option. Almost 88% of abortions in the United States are performed during the first 12 weeks of pregnancy, 10.4% from 13 to 20 weeks, and 1.5% after 21 weeks (Guttmacher Institute, 2013b). Recent controversy regarding procedures for terminating a pregnancy after fetal viability has called attention to ethical and legal dilemmas that are being addressed in the legal system, by most religions, and in other parts of U.S. culture. Opinion polls reveal, however, that like Hazel Gereke, the majority of Americans favor abortion as an option under specified conditions. May 2013 polling data indicate that 26% of the population in the United States think abortion should be legal under any circumstances, 52% think it should be legal under certain circumstances, 20% think it should be illegal in all circumstances, and 2% had no opinion (Gallup.com, 2013). These attitudes have been relatively consistent since 1975. According to the Guttmacher Institute (2013b), 18% of women obtaining an abortion in the United States are teenagers, and 57% are in their 20s. Non-Hispanic White women receive 36% of abortions, non-Hispanic Black women receive 30%, and Hispanic women receive 25%. Women who have never married and are cohabiting receive 45%, and 61% are obtained by women who have one or more children. About two fifths, 42%, of women obtaining abortions have incomes 100% below the federal poverty level.

Abortion procedures fall into three categories:

1. *Medical abortion.* Also known as chemical or nonsurgical abortion, medical abortion uses the drugs methotrexate, misoprostol, and/or mifepristone followed by prostaglandin. This procedure was used in 17.1% of all U.S. abortions in 2009 (Centers for Disease Control and Prevention, 2012a) with 98.5% effectiveness for mifepristone (Fjerstad, Truissell, Sivin, Lichtenberg, & Cullins, 2009). The combined mifepristone/prostaglandin regimen has 92% efficacy if used within 49 days of gestation. The use of medical abortion increased 10% from 2008 to 2009 and 350% from 2001 to 2009 (Centers for Disease Control and Prevention, 2012a).

2. *Instrumental or surgical evacuation.* One of two types of procedures was used in 82.3% of all U.S. surgical abortions in 2009 (Centers for Disease Control and Prevention, 2012a). The standard first-trimester vacuum curettage, also called manual vacuum aspiration or MVA, is the type most frequently performed in an outpatient clinic. A suction device is threaded through the cervix to remove the contents of the uterus. The use of this procedure decreased by 14% from 2001 to 2009. The second-trimester curettage abortion, accounting for 8.1% of U.S. abortions in 2009 (Centers for Disease Control and Prevention, 2012a), uses a surgical instrument to scrape the walls of the uterus. Risks for both procedures include bleeding, infection, and subsequent infertility. Abortion from 18 weeks (or 20 weeks, depending on source) to 26 weeks' gestation is referred to as "late-term abortion." The Partial-Birth Abortion Ban Act was introduced in the United States in 1995, passed in 2003, and was reaffirmed in federal court in 2007. This legislation bans a procedure called intact dilation and extraction, not abortion per se, with no health exceptions (Haddad, Yanow, Delli-Bovi, Cosby, & Weitz, 2009).

3. *Intrauterine Instillation.* In the second trimester, a chemical solution, usually saline, can be infused into the uterus to end the pregnancy. This is used in less than 0.01% of abortions due to the increase in medical abortion, which is more effective and has fewer risks (Centers for Disease Control and Prevention, 2012a).

Regardless of the timing or type of abortion, all women should be carefully counseled before and after the procedure. Unplanned pregnancies typically create considerable psychological stress, and social workers can help pregnant women consider all alternatives to an unwanted pregnancy—including abortion—consistent with the woman's personal values and beliefs. Following an abortion, most women have both negative and positive reactions. One research team (Fergusson, Horwood, & Boden, 2009) found that more than 85% of women reported feeling at least one negative reaction, such as grief, guilt, sadness, or sorrow, after having an abortion. These negative reactions were offset by positive reactions, and over 85% of the women also reported feeling relief, happiness, and satisfaction. The researchers also found that looking back at the abortion decision at a later date, nearly 90% reported that the decision to have an abortion was the correct decision, and only 2% reported that it was the wrong decision. Women who reported more negative reactions were more likely to have later mental health problems. Another research team (Steinberg & Finer, 2011) found that women who had risk factors such as physical or sexual abuse prior to abortion were more likely to have mental health issues after abortion. They also found that women with prior mood and anxiety disorders were more likely to have multiple abortions. It is important for the social worker working with clients with unintended pregnancy to assess for prior traumatic experiences as well as know the current federal and state legalities and resources, especially when clients have limited income. They also need to be mindful of their personal views about abortion in order to help clients make informed decisions that reflect their own values, religious beliefs, and available options as well as agency/organization policy related to abortion.

Infertility Treatment

Infertility, the inability to create a viable embryo after 1 year of intercourse without contraception (Centers for Disease Control and Prevention, 2013c), is a major life stressor. Because both male and female factors are involved, determining infertility prevalence rates is challenging. It is estimated that one in four couples in developing countries struggle with infertility (Mascarenhas, Flaxman, Boerma, Vanderpoel, & Stevens, 2012); it is also estimated that 10.9% of women in the United States have reduced fertility and 6.0% (1.5 million) are infertile (Centers for Disease Control and Prevention, 2013c). One research team (Mascarenhas et al., 2012) found a smaller rate of infertility when a 5-year, rather than a 1-year, period of unprotected sex was analyzed, meaning that many couples who have trouble getting pregnant within 1 year are successful at a later date. It is estimated that 40% of infertility problems reside with the female, 45% with the male, and 25% of the time both contribute to the problem (Center for Human Reproduction, 2013a). Approximately 1% of infants born in the United States are the result of assisted reproductive technology (ART), with 451 clinics providing treatment (Centers for Disease Control and Prevention, 2013c). Jennifer and Allan Bradshaw are struggling to find a way to afford infertility treatment as they encounter staggering costs.

Jennifer Bradshaw poignantly conveys her emotional distress about infertility, but we don't know much about what her husband was experiencing. While it is thought that infertility causes emotional distress to both women and men (Mascarenhas et al., 2012), little is known about the impact on men. Available research indicates that infertility places women at risk for depression, anxiety, substance abuse, social stress, isolation, and marital dissatisfaction (see, e.g., Baldur-Felskov et al., 2013; Karjane, Stovall, Berger, & Svikis, 2008). Women have traditionally sought informal support whereas men have focused on the financial impact of infertility. Social support, specifically a positive marital relationship, has been found to be positively associated with increased coping skills, but the process of disclosing one's infertility to others can increase anxiety (Martins, Peterson, Almeida, & Costa, 2011; Martins et al., 2013). One qualitative research team (Hinton, Kurinczuk, & Ziebland, 2010) found that women are more likely than men to seek support for coping with infertility from the Internet. Both the experience of infertility and the treatment of infertility can cause emotional distress (Greil, McQuillan, Lowry, & Shreffler, 2011). Narrative, existential, and cognitive behavioral approaches have been shown to be effective for this population (Ridenour, Yorgason, & Peterson, 2009; Stark, Keathley, & Nelson, 2011).

The causes of infertility are many and complex. Infertility, like other aspects of human behavior, is multidetermined. Exhibit 2.2, which draws on numerous sources to identify medical causes, environmental causes, and health and lifestyle causes, demonstrates this complexity. New research is also indicating that some men have a genetic factor that intersects with environmental factors to increase the risk of infertility (Hamada, Esteves, & Agarwai, 2011; Miyamoto et al., 2012). Medical causes have received more research attention than other causes; consequently, there is clearer evidence for the medical causes. Fertility decreases as men and women age (Amudha, Rani, Kannan, & Manavalan, 2013). There are racial differences in infertility in the United States, with Black and Hispanic women having twice the rate but using infertility services significantly less (Greil, McQuillan, Shreffler, Johnson, & Slauson-Blevins, 2011).

In the past, infertile couples could keep trying and hope for the best, but medical technology has given today's couples a variety of options, summarized in Exhibit 2.3. Women may be advised to lose or gain weight or to modify exercise habits to maximize the chances of ovulation and pregnancy. Medications may be used to help women ovulate, to treat infections in both men and women, and to treat ejaculation problems in men (Amudha et al., 2013). Surgeries may be used to correct structural problems in the reproductive systems of both men and women (Mayo Clinic, 2013a). Intrauterine insemination (IUI), traditionally known as artificial insemination, has a long history of use in animal

Exhibit 2.2   Possible Causes of Male and Female Infertility

MALE CAUSES	FEMALE CAUSES
Medical Causes	*Medical Causes*
• Varicocele (swelling of the veins that drain the testicle) • Infection (sexually transmitted infections, inflamed testicles due to mumps) • Antibodies that attack sperm • Tumors and treatments for tumors (surgery, radiation, and chemotherapy) • Undescended testicles • Hormone imbalances • Sperm duct defects • Chromosome defects (examples: Klinefelter's syndrome, cystic fibrosis) • Problems with sexual intercourse (erectile dysfunction, premature ejaculation) • Celiac disease • Medications (testosterone replacement therapy, anabolic steroids, antifungal medications, some ulcer drugs)	• Ovulation disorders (polycystic ovary syndrome [PCOS], hypothalamic dysfunction, premature ovarian insufficiency, too much prolactin) • Damage to fallopian tubes (caused by pelvic inflammatory disease, previous surgery in abdomen or pelvis, pelvic tuberculosis) • Endometriosis • Uterine or cervical causes (uterine polyps or tumors, abnormally shaped uterus, cervical stenosis, cervical mucus insufficiency) • Sexually transmitted infections
Environmental Causes	*Environmental Causes*
• Industrial chemicals (benzenes, toluene, xylene, pesticides, herbicides, painting material, lead) • Heavy metal exposure • Radiation or X-rays • Overheating the testicles (frequent use of saunas and hot tubs, sitting for long periods, wearing tight clothing, working on laptop computer for long stretches)	• Industrial chemicals • Radiation • Chemotherapy
Health, Lifestyle, and Other Causes	*Health, Lifestyle, and Other Causes*
• Illegal drug use (cocaine or marijuana) • Alcohol use • Tobacco smoking • Occupation (those involving extended use of computers, shift work, work-related stress) • Emotional stress • Obesity • Prolonged bicycling	• Illegal drug use • Alcohol use • Tobacco smoking • Physical and emotional stress • Eating disorders, obesity

husbandry and is now used to stimulate human reproduction (Bullough, 2005). IUI involves placing fresh or frozen sperm directly into the uterus using a long narrow tube around the time the ovary releases one or more eggs. It is the primary treatment for male infertility. It is also the treatment of choice for lesbian couples and single parents, using sperm of a male donor (De Brucker et al., 2009). The sperm of the male partner of a couple may also be placed in the uterus of a surrogate who gestates and carries the pregnancy for the couple. The resulting child will be biologically related to the male partner and the surrogate, but not to the female partner in the couple. The cost of IUI is approximately $1,200 to $1,500 per cycle (IVF Informant, 2012). The success rate depends on the quality of the sperm (Simonsen, Baksh, & Stanford, 2012).

The birth of the first "test tube baby" in 1978, the first of many assisted reproductive technologies, initiated a new era in infertility management and research. Today, approximately 1% of infants born in the United States are the result of **assisted reproductive technologies** (ART), with 451 clinics providing treatment (Centers for Disease Control and Prevention, 2013d). ART is any procedure that involves removing eggs from a woman's ovaries, combining them with sperm in the laboratory, and returning them to the woman's body or donating them to another woman. The eggs are recovered following hormonal treatment to induce ovulation. Previously frozen eggs may also be used; this is a less expensive and less invasive technique because it does not require egg removal or hyperstimulation of the ovary, but the rate of success decreases. For a woman younger than age 35, the success rate for nonfrozen eggs with the first cycle is 37.4%, whereas if frozen eggs are used the rate is 27.4% (Centers for Disease Control and Prevention, 2013d, 2013e). Women who are older have increased risks of complications and death with ART, but ART has been

Exhibit 2.3 Treatments for Infertility

Male Infertility		Female Infertility	
Problem	**Treatment**	**Problem**	**Treatment**
Low sperm count	Change of environment; antibiotics; surgery; hormonal therapy; artificial insemination	Vaginal structural problem	Surgery
		Abnormal cervical mucus	Hormonal therapy
Physical defect affecting transport of sperm	Microsurgery	Abnormal absence of ovulation	Antibiotics for infection; hormonal therapy
Genetic disorder	Artificial insemination	Blocked or scarred fallopian tubes	Surgery; IVF
Exposure to work environment substances	Early detection and changes in work environment	Uterine lining unfavorable to implantation	Hormone therapy; antibiotics; surgery
Alcohol and caffeine use and cigarette smoking	Reduction or abstinence preconception	Obesity	Weight reduction
Advancing age	Sperm banking at younger age; artificial insemination	Alcohol and caffeine use and cigarette smoking	Abstinence preconception (and postconception to maximize pregnancy outcome)

shown to offer the best chance of having a baby in this population (Armstrong & Akande, 2013; Segev, Riskin-Mashiah, Lavie, & Auslender, 2011). Other risks of ART include prematurity (33.4% for ART vs. 12.2% for general population) and extremely low birth weight (6.1% vs. 2.0%) (Sunderam et al., 2012).

As demonstrated by the Jennifer Bradshaw case, by the time a couple considers the use of ART, they have often struggled with infertility for some time, emotionally and physically, and may be desperate. But the high cost and limited success rate deter some prospective candidates. There are significant disparities in the availability and use of ART. Although women of lower socioeconomic status are exposed to more of the environmental and lifestyle causes for infertility, the high cost of ART is prohibitive for them, particularly if they do not have health insurance or live in a state that does not require coverage for infertility treatment (Kissil & Davey, 2012; Smith et al., 2011). Obviously, in impoverished countries where childlessness is a crippling social taboo, this procedure is beyond the reach of most of the population. Research indicates that health care provider biases about parenthood for gay males, lesbians, minorities, single persons, and women with HIV can be a barrier to access to ART (Kissil & Davey, 2012). In the United States, there are also geographic disparities in access to ART centers, with the greatest access in the Northeast and Alaska, Montana, Wyoming, and West Virginia as particularly underserved states (Nangia, Likosky, & Wang, 2010). Fifteen states have passed legislation that mandates coverage of infertility treatment in private insurance plans, but only 25% of plans in the United States cover infertility treatment (Bitler & Schmidt, 2012; Granger, 2013). The Affordable Care Act provides coverage to all women for obstetric and gynecological care but omits discussion of funding for infertility (Wilemon, 2013). It does allow an increase in flexible spending accounts to $2,500 and increases the tax deduction for infertility treatments from 7.5% to 10%, but this will not bring ART within the reach of women with low economic resources.

The most common types of ART include the following:

- *IVF.* In virto fertilization (IVF) is the most common and most effective ART used today. The woman is treated with a drug that causes the ovaries to produce multiple eggs. Mature eggs are surgically removed from the woman and combined with sperm in a dish in the lab. Healthy embryos are then implanted in the woman's uterus. This method is often used when a woman's fallopian tubes are blocked or a man produces too few sperms. Treatment costs may vary widely among clinics and states, with one cycle of IVF costing approximately $10,000 to $15,000 (Gurevich, 2011). Some clinics allow partial or complete refunds if pregnancy does not occur with higher-priced multiple-cycle plans, a practice referred to as "shared risk" (Advanced Fertility Center of Chicago, 2014). Success rates vary, but most clinics suggest that with a single cycle of IVF, there is a 30% to 40% success rate for women younger than age 34, to less than 5% for women older than 40 (Center for Human Reproduction, 2013b; Gordon et al., 2013), odds slightly lower than what Jennifer Bradshaw was told.

- *Intracytoplasmic sperm injection (ICSI).* ICSI is typically used for couples when there are serious problems with the sperm. In ICSI, rather than mixing egg and sperm in a dish, a single sperm is injected into a single mature egg.

- *GIFT, ZIFT, and PROST.* Gamete intrafallopian tube transfer (GIFT), zygote intrafallopian transfer (ZIFT), and pronuclear stage tubal transfer (PROST) all involve transferring the fertilized egg or eggs and the sperm into the woman's fallopian tube rather than the uterus. Although they were once more commonly used, these methods now represent only about 1% of ART procedures (Infertility & Reproduction Health Center, 2010).

- *Egg donors and gestational carriers.* A couple may use donor eggs to be fertilized with the sperm of the male partner and then have the fertilized egg placed in the uterus of the female partner. The resulting child will be genetically related to the egg donor and the male partner. Donor eggs are often used for women over the age of 40 because the rate of live births using ART decreases with age, from more than 40% for a woman in her late 20s to 30% at the age of 38 and 10% at the age of 40 (WebMD, 2010). Another option is to implant a gestational carrier with the couple's embryo produced through IVF. This option may be used when the woman can produce healthy eggs but is unable to carry a pregnancy to term. Donor eggs or sperm may also be used in IVF to produce the embryo, which is then placed in the gestational carrier. The resulting child has no genetic relationship to the gestational carrier (American Society for Reproductive Medicine, 2013). The costs of using a gestational carrier can easily reach $100,000 because insurance usually does not cover the medical costs of the pregnancy (Herron, 2013).

• *Uterine transplantation.* Uterine transplantation is on the frontier of infertility treatment. It has been tried in a number of animals and with varying degrees of success. One human transplant was tried in Saudi Arabia in 2000 but was unsuccessful. However, uterine transplantation is currently being studied in research centers in the United States and Europe (Catsanos, Rogers, & Lotz, 2013).

Each ART procedure carries risks. These include multiple gestations, which carry higher risks of maternal and neonate complications. In 2009, almost half of ART births resulted in more than one neonate (Centers for Disease Control, 2013d, 2013e). Sometimes IVF-conceived children have rare genetic malformations (Ceelen, van Weissenbruch, Vermeiden, van Leeuwen, & Delemarre-van de Waal, 2008), and genetic counseling is strongly encouraged for this population (Geary & Moon, 2006).

The new technologies for assisting reproduction are raising a number of ethical and legal issues. A major issue relates to the disparities in access to these technologies and the related question of whether some groups should be refused access (Brezina & Zhao, 2012). Another issue is what should happen to unused embryos created by IVF (Clark, 2009). There are also questions about whether embryos created by IVF should be genetically tested before implantation and whether they should be allowed to be selected on the basis of gender. There are many questions about the roles, rights, and responsibilities of surrogates and gestational carriers (Frith & Blyth, 2013; James, Chilvers, Havermann, & Phelps, 2010). Uterine transplantation carries many questions about access, risks, and costs (Catsanos et al., 2013). Questions are also raised about the costs of reproductive technologies in light of the need for adoptive families.

Adoption is another alternative for the infertile couple. From 2007 to 2008, 136,000 children were adopted in the United States, a 6% increase since 2000 and a 15% increase since 1990. Over half of these adoptions were private or tribal, about 40% were accomplished through public agency, and the remainder were intercountry (Child Welfare Information Gateway, 2011). Adoption is almost as emotionally daunting as infertility treatment. A time-consuming multiphase evaluation, which includes a home study, is required before finalization of custody. The idea of parenting an infant with an unknown genetic heritage may be a challenge for some people, particularly because an increasing number of problems previously thought to be environmentally induced are being linked—at least in part—to genetics. On the positive side, however, some individuals and couples prefer adoption to the demands and uncertainties of ART, and some adoptive parents are also committed to giving a home to children in need of care.

Critical Thinking Questions 2.2

In recent years, there has been much controversy about sex education in public schools. Some people argue that there should be no sex education in public schools. What is your opinion on this topic? If you think there should be sex education in public schools, at what age do you think it should start? If you think there should be sex education in public schools, what should it cover?

FETAL DEVELOPMENT

The 40 weeks of **gestation**, during which the fertilized ovum becomes a fully developed infant, are a remarkable time. **Gestational age** is calculated from the date of the beginning of the woman's last menstrual period, a fairly easy time for the woman to identify. In contrast, **fertilization age** is measured from the time of fertilization, approximately 14 days after the beginning of the last menstrual period. The average pregnancy lasts 280 days when calculated from gestational age and 266 days from the time of fertilization. Conventionally, the gestation period is organized by trimesters of about 3 months each. This is a convenient system, but note that these divisions are not supported by clearly demarcated events.

First Trimester

In some ways, the first 12 weeks of pregnancy are the most remarkable. In an amazingly short time, sperm and ovum unite and are transformed into a being with identifiable body parts. The mother's body also undergoes dramatic changes.

Fertilization and the Embryonic Period

Sexual intercourse results in the release of an average of 200 million to 300 million sperm. Their life span is relatively short, and their journey through the female reproductive tract is fraught with hazards. Thus, only about one or two in 1,000 of the original sperm reach the fallopian tubes, which lead from the ovaries to the uterus. Typically, only one sperm penetrates the ripened ovum, triggering a biochemical reaction that prevents entry of any other sperm. The **zygote** (fertilized egg) continues to divide and begins an approximately 7-day journey to the uterus.

Following implantation in the uterine wall, the zygote matures into an **embryo**. The placenta, which acts like a filter between the mother and the growing embryo, also forms. The umbilical cord connects the fetus to the placenta. Oxygen, water, and glucose, as well as many drugs, viruses, bacteria,

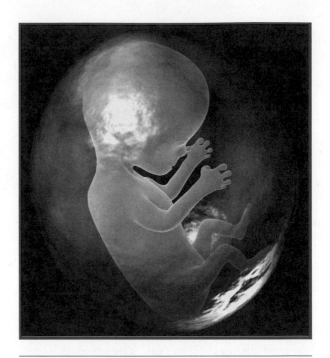

Photo 2.3 After week 8, the embryo is mature enough to be called a fetus.

© iStockphoto.com

vitamins, and hormones, pass through the placenta to the embryo. Amniotic fluid in the uterus protects the embryo throughout the pregnancy.

By the 3rd week, tissue begins differentiating into organs. During this period, the embryo is vulnerable to **teratogens**—substances that may harm the developing organism—but most women do not know they are pregnant. Exhibit 2.4 shows how some relatively common drugs may have a teratogenic effect in the earliest stage of fetal development. Exposure to bisphenol A (BPA) (found in, e.g., plastic materials, toy packaging, and water pipes), especially in the first trimester, has been shown to harm the mammary glands, the immune system, the brain, and the male and female reproductive tract development (Kaur, Shorey, Ho, Dashwood, & Williams, 2013). The importance of a healthy diet cannot be overestimated for the pregnant woman because her choices

> What do social workers need to know about the effects that different aspects of fetal development can have on subsequent development?

can have a lifelong impact on her baby (Anderson, 2010). Studies have found that nutritional deficiency in the first trimester results in an increase in brain abnormalities. High-fat diets negatively affect the development of the hippocampus, which helps control long-term memory and spatial navigation. Researchers have discovered that offspring of women who were either obese or pregnant during a famine were at significantly increased risk for developing schizophrenia (Khandaker, Dibben, & Jones, 2012; Roseboom, Painter, van Abeelen, Veenendall, & de Rooij, 2011). Ongoing research seems to support the interaction of environment and the nutritional status of the pregnant woman as a risk factor for the child developing cancer in later years. Isothiocyanate and cruciferous vegetables (such as broccoli, brussels sprouts, radishes, turnips), betacarotines (found in yellow, red, and orange fruits, vegetables and whole grains), and carotenoid lycopenes (found in tomatoes, guava, apricots, watermelons, papaya) have been found to promote healthy cellular growth in the fetus

(Kaur et al., 2013). The development of a healthy cellular structure promotes health throughout the life span, and the positive effects appear to extend into future generations because the change occurs at the cellular level (Kaur et al., 2013). Moreover, a protein supplement used throughout the pregnancy has been shown to reduce the incidence of small-for-gestational-age babies, especially among undernourished women (Imdad & Bhutta, 2012).

Ectopic pregnancy is one type of mishap that occurs during this period. An ectopic pregnancy occurs if the zygote implants outside the uterus, 93% of the time in the fallopian tubes (Murano & Cocuzza, 2009) and sometimes in the ovaries. Approximately 1% to 2% of pregnancies in the United States result in an ectopic pregnancy, with African American women experiencing 6.8% greater incidence than White women. Women older than 35 have a 3.5% greater chance of an ectopic pregnancy. Women who experience one ectopic pregnancy have higher rates of future ectopic pregnancies (5% to 20%) and infertility (ranging from

Exhibit 2.4   Potential Teratogens During the First Trimester

Substance	Effects on Fetal Development
Antacids	Increase in anomalies
Antianxiety medications	Cranial facial
Anticonvulsant medications	Facial defects, neural tube defects
Barbiturates	Increase in anomalies
Bisphenol A (BPA)	Mammary glands, immune system, brain, reproductive tract
Glucocorticoids (steroids)	Cleft palate, cardiac defects
Haloperidol	Limb malformations
Insulin	Skeletal malformations
Lithium	Goiter, eye anomalies, cleft palate
LSD	Chromosomal abnormalities
Podophyllin (in laxatives)	Multiple anomalies
Selective serotonin reuptake inhibitors (SSRIs)	May lead to neurobehavioral disturbances
Tetracycline (antibiotic)	Inhibition of bone growth, discoloration of teeth
Tricyclic antidepressants	Central nervous system and limb malformations

20% to 70%) (Sepilian, 2013). Chlamydia, the most commonly occurring sexually transmitted disease, increases the risk for an ectopic pregnancy (Centers for Disease Control and Prevention, 2013f).

With advancements in ultrasound technology and microsurgery, the maternal mortality rates in cases of ectopic pregnancy have decreased (Creanga et al., 2011). In early pregnancy, the drug methotrexate is used to terminate the pregnancy (Ehrenberg-Buchner, Sandadi, Moawad, Pinkerton, & Hurd, 2009). Surgery by laparoscopy or laparotomy is required in all cases of ovarian pregnancy (Gupta et al., 2012) and is the standard intervention for ectopic pregnancy in other locations.

The Fetal Period

By about the 8th week after fertilization, the embryo implanted in the uterine wall is mature enough to be called a **fetus**, or unborn baby, and the mother is experiencing signs of her pregnancy. Usually the mother has now missed one or two menstrual periods, but if her cycle was irregular, this may not be a reliable sign. A **multigravida**, or woman who has had a previous pregnancy, often recognizes the signs of excessive fatigue and soreness in her breasts as a sign of pregnancy. Approximately 80% of women experience nausea and vomiting (morning sickness) during the first trimester, as was the case for Felicia Thompson. It has been found that women are at a greater risk for morning sickness if there is a low protein intake. Some early studies have demonstrated that there may be positive benefits in stabilizing early fetal nutrition when a woman experiences morning sickness (Patil, Abrams, Steinmetz, & Young, 2012). Ginger, which has been used for more than 2,000 years to treat morning sickness, has been scientifically shown to reduce vomiting (Ozgoli, Goli, & Simbar, 2009). A few women experience vomiting so severe that it causes dehydration and metabolic changes requiring hospitalization. Hyperemesis gravidarum (HG) occurs in 0.3% to 2% of all pregnant women (more often in young women of lower socioeconomic class with preexisting medical and psychiatric conditions) and is characterized by unexplained cyclic vomiting and dehydration (Gawande, Vaidya, Tadke, Kirpekar,

& Bhave, 2011). It can last through all three trimesters and has been associated with prematurity, low birth weight, preeclampsia, placental abruption, and stillbirth (Bolin, Akerud, Cnattingius, Stephansson, & Wikstrom, 2013; Roseboom, Ravelli, van der Post, & Painter, 2011). Furthermore, HG can disrupt maternal-fetal attachment, and even after HG is resolved, these mothers have a higher risk of mental health issues (McCormack, Scott-Heyes, & McClusker, 2011). Teaching the mother progressive muscle relaxation along with medication management has been shown to reduce HG (Gawande et al., 2011).

From the 7th to 12th week, the fetal heart rate can be heard using a Doppler fetal monitor (Merce, Barco, Alcazar, Sabatel, & Trojano, 2009). Early ultrasounds are being used to predict prenatal complications (Parra-Cordeno et al., 2013). At 12 weeks, the sex of the fetus usually can be detected, and the face is fully formed. The fetus is moving within the mother, but it is still too early for her to feel the movement.

Newly pregnant women often feel ambivalence. Because of hormonal changes, they may experience mood swings and become less outgoing. Anxiety and depression have been found to be higher during the first trimester and in the postpartum period than the subsequent two trimesters and can affect attachment to the fetus (Fan et al., 2009; Figueiredo & Conde, 2011). Concerns about the changes in their bodies, finances, the impact on their life goals, lifestyle adjustments, and interpersonal interactions may cause anxiety. Often the father experiences similar ambivalence, and he may be distressed by his partner's mood swings. Parents who have previously miscarried may have a heightened concern for the well-being of this fetus.

Miscarriage, or **spontaneous abortion**, is a pregnancy loss prior to 20 weeks of gestation and is most prevalent in the first trimester. Approximately 10% to 15% of all clinically recognized pregnancies end in spontaneous abortion, often unrecognized by the mother and without a discernible cause (American College of Nurse-Midwives, 2013). Recurrent miscarriage, three or more consecutive miscarriages, occurs in 1% of women (Horn & Alexander, 2005). Sometimes the causes of miscarriage are not clear, but researchers have identified a number of potential causes. It is estimated that about half of all miscarriages are caused by abnormalities in the genetic makeup of the fetus. Chronic conditions such as uncontrolled diabetes, thyroid disease, and other underlying maternal health conditions increase the risk of miscarriage, as do smoking and alcohol use (American College of Nurse-Midwives, 2013; Medical News Today, 2013). Other potential causes are problems in placental development, womb structure abnormalities, polycystic ovary syndrome, obesity and underweight, environmental toxins, and some medications (Medical News Today, 2013).

The signs and symptoms of miscarriage include vaginal spotting or bleeding, cramping or pain in the abdomen, lower backache, fluid or tissue discharge from the vagina, and feeling faint or light-headed (Medical News Today, 2013). These symptoms do not always mean a woman is having a miscarriage, and sometimes miscarriage happens with no symptoms (American College of Nurse-Midwives, 2013). Miscarriage is most commonly diagnosed these days by ultrasound; blood tests may also be done. Some women choose to allow the miscarriage to pass naturally; this may take 2 weeks. Sometimes it is not possible to pass all of the pregnancy without further assistance. Women may take medication to help the body pass the miscarriage, and sometimes surgery is needed to complete the miscarriage (American College of Nurse-Midwives, 2013). Counseling of women who struggle with miscarriages focuses on genetics and the biopsychological needs of the woman and her family (Price, 2008a). Social workers need to understand the possibility of both short-term and long-term grief following a pregnancy loss and be prepared to talk with women about whether a subsequent pregnancy is planned, the importance the mother attributes to motherhood, and fertility issues (Price, 2008b; Shreffler, Greil, & McQuillan, 2011; Wright, 2011).

Second Trimester

By the 16th week, the fetus is approximately 19 centimeters (7.5 inches) long and weighs 100 grams (3.3 ounces). The most rapid period of brain development is during the second trimester (van de Beek, Thijssen, Cohen-Kettenis, van Goozen, & Buitelaar, 2004). Recent evidence cautions pregnant women to monitor the eating of fish with higher levels of mercury to avoid negative impact on the infant's cognitive skills (Jain, 2013; Zeilmaker et al., 2013). Insufficient weight gain by the pregnant woman during this trimester has been shown to be associated with a small-for-gestational-age (SGA) neonate (Drehmer, Duncan, Kac, & Schmidt, 2013). The second trimester is generally a period of contentment and planning for most women, as it seems to have been for Felicia Thompson. For problem pregnancies, or in troubled environments, quite the opposite may occur. However, the fatigue, nausea and vomiting, and mood swings that often accompany the first few weeks usually disappear in the second trimester.

Hearing the heartbeat and seeing the fetus via ultrasound often bring the reality of the pregnancy home. As seen in the story of the Thompsons, *quickening*—the experience of feeling fetal movement—usually occurs around this time, further validating the personhood of the fetus. *Fetal differentiation*, whereby the mother separates the individuality of the fetus from her own personhood, is usually completed by the end of this trimester. Many fathers too begin to relate to the fetus as a developing offspring.

Some fathers enjoy the changing shape of the woman's body, but others may struggle with the changes. Unless there are specific contraindications, sexual relations may continue throughout the pregnancy, and some men find the second trimester a period of great sexual satisfaction. Often during the second trimester the pregnant woman also experiences a return of her prepregnancy level of sexual desire.

Third Trimester

The third trimester is critical for continued fetal development and preparation for birth. The mother must be able to effectively meet both her nutritional needs and those of the growing fetus. Women who have an excessive weight gain are at risk for preterm delivery and higher rates of cesarean section (Drehmer et al., 2013). Maternal smoking decreases fetal circulation and has been correlated with lower birth weight (Lindell, Marsal, & Kallen, 2012). Spouses who smoke increase the nicotine level in the nonsmoking pregnant woman, even if the spouse smokes outside (Sang-Ho, 2010). The provision of in-home services early in the pregnancy to encourage smoking cessation has been shown to be effective in reducing the incidence of smoking during the third trimester (Matone, O'Reilly, Xianquin, Localio, & Rubin, 2012).

More than 30% of women are iron-deficient by the third trimester, placing the neonate at risk for anemia. Low iron levels can result in permanently altered developmental and metabolic processes and negatively impact brain development (Cao & O'Brien, 2013). In addition, maternal stress can reduce fetoplacental blood flow and fetal weight gain (Helbig, Kaasen, Mait, & Haugen, 2013). Today, a transvaginal neurosonography can visualize the fetal brain anatomy and identify specific neurological problems, including some trisomy patterns that are lethal to the neonate (Ginath et al., 2013; Loureiro, Ferreira, Ushokov, Montenegro, & Nicolaides, 2012). By 24 weeks, the fetus is considered viable in many hospitals. In spite of fetal viability, parents are not usually prepared for childbirth early in the third trimester. Felicia Thompson, for instance, was not prepared for the birth of her son, Paul, who at 26 weeks' gestation struggled to survive.

The tasks of the fetus during the third trimester are to gain weight and mature in preparation for delivery. As delivery nears, the increased weight of the fetus can cause discomfort for the mother, and often she looks forward to delivery with increasing anticipation. Completing preparations for the new baby consume much of her attention.

Labor and Delivery of the Neonate

Predicting when labor will begin is impossible. However, one indication of imminent labor is *lightening* (the descent of the fetus into the mother's pelvis). For a **primipara**—a first-time mother—lightening occurs approximately 2 weeks before delivery. For a **multipara**—a mother who has previously given birth—lightening typically occurs at the beginning of labor. Often the mother experiences Braxton Hicks contractions, brief contractions that prepare the mother and fetus for labor—what is often referred to as "false labor." Usually, true labor begins with a show or release of the mucous plug that covered the cervical opening.

Labor is divided into three stages:

1. In the first stage, the cervix thins and dilates. The amniotic fluid is usually released during this stage ("water breaking"), and the mother feels regular contractions that intensify in frequency and strength as labor progresses. Many factors determine the length of this stage, including the number of pregnancies the mother has experienced, the weight of the fetus, the anatomy of the mother, the strength of the contractions, and the relaxation of the mother in the process. Despite the stories that abound, most mothers have plenty of time to prepare for the upcoming birth. Near the end of this phase, "transition" occurs, marked by a significant increase in the intensity and frequency of the contractions and by heightened maternal emotionalism. The head crowns (is visible at the vulva) at the end of this stage.

2. The second stage is delivery, when the neonate is expelled from the mother. If the newborn is born breech (feet or buttocks first) or is transverse (positioned horizontally in the birth canal) and cannot be turned prior to birth, the mother may require a cesarean section.

3. Typically, within 1 hour after delivery, the placenta, the remaining amniotic fluid, and the membrane that separated the fetus from the uterine wall are delivered with a few contractions. If the newborn breastfeeds immediately, the hormone oxytocin is released to stimulate these contractions.

Following birth, the neonate undergoes rapid physiological changes, particularly in its respiratory and cardiac systems. Prior to birth, oxygen is delivered to the fetus through the umbilical vein, and carbon dioxide is eliminated by the two umbilical arteries. Although the fetus begins to breathe prior to birth, breathing serves no purpose until after delivery. The neonate's first breath, typically in the form of a cry, creates tremendous pressure within the lungs, which clears amniotic fluid and triggers the opening and closing of several shunts and vessels in the heart (Petty, n.d.). The blood flow is rerouted to the lungs.

Many factors, such as maternal exposure to narcotics during pregnancy or labor, can adversely affect the neonate's attempts to breathe—as can prematurity, congenital anomalies, and neonatal infections. Drugs and other interventions may be administered to maintain adequate respiration. To measure the neonate's adjustment to extrauterine life, Apgar scores—simple measures of breathing, heart rate, muscle tone, reflexes, and skin color—are assessed at 1, 5, and 10 minutes after birth. Apgar scores determine the need for resuscitation and indicate whether there are heart problems. The other immediate challenge to the newborn is to establish a stable temperature. Inadequately maintained body temperature creates neonatal stress and thus increased respiratory and cardiac effort, which can result in respiratory failure. Close monitoring of the neonate during the first 4 hours after birth is critical to detect any such problems in adapting to extrauterine life.

Sometimes the baby is born showing no signs of life; this is known as stillbirth. The World Health Organization (WHO, 2013b) defines stillbirth as "a baby born with no signs of life at or after 28 weeks' gestation." The WHO reports that in 2009, there were more than 2.6 million stillbirths around the world, the majority occurring in impoverished countries (World Health Organization, 2013b). In the United States one in 160 pregnancies ends in stillbirth, a statistic that has stabilized over the past 10 years yet remains higher compared with other developed countries (Stillbirth Collaborative Research Network Writing Group, 2011). In up to 50% of stillbirths, the causes are not determined. For those where a possible or probable cause is found, approximately 15% to 20% are caused by chromosomal and genetic abnormalities; placental abruption accounts for 25%; infection 10% to 20%; maternal illness 8% to 10%; and birth trauma 2% to 4% (March of Dimes, 2010; Stillbirth Collaborative Research Network Writing Group, 2011). There is a greater chance of subsequent pregnancies ending in stillbirth once this has occurred (Barclay, 2009). In cases of fetal death, labor generally proceeds immediately and is allowed to occur naturally. But the pregnancy may continue for several days following cessation of movement. Although this wait can be distressing for the mother, cesarean sections are usually avoided because of the potentially high number of complications for the mother (Barclay, 2009). Stillbirths are often unexpected, resulting in great stress and anguish for parents, who blame themselves and struggle with unresolved guilt. Social workers can help parents understand and cope with the strong emotions they are experiencing due to such a significant loss (Price, 2008a, 2008b).

> ### Critical Thinking Questions 2.3
>
> How is ultrasound technology changing the process of fetal development for the mother? What are the benefits to these technologies? What ethical issues are raised by the use of these technologies?

PREGNANCY AND THE LIFE COURSE

The childbearing age for women is usually listed as 15 to 44, but physiologically, women are considered to be at the optimal age for pregnancy from the ages of 20 to 35. Pregnant women of every age need the support of caring family members, friends, and health providers, but women of different ages face pregnancy with different biological bodies and different psychological and social resources. The special circumstances and needs of pregnant adolescents are discussed in Chapter 6, and this section considers pregnancy during young adulthood as well as what is referred to as delayed pregnancy after age 35.

> Under what conditions might the transition to parenthood become a turning point?

Pregnancy during young adulthood is a normative event in most cultures. Psychosocially, young adults are involved in establishing life goals, and both parenthood and employment are often a part of those goals. Women in young adulthood are trying to balance love and work, become more financially secure, and develop a career path or other positive work trajectory (Fulmer, 2011). Over the last three decades, pregnant women's employment patterns have seen major changes, with more women working at all and longer into the pregnancy cycle. From 2006 to 2008, two thirds of first-time mothers in the United States worked during their pregnancy, up from 44% from 1961 to 1965 (U.S. Census Bureau, 2008). There are legal, physical, and psychosocial considerations for maintaining employment during pregnancy. Salihu and colleagues (Salihu, Myers, & August, 2012) have done an in-depth review of research related to these considerations. The following three paragraphs summarize the important findings.

In terms of the legal considerations, a number of countries have laws to protect the rights of pregnant women in the workplace. In the United States, the Pregnancy Discrimination Act (PDA), passed in 1978, established that organizations cannot refuse to hire a woman because she is pregnant, cannot fire a woman or force her to leave because she is pregnant, cannot take away credit for previous years of work during maternity leave, and cannot fire or refuse to hire a woman because she had an abortion. It further states that a pregnant woman may be eligible for temporary job reassignment if she is unable to perform current duties during pregnancy. Other countries have laws that provide additional financial and legal protections. In spite of these laws, researchers have found that pregnant women experience a large amount of discrimination. One survey of employers found that pregnant women are seen as a liability in the workplace. Pregnant women continue to be terminated and demoted when their employers learn they are pregnant.

In terms of physical considerations, most of the available studies have found little or no negative physical effects on either the fetus or the mother from typical job activity, but high levels of physical labor may be associated with preeclampsia in the mother or small-for-gestation-age births. There is also some evidence that exposure to solvents and radiation in the workplace is hazardous to the fetus.

In terms of psychosocial considerations, the research has found no differences in stress, depression, and anxiety between pregnant homemakers, part-time workers, and full-time workers. Some researchers have found, however, that some pregnant women face negative stereotypes about pregnant women from their work colleagues. They also found that pregnant women tend to respond by delaying informing the workplace that they are pregnant and by refusing special accommodations or special time off.

An increasing number of women are delaying childbirth until their late 30s and 40s, even into their 50s and 60s. In the United States, the average age of first-time mothers has increased from 21.4 in 1970 to 25.8 in 2012. For all births in 2012, 14.9% were to women older than 34 (Martin, Hamilton, Osterman, Curtin, & Mathews, 2013). Many women have been struggling with infertility for several years before becoming pregnant; others, like Jennifer Bradshaw, deliberately have chosen to wait until their careers are established. Other women are choosing to have children with a new partner. Some single women, driven by the ticking of the so-called biological clock, may decide to have a child on their own, often using artificial insemination or, more recently, banking their eggs for a future pregnancy.

> What cohort effects can you recognize in attitudes toward delayed pregnancy?

At birth a woman has 6 to 7 million oocytes, but at menarche these decrease to 250,000, declining to only 25,000 at age 37 and declining again at age 38 to a few hundred to 1,000. While there is no absolute fertility age for men, semen volume and sperm motility decrease with age, and there are some changes in sperm cell morphology (Balasch & Gratacos, 2011). Despite decreasing odds of conception as one ages, as a result of the increasing success rate of infertility treatment, there are reports of women bearing their own child or grandchild(ren) at an elderly age (Hale & Worden, 2009; Weingartner, 2008). However, waiting until later in the life course to reproduce increases pregnancy risks.

Although most women acknowledge that they may encounter fertility issues if pregnancy is delayed, many women who know they have fertility problems and are older than age 30 believe that IVF will overcome the effects of age (Balasch & Gratacos, 2011). As with Jennifer and Allan Bradshaw, they may be faced with a rude awakening when they start the process. If pregnancy is successful, the risks are substantial for prematurity and genetic anomalies. Although non-Hispanic White women make up the largest proportion of women who deliver after the age of 35, 15.3% of older non-Hispanic Black women deliver low-birth-weight babies (compared with 8.4% for non-Hispanic White women, 8.4% for all Hispanic women, and 9.3% overall) (Martin et al., 2012). Women older than 30 have increased risk of cesarean delivery and preterm labor, but women who have already had a delivery have fewer complications than women with their first pregnancy at this time of life (Brunner, Larisswa, & Huber, 2009). The likelihood of maternal and infant mortality increases as maternal age increases (Joseph et al., 2005). Finally, advanced paternal age increases the risk of prematurity, with fathers older than age 34 more likely to have a premature baby than a teenaged father, when controlled for maternal age. No race or ethnicity differences were found in risk for the fathers (Reichman & Teitler, 2006).

Women with delayed pregnancy have increased challenges but also some protective factors. They have higher incidences of preconceptual complications such as diabetes, hypertension, and high cholesterol, but this may be counterbalanced by healthier behaviors, fewer gynecological infections, and fewer psychosocial stressors than experienced by younger women (Weisman et al., 2006). For women in their early 30s, there is a 15% chance of pregnancy each month with a miscarriage risk of 20%; for women older than 35, there is a 10% chance of pregnancy each cycle with a 25% chance of miscarriage and a 1 in 350 chance of Down syndrome. For women older than 40, the rates of pregnancy per month drop to less than 5% naturally (about 10% with IVF), the rate of miscarriage is about 33%, and 1 in 38 babies is born with genetic anomalies. It is expected that all of the

eggs of women older than 45 are abnormal, and there is less than a 1% chance of pregnancy in one month, with a miscarriage rate of more than 50% and genetic problems in about 1 in 12 pregnancies (Southern California Center for Reproductive Medicine, 2013).

AT-RISK NEWBORNS

Not all pregnancies proceed smoothly and end in routine deliveries. There are 15 million preterm births per year worldwide, and this rate is increasing (World Health Organization, 2013c). One in nine births in the United States is premature, defined as before 37 weeks' gestation, with prematurity the leading cause of nenonatal illness and responsible for 35% of infant deaths (March of Dimes, 2012a). More than 90% of babies born at less than 28 weeks' gestation (the smallest and most vulnerable of preemies) die in the first days of life in low-income countries, whereas in high-income countries (like the United States), the survival rate for these fragile neonates is more than 90% (March of Dimes, 2012a). Seventy-five percent of the deaths of premature infants are preventable with low-cost interventions such as providing warmth, basic care, and breastfeeding (Hamilton, Martin, and Ventura, 2013; March of Dimes, 2012a; World Health Organization, 2013c). Compared with 34 developed countries, the United States ranks 31st in infant mortality, despite having state-of-the-art medical services (Heisler, 2012). There is a global initiative to lower premature births by expanding birth control options and addressing adolescent pregnancy, preventing and treating STIs, increasing prenatal education, and enhancing prenatal nutrition (World Health Organization, 2013a, 2013c).

Prematurity and Low Birth Weight

The World Health Organization estimated that 9.6% of all global births were preterm in 2005. Approximately 85% of the preterm births occurred in Africa and Asia, but the highest rates of prematurity were in Africa and North America (Beck et al., 2010). Prematurity has a profound long-term effect on the family, including parental mental health problems related to parental stress (Mathews & MacDorman, 2013; Treyvaud et al., 2011). Prematurity costs more than $26 billion per year in the United States, with the average cost of a premature neonate 10 times greater than a full-term neonate (Centers for Disease Control and Prevention, 2013g; National Business Group on Health, 2009). It is estimated that the care of one preemie costs $51,600, with 65% covering medical costs, 22% representing lost wages, and the remaining costs covering maternal care, special education services, and early intervention programs (Centers for Disease Control and Prevention, 2013g).

Approximately 70% of premature births (8% of all births) occur from 34 to 36 weeks (40 weeks is full gestation), and the rate of these late-term preterm births has increased by 25% since 1990 (Loftin, Habli, & DeFranco, 2010). Most of these **late preterm births** are precipitated by induced labor, an elective cesarean, or maternal medical complications (including incorrect gestational estimation) (Loftin et al., 2010; March of Dimes, 2012b). These babies may weigh more than 2,500 grams (5.5 pounds) but are still premature. They are at risk for respiratory distress during the neonatal period as well as increased respiratory problems during the first year of life, feeding problems, hypoglycemia (low blood sugar), hypothermia (low body temperature), and hyperbilirubinemia (jaundice) (Cohen, McEnfoy, & Castile, 2010; Loftin et al., 2010). These babies have a threefold greater chance of dying than a full-term infant (McFarlin, 2009).

Low-birth-weight (LBW) neonates (weighing from 1,500 to 2,500 grams, 3.3 to 5.5 pounds) account for 8.2% of preterm births. Sometimes the LBW infant is **small for gestational age (SGA)**, generally weighing below the 10th percentile for sex and gestational age (Mandy, 2013; MedlinePlus, 2011). In other situations, the LBW infant is premature. These neonates have an increased risk for death in the neonatal period when they need support in feeding, temperature maintenance, and respiration (Cohen et al., 2010). Later, they have a

7% increased risk for developing asthma, showing delayed growth patterns, developing eye problems, and experiencing cardiovascular and renal disorders (McCormick, Litt, Smith, & Zupancic, 2011; Simeoni, Ligi, Buffat, & Boubred, 2011). Additionally, they are at higher risk for depression, anxiety, and inattention/hyperactivity than are full-term infants (Hall, Jaekel, & Wolke, 2012; Sullivan, Msall, & Miller, 2012). The risks continue into the next generation; it has been shown that women who themselves were premature or SGA had a higher risk for pregnancy complications (Boivin et al., 2012). Depression prior to pregnancy has been associated with the delivery of a LBW neonate, and the social worker needs to be aware of the multiple stressors these mothers face (Witt, Wisk, Cheng, Hampton, & Hagen, 2012).

The rate of **very-low-birth-weight (VLBW)** infants—infants weighing less than 1,500 grams (3 pounds, 3 ounces)—increased from 1.2% to 1.5% from 1983 to 2005 and remains at 1.5%. These neonates have a 100 times greater risk of death than a full-term neonate (U.S. Department of Health and Human Services, Maternal and Child Health Bureau, 2011) and are at greater risk for poor physical growth, a lower IQ, learning problems, and dropping out of high school (Child Trends Data Bank, 2013; Tamaru et al., 2011). Some will develop cerebral palsy (2 to 3 per 1,000 live births) (Lie, Groholt, & Eskild, 2010) and experience a lower quality of life (McCormick et al., 2011). There is a higher incidence of anxiety disorder and attention deficit/hyperactivity disorder in VLBW and SGA children compared with their full-term counterparts (Lund et al., 2011). While the cause(s) of all LBWs may not be known, maternal smoking, low prepregnancy weight, infection, increased maternal weight gain during pregnancy, and domestic violence have been shown to be contributors, as have multiple pregnancies. When a neonate is both premature and SGA, there are additive negative physiological and neurological effects (Boulet, Schieve, & Boyle, 2011).

Extremely low-birth-weight (ELBW) infants—infants weighing less than 1,000 grams (2.2 pounds)—add dramatically to the neonatal and infant mortality rates. The birth rate of neonates weighing less than 500 grams (1.1 pounds) has increased from 1.2% to 1.5% while the number of deaths increased from 42.9% to 54.8% from 1983 to 2005 (Lau, Ambalavanan, Chakraborty, Wingate, & Carlo, 2013). The smallest survivors have a very high risk of lifelong neurological, psychological, and physical problems, including cerebral palsy, blindness, deafness, cognitive delays, feeding intolerance, chronic lung disease, failure to thrive, anxiety, and attention deficit/hyperactivity disorder (Boat, Sadhasivam, Loepke, & Kurth, 2011; Boyle et al., 2011; Dewey et al., 2011). We know that most of the ELBW births are due to obstetric complications (especially placental insufficiency due to hypertension) (Claas, de Vries, & Bruinse, 2011). Social workers have an essential role in helping the family because most parents are not aware of the long-term implications of an ELBW neonate and are often asked to make decisions regarding interventions that may involve ethical consideration during a time of crisis (Govande et al., 2013). Paul Thompson is considered an ELBW newborn, and at approximately 540 grams, he has a 50% chance of survival.

The social worker needs to be familiar with some of the key risk factors for prematurity and low birth weight. Smoking during pregnancy increases the risks of ectopic pregnancy, placental abruption, stillbirth, and LBW. Women who abuse substances, including alcohol, are among the heaviest cigarette smokers, compounding risks (Burns, Mattick, & Wallace, 2007; Raatikainen, Huurinainen, & Heinonen, 2007). Advanced maternal age (greater than 30), high blood pressure (Laskov et al., 2012), and obesity also are associated with higher rates of prematurity (Aly et al., 2010). A variety of other factors have been shown to increase the risk of prematurity, including exposure to air pollution (Malmqvist et al., 2011); diabetes (Bener, Salameh, Yousafzal, & Saleh, 2012); male neonate (Aibar, Puertas, Valverde, Carrilo, & Montoya, 2012); feelings of unhappiness during the pregnancy (Chao et al., 2010); STIs, especially in adolescent pregnancy (Borges-Costa, Matos, & Pereira, 2012); intrauterine infections (Claas et al., 2011); and

shorter periods of cohabitation between the parents (Krupitzki et al., 2013). Mothers enrolled in the Medicaid program have increased rates of prematurity and infant death compared with mothers enrolled in nonpublic insurance plans (Eisenhauer, Uddin, Albert, Paton, & Stoughton, 2011), a factor no doubt related to economic status. The mother's adequate nutrition prior to conception, as well as during pregnancy, is another important factor in fetal health. Worldwide, more than one third of infant deaths are related to maternal and child malnutrition (Zerfu & Ayele, 2013).

Several policy initiatives in the United States address the issue of prematurity. Passage of the Prematurity Research Expansion and Education for Mothers who Deliver Infants Early (PREEMIE) Act in 2006 (Pub. L. No. 109-450) mandated interagency coordination, improved data collection, and education for health care professionals. In 2013, the PREEMIE Reauthorization Act (S-252, 113th Congress) was passed to promote further federal funding and awareness campaigns (Congress.gov, 2013). The March of Dimes has promoted a National Prematurity Campaign since 2003 and has been at the forefront in bringing attention to this serious health problem (March of Dimes, 2012c). The Affordable Care Act of 2010 has a provision for in-home services for pregnant women and mothers, but the states have the option to opt out of the block grants that fund this initiative (Affordable Care Act Maternal, Infant, and Early Childhood Home Visiting Program, 2010).

Newborn Intensive Care

The survival rates of premature infants in high-income countries have improved largely because of explosive growth in the field of neonatal medicine and the establishment of regional Neonatal Intensive Care Units (NICUs). Studying the long-term effects of prematurity is difficult because today's 5-year-old who was born at LBW received significantly less sophisticated care than will the current patients in the NICU.

As the Thompsons know all too well, parents' expectations for a healthy newborn are shattered when their child is admitted to an NICU. Their fear and anxiety often make it hard for them to form a strong emotional bond with their newborn. About 90% of mothers and 80% of fathers report that they develop an attachment to the infant during the third trimester of pregnancy (Latva, Lehtonen, Salmelin, & Tamminen, 2007). But when an infant is premature, the parents have not had the same opportunity. In addition, the fear that a sickly newborn may die inhibits some parents from risking attachment. Mothers of VLBW infants visit the newborn significantly less than do mothers of infants who weigh more; for fathers, visitation is influenced by geographical distance and the number of other children in the home (Latva et al., 2007). Some parents are consumed with guilt about their baby's condition and believe that they will only harm the newborn by their presence. The NICU experience places the mother at risk of depression, but it also has been found that short-term psychotherapy can reduce stress and promote visitation (Friedman, Kessler, & Martin, 2009). Felicia and Will Thompson had to work hard to contain their anxiety about Paul's frailties.

Early disruption in bonding may have a larger long-term impact on the child than the infant's actual medical condition (Wigert, Johannson, Berg, & Hellstrom, 2006). The response has been a movement toward family-centered NICU environments, which are structured to promote interaction between the infant and the parents, siblings, and others in the family's support system. Mothers seem to more readily engage in caring for their infants in this environment than fathers (Johnson, 2008). Ample opportunity to interact with Paul facilitated Felicia and Will Thompson's attempts to bond with him.

Neuroscientists have recently called attention to the physical environment needs of prematurely born babies, noting the competing needs of these vulnerable babies and the medical staff that care for them in NICUs. The medical staff need lights, noisy equipment, and alarms to signal physiological distress. The vulnerable baby needs a physical environment that more nearly approximates the uterus, without bright lights and stressful noise stimulation, and the premature brain is negatively affected by the stressful neonatal environmental conditions (Xiong & Zhang, 2013; Zeisel, 2006). The neonatal environmental conditions may be as much a risk factor for negative pregnancy outcomes as prematurity (Als, Heidelise, & Butler, 2008). With this discrepancy in mind, NICUs are being modified to accommodate the neurological needs of the vulnerable newborns.

Neonatology, the care of critically ill newborns, has only recently been recognized as a medical specialty. It is a much-needed specialty, however. Since the advent of the NICU in the 1970s, the survival rate of critically ill neonates has continued to increase. It is highly unlikely that Paul Thompson would have survived in 1970. Social workers in an NICU must negotiate a complex technological environment requiring specialized skill and knowledge while attempting to respond with compassion, understanding, and appropriate advocacy. Research has clearly shown the need for social work intervention that enables the parents to bond with their children and decreases the level of stress (Spielman & Taubman-Ben-Ari, 2009). It helps to remember that the effort could affect a neonate's complete life course.

Major Congenital Anomalies

Overall, only 2% to 4% of all surviving newborns have a birth defect. However, the number of neonates born with anomalies caused by genetics, exposure to teratogens, or nonhereditary factors that affect development of the fetus does not reflect the number of abnormal embryos. Fewer than half of all fertilized ova result in a live birth; the rest are spontaneously aborted, oftentimes before a woman knows she is pregnant. Based on data from a 10-year study of placental tissue following pregnancy loss, 80.5% of these spontaneous abortions were caused by a genetic anomaly (Osterweil, 2013). Another study of subsequent pregnancy outcomes after a pregnancy loss attributed to a genetic anomaly revealed that two thirds of these women had a live birth (Osterweil, 2013). Social workers need to be mindful of the low probability that a child will be born with a genetic disorder or congenital anomaly when responding to parental fears.

In 2006 the American College of Medical Genetics with the March of Dimes established a recommended list of 28 core metabolic, endocrine, and hemoglobin disorders for which newborns should be screened because early intervention for these hereditary yet rare diseases is essential (Watson, Mann, Lloyd-Puryear, Rinaldo, & Howell, 2006). Twenty-one of these tests are required in all states while some states screen for more than 30 disorders. The National Newborn Screening and Global Resource Center (NNSGRC) provides genetic and newborn screening information, including resources for parents and providers to respond to positive testing results (National Newborn Screening and Global Resource Center, 2013). A *screening* test may not be definitive, however, and, if positive, is usually followed by a *diagnostic* test to confirm a genetic mishap. Some screening may be done before birth (Centers for Disease Control, 2011).

Preventing, diagnosing, and predicting the outcome of genetic disorders are very difficult because of the complexities of many genetic processes, including the following (Genetics Home Reference, 2013):

- *Variable expressivity.* Genes manifest differently in different people. For example, persons with cystic fibrosis, caused by a recessive gene, display wide variability in the severity of symptoms. The expression of the disorder appears to be influenced by the interplay of psychological, social, political, economic, and other environmental factors. The effects can be exacerbated by maternal substance abuse, inadequate maternal nutrition, birth trauma, and poverty.

- *Genetic heterogeneity.* The same characteristic may be a consequence of one of a number of genetic anomalies. For example, neural tube defects may result either from gene mutations or from exposure to specific teratogens.

- *Pleiotropy principle.* The same gene may influence seemingly unrelated systems. Hair color, for example, is typically linked to a particular skin color (such as blonde hair with light complexion, black hair with olive complexion).

- *Epigenetics.* Environmental factors may influence gene expression (phenotype) without changing the genetic makeup of a person (genotype). These factors influence the chemicals that trigger (methyl groups) or inhibit (acetyl groups) genetic expression. Furthermore, these chemicals appear to have a generational influence without genetic alterations. Examples of these epigenetic environmental influences include nutrition, trauma such as childhood abuse, and teratogens (Kubota & Hata, 2013). The epigenetic influences in many cases are preventable and treatable, especially if identified early in development.

Congenital anomalies fall into four categories, summarized in Exhibit 2.5, which includes examples of the most prevalent anomalies (Pierce, 2012).

1. *Inheritance of a single abnormal gene.* An inherited anomaly in a single gene may lead to a serious disorder. The gene may be recessive, meaning that both parents must pass it along, or it may be dominant, in which case only one parent needs to have the gene in order for it to be expressed in the child. A third possibility is that the disorder is sex-linked, meaning that it is passed along by either the father or the mother (American College of Obstetricians and Gynecologists, 2013; National Human Genome Research Institute, 2013b; Pierce, 2012).

2. *Multifactorial inheritance.* Some genetic traits, such as height and intelligence, are influenced by environmental factors such as nutrition. Their expression varies because of **multifactorial inheritance**, meaning they are controlled by multiple genes. Multifactorial inheritance is implicated in traits that predispose a person to mental illnesses, such as depression. However, these traits are merely predisposing factors, creating what is called **genetic liability**. Siblings born with the same genetic traits thus may vary in the likelihood of developing a

specific genetically based disorder, such as alcoholism or mental illness (American College of Obstetricians and Gynecologists, 2013; National Human Genome Research Institute, 2013b).

3. *Chromosomal aberration.* Some genetic abnormalities are not hereditary but rather caused by a genetic mishap during development of the ovum or sperm cells. Sometimes the cells end up missing chromosomes or having too many. When the ovum or sperm cell has fewer than 23 chromosomes, the probability of conception and survival is minimal. But in the presence of too many chromosomes in the ovum or the sperm, various anomalies occur (American College of Obstetricians and Gynecologists, 2013; National Human Genome Research Institute, 2013b). Down syndrome, or trisomy 21, the most common

chromosomal aberration, is the presence of 47 chromosomes—specifically, an extra chromosome in the 21st pair. Its prevalence is 1 in 691 live births overall as with Cecelia Kin, but as seen in Hazel Gereke's story, it increases to 1 in 214 for women over age 35, and to 1 in 25 for women over the age of 45. Yet, while the prevalence increases with maternal age, 80% of children born with Down syndrome are to mothers under the age of 35 (National Down Syndrome Society [NDSS], 2013).

4. *Exposure to teratogens.* Teratogens can be divided into four categories: radiation, infections, maternal metabolic imbalance, and drugs and environmental chemicals. In the Thompson story, Felicia wondered if Paul's premature birth was a result of prenatal exposure to paint fumes. It may have been, depending on what specific chemicals

Exhibit 2.5 Four Categories of Congenital Anomalies

Inheritance of Single Abnormal Gene		
Recessive	**Dominant**	**Sex-Linked**
Sickle-cell anemia Tay-Sachs disease Cystic fibrosis	Neurofibromatosis Huntington's disease	Hemophilia Duchenne muscular dystrophy

Multifactorial Inheritance			
Possible mental illness	Alcoholism	Heart disease	Diabetes

Chromosomal Aberration		
Down syndrome (additional 21st chromosome)	Turner syndrome (X)	Klinefelter syndrome (XXY)

Exposure to Teratogens			
Radiation	**Infections**	**Maternal Metabolic Imbalance**	**Drugs and Environmental Chemicals**
Neural tube defects	Rubella: deafness, glaucoma Syphilis: neurological, ocular, and skeletal defects	Diabetes: neural tube defects Folic acid deficiency: brain and neural tube defects Hyperthermia (at 14–28 days): neural tube defects	Alcohol: intellectual disability Heroin: attention deficit disorder Amphetamine: congenital defects

were involved, when exposure occurred, and to what degree. Parents who, like the Thompsons, are experiencing considerable guilt over their possible responsibility for their baby's problems may take comfort from the knowledge that the impact of exposure to teratogens can vary greatly. Much depends on the timing of exposure. The various organ systems have different critical or **sensitive periods,** summarized in Exhibit 2.6.

Today most pregnant women in the United States undergo a maternal blood screen and ultrasound between week 11 and week 13. Most recently recommended is the noninvasive prenatal screening, or NIPS (American College of Medical Genetics, 2013). Second trimester screening, weeks 15 to 20, includes a maternal serum screen and an anomaly ultrasound (18 to 20 weeks), which produces a visual image of the developing fetus. Based on these results, the doctor may offer diagnostic tests such as high-resolution ultrasound and chorionic villi testing (CVT). CVT involves the insertion of a catheter through the cervix into the uterus to obtain a sample of the developing placenta and can be done as early as 10 to 12 weeks. *Amniocentesis* is the extraction of amniotic fluid for chromosomal analysis; it involves inserting a hollow needle through the abdominal wall during the second trimester. At greater risk of a genetic anomaly are women older than age 35, carriers of sex-linked genetic disorders and single gene defects, parents with chromosomal disorders, and women who have had previous and recurring pregnancy loss. When any of these risks is present, screening or diagnostic tests may be offered earlier in pregnancy (American Pregnancy Association, 2012; Centers for Disease Control, 2011).

Exhibit 2.6   Critical Periods in Prenatal Development

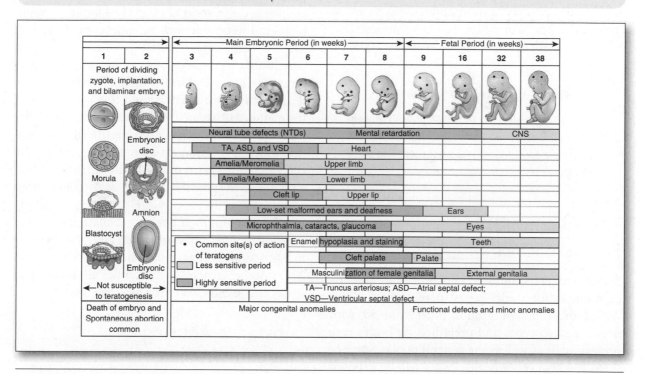

SOURCE: Moore, K. L., Persaud, T. V. N., & Torchia, M. G. (2013). *Before we were born: Essentials of embryology and birth defects* (8th ed.). Philadelphia: Saunders/Elsevier, Figure 19-11.

If an anomaly is detected, the decisions that need to be made are not easy ones. The possibility of false readings on these tests makes the decisions even more complicated. Should the fetus be aborted? Should fetal surgery be undertaken? Could gene replacement therapy, implantation of genetic material to alter the genotype—still a costly experimental procedure—prevent an anomaly or limit its manifestation? Do the parents have the financial and psychological means to care for a neonate with a disability? What is the potential impact on the marriage and extended family system? What is the potential long-term impact of knowing one's genetic makeup? For example, the 2008 Genetic Information Nondiscrimantion Act (GINA) prohibits insurance companies and employers from using genetic information in discriminatory ways (National Human Genome Research Institute [NIH], 2012). However, as the U.S. health care system undergoes change and new knowledge about genetic engineering emerges, this is an issue that should be considered by social workers. We do know that nonurgent decisions should be postponed until parents have an opportunity to adjust to the crisis and acquire the necessary information (National Association of Social Workers, 2003).

Critical Thinking Questions 2.4

Why do you think the rate of prematurity is higher in the United States than in most other industrialized countries? How could you go about learning more about the answer to this question?

SPECIAL PARENT POPULATIONS

Social workers should recognize the unique circumstances for some special parent populations. All of these parent groups must contend with negative stereotypes and prejudice, by health care professionals as well as the general public. Some of them fear that other health issues will be exposed by their participation in maternity care. Some need assistance to manage other health problems in the context of maternity care. Six special parent populations are briefly discussed here.

Gay and Lesbian Parents

At the time this is being written, same-sex marriage is legal in 15 countries and several subnational jurisdictions. In the United States, 16 states plus the District of Columbia authorize same-sex marriage, and with the 2013 repeal of one section of the Defense of Marriage Act by the U.S. Supreme Court, same-sex couples must receive the same federal benefits as heterosexual couples in those states where same-sex marriage is recognized. Increasingly, both gay male and lesbian couples are choosing to become parents. There have been great gains for marriage and adoption rights of same-sex couples in Europe and North America in recent years, but these couples continue to face much prejudice and discrimination when they wish to become parents (Pennings & Mertes, 2012).

Some same-sex couples may have children from prior relationships. Gay or lesbian individuals and couples are also seeking to create a family through biological reproduction, adoption, or fostering. There is some evidence that gay male and lesbian parenting faces more resistance than same-sex marriage (Pennings & Mertes, 2012). When a couple decides to have a biological child, they can use one of the methods of assisted reproduction discussed earlier. Lesbian couples typically use artificial insemination with a sperm donor. Gay male couples typically contribute the sperm of one of the fathers and find a surrogate to carry the pregnancy. Although more and more birth parents are choosing same-sex couples to adopt their babies, gay male and lesbian individuals and couples are often given low priority in agency adoptions (Human Rights Campaign, 2013). Some agencies and localities are more open to gay and lesbian foster parents than others.

Substance-Abusing Pregnant Women

Our knowledge of the developmental impact of maternal use of illegal and legal substances is rapidly increasing. The good news is that health care professionals are increasingly able to avoid prescribing legal drugs that might harm the developing fetus, once pregnancy is confirmed. The bad news is that too many pregnant women are still harming their babies through use of illegal drugs or abuse of legal substances. And, unfortunately, many women do not know they are pregnant during the first trimester, a period when the fetus is very vulnerable to teratogens.

The 2010 National Survey on Drug Use and Health (NSDUH) found that 4.4% of pregnant women aged 15 to 44 reported using illicit substances in the past month, an increase from 3% in 2002 (Wendell, 2013). These figures are considered to be a low estimate because drug use during pregnancy is underreported. The rate of illicit drug use by pregnant women was 16.2% among pregnant women aged 15 to 17, 7.4% aged 18 to 25, and 1.9% aged 26 to 44. There is also an epidemic of prescription drug abuse, and this is an issue that needs further attention (Sheehan & Sheehan, 2013).

Possible effects of commonly abused legal and illegal substances are presented in Exhibit 2.7. Fetal alcohol spectrum disorders (FASD) include fetal alcohol effects (FAE) and fetal alcohol syndrome (FAS), which are caused by alcohol consumption during pregnancy. FASD is associated with preterm birth, low birth weight, intrauterine growth restriction, and failure to thrive. It increases the likelihood of cognitive disability, malformations of the skeletal system and major organ systems, central nervous system defects, facial abnormalities, and vision and hearing problems (Wendell, 2013). FASD are 100% preventable with alcohol abstinence. Cocaine and crack use is connected with increased chances of preterm birth, low birth weight, small head circumference, and intrauterine growth restriction. It can also lead to the placenta separating from the uterine wall, which can lead to maternal and fetal death, premature rupture of the membranes, and maternal migraines and seizures (Wendell, 2013). Marijuana is the most commonly used illicit drug among pregnant women (although its illegal status is being challenged), with 11% of pregnant women reporting recent marijuana use. There is no consensus in the literature about the effects of prenatal exposure to marijuana (Wendell, 2013).

Exhibit 2.7   Commonly Abused Drugs and Fetal Effects

	Alcohol	Cocaine	Amphetamines	Cigarettes	Heroin
Abortion	X	X	X		X
Stillbirth	X	X	X		X
Prematurity	X	X	X	X	X
Low birth weight	X	X	X	X	X
Intrauterine growth restriction	X	X	X	X	X
Respiratory distress	X	X			X
Withdrawal	X	X	X		X
Fine motor problems	X				X
Malformations	X	X	X		X
Developmental delays	X	X	X		X

Social workers are collaborating with other professionals to provide public education to women in the childbearing years about the teratogenic effects of alcohol, tobacco, and other drugs. Because fathers are known to influence the substance use by mothers, and there is increasing evidence that paternal use impacts sperm, fathers increasingly are included in preventive efforts (Bertrand, Floyd, & Weber, 2005; Chang, McNamara, Orav, & Wilkins-Haug, 2006). It is important that substance-abusing pregnant women receive comprehensive and compassionate maternity care aimed at helping them manage the complex physical, emotional, and social challenges associated with addiction (Wendell, 2013).

Pregnant Women With Eating Disorders

There was an increase in eating disorders, primarily anorexia nervosa (self-imposed starvation) and bulimia (binging and purging), among U.S. teenagers and women in the United States during the past century, but the rate has stabilized in the last two decades (Smink, vanHoeken, & Hoek, 2012). Binge eating disorder is now recognized in DSM-5 as a separate category and is more common in older individuals. Eating disorders are most commonly found in women of childbearing age and are estimated to be an issue for 5.9% of women in the United States, but incidence among pregnant women is reported to be lower than that (Broussard, 2012). Several researchers have found that women with eating disorders reduce or suspend symptoms while pregnant and return to disordered eating after giving birth (Broussard, 2012).

An eating disorder during pregnancy is of concern because nutrition plays an important role in maternal health and pregnancy outcomes. Maternal outcomes can include poor nutrition, dehydration, cardiac irregularities, gestational diabetes, depression, labor complications, and nursing difficulties (National Eating Disorders Association, n.d.). Restricting caloric intake, binge eating, purging, or any combination of these behaviors can lead to nutritional insufficiency for both the mother and the fetus. Diets lacking in essential nutrients

have been associated with infertility, spontaneous abortion, preterm birth, low birth weight, and SGA neonates. SGA neonates are at great risk for perinatal death, congenital anomalies, impaired postnatal growth, and neurological disabilities (Broussard, 2012). It is critical that maternity care providers screen for eating disorders.

Pregnant Women With Disabilities

More than 27 million women in the United States have a disability, and, due to longer life expectancy, that number is growing, especially for those who reach childbearing age (Centers for Disease Control and Prevention, 2012b). For example, women with spina bifida are a population that, because of medical advances, only recently is living beyond sexual maturity (Jackson & Mott, 2007). People with physical or mental disabilities may be perceived as "asexual," and health care providers may not consider conception, pregnancy, and childbirth as relevant issues for them (Sawin, 1998). Health care providers may communicate unwarranted negative expectations about pregnancy outcomes or not take the woman's disability into consideration when providing contraceptive options. For example, women with spinal cord injury should not use IUDs due to an increased risk of bleeding, and barrier methods requiring manual dexterity may not be feasible. This is an issue worldwide and is perhaps even more pervasive in nonindustrialized countries (Emmett & Alant, 2006; Kristof & WuDunn, 2009).

Most women with disabilities can manage pregnancy and give birth to healthy babies if they have a health provider familiar with the disability and related risks, and they are monitored more closely than are women without disabilities (Center for Research on Women With Disabilities, 2013). Some risks include increased blood clots for women who use wheelchairs, risk of pneumonia when a respiratory impairment preexists, bladder infections that can lead to spontaneous abortion and miscarriage, and preterm labor and low-birth-weight babies. Women with spinal cord injury may have more spasticity, seizures, and a life-threatening sudden rise in blood pressure that is not related to pregnancy, per se (Center for Research on Women With Disabilities, 2013).

Despite public distaste for the practice, some persons with disabilities continue to be targets of involuntary sterilization (International Federation of Persons With Physical Disability, 2011). Professionals do not agree about how to handle the reproductive rights of individuals with severe inheritable disorders or with limited capacity to care for a child. Many do agree, however, that physical, environmental, interpersonal, informational, and policy barriers leave people with disabilities disenfranchised from both the reproductive health system and other reproductive options. As society slowly begins to recognize persons with disabilities as full members of society, some of the negative implications of conception, pregnancy, and childbirth with this population may decline. Social workers can be partners in this quest.

Incarcerated Pregnant Women

In 2009, 200,000 women were incarcerated in U.S. jails and prisons (Association of Women's Health, Obstetric and Neonatal Nurses [AWHONN], 2011). Although women are still a minority, about 7.5%, of the U.S. jail and prison population, the number has risen by 832% since the 1970s. This dramatic increase is largely due to mandatory drug sentencing laws, and most of the women are incarcerated for nonviolent offenses (AWHONN, 2011). The United States has the highest incarceration rate in the world and also incarcerates women at a higher rate than any other country (Hartny, 2006). Approximately 6% to 10% of incarcerated women in the United States are pregnant. Prior to entering the criminal justice system, these women are less likely than other pregnant women to receive prenatal care and more likely to have experienced poor nutrition, chronic disease, infectious disease, mental illness, drug and alcohol abuse, and intimate partner violence (Clarke & Adashi, 2011).

In 2011, the National Women's Law Center reported that 43 states in the United States do not require medical examinations as a part of prenatal care for incarcerated pregnant women, 41 states do not require prenatal nutrition counseling or provide appropriate nutrition, 34 do not require screening and treatment for women with high-risk pregnancies, and 48 do not require screening for HIV. Both the National Women's Law Center (2011) and AWHONN (2011) have protested the routine shackling of pregnant women that continues to go on in some state prisons. These mothers and babies are a particularly vulnerable group. Social workers working in prisons and jails can advocate for conditions to improve birth outcomes for the infants and pregnancy circumstances of the mothers as well as their extended families.

HIV-Infected Pregnant Women

Worldwide, women are more than half of all people living with HIV/AIDS, and young women aged 15 to 24 have twice the prevalence rate of young men of the same age (amfAR, The Foundation for AIDS Research, 2013). In the United States, women accounted for 20% of new HIV diagnoses in 2010, with the great majority of these new cases resulting from heterosexual contact (Centers for Disease Control and Prevention, 2013i). In that same year, the rate of new HIV infections among Black women was 20 times that of White women, and the rate among Hispanic/Latino women was 4 times the rate of White women (Centers for Disease Control and Prevention, 2013i). The number of women with HIV giving birth in the United States increased by approximately 30% from 2000 to 2006, but the estimated number of infections to newborn babies continues to decline (Centers for Disease Control and Prevention, 2012c). Women with HIV who take antiretroviral (ARV) medications and refrain from breastfeeding can reduce the risk of transmitting the disease to their babies to less than 1%. It should be noted, however, that in low-income countries without potable water, formula feeding may be more dangerous than breastfeeding with an HIV-infected mother (Centers for Disease Control and Prevention, 2013i).

In 2003 a coordinated response of multinational and U.S. agencies to the worldwide HIV/AIDS epidemic was launched, the President's Emergency Plan for AIDS Relief, or PEPFAR, with promising results. From 2001 to 2011, a 50% decrease in new HIV infections was reported in 25 countries, along with a 43% decrease in new infections in children from 2003 to 2011. Since 2011 there has been a 60% increase in the number of people accessing treatment worldwide (Centers for Disease Control and Prevention, 2013i). Currently the WHO recommends early HIV testing of all pregnant women and provision of antiretroviral drugs (ARVs) to all HIV-positive mothers, along with infant prophylaxis, to prevent mother-to-child HIV transmission (World Health Organization, 2013d, 2013e). However, in 2011, only about 57% of pregnant women with HIV in low- and middle-income countries received the most effective ARV medicines to prevent mother-to-child transfer of HIV (World Health Organization, 2012c). In spite of decreasing treatment costs, treatment barriers continue, including the stigma of HIV/AIDS paired with low status of women in many countries (Gable, Gostin, & Hodge, 2008; Kristoff & WuDunn, 2009). Treatment barriers in the United States include the lack of financial resources and health insurance, limited transportation, and responsibilities to care for others, especially children (American College of Obstetrics and Gynecology, 2012). Working to increase HIV awareness and promote clear notification of HIV status will continue to be important social work roles.

RISK AND PROTECTIVE FACTORS IN CONCEPTION, PREGNANCY, AND CHILDBIRTH

As the life course journey begins, human behavior is being shaped by risk factors and protective factors. Throughout this chapter, you have read about factors that either increase risk or offer protection for healthy processes of conception, pregnancy, and childbirth. Selected factors are summarized in Exhibit 2.8. A confluence of biological, psychological, and social factors determines whether a couple can conceive. Once the woman is pregnant, an interplay of biological, psychological, and social factors influence the growth and development of the fetus, the childbirth experience, and the health of the new baby. You also read about how the health of the new baby has long-term implications across the life course.

There is growing evidence from life course epidemiological research that experiences in these earliest days of a human life course have health impacts at every stage of the life course. This has led to a new "developmental" model for the origins of disease (for an overview of this model, see Barker & Thornburg, 2013). This model proposes that nutrition during fetal life is a key factor in later chronic disease. The fetal response to malnutrition is to slow growth and alter the metabolism in order to survive. It is not just the mother's diet during pregnancy that matters, but also her nutrient stores at the time of conception. There is much research evidence that a range of chronic diseases have their origin in malnutrition during fetal life and infancy, including cardiovascular disease, type 2 diabetes, some cancers, and chronic infections. Research also indicates that a baby's birth weight is affected not only by maternal nutrition before and during pregnancy but also by the shape and size of the placenta at birth. And certain patterns of shape and size of the placenta have been found to be a risk factor for heart disease, hypertension, and some forms of cancer. How and why the placenta develops a particular shape and size is not well understood, but animal research has found that the placenta enlarges in response to malnutrition in midpregnancy. Barker and Thornburg (2013) conclude that this research on fetal nutrition indicates that "protecting the nutrition and health of girls and young women should be the corner stone of public health" (p. 518).

Seldom is one environmental, social, or biological risk factor solely responsible for an

---

Critical Thinking Questions 2.5

Pregnancy is a powerful experience for the pregnant woman as well as for her partner. What are the biological needs of the pregnant woman? The psychological needs? The social needs? Where there is an involved father, what are the biological needs of the father? The psychological needs? The social needs?

outcome (Epps & Jackson, 2000). As you review the selected risk and protective factors (Exhibit 2.8), keep in mind that most outcomes are influenced by several factors, and ongoing research is showing an ever-increasing complexity of interacting factors.

Exhibit 2.8 Selected Risk and Protective Factors for Conception, Pregnancy, and Birth

	Risk Factors	Protective Factors
Conception	Low sperm count	Father drug abstinence (marijuana)
	Fallopian tubal factors	Gynecological care
	Genetic abnormality	Genetic counseling
	Adolescent promiscuity	Family life education; contraception; abstinence
	Endometriosis	Hormone therapy; surgery
	Inadequate nutrition for sexually active women of childbearing age	Folic acid supplement
	Obesity	
Pregnancy	Obesity	Normal weight maintenance
	Sexually transmitted diseases	Barrier birth control methods
	Female age (<18 or >35)	Family life education; birth control
	Delivery before 38 weeks	Women, Infants, and Children program
	Gestation, toxemia, diabetes	Prenatal care
	Stress because of inadequate resources	Social and economic support
	Trauma	Accident prevention (falls, fire, car)
	Smoking	Smoking cessation program
Birth	Venereal diseases such as gonorrhea and positive Group B strep	Prenatal care; antibiotic eye drops for neonate; maternal testing
	Meconium aspiration; anoxia	C-section delivery; drugs during pregnancy; well-managed labor and delivery
	Prolonged and painful labor	Birthing classes; social support; father's presence at birth; adequate pain control
	Obesity	Newborn screening tests

Implications for Social Work Practice

Social workers practicing with persons at the stage of life concerned with conception, pregnancy, and childbirth should follow these principles:

- Respond to the complex interplay of biopsychosocial and spiritual factors related to conception, pregnancy, and childbirth.
- When working with clients, both females and males, of childbearing age, always consider the possibility of conception, pregnancy, and childbirth; their potential outcomes; and their impact on the changing person/environment configuration.
- Identify the needs of vulnerable or at-risk groups and work to provide services for them. For example, structure birth education classes to include not only family but family-like persons and provide interpreters for the hearing impaired or use appropriate technology to deliver content.
- Actively pursue information about particular disabilities and their impact on conception, pregnancy, and childbirth and include this topic in client assessment.
- Acquire and apply skills in advocacy, education about reproductive options, consumer guidance in accessing services, and case management.
- Assume a proactive stance when working with at-risk populations to limit undesirable reproductive outcomes and to help meet their reproductive needs. At-risk groups include adolescents, low-income women, women involved with substance abuse, women with eating disorders, and women with disabilities who lack access to financial, physical, psychological, and social services.
- Assist parents faced with a potential genetic anomaly to gain access to genetic screenings, prenatal diagnosis, postnatal diagnosis, treatment, and genetic counseling.
- Involve parents in decision making to the greatest extent possible by delaying nonurgent decisions until parents have had a chance to adjust to any crisis and acquire the necessary information to make an informed decision.
- Establish collaborative relationships with other professionals to enhance and guide assessment and intervention.
- Identify and use existing programs that provide education and prenatal services to women, particularly for those most at risk of undesirable outcomes.

Key Terms

assisted reproductive technologies (ART)
chromosomes
dominant genes
embryo
extremely low birth weight (ELBW)
family pluralism
fertilization
fertilization age
fetal viability
fetus
genes

genetic liability
genotype
germ cell
gestation
gestational age
infertility
interactive genes
late preterm birth
low birth weight (LBW)
miscarriage
multifactorial inheritance
multigravida
multipara

neonate
phenotype
primipara
recessive genes
sensitive period
sex chromosomes
sex-linked trait
small for gestational age (SGA)
spontaneous abortion
teratogens
very low birth weight (VLBW)
zygote

1. Locate the National Association of Social Workers Code of Ethics on the organization's website at www.naswdc .org. Choose an ethical issue from the following list. Using the Code of Ethics as a guide, what values and principles can you identify to guide decision making related to the issue you have chosen?

   - Should all women and men, regardless of marital status or income, be provided with the most current technologies to conceive when they are unable to do so?
   - What are the potential issues of preservation and gestational surrogacy in terms of social justice and diversity?
   - Should pregnant women who abuse substances be incarcerated to protect the developing fetus?
   - Do adoptive parents have the right to know the genetic background of an adoptee?
   - Which genes, if any, should be selected for reproduction?
   - Will persons who are poor be economically disadvantaged in the use of genetic information?

2. Select one of the four life journeys that introduced this chapter: Jennifer Bradshaw's, the Thompsons', the Gerekes', or Cecelia Kin's. Identify the risk and protective factors related to their conception, pregnancy, and childbirth experience. Then change one factor in the story; for example, assume that Cecelia Kin's income was not needed. How might that alter her life course? Then try changing one factor in another story; for example, assume Jennifer had only a 10th-grade education. How does that change the trajectory of her story? Try again; for example, assume Felicia Thompson was being treated for depression when she became pregnant. Again, how does that factor alter her life course and that of her child?

3. In student groups of three or four, review the list of contraception options presented in this chapter. With each group representing a different 3- to 5-year age range of the childbearing age spectrum (ages 15 to 44), discuss the potential access and use or misuse of each form of contraception. Also, consider the role of a social worker in various social welfare settings in helping women (who represent different age, religious, and ethnic groups) select a form of birth control.

The American Congress for Obstetricians and Gynecologists (ACOG): www.acog.org

Site provides educational information and resources related to sexuality and women's health, including a section for patients, and offers materials in both Spanish and English.

The American Pregnancy Association: americanpregnancy.org

Site presented by the American Pregnancy Association contains information on a number of pregnancy-related topics, including infertility, adopting, pregnancy options, multiples pregnancy, and the developing baby.

Center for Research on Women With Disabilities (CROWD): www.bcm.edu/crowd

Site presented by the Center for Research on Women With Disabilities contains reports on sexual and reproductive health for women with disabilities, educational materials, and links to other related research.

Centers for Disease Control and Prevention: www.cdc.gov

U.S. government site contains public health information, current research, and health census data that include diseases and conditions related to conception, pregnancy, and childbirth with a focus on prevention; materials in both Spanish and English.

Childbirth.org: www.childbirth.org

Award-winning site maintained by Robin Elise Weiss contains information on conception, pregnancy, and birth, including recommended pregnancy books and access to a free online childbirth class.

National Healthy Mothers, Healthy Babies Coalition (HMHB): www.hmhb.org

Site maintained by HMHB, an informal coalition dedicated to improving the quality and reach of public education about prenatal and infant care, contains a blog, newsroom, and virtual library.

The National Human Genome Research Institute (NHGRI): www.genome.gov

Site maintained by NHGRI, which oversaw the Human Genome Project completed in 2003, provides quick access to recent news, including legislation related to genetics for use by students, educators, researchers, and the general public; available in both Spanish and English.

Planned Parenthood: www.plannedparenthood .org

Official site of the Planned Parenthood Federation of America Inc. contains information about Planned Parenthood, health and pregnancy, birth control, abortion, STDs, prochoice advocacy, educational tools for parents and educators, and information for teens.

Student Study Site

$SAGE edge™

Sharpen your skills with SAGE edge at **edge.sagepub.com/hutchisonclc5e**

SAGE edge for students provides a personalized approach to help you accomplish your coursework goals in an easy-to-use learning environment.

CHAPTER 3

Infancy and Toddlerhood

Debra J. Woody and Cara L. Wallace

CHAPTER OUTLINE

- What is important for social workers to know about brain development during infancy and toddlerhood?

- Why is it important for social workers to understand attachment issues between infants and toddlers and their parents?

- How do child care provisions in the United States compare with those in other countries?

Key Ideas

As you read this chapter, take note of these central ideas:

1. Although growth and development in young children have some predictability and logic, the timing and expression of many developmental skills vary from child to child and depend in part on the environment and culture in which the child is raised.

2. Physical growth, brain development, and the development of sensory abilities and motor skills are all important aspects of physical development in infants and toddlers.

3. According to Piaget, infants and toddlers are in the sensorimotor stage of cognitive development, responding to what they hear, see, taste, touch, smell, and feel.

4. Erikson describes two stages of psychosocial development relevant to infants and toddlers, each with its own central task: trust versus mistrust (birth to age 1½) and autonomy versus shame and doubt (1½ to 3 years).

5. The attachment relationship between infants and toddlers and their caregivers can affect brain development.

6. Researchers have found that children who live in poor economic conditions face serious risks to development in all dimensions.

7. Infant and toddler adversities have been found to have a negative effect on health across the life course.

8. Policies and programs that promote early intervention may be the key to increasing positive developmental outcomes for infants and toddlers.

CASE STUDY 3.1

Holly's Early Arrival

Although Marilyn Hicks had been very careful with her diet, exercise, and prenatal care during pregnancy, Holly arrived at 26 weeks' gestation, around 6 months into the pregnancy. Initially she weighed 3 pounds, 11 ounces, but she quickly lost the 11 ounces. Immediately after birth, Holly was whisked away to the neonatal unit in the hospital, and her parents had just a quick peek at her. The assigned social worker's first contact with Marilyn and

Martin Hicks, an Anglo couple, was in the neonatal unit. Although Marilyn Hicks began to cry when the social worker first spoke with her, overall both parents seemed to be coping well and had all their basic needs met at that time. The social worker left his business card with them and instructed them to call if they needed anything.

Despite her early arrival, Holly did not show any signs of medical problems, and after 6 weeks in the neonatal unit, her parents were able to take her home. The social worker wisely allowed the newly formed Hicks family time to adjust and, in keeping with the policy of the neonatal program, scheduled a follow-up home visit within a few weeks.

When the social worker arrives at the house, Marilyn Hicks is at the door in tears. She states that taking care of Holly is much more than she imagined. Holly cries "constantly" and does not seem to respond to Mrs. Hicks's attempts to comfort her. In fact, Mrs. Hicks thinks that Holly cries even louder when her mother picks her up or tries to cuddle with her. Mrs. Hicks is very disappointed, because she considers herself to be a nurturing person. She is unsure how to respond to Holly's "rejection of her." The only time Holly seems to respond positively is when Mrs. Hicks breastfeeds her.

Mrs. Hicks has taken Holly to the pediatrician on several occasions and has discussed her concerns. The doctor told her that nothing is physically wrong with Holly and that Mrs. Hicks has to be more patient.

Mrs. Hicks confides during this meeting that she read some horrifying material on the Internet about premature infants. According to the information she read, premature infants often have difficulty bonding with their caretaker, which in some children may ultimately result in mental health and emotional problems. Mrs. Hicks is concerned that this is the case with Holly.

The social worker must take into consideration that in addition to her fears, Mrs. Hicks must be exhausted. Her husband returned to work shortly after the baby came home, and Mrs. Hicks has not left the house since then. She tried taking a break once when her aunt came for a visit, but Holly cried so intensely during this time that her aunt refused to be left alone with Holly again. The social worker must now help Mrs. Hicks cope with the powerful feelings that have been aroused by Holly's premature birth, get any needed clarification on Holly's medical condition, and find ways to get Mrs. Hicks a break from caregiving. He will also want to help her to begin to feel more confident about her ability to parent Holly.

CASE STUDY 3.2

Sarah's Teen Dad

Chris Johnson is the only dad in the teen fathers group, facilitated by the social worker at a local high school, who has sole custody of his infant daughter. Initially Sarah, Chris's infant daughter, lived with her mom and maternal grandparents. Chris was contacted by the social worker from Child Protective Services (CPS), who informed him that Sarah was removed from the mom's care because of physical neglect. The referral to CPS was made when Sarah was seen in a pediatric clinic and the medical staff noticed that she had not gained weight since the last visit and was generally unresponsive in the examination. Further investigation by the CPS worker revealed that Sarah was left in her crib for most of the day, and few of Sarah's basic daily care needs were being fulfilled. Although Chris's contact with Sarah had been sporadic since her birth, he did not hesitate to pursue custody, especially given that

(Continued)

(Continued)

the only other alternative was Sarah's placement in foster care. Chris's parents were also supportive of Chris's desire to have Sarah live with all of them. However, although they were willing to help, they were adamant that the responsibility for Sarah's care belonged to Chris, not them. They were unwilling to raise Sarah themselves and in fact required Chris to sign a written statement indicating that he, not they, would assume primary responsibility for Sarah's care. Chris's parents also insisted that he remain in school and earn his high school diploma.

Thus far the situation seems to be working well. At the last medical appointment, Sarah's weight had increased significantly and she responded to the nurse's attempts to play and communicate with her. Chris is continuing his education at the alternative high school, which also has a day care for Sarah. Chris admits that it is much more difficult than he anticipated. He attends school for half the day, works a part-time job the other half, and then has to care for Sarah in the evenings. Chris has shared several times in the group that it is a lot for him to juggle. He still mourns the loss of his freedom and "carefree" lifestyle. Like most of the other teens in the group, whether they physically live with the child or not, Chris is concerned about doing the best he can for Sarah; he states that he just wants to be a good dad.

CASE STUDY 3.3

Overprotecting Henry

Irma Velasquez is still mourning the death of her little girl Angel, who was 2 years old when she was killed by a stray bullet that came into their home through the living room window. Although it has been about a year since the incident, no one has been arrested. The police do know, however, that neither Ms. Velasquez's daughter nor her family was the intended victim. The stray bullet was the result of a shoot-out between two rival drug dealers in the family's neighborhood.

Ms. Velasquez is just glad that now 14-month-old Henry was in his crib in the back of the house instead of in the living room on that horrible evening. He had fallen asleep in her lap a few minutes before, but she had just returned from laying him in his crib when the shooting occurred. Irma Velasquez confides in her social worker at Victim Services that her family has not been the same since the incident. For one thing, she and her husband barely speak. His method of dealing with the tragedy is to stay away from home. She admits that she is angry with her husband because he does not make enough money for them to live in a safer neighborhood. She thinks that he blames her because she did not protect Angel in some way.

Ms. Velasquez admits that she is afraid that something bad will also happen to Henry. She has limited their area in the home to the back bedroom, and they seldom leave the house. She does not allow anyone, even her sister, to take care of him and confesses that she has not left his side since the shooting. Even with these restrictions, Ms. Velasquez worries. She is concerned that Henry will choke on a toy or food or become ill. She still does not allow him to feed himself, even dry cereal. He has just begun walking, and she severely limits his space for movement. Ms. Velasquez looks worn and exhausted. Although she knows these behaviors are somewhat irrational, she states that she is determined to protect Henry. She further states that she just could not live through losing another child.

DEVELOPMENTAL NICHE AND TYPICAL INFANT AND TODDLER DEVELOPMENT

What happens during the prenatal period and the earliest months and years of a child's life has a lasting impact on the life course journey. In the earliest moments, months, and years, interactions with parents, family members, and other adults and children influence the way the brain and the rest of the body develop, as do such factors as nutrition and environmental safety. Although it is never too late to improve health and well-being, what happens during infancy and toddlerhood sets the stage for the journey through childhood, adolescence, and adulthood. We were all infants and toddlers once, but sometimes, in our work as social workers, we may find it hard to understand the experience of someone 2 years old or younger. (Young children are typically referred to as **infants** in the first year, but as they enter the second year of life and become more mobile, they are usually called **toddlers**, from about 12 to 36 months of age.) As adults, we have become accustomed to communicating with words, and we are not always sure how to read the behaviors of the very young child. And we are not always sure how we are to behave with them. The best way to overcome these limitations, of course, is to learn what we can about the lives of infants and toddlers.

> What must social workers know about biological age, psychological age, and social age to understand whether an infant's or toddler's behavior indicates a need for early intervention?

Photo 3.1 Babies depend on others for basic physical and emotional needs. Family support and affection are important factors in healthy development.

© iStockphoto.com

In all three of the case studies at the beginning of this chapter, factors can be identified that may adversely affect the children's development. However, we must begin by understanding what is traditionally referred to as "normal" development. But because *normal* is a relative term with some judgmental overtones, we will use the term *typical* instead, meaning typical in a statistical sense.

Social workers employed in schools, hospitals, community mental health centers, and other public health settings are often approached by parents and teachers with questions about development in young children. To assess whether any of the children they bring to your attention require intervention, you must be able to distinguish between healthy and problematic development in three areas: physical, cognitive, and socioemotional development. As you will see, young children go through a multitude of changes in all three areas simultaneously. Inadequate development in any one of them—or in multiple areas—may have long-lasting consequences for the individual.

Keep in mind, however, that what is considered to be healthy is relative to environment and culture. Every newborn enters a world with distinctive features structured by the social setting that he or she encounters (Gardiner & Kosmitzki, 2011). Therefore, all aspects of development must be considered in cultural context. Each newborn enters a **developmental niche**, in which culture guides every aspect of the developmental process (Harkness & Super, 2003, 2006). Parents get their ideas about parenting and about the nature of children from the cultural milieu, and parents' ideas are the dominant force in how the infant and toddler develop. Harry Gardiner and Corinne Kosmitzki (2011) identify three interrelated components of the developmental niche: physical and social settings of everyday life, child-rearing customs, and caretaker psychology. Exhibit 3.1 provides an overview of these three important components of the developmental niche encountered by every newborn. As you review this exhibit, think about the developmental niches encountered by Holly Hicks, Sarah Johnson, and Henry Velasquez as they begin their life journeys.

Exhibit 3.1   Components of Developmental Niche

PHYSICAL AND SOCIAL SETTINGS OF DAILY LIFE

Size, shape, and location of living space

Objects, toys, reading materials

Ecological setting and climate

Nutritional status of children

Family structure (e.g., nuclear, extended, single parent, blended)

Presence of multiple generations (e.g., parents, grandparents, other relatives)

Presence or absence of mother or father

Presence of multiple caretakers

Role of siblings as caretakers

Presence and influence of peer group members

CUSTOMS OF CHILD CARE AND CHILDREARING

Sleeping patterns (e.g., co-sleeping vs. sleeping alone)

Dependence versus independence training

Feeding and eating schedules

Handling and carrying practices

Play and work patterns

Initiation rites

Formal versus informal learning

PSYCHOLOGY OF THE CARETAKERS

Parenting styles (e.g., authoritarian, authoritative, laissez-faire)

Value systems (e.g., dependence, independence, interdependence)

Parental cultural belief systems or ethnotheories

Developmental expectations

SOURCE: Gardiner, H., & Kosmitzki, C. (2011). *Lives across cultures: Cross-cultural human development* (5th ed.), p. 31. Reprinted by permission of Pearson Education, Inc., Upper Saddle River, NJ.

In the United States and other wealthy postindustrial societies, many newborns enter a developmental niche in which families have become smaller than in earlier eras. This results in a great deal of attention being paid to each child. Parents take courses and read books about how to provide the best possible care for their infants and toddlers. Infant safety is stressed, with laws about car seats, guidelines about the position in which the baby should sleep, and a "baby industry" that provides a broad range of safety equipment (baby monitors, baby gates, and so on) and toys, books, and electronics to provide sensory stimulation. Of course this developmental niche requires considerable resources, and many families in wealthy nations cannot afford the regulation car seat or the baby monitor. Chris Johnson is attending school, working, and caring for Sarah; he probably would be hard-pressed to find time to read parenting books, but he does find time to attend a group for teen fathers. Irma Velasquez's concern for Henry's safety focuses on protecting him from stray bullets rather than on baby monitors and baby gates. And, of course, the developmental niches in nonindustrial and newly industrializing countries are very different from the niche described earlier. For example, African pygmy newborns will be introduced to multiple caregivers who will help protect them from danger and prepare them to live an intensely social life (Gardiner & Kosmitzki, 2011). Unfortunately, many infants of the world live in developmental niches characterized by infection and malnutrition. Please keep these variations in mind as you read about infant and toddler development.

To make the presentation of ideas about infancy and toddlerhood manageable, this chapter follows a traditional method of organizing the discussion by type of development: physical development, cognitive development, emotional development, and social development. In this chapter, emotional development and social development are combined under the heading Socioemotional Development. Of course, all these types of development and behavior are interdependent, and often the distinctions blur.

PHYSICAL DEVELOPMENT

Newborns depend on others for basic physical needs. They must be fed, cleaned, and kept safe and comfortable until they develop the ability to do these things for themselves. At the same time, however, newborns have an amazing set of physical abilities and potentials right from the beginning.

In Case Study 3.2, the pediatrician and CPS social worker were concerned that Sarah Johnson was not gaining weight. With adequate nourishment and care, the physical growth of the infant is quite predictable. Infants grow very rapidly throughout the first 2 years of life, but the pace of growth slows a bit in toddlerhood. The World Health Organization (WHO) undertook a project, called the Multicentre Growth Reference Study (MGRS), to construct standards for evaluating children from birth through 5 years of age. One part of that project was to construct growth standards to propose how children *should* grow in *all* countries, of interest because of WHO's commitment to eliminate global health disparities. MGRS collected growth data from 8,440 affluent children from diverse geographical and cultural settings, including Brazil, Ghana, India, Norway, Oman, and the United States. To be eligible for the study, mothers needed to be breastfeeding and not smoking, and the environment needed to be adequate to support unconstrained growth.

The researchers found that there were no differences in growth patterns across sites, even though there were some differences in parental stature. Given the striking similarity in growth patterns across sites, they concluded that the data could be used to develop an international standard. Across sites, the average length at birth was 19.5 inches (49.5 cm), 26.3 inches (66.7 cm) at 6 months, 29.5 inches (75.0 cm) at 12 months, and 34.4 inches (87.4 cm) at 24 months (WHO Multicentre Growth Reference Study Group, 2006a). By 1 year of age, infant height was about 1.5 times birth height, and by 2 years, the toddler had nearly doubled the birth height.

Most newborns weigh from 5 to 10 pounds at birth. Infants triple their weight in the first year, and by age 2 most infants are quadruple their original weight. Thus, the average 2-year-old weighs 20 to 40 pounds. Evidently, the size of individual infants and toddlers can vary quite a bit. Some of the difference is the result of nutrition, exposure to disease, and other environmental factors; much of it is the result of genetics. Some ethnic differences in physical development have also been observed. For example, Asian American children tend to be smaller than average, and African American children tend to be larger than average (Tate, Dezateux, Cole, and the Millennium Cohort Study Child Health Group, 2006). In the past decade there has been a great deal of concern about rapid weight gain during the first 6 months, which has been connected to overweight by age 4 and to several chronic diseases in adulthood, but recent longitudinal research suggests that rapid weight gain in infancy is just as often associated with later height as with later obesity (Wright, Cox, & Couteur, 2011). The WHO child growth standards, calculated by different methods, can be found at www .who.int/childgrowth/standards.

The importance of nutrition in infancy cannot be overstated. Nutrition affects physical stature, motor skill development, brain development, and most every other aspect of development. A 2013 report by the Lancet Maternal and Child Nutrition series (2013) indicates that, globally, malnutrition contributes to 3.1 million deaths of children age 5 and younger each year. In 2011, 26% of children in low-income countries suffered from stunted growth because of chronic maternal and child undernutrition. This was down from 40% in 1990, but still a serious global public health problem. Eastern and western Africa and south-central Asia have the highest prevalence of stunting. Nutritional deficiencies during the first 1,000 days of the child's life can result in damage to the immune system and impair social and cognitive capacities.

Self-Regulation

Before birth, the bodily functions of the fetus are regulated by the mother's body. After birth, the infant must develop the capacity to engage in self-regulation (Davies, 2011). At first, the challenge is to regulate bodily functions, such as temperature control, sleeping, eating, and eliminating. That challenge is heightened for the premature or

medically fragile infant, as Holly Hicks's mother is finding. Growing evidence indicates that some self-regulatory functions that allow self-calming and organize the wake-sleep cycles get integrated and coordinated during the third trimester, from 30 to 34 weeks' gestation (Institute of Medicine, 2006). Born at 26 weeks' gestation, Holly Hicks did not have the benefit of the uterine environment to support the development of these self-regulatory functions.

As any new parent will attest, however, infants are not born with regular patterns of sleeping, eating, and eliminating. With maturation of the central nervous system in the first 3 months, and with lots of help from parents or other caregivers, the infant's rhythms of sleeping, eating, and eliminating become much more regular (Davies, 2011). A newborn usually sleeps about 16 hours a day, dividing that time evenly between day and night. Of course, this is not a good fit with the way adults organize their sleep lives. At the end of 3 months, most infants are sleeping 14 to 15 hours per day, primarily at night, with some well-defined nap times during the day. Parents also gradually shape infants' eating schedules so that they are eating mainly during the day.

There are cultural variations in, and controversies about, the way caregivers shape the sleeping and eating behaviors of infants. The management of sleep is one of the earliest culturally influenced parenting behaviors. In some cultures, infants sleep with parents, and in other cultures, infants are put to sleep in their own beds and often in their own rooms. In some cultures, putting an infant to sleep alone in a room is considered to be neglectful (Gardiner & Kosmitzki, 2011). Co-sleeping, the child sleeping with the parents, is routine in most of the world's cultures (McKenna, 2002). Japanese and Chinese children often sleep with their parents throughout infancy and early childhood (Iwata, Iwata, & Matsuishi, 2013). There are also cultural variations and controversies about breastfeeding versus bottle feeding. It is interesting to note that both

> What have you observed about how culture influences the parenting of infants and toddlers?

breastfeeding and sleeping with parents induce shorter bouts of sleep and less sound sleep than the alternatives (Blunden, Thompson, & Dawson, 2011). Some researchers have speculated that the infant's lighter and shorter sleep pattern may protect against sudden infant death syndrome (SIDS). The connection between co-sleeping and SIDS has been a controversial research issue. One research team conducted a meta-analysis of research of the issue published from 1970 to 2010; they found that co-sleeping increased the risk for SIDS, and the risk is highest for infants younger than 12 weeks and when parents smoke (Vennemann et al., 2012).

Parents become less anxious as the infant's rhythms become more regular and predictable. At the same time, if the caregiver is responsive and dependable, the infant becomes less anxious and begins to develop the ability to wait to have needs met.

Cultural variations exist in beliefs about how to respond when infants cry and fuss, whether to soothe them, or leave them to learn to soothe themselves. When parents do attempt to soothe infants, interestingly, they seem to use the same methods across cultures: "They say something, touch, pick up, search for sources of discomfort, and then feed" (Shonkoff & Phillips, 2000, p. 100). Infants who have been consistently soothed usually begin to develop the ability to soothe themselves after 3 or 4 months. This ability is the precursor to struggles for self-control and mastery over powerful emotions that occur in toddlerhood. More is said about emotion self-regulation in a later section.

Sensory Abilities

Full-term infants are born with a functioning **sensory system**—the senses of hearing, sight, taste, smell, touch, and sensitivity to pain—and these abilities continue to develop rapidly in the first few months. Indeed, in the early months the sensory system seems to function at a higher level than the motor system, which allows movement. The sensory system allows infants, from the time of birth, to participate in and adapt to their environments. A lot of their learning happens through listening and watching (Newman & Newman, 2012). The sensory system is interconnected, with various sensory abilities working together to give the infant multiple sources of information about the world.

Hearing is the earliest link to the environment; the fetus is sensitive to auditory stimulation in the uterus (Moraru et al., 2011). The fetus hears the mother's heartbeat, and this sound is soothing to the infant in the early days and weeks after birth. Newborns show a preference for their mother's voice over unfamiliar voices, but one research team found that this is not the case for newborns whose mothers were anxious or depressed during the third trimester (Figueiredo, Pacheco, Costa, Conde, & Teixeira, 2010). Early infants can also distinguish changes in loudness, pitch, and location of sounds, and they can use auditory information to differentiate one object from another and to track the location of an object (Bahrick, Lickliter, & Flom, 2006). These capacities grow increasingly sensitive across the first 6 months after birth. Infants appear to be particularly sensitive to language sounds, and the earliest infant smiles are evoked by the sound of the human voice (Benasich & Leevers, 2003). Unfortunately, research indicates that malnutrition during the infant's first 3 months increases the likelihood of early onset hearing loss (Olusanya, 2010).

The newborn's vision improves rapidly during the first few months of life. By about the age of 4 months, the infant sees objects the same way an adult does. Of course, infants do not have cognitive associations with objects as adults do. Infants respond to a number of visual dimensions, including depth, brightness, movement, color, and distance. Human faces have particular appeal for newborns. Although conflicting evidence exists, research suggests that several days after birth infants are able to discriminate between facial expressions (Farroni, Menon, Rigato, & Johnson, 2007). From 4 to 7 months, infants are able to recognize expressions, particularly happiness, fear, and anger (McClure, 2000). Infants show preference for faces, and by 3 months, most infants are able to distinguish a parent's face from the face of a stranger (Nelson, 2001). Ability to recognize familiar faces is enhanced through positive expression, suggesting an interaction between expression and infants' recognition of a familiar face (Turati, Montirosso, Brenna, Ferrara, & Borgatti, 2011). Some researchers have found that infants are distressed by a lack of facial movement in the people they look at, showing that they prefer caregivers to have expressive faces (Muir & Lee, 2003).

Taste and smell begin to function in the uterus, and newborns can differentiate sweet, bitter, sour, and salty tastes. A preference for sweet tastes is innately present for both preterm and full-term newborns (Pepino & Mennella, 2006). Research suggests that the first few minutes after birth is a particularly sensitive period for learning to distinguish smells (Delaunay-El Allam, Marlier, & Schaal, 2006). Breastfed babies are particularly sensitive to their mother's body odors. One research team found that newborns undergoing a heel prick were soothed by the smell of breast milk, but only if the milk came from the mother's breast (Nishitani et al., 2009).

Both animal and human research tells us that touch plays a very important role in infant development. In many cultures, swaddling, or wrapping a baby snugly in a blanket, is used to soothe a fussy newborn. We also know that gentle handling, rocking, stroking, and cuddling are all soothing to an infant. Regular gentle rocking and stroking are very effective in soothing low-birth-weight (LBW) babies, who may have underdeveloped central nervous systems. Skin-to-skin contact between parents and their newborns has been found to have benefits for both infants and their parents. Preterm babies who have lots of skin contact with their parents, including gentle touching and massage, gain weight faster, have better temperature regulation, have better capacity for self-soothing, and are more alert compared with preterm babies who do not receive extensive skin contact (Feldman, 2004; Jean & Stack, 2012). Infants also use touch to learn about their world and their own bodies. Early infants use their mouths for exploring their worlds, but by 5 or 6 months of age, infants can make controlled use of their hands to explore objects in their environment. They learn about the world and keep themselves entertained by exploring small details, transferring objects from one hand to the other, and examining the differences in surfaces and other features of the object (Streri, 2005).

Clear evidence exists that from the first days of life, babies feel pain. Recently, pediatric researchers have been studying newborn reactions to medical procedures such as heel sticks, the sticks used to draw blood for lab analysis. One researcher found that newborns who undergo repeated heel sticks learn to anticipate pain and develop a stronger reaction to pain than other infants (Taddio, Shah, Gilbert-Macleod, & Katz, 2002). These findings are leading pediatricians to develop guidelines for managing pain in newborns (Spence et al., 2010).

Reflexes

Although dependent on others, newborns are equipped from the start with tools for survival that are involuntary muscle responses to certain stimuli, called **reflexes**. Reflexes aid the infant in adapting to the environment outside the womb. The presence and strength of a reflex is an important sign of neurological development, and the absence of reflexes can indicate a serious developmental disorder (Goldenring, 2011). Given Holly Hicks's early arrival, her reflex responses were thoroughly evaluated.

Newborns have two critical reflexes:

1. *Rooting reflex.* When infants' cheeks or the corners of their mouths are gently stroked with a finger, they will turn their head in the direction of the touch and open their mouths in an attempt to suck the finger. This reflex aids in feeding, because it guides the infants to the nipple.

2. *Sucking reflex.* When a nipple or some other suckable object is presented to the infant, the infant sucks it. This reflex is another important tool for feeding.

Many infants would probably perish without the rooting and sucking reflexes. Imagine the time and effort it would require for one feeding if they did not have them. Instead, infants are born with the ability to take in nutriment.

Exhibit 3.2   Infant Reflexes

Reflex	Description	Visible
Sucking	The infant instinctively sucks any object of appropriate size that is presented to the infant.	First 2 to 4 months
Rooting	The head turns in the direction of a stimulus when the cheek is touched. The infant's mouth opens in an attempt to suck.	First 4 months
Moro/startle	The arms thrust outward when the infant is released in midair, as if attempting to regain support.	First 2 months
Swimming	When placed facedown in water, the infant makes paddling, swimlike motions.	First 3 months
Walking/stepping	When the infant is held in an upright position with the feet placed on a firm surface, the infant moves the feet in a walking motion.	First 2 months
Grasping	The infant grasps objects placed in his or her hand.	First 4 months
Babinski	The toes spread when the soles of the feet are stroked.	First year
Blinking	The eyes blink when they are touched or when sudden bright light appears.	Lifetime
Cough	Cough occurs when airway is stimulated.	Lifetime
Gag	Gagging occurs when the throat or back of mouth is stimulated.	Lifetime
Sneeze	Sneezing occurs when the nasal passages are irritated.	Lifetime
Yawn	Yawning occurs when the body needs additional oxygen.	Lifetime

A number of reflexes disappear at identified times during infancy (see Exhibit 3.2) but in some cases change into voluntary behavior; others persist throughout adulthood (Goldenring, 2011; healthychildren.org, 2013). Both the rooting reflex and sucking reflex disappear at 2 to 4 months. By this time, the infant has mastered the voluntary act of sucking and is therefore no longer in need of the reflexive response. Several other infant reflexes appear to have little use now but probably had some specific survival purposes in earlier times. The presence of an infant reflex after the age at which it typically disappears can be a sign of damage to the brain or nervous system (Goldenring, 2011).

Motor Skills

The infant gradually advances from reflex functioning to motor functioning. The development of **motor skills**—the ability to move and manipulate—occurs in a more or less orderly, logical sequence. It begins with simple actions such as lifting the chin and progresses to more complex acts such as walking, running, and throwing. Infants usually crawl before they walk.

Motor development is somewhat predictable, in that children tend to reach milestones at about the same age and in the

> How do these motor skills help to promote a sense of human agency in making choices?

same sequence. As a part of the MGRS, WHO undertook a project to construct standards for evaluating the motor development of children from birth through 5 years of age. MGRS collected longitudinal data on six gross motor milestones of children ages 4 to 24 months in Ghana, India, Norway, Oman, and the United States. The milestones studied were sitting without support, standing with assistance, hands-and-knees crawling, walking with assistance, standing alone, and walking alone. Because WHO was trying to establish standards for evaluating child development, healthy children were studied in all five study sites. The researchers found that 90% of the children achieved five of the six milestones in the same sequence, but 4.3% of the sample never engaged in hands-and-knees crawling (WHO Multicentre Growth Reference Study Group, 2006b).

Based on the data collected, MGRS developed "windows of milestone achievement" for each of the six motor skills, with achievement at the 1st and 99th percentiles as the window boundaries. All motor achievement within the windows is considered normal variation in ages of achievement for healthy children. The windows of achievement for the six motor skills studied are reported in Exhibit 3.3. The results reveal that the range of the windows vary from 5.4 months for sitting without support (from 3.8 months at the 1st percentile to 9.2 months at the 99th percentile) to 10.0 months for standing alone (from 6.9 at the 1st percentile to 16.9 at the 99th percentile). This is quite a wide range for normal development and should be reassuring to parents who become anxious if their child is not at the low end of the window. Many parents, for example, become concerned if their child has not attempted to walk unassisted by age 1. However, some children walk alone at age 9 months; others do not even attempt to walk until almost 18 months. It is important to note, however, that delays in infant motor development have been found to be a risk factor for adult diagnosis of schizophrenia, particularly in cases where there were also obstetric complications (Clarke et al., 2011).

Culture and ethnicity appear to have some influence on motor development in infants and

Exhibit 3.3 Windows of Milestone Achievement in Months

Motor Milestone	Window of Milestone Achievement
Sitting without support	3.8–9.2 months
Standing with assistance	4.8–11.4 months
Hands-and-knees crawling	5.2–13.5 months
Walking with assistance	5.9–13.7 months
Standing alone	6.9–16.9 months
Walking alone	8.2–17.6 months

SOURCE: WHO Multicentre Growth Reference Study Group, 2006b

toddlers. MGRS found that girls were slightly ahead of boys in gross motor development, but the differences were not statistically significant. They did find small, but statistically significant, differences between sites of the study, however. The researchers speculate that these differences probably reflect culture-based child care behaviors, but the cause cannot be determined from the data, and a genetic component is possible. The earliest mean age of achievement for four of the six milestones occurred in the Ghanaian sample, and the latest mean age of achievement for all six milestones occurred in the Norwegian sample (WHO Multicentre Growth Reference Study Group, 2006c). The U.S. sample mean was in the middle range on all milestones except for hands-and-knees crawling, where it had the lowest mean achievement.

A longitudinal study of almost 16,000 infants in the United Kingdom took up this issue of cultural differences in developmental motor milestones. In this study, Black Caribbean infants, Black African infants, and Indian infants were, on average, more advanced in motor development than White infants. Pakistani and Bangladeshi infants were more likely than White infants to show motor delays. Although the delays among Pakistani

Photo 3.2   Fine motor skills, the ability to move and manipulate objects, develop in a logical sequence.
© iStockphoto.com

and Bangladeshi infants appear to be explained by factors associated with poverty, the earlier development of Black Caribbean, Black African, and Indian infants could not be explained by economic advantage. The researchers suggest that parental expectations and parenting practices play a role in cultural differences in motor development (Kelly, Sacker, Schoon, & Nazroo, 2006).

The development of motor skills (and most other types of skills, for that matter) is a continuous process. Children progress from broad capacities to more specific refined abilities. For example, toddlers progress from eating cereal with their fingers to eating with a spoon.

Parents are usually quite patient with their child's motor development. However, toilet training (potty training) is often a source of stress and uncertainty for new parents. Every human culture

has mechanisms for disposing of human waste and socializes infants and toddlers to that method. One of the basic issues in this socialization is whether it should be in the hands of the child or the caregiver (Valsiner, 2000). In places in the world where there are no disposable diapers and no access to a washing machine, parents, even in the early months, become sensitive to signs that the infant is about to defecate or urinate and hold him or her over whatever type of toilet is available. This method, referred to as "assisted infant toilet training," is expected to work by about age 6 months. Although this method is not typically followed in the middle- to high-income countries, there is a current movement in the United States to raise diaper-free babies by using "elimination communication," based on timing, cues, and intuition (see the website www.diaperfreebaby.org). There is no clear consensus in the United States about the best method for toilet training (Howell, Wyosocki, & Steiner, 2010). The U.S. American Academy of Pediatrics recommends a child-oriented approach that emphasizes the child's interest in toilet training and tries to minimize the demands made by parents. Toddlers are introduced to a potty-chair and gradually encouraged to sit on it and over time actually use it, followed by positive rewards. Reprimands or punishments are to be avoided. This can take weeks or months. In contrast, some parents use the train-in-a-day method developed by Azrin and Foxx (1989), which is recommended to start about the age of 20 months. Researchers have found that both the child-centered and the train-in-a-day method can lead to successful toilet training (Howell et al., 2010).

In the United States, the average age to complete toilet training has increased steadily over the past few decades, from 18 months in the 1940s to 27 months in 1980, and 37 months in 2003. There are subcultural variations, however. On average, girls achieve toilet training 2 to 3 months ahead of boys. Family stressors such as divorce, death, or birth of a new baby may lead to a delay in toilet training (Howell et al., 2010).

The Growing Brain

We are living in the midst of a neuroscientific revolution clarifying the important role of the brain in helping to shape human behavior (Matto, Strolin-Goltzman, & Ballan, 2014). Like the brains of other primates, human brains contain **neurons**, or specialized nerve cells that store and transmit information; they carry sensory information to the brain, and they carry out the processes involved in thought, emotion, and action. Between the neurons are **synapses**, or gaps that function as the site of information exchange from one neuron to another. **Synaptogenesis**, the creation of synapses, begins to accelerate during the last trimester of pregnancy and peaks at 2 to 3 years of age, when the brain has about twice the synapses it will have in adulthood (Pierce, 2011; Urban Child Institute, 2013). This rapid synaptogenesis results in an overabundance

of synapses and a tripling in brain weight during the first 3 years. The period of overproduction of synapses, or **blooming**, is followed by a period of **pruning**, or reduction, of the synapses to improve the efficiency of brain functioning. It is through this process of creating elaborate communication systems between the connecting neurons that more and more complex skills and abilities become possible. Thus, during these early years of life, children are capable of rapid new learning. The blooming and pruning of synapses process continues well into childhood and adolescence at different timetables in different regions of the brain.

The available evidence suggests that both genetic processes and early experiences with the environment influence the timing of brain development. Brain plasticity has been a major finding of neuroscientific research of the past few decades. There are two elements of **brain plasticity**: first, research indicates that the brain changes throughout life; and second, the brain changes in response to what it experiences—it is shaped by experience (Farmer, 2009). The human brain is genetically designed to accommodate an incredibly wide range of human experiences, and the environmental context helps to shape the brain for life in a particular developmental niche. What is used gets strengthened, and what is not used gets pruned. The infant and toddler contribute to their own brain development by repeating certain actions, attending to certain stimuli, and responding in particular ways to caregivers.

Exposure to speech in the first year expedites the discrimination of speech sounds; exposure to patterned visual information in the first few years of life is necessary for normal development of some aspects of vision. Some suggest that the entire infancy period is a crucial and sensitive time for brain development, given the quantity and speed at which the neurons develop and connect (Pierce, 2011). Positive physical experiences (feeding, safety, and so on) and positive psychological experiences (touching, cooing, and playing) activate and stimulate brain activity (Davies, 2011). Good nutrition and infant stimulation are essential for brain development, and exposure to environmental toxins, abuse, emotional trauma, and deprivation is hazardous. Persistent stress for the infant or toddler has been found to result in overdevelopment of areas of the brain that process anxiety and fear and underdevelopment of other brain areas, particularly the frontal cortex (Schore, 2002).

Certain risks to brain development are associated with prematurity. Premature infants like Holly Hicks, born at 24 to 28 weeks' gestation, have high rates of serious intracranial hemorrhage, which can lead to problems in cognitive and motor development, including cerebral palsy and mental retardation. Less serious intracranial hemorrhage can lead to later behavioral, attentional, and memory problems (Tam et al., 2011). It is not yet clear whether Holly Hicks suffered any type of brain hemorrhage and what impact it will have on her future development if she did.

Critical Thinking Questions 3.1

Revisit Exhibit 3.1, which lays out the components of the developmental niche. What do we know about the developmental niches involved in the three case studies at the beginning of the chapter, Holly, Sarah, and Henry? What strengths do you see in each of these developmental niches? What potential problems do you see?

COGNITIVE DEVELOPMENT

How do the drives to learn and be in interaction with the environment promote interdependence?

As the brain develops, so does its ability to process and store information and to solve problems. These abilities are known as **cognition**. When we talk about how fast a child is learning, we are talking about cognitive development. Researchers now describe the infant as "wired to learn" and agree that infants have an intrinsic drive to learn and to be in interaction with their environments. A central element of cognition is language, which facilitates both thinking and communicating. Exhibit 3.4 lists some milestones in cognitive development.

Exhibit 3.4   Selected Milestones in Cognitive Development

Milestone	Age of Onset
Coos responsively	Birth–3 months
Smiles responsively	3–4 months
Smiles at self in mirror	3–4 months
Laughs out loud	3–4 months
Plays peek-a-boo	3–4 months
Shows displeasure	5–6 months
Babbles	6–8 months
Understands simple commands	12 months
Follows directions	2 years
Puts two to three words together	2 years
Uses sentences	2–3 years

Piaget's Stages of Cognitive Development

To assess children's cognitive progress, many people use the concepts developed by the best-known cognitive development theorist, Jean Piaget (1936/1952). Piaget believed that cognitive development occurs in successive stages, determined by the age of the child. His overall contention was that as a child grows and develops, cognition changes not only in quantity but also in quality.

Piaget used the metaphor of a slow-motion movie to explain his theory, which is summarized in Exhibit 3.5 as follows:

1. **Sensorimotor stage** (ages birth to 2 years). Infants at this stage of development can look at only one frame of the movie at a time. When the next picture appears on the screen, infants focus on it and cannot go back to the previous frame.

2. Preoperational stage (ages 2 to 7). Preschool children and children in early grades can remember (recall) the sequence of the pictures in the movie. They also develop **symbolic functioning**—the ability to use symbols to represent what is not present. However, they do not necessarily understand what has happened in the movie or how the pictures fit together.

3. Concrete operations stage (ages 7 to 11). Not until this stage can children run the pictures in the movie backward and forward to better understand how they blend to form a specific meaning.

4. Formal operations stage (ages 11 and beyond). Children gain the capacity to apply logic to various situations and to use symbols to solve problems. Adding to Piaget's metaphor, one cognitive scientist describes formal operations as the ability of the adolescent not only to understand the observed movie but also to add or change characters and create an additional plot or staging plan (Edwards, 1992).

The first of Piaget's stages applies to infants and toddlers. During the sensorimotor period, they respond to immediate stimuli—what they see, hear, taste, touch, and smell—and learning takes place through the senses and motor activities. Piaget suggests that infant and toddler cognitive development occurs in six substages during the sensorimotor period.

Substage 1: Reflex Activity (birth to 1 month). Because reflexes are what the infant can "do," they become the foundation to future learning. Reflexes are what infants build on.

Substage 2: Primary Circular Reactions (1 to 4 months). During this stage, infants repeat (thus the term circular) behaviors that bring them a positive response and pleasure. The infant's body is the focus of the response, thus the term primary. If, for example, infants by chance hold their head erect or lift their chest, they will continue to repeat these acts because they are pleasurable. Infants also have limited anticipation abilities.

Substage 3: Secondary Circular Reactions (4 to 8 months). As in the second substage, the focus is on performing acts and behaviors that bring about a response. In this stage, however, the infant reacts to responses from the environment. If, for example, 5-month-old infants cause the rattle to sound inadvertently as their arms move, they will continue attempts to repeat this occurrence.

Exhibit 3.5 Piaget's Stages of Cognitive Development

Stage	Characteristics
Sensorimotor (birth–2 years)	Infant is egocentric; he or she gradually learns to coordinate sensory and motor activities and develops a beginning sense of objects existing apart from the self.
Preoperational (2–7 years)	The child remains primarily egocentric but discovers rules (regularities) that can be applied to new incoming information. The child tends to overgeneralize rules, however, and thus makes many cognitive errors.
Concrete operations (7–11 years)	The child can solve concrete problems through the application of logical problem-solving strategies.
Formal operations (11 years and beyond)	The person becomes able to solve real and hypothetical problems using abstract concepts.

Substage 4: Coordination of Secondary Circular Reactions (8 to 12 months). The mastery of **object permanence** is a significant task during this stage. Piaget contended that around 9 months of age, infants develop the ability to understand that an object or a person exists even when they don't see it. Piaget demonstrated this ability by hiding a favored toy under a blanket. Infants are able to move the blanket and retrieve the toy. Object permanence is related to the rapid development of memory abilities during this period and is necessary for mental representation to develop (Bruce & Vargas, 2013). Two other phenomena are related to this advance in memory. **Stranger anxiety**, in which the infant reacts with fear and withdrawal to unfamiliar persons, has been found to occur at about 9 months across cultures. Many first-time parents comment, "I don't know what has gotten into her; she has always been so outgoing." Babies vary in how intensely they react to the strange situation and in how they express their anxiety (Rieser-Danner, 2003). **Separation anxiety** also becomes prominent in this period. The infant is able to remember previous separations and becomes anxious at the signs of an impending separation from parents. With time, the infant also learns that the parent always returns.

Substage 5: Tertiary Circular Reactions (12 to 18 months). During this stage, toddlers become more creative in eliciting responses and are better problem solvers. For example, if the first button on the talking telephone does not make it talk, they will continue to press other buttons on the phone until they find the correct one.

Substage 6: Mental Representation (18 months to 2 years). Piaget described toddlers in this stage as actually able to use thinking skills in that they retain mental images of what is not immediately in front of them. For example, the toddler will look in a toy box for a desired toy and move other toys aside that prohibit recovery of the desired toy. Toddlers can also remember and imitate observed behavior. For example, toddlers roll their toy lawn mower over the lawn, imitating their parents' lawn mowing.

As much as Piaget's work has been praised, it has also been questioned and criticized. Piaget constructed his theory based on his observations of his own three children. Thus, one question has been how objective he was and whether the concepts can really be generalized to all children. Also, Piaget has been criticized for not addressing the influence of environmental factors—such as culture, family, and significant relationships and friendships—on cognitive development. However, for the past 30 years, researchers around the world have put Piaget's theory to the test. This research literature is immense but has been summarized by several reviewers (see, for example, Bronfenbrenner, 1993; Rogoff & Chavajay, 1995; Segall, Dasen, Berry, & Poortinga, 1999). Piaget's sensorimotor stage has been studied less than his other cognitive stages, but the existing research tends to support Piaget's theory, even though some minor cultural differences are noted (Gardiner & Kosmitzki, 2011). For example, some research has found that African infants receive more social stimulation and emotional support than European and American infants, while European and American infants get more experience with handling objects. This leads to African infants and toddlers developing more social intelligence and European and American children developing more technological intelligence (cited in Gardiner & Kosmitzki, 2011). This supports the idea of the importance of the developmental niche but, overall, suggests much more similarity than difference in cognitive development across developmental niches during infancy and toddlerhood.

Research findings have called into question some aspects of Piaget's theory. For example, Piaget described young children as being incapable of object permanence until at least 9 months of age. However, infants as young as 3½ and 4½ months of age have been observed who are already proficient at object permanence (Ruffman, Slade, & Redman, 2005). Other researchers (Munakata, McClelland, Johnson, & Siegler, 1997) have found that although infants seem aware of hidden objects at 3½ months, they fail to retrieve those objects until about 8 months of age. These researchers suggest that cognitive skills such as object permanence may be multifaceted and gradually developed (Baillargeon, 2004). Cognitive researchers have been interested in the development of object permanence in children with very low birth weight and in children with a range of intellectual and physical disabilities. One research team found that toddlers born full-term were more than six times more likely to have developed object permanence than children born prematurely with very low birth weight (Lowe, Erickson, MacLean, & Duvall, 2009). Susan Bruce and Zayyad Muhammad (2009) reviewed the research on the development of object permanence in children with intellectual disability, physical disability, autism, and blindness. They concluded that this research indicates that children with these disabilities develop object permanence in a similar sequence as children without disabilities, but at a slower rate. They also found evidence that children with severe disability benefit from systematic instruction in object permanence. Bruce and Vargas (2013) provide a case example of a successful team effort to teach object permanence to a 4-year-old girl with severe multiple developmental delays and visual impairment. It is interesting to note that much of the recent research on object permanence studies nonhuman animals. For example, one research team who studied Piagetian object permanence in carrion crows found support for Piagetian stages of cognitive development in this avian species (Hoffman, Rüttler, & Nieder, 2011).

Categorization is a cognitive skill that begins to develop in the first year of life. Categorization, or recognizing similarities in groups of objects, is a fundamental element of information processing. There is evidence that by 6 months, infants begin to see patterns in and make distinctions about human faces (Ramsey, Langlois, Hoss, Rubenstein, & Griffin, 2004). There is also evidence that by 3 months of age, infants can make a distinction between people and inanimate objects. They have been observed to smile and vocalize more and become more active when they are interacting with people than when interacting with inanimate objects (Rakison & Poulin-Dubois, 2001). Research has also found that 4½-month-old babies indicate

recognition when two objects are different from each other (Needham, 2001). As toddlers develop language skills, they use language as well as visual cues to categorize objects (Nazzi & Gopnik, 2001).

Prelanguage Skills

Some of the developmental milestones for language development are listed in Exhibit 3.4. It is hypothesized that the left hemisphere of the human brain is the part poised to receive and produce language. There is some research evidence for this hypothesis and also some evidence that, compared with other toddlers, the large majority of toddlers diagnosed with autism exhibit right hemisphere dominance in responses to language (Pierce, 2011). Although babies seem to be born ready to begin processing language and infants communicate with their caretakers from the beginning (primarily by crying), language development truly begins around 2 months of age. The first sounds, cooing, are pleasing to most parents. By age 4 months, infants babble. Initially, these babbles are unrecognizable. Eventually, at about 8 to 12 months, infants make gestures to indicate their desires. The babble sounds and gestures together, along with caretakers' growing familiarity with the infant's "vocabulary," make it easier for infants to communicate their desires. For example, 12-month-old infants may point to their bottle located on the kitchen cabinet and babble "baba." The caretaker soon learns that "baba" means "bottle."

By the age of 18 to 24 months, the toddler learns about one new word each week (CTParenting .com, 2014). Piaget asserts that children develop language in direct correlation to their cognitive skills. Thus, most of the words spoken at this age relate to people and significant objects in the toddler's environment. These include words such as "mama," "dada," "cat," and "sissy" (sister), for example. Across cultures, there is an overall bias in infancy to use nouns (Gardiner & Kosmitzki, 2011). Toddlers' first words also include situational words such as "hot," "no," and "bye." Around the age of 2, toddlers have a vocabulary of about 50 to 100 words and begin to combine two words together, also in tandem with growing cognitive abilities (CTParenting.com, 2014). For example, children can say "all gone" as they develop an understanding of object permanence (Berk, 2005). Even with these skills, toddlers may be difficult to understand on occasion. At 2 toddlers can be understood by adults about half of the time (CTParenting.com, 2014).

Cindy, the mom of 24-month-old Steven, describes collecting her son from day care. During the trip home, Steven initiated conversation with Cindy by calling out "Mama." He began to "tell" her about something that Cindy assumes must have occurred during the day. Steven continued to babble to his mother with animation and laughs and giggles during the story. Although Cindy laughed at the appropriate moments, she was unable to understand most of what Steven was sharing with her.

The most important thing that adults can do to assist with language development is to provide opportunity for interactions. Adults can answer questions, provide information, explain plans and actions, and offer feedback about behavior. Adults can also read to infants and toddlers and play language games. The opportunity for interaction is important for deaf children as well as hearing children, but deaf children need interaction that involves hand and eye, as with sign language (Shonkoff & Phillips, 2000). Researchers have found that when talking with infants and toddlers, adults and even older children will engage in behaviors that facilitate language development; they tend to speak in a high pitch, use shorter sentences, and speak slowly (Singh, Morgan, & Best, 2002). However, there appear to be cultural differences in how adults communicate with infants and toddlers, and it is not clear how these differences affect language acquisition (Sabbagh & Baldwin, 2001).

Research indicates that early infants are capable of recognizing and making sounds from a wide range of languages. However, as they have repeated interactions with caregivers and family members, they strengthen the neural connections for the sounds of the language(s) spoken in the home environment, and the neural connections

for sounds from other languages are lost (Hoff, 2009). Miraculously, infants and toddlers who are bilingual from birth learn two languages as fast as monolingual infants learn one (Kovács & Mehler, 2009). Of course, ability in any language is not retained unless the environment provides an opportunity for using the language.

SOCIOEMOTIONAL DEVELOPMENT

Infants and toddlers face vital developmental tasks in the emotional arena (some of which are listed in Exhibit 3.6), as well as in the social arena. Development during these early ages may set the stage for socioemotional development during all other developmental ages. This section addresses these tasks.

Exhibit 3.6   Selected Milestones in Emotional Development

Milestone	Age
Emotional life centered on physical states. Exhibits distress, fear, and rage.	Newborn
Emotional life begins to be centered on relationships. Exhibits pleasure and delight.	3 months
Emotional life continues to be relational, but distinctions are made between those relationships, as in stranger anxiety and separation anxiety. Exhibits joy, fear, anxiety, and anger.	9 months
Emotional life becomes sensitive to emotional cues from other people. Exhibits a range of emotion from joy to rage.	End of first year
Emotional life becomes centered on regulation of emotional states.	Second and third year

SOURCES: Based on Davies, 2011, and Shonkoff & Phillips, 2000

Erikson's Theory of Psychosocial Development

Erik Erikson's (1950) theory explains socioemotional development in terms of eight consecutive, age-defined stages. Each stage requires the mastery of a developmental task. Mastery at each stage depends on mastery in the previous stages. If the "task facilitating factors" for a stage are absent, the individual will become stuck in that stage of development.

Each of Erikson's stages is overviewed in Exhibit 3.7 and discussed in the chapter regarding the part of the life course to which it applies. The following two stages are relevant to infants and toddlers.

> How does the development of trust during infancy affect future relationships?

1. *Trust versus mistrust* (ages birth–1½). The overall task of this stage is for infants to develop a sense that their needs will be met by the outside world and that the outside world is an okay place to be. In addition, the infant develops an emotional bond with an adult, which Erikson believes becomes the foundation for being able to

Exhibit 3.7   Erikson's Stages of Psychosocial Development

Life Stage	Psychosocial Challenge	Characteristic
Infancy (birth to about 1 year)	Basic trust versus basic mistrust	Infants must form trusting relationships with caregivers or they will learn to distrust the world.
Toddlerhood (about 1–3 years)	Autonomy versus shame and doubt	Toddlers must develop self-confidence and a sense of mastery over themselves and their worlds and they must use newly developed motor skills, or they will develop shame and doubt about their inability to develop control.
Early childhood (3–5 years)	Initiative versus guilt	Young children must develop a growing capacity to plan and initiate actions or they may feel guilt about their taking initiative.
Middle childhood (6–11 years)	Industry versus inferiority	School-aged children must develop a sense of competence to master and complete tasks or they learn to feel inferior or incompetent.
Adolescence (11–20 years)	Identity versus role diffusion	Adolescents must develop a sense of who they are and where they are going in life or they become confused about their identity.
Young adulthood (21–40 years)	Intimacy versus isolation	Young adults must develop the capacity to commit to deep associations with others or they feel a sense of isolation.
Middle adulthood (40–65 years)	Generativity versus stagnation	Midlife adults must develop the capacity to transcend self-interest to guide the next generation or they feel stagnated.
Late adulthood (over 65 years)	Ego integrity versus despair	Older adults must find integrity and contentment in their final years by accepting their life as it has been or they feel a sense of despair.

SOURCE: Based on Erikson, 1950, 1978

form intimate, loving relationships in the future. Erikson argues the need for one consistent mother figure. The most important factor facilitating growth in this stage is consistency in having physical and emotional needs met: being fed when hungry, being kept warm and dry, and being allowed undisturbed sleep. In addition, the infant has to be protected from injury, disease, and so on and receive adequate stimulation. Infants who develop mistrust at this stage become suspicious of the world and withdraw, react with rage, and have deep-seated feelings of dependency. These infants lack drive, hope, and motivation for continued growth. They cannot trust their environment and are unable to form intimate relationships with others. Given Ms. Velasquez's view that the outside world is not a safe place, described at the beginning of the chapter, her young son, Henry, is at risk of developing feelings of mistrust.

2. *Autonomy versus shame and doubt* (ages 1½–3). A child with autonomy has a growing sense of self-awareness and begins to strive for independence and self-control. These children feel proud that they can perform tasks and exercise control over bodily functions. They relate well with close people in the environment and begin to exercise self-control in response to parental limits. To develop autonomy, children need firm limits for controlling impulses and managing anxieties but at the same time still need the freedom to explore their environment. Exhibit 3.8 summarizes possible sources of anxiety for toddlers (Davies, 2011). Toddlers also need an environment rich with stimulating and interesting objects and with opportunities for freedom of choice. Adults must accept the child's bodily functions as normal and good and offer praise and encouragement to enhance the child's mastery of self-control. At the other end of the spectrum are children who doubt themselves. They fear a loss of love and are overly concerned about their parents' approval. These children are ashamed of

> How does the toddler's experience with autonomy contribute to the capacity for human agency?

Exhibit 3.8 Some Possible Sources of Anxiety for Toddlers

Difficulty understanding what is happening

Difficulty communicating

Frustration over not being able to do what others can do or what they imagine others can do

Conflicts between wanting to be independent and wanting their parents' help

Separation or threat of separation from caregivers

Fears of losing parental approval and love

Reactions to losing self-control

Anxieties about the body

SOURCE: Adapted from Davies, 2011

their abilities and develop an unhealthy kind of self-consciousness.

Erikson does not address whether tasks that should be mastered in one stage can be mastered later if the facilitating factors—such as a dependable, nurturing caregiver—are introduced. For example, we know that Sarah suffered some neglect until Chris Johnson and his parents provided a dependable, nurturing environment for her. At what point is it too late to undo psychosocial damage? Critics also question Erikson's emphasis on the process of individualization, through which children develop a strong identity separate from that of their family. Many believe this to be a North American, Western value and therefore not applicable to collectivistic societies such as many African, Latin, and Asian societies or to collectivistic subcultures in the United States.

Emotional Control

Researchers have paid a lot of attention to the strategies infants develop to cope with intense emotions, both positive and negative. They have noted that infants use a range of techniques to cope with intense emotions, including turning the head away, sucking on hands or lips, and closing their eyes. By the middle of the second year, toddlers have built a repertoire of ways to manage strong emotions. They make active efforts to avoid or disregard situations that arouse strong emotions; they move away or they distract themselves with objects. They soothe themselves by thumb sucking, rocking, or stroking; they also engage in reassuring self-talk. In addition, they develop substitute goals if they become thwarted in goal-directed behavior (Shonkoff & Phillips, 2000). However, researchers who do experimental infant research note that a number of infants must be discontinued from the research process because they cannot be calmed enough to participate (Newman & Newman, 2012). The ability to control the intensity of emotional states has important implications for early childhood school performance and social relationships (Davidson & Begley, 2012).

You may not be surprised to learn that researchers have found that one of the most important elements in how an infant learns to manage strong emotions is the assistance provided by the caregiver for emotion management (see, for example, Lowe et al., 2012). Caregivers may offer food or a pacifier, or they may swaddle, cuddle, hug, or rock the infant. By the time the infant is 6 months old, caregivers often provide distraction and use vocalization to soothe. One research team found that for all levels of infant distress, the most effective methods of soothing were holding, rocking, and vocalizing. Feeding and offering a pacifier were effective when the infant was moderately distressed but not at times of extreme distress (Jahromi, Putnam, & Stifter, 2004). Infants who demonstrate greater emotion regulation are much more likely to have parents who use higher levels of positive parenting behaviors, such as sensitivity, positive regard, stimulation, and animation (Ursache, Blair, Stifter, & Voegtline, 2013). Another important element that impacts an infant's ability to manage emotions is whether or not the infant is receiving an adequate amount of sleep (Kurcinka, 2006). The child's temperament also makes a difference, as you will see in the next section.

Photo 3.3   Toddlers begin to build a repertoire of ways to manage strong emotions. The ability to control the intensity of emotional states has important implications for early childhood school performance and social relationships.

© Oleg Kozlov/iStockphoto.com

Finally, there are cultural differences in expectations for management of emotions in infants. For example, Japanese parents try to shield their infants from the frustrations that would invite anger. In other words, some emotions are regulated by protecting the child from situations that would arouse them (Kitayama, Karasaw, & Mesquita, 2004). Cultural differences also exist in how much independence infants and toddlers are expected to exercise in managing emotions. In one study comparing Anglo and Puerto Rican mothers, Harwood (1992) found that Anglo mothers expected their infants to manage their stranger anxiety and separation anxiety without clinging to the mother. The Puerto Rican mothers, conversely, expected their infants to rely on the mother for solace.

Temperament

Another way to look at emotional development is by evaluating **temperament**—the individual's innate disposition. The best-known study of temperament in infants and young children was conducted by Alexander Thomas, Stella Chess, and Herbert Birch (1968, 1970). They studied nine components of temperament: activity level, regularity of biological functions, initial reaction to any new stimulus, adaptability, intensity of reaction, level of stimulation needed to evoke a discernible response, quality of mood, distractibility, and attention span or persistence. From their observations, the researchers identified three types of temperament: easy, slow to warm up, and difficult. The *easy* baby is characterized by good mood, regular patterns of eating and sleeping, and general calmness. The *slow to warm up* baby has few intense reactions, either positive or negative, and tends to be low in activity level. The *difficult* baby is characterized by negative mood, irregular sleeping and eating patterns, and difficulty adapting to new experiences and people. There is a tendency for recent researchers to focus on two clusters of temperamental traits, negative emotions (irritability, fear, sadness, shyness, frustration, and discomfort) and regulatory capacity (ability to self-regulate behavior and engage in self-soothing), as important to parent-infant relationships as well as to future personality and behavior development (see Bridgett et al., 2009).

For an idea of the differences in infant temperament, consider the range of reactions you might see at a baptism service. One infant might scream when passed from one person to the other and when water is placed on his or her forehead. The mother might have difficulty calming the infant for the remainder of the baptism service. At the other extreme, one infant might make cooing noises throughout the entire service and seem unbothered by the rituals. The slow-to-warm-up infant might cautiously check out the clergy administering the baptism and begin to relax by the time the ritual is completed.

Thomas and his colleagues believed that a child's temperament appears shortly after birth and is set, or remains unchanged, throughout life. Whether temperament is permanent or not is still unresolved. Neurobiologists are suggesting that infants come into the world with preexisting temperaments or emotional styles (Davidson & Begley, 2012). They report strong evidence for a genetic basis of emotional styles, with the genetic contribution varying from 20% to 60% for different emotional style traits. But even traits with a strong genetic base can be modified by how parents, teachers, and other caregivers interact with the child. After several decades of study of the neuroscience of emotional style, Richard Davidson and colleagues (see Davidson & Begley, 2012) identify six dimensions of emotional style that have a strong neurobiological basis:

- *Resilience:* how quickly one recovers from adversity
- *Outlook:* how long one can sustain positive emotion
- *Social intuition:* how good one is at picking up social signals
- *Self-awareness:* how well one perceives bodily indications of emotions
- *Sensitivity to context:* how good one is at taking the context into account in regulating emotions
- *Attention:* how sharply and clearly one uses focused attention

Although most of these dimensions of emotional style will not become evident in the early months, there are early signs of a number of them.

Families like the Hicks family who have an infant with negative emotion and poor regulatory capacity may be in special need of social work interventions to prevent a troubling developmental trajectory for the infant and the relationship between the parents. Recent research provides some insight about what could happen between Holly and Mrs. Hicks, as well as between Mr. and Mrs. Hicks, over time. Researchers are finding that negative emotion in the first 3 months is related to decreases in regulatory capacity from 4 to 12 months. And decreases in regulatory capacity in the infant from 4 to 12 months predict poor parent-child relationships when the child is 18 months old (Bridgett et al., 2009). Another research team found a relationship between infant regulatory capacity and marital satisfaction. Following a group of infants and their families from the time the infants were 7 months old until they were 14 months, these researchers found that marital satisfaction increased as infants developed greater regulatory capacity and decreased when infants failed to gain in regulatory capacity (Mehall, Spinrad, Eisenberg,

& Gaertner, 2009). The good news is that neuroscience research suggests that how easily a baby can be soothed has little or no genetic contribution (Davidson & Begley, 2012), so the important thing is for Mrs. Hicks to find the types of caregiving most soothing to Holly.

As parents discipline infants and toddlers to help them gain self-control, different methods of discipline are indicated for children of different temperaments. Infants and toddlers who are fearful and inhibited respond best to gentle, low-power discipline techniques, but these techniques do not work well with fearless infants and toddlers who do best when positive feelings between the caregiver and child are emphasized (Kochanska, Aksan, & Joy, 2007).

Researchers have also been interested in whether there are cultural and socioeconomic differences in infant temperament. Several studies have found small to moderate cross-cultural differences in infant temperament and have attributed these differences mainly to genetics (see Gartstein, Knyazev, & Slobodskaya, 2005; Gartstein et al., 2006). To begin to examine the contributions of the role of genetics and environment to temperament, one research team compared three groups of Russian infants aged 3 to 12 months: infants living in Russia, infants of parents who immigrated to Israel, and infants of parents who immigrated to the United States. They found some differences in temperament across these three situations and concluded that the differences in temperament between the Russian Israeli infants and the Russian American infants probably reflect the different acculturation strategies used to adapt to different host societies (Gartstein, Peleg, Young, & Slobodskaya, 2009). Findings about the relationship between socioeconomic status and temperament are contradictory. Some researchers find no socioeconomic differences (Bridgett et al., 2009) while other researchers find that infants in more economically disadvantaged families have more difficult temperaments and conclude that this difference is largely explained by family stress (Jansen et al., 2009). The difference in findings about socioeconomic status and temperament could be caused by different samples, with socioeconomic variations in temperament more likely to show up when the sample includes greater income variability.

Bowlby's Theory of Attachment

Another key component of emotional development is **attachment**—the ability to form emotional bonds with other people. Many child development scholars have suggested that attachment is one of the most important issues in infant development, mainly because attachment is the foundation for emotional development and a predictor of later functioning. Note that this view of attachment is similar to Erikson's first stage of psychosocial development. This perspective is similar to the one Mrs. Hicks found on the Internet, which raised issues of concern for her.

> How important is the early attachment relationship for the quality of future relationships?

The two most popular theories of attachment were developed by John Bowlby (1969) and Mary Ainsworth and colleagues (Ainsworth, Blehar, Waters, & Wall, 1978). Bowlby, who initially studied attachment in animals, concluded that attachment is natural, a result of the infant's instinct for survival and consequent need to be protected. Attachment between infant and mother ensures that the infant will be adequately nurtured and protected from attack or, in the case of human infants, from a harsh environment. The infant is innately programmed to emit stimuli (smiling, clinging, and so on) to which the mother responds. This exchange between infant and mother creates a bond of attachment. The infant initiates the attachment process, but later the mother's behavior is what strengthens the bond.

Bowlby hypothesized that attachment advances through four stages: preattachment, attachment in the making, clear-cut attachment, and goal-corrected attachment. This process begins in the first month of life, with the infant's ability to discriminate the mother's voice. Attachment becomes fully developed during the second year of life, when the mother and toddler develop a partnership.

During this later phase of attachment, the child is able to manipulate the mother into desired outcomes, but the child also has the capacity to understand the mother's point of view. The mother and the child reach a mutually acceptable compromise.

Bowlby contends that infants can demonstrate attachment behavior to others; however, attachment to the mother occurs earlier than attachment to others and is stronger and more consistent. It is thought that the earliest attachment becomes the child's **working model** for subsequent relationships (Bowlby, 1982).

Attachment explains the child's anxiety when the parents leave. However, children eventually learn to cope with separation. Toddlers often make use of a **transitional object**, or comfort object, to help them cope with separations from parents and to handle other stressful situations. During such times, they may cuddle with a blanket, teddy bear, or other stuffed animal. The transitional object is seen as a symbol of the relationship with the caregiver, but toddlers also see it as having magic powers to soothe and protect them (Davies, 2011).

Ainsworth's Theory of Attachment

One of the most widely used methods to investigate infant attachment, known as the strange situation procedure, was developed by Ainsworth and colleagues (Ainsworth et al., 1978). The Ainsworth group believed that the level of infant attachment to the mother could be assessed through the infant's response to a series of "strange" episodes. Basically, the child is exposed over a period of 25 minutes to eight constructed episodes involving separation and reunion with the mother. The type of child attachment to the mother is measured by how the child responds to the mother following the "distressing" separation.

Ainsworth and her colleagues identified three types of attachment:

1. *Secure attachment.* The child uses the mother as a home base and feels comfortable leaving this base to explore the playroom. The child returns to the mother every so often to ensure that she is still present. When the mother leaves the room (act of separation), the securely attached child will cry and seek comfort from the mother when she returns. But this child is easily reassured and soothed by the mother's return.

2. *Anxious attachment.* The child is reluctant to explore the playroom and clings to the mother. When the mother leaves the room, the child cries for a long time. When the mother returns, this child seeks solace from the mother but continues to cry and may swat at or pull away from the mother. Ainsworth and colleagues described these infants as somewhat insecure and doubted that their mothers would ever be able to provide the security and safety they need.

3. *Avoidant attachment.* Some infants seem indifferent to the presence of their mother. Whether the mother is present or absent from the room, these children's responses are the same.

More recent scholars have added a fourth response, known as the *insecure disorganized/disoriented* response (Belsky, Campbell, Cohn, & Moore, 1996; Main & Hesse, 1990). These children display contradictory behavior: They attempt physical closeness, but retreat with acts of avoidance. These infants often have mothers who are depressed, have a history of being abused, or continue to struggle with a traumatic experience in their own lives. Observations of mothers of infants with disorganized attachment style reveal two patterns of parenting. Some mothers are negative and intrusive and frighten their babies with intense bursts of hostility. Other mothers are passive or helpless; they rarely comfort their babies and may actually appear afraid of their babies (Lyons-Ruth & Jacobvitz, 2008). As a result, the infants become confused in the "strange" situation. They fear the unknown figure and seek solace from the mother but retreat because they are also fearful of the mother (Abrams, Rifkin, & Hesse, 2006). Some authors have suggested that the behavior associated with the disorganized style is actually an adaptive response to harsh caregiving (Stovall & Dozier,

1998). However, research suggests a link between disorganized attachment and serious mental health problems in later childhood and beyond (Lyons-Ruth & Jacobvitz, 2008).

According to Ainsworth's attachment theory, children whose mothers are consistently present and responsive to their needs and whose mothers exhibit a warm, caring relationship develop an appropriate attachment. Findings from studies indicate that this is true, even when there are negative family issues such as alcoholism by the father (Edwards, Eiden, & Leonard, 2006). However, the implication is that only mother-infant attachment exists or is relevant to healthy infant development. This assumption probably seemed unquestionable when these theories were constructed. Today, however, many fathers have prominent, equal, and/or primary responsibilities in child rearing and child care, sometimes by choice and other times because of necessity. Sarah Johnson's dad, for example, became the primary caretaker for Sarah out of necessity. The gender of the parent is irrelevant in the development of secure infant attachment. Rather, it is the behavior of the primary caregiver, regardless of whether it is mother or father, that has the most influence on infant attachment (Geiger, 1996). When fathers who are the primary caregivers are able to provide infants with the warmth and affection they need, infants develop secure attachments to their fathers. In fact, under stress, fathers become a greater source of comfort to their infants than the mothers who are the secondary caregivers (Geiger, 1996). Perhaps the best scenario is when infants develop secure attachments to both parents. In one study, infants with secure attachments to both parents demonstrated fewer behavioral difficulties as toddlers, even fewer problems than toddlers with only secure mother-infant attachment (Volling, Blandon, & Kolak, 2006).

In addition to a more prominent role by fathers over the past 20 to 30 years, more women have entered the workforce, and many more children experience alternative forms of child care, including day care. The effect day care has on the development of attachment in young children continues to be a hotly debated topic. Some argue that day care has a negative effect on infant attachment and increases the risk of the infant developing insecure and avoidant forms of attachment (see, e.g., Belsky, 1987; Belsky & Braungart, 1991). The risks are thought to be especially high if the infant attends day care during the first year of life. Others argue that day care does not have a negative effect on infant and early childhood attachment (Shonkoff & Phillips, 2000). Friedman and Boyle (2008) reviewed 23 studies based on the National Institute of Child Health and Human Development (NICHD) data that tracked 1,000 children from birth through age 15. These studies found that the number of hours infants spend in nonmaternal care is not associated with the infants' security of attachment at age 15; they also found that working mothers interact with their infants almost as much as mothers who are not employed. The most robust finding was that mothers' sensitivity to their infants during interaction is a consistent predictor of secure attachment and positive child development. No main effects were found between the quality and type of child care and mother-infant attachment. However, hours in alternative child care was a risk factor for mother-infant attachment if combined with other risk factors such as maternal insensitivity and poor quality of child care.

A study in the Netherlands found that professional caregivers may be alternative attachment figures for children when their parents are not available, but it is the professional caregivers' group-related sensitivity, rather than the child's individual relationship with one professional caregiver, that promotes a sense of security and safety in children. Girls were found to be more securely attached to their professional caregivers than boys, however (De Schipper, Tavecchio, & Van IJzendoorn, 2008). In one study in the United States, day care was found to mitigate the adverse effects of insecure mother-infant attachment (Spieker, Nelson, & Petras, 2003).

Recently, researchers have begun to study attachment among children in foster care. In 2011 an estimated 400,540 children were in foster care (Child Welfare Information Gateway, 2013a). Most of these children come into foster care without secure attachments. Once in foster care, many children are subjected to frequent changes in their foster homes. Problems with attachment may contribute to foster home disruptions, but foster home disruptions also contribute to attachment problems. Others conclude that institutional care can also have the same devastating effects on attachment (Johnson, Browne, & Hamilton-Giachritsis, 2006).

Let's look at one other issue concerning attachment. The manner in which infant attachment is measured raises some concerns. Most studies of attachment have used the Ainsworth group's strange situation method. However, this measure may not yield valid results with some groups or under certain conditions. For example, the avoidant pattern of attachment some investigators have noted among children in day care may not indicate lack of attachment, as some have concluded. These children may be securely attached but seem indifferent to the exit and return of the mother simply because they have become accustomed to routine separations and reunions with their mother.

The appropriateness of using the strange situation method with certain ethnic groups has also been questioned. An early study found Japanese infants to demonstrate more anxious attachment style than infants in other parts of the world and attributed this finding to the fact that Japanese mothers left their infants in the care of others much less often than mothers in a number of other cultures (Takahashi, 1990). A more recent study found that the distribution of attachment styles of Japanese infants was consistent with worldwide norms when the researchers controlled for the unfamiliarity of separation from the mother (Behrens, Hesse, & Main, 2007).

Conversely, in many cultures infants are cared for by a collective of mothers, older siblings, cousins, fathers, aunts, uncles, and grandparents. The level of sense of security in these infants depends on coordinated care of a number of caregivers. The strange situation does not capture the fluid nature of caregiving and the degree to which it supports infants' feelings of security and safety (Lewis, 2005). One study found that in Israeli kibbutz-reared

> In what other ways does culture affect infant and toddler development?

children, one negative caregiving relationship could negatively affect other attachment relationships (Sagi, Koren-Karie, Gini, Ziv, & Joels, 2002).

In spite of these concerns, findings from a large number of studies using the strange situation in Europe, Africa, Asia, and the Middle East as well as North America indicate that the attachment patterns identified by Ainsworth occur in many cultures (Gardiner & Kosmitzki, 2011). It is important to remember that attachment theory was developed by European American theorists who conceptualized attachment as the basis for developing subsequent independence. However, in more collectivist cultures, attachment is seen as the basis for developing obedience and harmony (Weisner, 2005).

Attachment and Brain Development

Attachment directly affects brain development (Gerhardt, 2004; Perry, 2002). Gerhardt concludes that without emotional bonding with an adult, the orbitofrontal cortex in the brain of infants (the part of the brain that allows social relationships to develop) cannot develop well. During the first year of life, the infant must develop the capacity to tolerate higher and higher levels of emotional arousal. The caregiver helps the infant with this by managing the amount of stimulation the infant receives. As the right orbitofrontal cortex develops, the infant is able to tolerate higher levels of arousal and stimulation. However, when the caregiver is not attuned to the needs of the infant in regard to managing stimulation during the first year of life, negative emotions result and growth of the right orbitofrontal cortex is inhibited (Farmer, 2009). This process has been called the social brain. Supporters of this perspective cite several studies to support these conclusions, including an investigation of infants reared in orphanages in Romania conducted by Chugani et al. (2001). The infants had little contact with an adult, were left in their cots for most of the day, were fed with propped-up bottles, and were never smiled at or hugged. Research with these infants found that their brain development was severely impaired.

One question of concern is whether these deficiencies in brain development are permanent. Some suggest that the brain impairments can be reversed if changes in care and attachment occur early enough (Zigler, Finn-Stevenson, & Hall, 2002). They highlight the strides in brain development made by the Romanian orphans who were adopted into caring homes before they were 6 months of age. Perhaps Sarah Johnson's improvement was the result of early intervention and moving her quickly to live with her dad. Others suggest that the brain impairments caused by lack of attachment with a primary caregiver are permanent (Perry, 2002). Regardless, the implication is that future brain growth is seriously jeopardized if brain development is not adequately nurtured in the first 2 to 3 years. We have clear evidence that the human brain is plastic and changes over time with new experiences, but we also know that it is not completely plastic; brain vulnerabilities in early childhood predispose one to difficulties in managing social relationships, and social relationship problems affect ongoing brain development (Farmer, 2009). Gerhardt concludes that the best advice we can offer parents of newborns is to forget about holding flashcards in front of their babies but instead, hold and cuddle the infants and simply enjoy them.

Critical Thinking Questions 3.2

What have you seen the adults in your family, or other families you know, do to support language development in infants and toddlers? Do you know any bilingual infants and toddlers? If so, what have you observed about their language development? In your multigenerational family, what have you observed about the expectations parents have for how infants and toddlers should manage emotions?

THE ROLE OF PLAY _____

Play is crucial to child development. Play allows infants and toddlers to enhance motor, cognitive, language, emotional, social, and moral development.

Because of their differences in development in all areas, infants and toddlers play in different ways. Exhibit 3.9 describes four types of infant play and three types of play observed in very young children. These later types of play begin in toddlerhood and develop in union with cognitive and motor development. For example, young toddlers will play with a mound of clay by hitting and perhaps squishing it. More developed toddlers will mold the clay into a ball, and older toddlers will try to roll or throw the molded ball.

One zealous mother describes joining the "toy of the month club" in which she received developmental toys through the mail each month for the first 2 years of her child's life. This mother wanted to be sure that her child had every opportunity to advance in terms of motor and cognitive skills. Although this mother's efforts are to be applauded, she admits that these toys were very costly and that perhaps she could have achieved the same outcome with other less costly objects. For example, there is no evidence that a store-bought infant mobile is any more effective than a homemade paper one hung on a clothes hanger. The objective is to provide stimulation and opportunities for play. Fergus Hughes (2010, p. 68) makes the following suggestions about the appropriate toys for infants and toddlers during the first 2 years of life:

- *Birth to 3 months:* toys for sensory stimulation, such as rattles, bells, colorful pictures and wallpaper, crib ornaments, mobiles, music boxes, and other musical toys
- *3–6 months:* toys for grasping, squeezing, feeling, and mouthing, such as cloth balls, soft blocks, and teething toys
- *6–12 months:* colorful picture books, stacking toys, nesting toys, sponges for water play, mirrors, toy telephones, toys that react to the child's activity
- *12–18 months:* push toys; pull toys; balls; plain and interlocking blocks; simple puzzles with large, easy-to-handle pieces; stacking toys; riding toys with wheels close to the ground
- *18–24 months:* toys for the sandbox and water play; spoons, shovels, and pails; storybooks; blocks; dolls, stuffed animals, and puppets

Exhibit 3.9   Types of Play in Infancy and Toddlerhood

	Types of Infant Play
Vocal play	Playful vocalizing with grunts, squeals, trills, vowels, and so on to experiment with sound and have fun with it
Interactive play	Initiating interactions with caregivers (at about 4–5 months), by smiling and vocalizing, to communicate and make connection
Exploratory play with objects	Exploring objects with eyes, mouth, and hands to learn about their shape, color, texture, movement, and sounds and to experience pleasure
Baby games	Participating in parent-initiated ritualized, repetitive games, such as peek-a-boo, that contain humor, suspense, and excitement and build an emotional bond
	Types of Toddler Play
Functional play	Engaging in simple, repetitive motor movements
Constructive play	Creating and constructing objects
Make-believe play	Acting out everyday functions and tasks and playing with an imaginary friend

SOURCE: Based on Davies, 2011

Recently, researchers have become interested in the impact of new technologies and the effect they have on type of play, types of toys, and the amount of time spent in play (Bergen & Davis, 2011). It is not uncommon for children as young as several months old to be seen playing with technology-augmented toys or with apps on their parents' cell phones or tablets. The impact of this technology on young children and familial relationships is a needed area of research (Lombardi, 2012). One research team found that mothers interact less with their toddlers while engaged in play with electronic toys than when engaged in other types of play (Woolridge & Shapka, 2012). How this technology-based play affects moral development is another area for further exploration (Bergen & Davis, 2011). The American Academy of Pediatrics and the government of Australia recommend that children under the age of 2 should not watch any television or video material (cited in Courage & Howe, 2010). Courage and Howe (2010) reviewed the empirical literature on the effects of screen time on infant and toddler development and found the evidence was not all bad. They found evidence for the following statements:

- Infants do not learn as readily from screen materials as do older children and adults.
- Infants learn more readily from people than from television and videos.
- Infants and toddlers are not passive when viewing television or videos; they engage more with screen material that is interesting to them.
- Excessive screen time can interfere with time spent on physical activities and creative play.
- Television and videos do not cause ADHD, but extremely high levels of viewing are associated with ADHD symptoms; parents may seek relief from constant interaction with a child with ADHD symptoms by encouraging screen time.
- Background television distracts the play of infants and toddlers.
- Infants spend more time looking at a video if a parent views it with them and talks with them about it.
- Television can provide a route to early language development in impoverished environments.

Another important aspect of play is parent/child interaction. Parent/infant play may increase the likelihood of secure attachment between the parent and child (Davies, 2011; Hughes, 2010). The act of play at least provides the opportunity for infants and parents to feel good about themselves by enjoying each other and by being enjoyed. Even before infants can speak or understand language spoken to them, play provides a mechanism of communication between the parent and infants. Infants receive messages about themselves through play, which promotes their sense of self (Scarlett, Naudeau, Salonius-Pasternak, & Ponte, 2005).

Many similarities exist in the way that mothers and fathers play with infants and toddlers but also some differences. Both mothers and fathers are teachers and sensitive communicators, and both enjoy rough-and-tumble play with their babies (Roggman, Boyce, Cook, Christiansen, & Jones, 2004). But research has also noted some differences in the ways that mothers and fathers play with infants and toddlers. Fathers engage in more rough-and-tumble play; they are more likely to lift their babies, bounce them, and move their legs and arms. Mothers are more likely to offer toys, play conventional games of peek-a-boo and pat-a-cake, and engage in constructive play. However, mothers have been found to play differently with infant sons than with infant daughters, engaging in more conversation with daughters and making more statements about the baby's feelings when talking with daughters; conversely, they engage in more direction with sons and make more comments to call the baby's attention to his surroundings (Clearfield & Nelson, 2006). Mothers have also been found to be more likely to follow the child's lead, while fathers are more likely to steer play activity according to their preferences. It is important to note, however, that these mother/father differences have not been found in Sweden and Israel, both societies with more egalitarian gender roles than found in the United States (Hughes, 2010).

Play also is a vehicle for developing peer relations. A few decades ago, it was thought that babies really weren't interested in each other and could not form relationships with each other. Recent research challenges this view (Hughes, 2010). The peer group becomes more important at earlier ages as family size decreases and siblings are no longer available for daily social interaction. Researchers have found that very young infants, as young as 2 months, get excited by the sight of other infants; by 6 to 9 months, infants appear to try to get the attention of other infants; and by 9 to 12 months infants imitate each other (Hughes, 2010). Although toddlers are capable of establishing relationships, their social play is a struggle, and a toddler play session is quite a fragile experience. Toddlers need help in structuring their play with each other. And yet researchers have found that groups of toddlers in preschool settings develop play routines that they return to again and again over periods of months (Corsaro, 2011). These toddler play routines are primarily nonverbal, with a set of ritualized actions. For example, Corsaro (2011) notes a play routine in one Italian preschool in which a group of toddlers would rearrange the chairs in the room and work together to move them around in patterns. They returned to this routine fairly regularly over the course of a year, modifying it slightly over time. Peer relations are being built by "doing things together."

DEVELOPMENTAL DISRUPTIONS

Developmental delay is the name given to a situation in which an infant or toddler has a significant lag in development in any of the dimensions discussed earlier (Rosenberg, Ellison, Fast, Robinson, & Lazar, 2013). The delay may be temporary or may be a symptom of a lifelong condition. **Developmental disability** is the name given when a child has a lifelong impairment that results in functional limitations in some dimensions, including such conditions as intellectual disabilities, autism, or cerebral palsy (Parish, Saville, & Swaine, 2011). Part C of the Individuals with Disabilities Act (IDEA) is a nationwide program that provides services to infants and toddlers with developmental delays in cognitive, motor, communication, and social and emotional development, but there is no standard definition of what constitutes a developmental delay (Rosenberg et al., 2013). Premature infants like Holly Hicks, for example, often need time to catch up in terms of physical, cognitive, and emotional development. At what point does Holly's social worker decide that she is not developing fast enough and label her developmentally delayed? At what point would it be appropriate to decide that she has a lifelong developmental disability?

Because early interventions for infants and toddlers produce better outcomes in comparison with interventions for school-aged children (Matson, Fodstad, & Dempsey, 2009; McMahon, 2013), early detection and diagnosis is key. The Centers for Disease Control and Prevention (2012d), along with the American Academy of Pediatrics, recommends screening for all types of developmental delays and disabilities at 9, 18, and 24 or 30 months of age.

In recent years, researchers have been studying the early impairments of developmental disabilities such as cerebral palsy, Down syndrome, and seizure disorder (Hattier, Matson, Sipes, & Turygin, 2011). A more aggressive research agenda has focused on early identification of autism spectrum disorders (ASD), because early intervention is seen as so critical for this developmental disability. Typical behaviors with these disorders include impairments in social and communication development and restricted and repetitive behaviors. Barbaro and Dissanayake (2012) investigated the early markers of ASD at the ages of 12, 18, and 24 months in an attempt to understand how infants and toddlers with ASD could be distinguished from infants and toddlers with developmental delays that would disappear with time and early intervention. They found that infants with the most severe symptoms at 24 months had pervasive impairment on all social and communication items at 12 and 18 months. There was more variability in the impairments of 12- and 18-month-old infants who would later demonstrate less severe impairments at 24 months but were still on the autism spectrum. The infants and toddlers with developmental delays at 12 and 18 months had typical development in every area but language at 24 months. At 12 months the

markers of later ASD were deficits in pointing, waving, imitation, eye contact, and response to name. At 18 months, the key markers were deficits in pointing, eye contact, and showing items to a communication partner. The same markers were present at 24 months, plus an added marker of deficits in pretend play. The children with developmental delay showed earlier deficits in pretend play but were performing at the typical level by age 24 months.

Critical Thinking Questions 3.3

Why is play crucial to infant and toddler development? What do you think about infant and toddler use of television and videos? What do you think about toddler use of parents' cell phone and tablet apps? What have you observed about infant and toddler use of these technologies? Why do you think professionals and researchers recommend early intervention with infants and toddlers with developmental delays and disabilities?

CHILD CARE ARRANGEMENTS IN INFANCY AND TODDLERHOOD

Human infants start life in a remarkably dependent state, in need of constant care and protection. On their own, they would die. Toddlers are full of life and are making great strides in development in all areas, but they are also "not ready to set out for life alone in the big city" (Newman & Newman, 2012, p. 197). Societal health is dependent on finding good solutions to the question of who will care for infants and toddlers.

With large numbers of mothers of infants and toddlers in the paid workforce and not at home, this question becomes a challenging one. The United States seems to be responding to this challenge more reluctantly than other highly industrialized countries are. This difference becomes clear in comparative analysis of two solutions for early child care: family leave and paid child care.

Family Leave

Because of changes in the economic institution in the United States from 1975 to 1999, the proportion of infants with mothers in paid employment increased from 24% to 54% and leveled off at 57% by 2012 (Bureau of Labor Statistics, 2013; Shonkoff & Phillips, 2000). A similar trend is occurring around the world.

> What impact might this trend have over time on the current cohort of infants and toddlers?

In response, most industrialized countries have instituted social policies that provide for job-protected leaves for parents to allow them to take off from work to care for their infants. Sweden was the first country to develop such a policy in 1974. The Swedish policy guaranteed paid leave.

By the early 1990s, the United States was the only industrialized country without a family leave policy (Kamerman, 1996). But in 1993, the U.S. Congress passed the Family and Medical Leave Act (FMLA) of 1993 (Pub. L. No. 103-3). FMLA requires businesses with 50 or more employees to provide up to 12 weeks of unpaid, job-protected leave during a 12-month period for workers to manage childbirth, adoption, or personal or family illness. Eligible workers are entitled to continued health insurance coverage during the leave period, if such coverage is a part of their compensation package.

Exhibit 3.10 highlights the maternal leave policies in selected wealthy countries. Most of the countries listed, including the United States, require that fathers are entitled to the same leave as mothers. That means, for example, that mother and father could each take a 12-week leave in the United States, or 24 weeks total. In 2009, the United States and Australia were the only affluent countries of the world that did not offer some paid parental leave at the time of birth and adoption. Australia does, however, provide families with a universal, flat-rate maternity grant of $5,000 for each new child to assist with the costs of birth or adoption. European countries also provide birth or maternity

Exhibit 3.10

Country	Paid	Unpaid
France	20	142
Austria	16	96
Sweden	40	45
United Kingdom	12	53
Australia	0	52
Canada	29	23
Denmark	19	31
Greece	34	13
Netherlands	16	13
Switzerland	11	3
United States	0	12

SOURCE: Center for Economic and Policy Research, 2009

grants and family allowances. This is an area for social work advocacy in the United States.

Paid Child Care

Historically in the United States, mothers were expected to provide full-time care for infants and toddlers at home. If mothers were not available, it was expected that children would be cared for by domestic help or a close relative but still in their home setting. Even in the 1960s, with the development of Head Start programs, the focus was on preschool-age children; infants and toddlers were still expected to be cared for at home. Thus, historically there was very little provision of alternative child care for most children younger than school age.

This phenomenon has changed dramatically, however, over the last 30 years. As noted earlier, in 2013, 57% of mothers with children younger than 1 year of age were employed. The rate for mothers of children younger than 6 years of age was 64.8% (Bureau of Labor Statistics, 2013). Therefore, alternative child care has become a necessity in the United States. In 2010, about 68% of children younger than age 5 with employed mothers were involved in some type of nonparental care; 48% of those were in organized care settings, either in child care centers or family care homes; 40% were cared for by relatives; 12% were cared for by nonrelatives other than in organized care settings; about 11% had no regular child care arrangement; and about 7% went to work with their mothers. The numbers don't total 100% because 29% of these children are cared for in multiple arrangements (U.S. Census Bureau, 2011b).

Many advocates for day care refer to the European model as an ideal for the United States. Countries in Europe provide "universal" child care for all children, regardless of the parents' income, employment status, race, age, and so forth. These programs are supported through national policy and funded through public funds. If they pay at all, parents pay no more than a quarter of the monies needed. Parents in Europe thus pay far less than parents in the United States typically pay. For parents in the United States, only 1 in 6 eligible low-income families is receiving federal child care assistance (Lombardi, 2012).

As suggested earlier, there are controversies about whether child day care centers are harmful to infants and toddlers, but there is growing consensus that nonparental child care is not inherently harmful. The type of nonparental child care must be put in ecological context and considered along with other variables such as the quality of the child care, the amount of time spent in nonparental care, the sensitivity of both parental and nonparental care providers, and characteristics of the child.

INFANTS AND TODDLERS IN THE MULTIGENERATIONAL FAMILY

Maria, a new mom, describes the first visit her mother and father made to her home after the birth of Maria's new infant. "Mom and Dad walked right past me as if I was not there, even though we had not seen each other for 6 months. I quickly realized that my status as their 'princess' was now replaced with a new little princess. During their visit, my husband and I had to fight to see our own child. When she cried, they immediately ran to her. And my mother criticized everything I did—she didn't like the brand of diapers I used, she thought the color of the room was too dreary for an infant—and she even scolded my husband at one point for waking the baby when he went to check on her. I appreciated their visit, but I must admit that I was glad when it was time for them to leave." Maria's description is not unique. The involvement of grandparents and other extended family members in the care of infants and toddlers may be experienced either as a great source of support or as interference and intrusion (and sometimes as a little of each). And, of course, cultures of the world have different norms about who is involved, and in what ways, in the care of infants and toddlers.

Yet the specific roles of grandparents and other extended family members are rarely discussed within the family, which is why conflicts often occur (Carter, McGoldrick, & Petkov, 2011). When these roles are clearly articulated and agreed on, extended family members can provide support that enhances infant and toddler development. Family involvement as a form of social support is further discussed as a "protective factor" later in this chapter.

> What have you observed about how family relationships change when a baby is born?

The birth of a child, especially of a first child, brings about a major transition not only for parents but also for the entire kin network. Partners become parents; sons and daughters become fathers and mothers; fathers and mothers become grandfathers and grandmothers; and brothers and sisters become aunts and uncles. The social status of the extended family serves as the basis of the social status of the child, and the values and beliefs of the extended family will shape the way they care for and socialize the child (Newman & Newman,

2012). In addition, many children's names and child-rearing rituals, decisions, and behaviors are passed from past generations to the next.

To illustrate this point, there is an old joke about a mother who prepared a roast beef for most Sunday family dinners. She would always cut the roast in half and place it in two pans before cooking it in the oven. Observing this behavior, her young daughter asked her why she cut the roast in half. After some thought she told her daughter that she did not know for sure; she remembered that her mother had always cut her roast in half. Later the mother asked her mother why she had cut her roast in half before cooking it. The senior mother explained that she did not have a pan large enough for the size roast she needed to feed her family. Thus, she would cut the roast in half in order to fit it into the two pans that she did own.

Here is another example. One mother reports giving her infant daughter herb tea in addition to an ointment provided by her physician for a skin rash. It seems that this skin rash was common among infant girls in each generation in this family. A specific herb tea was traditionally used to treat the rash. This mother confesses that she did not tell her mother or grandmother that she used the ointment prescribed by her doctor. It is interesting for us to note that although the mother did not have complete faith in the tea, she also did not have complete faith in the ointment. The mother states that she is not sure which one actually cured the rash. Violation of family and cultural rituals and norms can be a source of conflict between new parents and other family members (Carter et al., 2011). For example, differences of opinion about baptism, male circumcision, and even child care arrangements can create family disharmony. One decision that often involves the multigenerational family is whether to breastfeed or bottle feed the infant.

The Breastfeeding Versus Bottle Feeding Decision

Throughout history, most infants have been breastfed. However, alternatives to breastfeeding by the mother have always existed, sometimes in the form of a wet nurse (a woman employed to breastfeed someone else's infant) or in the form of animal milks. Following World War II, breastfeeding ceased to be the primary nutritional source for infants because of the promotion of manufactured formula in industrialized and nonindustrialized countries. Since the 1980s, cultural attitudes have shifted again in favor of breastfeeding. The American Academy of Pediatrics (AAP) argues that infant nutrition should be considered a public health issue, not a lifestyle choice (Eidelman & Schanler, 2012). The AAP recommends that infants be breastfed, or fed with human milk, exclusively for the first 6 months, followed by continued breastfeeding with some supplementary use of foods until the infant is at least 1 year old.

In 2010, 76% of new mothers in the United States initiated breastfeeding, but only 13% breastfed exclusively for 6 months. The extended family could play a role in supporting mothers to persist with breastfeeding. There are racial, ethnic, and social class differences in the rate of breastfeeding, suggesting that family and culture play a role in the breastfeeding decision. The rate of breastfeeding initiation is 80.6% for Latina mothers and 58.1% for African American mothers. It is 67.5% for low-income mothers. Some employed mothers of infants are provided a space and flexible schedule for milk expression while at work, but workplace policies can be a barrier to breastfeeding for other mothers. Societal customs can support or discourage breastfeeding. In Saudi Arabia, a woman may breastfeed her infant openly and receive no notice, although otherwise she is fully veiled. In France, topless swimming is culturally acceptable, but breastfeeding in public is not (Riordan & Auerbach, 1999).

Postpartum Depression

Family dynamics are often altered when mothers are depressed following childbirth. There is evidence that, around the world, 10% to 15% of mothers will have postpartum depression in the first year of the infant's life (Pearlstein, Howard, Salisbury, & Zlotnick, 2009; Wisner, Chambers, & Sit, 2006). Although social factors no doubt contribute to postpartum depression, it is generally accepted that the precipitous hormonal changes at birth, to which some women seem especially sensitive, play a large role. Postpartum depression often goes undiagnosed and untreated across cultural groups (Dennis & Chung-Lee, 2006), but it is more likely to receive attention in societies that have regular postpartum visits from midwives or nurses. For example, in the United Kingdom, new parents receive seven visits from midwives in the first 2 weeks postpartum (Posmontier & Horowitz, 2004). Postpartum depression can be very disruptive to the early mother-infant relationship and, as discussed shortly, increases risk of impaired cognitive, emotional, and motor development (Wisner et al., 2006). Both social support and pharmacological interventions have been found to be helpful (Sword, Watt, & Krueger, 2006). Different cultures have different expectations for maternal adaptation, and it is important for health providers to recognize these cultural influences (Posmontier & Horowitz, 2004).

Very little research exists on psychosocial and mental health issues for new fathers, but the Australian First Time Fathers Study attempted to address this gap in knowledge (Condon, 2006). This study found no evidence of male postnatal depression but did find that male partners of women with postpartum depression are at risk of depression, anxiety, and abusing alcohol. At first, most men are confused by their wives' depression but supportive. If the depression lasts for months, which it often does, support is usually gradually withdrawn. Men report that they find their wives' irritability and lack of physical affection more troubling than the sadness and tearfulness. This study also found that male partners and other family members of depressed mothers often take on more and more of the care of the infant over time, which reinforces the mother's sense of incompetence. Communication breakdowns are very common in these situations.

> ### Critical Thinking Questions 3.4
>
> Why do you think that the United States was slower than other advanced industrial countries to develop family leave policies? Why do you think the United States' policy does not include paid family leave as is the case in almost all other advanced industrial societies? Do you think the United States should have "universal" child care for all children, regardless of parents' income, as they do in Europe? Why or why not?

RISKS TO HEALTHY INFANT AND TODDLER DEVELOPMENT

Unfortunately, not all infants and toddlers get the start they need in life. Millions of infants and toddlers around the world are impoverished, abandoned, neglected, and endangered. Collectively, the adults of the world have not ensured that every child has the opportunity for a good start in life. Not only do these adversities have consequences for the infant's or toddler's immediate development but research indicates that adversities experienced in childhood can also have negative consequences throughout the individual's life span. In a large, well-known study referred to as the adverse childhood experience (ACE), study investigators examined the consequences of adverse childhood experiences, including abuse, family violence, and parental substance abuse, mental illness, or imprisonment on the infant's later adult physical and mental health outcomes (Felitti et al., 1998). Not only did they find a relationship between the two but they also concluded that exposure to adversities during childhood, especially abuse and household dysfunction, increased the likelihood of developing a potentially fatal disease in adulthood. You have probably already surmised what some of the environmental factors are that inhibit healthy growth and development in infants and toddlers. This section addresses a few of those factors that social workers are especially likely to encounter: poverty, inadequate caregiving, and child maltreatment.

Poverty

Examining the social science evidence about the effects of family life on physical and mental health, Repetti, Taylor, and Seeman (2002, p. 359) made the following observation: "The adverse effects of low SES [socioeconomic status] on mental and physical health outcomes are as close to a universal truth as social science has offered." When a family is impoverished, the youngest are the most vulnerable, and, indeed, children birth to age 3 have the highest rates of impoverishment around the world (Addy & Wight, 2012; UNICEF, 2012a). Although there are many different ways of measuring poverty, it is generally agreed that 1 billion children across the world live in poverty, representing 1 in 2 children (Global Issues, 2013). Although children living in the poorest countries are much more likely than children living in wealthy countries to be poor, the proportion of children living in poverty has been rising in many of the wealthiest nations (UNICEF, 2012a). Using a relative measure of poverty as income below 50% of the national median income, the UNICEF researchers found that the percentage of children living in poverty in 35 economically advanced countries ranged from 4.7% in Iceland to 25.5% in Romania. The United States had the second highest rate, 23.1%. Fourteen countries, including most European countries, had child poverty rates of less than 10%.

> In what ways does social class affect the development of infants and toddlers?

In the United States, the National Center for Children in Poverty (NCCP) (Addy & Wight, 2012) estimates that families need an income about two times the U.S. federal poverty level to meet basic needs, and they refer to families below this level as low income. NCCP (Addy & Wight, 2012) reports that, in 2010, of the more than 11 million infants and toddlers in the United States, 5.7 million (48%) lived in low-income families, and 3.0 million (25%) lived in families below the poverty level. The percentage of infants and toddlers living in low-income families increased during the recession that began in 2007, from 44% in 2005 to 48% in 2010. There are racial and ethnic differences in the rates: 70% of Native American and Black infants and toddlers live in low-income families, compared with 66% of Latino infants and toddlers, 35% of White infants and toddlers, and 30% of Asian infants and toddlers. Infants and toddlers with immigrant parents are more likely than infants and toddlers with native-born parents to live in low-income families, 63% compared with 46%. Geographical differences also exist in the rates of infants and toddlers in low-income families: 58% of infants and toddlers living in rural areas live in low-income families, compared with 47% of infants and toddlers in urban areas. Forty percent of infants and toddlers living in low-income families have at least one parent who works full-time, year-round.

Although some young children who live in poverty flourish, poverty presents considerable risks to children's growth and development. (That risk continues from infancy and toddlerhood into early and middle childhood, as Chapters 4 and 5 explain.) Children living in poverty often suffer the consequences of poor nutrition and inadequate health care. Undernutrition in infancy and toddlerhood is a major risk factor for serious health problems at later stages of life, especially if it is combined with prenatal undernutrition (Barker & Thornburg, 2013).

Negative associations between family poverty and children's cognitive development begin to emerge by the end of the second year of life. By age 2, poor toddlers score 4.4 points lower on IQ tests than nonpoor toddlers. In addition, poor infants and toddlers are more likely to demonstrate emotional and behavioral problems than nonpoor infants and toddlers. Three-year-olds who live in deep poverty have been found to display more internalizing behavior symptoms, such as anxiety, withdrawal, and depression, than other children of the same age (Barajas, Philipsen, & Brooks-Gunn, 2008). Children are affected not only by the direct consequences of poverty but also by indirect factors such as family stress, parental depression, and inadequate or nonsupportive parenting (Davies, 2011). Irma Velasquez's depression and anxiety will affect her relationship with Henry. Poor children are also more likely to be exposed to environmental toxins (Hetherington & Boddy, 2013).

Most disturbing is the link between poverty and **infant mortality**—the death of a child before his or her first birthday. In general, infant mortality rates are the highest in the poorest countries (UNICEF, 2013a). Infant mortality rates in the United States are high compared with other economically advanced nations (World Bank, 2013a), but Bosnia and Herzegovina, a country with less than one fifth the average income of the United States, has achieved the same infant mortality rate as the United States (Central Intelligence Agency, 2012). Within the United States, mortality rates for infants are higher among the poor, and the rate among African American infants is over twice that of Hispanic and non-Hispanic White infants (Centers for Disease Control and Prevention, 2013j).

Inadequate Caregiving

Because they are so dependent on caregiver assistance in all areas of their lives, infants and toddlers' developmental risk is heightened when parents fail to carry out caregiving functions. The most pervasive response to inadequate caregiving is nonorganic failure to thrive (NOFTT). This diagnosis is used to describe infants, usually aged 3 to 12 months, who show poor development, primarily in terms of weight gain. These infants weigh less than 80% of the ideal weight for their age. The "nonorganic" feature refers to the lack of medical causes for the poor development and is thought to be a consequence of environmental neglect (lack of food), stimulus deprivation, and problems in the child-caregiver relationship (Kaneshiro, 2011). Overall, NOFTT is a consequence of the infant's basic needs going unmet, primarily the needs for feeding and nurturing.

Ongoing parental conflict, harsh parenting, and parental mental illness and substance abuse are also risk factors for infant and toddler development. When there is a high level of parental anger and conflict, parents typically become less available to the infant or toddler, creating an insecure home environment (Struge-Apple, Davies, & Cummings, 2006). Research indicates that infants and toddlers raised with high parental conflict have more active stress response systems. Parents who react to a toddler's assertive and limit-testing behavior with harsh discipline provide a model of aggression for solving relationship issues (Bayer et al., 2011). Serious parental mental illness, including chronic depression, bipolar disorder, posttraumatic stress disorder (PTSD), and schizophrenia, often compromise the ability of parents to meet the needs of infants and toddlers (Goodman & Brand, 2009; Natsuaki et al., 2010). Severe and chronic maternal depression has been associated with insecure attachment (Goodman & Brand, 2009). Parents whose lives are organized around accessing and abusing legal and illegal substances are four times more likely than other parents to neglect their infants and toddlers (Street, Whitlingum, Gibson, Cairns, & Ellis, 2008).

Child Maltreatment

National data indicate that in 2011, 681,000 children in the United States were assessed to be victims of abuse or neglect. (It is important to note that it is generally assumed that many abused and neglected children never come to the attention of government authorities.) Infants from birth to 1 year of age have the highest rate of victimization, at 1.2 per 1,000 (Child Welfare Information Gateway, 2013b). For all age groups, 78.5% of confirmed cases of child maltreatment involved neglect, 17.6% involved physical abuse, 9.1% involved sexual abuse, and 9% involved psychological abuse.

The effect of child maltreatment and other trauma on the brain during the first 3 years of life has been the subject of considerable study in recent years (Farmer, 2009; Fawley-King & Merz, 2014). Remember that neuroscientific research has clearly demonstrated that the brain is plastic throughout life, which means it is shaped by

> How might child abuse or neglect experienced as an infant or toddler affect later development?

experiences across the life course. Research indicates that several brain parts involved in responses to stress are especially disrupted and changed by traumatic events during the first 3 years of life. They include the brain parts that regulate homeostasis (brain stem and locus coeruleus), form memory systems and regulate emotion (hippocampus, amygdala, and frontal cortex), and regulate the executive functions of planning, working memory, and impulse control (orbito-frontal cortex, cingulate and dorsolateral prefrontal cortex). In addition, the major neuroendocrine stress response system, the hypothalamic-pituitary-adrenal (HPA) axis, is also impacted by trauma. Research indicates that early life stress, such as child maltreatment, can lead to disruptions in HPA axis functioning and result in anxiety disorders and depression in adulthood (see Fawley-King & Merz, 2014).

The child who experiences child maltreatment or other trauma at the ages of 2, 3, or 4 is at risk of developing memory problems, difficulty regulating emotions, and problems integrating sensory experiences. Research shows that people who experience childhood trauma are more likely to develop decreased volume in the hippocampus, a brain characteristic also found with adults experiencing PTSD. Injuries to the hippocampus have been found to be associated with cognitive impairments, memory deficits, poor coping responses, and dissociation (Farmer, 2009). When a child is exposed to extreme stress or trauma, the autonomic nervous system is activated, resulting in increased heart rate, respiration, and blood pressure. The child may freeze in place before beginning to fight. In the case of child sexual abuse, the child may dissociate, or detach from what is happening, becoming compliant and emotionally numb (Fawley-King & Merz, 2014).

As noted, 78.5% of all confirmed cases of child maltreatment involve neglect. Child neglect is thought to occur when caregivers are ignorant of child development, overwhelmed by life stresses, or struggling with mental health or substance abuse problems. Children who experience neglect in the early years of life often do not thrive. Much of the early human research on child neglect focused on

Romanian children who were placed in state-run institutions with few staff (staff-child ratio of 1:60) and very little sensory and emotional stimulation. At 3 years of age, these children were found to have delays in physical growth as well as in motor, cognitive, and language skills; they also had poor social skills. Preliminary research suggests that neglect leads to deficits in prefrontal cortex functioning (attention and social deficits) and executive functioning (planning, working memory, and impulse control). Working memory is key to learning. Early evidence suggests that these changes in brain functioning are related to difficulties managing emotions, problem solving, and social relationships. Most troubling is the finding that children who are neglected early in life have smaller brains than other children; they have fewer neurons and fewer connections between neurons.

An association has been found between infant temperament and abuse (Grogan-Kaylor & Otis, 2007). Infants who have "difficult" temperament are more likely to be abused and neglected. The combination of difficult temperament and environmental stress increases the risk of child abuse. Infants and toddlers with mental, physical, or behavioral abnormalities are also at a higher risk for abuse (Guterman & Embry, 2004).

Social workers need to keep abreast of the developing neuroscience research on the effects of child maltreatment on brain development, but we must also remember to put the brain in context. We must advocate for policies that ensure parents have the best available resources to provide the type of parenting infants and toddlers need. We must also encourage research that examines how to heal the disrupted brain.

PROTECTIVE FACTORS IN INFANCY AND TODDLERHOOD

Many young children experience typical growth and development despite the presence of risk factors. They are said to have resilience. Several factors have been identified as mediating between the risks children experience and their growth and development. These factors are "protective" in the sense that they shield the child from the consequences of potential hazards. Following are some protective factors that help diminish the potential risks to infants and toddlers.

Maternal Education

International research indicates that the education of the mother directly affects the outcome for infants and toddlers. This effect has been found in very poor populations in low-income countries. Longitudinal research of families in the poorest parts of Ecuador found that maternal education was a strong predictor of children's cognitive development at 36 months (Schady, 2011). Longitudinal research of a birth cohort from one Brazilian city measured the social, motor, communication, and cognitive development of infants and toddlers at 3, 12, and 24 months of age and found the level of maternal schooling to be associated with developmental outcomes at all three ages (Barros, Matijasevich, Santos, & Halpern, 2010). Another research team investigated the risk and protective factors for child health in 42 developing countries and found that maternal education has a substantial influence on child health (Boyle et al., 2006). Given these findings, it is not surprising that all of the researchers cited in this paragraph recommend education of girls and women as a protective factor for children.

Similar results have been found for another group of high-risk infants and toddlers—those born at very low birth weight (VLBW). One research team followed a group of VLBW infants in Taiwan during the first 2 years of life and found that maternal education and 6-month neurological status were the most significant predictors of the developmental trajectory from birth to age 2 (Wang, Wang, & Huang, 2008).

Social Support

Social support is often found in informal networks, such as friends and extended family members, or in formal support systems, such as the church, community agencies, day care centers, social workers, and other professionals. The availability of social support seems to buffer many risk factors, such as stress experienced by parents (Werner & Smith, 2001). For example, Mrs. Hicks could truly benefit from having the opportunity to take a break from the stresses of caring for Holly. Both formal and informal social support can fill this gap for her. One research team found that a combination of formal and informal social support, including both instrumental and emotional support, enhanced the ability of homeless mothers to provide consistent parenting (Marra et al., 2009).

Extended family members often serve as alternative caregivers when parents cannot provide care because of physical or mental illness or job demands. Reliance on an extended family is particularly important in some cultural and socioeconomic groups. In cultures where families live in multigenerational households, shared caregiving has been found to serve as a protective factor in situations where risk factors are involved (Feldman & Masalha, 2007). Sarah's dad, Chris Johnson, probably would not have been able to care for her without the support of his family. And it is through the support of his family that he has been able to continue his education.

Easy Temperament

There is evidence that infants with a positive, or easy, temperament are less likely to be affected by risk factors. In a study of resilience in children exposed to domestic violence, one research team (Martinez-Torteya, Bogat, von Eye, & Levendosky, 2009) found that easy temperament was a significant predictor of resilience in 2-, 3-, and 4-year-old children. Another research team (Derauf et al., 2011) found that easy infant temperament was associated with better behavioral outcomes in 3-year-old toddlers who had been exposed prenatally to methamphetamine. The association between easy temperament and "protection" is both direct and indirect. Infants with a positive temperament may simply perceive their world more positively. Infants with a positive temperament may also induce more constructive and affirming responses from those in their environment. Researchers have found that mothers of infants with easy temperament are less likely than mothers of infants with difficult temperament to become depressed (Montirosso et al., 2012; Solmeyer & Feinberg, 2011).

National and State Policy

Many social workers and others advocate for better national and state policies that will enhance good health among infants and toddlers, build and support strong families, promote positive early learning experiences, and create systems that advance the development and well-being of infants and toddlers (Zero to Three, 2013). This includes legislation and financial support to ensure things such as adequate health coverage for infants and toddlers, improved polices and programs that prevent child abuse, and development of programs and policies that promote parental and infant mental health. Also, continued support of national programs like the Women, Infants, & Children (WIC) program and the Child and Adult Care Food Program (CACFP) are considered crucial to promoting healthy physical development in infants and toddlers. Other advocates promote improving existing social and educational

programs. Knitzer (2007), for example, identifies what she wittingly refers to as legislation to improve the odds for young children. She suggests investing more federal and state financial resources to extend programs such as Early Head Start to incorporate home visiting, center-based instruction, and family support for all low-income babies and toddlers through (instead of up to) age 3. There is strong evidence that the tax and social welfare policies of other economically advanced countries are doing a better job of alleviating child poverty than the policies in the United States (UNICEF, 2013b). This has long-term consequences for the health of a society.

> ### Critical Thinking Questions 3.5
>
> Why do you think that researchers consistently find a negative association between family poverty and children's cognitive development? What biological, psychological, and social factors might be involved in that association? There is growing evidence that child maltreatment has a negative impact on brain development. What role can social workers play in informing the public about the impact of the environment on brain development?

Implications for Social Work Practice

In summary, knowledge about infants and toddlers has several implications for social work practice:

- Become well acquainted with theories and empirical research about growth and development among infants and toddlers.
- Assess infants and toddlers in the context of their environment, culture included.
- Promote continued use of formal and informal social support networks for parents with infants and toddlers.
- Continue to promote the elimination of poverty and the advancement of social justice.
- Advocate for compulsory health insurance and quality health care.
- Advocate for more affordable, quality child care.
- Collaborate with news media and other organizations to educate the public about the impact of poverty and inequality on early child development.
- Learn intervention methods to prevent and reduce substance abuse.
- Help parents understand the potential effects of inadequate caregiving on their infants, including the effects on brain development.

- Help parents and others understand the association between child development and consequential outcomes during adulthood.
- Provide support and appropriate intervention to parents to facilitate effective caregiving for infants and toddlers.

Key Terms

attachment
blooming
brain plasticity
cognition
concrete operations stage
developmental delay
developmental disability
developmental niche
formal operations stage
infant

infant mortality
motor skills
neurons
object permanence
preoperational stage
pruning
reflex
sensorimotor stage
sensory system
separation anxiety

stranger anxiety
symbolic functioning
synapses
synaptogenesis
temperament
toddler
transitional object
working model

Active Learning

1. Spend some time at a mall or other public place where parents and infants frequent. List behaviors you observe that indicate attachment between the infant and caretaker. Note any evidence you observe that may indicate a lack of attachment.

2. Ask to tour a day care facility. Describe the things you observe that may have a positive influence on cognitive development for the infants and toddlers who spend time there. List those things you think are missing from that setting that are needed to create a more stimulating environment.

3. Social support is considered to be a protective factor for individuals throughout the life course. List the forms of social support available to Marilyn Hicks, Chris Johnson, and Irma Velasquez. How do they help them with their parenting? In what ways could they be more helpful? How do they add to the level of stress?

Web Resources

The Clearinghouse on International Developments on Child, Youth and Family Policies: www.childpolicyintl.org

Site maintained at Columbia University contains international comparisons of child and family policies.

The Jean Piaget Society: www.piaget.org

Site presented by the Jean Piaget Society, an international interdisciplinary society of scholars, teachers, and researchers, contains information on the society, a student page, a brief biography of Piaget, and Internet links.

National Center for Children in Poverty (NCCP): www.nccp.org

Site presented by the NCCP of the Mailman School of Public Health of Columbia University contains media resources and child poverty facts as well as information about child care and early education, family support, and public welfare.

Zero to Three: www.zerotothree.org

Site presented by Zero to Three: National Center for Infants, Toddlers, and Families, a national nonprofit charitable organization with the aim to strengthen and support families, contains information about infant and toddler behavior and development, child maltreatment, child care and education, and public policy.

Student Study Site

$SAGE edge™

Sharpen your skills with SAGE edge at **edge.sagepub.com/hutchisonclc5e**

SAGE edge for students provides a personalized approach to help you accomplish your coursework goals in an easy-to-use learning environment.

CHAPTER 4

Early Childhood

Debra J. Woody and David Woody III

Chapter Outline

Opening Questions

- Why do social workers need to know about the ability of young children (ages 3 to 6) to express emotions and feelings?

- What is the process of gender and ethnic recognition and development among young children?

- What do social workers need to know about play among young children?

Key Ideas

As you read this chapter, take note of these central ideas:

1. Typical development is in many ways defined by the environment and culture in which the child is raised. In addition, although growth and development in young children have some predictability and logic, the timing and expression of many developmental skills vary from child to child.

2. According to Piaget, preschoolers are in the preoperational stage of cognitive development and become capable of cognitive recall and symbolic functioning.

3. Erikson describes the task of children ages 3 to 6 as the development of initiative versus guilt.

4. As young children struggle to discover stability and regularity in the environment, they are often rigid in their use of rules and stereotypes.

5. Regardless of country of residence or culture, all children ages 3 to 6 engage in spontaneous play.

6. Three types of parenting styles have been described: authoritarian, authoritative, and permissive. Parenting styles are prescribed to some extent by the community and culture in which the parent resides, and researchers are beginning to examine the appropriateness of using this parenting style typology across cultural groups.

7. Poverty, homelessness, ineffective discipline, divorce, and exposure to violence all pose special challenges for early childhood development.

CASE STUDY 4.1

Terri's Terrible Temper

Terri's mother and father, Mr. and Mrs. Smith, really seem at a loss about what to do. They adopted Terri, age 3, when she was an infant. They describe to their social worker how happy they were to finally have a child. They had tried for many years, spent a lot of money on fertility procedures, and had almost given up on the adoption process when Terri seemed to be "sent from heaven." Their lives were going well until a year ago, when Terri turned 2. Mrs. Smith describes an overnight change in Terri's behavior. Terri has become a total terror at home and at preschool. In fact, the preschool has threatened to dismiss Terri if her behavior does not improve soon. Terri hits and takes toys from other children, she refuses to cooperate with the teacher, and she does "what she wants to do."

Mr. and Mrs. Smith admit that Terri runs their household. They spend most evenings after work coaxing Terri into eating her dinner, taking a bath, and going to bed. Any attempt at a routine is nonexistent. When the Smiths try to discipline Terri, she screams, hits them, and throws things. They have not been able to use time-outs to discipline her because Terri refuses to stay in the bathroom, the designated time-out place. She runs out of the bathroom and hides. When they attempt to hold her in the bathroom, she screams until Mr. Smith gets too tired to continue to hold her or until she falls asleep. Mr. and Mrs. Smith admit that they frequently let Terri have her way because it is easier than saying no or trying to discipline her.

The "straw that broke the camel's back" came during a family vacation. Mrs. Smith's sister and family joined the Smiths at the beach. Mr. Smith describes the vacation as a total disaster. Terri refused to cooperate the entire vacation. They were unable to eat at restaurants because of her tantrums, and they were unable to participate in family activities because Terri would not let them get her ready to go. They tried allowing her to choose the activities for the day, which worked until other family members tired of doing only the things that Terri wanted to do. Terri would scream and throw objects if the family refused to eat when and where she wanted or go to the park or the beach when she wanted. Mrs. Smith's sister became so frustrated with the situation that she vowed never to vacation with them again. In fact, it was the sister who insisted that they get professional help for Terri.

CASE STUDY 4.2

Jack's Name Change

Until last month, Jack Lewis, age 4, lived with his mother, Joyce Lewis, and father, Charles Jackson Lewis, in what Joyce describes as a happy home. She was shocked when she discovered that her husband was having an affair with a woman at work. She immediately asked him to leave and has filed for divorce. Charles moved in with his girlfriend and has not contacted Joyce or Jack at this point. Joyce just can't believe that this is happening to her. Her mother had the same experience with Joyce's father but had kept the marriage going for the sake of Joyce and her siblings. Joyce, conversely, is determined to live a different life from the life her mother chose. She saw how depressed her mother was until her death at age 54. Joyce states that her mother died of a broken heart.

Although Joyce is determined to live without Charles, she is concerned about how she and Jack will live on her income alone. They had a comfortable life before the separation, but it took both incomes. Although she plans to seek child support, she knows she will need to move, because she cannot afford the mortgage on her own. Joyce would prefer for Jack not to have contact with his father. In fact, she is seriously considering changing Jack's name because he was named after his father. Joyce has tried to explain the situation to Jack as best she can. However, in the social worker's presence, she told Jack that she hopes he does not grow up to be like his father. She also told Jack that his father is the devil and is now living with a witch.

Joyce also shares that Jack has had difficulty sleeping and continues to ask when his father is coming home. Joyce simply responds to Jack by telling him that they probably will never see Charles again.

CASE STUDY 4.3

A New Role for Ron and Rosiland's Grandmother

Ron, age 3, and Rosiland, age 5, have lived with Ms. Johnson, their grandmother, for the last year. Their mother, Shirley, was sent to prison a year ago after conviction of drug trafficking. Shirley's boyfriend is a known drug dealer and had asked Shirley to make a "delivery" for him. Shirley was arrested as she stepped off the bus in another state where she had taken the drugs for delivery. Ron and Rosiland were with her when she was arrested, because she had taken them with her. Her boyfriend thought that a woman traveling with two young children would never be suspected of delivering drugs.

Ron and Rosiland were put into foster care by Child Protective Services until Ms. Johnson arrived to pick them up. It had taken her 2 weeks to save enough money to get to the children and fly them all home. Ms. Johnson shares with the social worker how angry she was that Shirley's boyfriend refused to help her get the children home. Shirley calls the children when she can, but because her crime was a federal offense, she has been sent to a prison far away from home. The children ask about her often and miss her terribly. Ms. Johnson has told the children that their mom is away but has not told them that she will be away for some time. She is also unsure how much they understand about what happened, even though they were present when their mom was arrested.

Ms. Johnson shares that she has no choice but to care for the children, although this is definitely not the life she had planned. She was looking forward to living alone; her husband died several years ago. With her small savings, she was planning to visit her sister in another state for an extended visit. But that money is gone now, because these funds were used to help get the children home. She seems to love both of the children but confides that the children "drive her crazy." She is not accustomed to all the noise, and they seem to need so much attention from her. Getting into the habit of having a scheduled day is also difficult for Ms. Johnson. Both children attend preschool, an arrangement Shirley made before her incarceration. Ms. Johnson describes the fact that the children attend preschool as a blessing, because it gives her some relief. Her social worker suspects that preschool is a blessing for the children as well.

TYPICAL DEVELOPMENT IN EARLY CHILDHOOD

As children like Terri Smith, Jack Lewis, and Ron and Rosiland Johnson emerge from toddlerhood, they turn their attention more and more to the external environment. Just as when in infancy and toddlerhood they worked at developing some regularity in their body rhythms, attachment relationships, and emotional states, they now work to discover some stability and regularity in the external world. That is not always an easy task, given their limitations in cognitive and language development. Some children emerge from toddlerhood with a sense of confidence in the availability of support and a beginning sense of confidence in themselves. Other children, unfortunately, leave toddlerhood more challenged than when they entered that stage (Sroufe, Egeland, Carlson, & Collins, 2005). Much happens in all interrelated dimensions of development from age 3 to 6, however, and most children emerge from early childhood with a much more sophisticated ability to understand the world and their relationships to it. They work out this understanding in an increasingly wider world, with major influences coming from family, school, peer groups, neighborhood, and the media (Mokrova, O'Brien, Calkins, Leerkes, & Marcovitch, 2012).

Some child development scholars still refer to the period from age 3 to 6 as the preschool age, but others have recently begun to refer to this

What historical trends are influencing our understanding of social age in early childhood?

period as early school age, reflecting the fact that a large number of children are enrolled in some form of group-based experience during this period. In 2011, 48% of 3- and 4-year-olds in the United States were enrolled in nursery school, at least part time, compared with 10% in 1965 (Davis & Bauman, 2013). We simply refer to this period from 3 to 6 years of age as early childhood. Remember as you read that the various types of development discussed in this chapter under separate headings actually are interdependent, and sometimes the distinctions between the dimensions blur.

International literature criticizes the notion of a universal early childhood. It suggests, instead, multiple and diverse early childhoods, based on class, race, gender, geography, and time (see Dahlberg, Moss, & Pence, 2007; Waller, 2009). Cultural psychologists report that 96% of participants in research studies about human behavior come from Western industrialized countries, countries whose populations make up only 12% of the world (Henrich, Heine, & Norenzayan, 2010). There are growing criticisms that all children of the world are evaluated against Western developmental psychology science, which is a mix of statistical averages and historically and culturally specific value judgments (Dahlberg et al., 2007; Nybell, Shook, & Finn, 2009). In this chapter, we have tried to broaden the view of early childhood, where the literature allows, but please keep this criticism in mind as you read. Also keep in mind the great inequity in the environments children are born into. Many children of the world are still reared in households without access to even basic necessities such as safe drinking water and sanitation (UNICEF, 2012b).

Physical Development in Early Childhood

As Chapter 3 explained, infants and toddlers grow rapidly. From ages 3 to 6, physical growth slows. On average, height during this stage increases about 2 to 3 inches per year, and the young child adds about

5 pounds of weight per year. As a result, young children look leaner. However, globally, one quarter of children younger than 5 years of age are stunted in growth due to malnutrition, with the highest prevalence in Sub-Saharan Africa and South Asia, where about 38% of children younger than 5 have stunted growth. At the same time, increasing rates of children have been found to be overweight in most regions of the world. Globally, 7% of children younger than 5 years of age were overweight in 2012, a 43% increase since 1990 (UNICEF, 2013b). There are two forms of malnutrition: undernutrition caused by inadequate intake of nutrients and obesity caused by excessive intake of foods high in calories (Ritzer, 2013). As suggested in the previous chapter, the importance of adequate nutrition cannot be overemphasized; poor nutrition is involved in at least half of the child deaths in the world each year. It magnifies the effect of every disease.

Great variation exists in the height and weight of young children, and racial and ethnic differences in height and weight are still evident in the early childhood years. For example, in the United States, African American children in early childhood on average are taller than White and Hispanic children of the same age, and there is some evidence that Hispanic American children weigh more on average than other young children (Dennison, Edmunds, & Stratton, 2006). Children of low economic status are more likely than other children to be overweight during early childhood, but severe food insecurity may lead to growth inhibition (Wang & Zhang, 2006).

As noted in Chapter 3, the brain continues to be shaped by experience throughout early childhood and beyond. Brain growth continues at a rapid pace but is slower than in infancy. By age 5, the brain is 90% of its adult size (Christen & Narvaez, 2012). Synaptic pruning and myelination continue, and motor and cognitive abilities increase by leaps and bounds because of increased interconnections between brain cells, which allow for more complex cognitive and motor capability (Davies, 2011). These abilities are perhaps even more accelerated with the availability of technology and media appropriate for young children that further stimulate brain development (Courage & Setliff, 2009). There is little research to date to clarify the benefits of and drawbacks to use of information and communication technology with young children, but what little research there is suggests that brain development may be enhanced with the use of interactive technologies that help children develop curiosity, problem solving, and independent thinking skills but hampered by passive engagement with technology (Mercer, 2013). Because of the great plasticity of the brain, each new wave of technological advancement, like earlier development of written language, results in new brain-mediated capabilities that had previously been unexpressed (Kneas & Perry, 2011).

Through a process called **lateralization**, the two hemispheres of the brain begin to operate slightly differently, allowing for a wider range of activity. Simply stated, brain functioning becomes more specialized. The left hemisphere is activated during tasks that require analytical skills, including speaking and reading. Tasks that involve emotional expression and spatial skills, such as visual imagery, require response from the right hemisphere. With the development of the right hemisphere and the social-emotional components there, young children develop the ability to reflect on the feelings and thoughts of others (James & Bose, 2011). Brain lateralization was identified early in neuroscientific research, but current thinking is that we should avoid applying the right hemisphere/left hemisphere paradigm too rigidly. The hemispheres are in constant communication, and the tasks performed by each hemisphere are much more complex than once thought (Fogarty, 2009; Peng & Wang, 2011).

Because of other developments in the brain, children also obtain and refine some advanced motor skills during this time, such as running, jumping, and hopping, but less is known about motor development in early childhood compared with infancy and toddlerhood (Keenan & Evans, 2009). Early intervention specialists suggest the gross motor milestones presented in Exhibit 4.1. In addition to these **gross motor skills**—skills that require use of the large muscle groups—young

children develop **fine motor skills**, including the ability to scribble and draw and cut with scissors. Suggested fine motor milestones are also presented in Exhibit 4.1. As you review these suggested milestones, remember that there is much variability in motor development in early childhood. For example, one child may be advanced in gross motor skills and lag in fine motor skills, or the opposite. In addition, different motor skills are valued in different developmental niches, and the expression of motor skills will depend on the tools available to the child. With these cautions, parents and other adults who spend time with young children will find the milestones presented in Exhibit 4.1 to be helpful to keep in mind as they interact with young children.

Photo 4.1 During early childhood, young children make advancements in the development of fine motor skills, including the ability to draw.

© iStockphoto.com

Exhibit 4.1   Gross Motor and Fine Motor Skills in Early Childhood

	Gross Motor Skills	Fine Motor Skills
Most 3-year-olds can	Run forward Jump in place Stand on one foot with support Walk on tiptoe Avoid obstacles in path Catch an 8-inch ball Climb and walk up stairs with alternating feet Kick a ball forward Ride a tricycle Climb a ladder	Turn single pages Snip with scissors Hold crayons with thumb and finger Use one hand consistently Imitate circular, vertical, and horizontal strokes Paint with some wrist action Make dots, lines, and circular strokes Roll, pound, squeeze, and pull clay Build a tower of up to nine cubes String ½-inch beads Cut along a line Use a fork Manage large buttons Dress self with supervision
Most 4-year-olds can	Run around obstacles Walk on a line Balance on one foot for 5–10 seconds Hop on one foot Push, pull, and steer wheeled toys Use a slide independently Jump over a 6-inch-high object and land on both feet Throw a ball overhead Catch a bouncing ball	Copy crosses and squares Print some letters Use table utensils Cut on a line Build a tower of nine small blocks
Most 5-year-olds can	Walk backward toe to heel Jump forward 10 times without falling Walk up and down stairs independently with alternating feet Turn a somersault Walk on tiptoes Walk on a balance beam Jump rope	Lace shoes but not tie Grasp pencil like an adult Color within lines Cut and paste simple shapes

SOURCE: Based on Destefanis & Firchow, 2013; Early Intervention Support, 2013

Increases in fine motor skills allow young children to become more self-sufficient. However, allowing the extra time needed for young children to perform self-care tasks can be frustrating to adults. Ms. Johnson, for example, has lived alone for some time now and may need to readjust to allowing extra time for the children to "do it themselves." Spills and messes, which are a part of this developmental process, are also often difficult for adults to tolerate.

Cognitive and Language Development

A few years ago, the first author of this chapter was at a doctor's office when a mother walked into the waiting area with her son, about age 3. The waiting area was very quiet, and the young child's voice seemed loud in the silence. The mother immediately began to "shh" her son. He responded by saying, "I don't want to shh, I want to talk." Of course, everyone laughed, which made the child talk even louder. The mother moved immediately to some chairs in the corner and attempted to get her son to sit. He refused, stating that he wanted to stand on one foot. The mother at once attempted to engage him with the toys she had with her. They played with an electronic game in which the child selects pieces to add to a face to make a complete face. This game kept the child's attention for a while until he became bored. The mother told him to "make the game stop." The child responded by yelling at the game, demanding that it stop making the face. The mother, understanding that her son had taken a literal interpretation of her comments, rephrased her directions and showed her son how to push the stop button on the game.

Next, the two decided to read *The Lion King*. The child became very confused, because in the book, different from his memory of the movie, the main character, Simba, was already an adult at the beginning. The child, looking at the pictures, argued that the adult lion was not Simba but instead was Simba's father. The mother attempted to explain that this book begins with Simba as an adult. She stated that just as her son will grow, Simba grew from a cub to an adult lion. The son looked at his mother bewildered, responding with, "I am not a cub; I am a little boy." The mother then tried to make the connection that just like the son's daddy was once a boy, Simba grew up to be a lion. The boy responded by saying that men and lions are not the same. Needless to say, the mother seemed relieved when her name was called to see the doctor.

This scene encapsulates many of the themes of cognitive and moral development in early childhood. As memory improves, and the store of information expands, young children begin to think much more in terms of categories, as the little boy in the doctor's office was doing (Davies, 2011; Newman & Newman, 2012). He was now thinking in terms of cubs, boys, lions, and men. They also begin to recognize some surprising connections between things. No doubt, in a short time, the little boy will recognize a connection between boys and cubs, men and lions, boys and men, as well as cubs and lions. Young children are full of big questions such as where do babies come from, what happens to people when they die, where does the night come from, and so on. They can think about themselves and about other people. They engage in creative and imaginative thought and begin to develop humor, empathy, and altruism. They make great strides in language development and the ability to communicate. And they make gradual progress in the ability to judge right and wrong and to regulate behavior in relation to that reasoning.

Piaget's Stages of Cognitive Development

In early childhood, children fit into the second stage of cognitive development described by Piaget, the preoperational stage. This stage is in turn divided into two substages:

Substage 1: Preconceptual stage (ages 2 to 3). The most important aspect of the preoperational stage is the development of symbolic representation, which occurs in the preconceptual stage. Through play, children learn to use symbols and actively engage in what Piaget labeled deferred imitation.

Deferred imitation refers to the child's ability to view an image and then, significantly later, recall and imitate the image. For example, 3-year-old Ella, who watches the *Dora the Explorer* cartoon on TV, fills her backpack with a pretend map and other items she might need, such as a blanket and a flashlight, puts it on, creates a pretend monkey companion named Boots, and sets off on an adventure, using the kitchen as a barn, the space under the dining table as the woods, and keeping her eyes open all the while for the "mean" Swiper the Fox. Ella's cousin, Zachery, who is enthralled with the *Bob the Builder* cartoon, often pretends that he is Bob the Builder when he is playing with his toy trucks and tractors. Whenever Zachery encounters a problem, he will sing Bob's theme song, which is "Bob the Builder, can we fix it, yes we can!!"

Substage 2: Intuitive stage (ages 4 to 7). During the second part of the preoperational stage, children use language to represent objects. During the preconceptual stage, any object with long ears may be called "bunny." However, during the intuitive stage, children begin to understand that the term *bunny* represents the entire animal, not just a property of it. However, although young children are able to classify objects, their classifications are based on only one attribute at a time. For example, given a set of stuffed animals with various sizes and colors, the young child will group the animals either by color or by size. In contrast, an older child who has reached the intuitive stage may sort them by both size and color.

In early childhood, children also engage in what Piaget termed **transductive reasoning**, or a way of thinking about two or more experiences without using abstract logic. This can be explained best with an illustration. Imagine that 5-year-old Sam immediately smells chicken when he enters his grandmother's home. He comments that she must be having a party and asks who is coming over for dinner. When the grandmother replies that no one is coming over and that a party is not planned, Sam shakes his head in disbelief and states that he will just wait to see when the guests arrive. Sam recalls that the last time his grandmother cooked chicken was for a party. Because grandmother is cooking chicken again, Sam thinks another party is going to occur. This type of reasoning is also evident in the example of the mother and child in the doctor's office. Because the child saw Simba as a cub in the movie version of *The Lion King*, he reasons that the adult lion in the picture at the beginning of the book cannot possibly be Simba.

One last related preoperational concept described by Piaget is **egocentrism**. According to Piaget, in early childhood, children perceive reality only from their own experience and believe themselves to be at the center of existence. They are unable to recognize the possibility of other perspectives on a situation. For example, a 3-year-old girl who stands between her sister and the television to watch a program believes that her sister can see the television because she can. This aspect of cognitive reasoning could be problematic for most of the children described in the case examples. Jack may believe that it is his fault that his father left the family. Likewise, Ron and Rosiland may attribute their mother's absence to their behavior, especially given that they were present when she was arrested. More recent experimental research has found that the ability to see another's point of view begins to develop by age 2 and continues to develop throughout early childhood (Davies, 2011). Researchers are finding that young children have the capacity for nonegocentric thinking but do not consistently demonstrate that capacity (Engel, 2005).

Language Skills

Language development is included under cognitive development because it is the mechanism by which cognitive interpretations are communicated to others. For language to exist, children must be able to "organize" their experiences. At the end of toddlerhood, on average, young children have a vocabulary of about 1,000 words, and they are increasing that store by about 50 words each month (Davies, 2011). They can speak in two-word sentences, and they have learned the question form of language. They are asking "why" questions, persistently and often assertively, to learn about the world. Three-year-old speech is generally clear and easy to understand. At every point in development, however, children differ in the size of the vocabularies they command, the complexity of the language structure used, and the skill with which they communicate (Hoff, 2006).

How does language development in early childhood promote human agency in making choices?

By the fourth year of life, language development is remarkably sophisticated. The vocabulary is becoming more and more adequate for communicating ideas, and 4-year-olds are usually speaking in sentences of 8 to 10 words. They have mastered language well enough to tell a story mostly in words, rather than relying heavily on gestures, as toddlers must do. But perhaps the most remarkable aspect of language development in early childhood is the understanding of grammar rules. By age 4, young children in all cultures understand the basic grammar rules of their language (Gardiner & Kosmitzki, 2011). They accomplish this mostly by a figuring-out process. As they figure out new grammar rules, as with other aspects of their learning, they are overly regular in using those rules, because they have not yet learned the exceptions. So we often hear young children make statements such as "she goed to the store," or perhaps "she wented to the store."

There are two different approaches to studying language development. One approach focuses on the mental processes by which language is acquired and conceptualizes language ability as primarily a function of genetics. Although somewhat influenced by the environment, children are thought to develop language skills as long as the appropriate genetic material is in place (Chomsky, 1968; Hoff, 2005). The other approach focuses on the way that the social contexts in which children live shape language acquisition (Bronfenbrenner & Morris, 1998). Erika Hoff (2006) proposes a model that synthesizes these two approaches, a model that considers both "how the mind acquires language" and "how the social context shapes language development" (p. 56). She argues that children need both a language model and opportunities for communicative interaction to support language development. Language is not learned simply by overhearing it, as many of us have learned from our efforts to learn a new language in adolescence or adulthood. Language development is a social process; children learn language by listening to others speak and by asking questions. Past toddlerhood, children increasingly take charge of their own language acquisition by asking questions and initiating dialogues (Hoff, 2006). Parents can assist children by asking questions, eliciting details, and encouraging children to reflect on their experiences. As children grow older, they are often corrected by caregivers and preschool teachers in the misuse of words or phrases (Chapin & Altenhofen, 2010).

How do social class, culture, and gender affect the "developmental niche" during early childhood?

It appears that the developmental niche has an impact on the development of language skills. Children are talked to a great deal in some cultures and very little in other cultures (Hoff, 2006). North American parents tend to talk a lot about objects when speaking to their infants and toddlers, while Asian parents tend to use more verbs and fewer nouns. Considerable research indicates that infants and toddlers who are talked to a great deal acquire language skills earlier than infants and toddlers who are talked to less (Hoff, 2006). Across cultures, there is consistent evidence that parents with higher socioeconomic status, on average, speak more to their children, elicit more conversations with their children, use larger vocabularies in conversations with their children, and engage in fewer verbal behavioral prohibitions than parents with lower socioeconomic status (Hoff, 2006; Zhang, Jin, Shen, Zhang, & Hoff, 2008). This means that many low-income children enter elementary school with smaller vocabularies than their more privileged peers unless they are provided with support for language development. Some research indicates that both low-income and high-income mothers use more complex speech when reading books to their children, and book reading can attenuate the language disadvantage of low-income children (Hoff, 2003).

From observation of their environment—physical and social surroundings, child-rearing customs, and caregiver personality—children learn a set of regulations, or rules for communication, that shape their developing language skills. Children have an innate capacity for language, but the structuring of the environment through culture is what allows language development to occur. Two special types of language learners deserve greater attention: multilingual language learners and deaf and hard-of-hearing language learners.

Hoff (2006) reports that half of the children in the world live in multilingual situations. And yet research on language acquisition among multilingual children is very young. There is some evidence that children learning two languages tend to have smaller vocabularies in each language than monolingual children, but vocabulary size depends on the amount of exposure to each language and the opportunities to speak each language (Hoff, 2006). Recent research indicates, however, that learning two languages simultaneously in the first 3 years of life lays down the brain structures for later language learning (Klein, Mok, Chen, & Watkins, 2013).

Language development is a particularly important area of development for deaf and hard-of-hearing (DHH) children. Unless they have deaf parents, who will teach them sign language, these children require intervention to acquire language. Three common methods provide DHH children with access to language: sign language, simultaneous communication, and spoken language. Various sign languages, using manual signs, have developed in deaf communities around the world. Simultaneous communication uses signs from traditional sign languages plus newly created signs to correspond to spoken language. These new sign systems can theoretically be used simultaneously with speech, but in reality, this is very challenging because signs are longer in duration than words. Some children are exposed to spoken language only, and technological innovations, such as hearing aids and cochlear implants, are making that a more realistic choice for children with less severe hearing loss. The choice of method is influenced by attitudes about how important it is for children to fit into a mainstream hearing world. What is of paramount importance is that hearing loss be detected at birth or shortly after, which is now possible, and that access to language begin in the early days and weeks. There is strong evidence that not having access to language in the early months has long-term negative consequences for language development. The method of language exposure should fit the specific nature of the hearing loss (Lederberg, Schick, & Spencer, 2013).

Moral Development

During early childhood, children move from a moral sense based on outside approval to a more internalized moral sense, with a rudimentary moral code. They engage in a process of taking society's values and standards as their own. They begin to integrate these values and standards into both their worldview and their self-concept. There are three components of moral development during early childhood (Newman & Newman, 2012):

1. *Knowledge* of the moral code of the community and how to use that knowledge to make moral judgments

2. *Emotions* that produce both the capacity to care about others and the capacity to feel guilt and remorse

3. *Actions* to inhibit negative impulses as well as to behave in a **prosocial** or helpful and empathic manner

Understanding Moral Development

Moral development has been explored from several theoretical perspectives found to have merit. Three of these approaches to moral development are explored here.

1. *Psychodynamic approach.* Sigmund Freud's psychoanalytic theory proposed three distinct structures of the personality: id, ego, and superego.

According to Freud, the superego is the personality structure that guides moral development. There are two aspects to the superego: the *conscience*, which is the basis of a moral code, and the *ego ideal*, which is a set of ideals expected in a moral person. Freud (1927) thought the superego is formed from the ages of 4 to 7, but more recent psychodynamic formulations suggest that infancy is the critical time for the beginning of moral development (Kohut, 1971). Freud thought children would have more highly developed superegos when their parents used strict methods to inhibit the children's impulses. Contemporary research indicates the opposite, however, finding that moral behavior is associated with parental warmth, democratic decision making, and modeling of temptation resistance (Kochanska, Forman, Aksan, & Dunbar, 2005). New psychodynamic models emphasize a close, affectionate bond with the caregiver as the cornerstone of moral development. This is supported by recent neuroscience research that finds these caregiving practices to foster the type of brain development that underlies moral behaviour in adults: breastfeeding, prompt response to needs, touch, play, and support (see Christen & Narvaez, 2012). Freud also believed that males would develop stronger superegos than females, but research has not supported this idea.

2. *Social learning approach.* From the perspective of social learning theory, moral behavior is shaped by environmental reinforcements and punishments. Children are likely to repeat behaviors that are rewarded, and they are also likely to feel tension when they think about doing something that they have been punished for in the past. From this perspective, parental consistency in response to their children's behavior is important. Social learning theory also suggests that children learn moral conduct by observing models. Albert Bandura (1977) found that children are likely to engage in behaviors for which they see a model rewarded and to avoid behaviors that they see punished. This can be problematic for children who watch a lot of television, because they may come to view violence as an acceptable way to solve interactional conflict if they see violence go unpunished.

3. *Cognitive developmental approach.* Piaget's theory of cognitive development has been the basis for stage models of moral reasoning, which assume that children's moral judgments change as their cognitive development allows them to examine the logical and abstract aspects of moral dilemmas. Moral development is assisted by opportunities to encounter new situations and different perspectives. The most frequently researched stage model is that presented by Lawrence Kohlberg (1969, 1976) and summarized in Exhibit 4.2. Kohlberg described three levels of moral reasoning, with two stages in each level. It was expected that in early childhood, children will operate at the **preconventional level of moral reasoning**, with their reasoning about moral issues based, first, on what gets them rewarded or punished. This type of moral reasoning is thought to be common among toddlers. In the second stage, moral reasoning is based on what benefits either the child or someone the child cares about. This is consistent with the child's growing capacity for attachments. There is some empirical evidence that children ages 3 to 6 do, indeed, begin to use the type of moral reasoning described in Stage 2 (Walker, 1989). The idea of a hierarchical sequence of stages of moral development has been challenged as being based on a Western cultural orientation, but longitudinal studies in a variety of countries have produced support for the idea of evolution of moral reasoning (Gielen & Markoulis, 2001).

> Why is the development of empathy important for future capacity for relationships?

All of these approaches to moral development in early childhood have been criticized for leaving out two key ingredients for moral development: **empathy**, or the ability to understand another person's emotional condition, and **perspective taking**, or the ability to see a situation from another person's point of view (Eisenberg, 2000). Neuroscientific research is currently suggesting that a special type of brain cell, called a *mirror neuron*, is key to the

Exhibit 4.2 Kohlberg's Stages of Moral Development

Level I	**Preconventional**
	Stage 1: Moral reasoning is based on whether behavior is rewarded or punished.
	Stage 2: Moral reasoning is based on what will benefit the self or loved others.
Level II	**Conventional**
	Stage 3: Moral reasoning is based on the approval of significant others.
	Stage 4: Moral reasoning is based on upholding societal standards.
Level III	**Postconventional**
	Stage 5: Moral reasoning is based on social contracts and cooperation.
	Stage 6: Moral reasoning is based on universal ethical principles.

SOURCE: Based on Kohlberg, 1969, 1976

development of empathy. Have you ever noticed how you instinctively smile when you see someone else smiling? Mirror neurons allow us to sense the move another person is about to make and the emotions he or she is experiencing. Emotion is contagious, because mirror neurons allow us to feel what the other person feels through a brain-to-brain connection. Daniel Goleman (2006) calls this primal empathy; it is based on feelings, not thoughts. He has coined the phrase *social intelligence* to refer to this ability to be attuned to another person. It appears that humans have multiple systems of mirror neurons, and scientists are in the early stages of learning about them. Studies have found that people with autism have a dysfunctional mirror neuron system (Goleman, 2006).

There is growing agreement that empathy begins in infancy and grows throughout early childhood (Meltzoff, 2002). By age 3 or 4, children across cultures have been found to be able to recognize the type of emotional reaction that other children might have to different situations. Perspective taking, which is a thinking rather than feeling activity, grows in early childhood and is another important ingredient in moral development. One research team studied children at ages 3½ years and

5½ years and found that a sophisticated understanding of both emotional and mental states was associated with increased consideration of the emotional and mental states of others (Lane, Wellman, Olson, LaBounty, & Kerr, 2010). Longitudinal research has found that children who show empathy and perspective taking at 4 and 5 years of age are more likely to exhibit prosocial behavior and sympathy during adolescence and early adulthood (Eisenberg et al., 1999).

In addition, there has been considerable examination of the degree to which Kohlberg's model is responsive to gender and cultural experience, in view of the study population on which his theory is based—Harvard male undergraduates (Donleavy, 2008; Sherblom, 2008). Carol Gilligan (1982) notes that gender plays a significant role in how one experiences and acts on themes of ethical thinking, justice, and notions of individuality and connectedness. She suggests strong gender bias in Kohlberg's theory, and her research indicated that women's moral thought is guided by caring and maintaining the welfare of others while men use more abstract principles of justice. As you can see from Exhibit 4.2, caring for others and maintaining harmony in relationships would put women in

Stage 3, at the highest. A similar criticism has been lodged about the poor fit of Kohlberg's theory with many non-European cultures that are more collectivist oriented than European and North American societies. Indeed, studies of Buddhist monks find that older monks barely reach Kohlberg's Stage 4, indicating that their moral reasoning is not as well developed as Western male adolescents, according to Kohlberg's model (Huebner & Garrod, 1993). The researchers suggest that the moral ideal in Western cultures is an autonomous individual with strong convictions who sticks up for those convictions. In contrast, the Buddhist moral ideal is guided by compassion and detachment from one's own individuality. How such themes are transmitted to young children can be indelible guideposts for managing and participating in interpersonal relationships.

One aspect of moral reasoning is *distributive justice*, or the belief about what constitutes a fair distribution of goods and resources in a society. Cross-cultural studies suggest that cultures hold different views on what constitutes a "fair" distribution of resources. Some societies see fairness in terms of need while other societies see fairness in terms of merit. Reasoning about distributive justice starts in early childhood but is not well articulated until middle childhood (Gardiner & Kosmitzki, 2011).

Helping Young Children Develop Morally

Growing evidence indicates that some methods work better than others for helping children develop moral reasoning and conduct. Particularly helpful activities are those that help children control their own behavior, help them understand how their behavior affects others, show them models of positive behavior, and get them to discuss moral issues (Arsenio & Gold, 2006). It is important, however, to consider a child's temperament when undertaking disciplinary actions. Some children are more sensitive to messages of disapproval than others; sensitive children require a small dose of criticism, and

less sensitive children usually require more focused and directive discipline (Kochanska, 1997). Brian Edmiston (2010) suggests that one important way for adults to assist young children to develop morally is to engage in dramatic play that helps children develop ethical identities.

Although religious beliefs play a central role in most societies in clarifying moral behavior, little research has been done to explore the role of religion in moral development in young children. Research (Roof, 1999) has indicated that adults often become affiliated with a religious organization when their children are in early childhood, even if the parents become "religious dropouts" after the children are out of the home. Religious rituals link young children to specific actions and images of the world as well as to a community that can support and facilitate their moral development. The major world religions also teach parents about how to be parents. Young children, with their comfortable embrace of magic, easily absorb religious stories on topics that may be difficult for adults to explain. Religion that emphasizes love, concern, and social justice can enrich the young child's moral development. Conversely, religion that is harsh and judgmental may produce guilt and a sense of worthlessness, which do not facilitate higher levels of moral reasoning.

Critical Thinking Questions 4.1

What have you observed about the differences in gross and fine motor development among young children, as outlined in Exhibit 4.1? How do you think culture and social class affect gross and fine motor development during this period? What types of social policies might help to narrow the social class disparities in language development? What do you see as the benefits and drawbacks to being multilingual during early childhood? What special challenges might caregivers face in their attempts to assist Terri Smith, Jack Lewis, and Ron and Rosiland Johnson with moral development?

Personality and Emotional Development

The key concern for Jack Lewis and for Ms. Johnson's grandchildren—Ron and Rosiland—is their emotional development. Specifically, will they grow into happy, loving, well-adjusted people despite the disruptions in their lives? Writing about the early childhood years, Sroufe and colleagues (2005) suggest this as the period of life when a coherent personality emerges: "It is no exaggeration to say that the person emerges at this time" (p. 121). Based on a longitudinal study of 180 children born into poverty, they conclude that behavior and adaptation during early childhood predict later behavior and adaptation, something they did not find to be the case with the predictive power of behavior and adaptation in infancy and toddlerhood. They suggest that the important themes of development during this period are self-direction, agency, self-management, and self-regulation. Young children do face important developmental tasks in the emotional arena. This section addresses these tasks, drawing on Erikson's theory of psychosocial development.

Erikson's Theory of Psychosocial Development

Erikson labeled the stage of emotional development that takes place during the early childhood years as *initiative versus guilt* (ages 3 to 6). (Refer back to Exhibit 3.7 for the complete list of Erikson's stages.) Children who pass successfully through this stage learn to get satisfaction from completing tasks. They develop imagination and fantasies and learn to handle guilt about their fantasies.

At the beginning of this stage, children's focus is on family relationships. They learn what roles are appropriate for various family members, and they learn to accept parental limits. In addition, they develop gender identity through identification with the parent of the same sex. Age and sex boundaries must be appropriately defined at this stage, and parents must be secure enough to set limits and resist the child's possessiveness.

By the end of this stage, the child's focus turns to friendships outside the family. Children engage in cooperative play and enjoy both sharing and competing with peers. Children must also have the opportunity to establish peer relationships outside the family. This is one of the functions the preschool program serves for Ms. Johnson's grandchildren.

Children who become stuck in this stage are plagued with guilt about their goals and fantasies. They become confused about their gender identity and about family roles. These children are overly anxious and self-centered.

Emotions

Growing cognitive and language skills give young children the ability to understand and express their feelings and emotions. Children ages 3 to 5 can recognize and label simple emotions, and they learn about themselves when they talk about their anxieties and fears (Hansen & Zambo, 2007). Children in early childhood can also identify feelings expressed by others—as the earlier discussion of empathy illustrated—and use creative ways to comfort others when they are upset. A friend describes the response of her 5-year-old son Marcus when he saw her crying about the sudden death of her brother in a car accident. Marcus hugged his mom and told her not to cry, because, although she was sad about Uncle Johnny, she still had Marcus. Marcus promised his mother to never drive a car so she would not have to worry about the same thing happening to him. This attempt to reduce his mother's sadness is a typical response from a child of this age (Findlay, Girardi, & Coplan, 2006).

The ability to understand emotion continues to develop as young children have more opportunity to practice these skills. Children reared in homes in which emotions and feelings are openly discussed are better able to understand and express feelings (Bradley, 2000). Early childhood educators Cory Cooper Hansen and Debby Zambo (2007) recommend the use of children's literature to help children understand and manage emotions. Here are some of their recommendations for how to do that (p. 277):

- Respect all responses to talks about emotions.
- Ask children to describe the emotions of story characters.
- Talk about your own emotions about story characters.
- Encourage children to draw, write, or paint about the emotions of story characters as well as their own emotional reactions.
- Sing or chant about emotions and how to handle them.
- Brainstorm ways that story characters can handle their emotions.
- Practice reading emotions from pictures in books.
- Use stuffed animals to "listen" to children's stories.

What are our societal expectations for regulation of emotions during early childhood?

Most child development scholars agree that all emotions, including those that have been labeled "negative" (anger, sadness, guilt, disgust), are adaptive, but more needs to be learned about how the "negative" emotions can become problematic for children (Cole, Luby, & Sullivan, 2008). We know that by the first grade, most children can regulate their emotions well enough to learn, obey classroom rules, and develop friendships (Calkins & Hill, 2007). But we also know that emotional receptivity makes young children vulnerable to environmental stress, and early exposure to adverse situations can have a negative effect on the brain, cardiovascular, and endocrine processes that support emotional development (Gunnar & Quevedo, 2007). It is important to recognize when emotional development is getting off course, and researchers are at work to develop understanding of that issue. For example, we know that most young children have tantrums. For most children, anger and distress are expressed in quick peaks in anger intensity that decline into whining and comfort-seeking behavior. Researchers are finding, however, that the tantrums of depressed young children are more violent, destructive, verbally aggressive, and self-injurious; they also have a longer recovery time (Belden, Thompson, & Luby, 2008). It is important to avoid both overreacting and underreacting to children's difficulties in regulating their emotions (Hane, Cheah, Rubin, & Fox, 2008).

Aggression

One behavior that increases during the early childhood years is aggression. Two types of aggression are observed in young children: **instrumental aggression**, which occurs while fighting over toys and space, and **hostile aggression**, which is an attack meant to hurt another individual. Recently, researchers have studied another typology of aggression: physical aggression and relational aggression. **Physical aggression**, as the name suggests, involves using physical force against another person. **Relational aggression** involves behaviors that damage relationships without physical force, behaviors such as threatening to leave a relationship unless a friend complies with demands or using social exclusion or the silent treatment to get one's way. Researchers are finding that boys make greater use of physical aggression than girls, and girls make greater use of relational aggression (Ostrov, Crick, & Stauffacher, 2006).

Although some children continue high levels of aggression into middle childhood, usually physical aggression peaks early in the early childhood years (Alink, Mesmon, & van Zeijl, 2006). By the end of the early childhood years, children learn better negotiation skills and become better at asking for what they want and using words to express feelings. Terri Smith, in the first case study in this chapter, obviously has not developed these moderating skills.

Attachment

In early childhood, children still depend on their attachment relationships for feelings of security. In particularly stressful times, the attachment behavior of the young child may look very much like the clinging behavior of the 2-year-old. For the most part, however, securely attached children will handle their anxieties by verbalizing their needs. For example, at bedtime, the 4-year-old child may say, "I would like you to read one more story before you go." This increased ability to verbalize wants is a source of security. In addition, many young children continue to use transitional objects, such as blankets or a favorite teddy bear, to soothe themselves when they are anxious (Davies, 2011).

In their longitudinal study of 180 children born into poor families, Sroufe et al. (2005) examined, among other things, how attachment style in infancy and toddlerhood affected the developmental trajectory into early childhood. Here are some of the findings:

- Anxiously attached infants and toddlers were more dependent on their mothers and performed more poorly on teaching tasks at age 3½ than either securely or avoidant attached toddlers.
- Securely attached infants and toddlers rated higher on curiosity, agency, activity, self-esteem, and positive emotions at age 4½ than either anxiously or avoidant attached toddlers.
- Securely attached infants and toddlers had better emotion regulation in early childhood than anxiously attached toddlers.

Sroufe and colleagues also found that temperament was not a powerful predictor of early childhood behavior.

Social Development

In early childhood, children become more socially adept than they were as toddlers, but they are still learning how to be social and how to understand the perspectives of other people. The many young children who enter group care face increasing demands for social competence.

Peer Relations

In early childhood, children form friendships with other children of the same age and sex; boys gravitate toward male playmates and girls choose girls. Across cultures, young children's friendship groups are likely to be segregated by sex (Barbu, Le Maner-Idrissi, & Jouanjean, 2000; Maccoby, 2002a). When asked about the definition of a friend, most children in this age group think of someone with whom they play (Corsaro, 2011). Our neighbor children, for example, made their initial approach to our young son by saying, "Let's be friends; let's play" and "I'll be your friend if you will be mine." Young children do not view friendship as a trusting, lasting relationship, but even this limited view of friendship is important for this age group. As peer relationships become more important, around age 3, children are motivated to be accepted by peers. This motivation is the incentive for development of such skills as sharing, cooperating, negotiating, and perspective taking. Nevertheless, peer relations in early childhood are often marked by conflict and falling-outs (Davies, 2011).

Research indicates that young children are at a higher risk of being rejected by their peers if they are aggressive and comparatively more active, demonstrate a difficult temperament, are easily distracted, and demonstrate lower perseverance (Campbell, 2002). One would wonder, then, how young peers respond to Terri Smith. The rejection of some children is long lasting. It is important, therefore, to intervene early to help children like Terri Smith learn more prosocial behavior.

Peer relationships in early childhood are associated with early attachments. A child who has had secure relationships with parents in the first 3 years is likely to have good social skills and to expect peer relations to be positive. In contrast, peer interactions are often difficult for young children with insecure working models.

Self-Concept

In early childhood, the child seems to vacillate between grandiose and realistic views of the self (Davies, 2011). Children are aware of their growing competence, but at the same time, they have normal doubts about the self, based on realistic comparisons of their competence with the competence of adults. In early childhood, children begin to develop a self-concept, which includes a perception of oneself as a person who has desires, attributes, preferences, and abilities.

Some investigators have suggested that during early childhood, the child's ever-increasing understanding of the self in relation to the world begins to become organized into a **self-theory** (Epstein, 1973, 1991, 1998). As children develop the cognitive ability to categorize, they use categorization to think about the self. By age 2 or 3, children can identify their gender and race (discussed in greater detail shortly) as factors in understanding who they are. From ages 4 to 6, young children become more aware that different people have different perspectives on situations (Ziv & Frye, 2003). This helps them to begin to understand cultural expectations and sensitizes them to the expectations that others have for them.

This growing capacity to understand the self in relation to others leads to self-evaluation, or **self-esteem**. Very early interpersonal experiences provide information that becomes incorporated into self-esteem. Messages of love, admiration, and approval lead to a positive view of the self (Brown, Dutton, & Cook, 2001). Messages of rejection or scorn lead to a negative view of the self (Heimpel, Wood, Marshall, & Brown, 2002). In addition to these interpersonal messages, young children observe their own competencies and attributes and compare them with the competencies of other children as well as adults. And they are very aware of being evaluated by others, their peers as well as important adults (Newman & Newman, 2012).

Of course, a young child may develop a positive view of the self in one dimension, such as cognitive abilities, and a negative view of the self in another dimension, such as physical abilities. Children also learn that some abilities are more valued than others in the various environments in which they operate. For example, in individualistic-oriented societies, self-reliance, independence, autonomy, and distinctiveness are valued while interdependence and harmony are valued in most collectivistic-oriented societies. Self-esteem is based on different values in these different types of cultures (Brown, 2003). It is probably the case that every culture includes both individualistic and collectivistic beliefs (Turiel, 2004), but the balance of these two belief systems varies greatly from culture to culture. An example of the way these beliefs play out and influence self-development from an early age was described by Markus and Kitayama (2003), who noted that in U.S. coverage of the Olympics, athletes are typically asked about how they personally feel about their efforts and their success. In contrast, in Japanese coverage, athletes are typically asked "Who helped you achieve?" This idea of an interdependent self is consistent with cultural relational theory as well as feminist and Afro-centric perspectives on relationships.

Recently, cognitive neuroscientists have been exploring the ways the brain gives rise to development of a sense of self. They have found that a right fronto-parietal network, which overlaps with mirror neurons, is activated during tasks involving self-recognition and discrimination between the self and the other (Kaplan, Aziz-Zadeh, Uddin, & Iacoboni, 2008). Viewing one's own face leads to greater signal changes in the inferior frontal gyrus (IFG), the inferior occipital gyrus, and the inferior parietal lobe. In addition, there is greater signal change in the right IFG when hearing one's own voice compared with hearing a friend's voice (Kaplan et al., 2008). Beginning evidence also indicates that the cortical midline structures (CMS) of the brain are involved in self-evaluation and in understanding of others' emotional states. In addition, there is beginning evidence of at least one pathway that connects the mirror neurons and the CMS, allowing for integration of self and other understanding (Uddin, Iacoboni, Lange, & Keenan, 2007).

Gender Identity and Sexual Interests

During early childhood, gender becomes an important dimension of how children understand themselves and others.

> How does gender influence early childhood development?

Researchers have suggested four components to gender identity during early childhood (Newman & Newman, 2012):

1. *Making correct use of the gender label.* By age 2, children can usually accurately identify others as either male or female, based on appearance.

2. *Understanding gender as stable.* Later, children understand that gender is stable, that boys grow up to be men and girls to be women.

3. *Understanding gender constancy.* Even with this understanding of gender stability, young children, with their imaginative thinking, continue to think that girls can turn into boys and boys into girls by changing appearance. For example, a 3-year-old given a picture of a girl is able to identify the person as a girl. But if the same girl is shown in another picture dressed as a boy, the 3-year-old will label the girl a boy. It is not until sometime from ages 4 to 7 that children understand *gender constancy*, the understanding that one's gender does not change, that the girl dressed as a boy is still a girl.

4. *Understanding the genital basis of gender.* Gender constancy has been found to be associated with an understanding of the relationship between gender and genitals (Bem, 1998).

Before going further, it is important to differentiate among four concepts: sex, gender, gender identity, and sexual orientation. *Sex* refers to biologically linked distinctions determined by chromosomal information. An infant's external genitalia are usually used as the determinant of sex. In most humans, chromosomes, hormones, and genitalia are consistent, and determining sex is considered unambiguous. However, this is not always the case. Chromosomal, genetic, anatomical, and hormonal aspects of sex are sometimes not aligned. *Gender* includes the cognitive, emotional, and social schemes associated with being female or male. *Gender identity* refers to one's sense of being male or female, a topic that receives more attention in the chapter on adolescence. *Sexual orientation* refers to one's preference for sexually intimate partners. It appears that gender identity development begins with a recognition of sex differences.

There is evidence of gender differences in multiple dimensions of human behavior but also much debate about just how pervasive these differences are and, if they exist, how to explain them. In terms of the pervasiveness of gender differences, the findings are not at all consistent. In 1974, Eleanor Maccoby and Carol Jacklin reviewed more than 2,000 studies that included sex differences and found evidence of four sex differences: (1) girls have greater verbal abilities than boys, (2) boys excel in visual-spatial ability, (3) boys excel in mathematical ability, and (4) boys are more aggressive. Thirty years later, Janet Hyde (2005) reviewed a large number of studies and found that in 78% of them, gender differences were close to zero or quite small and that there was evidence of much within-group difference. In other words, the differences among girls were as great or greater than the differences between boys and girls. There were substantial gender differences in a few areas, however: some aspects of motor performance, some sexual attitudes and behaviors, and physical aggression. Indeed, the research subsequent to the Maccoby and Jacklin review has found that the cognitive differences they reported are very limited. Females do seem to have an advantage in verbal fluency and writing, but not in reading comprehension. Males' visual-spatial advantage seems to occur only in tasks requiring mental rotation of a three-dimensional object. Although males perform better on tests of broad mathematical ability, females score better on computation (Garrett, 2009).

In terms of the debate about the causes of gender differences, there are two competing perspectives: the biological determination perspective and the socially constructed perspective. There is some evidence to support each of these perspectives, suggesting, not surprisingly, that behavior is multiply determined. In terms of verbal ability, there is some evidence that females use both hemispheres of the brain for solving verbal problems while males use mostly the left hemisphere, but the findings in this regard are not consistent. Relatively strong evidence indicates that estrogen probably does contribute to women's verbal advantage. Men who take estrogen in their transsexual treatments to become female score higher on verbal learning than men who do not take estrogen as part of their transsexual transformation. Testosterone appears to play a role in spatial ability. Males who produce low levels of testosterone during the developmental years have less well-developed spatial ability; in addition, testosterone replacement therapy in older men improves their spatial functioning. Interestingly, there is only a small sex difference in aggression when behavior is studied in the laboratory, but a very large difference outside the laboratory. That is not convincing evidence for a biological basis for the gender differences in aggression (Garrett, 2009).

In terms of the socially constructed perspective, we know that human societies use gender as an important category for organizing social life. There are some rather large cultural and subcultural variations in gender role definitions, however. Existing cultural standards about gender are pervasively built into adult interactions with young children and into the reward systems that are developed for shaping child behavior. Much research indicates that parents begin to use gender stereotypes to respond to their children from the time of birth (Gardiner & Kosmitzki, 2011). They cuddle more with infant girls and play more actively with infant boys. Later, they talk more with young girls and expect young boys to be more independent. Recent studies have found that the nature of parental influence on children's gender role development is more complex than this. Parents may hold to stereotypical gender expectations in some domains but not in others. For example, parents may have similar expectations for boys and girls in terms of sharing or being polite (McHale, Crouter, & Whiteman, 2003). (Note: Unless otherwise specified by researchers, we have used the language of "gender difference" rather than "sex difference" because research indicates that these differences are both biologically and socially constructed.)

Once toddlers understand their gender, they begin to imitate and identify with the same-sex parent, if he or she is available. Once young children begin to understand gender role standards, they become quite rigid in their playing out of gender roles—only girls cook, only men drive trucks, only girls wear pink flowers, only boys wear shirts with footballs. This gender understanding also accounts for the preference of same-sex playmates and sex-typed toys (Davies, 2011). Remember, though, that the exaggeration of gender stereotypes in early childhood is in keeping with the struggle during this period to discover stability and regularity in the environment.

Evidence that gender differences in verbal, visual, and mathematical skills are at least partially socially constructed can be found in data that indicate that differences in all three areas have decreased over the same time period that gender roles have changed toward greater similarity. The dramatic difference in murder rates across societies suggests a strong cultural influence on aggression (Garrett, 2009).

During early childhood, children become increasingly interested in their genitals. They are interested, in general, in how their bodies work, but the genitals seem to hold a special interest as the young child learns through experimentation that the genitals can be a source of pleasure. From 3 to 5, children may have some worries and questions about genital difference; little girls may think they once had a penis and wonder what happened to it. Little boys may fear that their penises will disappear, like their sister's did. During early childhood, masturbation is used both as a method of self-soothing and for pleasure. Young children also "play doctor" with each other, and often want to see and touch their parents' genitals. Many parents and other caregivers are confused about how to handle this behavior, particularly in our era of heightened awareness of childhood sexual abuse. In general, parents should not worry about genital curiosity or about children experimenting with touching their own genitals. They should remember, however, that at this age children may be overstimulated by seeing their parents' genitals. And we should always be concerned when children want to engage in more explicit adultlike sexual play that involves stimulation of each other's genitals (Davies, 2011; Newman & Newman, 2012).

Racial and Ethnic Identity

How important are racial and ethnic identity in early childhood?

Findings from research suggest that children first learn their own racial identity before they are able to identify the race of others (Kowalski, 2003). Elements of racial and ethnic identity awareness have been found to occur as early as age 3. Most children begin to self-identify as a member of a racial group by age 3 to 4, but identification with an ethnic group does not usually occur until later in childhood, from 5 to 8 years of age (Blackmon & Vera, 2008). Early identification of others by race is limited to skin color, which is more easily recognized than ethnic origin. Young children may label a Latino/Latina individual, for example, as either African American or White, depending on the individual's skin color. Young children also show a preference for members of their own race over another, but they do not reject others on the basis of race (Brewer, 1999). Perhaps this choice is similar to the preference for same-sex playmates, a result of young children attempting to learn their own identity.

Social scientists concerned about the development of self-esteem in children of color have investigated racial bias and preference using children in early childhood as research participants. The most famous of these studies was conducted by Kenneth Clark and Mamie Clark in 1939. They presented African American children with Black dolls and White dolls and concluded that African American children responded more favorably to the White dolls and had more negative reactions to the Black dolls. A similar study 40 years later, observing young Black children in Trinidad and African American children in New York, reported similar results (Gopaul-McNicol, 1988). The young children from both New York and Trinidad preferred and identified with the White dolls. Interestingly, the same results have been reported more recently

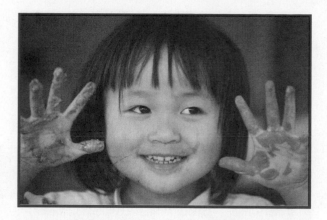

Photo 4.2 Play is one of the few elements in the development of children that is universal—regardless of culture.

© iStockphoto.com

in studies of Taiwanese young children (Chang, 2001). Most of the Taiwanese children in the study indicated a preference for the White dolls and demonstrated a "pro-white attitude." Another more recent study found that African American children growing up in a mainly European American community tend to choose White images or dolls, but those growing up in a predominantly African American community tend to choose Black images or dolls (Cameron, Alvarez, Ruble, & Fuligni, 2001). Furthermore, when young children were not asked to make a preference between images, they showed interest in Asian, White, and Black images or dolls and did not make judgments based on race or ethnicity (Kowalski, 2003).

It is questionable, however, whether preferences and biases found in research are equated with self-concept and low self-esteem for children of color. Most argue that they are not. For example, racial bias and self-concept were not related among the young Taiwanese children (Chang, 2001). Likewise, findings from studies about young African American children indicate high levels of self-concept despite the children's bias in favor of the White culture and values (Crain, 1996; Spencer, 1984). Spencer concludes that young Black children compartmentalize personal identity (self-concept) from knowledge about racial stereotypes in the dominant culture.

Photo 4.3   During early childhood, children engage in cooperative play and enjoy sharing and competing with peers.

© iStockphoto.com

The Role of Play

The young child loves to play, and play is essential to all aspects of early child development. We think of the play of young children as fun-filled and lively. And yet it serves a serious purpose. Through play, children develop the motor skills essential for physical development, learn the problem-solving skills and communication skills fundamental to cognitive development, express the feelings and gain the self-confidence needed for emotional growth, and learn to cooperate and resolve social conflicts. Essentially, play is what young children are all about; it is their work.

As children develop in all areas during early childhood, their play activities and preferences for play materials change over time. Hughes (2010) makes the following recommendations about the preferred play materials at different ages during early childhood:

- *Three-year-olds:* props for imaginative play, such as dress-up clothes, doctor kits, and makeup; miniature toys that represent adult models, such as toy trucks, gas stations, dolls, doll houses, and airplanes; art materials, such as paint brushes, easels, marker pens, and crayons

- *Four-year-olds:* vehicles, such as tricycles and wagons; play materials to develop fine motor skills, such as materials for sewing, stringing beads, coloring, painting, and drawing; books that involve adventure

- *Five-year-olds:* play materials to develop precision in fine motor skills, such as coloring books, paints and brushes, crayons, marker pens, glue, scissors, stencils, sequins and glitter, clay, and Play-Doh; play materials that develop cognitive skills, such as workbenches, play cards, table games, and board games

In recent years, there has been a dramatic increase in the availability of computers and other instructional technology. These technologies have made their way into early childhood education programs, but there is controversy among early childhood educators about the positive and negative aspects of these technologies for early childhood development. There is evidence of benefits of instructional technologies in the preschool classroom. For example, 4- and 5-year-old children can use technology to develop language, art, mathematics, and science skills. Conversely, some early childhood educators are concerned that computers and other instructional technologies contribute to social isolation and limit children's creative play (Hughes, 2010). Adults must give serious consideration to how to balance the positive and negative aspects of these technologies.

The predominant type of play in early childhood, beginning around the age of 2, is **symbolic play**, otherwise known as fantasy play, pretend play, or imaginary play (Hughes, 2010). Children continue to use vivid imaginations in their play, as they did as toddlers, but they also begin to put more structure into their play. Thus, their play is intermediate between the fantasy play of toddlers and the structured, rules-oriented play of middle childhood. Although toddler play is primarily nonverbal, the play of young children often involves highly sophisticated verbal productions. There is some indication that this preference for symbolic play during early childhood exists across cultures, but the themes of the play reflect the culture in which it is enacted (Roopnarine, Shin, Donovan, & Suppal, 2000).

Symbolic play during early childhood has six primary functions: providing an opportunity to explore reality, contributing to cognitive development, practicing for morality, allowing young children to gain control over their lives, serving as a shared experience and opportunity for development of peer culture, and as the route to attachment to fathers. These functions are now explained in more detail.

Play as an Opportunity to Explore Reality

Young children imitate adult behavior and try out social roles in their play (Davies, 2011; Hughes, 2010). They play house, school, doctor, police, firefighter, and so on. As they "dress up" in various guises of adult roles, or even as spiders and rabbits, they are using fantasy to explore what they might become. Their riding toys allow them to play with the experience of having greater mobility in the world.

Play's Contribution to Cognitive Development

The young child uses play to think about the world, to understand cause and effect (Roskos & Christie, 2000). Throughout early childhood, young children show increasing sophistication in

Photo 4.4 Young children use play to think about the world and to understand cause and effect.

© Erna Vader/iStockphoto.com

using words in their dramatic play. Some researchers have asked this question: Does symbolic play facilitate cognitive development, or does symbolic play require mature cognitive abilities? The question is unresolved; the available evidence indicates only that cognitive development is connected with play in early childhood (Roopnarine et al., 2000). Childhood sociologists have found that children create sophisticated language games for group play that facilitate the development of language and logical thinking (Corsaro, 2011). A number of researchers have studied how young children build literacy skills through play, particularly play with books (Roskos & Christie, 2000). Play that is focused on language and thinking skills has been described as **learning play** (Meek, 2000).

Play as Practice for Morality

In their fantasy play, young children begin to think about "good" and "bad" behavior and to try out roles of superheroes and "bad guys." They can discharge aggressive impulses in the relative safety of pretend play (Davies, 2011).

Play as an Opportunity to Gain Control

In his cross-cultural study of play, childhood sociologist William Corsaro (2011) demonstrates that young children typically use dramatic play to cope with fears. They incorporate their fears into their group play and thus develop some mastery over stress and anxiety. This perspective on young children's play is the cornerstone of play therapy (Chethik, 2000). Anyone who has spent much time in a child care center has probably seen a group of 4-year-olds engaged in superhero play, their flowing capes improvised with towels pinned on their shirts. Such play helps the child compensate for feelings of inadequacy and fear that come from recognizing that one is a small person in a big world (Davies, 2011). Corsaro (2011) suggests that the love for climbing toys that bring small children high over the heads of others serves the same purpose.

How does play develop skills for human agency in making choices?

Children in preschool settings have also been observed trying to get control over their lives by subverting some of the control of adults. Corsaro (2011) describes a preschool where the children had been told they could not bring any play items from home. The preschool teachers were trying to avoid the kinds of conflicts that can occur over toys brought from home. The children in this preschool found a way to subvert this rule, however; they began to bring in very small toys, such as matchbox cars, that would fit in their pockets out of sight when teachers were nearby. Corsaro provides a number of other examples from his cross-cultural research of ways that young children use play to take some control of their lives away from adults.

Play as a Shared Experience

Increasing emphasis is placed on the way that play in early childhood contributes to the development of peer culture. Many researchers who study the play of young children suggest that **sociodramatic play**, or group fantasy play in which children coordinate their fantasy, is the most important form of play during this time. Young children are able to develop more elaborate fantasy play and sustain it by forming friendship groups, which in turn gives them experience with group conflict and group

problem solving that carries over into the adult world (Corsaro, 2011). Group play also helps young children learn to understand and follow rules.

As young children play in groups, they attempt to protect the opportunity to keep the play going by restricting who may enter the play field (Corsaro, 2011). Young children can often be heard making such comments as, "We're friends; we're playing, right?" Or perhaps, "You're not our friend; you can't play with us." The other side of the coin is that young children must learn how to gain access to play in progress (Garvey, 1984). An important social skill is being able to demonstrate that they can play without messing the game up. Young children learn a set of do's and don'ts to accomplish that goal (see Exhibit 4.3) and develop complex strategies for gaining access to play.

Conflict often occurs in young children's play groups, and researchers have found gender and cultural variations in how these conflicts get resolved. Young girls have been found to prefer

Exhibit 4.3 Do's and Don'ts of Getting Access to Play in Progress

Do's
Watch what's going on
Figure out the play theme
Enter the area
Plug into the action
Hold off on making suggestions about how to change the action
Don'ts
Ask questions for information (if you can't tell what's going on, you'll mess it up)
Mention yourself or your reactions to what is going on
Disagree or criticize what is happening

SOURCE: Based on Garvey, 1984

dyadic (two-person) play interactions, and young boys enjoy larger groups (Benenson, 1993). These preferences may not hold across cultures, however. For example, White middle-class young girls in the United States are less direct and assertive in challenging each other in play situations than either African American girls in the United States or young girls in an Italian preschool (Corsaro, 2011). Greater assertiveness may allow for more comfortable play in larger groups.

Play as the Route to Attachment to Fathers

Most of the efforts to understand attachment focus on the link between mothers and children and the effect of the maternal relationship. More recently, though, there has been growing concern about and interest in the importance of fathers in the development of attachment for young children. Some suggest that father-child attachment may be promoted mainly through play, much like the mother-child relationship may be the result of caregiving activities (Laflamme, Pomerleau, & Malcuit, 2002; Roggman, 2004). Differences in play style noted for mothers versus that seen in fathers is of particular interest. Investigators conclude that more physical play is seen between fathers and young children compared with more object play and conventional play interaction between mothers and children (Goldberg, Clarke-Stewart, Rice, & Dellis, 2002). Both forms of play can involve the display of affection by the parent. Thus, both forms of play contribute to the development of parent-child attachment. This research challenges the notion that only certain kinds of play have the potential to effect positive attachment and affirms the notion that there is developmental value for children in father-child physical play. In fact, physical play stimulates and arouses children and takes them out of their comfort zone. Roggman (2004) further notes that the style of play often ascribed to fathers provides opportunity for young children to overcome their limits and to experience taking chances in a context where there is some degree of confidence that they will be protected.

Developmental Disruptions

Children develop at different rates. Most developmental problems in infants and young children are more accurately described as developmental delays, offering the hope that early intervention, or even natural processes, will mitigate the long-term effects. Developmental delays may exist in cognitive skills, communication skills, social skills, emotion regulation, behavior, and fine and gross motor skills. Developmental problems in school-age children are typically labeled disabilities and classified into groups, such as cognitive disability, learning disabilities, and motor impairment (Parish, Saville, & Swaine, 2011).

Many young children with developmental difficulties, including emotional and behavioral concerns, are inaccurately assessed and misdiagnosed. In fact, the American Academy of Pediatrics encourages rigorous screening for developmental delays and other developmental difficulties during well-child checkups, including the use of standardized assessment tools (Glascoe, 2005). After interviewing professionals who work with children age 6 and younger, one research team compiled a list of traits observed in young children that indicate emotional and behavioral problems: extreme aggressive behavior, difficulty with change, invasion of others' personal space, compulsive or impulsive behavior, low ability to trust others, lack of empathy or remorse, and cruelty to animals (Schmitz & Hilton, 1996). Parents and teachers often handle these behaviors with firmer limits and more discipline. However, environmental risk factors, such as emotional abuse or neglect and domestic violence, may be the actual cause.

Given the difficulty of accurate assessment, assessment in young children should include many disciplines to gain as broad an understanding as possible (Parish et al., 2011). Assessment and service delivery should also be culturally relevant. In other words, culture and other related issues—such as family interaction patterns and stress, the social environment, ethnicity, acculturation, social influences, and developmental expectations—should all be considered when evaluating a child's developmental abilities.

For those children who have been labeled developmentally delayed, the main remedy has been social skill development. In one such program, two types of preschool classrooms were evaluated (Roberts, Burchinal, & Bailey, 1994). In one classroom, young developmentally delayed children were matched with nondelayed children of the same age; in another classroom, some of the "normal" children were the same age as the developmentally delayed children and some were older. Social exchange between the children with delays and those without delays was greater in the mixed-aged classroom. Another study evaluated the usefulness of providing social skills training to children with mild developmental disabilities (Lewis, 1994). In a preschool setting, developmentally delayed children were put in situations requiring social interaction and were praised for successful interaction. This method increased social interaction between the young children.

It is also important to recognize the parental stress that often accompanies care of children with developmental disabilities. Researchers have found that an educational intervention with parents that teaches behavioral management and how to plan activities that minimize disruptive behavior results in improved child behavior, improved parent-child relationship, and less parental stress (Clare, Mazzucchelli, Studman, & Sanders, 2006).

In the 1980s, concern about the quality of education in the United States led to upgrades in the elementary school curriculum. Many skills previously introduced in the first grade became part of the kindergarten curriculum. This has led to increased concern about kindergarten readiness, the skills that the young child should have acquired before entering kindergarten, as well as how to provide for the needs of developmentally delayed children in the kindergarten classroom. It has also led to controversies about when to begin to think of developmental delays as disabilities. A growing concern is that children with developmental problems should not be placed in kindergarten classrooms that do not provide support for their particular developmental needs (Litty & Hatch, 2006). States vary in how much support they provide to children with developmental delays to allow them to participate in fully inclusive classrooms (classrooms where they are mainstreamed with children without developmental delays), but a growing group of children with developmental delays in the United States are participating as full citizens in inclusive classrooms during preschool and kindergarten (Guralnick, Neville, Hammond, & Connor, 2008). Before leaving this discussion, we would like to emphasize one important point. When working with young children, we want to recognize and respect the variability of developmental trajectories. At the same time, however, we want to be attentive to any aspects of a child's development that may be lagging behind expected milestones so that we can provide extra support to young children in specific areas of development (Spinrad et al., 2007).

> ### Critical Thinking Questions 4.3
>
> How can play be used to help Terri Smith, Jack Lewis, and Ron and Rosiland Johnson in their multidimensional development? What do you see as particular needs each of them have that could be at least partially addressed with play?

EARLY CHILDHOOD EDUCATION

It is a relatively new idea to provide formalized education for young children, but three strands of research are indicating the importance of formal education to support social awareness, group interaction skills, and cognitive development during early childhood to prepare children to live in contemporary knowledge-driven economies. First, neuroscientific research indicates the critical importance of brain development in the early years. Second, social science research indicates that high-quality early childhood education programs improve readiness for primary school. And third, econometric research indicates that high-quality early childhood education programs save societies significant amounts of money over time (Economist Intelligence Unit, 2012). Early childhood education has been found to be especially important for children from low-income households in highly unequal societies who are likely to enter primary school far behind their peers and experience an achievement gap throughout their schooling years (Heckman, 2006, 2008). President Barack Obama (2014) has promoted early childhood education on the basis that it reduces inequality while also fostering economic efficiency. In spite of mounting evidence that greater investment in early childhood education reduces costs at later stages of education, most societies continue to prioritize tertiary, secondary, and primary education over early childhood education (Economist Intelligence Unit, 2012).

Rates of enrollment in early childhood education vary across the world, and program quality varies as well. In 2011, 47% of 3- and 4-year-olds in the United States were involved in formal education, compared with 100% in France, Germany, and Italy; 95% in the United Kingdom; and 86% in Japan (Miller, Warren, & Owen, 2011). With increasing concern about the need for early childhood learning, the Lien Foundation of Singapore commissioned the Economist Intelligence Unit (EIU) to study "preschool education" (which we are calling early childhood education) on a global scale. The EIU developed an index, which they call the Starting Well Index, to rank early childhood education in 45 countries on four indicators: social context, availability, affordability, and quality (Economist Intelligence Unit, 2012). The United States, tied with the United Arab Emirates for an overall rank of 24th among the 45 countries, was ranked 28th for social context, 31st for availability, 16th for affordability, and 22nd for quality. The countries with the top five overall rankings were Finland, Sweden, Norway, the United Kingdom, and Belgium, all countries that put high value on state-supported early childhood education.

Much evidence indicates that low-income and racial minority students in the United States have less access to quality early childhood education than their age peers (Ravitch, 2013). Throughout the recession that started in 2008, funding for pre-kindergarten programs in the United States was weak, and in 2012, funding for these programs decreased for the first time in a decade. State spending per child for state-supported early childhood education programs decreased by $600 from 2008 to 2012, and some states began to lower their quality benchmarks for these programs. Head Start, the federally funded program that provides early childhood education for impoverished children, received a boost from the 2009 stimulus bill but faced later cuts from the 2013 sequestration, cuts that meant 57,000 children lost their Head Start slots (Guernsey, Bornfreund, McCann, & Williams, 2014). Wealthy families are competing for slots for their young children in expensive preschool programs, called the "baby ivies," that provide highly enriched early learning environments, further advancing opportunities for children in privileged families (Kozol, 2005). Middle-class families, as well as impoverished families, are increasingly unable to access quality early childhood education; 78% of families who earned more than $100,000 per year in 2004 sent their young children to early childhood educational programs compared with less than half of families earning less than $50,000 per year (Calman & Tarr-Whelan, 2005).

One longitudinal study followed a group of children who attended the High/Scope Perry Preschool Program in Ypsilanti, Michigan, until they reached the age of 40 (Schweinhart et al., 2005). From 1962 to 1967, the researchers identified a sample of 123 low-income African American children who had been assessed to be at high risk of school failure. They randomly assigned 58 of these children to attend a high-quality 2-year preschool program for 2- and 3-year-olds, while the other 65 attended no preschool program. The program met for 2½ hours per day, 5 days a week, and teachers made home visits every 2 weeks. The teachers in the preschool program had bachelor's degrees and education certification. No more than eight children were assigned to a teacher, and the curriculum emphasized giving children the opportunity to plan and carry out their own activities. By age 40, the preschool participants, on average, were doing better than the nonparticipants in several important ways:

- They were more likely to have graduated from high school (65% vs. 45%).
- They were more likely to be employed (76% vs. 62%).
- They had higher median annual earnings ($20,800 vs. $15, 300).
- They were more likely to own their own home (37% vs. 28%).
- They were more likely to have a savings account (76% vs. 50%).
- They had fewer lifetime arrests (36% vs. 55% arrested five or more times).
- They were less likely to have spent time in prison or jail (28% vs. 52% never sentenced).

The researchers report that the preschool program cost $15,166 per child and the public gained $12.90 for every dollar spent on the program by the time the participants were 40 years old. The savings came from reduced special education costs, increased taxes derived from higher earnings, reduced public assistance costs, and reduced costs to the criminal justice system. Nobel Prize–winning economist James Heckman and colleagues (Heckman, Moon, Pinto, Savelyev, & Yavitz, 2010) have reanalyzed the data to rule out alternative assumptions and concluded that the estimated rates of social return fall from 7% to 10%.

Another longitudinal study began in North Carolina in 1972, when 112 low-income infants were randomly assigned to either a quality preschool program or no program (Masse & Barnett, 2002). The group assigned to the preschool program was enrolled in the program for 5 years instead of the 2 years in the High/Scope Perry study. The participants in this study were followed to the age of 21. The children who participated in the preschool program were less likely to repeat grades, less likely to be placed in special education classes, and more likely to complete high school. It is important to note that the researchers in this study also investigated the impact of the preschool program on the mothers. They found that the preschool program mothers earned $3,750 more per year than the mothers whose children did not attend the program, for a total of $78,750 more over 21 years.

These two longitudinal studies investigated the impact of quality preschool education on low-income children, but there is also preliminary evidence of the benefit of early childhood education on all children. A study conducted at Georgetown University has examined the effect of prekindergarten (PK) programs in Tulsa, Oklahoma (Gromley, Gayer, Phillips, & Dawson, 2005). These programs are considered high quality because teachers are required to have a bachelor's degree, there are no more than 10 children per teacher, and teachers are paid on the same scale as public school teachers. The researchers found that children who attended PK scored better on letter-word identification, spelling, and applied problems than children of the same age who had not attended PK. This was true regardless of race or socioeconomic status. Results from other research indicate that public funding of early childhood education can help close the gap in preschool education between low-income and higher-income children (Greenberg, 2010).

These studies suggest that early childhood education programs are good for children, for families, for communities, and for society. With such evidence in hand, social workers can join with other child advocates to build broad coalitions to educate the public about the multilevel benefits and to push for public policy that guarantees universal quality early childhood education.

EARLY CHILDHOOD IN THE MULTIGENERATIONAL FAMILY

Curiosity and experimentation are the hallmarks of early childhood. Young children are sponges, soaking up information about themselves, their worlds, and their relationships. They use their families as primary sources of information and as models for relationships. Where there are older siblings, they serve as important figures of identification and imitation. Aunts, uncles, cousins, and grandparents may also serve this role, but parents are, in most families, the most important sources of information, support, and modeling for young children.

Parents play two very important roles for their 3- to 6-year-old child: educator and advocate (Newman & Newman, 2012). As educators, they answer children's big and little questions, ask questions to stimulate thinking and growth in communication skills, provide explanations, and help children figure things out. They teach children about morality and human connectedness by modeling honest, kind, thoughtful behavior and by reading to their children about moral dilemmas and moral action. They help children develop emotional intelligence by modeling how to handle strong feelings and by talking with children about the children's strong feelings. They take young children on excursions in their real physical worlds as well as in the fantasy worlds found in books. They give children opportunities to perform tasks that develop a sense of mastery.

Not all parents have the same resources for the educator role or the same beliefs about how children learn. And some parents take their role as educators too seriously, pushing their young children into more and more structured time with higher and higher expectations of performance. Many of these parents are pushing their own frustrated dreams onto their young children. The concern is that these children are deprived of time for exploration, experimentation, and fantasy.

In the contemporary era, children are moving into organized child care settings at earlier ages. As they do so, parents become more important as advocates who understand their children's needs. The advocate role is particularly important for parents of young children with disabilities. These parents may need to advocate to ensure that all aspects of early childhood education programs are accessible to their children.

For some children, like Ron and Rosiland Johnson, it is the grandparent and not the parent who serves as the central figure. Estimates are that in 2011, 7.7 million children were living with a grandparent or other relative, with 3 million of these children being cared for primarily by that grandparent. Both of these numbers rose rapidly after the recession of 2008. In 80% of the cases where children live with a grandparent, at least one of the child's parents is also living in the household. Many of the parents in these households are in need of assistance: 44% had a baby as a teen, 12% have a disability, 21% are unemployed, and 29% have less than a high school education (Livingston, 2013). Some custodial grandparents describe an increased purpose for living, but others describe increased isolation, worry, physical and emotional exhaustion, and financial concerns (Clarke, 2008). These are some of the same concerns expressed by Ms. Johnson. In addition, grandparents caring for children with psychological and physical problems experience high levels of stress (Sands & Goldberg, 2000).

The literature indicates that young children often do better under the care of grandparents than in other types of homes. However, children like Ron and Rosiland, who are parented by their grandparents, must often overcome many difficult emotions (Smith, Dannison, & Vach-Hasse, 1998). These children struggle with issues of grief and loss related to loss of their parent(s) and feelings of guilt, fear, embarrassment, and anger. These feelings may be especially strong for young children who feel they are somehow responsible for the loss of their parent(s). Although children in this age group are capable of labeling their feelings, their ability to discuss these feelings with any amount of depth is very limited. In addition, grandparents may feel unsure about how to talk about the situation with their young grandchildren. Professional intervention for the children is often recommended (Smith et al., 1998). Some mental health practitioners have had success providing group sessions that help grandparents gain control over their grandchildren's behavior, resolve clashes in values between themselves and their grandchildren, and help grandparents avoid overindulgence and set firm limits.

Grandparents are often important figures in the lives of young children even when they do not serve as primary caregivers; they provide practical support, financial support, and emotional support.

They may offer different types of practical support, coming to the aid of the family when needs arise. Or they may serve as the child care provider while parents work or provide babysitting services in the evening. They also provide financial support, depending on their financial circumstances. They may provide cash assistance or buy things such as clothes and toys for the children; it is distressing to some grandparents if they lack the financial resources to buy things for their grandchildren. Grandparents may also provide emotional support and advice to parents of young children; this is something that can be done at a distance by a variety of electronic technologies when grandparents live at some distance from the children (Clarke, 2008).

Critical Thinking Questions 4.4

Based on the research noted earlier, what types of social policies would you like to see enacted in early childhood education? The United States has less vigorous state support for early childhood education than many other wealthy nations. What factors do you think influence the policy decisions about early childhood education in the United States and other wealthy nations? How could a social worker help Ron and Rosiland Johnson and their grandmother to thrive while Ron and Rosiland's mother is incarcerated?

RISKS TO HEALTHY DEVELOPMENT IN EARLY CHILDHOOD

This section addresses a few risk factors that social workers are likely to encounter in work with young children and their families: poverty, homelessness, ineffective discipline, divorce, and violence (including child abuse). In addition, the section outlines the protective factors that ameliorate the risks.

Why is it important to recognize risk factors and protective factors in early childhood?

Poverty

As reported in Chapter 3, there are 1 billion children around the world living in poverty. In the United States, 6 million children (25%) younger than age 6 lived in poverty in 2011, and about 49% of children younger than age 6 lived in low-income families, with incomes below 200% of the poverty level. Seventy percent of American Indian and Black children younger than age 6 lived in low-income households, compared with 67% of Hispanic, 35% of White, and 30% of Asian children. These rates have been on the rise since 2006 (Addy, Engelhardt, & Skinner, 2013). Poverty—in the form of food insecurity, inadequate health care, and overcrowded living conditions—presents considerable risks to children's growth and development. In 2011, 22% of households with children younger than age 18 were food insecure for some part of the year. The research indicates that families with food insecurity usually attempt to provide adequate nutrition to the youngest children, with parents and older children making sacrifices to feed younger children (Child Trends, 2013a). A study of the Northern Cheyenne Indian reservation in southeastern Montana found that 70% of all households were food insecure (Whiting & Ward, 2008). Inadequate nutrition is a serious threat to all aspects of early childhood development. Inadequate health care means that many acute conditions become chronic. Overcrowding is problematic to young children in that it restricts opportunities for play, the means through which most development occurs.

Research indicates that young children reared in poverty are significantly delayed in language and other cognitive skills (Locke, Ginsborg, & Peers, 2002). The effects of poverty on children in early childhood appear to be long lasting. Children who experience poverty during their early years are less likely to complete school than children whose initial exposure to poverty occurred in the middle childhood years or during adolescence. Researchers have also found that children who live in poverty are at high risk for low self-esteem, peer conflict, depression, and childhood psychological disorders. Poverty is often associated with other risk factors such as overwhelmed parents, living in a violent setting or in deteriorated housing, and instability of frequent changes in residence and schools (Bartholomae & Fox, 2010).

Not all young children who live in poverty fare poorly, however. In their longitudinal study of 180 children born into poverty, Sroufe et al. (2005) report that four groups emerged by early childhood: They grouped 70 children into a very competent cluster who were high in enthusiasm, persistence, compliance, and affection for the mother. They grouped another 25 children into a very incompetent cluster characterized by high negativity and low compliance and affection. The other almost half of the children were grouped into two clusters that fell between very competent and very incompetent.

Homelessness

Families with children make up one third of the homeless population, and families became more and more vulnerable to home foreclosures and unemployment during the deep recession that started in late 2007. It is estimated that 42% of homeless families have children younger than age 6. Homeless children are sick more often, are exposed to more violence, and experience more emotional and behavioral problems and more delayed development than low-income housed children. Their school attendance is often disrupted because they need to change schools, but often because of transportation problems as well (Paquette & Bassuk, 2009).

Kristen Paquette and Ellen Bassuk (2009) note that parents' identities are often closely tied to relationships they maintain, especially with their children, and that homelessness undermines their ability to protect those they have a responsibility to protect. Like all parents, homeless parents want to provide their children with basic necessities. Being homeless presents dramatic barriers and challenges for parents, who too often lose the ability to provide essentials for their children, including shelter, food, and access to education. They must look for jobs and housing while also adhering to shelter rules. Their parenting is public, easily observed, and monitored by others. What they need is to be involved with a meaningful social support system that links them to organizations and professionals in the community who might offer resources and options that support them to engage in effective parenting.

Ineffective Discipline

A once-popular guidebook for parents declared, "Under no circumstances should you ever punish your child!!" (Moyer, 1974, p. 40). Punishment implies an attempt to get even with the child, whereas **discipline** involves helping the child overcome a problem. Parents often struggle with how forceful to be in response to undesired behavior. The Smiths are a good example of this struggle. And, indeed, the research on parental styles of discipline is finding that the question of the appropriate style of parenting young children is very complex.

A good place to begin this discussion is with the work of Diana Baumrind (1971), who, after extensive research, described three parenting styles—authoritarian, authoritative, and permissive—that use different combinations of two factors: warmth and control (see Exhibit 4.4). The **authoritarian parenting** style uses low warmth and high control. These parents favor punishment and negative reinforcement, and children are treated as submissive. Children reared under an authoritarian parenting style have been found to become hostile and moody and have difficulty managing stress (Carey, 1994). Baumrind considered the **authoritative parenting** style, in which parents consider the child's viewpoints but remain in control, to be the most desirable approach to discipline and behavior management. The authoritative parenting style has been found to be associated with academic achievement, self-esteem, and social competence (see Domenech Rodriguez, Donovick, & Crowley, 2009). The **permissive parenting** style accepts children's behavior without attempting to modify it. Baumrind suggested that children reared from the permissive parenting orientation are cheerful but demonstrate little if any impulse control. In

Exhibit 4.4 Three Parenting Styles

Parenting Style	Description	Type of Discipline
Authoritarian	Parents who use this type of parenting are rigid and controlling. Rules are narrow and specific, with little room for negotiation, and children are expected to follow the rules without explanation.	Cold and harsh Physical force No explanation of rules provided
Authoritative	These parents are more flexible than authoritarian parents. Their rules are more reasonable, and they leave opportunities for compromises and negotiation.	Warm and nurturing Positive reinforcement Set firm limits and provide rationale behind rules and decisions
Permissive	The parents' rules are unclear, and children are left to make their own decisions.	Warm and friendly toward their children No direction given

SOURCE: Adapted from Baumrind, 1971

addition, these children are overly dependent and have low levels of self-reliance. The Smiths' style of parenting probably fits here. Certainly, Terri Smith's behavior mirrors behavior exhibited by children reared with the permissive style. In later work, Baumrind (1991) presented a fourth parenting style, **disengaged parenting**, parents who are aloof, withdrawn, and unresponsive. Baumrind's typology of parenting styles has been the building block of much theorizing and research on parenting styles and child outcomes.

Stephen Greenspan (2006) questions Baumrind's suggestion that authoritative parenting is the best parenting. He suggests that Baumrind paid too little attention to the context in which parental discipline occurs, arguing that there are times to exercise control and times to tolerate a certain level of behavioral deviance and that a wise parent knows the difference between these types of situations. Greenspan proposes that another dimension of parenting should be added to Baumrind's two dimensions of warmth and control. He calls this dimension "tolerance" and recommends a style of parenting called "harmonious." He suggests that harmonious parents are warm and set limits when they feel they are called for,

overlooking some child behaviors in the interests of facilitating child autonomy and family harmony. It seems that many parents, like Terri Smith's parents, struggle with knowing which situations call for firm control and which ones call for tolerating some defiance.

Parenting styles are prescribed in part by the community and the culture; therefore, it is not surprising that there is growing sentiment that Baumrind's parenting typology may be a good model for understanding parenting in White, middle-class families, but may not work as well for understanding parenting in other cultural groups. We examine two streams of research that have explored racial and ethnic variations in parenting styles: research on Latino families and research on African American families.

Strong support has not been found for Baumrind's parenting typology in research on Latino parenting styles. Some researchers have described Latino parenting as permissive and others have described it as authoritarian. One research team (Domenech Rodriguez et al., 2009), like Greenspan, suggests that another dimension of parenting should be added to Baumrind's two-dimension model of warmth and control. They call this dimension "autonomy granting," which they describe as allowing children autonomy of individual expression in the family. This seems to be very close to what Greenspan meant by "tolerance," because he writes of tolerance of emotional expression in the spirit of autonomy. Domenech Rodriguez and colleagues (2009) suggest that these three dimensions—warmth, control, and autonomy granting—can be configured in different ways to produce eight different parenting styles:

Authoritative: high warmth, high control, high autonomy granting

Authoritarian: low warmth, high control, low autonomy granting

Permissive: high warmth, low control, high autonomy granting

Neglectful: low warmth, low control, low autonomy granting

Protective: high warmth, high control, low autonomy granting

Cold: low warmth, high control, high autonomy granting

Affiliative: high warmth, low control, low autonomy granting

Neglectful II: low warmth, low control, high autonomy granting

In their preliminary research, which involved direct observation of 56 first-generation Latino American families, they found that the majority (61%) used a protective parenting style but had different expectations for male and female children. There seems to be merit in adding the dimension of autonomy granting, because it may help to capture the parenting styles of cultural groups that are less individualistic than European American culture.

There is a relatively long line of research that has questioned the appropriateness of applying Baumrind's model to understand African American parenting, and the issues are proving to be complex. Much of this research has looked at the use of physical discipline, with the finding that physical discipline causes disruptive behaviors in White families but not Black families (see Lau, Litrownik, Newton, Black, & Everson, 2006, for a review of this research). Researchers have suggested that Black children may regard physical discipline as a legitimate parenting behavior because there is a culture of using physical discipline out of "concern for the child": high levels of firm control are used along with high levels of warmth and affection. Conversely, it is argued that White children may regard physical discipline as an act of aggression because it is often used when parents are angry and out of control (Lansford, Deater-Deckard, Dodge, Bates, & Pettit, 2004). The idea is that the context of the physical discipline and the meaning made of it will influence its impact. However, research by Lau et al. (2006) did not replicate earlier research that found that the effects of physical discipline differed by race. They found that for both Black and White children, physical discipline exacerbated impulsive, aggressive, and noncompliant behaviors for children who had exhibited behavioral problems at an early age. However, they also found that parental warmth protected against later problems in White children but seemed to exacerbate early problems in Black children. The researchers concluded that professionals must recognize that parenting may need to take different forms in different communities. Clearly, this is an issue that needs further investigation.

Research has also indicated differences in parenting style based on the socioeconomic environment in which parenting occurs (Slatcher & Trentacosta, 2012). Low-income parents have been noted to be more authoritarian than more economically advantaged parents. Using observation methods, one research team found that the socioeconomic differences in parenting styles is not that straightforward, however. They found that middle-class parents routinely use subtle forms of control while, at the same time, trying to instill autonomy in their children. Their children spend a large portion of their time under adult supervision, in one activity or another. The researchers also found that low-income parents tend to value conformity but allow their school-aged children to spend considerable leisure time in settings where they do not have adult supervision, consequently affording them considerable autonomy (Weininger & Lareau, 2009).

Findings from studies about punishment and young children indicate that punishment is often used in response to early childhood behavior that is age appropriate. So rather than encouraging the independence that is otherwise expected for a child, such age-appropriate behavior is discouraged (Culp, McDonald Culp, Dengler, & Maisano, 1999). In addition, evidence indicates that brain development can be affected by the stress created by punishment or physical discipline (Glaser, 2000). Harsh punishment and physical discipline interfere with the neural connection process that begins in infancy and continues throughout early childhood. But for many low-income parents, harsh punishment may be less an issue of control or "bad parenting" than an effort to cope with a desperate situation.

As you can see, there are many controversies about effective parenting for young children, and this is an issue about which parents and professionals often have strong feelings. Research is beginning to recognize that different parenting styles may work well in different developmental niches. To make the issue even more complicated, scholars such as Judith Rich Harris (1998) and Steven Pinker (2002) argue that behavioral traits have such a strong genetic component that we should avoid overemphasizing the role of parenting style in behavioral outcomes. In fact, they argue that we have overemphasized the role of families in shaping behavior, other than by providing genetic heritage. Harris also argues that the peer group and community have more impact on child identity and behavior than parents. No doubt, Harris and Pinker would argue that the inconsistent findings about the impact of parenting styles are evidence that parenting style is not a supremely important variable in child development. Of course, we are learning more about the genetic component of human behavior, but we are also learning about the plasticity of the brain to be affected by experience. Parents are a very large part of that experience throughout life, but in early childhood, other people come to be a part of the context of ongoing brain development. Recent research on *epigenetics* is uncovering how environments affect gene expression and providing convincing evidence of the important role of the social environment for turning genes on or silencing them (Combs-Orme, 2013). In an era of great advancements in the biological sciences, epigenetic research is reminding us that "social workers can have their biggest influence through social policies that work hand in hand with nature to prevent the development of many of the problems that plague our nation and world (Combs-Orme, 2013, p. 28).

Divorce

The divorce rate in the United States increased steadily from the mid-19th century through the 1970s, except for a steep drop in the 1950s; it stabilized in the 1980s and has declined slightly since then (Fine, Ganong, & Demo, 2010). It is estimated that more than half of the children born in the 1990s spent some of their childhood in a single-parent household (Anderson, 2005). Compared with parents in two-parent families, single parents work longer hours, experience greater stress, have more economic problems, and have less emotional support (Anderson & Anderson, 2011). Following divorce, about two thirds of children live with their mother, and most women and children experience a sharp and, unfortunately, long-term decline in economic well-being after divorce (Fine et al., 2010).

Researchers have come to very different conclusions about the effects of divorce on children. Some have found that children have severe and long-term problems following divorce (Wallerstein & Blakeslee, 1989). Others, using larger and more representative samples, have found less severe and more short-term effects of divorce on children (Barber & Demo, 2006). It has been suggested that the negative effects children experience may actually be the result of parents' responses to divorce rather than the divorce itself (Hetherington &

> How are young children affected by this historical trend toward high rates of divorce?

Kelly, 2002). After reviewing the disparate findings, Emery (1999) came to the following conclusions:

- Divorce is stressful for children.
- Divorce leads to higher levels of adjustment and mental health problems for children.
- Most children are resilient and adjust well to divorce.
- Children report considerable pain, unhappy memories, and continued distress about their parents' divorce.
- Postdivorce family interaction has a great influence on children's adjustment after divorce.

Several factors may protect children from long-term adjustment problems when their parents divorce. One significant parental issue is the relationship the parents maintain during and after the divorce. With minimal conflict between the parents about custody, visitation, and child-rearing issues, and with parents' positive attitude toward each other, children experience fewer negative consequences (Hetherington & Kelly, 2002). Unfortunately, many children, like Jack Lewis in the case study, end up as noncombatants in the middle of a war, trying to avoid or defuse raging anger and disagreement between the two parents. Other protective factors are higher levels of predivorce adjustment, adequate provision of economic resources, and nurturing relationships with both parents (Fine et al., 2010).

Children who live in families where divorce results in economic hardship are at special risk. Chronic financial stress takes its toll on the mental and physical health of the residential parent, who is usually the mother. The parent often becomes less supportive and engages in inconsistent and harsh discipline. In these situations, children become distressed, often developing difficulties in cognitive and social development (Fine et al., 2010).

In early childhood, children are more vulnerable than older children to the emotional and psychological consequences of separation and divorce (Wallerstein & Corbin, 1991). One reason may be that young children have difficulty understanding divorce and often believe that the absent parent is no longer a member of the family and will never be seen again. In addition, because of young children's egocentrism, they often feel that the divorce is a result of their behavior and experience the absent parent's leaving as a rejection of them. One wonders if Jack Lewis thinks he not only caused his father to leave but also caused him to become the devil.

Violence

Many parents complain that keeping violence away from children requires tremendous work even in the best of circumstances. Children witness violence on television and through video and computer games and hear about it through many other sources. In the worst of circumstances, young children not only are exposed to violence but become victims of it as well. This section discusses three types of violence experienced by many young children: community violence, domestic violence, and child maltreatment.

Community Violence

In some neighborhoods, acts of violence are so common that the communities are labeled "war zones." However, most residents prefer not to be combatants. When surveyed, mothers in a Chicago housing project ranked neighborhood violence as their number one concern and as the condition that most negatively affects the quality of their life and the lives of their children (Dubrow & Garbarino, 1989). Unfortunately, neighborhood violence has become a major health issue for children (Krug, Dahlberg, Mercy, Zwi, & Lozano, 2002).

A number of years ago, the first author (Debra) had the opportunity to observe the effects of community violence up close when she took her daughter to get her hair braided by someone who lived in a housing project, an acquaintance of a friend. Because the hair-braiding procedure takes several hours, she and her daughter were in the home for an extended period. While they were there, the news was released that Tupac Shakur (a popular rap singer) had died from gunshot injuries received earlier. An impromptu gathering of friends and relatives of the woman who was doing the braiding ensued. Ten men and women in their early 20s, along with their young children, gathered to discuss the shooting and to pay tribute to Tupac, who had been one of their favorite artists. As Tupac's music played in the background, Debra was struck by several themes:

- Many in the room told of a close relative who had died as a result of neighborhood violence. Debra noticed on the wall of the apartment three framed programs from funerals of young men. She later learned that these dead men were a brother and two cousins of the woman who lived in the apartment. All three had been killed in separate violent incidents in their neighborhood.

- A sense of hopelessness permeated the conversation. The men especially had little hope of a future, and most thought they would be dead by age 40. Clinicians who work with young children living in neighborhoods in which violence is prevalent relate similar comments from children (National Center for Clinical Infant Programs, 1992). When asked if he had decided what he wanted to be when he grew up, one child is quoted as saying, "Why should I? I might not grow up" (p. 25).

- Perhaps related to the sense of hopelessness was an embracing of violence. Debra observed that during lighter moments in the conversation, the guests would chuckle about physical confrontations between common acquaintances.

Ironically, as Debra and her daughter were about to leave, gunshots sounded and the evening get-together was temporarily interrupted. Everyone, including the children, ran out of the apartment to see what had happened. For Debra, the significance of the evening was summarized in one of the last comments she heard before leaving. One of the men stated, "If all that money didn't save Tupac, what chance do we have?" It is interesting to note that Tupac's music and poetry continue to be idolized. Many still identify with his descriptions of hopelessness.

These sorts of conditions are not favorable for adequate child development (Krug et al., 2002).

Investigations into the effects of living in violent neighborhoods support this claim. Children who grow up in a violent environment are reported to demonstrate symptoms of distress, deficient social skills and peer relationships, and difficulty in cognitive and school performance (Farver, Xu, Eppe, Fernandez, & Schwartz, 2005). When Debra and her daughter visited the housing project, for example, they witnessed a 3-year-old telling her mother to "shut up." The mother and child then began hitting each other. Yes, some of this behavior is a result of parenting style, but one cannot help wondering about the influence of living in a violent community.

For many children living in violent neighborhoods, the death of a close friend or family member is commonplace. When the second author (David) was employed at a community child guidance center, he found that appointments were often canceled so the parents could attend funerals. Living so intimately with death has grave effects on young children. In one study of young children whose older siblings had been victims of homicide, the surviving siblings showed symptoms of depression, anxiety, psychosocial impairment, and post-traumatic stress disorder (Freeman, Shaffer, & Smith, 1996). These symptoms are similar to those observed in young children in situations of political and military violence—for example, in Palestinian children in the occupied West Bank (Qouta, Punamaki, & El-Sarraj, 2003) and in children in Cape Town, South Africa (Shields, Nadasen, & Pierce, 2008). Perhaps the label "war zone" is an appropriate one for violent communities. However, positive, affectionate, caregiving relationships—whether by parents or other family members or individuals in the community—can play an important mediating role in how violence is managed by young children (Shields et al., 2008).

Domestic Violence

The family is the social group from whom we expect to receive our greatest love, support, nurturance, and acceptance. And yet family relationships are some of the most violent relationships in many societies. It is

How does psychological age affect children's responses to domestic violence?

estimated that wife beating occurs in about 85% of the world's societies, and husband beating occurs in about 27% (D. Newman, 2012). Some suggest that physical violence between siblings may be the most common form of family violence (Gelles, 2010). Domestic violence may take the form of verbal, psychological, or physical abuse, although physical abuse is the form most often implied. It is difficult to produce accurate statistics about the amount of family violence because what happens in families is usually "behind closed doors." An estimated 275 million children worldwide are exposed each year to violence in their home (UNICEF, 2006).

In early childhood, children respond in a number of ways during violent episodes (Smith, O'Connor, & Berthelsen, 1996). Some children display fright—that is, they cry and scream. Others attempt to stop the violence by ordering the abuser to stop, by physically placing themselves between the mother and the abuser, or by hitting the abuser. Many children attempt to flee by retreating to a different room, turning up the volume on the TV, or trying to ignore the violence.

The effects of domestic violence on children's development are well-documented. Distress, problems with adjustment, characteristics of trauma, and increased behavior problems have all been observed in children exposed to domestic violence (Turner, Finkelhor, & Ormrod, 2006). In addition, these children develop either aggressive behaviors or passive responses, both of which make them potential targets for abuse as teens and adults (Baldry, 2003). Unfortunately, researchers are finding that children who witness intimate partner violence at home are also more likely to be victimized in other ways, including being victims of child maltreatment and community violence. The accumulation of victimization produces great risk for a variety of mental health problems in children (Turner et al., 2006).

In early childhood, children are more vulnerable than school-age children to the effects of living with domestic violence (O'Keefe, 1994). Younger children simply have fewer internal resources to help them cope with the experience. In addition, older children have friendships outside the family for support, whereas younger children rely primarily on the family. Many parents who are victims of domestic violence become emotionally unavailable to their young children. Battered mothers, for example, often become depressed and preoccupied with the abuse and their personal safety, leaving little time and energy for the attention and nurturing needed by young children. Another reason that young children are more vulnerable to the effects of domestic violence is that children ages 3 to 6 lack the skills to verbalize their feelings and thoughts. As a result, thoughts and feelings about the violence get trapped inside and continually infringe on the child's thoughts and emotions. Finally, as in the case of divorce, because of their egocentrism, young children often blame themselves for the domestic abuse.

Domestic violence does not always affect children's long-term development, however. In one study, one third of the children seemed unaffected by the domestic violence they witnessed at home; these children were well adjusted and showed no signs of distress, anxiety, or behavior problems (Spilsbury et al., 2008). Two factors may buffer the effect domestic violence has on children (O'Keefe, 1994):

1. *Amount of domestic violence witnessed by the child.* The more violent episodes children witness, the more likely they are to develop problematic behavior.

2. *Relationship between the child and the mother,* assuming the mother is the victim. If the mother-child relationship remains stable and secure, the probability of the child developing behavioral difficulties decreases significantly— even when the amount of violence witnessed by the child is relatively high.

Interestingly, the father-child relationship in cases of domestic abuse was not found to be related to the child's emotional or psychological development (O'Keefe, 1994). However, this finding should be reviewed with caution because it is often difficult to find fathers to include in this type of research and then to accurately measure the quality of attachment a younger child in such a circumstance experiences with the father or father figure (Mackey, 2001).

Child Maltreatment

It is difficult to estimate the rate of **child maltreatment**, because many incidences are never reported and much that is reported is not determined to be child maltreatment. Approximately 3.4 million referrals were made to Child Protective Services in 2012 involving 6.3 million children (U.S. Department of Health and Human Services, Administration on Children, Youth, and Families, 2012). An estimated 1,640 children died as a result of abuse and/or neglect, and 70% of these victims were younger than 3 years of age. The most prevalent forms of child maltreatment described by the U.S. Children's Bureau include neglect, physical abuse, sexual abuse, and emotional maltreatment. Slightly more girls were victims of child maltreatment in 2012, but boys had a higher incidence of fatal injuries. National incidence data indicate that the majority of child victims in 2012 were either White (44%), African American (21%), or Hispanic (22%). Poverty and the lack of economic resources are correlated with maltreatment, especially physical abuse and neglect (Berger, 2005). In addition, family isolation and lack of a support system, parental drug and alcohol abuse, lack of knowledge regarding child rearing, and parental difficulty in expressing feelings are all related to child maltreatment (Berger, 2005). There is some indication that stress experienced by working parents is also related to child maltreatment (Prasad, 2001).

Child maltreatment creates risks to all aspects of growth and development, as shown in Exhibit 4.5, but children ages birth to 6 are at highest risk of having long-lasting damage (Pecora & Harrison-Jackson, 2011). In their longitudinal research of 180 children born into poverty, Sroufe et al. (2005) found that young children who had been physically abused as toddlers had higher levels of negativity, noncompliance, and distractibility than other children. Those whose mothers were psychologically unavailable demonstrated more avoidance of and anger toward the mother. Children with a history all types of maltreatment had lower self-esteem and agency and demonstrated more behavior problems than other children. Children with a history of neglect were more passive than other children.

PROTECTIVE FACTORS IN EARLY CHILDHOOD

Many of the factors listed in Chapter 3 that promote resiliency during the infant and toddler years are equally relevant during the early childhood years. Other protective factors also come into play (Jenson & Fraser, 2011):

- *Social support.* Social support mediates many potential risks to the development of young children. The presence of social support increases the likelihood of a positive outcome for children whose parents divorce (Garvin, Kalter, & Hansell, 1993), moderates the effects for children who experience violence (Nettles, Mucherah, & Jones, 2000), facilitates better outcomes for children of mothers with mental illness (Oyserman, Bybee, Mowbray, & MacFarlane, 2002), and is even thought to reduce the continuation of abuse for 2- and 3-year-olds who have experienced parental abuse during the first year of life (Kotch et al., 1997). Social support aids young children in several ways (Jenson & Fraser, 2011). Having a consistent and supportive aunt or uncle or preschool teacher who can set firm but loving limits, for example, may buffer the effects of a parent with ineffective skills. At the community level, preschools, religious programs, and the like may help to enhance physical and cognitive skills, self-esteem, and social development. Through social support from family and nonfamily relationships, young children can receive care and support, another identified protective factor.

- *Positive parent-child relationship.* A positive relationship with at least one parent helps children to feel secure and nurtured (Jenson & Fraser, 2011).

Exhibit 4.5   Some Potential Effects of Child Abuse on Growth and Development

Physical Impairments	Cognitive Impairments	Emotional Impairments
Physical Abuse and Neglect		
Burns, scars, fractures, broken bones, damage to vital organs and limbs	Delayed cognitive skills	Negative self-concept
Malnourishment	Delayed language skills	Increased aggressiveness
Physical exposure	Mental retardation	Poor peer relations
Poor skin hygiene	Delayed reality testing	Poor impulse control
Poor (if any) medical care	Overall disruption of thought processes	Anxiety
Poor (if any) dental care		Inattentiveness
Serious medical problems		Avoidant behavior
Serious dental problems		
Failure-to-thrive syndrome		
Death		
Sexual Abuse		
Trauma to mouth, anus, vaginal area	Hyperactivity	Overly adaptive behavior
Genital and rectal pain	Bizarre sexual behavior	Overly compliant behavior
Genital and rectal bleeding		Habit disorders (nail biting)
Genital and rectal tearing		Anxiety
Sexually transmitted disease		Depression
		Sleep disturbances
		Night terrors
		Self-mutilation
Psychological/Emotional Abuse		
	Pessimistic view of life	Alienation
	Anxiety and fear	Intimacy problems
	Distorted perception of world	Low self-esteem
	Deficits in moral development	Depression

Remember from Chapter 3 that a sense of security is the foundation on which young children build initiative during the early childhood years. Even if Jack Lewis never has contact with his father, Charles, a positive relationship with Joyce, his mother, can mediate this loss.

• *Effective parenting.* In early childhood, children need the opportunity to take initiative but also need firm limits, whether they are established by parents or grandparents or someone else who adopts the parent role. Terri Smith, for example, has not been able to establish self-control because her boundaries are not well defined. Effective parenting promotes self-efficacy and self-esteem and provides young children with a model of how they can take initiative within boundaries (Jenson & Fraser, 2011).

- *Self-esteem*. A high level of self-worth may allow young children to persist in mastery of skills despite adverse conditions. Perhaps a high level of self-esteem can enhance Ron's, Rosiland's, and Jack's development despite the disruptions in their lives. In addition, research indicates that self-esteem is a protective factor against the effects of child abuse (Jenson & Fraser, 2011).

- *Intelligence*. Even in young children, a high IQ serves as a protective factor. For example, young children with high IQs were less likely to be affected by maternal psychopathology (Tiet et al., 2001). Others suggest that intelligence results in

success, which leads to higher levels of self-esteem (Jenson & Fraser, 2011). For young children, then, intelligence may contribute to mastery of skills and independence, which may enhance self-esteem. Intelligence may also protect children through increased problem-solving skills, which allow for more effective responses to adverse situations.

Critical Thinking Questions 4.5

What type of parenting style do you think your parents used when you were a child? Did both parents use the same parenting style? Do you think the parenting style(s) used by your parents was effective? How do you think your parents' parenting style was affected by culture? Would you want to use the same parenting style that your parents used if you were a parent? Why or why not?

Implications for Social Work Practice

In summary, knowledge about early childhood has several implications for social work practice with young children:

- Become well acquainted with theories and empirical research about growth and development among young children.
- Continue to promote the elimination of poverty and the advancement of social justice.
- Collaborate with other professionals in the creation of laws, interventions, and programs that assist in the elimination of violence.
- Create and support easy access to services for young children and their parents.
- Assess younger children in the context of their environment.
- Become familiar with the physical and emotional signs of child abuse.
- Directly engage younger children in an age-appropriate intervention process.
- Provide support to parents and help facilitate positive parent-child relationships.
- Encourage and engage both mothers and fathers in the intervention process.
- Provide opportunities for children to increase self-efficacy and self-esteem.
- Help parents understand the potential effects of negative environmental factors on their children.

Key Terms

authoritarian parenting
authoritative parenting

child maltreatment
discipline

disengaged parenting
egocentrism

empathy
fine motor skills
gross motor skills
hostile aggression
instrumental aggression
lateralization
learning play

permissive parenting
perspective taking
physical aggression
preconventional level of moral
   reasoning
prosocial
relational aggression

self-esteem
self-theory
sociodramatic play
symbolic play
transductive reasoning

Active Learning

1. Watch any child-oriented cartoon on television. Describe the apparent and implied messages (both positive and negative) available in the cartoon about race and ethnicity and gender differences. Consider how these messages might affect gender and ethnic development in young children.

2. Observe preschool-age children at play. Record the types of play that you observe. How well do your observations fit with what is described about play in this chapter?

3. The case studies at the beginning of this chapter (Terri, Jack, and Ron and Rosiland) do not specify race or ethnicity of the families. How important an omission did that appear to you? What assumptions did you make about the racial and/or ethnic background of the families? On what basis did you make those assumptions?

Web Resources

American Academy of Child & Adolescent Psychiatry: www.aacap.org

Site presented by the American Academy of Child & Adolescent Psychiatry contains concise and up-to-date information on a variety of issues facing children and their families, including day care, discipline, children and divorce, child abuse, children and TV violence, and children and grief.

Children's Defense Fund: www.childrensdefense.org

Site presented by the Children's Defense Fund, a private nonprofit child advocacy organization, contains information on issues, the Black Community Crusade for Children, the Child Watch Visitation Program, and a parent resource network.

National Family Resiliency Center, Inc. (NFRC): www.divorceabc.com

Site presented by the NFRC contains information about support groups, resources for professionals, and frequently asked questions.

Play Therapy International: www.playtherapy.org

Site presented by Play Therapy International contains reading lists, articles and research, news, and information about training and careers in play therapy.

U.S. Department of Health & Human Services: www.dhhs.gov

Site maintained by the U.S. Department of Health & Human Services contains news and information on health topics, prevention, and safety.

⑤SAGE edge™

Sharpen your skills with SAGE edge at **edge.sagepub.com/hutchisonclc5e**

SAGE edge for students provides a personalized approach to help you accomplish your coursework goals in an easy-to-use learning environment.

CHAPTER 5

Middle Childhood

Leanne Wood Charlesworth

Chapter Outline

Acknowledgments: The author would like to acknowledge the past contributions of Jim Wood and Pamela Viggiani and would like to thank Meena Lall for assistance in writing this chapter.

Opening Questions

- How do our conceptions of middle childhood change over time?

- What types of individual, family, school, community, and other systemic qualities are most conducive to positive development during middle childhood?

- During middle childhood, what factors heighten developmental risk for children, and what supports resilience?

Key Ideas

As you read this chapter, take note of these central ideas:

1. Values and beliefs regarding childhood in general, and middle childhood specifically, are shaped by historical and sociocultural context.

2. During middle childhood, a wide variety of bio/psycho/social/spiritual changes take place across the developmental domains.

3. As children progress through middle childhood, the family environment remains extremely important, while the community environment—including the school—also becomes a significant factor shaping development.

4. During middle childhood, peers have a strong impact on development; peer acceptance is often very important to well-being.

5. Poverty and violence create developmental risk for many children.

CASE STUDY 5.1

Anthony Bryant's Impending Assessment

Anthony is a 6-year-old boy living in an impoverished section of a large city. Anthony's mother, Sephora, was 14 when Anthony was born. Anthony's father, James, 15 when Anthony was born, has always spent a great deal of time with Anthony. Although James now also has a 2-year-old daughter from another relationship, he has told Sephora that Anthony and Sephora are the most important people in his life. Once Anthony was out of diapers, James began spending even more time with him, taking Anthony along to visit friends and, occasionally, on overnight outings.

James's father was murdered when James was a toddler and he rarely sees his mother, who struggles with a serious substance addiction and is known in the neighborhood as a prostitute. James lived with his paternal grandparents until he was in his early teens, when he began to stay with a favorite uncle. Many members of James's large extended family have been incarcerated on charges related to their involvement in the local drug trade. James's favorite uncle is a well-known and widely respected dealer. James himself has been arrested a few times and is currently on probation.

Sephora and Anthony live with her mother. Sephora obtained her general equivalency diploma after Anthony's birth, and she has held a variety of jobs at local fast food chains. Sephora's mother, Cynthia, receives Supplemental Social Security Income/Disability because she has been unable to work for several years because of her advanced rheumatoid arthritis, which was diagnosed when she was a teenager. Sephora remembers her father only as a loud man who often yelled at her when she made noise. He left Cynthia and Sephora when Sephora was 4 years old, and neither has seen him since. Cynthia seemed pleased when Anthony was born and she has been a second mother to him, caring for him while Sephora attends school, works, and socializes with James and her other friends.

Anthony has always been very active and energetic, frequently breaking things and creating "messes" throughout the apartment. To punish Anthony, Cynthia spanks him with a belt or other object—and she sometimes resorts to locking him in his room until he falls asleep. Sephora and James are proud of Anthony's wiry physique and rough and tough play; they have encouraged him to be fearless and not to cry when he is hurt. Both Sephora and James use physical punishment as their main discipline strategy with Anthony, but he usually obeys them before it is needed.

Anthony entered kindergarten at a local public school last fall. When he started school, his teacher told Sephora that he seemed to be a very smart boy, one of the only boys in the class who already knew how to write his name and how to count to 20. It is now spring, however, and Sephora is tired of dealing with Anthony's teacher and other school staff. She has been called at work a number of times, and recently the school social worker requested a meeting with her. Anthony's teacher reports that Anthony will not listen to her and frequently starts fights with the other children in the classroom. Anthony's teacher also states that Anthony constantly violates school rules, like waiting in line and being quiet in the hallways, and he doesn't seem bothered by threats of punishment. Most recently, Anthony's teacher has told Sephora that she would like Anthony assessed by the school psychologist.

CASE STUDY 5.2

Brianna Shaw's New Self-Image

When Brianna was born, her mother, Deborah, was 31 years old with a 13-year-old daughter (Sienna) from a prior, short-lived marriage. Deborah and Michael's relationship was relatively new when Deborah became pregnant with Brianna. Shortly after Deborah announced the pregnancy, Michael moved into her mobile home. Michael and Deborah initially talked about setting a wedding date and pursuing Michael's legal adoption of Sienna, whose father had remarried and was no longer in close contact.

Michael made it clear throughout Deborah's pregnancy that he wanted a son. He seemed very content and supportive of Deborah until around the time the couple found out the baby was a girl. In Sienna's view, Michael became mean and bossy in the months that followed. He started telling Sienna what to do, criticizing Deborah's appearance, and complaining constantly that Deborah wasn't any fun anymore since she stopped drinking and smoking while she was pregnant.

During Brianna's infancy, the couple's relationship began to change even more rapidly. Michael was rarely home and instead spent most of his free time hanging out with old friends. When he did come by, he'd encourage Deborah to leave Brianna with Sienna so the two of them could go out like "old times." Even though her parents were Deborah's full-time day care providers and both Brianna and Sienna were thriving, Deborah was chronically

(Continued)

(Continued)

exhausted from balancing parenting and her full-time job as a nursing assistant. Soon, whenever Michael came by, the couple frequently argued and their shouting matches gradually escalated to Michael threatening to take Brianna away. Michael was soon dating another woman, and his relationship with Deborah and Sienna became increasingly hostile during the following 4 years.

The summer that Brianna turned 5, the local hospital closed down and Deborah lost her job. After talking with her parents, Deborah made the decision to move her daughters to Fairfield, a city 4 hours away from home. An old high school friend had once told Deborah that if she ever needed a job, the large hospital her friend worked for had regular openings and even offered tuition assistance. Within 2 months, Deborah had sold her mobile home, obtained a full-time position with her friend's employer, and signed a lease for a small townhouse in a suburb known for its high-quality school system.

When Brianna started kindergarten in their new town, her teacher described her to Deborah as shy and withdrawn. Deborah remembered reading something in the school newsletter about a social skills group run by a school social worker, and she asked if Brianna could be enrolled. Gradually, the group seemed to make a difference and Brianna began to act more like her old self, forming several friendships during the following 2 years.

Today, Brianna is 8 years old and has just entered third grade. Brianna usually leaves for school on the bus at 8:00 a.m., and Deborah picks her up from an afterschool program at 5:45 p.m. When possible, Sienna picks Brianna up earlier, after her own classes at a local community college are over. Brianna still spends summers with her grandparents in the rural area where she was born. Academically, she has thus far excelled in school, but a new concern is Brianna's weight. Brianna is 49 inches tall and weighs 72 pounds. Until the last year or so, Brianna seemed unaware of the fact that many people viewed her as overweight. In the last several months, however, Brianna has told Sienna and Deborah various stories about other children calling her "fat" and making other comments about her size. Deborah feels that Brianna is increasingly moody and angry when she is home. Brianna recently asked Deborah why she is "fat" and told Sienna that she just wishes she were dead.

CASE STUDY 5.3

Manuel Vega's Difficult Transition

Slightly built 11-year-old Manuel is in sixth grade in Greenville, Mississippi. He was born in Texas where his mother, Maria, and father, Estaban, met. For Estaban, it has been an interesting journey from his hometown in Mexico to Mississippi. For generations, Estaban's family lived and worked near Izucar de Matamoros, a small city in Mexico on the Inter-American Highway. By the time he was in his early 20s, Estaban began to look for better paying work and was able to get his license to haul products from Izucar de Matamoros to larger cities, including Mexico City. Estaban and one of his four brothers eventually moved to a medium-sized city where his employer, the owner of a small trucking company, provided an apartment for several of his single truckers.

After 3 productive years in the trucking industry, the company went bankrupt. Estaban wanted to pursue his dream of owning his own trucking company but instead began working as a day laborer and eventually made his way to Laredo, Texas, where he met and married Maria. Although both Maria and Estaban's formal schooling ended relatively early, both acquired a basic command of English while living in Laredo. Aware of the family's financial challenges, Maria's uncle Arturo urged the family to move to the Mississippi Delta where he owns a Mexican restaurant and wholesale business. Uncle Arturo was hopeful that Maria would enrich his menu with her mastery of Mexican cuisine, and he promised employment for Estaban, hauling Mexican specialty food staples to the growing number of Mexican restaurants in the Delta, ranging from Memphis to Biloxi.

Almost 3 years ago, Estaban and Maria decided to take Arturo up on his offer, and together with their two sons, they moved to Greenville. Their older son, Carlos, never adjusted to school life in Mississippi. Now 16, Carlos did not return to school this fall. Instead, he began working full-time for his father loading and unloading the truck and providing his more advanced English language capacity to open up new business markets. At first Maria and Estaban resisted the idea of Carlos dropping out of school, but he was insistent. Carlos knows the family finances are in peril and that he is needed. Manuel yearns to be like his older brother, but Carlos has always considered it his job to protect and care for his younger brother. He tells Manuel that he must stay in school to acquire the "book learning" that he could never grasp.

Leaving the warm embrace of their former neighborhood in Texas for the Mississippi Delta has been hard for Manuel. In Manuel's old school, most students and teachers spoke or knew how to speak Spanish, and Manuel always felt he fit in. Now, Manuel is one of a small percentage of Spanish-speaking students in his new school, where the vast majority of students and staff are African American and speak only English.

In the school setting, Manuel's new English as a second language (ESL) teacher, Ms. Jones, is concerned about him. His teacher reports that he often seems sullen. Ms. Jones has observed that Manuel frequently appears to be daydreaming, and when teachers try to talk with him, he seems to withdraw further. Ms. Jones knows that Manuel's records from Texas indicate that he was a successful, socially adjusted primary-school student. However, his records also show that his reading and writing performance was below grade level starting in first grade. Ms. Jones has found that if she speaks with Manuel in Spanish while taking a walk around the school, he will share stories about his family and his old neighborhood and friends.

HISTORICAL PERSPECTIVE ON MIDDLE CHILDHOOD

Historically, middle childhood represented a period during which children became increasingly able to play a role in maintaining or improving the economic status of the family and community (Fass & Mason, 2000). Beginning in the early 20th century, however, a radical shift occurred in the Western world's perceptions of children. Children passing through middle childhood became categorized as "school age," and their education became a societal priority. Child labor and compulsory education laws supported and reinforced this shift in societal values.

In parts of the United States and world, however, children continue to play important economic roles for families. Many children from the most impoverished families live and work on the streets, and in countries striving toward universal primary school education, children must balance their economic productivity with time spent in school (Karraker, 2013). Although this significant diversity exists among children, middle childhood is generally viewed in the United States as a time when education, play, and social activities should dominate daily life (Cole & Durham, 2008).

The age range classified as middle childhood is subject to debate. In the United States, it is most often defined as the period beginning at approximately ages 5 or 6 and ending at approximately ages 10 to 12 (Marotz & Allen, 2013). It is common to think of middle childhood as consisting of an early (ages 6 through 8) and later (ages 9 through 11) phase.

Images of middle childhood often include children who are physically active and intellectually curious, making new friends and learning new things. But as Anthony Bryant, Brianna Shaw, and Manuel Vega demonstrate, middle childhood is filled with both opportunities and challenges. For some children, it is a period of particular vulnerability. In fact, when we think of school-age children, images of child poverty and related school inequities, family and community violence, sexual victimization or **precociousness** (early development), learning challenges, and physical and emotional ailments such as anxiety, depression, asthma, and attention deficit/hyperactivity disorder (ADHD) may dominate our thoughts. In some parts of the world, children in this developmental phase are vulnerable to war, forced enlistment as soldiers, slave-like labor, and being sold as sex workers in an international child trafficking economy (Human Rights Watch, 2013).

MIDDLE CHILDHOOD IN THE MULTIGENERATIONAL FAMILY

During middle childhood, the child's social world expands dramatically. Although the family is not the only relevant force in a child's life, it remains an extremely significant influence on development. Families are often in a constant state of change, and so the school-age child's relationships with family members and the environment the family inhabits are likely to be different from the child's first experiences of family. For example, consider the changes in Anthony Bryant's, Brianna Shaw's, and Manuel Vega's families over time and the ways in which family relationships have been continually evolving.

How are Anthony, Brianna, and Manuel affected by their multigenerational families?

Despite the geographical distances that often exist between family members today, nuclear families are still emotional subsystems of extended,

multigenerational family systems. The child's nuclear family is significantly shaped by past, present, and anticipated future experiences, events, and relationships (McGoldrick, Carter, & Garcia-Preto, 2011b). Profoundly important factors such as historical events, culture, and social structure, as well as family members' experiences and characteristics, often influence children through their family systems. Relatives' experiences or characteristics may be biological and therefore fairly obvious, or they may include more nebulous qualities such as acquired emotional strengths or wounds. For example, consider Brianna's maternal grandfather, who is African American and grew up with the legacy of slavery under Jim Crow laws and legal segregation in the United States, or Anthony's maternal grandmother, who as a child was repeatedly victimized sexually. Children become connected to events or phenomena such as a familial history of child abuse or a group history of discrimination and oppression (restrictions and exploitation), even in the absence of direct experiences in the present generation (see Miller & Garran, 2008).

Thus, the developing school-age child is shaped not only by events and individuals explicitly evident in the present time and physical space but also by those events and individuals who have more directly influenced the lives of their parents, grandparents, great-grandparents, and beyond. These influences—familial, cultural, and historical—shape all aspects of every child's development in an abstract and complex fashion.

Critical Thinking Questions 5.1

When you think of middle childhood for Anthony Bryant, Brianna Shaw, and Manuel Vega, do you think of it as a time of promise or a time of vulnerability? Explain. What do you see as the strengths in their multigenerational families? What do you see as the special challenges in their multigenerational families?

DEVELOPMENT IN MIDDLE CHILDHOOD

New developmental tasks are undertaken in middle childhood, and development occurs within multiple dimensions. Although each developmental domain is considered separately for our analytical purposes, changes in the developing child reflect the dynamic interaction continuously occurring across these dimensions.

Physical Development

During middle childhood, physical development typically continues steadily, but children of the same chronological age may vary greatly in stature, weight, and sexual development. For most children, height and weight begin to advance less rapidly than during prior developmental phases, but steady growth continues. The nature and pace of physical growth during this period are shaped by both genetic and environmental influences in interaction (Jurimae, 2013).

> What impact do these differences in biological age have on psychological and social development during middle childhood?

As children progress from kindergarten to early adolescence, their fine and gross motor skills typically advance. In the United States today, children in this age range are often encouraged to gain a high level of mastery over physical skills associated with a particular interest such as dance, sports, or music. However, medical professionals caution that school-age children continue to possess unique physical vulnerabilities related to the growth process and thus are susceptible to injuries associated with excessive physical activity or training (Jurimae, 2013).

Middle childhood is a developmental phase of entrenchment or eradication of many potent risk or protective factors manifesting in this developmental domain (Mah & Ford-Jones, 2012). Focusing on risk, for children residing in chronically impoverished countries and communities, issues such as malnutrition and disease threaten physical health. Seemingly innocuous issues such as poor dental hygiene or mild visual impairment may become more serious as they begin to impact other areas of development such as cognitive, emotional, or social well-being. In the United States, health issues such as asthma and obesity are of contemporary concern and often either improve or become more severe during middle childhood. Susceptibility to risk varies across socioeconomic and ethnic groups. Unintentional death and physical injury (for example, motor vehicle injuries, drowning, playground accidents, and sports-related traumatic brain injury) represent a major threat to well-being among school-age children in general (Gilchrist, 2012). Moreover, as children move into middle childhood they gain other new risks: approximately one third of rapes occur before age 12, homicide risk increases, and among children ages 10 to 14, suicide is a leading cause of death (Black et al., 2011).

Some of the physical injuries unique to middle childhood may be indirectly facilitated by declines in adult supervision and adult overestimation of children's safety-related knowledge and ability to implement safety practices. In addition, children's continued physical and cognitive (specifically, judgment and decision-making processes) vulnerabilities combine, potentially, with an increasing propensity to engage in risk-taking activities and behaviors (Berk, 2012).

Many children experience puberty during middle childhood. Focusing on racial differences, several studies have found that in the United States, non-Hispanic African American girls begin puberty earlier than other children (National Institute of Health, 2013; Reynolds & Juvonen, 2012). A trend toward earlier age of puberty onset, particularly among girls, has brought much attention to the potential causes. Most recently, research on this topic has examined in more depth the linkages between obesity and puberty onset among girls (Aleccia, 2013) and has also begun to reflect new interest in early puberty onset among boys (American Academy of Pediatrics, 2012).

Photo 5.1 New developmental tasks are undertaken in middle childhood, and development occurs within interacting developmental domains.

© Bonnie Jacobs/iStockphoto.com

A wide variety of multidisciplinary researchers across the globe are examining available data regarding the causes of puberty onset. It is evident that a complex range of interacting factors, crossing the biopsychosocial spectrum, are relevant to understanding puberty onset. Wang, Needham, and Barr (2005) identify nutritional status; genetic predisposition, including race/ethnicity; and environmental chemical exposure as associated with age of puberty onset.

It should be noted that careful examination of puberty onset trends suggests that the "trend toward earlier onset of puberty in U.S. girls over the past 50 years is not as strong as some reports suggested" (Kaplowitz, 2006, p. 487). Specifically, the average age of menarche decreased from approximately 14.8 years in 1877 to about 12.8

years in the mid-1960s (Kaplowitz, 2006). Most researchers have concluded that the general trend observed during this broad historical time period is the result of health and nutrition improvement within the population as a whole. Recent examination of available data concludes that there is little evidence to support a significant continued decline in more recent years. Nevertheless, some have suggested that our public education and health systems should consider early health education for children because the onset of puberty may impact social and emotional development and has traditionally been associated with a variety of "risky and unhealthy behaviors" (Wang et al., 2005, p. 1101).

Indeed a relationship, albeit complex, appears to exist between puberty and social development for both boys and girls (Santrock, 2009).

During middle childhood, girls experiencing early onset puberty may be at particular risk (Mendle, Turkheimer, & Emery, 2007). Intervention focused on self-protection and individual rights and responsibilities may be beneficial, and schools committed to the safety of their students must diligently educate staff and students about sexual development and risk.

Middle childhood is the developmental phase when increased public attention and self-awareness is directed toward various aspects of physical growth, skill, or activity patterns and levels deemed outside the normal range. Because physical development is outwardly visible, it affects perceptions of self and the way a child is viewed and treated by peers and adults. School-age children constantly compare themselves with others, and physical differences are often the topic of discussion. Many children worry about being "normal." Reassurance by adults that physical development varies among people and that all development is "normal" is crucial.

Cognitive Development

For most children, the acquisition of cognitive abilities that occurs early in middle childhood allows the communication of thoughts with increasing complexity. Public education plays a major role in the cognitive development of children in the United States, if only because most children attend school throughout the formative years of such development. When Anthony Bryant, Brianna Shaw, and Manuel Vega first entered school, their readiness to confront the challenges and opportunities that school presents was shaped by prior experiences. Anthony, for example, entered school generally prepared for the academic emphases associated with kindergarten. He was perhaps less prepared for the social expectations present in the school environment.

Jean Piaget (1936/1952) played a significant role in our understanding of the cognitive development of children. In his terms, children start school during the second stage (preoperational thought) and finish school when they are completing the fourth and final stage of cognitive development (formal operations). In the third stage (concrete operations), children are able to solve concrete problems using logical problem-solving strategies. By the end of middle childhood, they enter the formal operations stage and become able to solve hypothetical problems using abstract concepts (refer back to Exhibit 3.5 for an overview of Piaget's stages of cognitive development). Examples of expanding cognitive capacity include pondering complex conceptual questions, advancing skill in categorizing and analyzing complicated systems of ideas or objects, and enhanced ability to solve problems. As you observe children moving into and through middle childhood, you will note these rapid gains in intellectual processes (Adler-Tapia, 2012). These brain-produced shifts in the child's understanding of himself or herself and the surrounding world are consistent with the transition into Piaget's concrete operational and formal operations stages of cognitive development.

Beyond Piaget's ideas, brain development and cognitive functioning during middle childhood traditionally received less attention than research devoted to brain development in prior developmental phases. Indeed, as pointed out in Chapter 3, infancy, toddlerhood, and early childhood appear to represent "sensitive periods" in brain development. By middle childhood, a child's brain development and functioning have been profoundly shaped by the nature of earlier experiences and development. And yet remarkable brain plasticity continues, with brain structure and functioning capable of growth and refinement throughout life (National Research Council, 2012). The conceptual framework perhaps most useful to understanding this potential and the processes at play is nonlinear dynamic systems theory, also known as complexity or chaos theory (Applegate & Shapiro, 2005). Applied to this context, this theoretical perspective proposes that changes in one area or aspect of the neurological system may stimulate or interact with other neurological or broader physiological system components in an unpredictable fashion, potentially leading to unanticipated outcomes. Brain development follows a coherent developmental

Photo 5.2   Middle childhood is a critical time for children to acquire a sense of self-confidence and develop conceptual thought.

© Josh Hodge/iStockphoto.com

process, but brain plasticity in particular demonstrates the role of complex nonlinear neurological system dynamics and processes.

At least two aspects of brain development are of particular interest when we focus on middle childhood. The first is the idea that different brain regions appear to develop according to different timelines. In other words, middle childhood may be a "sensitive period" for certain aspects of brain development not yet clearly understood. The second important idea is the notion that brain synapses (connections between cells in the nervous system) that are initially present as children enter this developmental phase may be gradually eliminated if they are not used. As reported in Chapter 3, there seems to be a pattern of *synaptogenesis*, or creation and fine-tuning of brain synapses, in the

human cerebral cortex during early childhood, which appears to be followed by a gradual pruning process that eventually reduces the overall number of synapses to their adult levels (National Research Council, 2012).

The **cerebral cortex** is the outer layer of gray matter in the human brain thought to be responsible for complex, high-level intellectual functions such as memory, language, and reasoning. Ongoing positive and diverse learning opportunities during middle childhood may help facilitate continued brain growth and optimal refinement of existing structures. Variations in brain development and functioning play a critical role in learning, emotional responses, and patterns of behavior (Davidson & Begley, 2012; Kahneman, 2011). During middle childhood, identification and potential diagnosis of special needs, including issues such as ADHD, typically peaks. In recent years, an area of public interest is gender- or sex-based differences in brain functioning and, possibly, learning styles. This interest has been stimulated in part by evidence suggesting that in some countries, such as the United States, boys are currently at higher risk than girls for poor literacy performance, special education placement, and school dropout (Weaver-Hightower, 2008).

It has been suggested that brain-based behavior and learning style differences may be responsible for the somewhat stable trends observed in gender differences in educational achievement (Gurian, 2011). The importance of sex or gender in shaping the human experience cannot be overstated. Gender is a profoundly influential organizing factor shaping human development, and its biological correlates may impact behavior and learning processes in ways we do not clearly understand. However, gender is but one of several personal and group characteristics relevant to understanding educational privilege specifically as well as risk and protection generally. Unfortunately, developmental research historically lacked rigor and did not devote sufficient attention to females and children belonging to nondominant groups.

A number of contemporary developmental theorists have focused on assessing the relevance and applicability of traditional developmental tasks to all children. Most agree that the central ideas of the theorists summarized in Exhibit 5.1 continue to be meaningful. For example, Erikson's thoughts remain widely recognized as relevant to our understanding of school-age children. In some areas, however, these developmental theories have been critiqued and subsequently expanded. This is particularly true in the area of moral development.

The best-known theory of moral development is Lawrence Kohlberg's stage theory (for an overview of this theory, refer back to Exhibit 4.2). Kohlberg's research on moral reasoning found that children do not enter the second level of *conventional moral reasoning*, or morality based on approval of authorities or upon upholding societal standards, until about age 9 or 10, sometime after they have the cognitive skills for such reasoning. Robert Coles (1987, 1997) expanded on Kohlberg's work and emphasized the distinction between moral imagination—the gradually

Exhibit 5.1 Phases and Tasks of Middle Childhood

Theorist	Phase or Task	Description
Freud (1938/1973)	Latency	Sexual instincts become less dominant; superego develops further.
Erikson (1950)	Industry versus inferiority	Capacity to cooperate and create develops; result is sense of either mastery or incompetence.
Piaget (1936/1952)	Concrete operational	Reasoning becomes more logical but remains at concrete level; principle of conservation is learned.
Piaget (1932/1965)	Moral realism and autonomous morality	Conception of morality changes from absolute and external to relative and internal.
Kohlberg (1969)	Preconventional and conventional morality	Reasoning based on punishment and reward is replaced by reasoning based on formal law and external opinion.
Selman (1976)	Self-reflective perspective taking	Ability develops to view one's own actions, thoughts, and emotions from another's perspective.

developed capacity to reflect on what is right and wrong—and moral conduct, pointing out that a "well-developed conscience does not translate, necessarily, into a morally courageous life" (p. 3). Analyses of the interplay of imagination and conduct within more recent research supports Coles's initial ideas in this area (Gutzwiller-Helfenfinger, Gasser, & Malti, 2010). Moral *behavior* is shaped by daily experiences, typically reflecting the way the child is treated in his or her various environments such as home and school. The school-age child often pays close attention to the discrepancies between the "moral voices" and actions of the adults in his or her world, including parents, friends' parents, relatives, teachers, and coaches. Each new and significant adult sets an example for the child, sometimes complementing and sometimes contradicting the values emphasized in the child's home environment.

Carol Gilligan (1982) extensively criticized Kohlberg's theory of moral development as paying inadequate attention to girls' "ethic of care" and the keen emphasis girls often place on relationships and the emotions of others. Consistent with Gilligan's ideas, a number of developmental theorists have argued that girls possess heightened **interrelational intelligence**, which is based on emotional and social intelligence and is similar to Howard Gardner's concept of interpersonal intelligence (Borysenko, 1996). Such developmentalists, drawing on feminist scholarship, point out that both girls and boys advance rapidly in the cognitive and moral developmental domains during middle childhood, but the sexes may be distinct in their approaches to social relationships and interactions, and such differences may shape the nature of development in all domains (Borysenko, 1996; Gilligan, 1982; Taylor, Gilligan, & Sullivan, 1995). It is also important to note that collectivist-oriented societies put a high value on connectedness, and research with groups from collectivist societies indicates that they do not score well on Kohlberg's model of moral development. Some scholars argue that moral development must be understood in cultural context (Gardiner & Kosmitzki, 2011; Haidt, 2013).

As children's cognitive abilities advance, understanding of group identities shifts. Children become much more aware of ethnic identities and other aspects of diversity (such as socioeconomic status and gender identities) during their middle childhood years. Cultural awareness and related beliefs are shaped by the nature of experiences such as exposure to diversity within the family and community, including school, contexts. Unlike the preschoolers' attraction to "black-and-white" classifications, children progressing through middle childhood are increasingly capable of understanding the complexities of group memberships; in other words, they are cognitively capable of rejecting oversimplistic stereotypes and recognizing the complexities present within all individuals and groups (Davies, 2011).

McAdoo (2001) asserts that, compared with children who identify with the majority group, children from nondominant groups are much more likely to possess awareness of their own group identity or identities as well as majority group characteristics. Thus, a now widely recognized developmental task associated with middle childhood is the acquisition of positive group identity or identities (Azzi, 2011). The terms *bicultural* or *multicultural competence* are used to refer to the skills children from nondominant groups must acquire in order to survive and thrive developmentally (Lum, 2011).

Manuel speaks English as a second language and in some ways is representative of many school-age children. In the United States, approximately 20% of all children ages 5 through 17 enrolled in school speak a language other than English at home; this figure is expected to continue to increase steadily in the future (Kominski, Shin, & Marotz, 2008). Multi- and bilingual children in the United States were traditionally thought to be at risk of developmental deficits. However, significant research demonstrates that bilingualism may have a positive impact on cognitive development. When controlling for socioeconomic status, bilingual children may perform better than monolingual children in certain areas of intellectual and academic performance (Korkman et al., 2012; Yow &

Markman, 2011). With growing understanding of the way that environmental demands change brain structures, researchers have begun to explore the relationship between bilingualism and the brain. They have found that learning a second language increases the density of gray matter in the left inferior parietal cortex. The earlier a second language is learned and the more proficient the person becomes, the more benefit to brain development (Levine & Munsch, 2011).

Cultural Identity Development

For many European American children, ethnicity does not lead to comparison with others or exploration of identity (Tatum, 2003). But for most children who are members of nondominant groups, ethnicity or race may be a central part of the quest for identity that begins in middle childhood and continues well into adolescence and young adulthood. During middle childhood, cognitive advances allow children to view themselves and others as capable of belonging to more than one "category" at once, as capable of possessing two or more heritages simultaneously (Butler-Sweet, 2011; Nuttgens, 2010). As children mature, they may become more aware not only of dual or multiple aspects of identity but also of the discrimination and inequality to which they may be subjected. Such issues may in fact present overwhelming challenges for the school-age child belonging to a nondominant group. At a time when development of a sense of belonging is critical, these issues set some children apart from members of dominant groups and may increase the challenges they experience.

> How can cultural identity serve as a protective factor for children from nondominant groups?

Segregation based on ethnicity/race and social class is common in friendships at all ages, including middle childhood. Like adults, children are more likely to hold negative attitudes toward groups to which they do not belong (Haidt, 2013). However, children, like adults, vary in the extent to which they hold ethnic and social class biases. Verbalized prejudice declines during middle childhood as children learn to obey social norms against overt prejudice. However, children belonging to nondominant groups continue to face institutional discrimination and other significant challenges throughout this period of the life course (Dulin-Keita, Hannon, Fernandez, & Cockerham, 2011; Harry & Klinger, 2006).

A particular challenge for children such as Anthony Bryant or Manuel Vega may be blending contradictory values, standards, or traditions. Some children respond to cultural contradictions by identifying with the mainstream American culture (*assimilation*) in which they are immersed or by developing negative attitudes about their subcultural group memberships either consciously or subconsciously (*stereotype vulnerability*). Individual reactions, such as those of Manuel, will be shaped by the child's unique experiences and social influences. It is a major developmental task to integrate dual or multiple identities into a consistent personal identity as well as a positive ethnic or racial identity (Vera et al., 2011). Many models of identity exist for children of mixed ethnicity, with new ideas and theories constantly emerging. It is clear that identity development for such children is diverse, extremely complex, and not well understood. As always, however, parents and professionals must start where the child is, with a focus on facilitating understanding and appreciation of heritage to promote development of an integrated identity and positive self-regard (Chung, Bemak, & Grabosky, 2011). Children should be provided with opportunities to explore their dual or multiple heritages and to select their own terms for identifying and describing themselves (Nuttgens, 2010; Rollins & Hunter, 2013). Although studies have produced diverse findings, the most positive outcomes seem to be associated with supportive family systems and involvement in social and recreational activities that expose children to their heritage and lead to self-affirmation (Hagelskamp, Suárez-Orozco, & Hughes, 2010; Lunkett, Behnke, Sands, & Choi, 2009). The family environment plays a critical role in shaping all aspects of development, and the family is the primary vehicle through which cultural identity is transmitted. Children typically learn, through their families, how to view their own ethnicity/race and that of others as well as coping strategies to respond to potential or direct exclusion, discrimination, or racism (Ponterotto, 2010).

Key tasks for all adults include educating children about family histories and supporting the creation of an integrated sense of self. Individuals and organizations within the child's social system can provide support by being sensitive to issues related to ethnic/racial origin and ethnic/racial distinctions; they can also help by celebrating cultural diversity and trying to increase the cultural sensitivity of all children. Such interventions appear to encourage fewer negative stereotypes of peers belonging to nondominant groups (Isenberg & Jolongo, 2003). In general, it is critical to the positive identity development of all children, but particularly those from nondominant groups, that schools value diversity and offer a variety of experiences that focus on positive identity development. Ensuring that schools respect nondominant cultures and diverse learning styles is an important step. For schools to do this, all school staff must develop self-awareness. A variety of materials have been designed to facilitate this process among educators (Banks & Banks, 2010).

Emotional Development

As most children move from early childhood into and through middle childhood, they experience significant gains in their ability to identify and articulate their own emotions as well as the emotions of others. Exhibit 5.2 summarizes several gains school-age children often make in the area of emotional functioning. It is important to recognize, however, that culture and other aspects of group identity may shape emotional development. For example, cultures vary in their acceptance of expressive displays of emotion.

Many children in this age range develop more advanced coping skills that help them when encountering upsetting, stressful, or traumatic situations. As defined by Daniel Goleman (2006),

emotional intelligence refers to the ability to "motivate oneself and persist in the face of frustrations, to control impulse and delay gratification, to regulate one's moods and keep distress from swamping the ability to think, to empathize and to hope" (p. 34). To Goleman (2006), emotional and social intelligence are inextricably linked, and many other developmentalists agree. As a result, interventions used with children experiencing social difficulties often focus on enhancing some aspect of emotional intelligence (see, for example, Birknerová, 2011).

> What are our societal expectations for emotional intelligence during middle childhood?

Goleman also asserts that social and emotional intelligence are key aspects of both moral reasoning and moral conduct. In other words, although often it may seem that advancing capacities in the moral domain occur naturally for children, positive conditions and interactions must exist in a child's life in order for optimal emotional and social competencies to develop. Thus, a child like Anthony Bryant,

Exhibit 5.2   Common Emotional Gains During Middle Childhood

- Ability to mentally organize and articulate emotional experiences
- Cognitive control of emotional arousal
- Ability to remain focused on goal-directed actions
- Ability to delay gratification based on cognitive evaluation
- Ability to understand and use the concept of planning
- Ability to view tasks incrementally
- Use of social comparison
- Influence of internalized feelings (e.g., self-pride, shame) on behavior
- Capacity to tolerate conflicting feelings
- Increasingly effective defense mechanisms

SOURCE: Davies, 2011, pp. 360–363

with seemingly great academic promise, may not realize his potential without timely intervention targeting the development of critical emotional and social competencies. These competencies include, for example, self-awareness, impulse control, and the ability to identify, express, and manage feelings, including love, jealousy, anxiety, and anger. Healthy emotional development can be threatened by a number of issues, including challenges such as significant loss and trauma. We increasingly recognize the vulnerability of school-age children to serious emotional and mental health issues. Assessment approaches that incorporate awareness of and attention to the possible existence of such issues are critical.

Fortunately, a substantial knowledge base regarding the promotion of positive emotional development exists. Richard Davidson and Sharon Begley (2012) have written extensively about the concept of "emotional style" and effective approaches to changing one's emotional style. Many emotion-focused intervention strategies appear effective, particularly when they are preventive and provided during or before middle childhood (see Colle & Del Giudice, 2011).

For example, Brianna Shaw, like too many children—particularly girls her age—is at risk of developing depression and could benefit from intervention focusing on the development of appropriate coping strategies. A number of interacting, complex biopsychosocial-spiritual factors shape vulnerability to ailments such as depression. Davidson and Begley assert that an individual's unique, brain-based emotional style reflects a combination of six concepts, or "sub-styles." These six (outlook, attention, sensitivity to context, social intuition, resilience, and self-awareness) interact to produce our emotional style, and although it is not easy, we are capable of changing our style.

Goleman (2006) specifically argues that many cases of depression arise from deficits in two key areas of emotional competence: relationship skills and cognitive, or interpretive, style. In short, many children suffering from—or at risk of developing—depression likely possess a depression-promoting

way of interpreting setbacks. Children with a potentially harmful outlook attribute setbacks in their lives to internal, personal flaws. Appropriate preventive intervention, based on a cognitive behavioral approach, teaches children that their emotions are linked to the way they think and facilitates productive, healthy ways of interpreting events and viewing themselves. For Brianna, such cognitive-behavioral-oriented intervention may be helpful. Brianna also may benefit from a gender-specific intervention, perhaps with a particular focus on relational resilience. Gender-specific interventions are often most appropriate when the social problem is experienced primarily by one gender (Perry-Parrish & Zeman, 2011; Potter, 2004). Eating disorders and depression are two examples of issues disproportionately impacting girls. Identifying the relevance of gender issues to Brianna's current emotional state and considering a gender-specific intervention strategy therefore may be appropriate. The concept of "relational resilience" is built on relational-cultural theory's belief that "all psychological growth occurs in relationships": the building blocks of relational resilience are "mutual empathy, empowerment, and the development of courage" (Jordan, 2005, p. 79).

Many school-age girls and boys also experience depression and other types of emotional distress because of a variety of factors, including **trauma** (severe physical or psychological injury) or significant loss. Children with close ties to extended family are particularly likely to experience loss of a close relative at a young age and therefore are more prone to this sort of depression. Loss, trauma, and violence may present serious obstacles to healthy emotional development. Research demonstrates the remarkable potential resilience of children (see Goldstein & Brooks, 2013; Luthar, 2003; Werner & Brendtro, 2012), but both personal and environmental attributes play a critical role in processes of resilience. To support the healthy emotional development of children at risk, appropriate multilevel prevention and intervention efforts are crucial.

Social Development

Perhaps the most widely recognized developmental task of this period is the acquisition of feelings of *self-competence*. Traditional developmentalists have pointed out that the school-age child searches for opportunities to demonstrate personal skills, abilities, and achievements. This is what Erik Erikson (1963) was referring to when he described the developmental struggle of middle childhood as industry versus inferiority (refer back to Exhibit 3.7 for a description of all eight of Erikson's psychosocial stages). *Industry* refers to a drive to acquire new skills and do meaningful "work." The experiences of middle childhood may foster or thwart the child's attempts to acquire an enhanced sense of *mastery* and self-efficacy. Family, peer, and community support may enhance the child's growing sense of competence; lack of such support undermines this sense. The child's definitions of self and accomplishment vary greatly according to interpretations in the surrounding environment. But superficial, external bolstering of self-esteem is not all that children of this age group require. External appraisal must be supportive and encouraging but also genuine for children to value such feedback.

Some theorists argue that children of this age must learn the value of perseverance and develop an internal drive to succeed (Seligman, Reivich, Jaycox, & Gillham, 2007; Snyder et al., 2013). Opportunities to both fail and succeed must be

How does a growing sense of competence promote the capacity for human agency in making choices?

provided, along with sincere feedback and support. Ideally, the developing school-age child acquires the sense of personal competence and tenacity that will serve as a protective factor during adolescence and young adulthood.

Families play a critical role in supporting development of this sense. For example, as the child learns to ride a bike or play a sport or musical instrument, adults can provide specific feedback and praise. They can counter the child's frustration by identifying and complimenting specific improvements and emphasizing the role of practice and perseverance in producing improvements. Failures and setbacks can be labeled as temporary and surmountable rather than attributed to personal flaws or deficits. The presence of such feedback loops is a key feature of high-quality adult-child relationships, in the family, at school, and beyond.

Middle childhood is a critical time for children to acquire a sense of competence, and yet children are not equally positioned to acquire feelings of self-competence as they enter this developmental phase, as Anthony Bryant's, Brianna Shaw's, and Manuel Vega's stories suggest. Developmental pathways preceding entry into middle childhood are extremely diverse. Children experience this phase of life differently based not only on differences in the surrounding environment—such as family structure and socioeconomic status—but also on their personality differences. A particular personality and learning style may be valued or devalued, problematic or nonproblematic, in each of the child's expanding social settings (Berk, 2012). Thus, although Anthony, Brianna, and Manuel are moving through the same developmental period and facing many common tasks, they experience these tasks differently and will emerge into adolescence as unique individuals.

Each individual child's identity development is highly dependent on social networks of privilege and exclusion. A direct relationship exists between the level of control and power a child experiences and the degree of balance achieved between feelings of power (privilege) and powerlessness (exclusion) (Johnson, 2006; Tatum, 2007). As children move toward adolescence and early adulthood, the amount of emotional, social, spiritual, and economic **capital**, or resources, acquired determines the likelihood of socioeconomic and other types of success as well as feelings of competence to succeed. Experiencing economically and socially just support systems is critical to optimum development.

Advancing language capability in middle childhood serves not only as a communication tool but also as a vehicle for more sophisticated introspection. Language is also a potential tool for positive assertion of self and more complex personal opinions as the child's social world expands (Coles, 1987, 1997; Gutzwiller-Helfenfinger et al., 2010). In recent years, many elementary schools have added **character education** to their curricula. Such education often consists of direct teaching and curriculum inclusion of mainstream moral and social values thought to be universal in a community (e.g., kindness, respect, honesty). Renewed focus on children's character education is in part related to waves of school violence, harassment, and bullying. Survey research with children suggests that, compared with children in middle and high school settings, children in elementary school settings are at highest risk of experiencing bullying, as either a perpetrator or a victim (Espelage & Swearer, 2011).

At a broader level, legislative initiatives have encouraged school personnel to confront bullying and harassment in the school setting (Piacenti, 2011). Schools have been particularly responsive to these initiatives in the wake of well-publicized incidents of school violence. Today, most schools have policies in place designed to facilitate efficient and effective responses to aberrant behavior, including bullying and violence. The content and implementation details of such policies, of course, vary widely.

During the late 20th century, changes occurred within our views and understanding of bullying (Espelage & Swearer, 2011). In general, the public has become less tolerant of bullying, perhaps because of a fairly widespread belief that school shootings (such as the Chardon, Ohio, school shootings and the Columbine High School massacre) can

be linked to bullying. Bullying is today recognized as a complex phenomenon, with both **direct bullying** (physical) and indirect bullying viewed as cause for concern. **Indirect bullying** refers to verbal, psychological, and social or "relational" bullying tactics and includes cyberbullying (Englander, 2013).

In recent years, new interest has centered on the ways in which technology influences social relationships among children and youth as well as gender differences in relationships and bullying. Initially, attention was drawn to the previously underrecognized phenomenon of girls experiencing direct bullying, or physical aggression and violence, at the hands of other girls (Garbarino, 2007). Although both direct and indirect bullying crosses genders, more recent attention has centered on the widespread existence of indirect, or relational, bullying among all children, but particularly among girls, and its potentially devastating consequences (Chesney-Lind & Jones, 2010; Pepler, 2012; Simmons, 2011). One positive outcome of recent attention to bullying is interest in establishing "best practices" in bullying prevention and intervention. The current knowledge base suggests that the most effective approach to reducing bullying within a school is implementation of a comprehensive, schoolwide prevention and intervention plan that addresses the contributing factors within all levels of the school and community environment (Klein, 2012).

Communities possess great potential to provide important support and structure for children. Today, however, many communities provide as many challenges as opportunities for development. Communities in which challenges outweigh opportunities have been labeled as "socially toxic," meaning they threaten positive development (Garbarino, 1995). In contrast, within a socially supportive environment, children have access to peers and adults who can lead them toward more advanced moral and social thinking. This development occurs in part through the modeling of *prosocial behavior*, which injects moral reasoning and social sensitivity into the child's accustomed manner of reasoning and behaving. Thus, cognitive and moral development is a social issue. The failure of adults to take on moral and spiritual mentoring roles contributes significantly to the development of socially toxic environments.

Mentoring takes place in the **zone of proximal development**—the theoretical space between the child's current developmental level and the child's potential level if given access to appropriate models and experiences in the social environment (Vygotsky, Hanfmann, Vakar, & Kozulin, 2012). The child's competence is ideally impacted through such interactions in a dynamic and positive fashion, resulting in developmental progress.

The Peer Group

Nearly as influential as family members during middle childhood are *peer groups*: collections of children with unique values and goals. As children progress through middle childhood, peers have an increasingly important impact on such everyday matters as social behavior, activities, and dress. By this phase of development, a desire for group belongingness is especially strong. Within peer groups, children potentially learn three important lessons. First, they learn to appreciate different points of view. Second, they learn to recognize the norms and demands of their peer group. And third, they learn to have closeness to a same-sex peer (Newman & Newman, 2012). Whereas individual friendships facilitate the development of critical capacities such as trust and intimacy, peer groups foster learning about cooperation and leadership.

Throughout middle childhood, the importance of *group norms* is highly evident (von Salisch, Haenel, & Freund, 2013). Children are sensitive, sometimes exceedingly so, to their peers' standards for behavior, appearance, and attitudes. Brianna Shaw, for instance, is beginning to devalue herself because she recognizes the discrepancy between her appearance and group norms. Often it is not until adolescence that group

> What role do peer groups play in developing the capacity for meaningful relationships in middle childhood?

norms may become more flexible, allowing for more individuality. This shift reflects the complex relationship among the developmental domains. In this case, the association between social and cognitive development is illustrated by simultaneous changes in social relationships and cognitive capacities.

Gains in cognitive abilities promote more complex communication skills and greater social awareness. These developments, in turn, facilitate more complex peer interaction, which is a vital resource for the development of **social competence**—the ability to engage in sustained, positive, and mutually satisfactory peer interactions. Positive peer relationships reflect and support social competence, as they potentially discourage egocentrism, promote positive coping, and ultimately serve as a protective factor during the transition to adolescence (Spencer, Harpalani, Fegley, Dell'Angelo, & Seaton, 2003).

Gender and culture influence the quantity and nature of peer interactions observed among school-age children (Perry-Parrish & Zeman, 2011). Sociability, intimacy, social expectations and rules, and the value placed on various types of play and other social activities are all phenomena shaped by both gender and culture.

Spencer et al. (2003) point out that children from nondominant groups are more likely to experience dissonance across school, family, and peer settings; for example, such children may experience language differences, misunderstandings of cultural traditions or expressions, and distinct norms, or rules, regarding dating behavior, peer intimacy, or cross-gender friendships. These authors also assert that although many youth experiencing dissonance across school, family, and peer systems may suffer from negative outcomes such as peer rejection or school failure, some may learn important coping skills that will serve them well later in life. In fact, the authors argue that given the clear trend toward increasing cultural diversity around the globe, "experiences of cultural dissonance and the coping skills they allow youth to develop should not be viewed as aberrant; instead, privilege should be explored as having a 'downside' that potentially compromises the development of coping and character" (p. 137).

However, a persistent finding is that, across gender and culture, peer acceptance is a powerful predictor of psychological adjustment. One well-known study asked children to fit other children into particular categories. From the results, the researchers developed five general categories of social acceptance: popular, rejected, controversial, neglected, and average (Coie, Dodge, & Coppotelli, 1982). Common predictors of popular status include physical appearance and prosocial behaviors in the social setting (Kupersmidt & Dodge, 2004; Rotenberg et al., 2004). Rejected children are those who are actively disliked by their peers. Rejected status is strongly associated with poor academic and social outcomes (Lev-Wiesel, Sarid, & Sternberg, 2013). For this reason, we should be concerned about Brianna Shaw's growing sense of peer rejection.

Support for rejected children may include interventions to improve peer relations and psychological adjustment. Most of these interventions are based on social learning theory and involve modeling and reinforcing positive social behavior—for example, initiating interaction and responding to others positively. Such programs are capable of helping children develop social competence and gain peer approval (Mikami et al., 2013; Mikami, Lerner, & Lun, 2010).

Friendship and Intimacy

Throughout middle childhood, children expand their ability to look at things from others' perspectives. In turn, their capacity to develop more complex friendships—based on awareness of others' thoughts, feelings, and needs—emerges (von Salisch et al., 2013; Zelazo, Chandler, & Crone, 2010). As a result, for many children, more complex and stable friendships begin to form for the first time in middle childhood. Although skills such as cooperation and problem solving are learned in the peer group, close friendships facilitate understanding and promote trust and reciprocity. Most

socially competent children maintain and nurture both close friendships and effective peer-group interaction.

As children move through middle childhood, friendship begins to entail mutual trust and assistance and acquires a more intense emotional component (Jobe-Shields, Cohen, & Parra, 2011). As children move toward adolescence, they may gain close friendships based on the emotional support provided for one another as much as, if not more than, common interests and activities. The concept of friend is transformed from the playmate of early childhood to the confidant of middle childhood. The role of emotional support and intimacy in friendship becomes even more pronounced, and children increasingly value mutual understanding and loyalty in the face of conflict among peers (Woods, 2013).

Team Play

The overall incidence of aggression during peer activities decreases during middle childhood, and friendly rule-based play increases. This transition is due in part to the continuing development of a perspective-taking ability, the ability to see a situation from another person's point of view. In addition, most school-age children are exposed to peers who differ in a variety of ways, including ethnicity and personality.

Developmental changes result in shifts in group communication and interaction, reflecting an enhanced ability to understand the role of multiple participants in activities. These developments facilitate the transition to participation in more complex rule-based activities, such as team sports. Despite occasional conflict with peers, involvement with team sports may provide great enjoyment and may have long-term benefits. Research suggests linkages between physical activity in adulthood and participation in sports and other forms of regular exercise during childhood and adolescence (Mäkinen et al., 2010; Ortega et al., 2013). While participating in team sports and other similar group activities, other potential positive outcomes include the capacity for interdependence, cooperation, comprehension of division of labor, and healthy competition (American Alliance for Health, Physical Education, Recreation and Dance, 2013).

Gender Identity and Gender Roles

Although most children in middle childhood have a great deal in common based on their shared developmental phase, girls and boys differ significantly in areas ranging from their self-understanding and social relationships to school performance, interests, and life aspirations (Perry-Parrish & Zeman, 2011). Among most school-age children, gender identity, or an "internalized psychological experience of being male or female," is quite well-established (Diamond & Savin-Williams, 2003, p. 105). This is not, however, the case for all children. Many children experience a fluid sense of gender identity, particularly prior to the onset of puberty. Research indicates that the greater the **gender dysphoria** experienced as a young child, the more likely it is that the child will continue to experience gender variance through adolescence (Wallien & Cohen-Kettenis, 2008). Transgender children and youth are particularly vulnerable to social isolation and other developmental challenges associated with negative experiences in family and school settings (Burgess, 2009).

Our understanding of the structure of gender roles is derived from various theoretical perspectives (Bromberg & O'Donohue, 2013). An anthropological or social constructionist orientation illuminates the ways in which gender shapes familial and societal systems and inevitably impacts individual development in an intangible yet profound fashion (Gardiner & Kosmitzki, 2011). Cognitive theory suggests that at the individual level, self-perceptions emerge. Gender, as one component of a psychological sense of self, joins related cognitions to guide children's gender-linked behaviors. A behavioral perspective suggests that gender-related behaviors precede self-perception in the development of gender role identity; in other words, at a very young age, girls start imitating feminine behavior and later begin thinking of themselves as distinctly female, and boys go through the same sequence in developing a masculine identity. Gender schema theory (see Bem, 1993, 1998), an information-processing approach to gender, combines behavioral and cognitive theories, suggesting that social influences and cognition work together to perpetuate gender-linked perceptions and behaviors.

Feminist psychodynamic theorists such as Nancy Chodorow (1991, 1999) have proposed that while boys typically begin to separate psychologically from their female caregivers in early childhood, most girls deepen their connection to and identification with their female caregivers throughout childhood. Such theorists propose, then, that as girls and boys transition into adolescence and face a new level of individuation, they confront this challenge from very different psychological places, and adolescent girls are more likely to find the task emotionally confusing if not deeply overwhelming. This feminist, psychoanalytic theoretical orientation represents one approach used to explain not only gender identity and role development but also differences between boys and girls in their approaches to relationships and emotional expressiveness.

Women's studies experts have pointed out that school-age girls often seem to possess a "confident understanding of self," which too often disintegrates as they increasingly "discredit their feelings and understandings, experiencing increased self-doubt" during early adolescence and subsequently becoming susceptible to a host of internalizing and externalizing disorders linked to poor self-esteem (Potter, 2004, p. 60). A number of studies and theories attempt to explain this shift in girls' self-image and mental health as they transition to adolescence (Perry-Parrish & Zeman, 2011; Simmons, 2011), but Potter (2004) cautions against overgeneralization of the phenomena and in particular suggests that the trend may not apply widely across girls from differing ethnic groups, socioeconomic statuses, and sexual orientations.

During middle childhood, often boys' identification with "masculine" role attributes increases while girls' identification with "feminine" role attributes decreases (Potter, 2004). For instance, boys are more likely than girls to label a chore as a "girl's job" or a "boy's job." As adults, females are the more androgynous of the two genders, and this movement toward androgyny appears to begin in middle childhood (Diamond & Savin-Williams, 2003).

These differences have multiple causes, from social to cognitive forces. In the United States, during middle childhood and beyond, cross-gender behavior in girls is more socially acceptable than such behavior among boys. Diamond and Savin-Williams (2003) use the term "gender typicality," or the "degree to which one's appearance, behavior, interests, and subjective self-concept conform to conventional gender norms" (p. 105). Research suggests that for both genders, a traditionally "masculine" identity is associated with a higher sense of overall competence and better academic performance (Boldizar, 1991; Newcomb & Dubas, 1992). Diamond and Savin-Williams (2003) also emphasize the role of culture in this relationship, pointing out that this is likely because the traits associated with male, or for girls, "tomboy," status are those most valued in many communities. These traits include qualities such as athleticism, confidence, and assertiveness. Indeed, local communities with "more entrenched sexist ideologies" regarding male versus female traits are those in which boys exhibiting feminine or "sissy" behaviors are likely to suffer (p. 107).

In general, because of expanding cognitive capacities, as children leave early childhood and progress through middle childhood, their gender stereotypes gradually become more flexible, and most school-age children begin to accept that males and females can engage in the same activities (Kahraman & Basal, 2012). The relationships between gender identity, gender stereotyping, and individual gender role adoption are not clear-cut. Even children well aware of community gender norms and role expectations may not conform to gender role stereotypes in their actual behavior (Brinkman, Jedinak, Rosen, & Zimmerman, 2011; Gerouki, 2010). Our understanding of the complexities of gender and sexual identity development—and the relationships between the two during the life course—is in its infancy.

Technology and Social Development

In recent years, there has been intense interest in the ways in which technology impacts child development. In affluent nations, many children are technologically savvy by the time they enter middle childhood. Technological advances in social media, gaming, television, and the music industry are just a few examples of the ways in which digital media impact children (Turkle, 2011). An extensive body of research suggests both positive and negative implications for child development.

Technology presents children and the adults in their lives with opportunities for social connection that did not exist in the past (Singer & Singer, 2011). Children can maintain and develop relationships despite geographical or other separations. Social support positively influences children, and these relationships may promote the development of communication skills not supported through relationships initiated or maintained solely through in-person interaction.

Some argue that technology presents children with positive opportunities for social interaction that does not "fit" in the busy weekly schedule of today's often overscheduled school-age child (Singer & Singer, 2011). In addition, some children report that use of technology allows them to explore aspects of their identity in a safe way not possible through in-person interactions. Indeed, personal identity development in areas such as sexuality and ethnicity can be informed in both positive and negative ways via media exposure. Some children also report that technology enables them to relax or escape from stressors associated with family, peer relationships, or other challenges (Singer & Singer, 2011).

Turkle (2011) explains the ways in which a variety of new toys and virtual creatures, enhanced by technology, promote prosocial behavior in young children. However, like the violent video game controversy, some question whether young children should be exposed to the complex ethical issues inherent in such toys or entertainment. In particular, is it appropriate to allow "tech creatures" to die when neglected, potentially harming children's developing capacity for empathy and understanding of the nature of human life? A related but distinct question to ponder is whether the attachments to "virtual" friends or creatures alter the nature of human attachment or attachment style among such children in some way.

Some children, like adults, report potentially unhealthy outcomes of technology use such as feeling more comfortable existing or interacting in a virtual rather than "real" environment and feeling more comfortable in a virtual identity (e.g., an avatar). Children are easily able to access an overwhelming quantity of media-based information, appropriate or inappropriate. Although there is evidence to support the harmful effects of such information access, evidence also supports the ways in which such media access can be positive, such as enhanced cognitive and moral development (Turkle, 2011). In addition, some research suggests that most children are more capable of strategizing through unwanted media-based information and messages than most adults think (Singer & Singer, 2011).

Children are impacted by technology in other less obvious ways as well. For example, parents are increasingly distracted by media, finding it difficult to "turn off" or "unplug" from work and social connections (Turkle, 2011). And yet information about effective parenting strategies and social support for isolated parents is facilitated by access to media and new technologies. Similarly, parents are capable of using technology to monitor or connect with their children more than ever before.

Focusing solely on the relationship between technology and social development, neuroscientists argue that children and adults struggle to "unplug" because of the dopamine release associated with human connection, and received texts and e-mails elicit this pleasure response to the point of addiction (Turkle, 2011). Our knowledge of neurobiology suggests that the human relationship with technology is shaping the development of school-age children in a complex and profound fashion.

Spiritual Development

Spiritual development, historically neglected or subsumed within other developmental domains, is now widely recognized as a critical aspect of child development. Robert Coles (1990) is identified as one of the first Western developmentalists to draw connections between moral and spiritual development. Benson, Scales, Syvertsen, and Roehlkepartain (2012) define spiritual development as comprising awareness or awakening, interconnecting and belonging, and a way of life; or more specifically a synergistic process of "becoming aware of one's potential and possibility; becoming aware of the intersection of one's life with others, nature, and the universe; connecting and linking the self and one's potentials to ideals and narratives; and developing a life orientation that generates hope, purpose, and compassion" (p. 457).

A significant body of research suggests that spirituality functions as a protective factor for children as well as adults. Spirituality has been established as supporting adaptive coping, and Clinton (2008) specifically found that among children suffering experiences of trauma in early childhood, higher levels of spiritual awareness are associated with more adaptive behavior, including more effective coping and resilience over time.

Holder, Coleman, and Wallace (2010) examined the differences between children's religiosity and spirituality as well as connections between spirituality and happiness within a sample of 8- to 12-year-old children. In their study, spirituality remained a significant happiness predictor even after removing the variance associated with individual temperament. Similar to scholars investigating adult spirituality and happiness, the researchers found that two particular aspects of spirituality—children's assessment of the value of life and the quality of interpersonal relationships (also labeled the "personal" and "communal" domains of spirituality)—were particularly good predictors of happiness.

Lipscomb and Gersch (2012) have engaged in qualitative research employing a spiritual listening approach, which they describe as an attempt to elicit children's views "about the meanings they attach to their lives, their essential drives, motivation and desires . . . a method of tapping into children's individual spiritual journey at a particular point in their lives" (p. 8). In a study with participants ages 10 and 11, Lipscomb and Gersch (2012) employed spiritual listening to inquire about identity, purpose, happiness, destiny, drive, and transition. Children shared views about identity, such as identity is "like an oyster" and "at first I was happy and I knew just what I was doing, but then people started bullying me just because of my skin colour and then I started to think, who am I, what am I and why am I in this world" (p. 12). They also spoke about purpose, with such comments as "My purpose of life is having a mission. I don't really know what it is but I know it's a mission. I think my mission is to help other people, which is like my identity" (p. 13). The researchers noted that all children in the study were able to relate to questions about these abstract and complex concepts in an individual and relevant way. It is interesting to note that one of the strategies children used to connect philosophical ideas back to their concrete experiences was by referencing popular culture, including themes they had observed in television and films. Of particular relevance to social work is the authors' conclusion that the technique of spiritual listening may support children's development as it facilitates children's ability to link the concrete nature of their lives to the metaphysical.

Critical Thinking Questions 5.3

Why do you think peer acceptance is a powerful predictor of psychological adjustment in middle childhood? Why do you think cross-gender behavior is more socially acceptable for girls than for boys in the United States? How do you think Anthony Bryant, Brianna Shaw, and Manuel Vega would respond to spiritual questioning?

MIDDLE CHILDHOOD AND FORMAL SCHOOLING

Before discussing the role of formal schooling in the life of the school-age child in the United States and other relatively affluent societies, it is important to note that there continue to be large global gaps in opportunities for education. Although educational participation is almost universal from ages 5 to 14 in affluent countries, many of the world's children do not receive even a primary education. In the current context of a knowledge-based global economy, the importance of formal schooling during middle childhood cannot be overstated, and yet a widening gap exists in average years of education between rich and poor countries (Gardiner & Kosmitzki, 2011; World Bank, 2013b).

Children entering school must learn to navigate a new environment quite different from the family. In school, they are evaluated on the basis of how well they perform tasks; people outside the family—teachers and other school staff as well as peers—begin shaping the child's personality, dreams, and aspirations. For children such as Manuel Vega, the environmental adjustment can be even more profound in part because the educational attainment of family members may be limited (Crouse, 2010). At the same time, the school environment has the potential to serve as an important resource for the achievement of the physical, cognitive, emotional, social, and spiritual developmental tasks of middle childhood for all children, regardless of the previous schooling available to their parents.

Success in the school environment is very important to the development of self-esteem. Anthony Bryant, Brianna Shaw, and Manuel Vega illustrate the potentially positive as well as painful aspects of schooling. Manuel and Brianna seem increasingly distressed by their interactions within the school environment. Often, difficulties with peers create or compound academic challenges. Brianna's school experience is becoming threatening enough that she may begin to withdraw from the environment, which would represent a serious risk to her continued cognitive, emotional, and

Photo 5.3 As children get older, schools are the primary context for development in middle childhood.

© Brand X Pictures/ThinkStock

social development. As children move through the middle years, they become increasingly aware that they are evaluated on the basis of what they are able to do. In turn, they begin to evaluate themselves based on treatment by teachers and peers and on self-assessments of what they can and cannot do well (Garralda & Raynaud, 2010).

How might increased emphasis on cognitive diversity alter the life course of students such as Anthony, Brianna, and Manuel?

In the past few decades, school-age children have benefited from new research and theory focusing on the concept of intelligence. Howard Gardner's work represented a paradigm shift

in the field of education. He proposed that intelligence is neither unitary nor fixed and argued that intelligence is not adequately or fully measured by IQ tests. More broadly, in his theory of **multiple intelligences**, intelligence is "the ability to solve problems or fashion products that are of consequence in a particular cultural setting or community" (Gardner, 1993, p. 15). Challenging the idea that individuals can be described, or categorized, by a single, quantifiable measure of intelligence, Gardner proposed at least eight critical intelligences: verbal/linguistic, logical/mathematical, visual/spatial, musical/rhythmic, bodily/kinesthetic, naturalist, interpersonal, and intrapersonal (Campbell, Campbell, & Dickinson, 2004; Zeidner, Matthews, & Roberts, 2012). In its practical application, multiple intelligence theory calls for the use of a wide range of instructional strategies that engage the range of strengths and intelligences of each student (Ghazi, Shahzada, Gilani, Shabbir, & Rashid, 2011). In addition to calling for innovative and diverse instructional strategies, multiple intelligence theory suggests achievement evaluation should consist of comprehensive assessments examining diverse areas of performance.

Many schools are ill-equipped to respond to the issues confronting children such as Manuel. If Manuel is not supported and assisted by his school system, his educational experience may assault his healthy development. But if Manuel's personal and familial support systems can be tapped and mobilized, they may help him overcome his feelings of isolation in his new school environment. Carefully constructed and implemented interventions must be used to help Manuel.

Today in the United States, Manuel's situation is not rare. About 1 in 5 U.S. students speak a language other than English at home (Skinner, Wight, Aratani, Cooper, & Thampi, 2010). Overall, the percentage of children living in the United States with at least one foreign-born parent rose from 15% in 1994 to 24% in 2012 (Federal Interagency Forum on Child and Family Statistics, 2013). In general, students in the United States are more diverse than ever before (U.S. Department of Health and Human Services, 2011). Many challenges face children who have recently arrived in the United States, particularly those fleeing war-torn countries. Research suggests that immigrant and refugee children are at heightened risk of experiencing mental health challenges and school failure (Briggs, 2011; Henderson, 2008).

Language difficulties and their consequences among such children are also increasingly recognized. It has been established that children are best served when they are able to speak both their native language and the language of their host country (Auerbach & Collier, 2012). The need for specific strategies to acknowledge and honor the "informal language register," while teaching the formal, has been identified by several literacy researchers (see Gee, 2012; Maier, Vitiello, & Greenfield, 2012). These researchers emphasize the importance of teaching children to recognize their internal, or natural, "speech" and the "register" they use in the school environment. Identifying and mediating these processes is best accomplished in the context of a caring relationship (Noddings, 2013). By sensitively promoting an awareness of such differences in the home and school, social workers and other adults can help children experience less confusion and alienation.

Other aspects of the link between school and home are important as well because school and home are the two major spheres in which children exist during middle childhood. The more similar these two environments are, the more successful the child will be at school and at home. Students who experience vastly different cultures at home and at school are likely to have difficulty accommodating the two worlds (Gregory, 2000). A great deal of learning goes on before a child enters school. By the time Anthony Bryant, Brianna Shaw, and Manuel Vega began school, they had acquired routines, habits, and cognitive, social, emotional, and physical styles and skills (Hayes, 2011). The transition to school is relatively easy for many students because schools typically present a mainstream model for behavior and learning. As most parents interact with their children, they model and promote the behavior that will be acceptable in school. Children are well prepared for the school environment when, quite simply, they understand the rules because the school is then accepting of them (Howard, 2010; Payne, 2013).

In contrast, children not fluent in mainstream speech patterns or not extensively exposed to school rules or materials such as scissors and books typically possess skills and curiosity but are often viewed as inferior in some way by school personnel (Crouse, 2010; Murillo, 2010). Because the school environment does not support the home environment and the home environment does not support the school environment, these children face an increased risk of poor school outcomes. Schools that recognize the contribution of home to school success typically seek family involvement (Constable, 2006; Fan, Williams, & Wolters, 2012). Indeed, parental involvement in school is associated with better school performance (Duncan & Murnane, 2011). Schools serving diverse populations are becoming increasingly creative in their approaches to encouraging parent involvement, including the development of sophisticated interpretation and translation infrastructures (McNeal, 2012).

> How can social workers help bridge the divide between school and home when the cultures of the two are different?

The U.S. educational system today struggles to correct its traditional structure, which both reflected and supported racial, ethnic, and class divisions within U.S. society (Darling-Hammond, 2010; Frankenberg & Debray, 2011; Kozol, 2005; Orfield, Kucsev, & Siegal-Harvey, 2012). For example, *full-service schools* attempt to provide school-based or school-linked health and social services for schoolchildren and their families (Dyson, 2011). This push for educational accountability and its impact on the lives of children is complex and highly controversial. The application of the No Child Left Behind Act's standards spurred a number of organizations and states to either sue the federal government or sharply criticize the act for raising state achievement requirements without adequate supporting funds or as a violation of states' rights.

No Child Left Behind reforms have gained momentum with the U.S. Department of Education

(2013) providing Race to the Top funds as an incentive to states to adopt particular programs designed to raise student achievement outcomes. Many states have won significant competitive grants for increasing charter school options and negotiating merit-based teacher contracts tied, in part, to students' achievement growth on standardized tests. Such tests are linked to the new national Common Core Curriculum that, as of 2013, had been adopted by 45 states. The testing regimen to assess student knowledge of the Common Core has created the most controversy, continuing age-old states' rights concerns (Rich, 2013). Many believe such reforms will ultimately benefit diverse students like Anthony, Brianna, and Manuel, while others are convinced that most of the reforms will leave struggling students further behind.

In recent years, funding from government and corporate sources is increasingly directed at poor, low-resourced school districts. The idea is to use such funding to increase community partnerships designed to serve historically excluded students and their families as well as expanding preschool options and building more instructional technology infrastructure. In addition, many schools have responded to calls for educational reform by implementing innovative practices designed to raise achievement of basic skills while attempting to meet the educational needs of all students (Sherer, 2009; U.S. Department of Education, 2010). However, educational research has not had time to conclusively measure the long-range effects of such practices on a wide range of students.

Critical Thinking Questions 5.4

Think about your own middle childhood years, ages 6 to 12. What are some examples of school experiences that helped you to feel competent and confident? What are some examples of school experiences that lead you to feel incompetent and inferior? What biological, family, cultural, and other environmental factors led to success and failure in school?

SPECIAL CHALLENGES IN MIDDLE CHILDHOOD

In the last several decades in the United States, family structures have become more diverse than ever. Although the percentage of children living with both parents has steadily declined during the last four to five decades, according to the U.S. Census Bureau, approximately two thirds of children live with married parents and one quarter live with one parent (Vespa, Lewis, & Kreider, 2013). Exhibit 5.3 shows trends in living arrangements of children from 1958 to 2008.

Social and economic trends require more parents of very young children to participate in the workforce in order to make ends meet. Legislation requires single parents who receive public assistance to remain engaged in or to reenter the workforce (Parham, Quadagno, & Brown, 2009). The school day often does not coincide with parents' work schedules, and recent research suggests that as a result of parental employment, more than half of school-age children regularly need additional forms of supervision when school is not in session. Most of these children either participate in a before- or afterschool program (also known as wrap-around programs) or receive care from a relative; many low- and middle-income families struggle to find affordable child care and often are forced to sacrifice quality child care for economic reasons (Lippman, Vandivere, Keith, & Atienza, 2008; National Association of Child Care Resources and Referral Agencies, 2012). Unfortunately, available data suggest that the quality of child care experienced by the average child in the United States is less than ideal (Lippman et al., 2008).

This fact is particularly troubling because child care quality has been linked to children's physical health as well as cognitive, emotional, and social development. These findings apply not only to early childhood programs but also to before- and afterschool programs for older children. Moreover, as children move from the early (ages 5 to 9) to later (10 to 12) middle childhood years, they are increasingly likely to take care of themselves during the

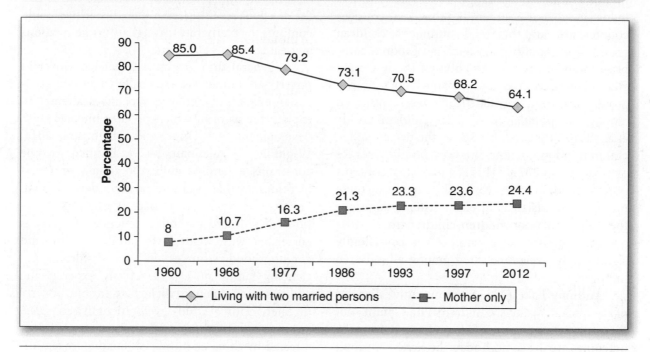

SOURCE: Based on Child Trends, 2013b

before- and afterschool hours. Regular participation in a high-quality before- and afterschool program is positively associated with academic performance, and a significant body of research suggests that how school-age children spend their afterschool hours is strongly associated with the likelihood of engaging in risky behaviors (Lyn, 2009).

Inadequate and low-quality child care is just one of the challenges facing school-age children—along with their families and communities—in the 21st century. Other challenges include poverty, family and community violence, mental and physical challenges, and family disruption.

Poverty

Poverty is the most significant human rights challenge facing the world community. Foremost among threats to children's healthy development is poverty, which potentially threatens positive development in all domains (see Ortiz, Daniels, & Engilbertsdóttir,

2012). It is estimated that half of the children of the world live in poverty, many in extreme poverty. That children should be protected from poverty is not disputed; in the United States, this societal value dates back to the colonial period (Trattner, 1998). The nature of policies and programs targeted at ensuring the minimal daily needs of children are met, however, has shifted over time, as has our success in meeting this goal (Bailey & Danzinger, 2013).

In the United States, the late 20th century brought a dramatic rise in the child poverty rate, which peaked in the early 1990s, declined for approximately a decade, and has gradually increased during the 21st century (Wight, Chau, & Aratani, 2011). The percentage of children living in low-income families (both poor and near poor) increased from 40% in 2006 to 45% in 2011 (Addy, Engelhardt, & Skinner, 2013).

> How does poverty serve as a risk factor in middle childhood?

As illustrated in Exhibit 5.4, children in the middle childhood age range are less likely to live in low-income or poor families than their younger counterparts, and this trend continues as children grow toward adulthood. Caucasian children comprise the majority of poor children in the United States. Young children and children from minority groups, however, are statistically overrepresented among the population of poor children (Addy et al., 2013). (See Exhibit 5.5 for the percentage of children in low-income and poor families by race or ethnicity in 2011.) This is a persistent contemporary trend; in other words, although in absolute numbers Caucasian children consistently comprise the majority of poor children, children from Latino and African American families are consistently significantly overrepresented among all children in poverty.

Anthony Lake (2013), the executive director of the United Nations' Children's Fund, points out that although the causes of inequality are many, the outcomes are the same. Today, the richest approximately 20% of the global population enjoy about 70% of the world's total income. These disparities exist in the United States as well. Lake warns that the divisions resulting from such disparities "could continue to reverberate through future generations at great cost to us all" (para. 36).

In general, the risk factors associated with child poverty are numerous, especially when poverty is sustained. A number of perspectives attempt to explain the ways in which poverty impacts child development (see Duncan & Magnuson, 2011; Wagmiller & Adelman, 2009). Limited income constrains a family's ability to obtain or invest in resources that promote positive development. Poverty detrimentally impacts caregivers' emotional health and parenting practices. Poverty is correlated with inadequate family, school, and neighborhood resources, and thus children experiencing family poverty are likely experiencing additional, cumulative risk factors. In sum, poverty threatens optimal child development in a complex, synergistic fashion. Research suggests that children affected by three or more risk factors are significantly more likely to experience school failure and

Exhibit 5.4 Percentage of Children in Low-Income and Poor Families by Age, 2011

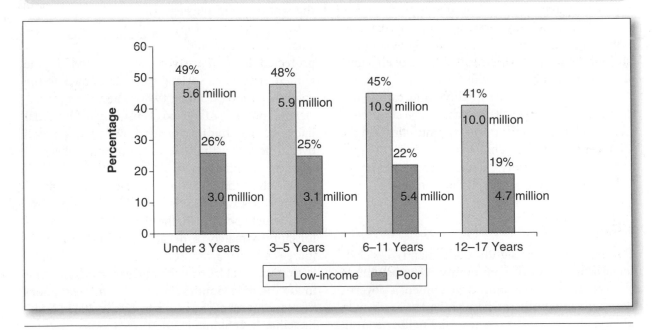

SOURCE: Addy et al., 2013

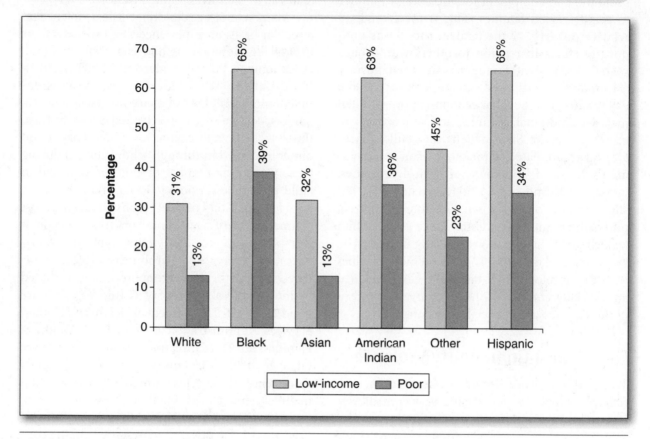

SOURCE: Addy et al., 2013

to employ maladaptive coping strategies associated with a variety of negative outcomes (Robbins, Stagman, & Smith, 2012). Children who have spent any part of their prenatal period, infancy, or early childhood in poverty have often already encountered several developmental challenges by the time middle childhood begins. Children who enter, progress through, and leave middle childhood in poverty are at much greater risk of negative developmental outcomes than those who briefly enter and then exit poverty while still in middle childhood (Moore, Redd, Burkhauser, Mbwana, & Collins, 2009).

Persistent and "deep," or extreme, poverty poses the most significant threat to healthy child development. For example, extreme family poverty

is correlated with homelessness, and poverty and homelessness combined increase a child's risk of abrupt family separation and experiencing or witnessing forms of trauma such as physical or sexual assault (Schneir, 2009).

But what does it actually mean, to a child, to be poor? Being poor is a relative concept, the meaning of which is defined by perceptions of and real exclusion (Dinitto, 2011; Kozol, 2005). In most communities, one must be *not* poor in order to be fully engaged and included. Lack of income and certain goods deprive poor people of what is expected among those who belong; thus, poverty results in perceived and real inabilities and inadequacies. For example, children often participate in extracurricular activities such as sports, music, or art. These programs often involve registration, program, and equipment fees that are prohibitive to impoverished families. This is the essence of **relative poverty**, or the tendency to define one's poverty status in relation to others within one's social environment. Fundamentally, then, poverty is as much a social as an economic phenomenon. Payne (2013) argues that economic poverty often includes emotional, spiritual, and support system impoverishment. Such deficits in a child's background accumulate and too often result in impediments to the development of critical capacities. James Garbarino (1995), a researcher who has studied causes of violent behavior among children, points to an innocent question once asked of him by a child: "When you were growing up, were you poor or regular?" (p. 137). As a child struggles with the developmental tasks of feeling included and socially competent, relative poverty sends a persistent message of social exclusion.

Family and Community Violence

Witnessing violence deeply affects children, particularly when the perpetrator or victim of violence is a family member. Children are increasingly witness or subject to violence in their homes, schools, and neighborhoods (Finkelhor, Turner, Ormrod, Hamby, & Kracke, 2009). Although child maltreatment and domestic violence have always existed, they have been recognized as social problems only recently. Community violence is slowly becoming recognized as a social problem of equal magnitude, affecting a tremendous number of children and families. Exposure to violence is a particular problem in areas where a lack of economic and social resources already produces significant challenges for children. Children are most likely to experience "polyvictimization" beginning in the middle childhood years (Finkelhor, Turner, Hamby, & Ormrod, 2011). The atrocities witnessed or experienced by children from war-torn countries are often unimaginable to

What protective factors can buffer the effects of neighborhood violence on school-age children?

children and adults who have resided in the United States all of their lives (United Nations, 2011).

Many school-age children witness violence on a regular basis, an experience that threatens their healthy development (Children's Defense Fund, 2012; Tomoda, Polcari, Anderson, & Teicher, 2012). In the United States, children appear most susceptible to nonfatal physical abuse from ages 6 to 12. Some speculate that in the United States, at least, this association may be due to increased likelihood of public detection through school contact during these years. The number of children reported to child protective services (CPS) agencies annually is staggering. Child neglect is consistently the most common form of documented maltreatment, but it is important to note that victims typically experience more than one type of abuse or neglect simultaneously and therefore are appropriately included in more than one category (Children's Defense Fund, 2013; U.S. Department of Health and Human Services Administration on Children, Youth, & Families, 2012). Maltreatment subtype trends are relatively stable over time; victims of child neglect consistently account for more than half of all child maltreatment victims (see Exhibit 5.6).

African American and Native American children are consistently overrepresented among confirmed maltreatment victims. Careful examination of this issue, however, has concluded that although children of color are disproportionately represented within the child welfare population, studies that are cognizant of the relationship between culture and parenting practices, that control for the role of poverty, and that examine child maltreatment in the general population find no association between a child's race or ethnicity and likelihood of child maltreatment. Thus, it is likely that the disproportionate representation of children of color within the child welfare system is caused by the underlying relationship between poverty and race or ethnicity (Derezotes, Testa, & Poertner, 2005; Martinez, Gudiño, & Lau, 2013).

A variety of factors contribute to child maltreatment and family violence (Institute of Medicine and National Research Council, 2012). These factors include parental, child, family, community,

Exhibit 5.6   Selected Maltreatment Types of Victims by Age, 2011

Age	Medical Neglect		Neglect		Physical Abuse		Psychological Maltreatment		Sexual Abuse	
	Number	%	Number	%	Number	%	Number	%	Number	%
<1–2	5,212	34.6	159,753	30.1	28,565	24.0	12,946	21.3	1,650	2.7
3–5	2,313	15.3	110,335	20.8	19,394	16.3	11,767	19.3	8,585	14.0
6–8	2,046	13.6	86,282	16.2	19,644	16.5	10,787	17.7	9,978	16.2
9–11	1,820	12.1	68,212	12.8	16,779	14.1	9,782	16.1	11,347	18.5
12–14	1,965	13.0	58,603	11.0	18,207	15.3	8,976	14.8	16,178	26.3
15–17	1,695	11.2	46,660	8.8	15,579	13.1	6,377	10.5	13,411	21.8
Unborn, Unknown, and 18–21	23	0.2	1,568	0.3	657	0.6	204	0.3	323	0.5
Total	15,074		531,413		118,825		60,839		61,472	
Percentage		100.0		100.0		100.0		100.0		100.0

SOURCE: U.S. Children's Bureau, 2012a

and cultural characteristics. Typically, the dynamic interplay of such characteristics leads to maltreatment, with the most relevant factors varying significantly depending on the type of maltreatment examined. Thus, multiple theoretical perspectives, particularly the life course, ecological, systems, and stress and coping perspectives, are helpful for understanding situations of child maltreatment.

The impact of child maltreatment varies based on a number of factors, including but certainly not limited to the type of maltreatment, the age of the child, and many other child, family, and community characteristics (Cicchetti, 2013). The Centers for Disease Control and Prevention (2013k) provides a helpful overview of child maltreatment consequences, pointing out that experiencing maltreatment as a child is associated with an overwhelming number of negative health outcomes as an adult. These outcomes include an increased likelihood of using or abusing alcohol and other substances,

disordered eating, depression, and susceptibility to certain chronic diseases.

Children who experience trauma, induced by either indirect or direct exposure to violence, may experience *post-traumatic stress disorder* (PTSD)—a set of symptoms that includes feelings of fear and helplessness, reliving of the traumatic experience, and attempts to avoid reminders of the traumatic experience (Foa, Keane, Friedman, & Cohen, 2010). Researchers have found changes in the brain chemistry of children exposed to chronic violence (Matto, Strolin-Goltzman, & Ballan, 2013). Witnessing or experiencing violence adversely affects children in a number of areas, including the ability to function in school and the ability to establish stable, healthy relationships (Lang et al., 2008; Tomoda et al., 2012). Children who directly experience violence are at high risk of negative outcomes, but secondary exposure to violence and trauma—such as when a child's parents are suffering from PTSD—also may lead to negative outcomes for children (Wasserman & McReynolds, 2011).

In general, the intergenerational nature of family violence has been established (Robboy & Anderson, 2011). Childhood exposure to violence significantly increases the likelihood of mental health difficulties and violence perpetration or revictimization. Currently, the focus is on understanding the specific pathways of intergenerational processes. It is clear that prolonged exposure to violence has multiple implications for child development. Children are forced to learn lessons about loss and death, perhaps before they have acquired the cognitive ability to understand. They may therefore come to believe that the world is unpredictable and violent, a belief that threatens children's natural curiosity and desire to explore the social environment. Multiple experiences in which adults are unable to protect them often lead children to conclude that they must take on such responsibility for themselves, a prospect that can easily overwhelm the resources of a school-age child. Experiencing such helplessness may also lead to feelings of incompetence and hopelessness, to which children who experience chronic violence react in diverse ways. Responses may be passive, including withdrawal symptoms and signs of depression; or they may be active, including the use of aggression as a means of coping with and transforming the overwhelming feelings of vulnerability (Charlesworth, 2007).

The emotional availability of a parent or other caretaker who can support the child's need to process traumatic events is critical. However, in situations of crisis stimulated by child maltreatment, domestic violence, and national or international violence, families are often unable to support their children psychologically. Even with the best of parental resources, moreover, children developing in violent and chronically dangerous communities continue to experience numerous challenges to development. The child's need for autonomy and independence is directly confronted by the parent's need to protect the child's physical safety. For example, hours spent indoors to avoid danger do not promote the much-needed peer relationships and sense of accomplishment, purpose, and self-efficacy so critical during this phase of development (Hutchison, 2007).

Mental and Physical Challenges

Although the term *disability* is still widely used in academic discourse and government policy, many are actively seeking to change popular discourse to reflect the need to see all children as possessing a range of physical and mental abilities. The use of the term *disability* establishes a norm within that range and labels those with abilities outside the norm as "disabled," which implies that group of individuals is "abnormal" and the group of individuals within the norm is "normal." These labels are not helpful to realizing a vision of a just and equal society, and yet information of relevance is shared within the confines of this terminology. In 2012, of the 62.2 million children younger than age 15, about 5.2 million or 8.4% had some kind of disability. Half of children with a disability were classified with severe disabilities (Brault, 2012). During the last several years in the United States, the prevalence of developmental disabilities has increased (Boyle et al., 2011). Of particular note, ADHD and autism prevalence continues to increase.

Attention Deficit Hyperactivity Disorder (ADHD)

ADHD is a commonly diagnosed childhood behavioral disorder impacting learning in the school environment. ADHD includes predominately inattentive, predominately impulsive-hyperactive, and combined inattentive-hyperactivity (American Psychiatric Association, 2013) (see Exhibit 5.7 for diagnostic criteria for ADHD). The Centers for Disease Control and Prevention (2013l) report that approximately 11% of children 4 to 17 years of age (6.4 million) have been diagnosed with ADHD as of 2011. In 2011, boys (13.2%) were more likely than girls (5.6%) to have ever been diagnosed with ADHD. The average age of ADHD diagnosis was 7, but children reported by their parents as having

A. Either (1) or (2):

1. **Inattention:** Six (or more) of the following symptoms have persisted for at least 6 months to a degree that is inconsistent with developmental level and that negatively impacts directly on social and academic/occupational activities: The symptoms are not solely a manifestation of oppositional behavior, defiance, hostility, or failure to understand tasks or instructions. For older adolescents and adults (age 17 and older), at least five symptoms are required.

    a. Often fails to give close attention to details or makes careless mistakes in schoolwork, at work, or during other activities.
    b. Often has difficulty sustaining attention in tasks or play activities.
    c. Often does not seem to listen when spoken to directly.
    d. Often does not follow through on instructions and fails to finish schoolwork, chores, or duties in the workplace.
    e. Often has difficulty organizing tasks and activities.
    f. Often avoids, dislikes, or is reluctant to engage in tasks that require sustained mental effort.
    g. Often loses things necessary for tasks or activities.
    h. Is often easily distracted by extraneous stimuli.
    i. Is often forgetful in daily activities.

2. **Hyperactivity and impulsivity:** Six (or more) of the following symptoms of hyperactivity-impulsivity have persisted for at least 6 months to a degree that is inconsistent with developmental level and that negatively impacts directly on social and academic/occupational activities. The symptoms are not solely a manifestation of oppositional behavior, defiance, hostility, or a failure to understand tasks or instructions. For older adolescents and adults (age 17 and older), at least five symptoms are required.

    a. Often fidgets with hands or feet or squirms in seat.
    b. Often leaves seat in situations when remaining seated is expected.
    c. Often runs about or climbs in situations where it is inappropriate (in adolescents or adults, may be limited to feelings of restlessness).
    d. Often unable to play or engage in leisure activities quietly.
    e. Is often "on the go," acting as if "driven by a motor."
    f. Often talks excessively.
    g. Often blurts out answers to questions before they have been completed.
    h. Often has difficulty waiting his or her turn.
    i. Often interrupts or intrudes on others.

B. Several inattentive or hyperactive-impulse symptoms were present prior to age 12.

C. Several inattentive or hyperactive-impulse symptoms are present in two or more settings.

D. There is clear evidence that the symptoms interfere with, or reduce the quality of, social, academic, or occupational functioning.

E. The symptoms do not occur exclusively during the course of schizophrenia or another psychotic disorder and are not better explained by another mental disorder.

SOURCE: Reprinted with permission from the *Diagnostic and Statistical Manual of Mental Disorders, Fifth Edition* (Copyright 2013), pp. 59–62. American Psychiatric Association. All Rights Reserved.

more severe ADHD are typically diagnosed earlier. Prevalence of ADHD diagnosis varied substantially by state, from a low of 5.6% in Nevada to a high of 18.7% in Kentucky.

ADHD is associated with school failure or academic underachievement, but the relationship is complex in part because of the strong relationship between ADHD and a number of other factors also associated with school difficulties (Foley, 2011; Rietz, Hasselhorn, & Labuhn, 2012). Also, several studies suggest that the interpretation and evaluation of ADHD behaviors are significantly influenced by culturally linked beliefs (Rohde et al., 2005). In other words, the extent to which ADHD-linked behaviors are perceived as problematic varies according to individual and group values and norms.

Autism Spectrum Disorder (ASD)

In recent years, controversy has surrounded autism spectrum disorder, including definitions, causes, and diagnostic criteria (Grandin & Panek, 2013; Shannon, 2011). According to the Centers for Disease Control and Prevention (2013m), autism spectrum disorder is typically diagnosed by age 3 in about 1 in 88 children, and boys are approximately 5 times more likely to be diagnosed (1 in 54) than girls (1 in 252). Although autism spectrum disorder typically manifests and is diagnosed during or before early childhood, some children may not receive formal assessment or diagnosis until their early or middle childhood years. In general, autism spectrum disorder consists of impairment within reciprocal social interaction, verbal and nonverbal communication, and range of activities and interests (Insel, 2013). Like children with any special need or disability, children diagnosed with autism spectrum disorder are extremely diverse; in particular, such children vary widely in terms of their intellectual and communicative abilities, the nature and severity of behavioral challenges, and appropriate interventions (Herbert & Weintraub, 2012). Exhibit 5.8 presents the diagnostic criteria for autism spectrum disorder.

Emotional/Behavioral Disorder

In many schools, the children perhaps presenting the greatest challenge to educators and administrators are those who consistently exhibit disruptive or alarming behavior yet do not clearly fit the criteria for a disability diagnosis. Although the U.S. Individuals with Disabilities Education Act (IDEA) includes a definition for "seriously emotionally disturbed" children, not all school professionals and government education agencies consistently agree with or use this definition. It is estimated that approximately 15% of children 4 to 17 years old have parents or guardians who have talked with a health care provider or school staff about the child's emotional or behavioral difficulties (Simpson, Cohen, Pastor, & Reuben, 2008). The National Mental Health and Special Education Coalition has publicized a definition of "emotionally/behaviorally disordered" children, suggesting that this term and a set of diagnostic criteria could be used in place of the IDEA definition (see Exhibit 5.9). This revised definition remains problematic, and because of definitional inconsistencies, it is extremely difficult to accurately estimate the number of school-age children falling within this population. Estimates range from 0.05% to 12% of preadolescent students (Bellenir, 2012; Walker & Melvin, 2010).

Early identification and intervention, or provision of appropriate supportive services, are key protective factors for a child with special needs. In addition, the social environment more generally may serve as either a risk or protective factor, depending on its response to the child with a special need. Although difference of any sort is often noticed by children and adults, students with special needs or chronic illness are at particular risk for being singled out by their peers, and middle childhood is a critical time for such children. For children to acquire a clear and positive sense of self, they need positive self-regard.

> What educational initiatives could minimize the risks associated with ADHD, autism spectrum disorder, and other emotional/behavioral disorders?

Exhibit 5.8 Diagnostic Criteria for Autism Spectrum Disorder

A. Persistent deficits in social communication and social interaction across multiple contexts, as manifested by the following, currently or by history (examples are illustrative, not exhaustive):

1. Deficits in social-emotional reciprocity, ranging, for example, from abnormal social approach and failure of normal back-and-forth conversation; to reduced sharing of interests, emotions, or affect; to failure to initiate or respond to social interactions.
2. Deficits in nonverbal communicative behaviors used for social interactions, ranging, for example, from poorly integrated verbal and nonverbal communication; to abnormalities in eye contact and body language or deficits in understanding and use of gestures; to a total lack of facial expressions and nonverbal communication.
3. Deficits in developing, maintaining, and understanding relationships, ranging, for example, from difficulties adjusting behavior to suit various social contexts; to difficulties in sharing imaginative play or in making friends; to absence of interest in peers.

B. Restricted, repetitive patterns of behavior, interests, or activities, as manifested by at least two of the following, currently or by history (examples are illustrative, not exhaustive):

1. Stereotyped or repetitive motor movements, use of objects, or speech.
2. Insistence on sameness, inflexible adherence to routines, or ritualized patterns of verbal or nonverbal behavior.
3. Highly restricted, fixated interests that are abnormal in intensity or focus.
4. Hyper- or hypoactivity to sensory input or unusual interest in sensory aspects of the environment.

C. Symptoms must be present in the early developmental period (but may not become fully manifest until social demands exceed limited capacities, or may be masked by learned strategies in later life).

D. Symptoms cause clinically significant impairment in social, occupation, or other important areas of current functioning.

E. These disturbances are not better explained by intellectual disability or global developmental delay. Intellectual disability and autism spectrum disorder frequently co-occur.

SOURCE: Reprinted with permission from the *Diagnostic and Statistical Manual of Mental Disorders, Fifth Edition* (Copyright 2013, pp. 53–55). American Psychiatric Association. All Rights Reserved.

The positive development of all children is facilitated by support at multiple levels to promote feelings of self-competence and independence. Educating all children and adults about special needs and encouraging the support of all students may help to minimize negative attitudes and incidents (Gargiulo & Kilgo, 2011; Painter, 2012).

Students who feel misunderstood by their peers are particularly likely to feel alone or isolated in the school setting. Students who are socially excluded by their peers often develop a dislike of school. Some students who are teased, isolated, or harassed on a regular basis may begin to withdraw or act out in order to cope with unpleasant experiences. Teachers, parents, and other school personnel who pay special attention to, and intervene with, students in this situation may prevent the escalation of such problems.

Children's adjustment to special needs is highly dependent on the adjustment of those around

Exhibit 5.9 Diagnostic Criteria for Emotional/Behavioral Disorder or Disturbance

Emotionally disturbed	1. A condition exhibiting one or more of the following characteristics over a long period of time and to a marked degree, which adversely affects educational performance:
	a. An inability to learn that cannot be explained by intellectual, sensory, or health factors
	b. An inability to build or maintain satisfactory interpersonal relationships with peers and teachers
	c. Inappropriate types of behavior or feelings under normal circumstances
	d. A general, pervasive mood of unhappiness or depression
	e. A tendency to develop physical symptoms or fears associated with personal or school problems
	2. Includes children who are schizophrenic (or autistic). The term does not include children who are socially maladjusted, unless it is determined that they are seriously emotionally disturbed.
Emotional/behavioral disorder	1. A disability characterized by behavioral or emotional responses in school programs so different from appropriate age, culture, or ethnic norms that they adversely affect educational performance, including academic, social, vocational, or personal skills, and that
	a. Is more than a temporary, expected response to stressful events in the environment
	b. Is consistently exhibited in two different settings, at least one of which is school-related
	c. Persists despite individualized interventions within the education program, unless, in the judgment of the team, the child or youth's history indicates that such interventions would not be effective
	2. May include children or youth with schizophrenia disorders, affective disorders, anxiety disorders, or other sustained disturbances of conduct or adjustment when they adversely affect educational performance in accordance with Section 1.

SOURCE: Young, K. R., Marchant, M., & Wilder, L. K. (2004). School-based interventions for students with emotional and behavioral disorders. In P. Allen-Meares & M. W. Fraser (Eds.), *Intervention with children and adolescents: An interdisciplinary perpective.* Boston: Allyn & Bacon, pp. 177–178. Reprinted by permission of Pearson Education, Inc., Upper Saddle River, NJ.

them. Families may respond in a number of ways to a diagnosis of a disability or serious illness. Often caregivers experience loss or grief stages; these stages may include the following: denial, withdrawal, rejection, fear, frustration, anger, sadness, adjustment, and acceptance (Ahmann, 2013; Richardson, Cobham, McDermott, & Murray, 2013). The loss and grief stages are not linear but can be experienced repeatedly as parents interface with educational, social, and medical institutions throughout their child's life. Awareness of and sensitivity to these stages and the ongoing nature of grief and loss is critical for those assessing the need for intervention. Typically, parents are helped by advocacy and support groups and access to information and resources (McMillan, 2011).

Families of children with special needs also typically desire independence and self-determination for their children. Family empowerment was an explicit focus of the Education for All Handicapped Children Act (Pub. L. No. 94-142) of 1975, which stresses parental participation in the development of an **individual education plan (IEP)** for each child. The IEP charts a course for ensuring that each child achieves as much as possible in the academic realm. The need to include the family in decision making and planning is also embodied in the IDEA of 1990 (reauthorized in 1997 and 2004), which replaced the Education for All Handicapped Children Act (National School Board Association, 2013). The IDEA requires that the IEP include specific educational goals for each student classified as in need of special educational services. In addition, the IDEA assures all children the right to a free and appropriate public education and supports the placement of children with disabilities into integrated settings.

Prior to this act, the education of children with disabilities was left to individual states. As a result, the population labeled "disabled" and the services provided varied greatly. Today, however, through various pieces of legislation and several court decisions, society has stated its clear preference to educate children with special needs in integrated settings (*least restrictive environment*) to the maximum extent possible.

A recent examination of the nature of inclusion nationwide concluded that during the last few decades, students with special needs (including learning disabilities) were much more likely to be formally identified, but many states are not aggressively pursuing the ability to educate students with special needs in less restrictive settings (Aron & Loprest, 2012). Evaluations of the impact of inclusive settings on children's school success suggest positive academic gains for children with special needs and neutral impact on academic performance for children without identified special needs (Weigert, 2012). However, some caution is in order against a "one size fits all" model of inclusion for all students with special needs, arguing that assessment of the optimal educational setting must be thorough and individualized (Goodfellow, 2012).

Family Disruption

Throughout history, most nuclear and extended families have succeeded in their endeavor to adequately protect and socialize their young. For too many children, however, the family serves as both a protective and risk factor because of unhealthy family attributes and dynamics. In the specific realm of family disruption, divorce was traditionally viewed as a developmental risk factor for children. Today, among U.S. children with married parents, approximately one half experience the divorce of their parents (American Academy of Child & Adolescent Psychiatry, 2013). Many parents marry a second time, and thus approximately 10% of U.S. children live in blended family situations (U.S. Census Bureau, 2013a; Miller, 2010). Many children experience the dissolution of their parents' nonmarital romantic relationships, and related attachments, without being counted in official "children of divorce" statistics or research. Although no reliable data on similar nonmarital relationship patterns exist, we can assume that similar trends exist among children's nonmarried parents and other caregivers.

Divorce and other types of family disruption lead to new situations, including the introduction of new people, new housing and income arrangements, and new family roles and responsibilities (Ahrons, 2011). Family disruption may also immerse the child in poverty (Ducanto, 2010). As the body of research on children and divorce has grown in depth and breadth, it has become apparent that divorce and other types of family disruption may detrimentally or positively impact children depending on the circumstances preceding and following the divorce (Stadelmann, Perren, Groeben, & von Klitzing, 2010). For example, if divorce brings an end to seriously dysfunctional spousal tension or violence and results in positive changes within the home environment, child outcomes may be positive. Alternatively, if the divorce disrupted a healthy, nurturing family system and led to declines in the emotional and financial health of the child's primary caregiver(s), child outcomes may be negative.

Marriage appears to protect children financially; approximately

> 70% of the children who lived with two married parents were in households that were at least 200 percent above the poverty level in 2013, but nearly 1 in 2 children who lived with their mother only, two unmarried parents, or no parents at all were living below the poverty level. Children living in these other family arrangements were also more likely than those living with two married parents to receive public assistance and food stamps, and to lack health insurance coverage. (Vespa et al., 2013, p. 23)

Historically, many children experienced family disruption because of the death of one or both parents (Amato, 2003). Although improvements in public health have significantly reduced the likelihood of parental death, a substantial number of children continue to experience the death of a primary caregiver. Compared with adults, children have fewer cognitive and other resources to cope with death and loss (Buchwald, Delmar, & Schantz-Laursen, (2012). For children coping with the death of a parent, the circumstances of the death and the adjustment of the remaining caregivers are critical variables impacting child outcomes. Also, in recent years, a number of studies have focused on "children of suicide." This literature notes the potential long-term impacts of parental suicide on surviving children and identifies the ways in which outcomes may be carried through generations (Bisagni, 2012).

Many school-age children experience disruption of attachment relationships through other means. Approximately 2 million children in the United States have one active-duty parent in the military. Children in military families are at heightened risk of frequent moves, parental absence, and parental emotional distress (Murphey, 2013). In any month in 2011, there were approximately 400,000 children in foster care (U.S. Children's

Bureau, 2013). Some children spend lengthy periods of time in some type of foster care setting, while some children enter and leave foster care rapidly and only once during their childhoods, and still other children cycle in and out of their home and foster care settings repeatedly. Approximately one third of the children in foster care at any time have been in substitute care for 3 years or more; approximately one fifth of children in foster care are identified as unlikely to ever return home and are awaiting a permanent plan (Downs, Moore, & McFadden, 2010).

Family disruption is stressful for all children. Great variation exists, however, in the circumstances preceding and following the family disruption, the nature of the changes involved, and how children respond to this type of stress. Critical factors in outcomes for children include social supports within the family and surrounding community, the child's characteristics, the emotional well-being of caregivers, and in general the quality of care received following the family disruption. In addition, because middle childhood spans a wide age range, school-age children exhibit a wide range of cognitive, emotional, and behavioral responses to divorce and other types of family disruption. They may blame themselves and experience anxiety or other difficult emotions, or they may demonstrate a relatively mature understanding of the reasons behind the events.

Children experiencing family disruption without supports or those who have experienced difficulties preceding the disruption are most likely to experience long-term emotional and behavioral problems. Children placed in foster care or otherwise exposed to traumatic or multiple losses are more likely to fall into this group (Webb & Dumpson, 2006). These children are likely to face additional stress associated with the loss of familiar space, belongings, and social networks (Mallon & Hess, 2014). However, with appropriate support and intervention as well as the presence of other protective factors, many children experiencing family disruption adjust over time (see Guest, 2012).

RISK FACTORS AND PROTECTIVE FACTORS IN MIDDLE CHILDHOOD _____

School-age children face a variety of risks that undermine their struggles to develop a sense of purpose and self-worth. Risk factors are anything that increases the probability of a problem condition, its progression into a more severe state, or its maintenance (Luthar, 2003). Risk factors are moderated, however, by protective factors, either internal or external, that help children resist risk (Werner & Brendtro, 2012). Risk and protective factors can be biological, psychological, social, and spiritual, and like all influences on development, they span the micro to macro continuum (Bronfenbrenner, 1996). Dynamic, always-evolving interaction occurs among risk and protective factors present in each dimension of the individual child and his or her environment.

Resilience—or "survival against the odds"— arises from an interplay of risk and protective factors and manifests as adaptive behavior producing positive outcomes (Jenson & Fraser, 2011). A variety of factors influence resilience during middle childhood. Whether a factor presents risk or protection often depends on its interaction with other factors influencing the individual child. For example, a highly structured classroom environment run by a "strict" teacher may function as a protective factor for one child while simultaneously functioning as a risk factor for another child.

The life course and systems perspectives provide tools for understanding positive development during middle childhood. These perspectives also facilitate assessment and intervention efforts. As social workers, we must recognize that resilience is rarely an innate characteristic. Rather, it is a process that may be facilitated by influences within the child's surrounding environment. Indeed, research suggests that high-risk behavior among children increases when they perceive declining family involvement and community support (Benson, Scales, & Roehlkepartain, 2011). A primary goal of the professions dedicated to child well-being must be facilitation of positive external supports for children and enhancement of the person/environment fit so as to maximize protective factors and minimize risk factors. Exhibit 5.10 summarizes major risk and protective factors identified as most relevant to childhood.

Exhibit 5.10 Potential Childhood Risk and Protective Factors

Risk	Protective
Child/Individual	**Child/Individual**
Prematurity, birth anomalies	Good health
Exposure to toxins in utero	
Chronic or serious illness	
Temperament: for example, difficult or slow to warm up	Personality factors: easy temperament; positive disposition; active coping style; positive self-esteem, good social skills; internal locus of control; balance between help seeking and autonomy
Cognitive delays, low intelligence	Above-average intelligence
Childhood trauma	History of adequate development
Antisocial peer group	Hobbies and interests
Gender	Good peer relationships

(Continued)

Exhibit 5.10   (Continued)

Risk	Protective
Parental/Family	**Parental/Family**
Insecure attachment	Secure attachment; positive and warm parent-child relationship
Parent: insecure adult attachment pattern	Parent: secure adult attachment pattern
Single parenthood (with lack of support)	Parent(s) supports child in times of stress
Harsh parenting, maltreatment	Effective/positive (authoritative) parenting
Family disorganization; low parental monitoring	Household rules and structure, parental monitoring of child
Social isolation, lack of support, domestic violence	Support/involvement of extended family, including help with caregiving
High parental/interparental conflict	Positive, stable relationship between parents
Separation/divorce, especially high-conflict divorce	
Parental psychopathology	Stable parental mental health; parent(s) models competence and good coping skills
Parental substance abuse	High parental expectations; family models aspects of prosocial behavior
Parental illness	
Death of a parent or sibling	
Foster care placement	Family residential stability; stable parental physical health
Social/Environmental	**Social/Environmental**
Poverty/collective poverty	Middle-class-or-above socioeconomic status
Lack of access to adequate medical care, health insurance, and social services	Access to adequate health care and social services
Parental/community unemployment	Consistent parental/community employment
Inadequate child care	Adequate child care
Inadequate housing	Adequate housing
Exposure to racism, discrimination, injustice	Family religious faith/participation
Low-quality schools	High-quality schools
Frequent change of residence and schools/transient community	Presence of caring adult(s); supportive adults outside family who serve as role models/mentors to child
Exposure to environmental toxins	Healthy physical environment
Exposure to dangerous neighborhood(s), community violence, media violence	Collective efficacy
Competence in normative roles	
Few opportunities for education or employment	Many opportunities for education and employment

SOURCES: Based on Davies, 2011, pp. 103–104; Fraser, Kirby, & Smokowski, 2004, pp. 36–49

Critical Thinking Questions 5.5

There is general agreement that poverty and child maltreatment are among the most serious threats to healthy child development. How does poverty threaten physical, cognitive, emotional, social, and spiritual development during middle childhood? How does child maltreatment threaten physical, cognitive, emotional, social, and spiritual development during middle childhood?

Implications for Social Work Practice

This discussion of middle childhood suggests several practice principles for social workers and other professionals working with children:

- Development is multidimensional and dynamic; recognize the complex ways in which developmental influences interact, and incorporate this understanding into your work with children.
- Support parents and other family members as critically important social, emotional, and spiritual resources for their children.
- Support family, school, and community attempts to stabilize environments for children.
- Incorporate identification of multilevel risk and protective factors into assessment and intervention efforts.
- Recognize and support resilience in children and families. Support the strengths of children and families and their efforts to cope with adversity.
- Recognize the critical influence of the school environment on growth and development, and encourage attempts by school personnel to be responsive to all children and families.
- Understand the important role of peer groups in social and emotional growth and development; facilitate the development and maintenance of positive peer and other social relationships.
- Understand the ways in which the organization of schools reflects and supports the social injustice present in society. Support schools in their efforts to end practices and policies that sustain or reinforce inequalities.
- Facilitate meaningful teacher-family-child communication and school responsiveness to children experiencing difficulties in the school environment.
- Understand the effects of family, community, and societal violence on children and establish prosocial, nurturing, nonviolent environments whenever possible; provide opportunities for positive nurturing and mentoring of children in the school and community environments.
- Become familiar with and implement best practices in areas such as trauma, loss and grief, social skill development, and character education.
- Promote cultural competency and help children and other adults recognize and respect all forms of diversity and difference.

Key Terms

capital	gender dysphoria	precociousness
cerebral cortex	indirect bullying	relative poverty
character education	individual education plan (IEP)	social competence
direct bullying	interrelational intelligence	trauma
emotional intelligence	multiple intelligences	zone of proximal development

1. In small groups, compare and contrast the risk and protective factors present for Anthony Bryant, Brianna Shaw, and Manuel Vega. Brainstorm multilevel interventions you would consider if you were working with each child.

2. Working in pairs, consider the story of Anthony Bryant, Brianna Shaw, or Manuel Vega (as assigned by the instructor). Each pair should identify the relevance of the various developmental theorists discussed in the chapter to the assigned child, focusing on the theorist(s) whose idea(s) seem particularly relevant to the selected child. After approximately 20 minutes, form three small groups consisting of the pairs focusing on the same child. After comparing the similarities and differences in their assessments of the different theories, each group should report back to the full class.

3. As a class, create a list of debate topics raised directly or indirectly in the chapter (e.g., educational assessment/ standardized testing, federal spending or programs to address child poverty, gun control to reduce violence against children, family structure and family disruption, inclusion for children with special needs). Debates can take place between teams or individuals. Each side will take 2 minutes to present their case, and each side will also have 1 minute for rebuttal.

4. Use task rotation for important chapter issues such as *family and community violence*: (1) How does child maltreatment or trauma impact childhood development? (2) How are child witnesses impacted by acts of violence? (3) What programs might schools employ to support students impacted by violence? (4) What interventions might a social worker pursue to help families impacted by violence? *Task rotation description*: Questions are posted on chart paper around the room. Each group starts at a question, discusses it, writes ideas in response on the chart paper, and then after a short time (less than 3 minutes) is stopped and rotated to the next chart. At the next chart, they are given a brief period of time to review the work of the previous group and add any ideas the first group missed. The groups are stopped and rotated until all groups have read and added to all issues listed on the charts. Whole-group review follows.

American Association of University Women: www.aauw.org

Site maintained by the American Association of University Women contains information on education and equity for women and girls, including a report card on Title IX, a law that banned sex discrimination in education.

Child Trauma Academy: www.childtraumaacad emy.com

Site presented by the Child Trauma Academy contains information on the impact of child maltreatment on the brain and the physiological and psychological effects of trauma on children.

Child Welfare Information Gateway: www .childwelfare.gov

Site presented by the Administration for Children and Families contains information and resources to protect children and strengthen families, including statistics, prevention information, state statutes, family-centered practice, and publications.

Forum on Child and Family Statistics: www .childstats.gov

Official website of the Federal Interagency Forum on Child and Family Statistics offers easy access to federal and state statistics and reports on children and families, including international comparisons.

Search Institute: www.search-institute.org

Site presented by the Search Institute, an independent, nonprofit, nonsectarian organization with the goal of advancing the well-being of adolescents and children, contains information on 40 developmental assets and methods for building assets for child and youth development.

Student Study Site

ⓈSAGE edge™

Sharpen your skills with SAGE edge at **edge.sagepub.com/hutchisonclc5e**

SAGE edge for students provides a personalized approach to help you accomplish your coursework goals in an easy-to-use learning environment.

Adolescence

Susan Ainsley McCarter

Opening Questions

- How do biological, psychological, social, cultural, and spiritual dimensions affect the adolescent phase of the life course?

- Why do social workers need to understand theories of identity formation when working with adolescents?

- What unique challenges do adolescents face when confronted with issues of sexuality, violence, and substance use and abuse?

Key Ideas

As you read this chapter, take note of these central ideas:

1. Adolescence is characterized by significant physical change, increased hormone production, sexual maturation, improved cognitive functioning, formative identity development, and increased independence.

2. During adolescence, increased hormone production results in a period called puberty, during which persons become capable of reproduction. Other visible physical changes during this period include skeletal, musculature, and fat distribution changes, as well as development of primary and secondary sex characteristics.

3. Unseen growth and pruning occurs in the adolescent brain.

4. Psychological changes during this period include reactions to physical, social, and cultural changes confronting the adolescent, as well as cognitive development, in which most individuals develop improved reasoning skills, abstract thinking, a sense of their own thinking, and the ability to consider potential future consequences of their actions.

5. The greatest task of adolescence is identity formation—determining who one is and where one is going.

6. Adolescents in the United States spend nearly a third of their waking hours at school, where they should receive skills and knowledge for their next step in life, but a school that follows a Eurocentric educational model without regard for other cultures, or one that "pushes" at-risk students out, may damage the self-esteem of students of color, those with disabilities, or sexual minority students.

7. Among the physical and mental health risks to today's adolescents are substance abuse, juvenile delinquency, bullying, violence, poverty, low educational attainment, eating issues, and depression and suicide.

CASE STUDY 6.1

David's Coming-Out Process

The social worker at Jefferson High School sees many facets of adolescent life. Nothing much surprises her—especially not the way some of the kids hem and haw when they're trying to share what's really on their mind. Take David Costa, for instance. When he shows up for his first appointment, he is simply asked to tell a bit about himself.

"Let's see, I'm 17," he begins. "I'm a center fielder on the varsity baseball team. What else do you want to know? My parents are from Bolivia and are as traditional as you can imagine. My dad, David Sr., teaches history and is the varsity soccer coach here at Jefferson. My mom is a geriatric nurse. I have a younger sister, Patti. Patti Perfect. She goes to the magnet school and is in the eighth grade."

"How are things at home?" his social worker asks.

"Whatever. Patti is perfect, and I'm a 'freak.' They think I'm 'different, arrogant, stubborn.' I don't know what they want me to be. But I don't think that's what I am. That may be because . . . because I'm gay. But I haven't come out to my parents. That's all I need!"

This is obviously a difficult confession for David to make to an adult, but with a little encouragement he continues: "There are a few other seniors at Jefferson who are out, but they aren't student athletes and so I don't really spend any time with them. Basically when the whole baseball team is together or when I'm with other kids from school, I just act straight. I talk about girls' bodies just like the other guys. I think that is the hardest, not being able to be yourself. It was really hard when I was about 13. I was so confused. I knew that men were supposed to be with women, not other men. What I was feeling was not 'normal,' and I thought I was the only one. I wanted to kill myself. That was a bad time."

David's tone changes. "Let's talk about something good. Let me tell you about Theo. I think Theo is hot! He's got a great body. I wonder if he'd like to hang out together—get to know me. He's a junior, and if we got together, I would hear about it. But I keep thinking about him and looking at him during school. I just need to say something to him. There's a club downtown that has over-18 night, maybe I could get him in."

CASE STUDY 6.2

Carl's Struggle for Identity

Whereas David seeks out the social worker, Carl Fleischer, another 17-year-old, is sent to the social worker's office at the high school. He matter-of-factly shares that he is "an underachiever." He used to get an occasional B in his classes, but now it's mostly C's with an occasional D.

When Carl is asked what he likes to do in his spare time, he replies, "I get high and play Xbox." Further probing elicits one-word answers until the social worker asks Carl about relationships. His face contorts as he slaps his ample belly: "I'm not exactly a sex symbol. According to my doctor, I'm a fatso. He says normal boys my age and height weigh at least 50 pounds less than I do. He also tells me to quit smoking and get some exercise. Whatever. My mom says I'm big-boned. She says my dad was the same way. I wouldn't know. I never met the scumbag. He left when my mom was pregnant. But you probably don't want to hear about that."

Carl won't say more on that topic, but with more prodding, he finally talks about his job, delivering pizzas two nights a week and on the weekends. "So if you need pizzas, call me at Antonio's. I always bring pies home for my mom on Tuesday and Friday nights. She works late those nights and so we usually eat pizza and catch the Tuesday and Friday night lineups on TV. She lets me smoke in the house—cigarettes, not weed. Although I have gotten high in the house a couple times. Anyway, I am not what you would call popular. I am just a fat, slow geek and a pizza guy. But there are some heads who come into Antonio's. I exchange pies for dope. Works out pretty well: They get the munchies, and the pies keep me in with the heads!"

Monica's Quest for Mastery

Monica Golden, a peer counselor at Jefferson High, hangs around to chat after a meeting of the peer counselors. Monica is the eldest and tallest daughter in a family of five kids. Monica's mother is the assistant principal at Grover Middle School, and her father works for the Internal Revenue Service. This year, in addition to being a Jefferson peer counselor, Monica is the vice president of the senior class, the treasurer for the Young Republicans, a starter on the track team, and a teacher at Sunday school.

When the social worker comments on the scope of these activities, Monica replies, "I really do stay busy. I worked at the mall last year, but it was hard to keep my grades up. I'm trying to get into college, so my family and I decided I shouldn't work this year. So I just babysit sometimes. A lot of my aunts and uncles have me watch their kids, but they don't pay me. They consider it a family favor. Anyway, I am waiting to hear back from colleges. They should be sending out the letters this week. You know, the fatter the envelope the better. It doesn't take many words to say, 'No. We reject you.' And I need to either get into a state school or get a scholarship so that I can use my savings for tuition."

Next they talk a little about Monica's options, and she shares that her first choice is Howard University. "I want to surround myself with Black scholars and role models, and my dream is to be a pediatrician, you know. I love kids," Monica says. "I tried tons of jobs—that's where I got the savings. And, well, those with kids I enjoyed the most. Like I said, I've worked retail at the mall. I've worked at the supermarket as a cashier. I've worked at the snack bar at the pool. And I've been babysitting since I was 12. That's what I like the most."

"I'd love to have kids someday. But I don't even have a boyfriend. I wear glasses. My parents say I don't need contacts; they think I'm being vain. Not that I don't have a boyfriend because I wear glasses. Guys think I'm an overachiever. They think I'm driven and demanding and incapable of having fun. That's what I've been told. I think I'm just ambitious and extroverted. But really, I just haven't had much time to date in high school. I've been so busy. Well, gotta run."

THE SOCIAL CONSTRUCTION OF ADOLESCENCE ACROSS TIME AND SPACE

If we were asked to describe David Costa, Carl Fleischer, and Monica Golden, attention would probably be drawn to their status as adolescents. Worldwide, the current generation of adolescents is the largest in history, and youth ages 10 to 24 comprise one quarter of the world's population. Nearly 90% of these youth live in low-income and middle-income countries, where they comprise a much larger proportion of the population than they do in high-income countries (Sawyer et al., 2012).

The adolescent status has changed across time and cultures. Adolescence was invented as a psychosocial concept in the late 19th and early 20th centuries as the United States made the transition from an agrarian to an urban-industrial society (Choudhury, 2010). Prior to this time, adolescents worked beside adults, doing what adults did for the most part (Leeder, 2004). This is still the case for adolescents in many nonindustrial societies today, and in some cultures, adolescence is not recognized as a stage at all (Gardiner & Kosmitzki, 2011). As the United States and other societies became urbanized and industrialized, child labor legislation and compulsory education policies were passed, and adolescents were moved from the workplace to

How have our views on adolescence changed over time?

the school and became economically dependent on parents. The juvenile justice system was created in the United States in 1899 because youthful offenders had come to be regarded as different from adult offenders, with less culpability for their crimes because of their immaturity.

In 1904, G. Stanley Hall, an American psychologist, published *Adolescence: Its Psychology and Its Relations to Physiology, Anthropology, Sociology, Sex, Crime, Religion, and Education.* Hall proposed that adolescence is a period of "storm and stress," a period when hormones cause many psychological and social difficulties. Hall was later involved in the eugenics movement, a movement that intended to improve the human population by controlled selective breeding, and there seems to be racist and classist bias in his work on adolescence, which was not unusual in his time. His discussion suggests that poor youth are at risk of trouble because of their heredity whereas middle-class youth are at risk of being corrupted by the world around them (Finn, 2009). Janet Finn argues that the public, professional, and scholarly conversations about adolescence in the 20th and beginning of the 21st century have focused on adolescents as "trouble."

Jane Kroger (2007) suggests that many societies are clear about what they want their adolescents to avoid (alcohol and other drugs, delinquency, and pregnancy) but not as clear about what positive things they would like their youth to achieve. There is growing agreement that the societal context in which adolescence is experienced in the United States and other wealthy nations is becoming increasingly less supportive for adolescent development (Choudhury, 2010). This concern has led, in recent years, to the construction of a positive youth development movement, which has focused on youth "as resources to be developed, and not as problems to be managed" (Silbereisen & Lerner, 2007a, p. 7).

Perhaps no life course phase has been the subject of more recent empirical research than adolescence. Most prominently, the National Longitudinal Study of Adolescent Health (Add Health) was initiated at the Carolina Population Center in 1994. It is a study of a representative sample of adolescents in Grades 7 through 12 during the 1994–1995 school year. This cohort was followed into young adulthood in 2008, when the sample was 24 to 32 years of age. The Add Health study includes measures of social, economic, psychological, and physical well-being as well as contextual information on the family, neighborhood, community, school, friendships, peer groups, and romantic relationships. Add Health data are now generating large numbers of research reports, a partial list of which can be retrieved at the website listed at the end of this chapter.

THE TRANSITION FROM CHILDHOOD TO ADULTHOOD

In many countries, adolescence is described as the transitional period between childhood and adulthood. It is more than that, of course. It is a very rich period of the life course in its own right. For many, it is a thrilling time of life full of new experiences. The word *adolescence* originates from the Latin verb *adolescere*, which means "to grow into maturity." It is a period of life filled with transitional themes in every dimension of the configuration of person and environment: biological, psychological, social, and spiritual. These themes do not occur independently or without affecting one another. For example, David Costa's experience may be complicated because he is gay and because his family relationships are strained, but it is also strengthened by his supportive friendships and his participation in sports. Carl Fleischer's transition is marked by several challenges—his weight, his substance use, his lack of a relationship with his father, his academic performance—but also by the promise of his developing computer expertise and entrepreneurial skills. Monica Golden's movement through adolescence may be eased by her academic, athletic, and social success, but it also could be taxed by her busy schedule and high expectations for herself.

Many cultures have specific **rites of passage**—ceremonies that demarcate the transition from childhood to adulthood. Often these rites include sexual themes, marriage themes, themes of becoming a man or a woman, themes of added responsibility, or themes of increased insight or understanding. Such rites of passage are found in most nonindustrialized societies (Gardiner & Kosmitzki, 2011). For example, among the Massai ethnic group in Kenya and Tanzania, males and females are both circumcised at about age 13, and males are considered junior warriors and sent to live with other junior warriors (Leeder, 2004). For the most part, the transition from adolescence to adulthood is not marked by such clearly defined rituals in North America and many other Western countries (Gardiner & Kosmitzki, 2011). Some scholars who study adolescence have suggested that where there are no clear-cut puberty rituals, adolescents will devise their own rituals, such as "hazing, tattooing, dieting, dress, and beautification rituals" (Kroger, 2007, p. 41).

Some groups in North America continue to practice rites of passage, however. In the United States, some Jews celebrate the bar mitzvah for boys and bat mitzvah for girls at the age of 13 to observe their transition to adulthood and to mark their assumption of religious responsibility. Many Latino families, especially of Mexican heritage, celebrate *quinceañera*, during which families attend Mass with their 15-year-old daughter, who is dressed in white and then presented to the community as a young woman. Traditionally, she is accompanied by her *padrinos*, or godparents, who agree to support her parents in guiding her during this time. The ceremony is followed by a reception at which

Photo 6.1 Adolescence is a period filled with transitional themes in every dimension of life: biological, psychological, social, and spiritual.

© Don Hammond/Design Pics/Corbis

her father dances with her and presents her to the family's community of friends (Garcia, 2001; Roma, Mireless-Rios, & Lopez-Tello, 2014). Among many First Nations/Native American tribes in North America, boys participate in a vision quest at age 14 or 15. The boy is taken into a "sweat lodge," where his body and spirit are purified by the heat. He is assisted by a medicine man who advises him and assists with ritual prayers. Later he is taken to another place where he is left alone to fast for 4 days. Similarly, some First Nations/Native American girls take part in a ritual that involves morning running and baking a ceremonial cake (see Gardiner & Kosmitzki, 2011).

Mainstream culture in the United States, however, has few such rites. Many young adolescents go through confirmation ceremonies in Protestant and Catholic churches. Otherwise, the closest thing to a rite of passage may be getting a driver's license, graduating from high school, registering to vote, graduating from college, or getting married. But these events all occur at different times and thus do not provide a discrete point of transition. Moreover, not all youth participate in these rites of passage. Even without a cultural rite of passage, all adolescents experience profound biological, psychological, social, and spiritual changes. In economically advanced societies, these changes have been divided into three phases: early adolescence (ages 11 to 14), middle adolescence (ages 15 to 17), and late adolescence (ages 18 to 22). Exhibit 6.1 summarizes the typical biological, psychological, and social developments in these three phases.

Exhibit 6.1   Typical Adolescent Development

Stage of Adolescence	Biological Changes	Psychological Changes	Social Changes
Early (11–14)	Hormonal changes Beginning of puberty Physical appearance changes Possible experimentation with sex and substances	Reactions to physical changes, including early maturation Concrete/present-oriented thought Body modesty Moodiness	Changes in relationships with parents and peers Less school structure Distancing from culture/tradition Seeking sameness
Middle (15–17)	Completion of puberty and physical appearance changes Possible experimentation with sex and substances	Reactions to physical changes, including late maturation Increased autonomy Increased abstract thought Beginning of identity development Preparation for college or career	Heightened social situation decision making Continue to renegotiate family relationships More focus on peer group Beginning of one-to-one romantic relationships Moving toward greater community participation
Late (18–22)	Slowing of physical changes Possible experimentation with sex and substances	Formal operational thought Continuation of identity development Moral reasoning	Very little school/life structure Beginning of intimate relationships Renewed interest in culture/tradition

Of course, adolescent development varies from person to person and with time, culture, and other aspects of the environment. Yet deviations from the normative patterns of adolescent change may have psychological ramifications, because adolescents are so quick to compare their own development with that of their peers and because of the cultural messages they receive about acceptable appearance and behavior.

BIOLOGICAL ASPECTS OF ADOLESCENCE

Adolescence is a period of great physical change, marked by a rapid growth spurt in the early years, maturation of the reproductive system, redistribution of body weight, and continuing brain development. Adequate care of the body during this exciting time is of paramount importance.

Puberty

Puberty is the period of the life course in which the reproductive system matures. It is a process that begins before any biological changes are visible and occurs through interrelated neurological and endocrinological changes that affect brain development, sexual maturation, levels and cycles of hormones, and physical growth. The hypothalamus, pituitary gland, adrenal glands, and **gonads** (ovaries and testes) begin to interact and stimulate increased hormone production. It is the increase of these hormones that leads to the biological changes. Although androgens are typically referred to as male hormones and estrogens as female hormones, males and females in fact produce all three major **sex hormones**: androgens, progestins, and estrogens. Sex hormones affect the development and functioning of the gonads (including sperm production and ova maturation) and mating and child-caring behavior.

During puberty, increased levels of androgens in males stimulate the development and functioning of the male reproductive system; increased levels of progestins and estrogens in females stimulate the development and functioning of the female reproductive system. Specifically, the androgen testosterone, which is produced in males by the testes, affects the maturation and functioning of the penis, prostate gland, and other male genitals; the secondary sex characteristics; and the sex drive. The estrogen estradiol, which is produced in females by the ovaries, affects the maturation and functioning of the ovaries, uterus, and other female genitals; the secondary sex characteristics; and child-caring behaviors.

Primary sex characteristics are those directly related to the reproductive organs and external genitalia. For boys, these include growth of the penis and scrotum. During adolescence, the penis typically doubles or triples in length. Girls' primary sex characteristics are not so visible but include growth of the ovaries, uterus, vagina, clitoris, and labia.

Secondary sex characteristics are those not directly related to the reproductive organs and external genitalia. Secondary sex characteristics are enlarged breasts and hips for girls, facial hair and deeper voices for boys, and hair and sweat gland changes for both sexes. Female breast development is distinguished by growth of the mammary glands, nipples, and areolae. The tone of the male voice lowers as the larynx enlarges and the vocal cords lengthen. Both boys and girls begin to grow hair around their genitals and then under their arms. This hair begins with a fine texture and light color and then becomes curlier, coarser, and darker. During this period, the sweat glands also begin to produce noticeable odors.

Puberty is often described as beginning with the onset of menstruation in girls and production of sperm in boys, but these are not the first events in the puberty process. Menstruation is the periodic sloughing off of the lining of the uterus. This lining provides nutrients for the fertilized egg. If the egg is not fertilized, the lining sloughs off and is discharged through the vagina. However, for a girl to become capable of reproduction, she must not only menstruate but also ovulate. Ovulation,

What is the impact of biological age on psychological age, social age, and spiritual age during adolescence?

the release of an egg from an ovary, usually does not begin until several months after **menarche**, the onset of menstruation. For boys to reproduce, **spermarche**—the onset of the ability to ejaculate mobile sperm—must occur. Spermarche does not occur until after several ejaculations.

Girls typically first notice breast growth, then growth of pubic hair, and then body growth, especially hips. They then experience menarche; then growth of underarm hair; and finally, an increase in production of glandular oil and sweat, possibly with body odor and acne. Boys typically follow a similar pattern, first noticing growth of the testes; then growth of pubic hair; body growth; growth of penis; change in voice; growth of facial and underarm hair; and finally, an increase in the production of glandular oil and sweat, possibly with body odor and acne. Girls experience the growth spurt before they have the capacity for reproduction, but the opposite is the case for boys (Kroger, 2007).

Pubertal timing varies greatly. Generally, girls begin puberty about 2 years earlier than boys. Normal pubertal rates (meaning those experienced by 95% of the population) are for girls to begin menstruating between the ages of 9 and 17 and for boys to begin producing sperm between the ages of 11 and 16 (Rew, 2005). The age at which puberty begins has been declining in this century, but there is some controversy about the extent of this shift. There is evidence that puberty arrives earlier in economically advanced countries than in low-income countries and that nutrition and other living conditions play a role (Newman & Newman, 2012).

In addition to changes instigated by sex hormones, adolescents experience growth spurts. Bones are augmented by cartilage during adolescence, and the cartilage calcifies later, during the transition to adulthood. Typically, boys develop broader shoulders, straighter hips, and longer forearms and legs; girls typically develop narrower shoulders and broader hips. These skeletal differences are then enhanced by the development of additional upper body musculature for boys and the development of additional fat deposits on thighs, hips, and buttocks for girls. These changes account for differences in male and female weight and strength.

The Adolescent Brain

As recently as 30 years ago, it was thought that human brain development was finalized by early childhood (Choudhury, 2010). In the past 15 years, however, neuroimaging techniques have allowed researchers to study how the brain changes across the life course, and there is no doubt that the brain changes a great deal during adolescence (Colver & Longwell, 2013). Researchers are now able to study the adolescent brain using both magnetic resonance imaging (MRI), which provides an image of brain structure, and functional magnetic resonance imaging (fMRI), which provides a picture of metabolic function under specific circumstances (Blakemore, 2012). As discussed in earlier chapters, researchers have known for some time that the brain overproduces gray matter from development in the womb to about the age of 3 years, is highly plastic and thus shaped by experience, and goes through a pruning process. The neural connections or synapses that get exercised are retained during pruning, whereas the ones that are not exercised are eliminated. New brain research suggests that the adolescent brain undergoes another period of overproduction of gray matter just prior to puberty, peaking at about 11 years of age for girls and 12 years for boys, followed by another round of pruning. This process, like the infant's, is also affected by the individual's interactions with the outside world (Colver & Longwell, 2013).

Much interest surrounds recent findings about frontal lobe development during adolescence. The pruning process just described allows the brain to be more efficient to change in response to environmental demands and also facilitates improved integration of brain activities. Recent research indicates that pruning occurs in some parts of the brain earlier than in others, in general progressing from the back to the front part of brain, with the frontal lobes among the latest to show the structural changes. The frontal lobes are key players in the "executive functions" of planning, working memory, and impulse control, and the latest research indicates that they may not be fully developed until about age 25 (Blakemore & Robbins, 2012). Because of the relatively late development of the frontal lobes, particularly the prefrontal cortex, different neuronal circuits are involved in the adolescent brain under different emotional conditions. The researchers make a distinction between "cold cognition" problem solving and "hot cognition" problem solving during adolescence. Cold-cognition problem solving occurs when the adolescent is alone and calm, as he or she typically would be in the laboratory. Conversely, hot-cognition problem solving occurs in situations where teens are with peers, emotions are running high, they are feeling sexual tension, and so on. The research indicates that in situations of cold cognition, adolescents or even preadolescents as young as 12 or 13 can reason and problem solve as well as or better than adults. However, in situations of hot cognition, adolescent problem solving is much more impulsive (Blakemore & Robbins, 2012).

Similar to all social mammals, human adolescents tend to demonstrate increased novelty seeking, increased risk taking, and greater affiliation with peers (Colver & Longwell, 2013). Yet, for most individuals, these activities peak in adolescence and then taper off as newly formed identities set and youth mature out of these tendencies (Spear, 2010; Steinberg, 2009). Brain research does not yet allow researchers to make definitive statements about the relationship between these adolescent behavior changes and changes in the brain, but these connections are being studied. Overall, as compared with adults, three themes have emerged: (1) adolescents do not yet have adult levels of maturity, responsibility, impulse control, and self-regulation; (2) adolescents are less autonomous and more susceptible to outside pressures (such as those from their peers) than adults; and (3) adolescents are less capable than adults of weighing potential consequences and considering future implications of their behavior (McCarter & Bridges, 2011; Spear, 2010). The emerging research on the adolescent brain is raising issues about

social policy related to adolescents and is being used in ways that may be both helpful and hurtful to adolescent development (Steinberg, 2009). This is illustrated by two examples from the past 10 years. In 2005, the U.S. Supreme Court heard the case of *Roper v. Simmons* (543 U.S. 551), involving 17-year-old Christopher Simmons, who had been convicted of murdering a woman during a robbery. He had been sentenced to death for his crime. His defense team argued that his still developing adolescent brain made him less culpable for his crime than an adult, and therefore he should not be subject to the death penalty. The neuroscience evidence may have tipped the scales in the Supreme Court's decision to overturn the death penalty for Simmons and all other juveniles (Haider, 2006). In another example, in 2006, the state of Kansas used an interpretation of neuroscience research to stipulate that "sexual acts with individuals under 16 years of age are illegal regardless of the age of the defendant." This would include any consensual touching by youth and classify such as criminal statutory rape except in instances where the individuals are married (Kansas Statutes, § 21-3502 and § 21-3504; Johnson, Blum, & Giedd, 2009).

The question being raised is, what is the extent of human agency, the capacity for decision making, among adolescents? The answer to that question will vary from adolescent to adolescent. There is great risk that neuroscience research will be overgeneralized to the detriment of adolescents. Johnson et al. (2009) caution that it is important to put the adolescent brain in context, remembering that there are complex interactions of the brain with other biological systems as well as with "multiple interactive influences including experience, parenting, socioeconomic status, individual agency and self-efficacy, nutrition, culture, psychological well-being, the physical and built environments, and social relationships and interactions" (p. 219). Johnson and colleagues also recommend that we avoid focusing on pathology and deficits in adolescent development and

> How do changes in the brain during adolescence affect the capacity to exercise human agency in making choices?

use neuroscience to examine the unique strengths and potentials of the adolescent brain. Colver and Longwell (2013) argue that though the adolescent brain leads to greater risk taking, it supports the challenges specific to adolescence and allows adolescents to "push ideas and boundaries to the limit" (p. 905). That perspective is in keeping with the increasing focus on positive psychology and the related positive youth development movement. Researchers at Duke University have created an interdisciplinary team whose mission is to educate society, especially young people, about the brain—how to use it effectively and how to keep it healthy. (A link to DukeLearn appears with the web resources at the end of this chapter.) Knowing more about the neurodevelopment of their own bodies may change the behaviors of some adolescents.

Nutrition, Exercise, and Sleep

At any stage along the life course, the right balance of nutrition, exercise, and sleep is important. As the transition from childhood to adulthood begins, early adolescent bodies undergo significant biological changes from their brains to the hair follicles on their legs and everywhere in between. Yet it appears that few adolescents maintain a healthy balance during their time in adolescent flux.

In many parts of the world, adolescents simply cannot get access to an adequate diet, resulting in high levels of anemia and youth who are underweight and overweight (Sawyer et al., 2012). In economically advanced nations, there is enough to eat, but adolescents often do not have a satisfactory diet to support the adolescent growth and development. In the United States, the Department of Health and Human Services (HHS) and the Department of Agriculture (USDA) worked together to develop the *Dietary Guidelines for Americans* (which is to be updated every 5 years; see www.dietaryguidelines .gov). For older children and adolescents (ages 4 to 18), they recommend that 45% to 65% of one's diet be from carbohydrates, 10% to 30% be from proteins, and 25% to 35% be from fats. Additionally, adolescents should consume 2 cups of fruit (not from juice) and 2½ cups of vegetables a day (for a

2,000-calorie intake); choose a variety of fruits and vegetables each day; choose from all five vegetable subgroups—dark green, orange, legumes, starchy vegetables, and other vegetables—several times a week; consume 3 or more ounce equivalents of whole-grain products per day; consume 3 cups per day of fat-free or low-fat milk or equivalent milk products; consume most of their fat intake from sources of polyunsaturated and monounsaturated fatty acids, such as fish, nuts, and vegetable oils; and consume less than 2,300 mg (approximately 1 teaspoon of salt) of sodium per day (U.S. Department of Agriculture & U.S. Department of Health and Human Services [USDA/USDHHS], 2010).

With obesity rates at profound proportions, food choices are being evaluated more seriously in the United States than ever before, and social workers can certainly help with this. Consider all of the factors that affect what you have for breakfast, lunch, and dinner. What factors might affect David Costa, Carl Fleischer, and Monica Golden's food choices?

The National Youth Risk Behavior Survey (YRBS) for 2011 (Eaton et al., 2012) suggests that in the United States only 22.4% of young people in Grades 9 to 12 had eaten at least five fruits and vegetables a day in the past 7 days, and 13.1% of students had not eaten breakfast at least once in the past 7 days. This is unfortunate, given the need for well-balanced diets and increased caloric intake during a period of rapid neurobiological and physical growth. Many U.S. youth say they don't have time to eat breakfast or that they aren't hungry in the morning. Yet the research is rather convincing, indicating that adolescent students who eat breakfast report higher energy and less fatigue and perform better on cognitive tests than students who do not eat breakfast (Cooper, Bandelow, & Nevill, 2011).

The recommendation is for most people of every age to engage in regular physical activity and reduce sedentary activities to promote health, psychological well-being, and a healthy body weight. Physical fitness should be achieved by including cardiovascular conditioning, stretching exercises for flexibility, and resistance exercises or calisthenics for muscle strength and endurance.

The specific recommendation for adolescents (6 to 17 years old) is to engage in at least 60 minutes of physical activity on most, preferably all, days of the week (USDA/USDHHS, 2010).

Again, the data are not promising. Nationwide, 49.5% of high school students reported being physically active for a total of at least 60 minutes a day on at least 5 of the 7 days preceding the survey. Conversely, 31.1% of students played video or computer games, or used the computer for something other than school work, for 3 hours or more on an average school day, and 32.4% watched television for 3 hours or more on an average school day (Eaton et al., 2012).

Along with other changes of puberty, there are marked changes in sleep patterns (National Sleep Foundation, 2013). Changes in circadian rhythms create a tendency to be more alert late at night and to wake later in the morning. Given the mismatch of these sleep patterns with the timing of the school day, adolescents often doze off during the school day. Sleep researchers suggest that adolescents require 8½ to 9¼ hours of sleep each night (National Sleep Foundation, 2013).

Researchers have found that typical adolescents in the United States are chronically sleep-deprived (Moreno, Furtner, & Rivara, 2010). Survey data show that only 15% of U.S. adolescents get at least 8½ hours of sleep on school nights (National Sleep Foundation, 2013).

Moreover, sleep deprivation has recently been linked to poor food choices. In their 2013 study of 13,284 teens, Krueger, Reither, Peppard, Krueger, and Hale found that 18% of youth slept less than 7 hours a night. Adolescents with sleep deprivation were less likely than well-slept adolescents to eat healthy food throughout the week and were more likely to eat fast food at least twice a week (Krueger et al., 2013). School performance is affected by insufficient sleep (Wong et al., 2013). One research team found that cognitive performance was impaired in Spanish male adolescents who slept less than 8 hours a day, but this was not found to be the case for female adolescents (Ortega et al., 2010). Mood is also improved by sufficient sleep (Wong et al., 2013). As suggested, the risks of

sleep deprivation are varied, and they can be serious (National Sleep Foundation, 2013). Drowsiness or falling asleep at the wheel is a principal cause of at least 100,000 U.S. police-reported traffic collisions annually. Sleep deficit contributes to acne, aggressive behavior, eating too much or unhealthy foods, illness, and unsafe use of equipment. It also heightens the effects of alcohol and can lead to increased use of caffeine and nicotine (National Sleep Foundation, 2013).

Critical Thinking Questions 6.1

What are the implications of recent research findings about the adolescent brain for social policy? This research is leading to a number of policy discussions about several issues, including the timing of the school day; regulations for adolescent driving, including the legal age of driving, whether evening driving should be allowed, whether other adolescents can be present in the car of an adolescent driver, and so on; the drinking age; and the age when a juvenile can be tried as an adult in a court of law. What opinions do you hold about these issues? How are those opinions shaped by recent brain research?

PSYCHOLOGICAL ASPECTS OF ADOLESCENCE

Psychological development in adolescence is multifaceted. Adolescents have psychological reactions, sometimes dramatic, to the biological, social, and cultural dimensions of their lives. They become capable of and interested in discovering and forming their psychological selves. They may show heightened creativity as well as interest in humanitarian issues; ethics; religion; and reflection and record keeping, as in a diary (Rew, 2005). There is evidence that adolescence is a time of increased emotional complexity and a growing capacity to understand and express a wider range of emotions and to gain insight into one's own emotions (Silvers et al., 2012). Three areas of psychological development are particularly noteworthy: psychological reactions to biological changes, changes in cognition, and identity development.

Psychological Reactions to Biological Changes

"Will my body ever start changing? Will my body ever stop changing? Is this normal? Am I normal? Why am I suddenly interested in girls? And why are the girls all taller (and stronger) than me? How can I ask Mom if I can shave my legs?" These are some of the questions mentioned when Jane Kroger (2007, pp. 33–34) asked a class of 12- and 13-year-old adolescents what type of questions they think most about. As you can see, themes of biological changes were pervasive. If you can remember your own puberty process, you probably are not surprised that researchers have found that pubertal adolescents are preoccupied with physical changes and appearances (Price, 2009). Young adolescents are able to reflect on and give meaning to their biological transformations. Of course, responses to puberty are influenced by the way other people, including parents, siblings, teachers, and peers, respond to the adolescent's changing body. In addition, reactions to puberty are influenced by other events in the adolescent's life, such as school transition, family conflict, and peer relationships. Media images also play an important role (Krayer, Ingledew, & Iphofen, 2008).

It appears that puberty is usually viewed more positively by boys than by girls, with boys focused on increased muscle mass and physical strength and girls focused on increased body weight and fat deposits (Price, 2009). These reactions are rooted in European culture that values muscular males and petite, shapely females. For girls, body dissatisfaction and self-consciousness peaks from ages 13 to 15. There is evidence that African American adolescent girls are more satisfied with their body image and less inclined to eating disorders than Caucasian American girls, most likely due to a different cultural valuing of thinness in females (Franko & Striegel-Moore, 2002). Reactions to menstruation are often mixed (Uskul, 2004). One study of Chinese American adolescent girls found 85% reported that they were annoyed and embarrassed by their first menstruation, but 66% also reported positive feelings (Tang, Yeung, & Lee, 2003). In a focus group of 53 women from 34 different countries, most of the participants had vivid memories of their first menstruation. They reported both positive and negative emotions, but negative reactions (such as embarrassment, shame, fear, shock, and confusion) were more often noted. Reactions to menarche were greatly affected by the type of information and level of support that the young women received from their mothers (Uskul, 2004). Research shows that pubescent girls talk with parents and friends about their first menstruation, but pubescent boys do not discuss with anyone their first ejaculation, an event sometimes seen as the closest male equivalent to first menstruation (Kroger, 2007). Pubescent boys may receive less information from adults about nocturnal ejaculations than their sisters receive about menarche.

Because the onset and experience of puberty vary greatly, adolescents need reassurance regarding their own growth patterns. Some adolescents will be considered early maturers, and some will be considered late maturers. Timing and tempo of puberty are influenced by genetics, and there are ethnic differences, as well. On average, African American adolescents enter puberty earlier than Mexican American adolescents, who enter puberty earlier than Caucasian Americans (Chumlea et al., 2003). There are psychological and social consequences of early maturing for both male and female adolescents, but the research findings are not always consistent. A recent longitudinal study of Australian children found that those who experienced early puberty had more adjustment problems than their age peers; this was true for both boys and girls (Mensah et al., 2013). The researchers found, however, that the children who entered puberty early demonstrated more adjustment problems from early childhood through early adolescence. They concluded that the data support a "life course hypothesis that differences in pubertal timing and childhood adjustment may at least in part result from genetic and environmental factors early in life" (p. 122). Further longitudinal research is needed to provide better understanding of the early risk factors for a difficult transition to puberty.

Changes in Cognition

Adolescence is considered to be a crucial phase in cognitive development, with development occurring in three main areas (Sanders, 2013):

1. *Improved reasoning skills*: the ability to consider a range of possibilities, to think hypothetically, and to engage in logical analysis

2. *Abstract thinking*: the ability to imagine things not seen or experienced

3. *Meta-cognition*: the ability to think about thinking

These abilities are components of Jean Piaget's fourth stage of cognitive development called formal operational thought (see Exhibit 3.5 for an overview of Piaget's stages of cognitive development). *Formal operational thought* suggests the capacity to apply hypothetical reasoning to various situations and the ability to use symbols to solve problems. David Costa, for example, demonstrated formal operational thought when he considered the possibility of getting to know Theo. He considered the reactions from his other friends if he were to get together with Theo, he examined his thoughts, and he formulated a strategy based on the possibilities and on his thoughts.

Whereas younger children focus on the here-and-now world in front of them, the adolescent brain is capable of retaining larger amounts of information. Thus, adolescents are capable of hypothesizing beyond the present objects. This ability also allows adolescents to engage in decision making based on a cost-benefit analysis. As noted, brain research indicates that adolescent problem solving is as good as adult problem solving in cold-cognition situations but is not equally sound in hot-cognition situations. Furthermore, brain development alone does not result in formal operational thinking. The developing brain needs social environments that encourage hypothetical, abstract reasoning and opportunities to investigate the world (Cohen & Sandy, 2007; Gehlbach, 2006). Formal operational thinking is more imperative in some cultures than in others but is most imperative in many fields in the changing economic base of postindustrialized societies. One research team found that Taiwanese adolescents, who are reared in a collectivist culture, exercise formal operational thinking but rely on parents and other important people to validate their thoughts (Lee & Beckert, 2012). More research is needed to explore cultural variations in cognitive autonomy. It is also important to remember that although contemporary education is organized to facilitate formal operational thinking, students in the United States and around the world do not have equal access to sound curriculum and instruction.

Recent research is suggesting that adolescence is a period of profound advancements in social cognition, which is the processing, storing, and using of information about other people. Brain researchers are identifying the brain regions that are involved in *mentalizing*, or the ability to think about the mental states and intentions of others, and finding that these regions of the brain continue to develop throughout adolescence (Blakemore & Robbins, 2012). They argue that this helps to explain why adolescents are more sociable, form more complex peer relationships, and are more sensitive to peer acceptance and rejection than younger children (Blakemore, 2012). One research team has investigated another way of thinking about changes in social cognition during adolescence. They found that group identity becomes a dominant theme in early adolescence, and automatic evaluations develop based on in-group and out-group memberships, with a tendency for positive evaluation of in-group members and negative evaluation of out-group members. They found that although younger children are aware of group identities, they do not develop automatic evaluations based on them (Degner & Wentura, 2010). This would suggest that early adolescence is a good time to help young people think about their automatic evaluations related to group identity.

Identity Development

There is growing agreement that identity is a complex concept. **Psychological identity** is a "person's self-definition as a separate and distinct individual" (Gardiner & Kosmitzki, 2011, p. 165). **Social identity** is the part of the self-concept that comes from knowledge of one's membership in a social group and the emotional significance of that membership (Gardiner & Kosmitzki, 2011). Lene Arnett Jensen (2003) suggests that adolescents increasingly develop multicultural identities as they are exposed to diverse cultural beliefs, either through firsthand experience or through the media. She argues that the process of developing an identity presents new challenges to adolescents in a global society. Jensen gives the example of arranged marriage in India, noting that on the one hand, Indian adolescents grow up with cultural values favoring arranged marriage, but on the other hand, they are increasingly exposed to values that emphasize freedom of choice. But identity is even more complex than that; it is increasingly examined from an *intersectional* perspective that recognizes the multiple social identities we must integrate, including gender identity, ethnic/racial identity, religious identity, social class identity, national identity, regional identity, and so on (see Shade, Kools, Weiss, & Pinderhughes, 2011).

> How do factors such as gender, race, ethnicity, and social class affect identity development?

Theories of Self and Identity

A number of prominent psychologists have put forward theories that address self or psychological identity development in adolescence. Exhibit 6.2 provides an overview of six theorists: Freud, Erikson, Kegan, Marcia, Piaget, and Kohlberg. All six help to explain how a concept of self or identity develops, and all six suggest that it cannot develop fully before adolescence. Piaget and Kohlberg suggest that some individuals may not reach these higher levels of identity development at all.

Exhibit 6.2 Theories of Self or Identity in Adolescence

Theorist	Developmental Stage	Major Task or Processes
Freud	Genital stage	To develop libido capable of reproduction and sexual intimacy
Erikson	Identity versus role diffusion	To find one's place in the world through self-certainty versus apathy, role experimentation versus negative identity, and anticipation of achievement versus work paralysis
Kegan	Affiliation versus abandonment (early adolescence)	To search for membership, acceptance, and group identity, versus a sense of being left behind, rejected, and abandoned
Marcia	Ego identity statuses	To develop one of these identity statuses: identity diffusion, foreclosure, moratorium, or identity achievement
Piaget	Formal operational thought	To develop the capacity for abstract problem formulation, hypothesis development, and solution testing
Kohlberg	Postconventional morality	To develop moral principles that transcend one's own society: individual ethics, societal rights, and universal principles of right and wrong

Sigmund Freud (1905/1953) thought of human development as a series of five psychosexual stages in the expression of libido (sensual pleasure). The fifth stage, the genital stage, occurs in adolescence, when reproduction and sexual intimacy become possible.

Building on Freud's work, Erik Erikson (1950, 1959, 1963, 1968) proposed eight stages of psychosocial development (refer back to Exhibit 3.7 for a summary of Erikson's eight stages). He viewed psychosocial crisis as an opportunity and challenge. Each Eriksonian stage requires the mastery of a particular developmental task related to identity. Erikson's fifth stage, identity versus role diffusion, is relevant to adolescence. The developmental task is to establish a coherent sense of identity; failure to complete this task successfully leaves the adolescent without a solid sense of identity.

Robert Kegan (1982, 1994) asserts that there should be another stage between middle childhood and adolescence in Erikson's model. He suggests that before working on psychological identity, early adolescents face the psychosocial conflict of affiliation versus abandonment. The main concern is being accepted by a group, and the fear is being left behind or rejected. Successful accomplishment of group membership allows the young person to turn to the question of "Who am I?" in mid- and late adolescence.

James Marcia (1966, 1980) expanded on Erikson's notion that adolescents struggle with the issue of identity versus role diffusion, and his theory is the most researched of adolescent identity. Marcia proposed that adolescents vary in how easily they go about developing a personal identity, and he described four identity statuses based on two aspects of identity development—the amount of exploration being done toward identity development and the amount of commitment to a particular identity:

1. *Identity diffusion*: no commitment made to roles and values, with or without exploration

2. *Foreclosure*: commitment made to roles and values without exploration

3. *Moratorium*: exploration of roles and values without commitment

4. *Identity achievement*: exploration of roles and values followed by commitment

Jean Piaget proposed four major stages leading to adult thought (refer back to Exhibit 3.5 for an overview of Piaget's stages). He expected the last stage, the stage of formal operations, to occur in adolescence, enabling the adolescent to engage in more abstract thinking about "who I am." Piaget (1972) also thought that adolescents begin to use formal operational skills to think in terms of what is best for society.

Lawrence Kohlberg (1976, 1984) expanded on Piaget's ideas about moral thinking to describe three major levels of moral development (refer back to Exhibit 4.2 for an overview of Kohlberg's stage theory). Kohlberg thought that adolescents become capable of **postconventional moral reasoning**, or morality based on moral principles that transcend social rules, but that many never go beyond conventional morality, or morality based on social rules.

These theories have been influential in conceptualizations of identity development. Morris Rosenberg (1986) provides another useful model of identity to keep in mind while working with adolescents—or perhaps to share with adolescents who are in the process of identity formation. His model includes both social identity and psychological identity but also incorporates physical traits, which taps into the important role that body image plays in adolescent development. Rosenberg suggests that identity comprises three major parts, outlined in Exhibit 6.3:

- *Social identity* is made up of several elements derived from interaction with other people and social systems, including social statuses, membership groups, and social types.
- *Dispositions* are self-ascribed aspects of identity.
- *Physical characteristics* are simply one's physical traits, which all contribute a great deal to sense of self.

Exhibit 6.3 Rosenberg's Model of Identity

Social Identity	Disposition	Physical Characteristics
Social statuses: basic classifications or demographic characteristics, such as sex, age, and socioeconomic status	Attitudes (e.g., conservatism, liberalism)	Height
	Traits (e.g., generosity, bravery)	Weight
Membership groups: groups with which the individual shares an interest, belief, origin, or physical or regional continuity (e.g., groups based on religion, political party, or race)	Abilities (e.g., musical talent, athletic skill)	Body build
		Facial features
	Values (e.g., efficiency, equality)	
Labels: identifiers that result from social labeling (as when the boy who skips school becomes a delinquent)	Personality traits (e.g., introversion, extroversion)	
	Habits (e.g., making lists, getting up early)	
Derived statuses: identities based on the individual's role history (e.g., veteran, high school athlete, or Harvard alumnus)	Tendencies (e.g., to arrive late, to exaggerate)	
	Likes or preferences (e.g., romance novels, pizzas)	
Social types: interests, attitudes, habits, or general characteristics (e.g., jock, geek, head, playboy, or go-getter)		
Personal identities: unique labels attached to individuals (e.g., first name, first and last names, social security number, fingerprints, or DNA)		

SOURCE: Based on Rosenberg, 1986

Exhibit 6.4 uses Rosenberg's model to analyze the identities of David Costa, Carl Fleischer, and Monica Golden. Notice that disposition is an element of identity based on self-definition. In contrast, a label is determined by others, and physical characteristics are genetically influenced. David has an athletic body and thinks of himself as athletic, but his parents—and perhaps others—label him as a freak. He is working to incorporate the fact that he is different into his identity. Carl has been labeled as a fatso, an underachiever, and a smoker. He seems to have incorporated these negative labels into his identity. Monica has been labeled as an overachiever, but she does not absorb the negative label, reframing it instead as ambitious.

Scholars generally agree that identity formation is structured by the sociocultural context (see Gardiner & Kosmitzki, 2011; Kroger, 2007). Thus, the options offered to adolescents vary across cultures. Societies such as North American and other Western societies that put a high value on autonomy offer more options for adolescents than more collectivist-oriented societies. Some writers suggest that having a large number of options increases stress for adolescents (Gardiner & Kosmitzki, 2011). Think about the case studies of David Costa, Carl Fleischer, and Monica Golden. What is the sociocultural context of their identity struggles? What choices do they have, given their sociocultural contexts?

Exhibit 6.4 Examples of Adolescent Identity

Element of Identity	David	Carl	Monica
Social Identity			
Social statuses	Male, 17, middle class	Male, 17, working class	Female, 17, upper-middle class
Membership groups	Bolivian American, gay	European American, heads	African American, Christian, Young Republicans
Labels	Freak, athlete	Fatso, underachiever, smoker	Overachiever, brain
Derived statuses	Baseball player	Pizza deliverer	Senior class vice president, babysitter, track athlete
Social types	Jock	Geek, head (affiliate)	Brain, go-getter
Personal identity	David Costa	Carl Fleischer	Monica Golden
Disposition	Athletic	Underachiever, not popular, fat, slow, likes to get high, likes to surf the Internet	Athletic, ambitious, extroverted, likes children
Physical characteristics	Athletic build	Overweight	Tall

For those aspects of identity that we shape ourselves, individuals have four ways of trying on and developing a preference for certain identities:

1. *Future orientation.* By adolescence, youth have developed two important cognitive skills: They are able to consider the future, and they are able to construct abstract thoughts. These skills allow them to choose from a list of hypothetical behaviors based on the potential outcomes resulting from those behaviors. David Costa demonstrates future orientation in his contemplation regarding Theo. Adolescents also contemplate potential future selves.

2. *Role experimentation.* According to Erikson (1963), adolescence provides a psychosocial moratorium—a period during which youth have the latitude to experiment with social roles. Thus, adolescents typically sample membership in different cliques, build relationships with various mentors, take various academic electives, and join assorted groups and organizations—all in an attempt to further define themselves. Monica Golden, for instance, sampled various potential career paths before deciding on becoming a pediatrician.

3. *Exploration.* Whereas role experimentation is specific to trying new roles, exploration refers to the comfort an adolescent has with trying new things. The more comfortable the individual is with exploration, the easier identity formation will be.

4. *Self-evaluation.* During the quest for identity, adolescents are constantly sizing themselves up against their peers. Erikson (1968) suggested that the development of identity is a process of personal reflection and observation of oneself in relation to

others. George Herbert Mead (1934) suggested that individuals create a **generalized other** to represent how others are likely to view and respond to them. The role of the generalized other in adolescents' identity formation is evident when adolescents act on the assumed reactions of their families or peers. For example, what Monica Golden wears to school may be based not on what she thinks would be most comfortable or look the best but rather on what she thinks her peers expect her to wear. Thus, she does not wear miniskirts to school because "everyone" (generalized other) will think she is "loose." Recent attention has been paid to identity as a life story that begins to be told in late adolescence, a story one tells oneself about one's past, present, and anticipated future (see McLean & Mansfield, 2012). This is called narrative identity.

Gender Identity

Adolescence, like early childhood, covered in Chapter 4, is a time of significant gender identification. **Gender identity**, the internalized understanding of one's gender, begins in early childhood but is elaborated on and revised during adolescence (Steensma, Kreukels, de Vries, & Cohen-Kettenis, 2013). Efforts are made to integrate the biological, psychological, and social dimensions of sex and gender. *Gender expression* refers to how individuals express their socially constructed gender and may include how they dress, their general appearance, the way they speak, or the way they carry themselves. *Gender roles* are societal expectations of how individuals should act, think, or feel based on their assigned gender or biological sex (and based on the predominant binary system: male/female). Culture plays a large role in gender identity, gender expression, and gender roles. Gender roles can be a source of painful culture clash for some immigrant groups who are migrating to North America and Europe, harder for some ethnic groups than for others. But there is evidence that many immigrant families and individuals learn to be bicultural in terms of gender expectations, holding on to some traditional expectations while also innovating some new ways of doing gender roles (see Denner & Dunbar, 2004).

In the majority of cases, gender identity develops in accordance with physical characteristics, but this does not always happen. Surprisingly little is known about the influences on adolescent gender identity development (Steensma et al., 2013). In recent years, the term *cisgender* has been used to describe situations in which people's gender identity matches their assigned gender or biological sex. *Trans* is an umbrella term used to include transgender, transsexual, and transvestite persons as well as other gender nonconformists. *Transgender* describes youth who have been assigned a gender (based on their biological sex) and identify as the "opposite" gender. These individuals may or may not alter their bodies through surgery or hormones. *Transsexuals* are folks who wish to alter their physical bodies through surgery and/or hormones to have their bodies match their internalized gender identities. *Transvestite* refers to people who wear the clothing of the "opposite" gender and may also identify as cross-dressers or drag kings/queens. One study followed the adjustment of 20 adolescent transsexuals who had sex-reassignment surgery. In the 1 to 4 years of follow-up, the adolescents were doing well, and none of them had regrets about the decision to undergo the sex change (Smith, van Goozen, & Cohen-Kettenis, 2001).

Gender identity is not the same as sexual orientation. Gender identity is how I consider myself, man, woman, somewhere in between or neither; and sexual orientation refers to whether I am sexually attracted to members of the same sex, the opposite sex, or both. As we work with adolescents and strive to be responsive to their stories, we must allow youth to share their identities (if they are known) with us and not assume that they are cisgender or heterosexual. Some adolescents will still be questioning and, thus, are unsure about their sexual orientation or gender identity. Sexual orientation is discussed later under the Adolescent Sexuality section.

Cultural Identity

Research indicates that ethnic origin is not likely to be a key ingredient of identity for Caucasian

North American adolescents, but it is often central to identity in adolescents of ethnic minority groups (Branch, Tayal, & Triplett, 2000). Considerable research indicates that adolescence is a time when young people evaluate their ethnic background and explore ethnic identity (see French, Seidman, Allen, & Aber, 2006; Phinney, 2006). The development of ethnic identity in adolescence has been the focus of research across Canada, the United States, and Europe in recent years as ethnic diversity increases in all of these countries (see, e.g., Street, Harris-Britt, & Walker-Barnes, 2009). Ethnic minority youth are challenged to develop a sense of themselves as members of an ethnic minority group while also coming to terms with their national identity (Lam & Smith, 2009). Adolescents tend to have wider experience with multicultural groups than when they were younger and may be exposed to ethnic discrimination, which can complicate the development of cultural pride and belonging (Costigan, Su, & Hua, 2009).

Consider Monica Golden, who is an upper-middle-class, African American teenager in a predominantly White high school. What are some of the potential added challenges of Monica's adolescent identity formation? Is it any wonder she is hoping to attend Howard University, a historically Black school, where she could surround herself with African American role models and professional support networks?

Researchers have found that ethnic minority adolescents tend to develop strong ethnic identity, but there is also variability within ethnic groups in terms of extent of ethnic identity. Costigan and colleagues (2009) reviewed the literature on ethnic identity among Chinese Canadian youth and concluded that the evidence indicates a strong ethnic identity among these youth. Conversely, there was much variability in the extent to which these youth reported a Canadian national identity. Adolescents negotiated ethnic identity in diverse ways across different settings, with different approaches being used at home versus in public settings. Lam and Smith (2009) studied how African and Caribbean adolescents (ages 11 to 16) in Britain negotiate ethnic identity and national identity and had similar findings to those for Chinese Canadian youth. They found that both groups of adolescents, African and Caribbean, rated their ethnic identity higher than their national identity and reported more pride in their ethnic heritage than in being British. The researchers found, however, that girls reported stronger ethnic identity than boys.

Using in-depth interviews rather than standardized instruments, Rivas-Drake (2008) found three different styles of ethnic identity among Latinos in one public university in the United States. One group reported high individualistic achievement motivation and alienation from other Latinos. A second group reported strong identification with Latinos and was motivated to remove perceived barriers for the group. A third group reported strong connection to Latinos but was not motivated to work to remove barriers for the group.

How can social workers use research like this to understand risk and protection in minority youth?

Cultural identity usually develops within the context of the family, and there has been a general belief that children of immigrants acculturate more quickly than their parents do, leaving parents with a stronger ethnic identity than their children. Some research in Canada questions that belief. Costigan and Dokis (2006) found that Chinese Canadian mothers and children indicated stronger ethnic identity than the fathers, and mothers and children did not differ from each other. Interestingly, they found that the adolescents tended to report stronger ethnic identity than their parents in families characterized by high levels of warmth. This finding may reflect the Canadian cultural context: Canada has an official policy of multiculturalism, which promotes the maintenance of one's cultural heritage. Conversely, researchers in the United States have found that African American parents are more likely than parents in other ethnic groups to feel the need to prepare their adolescents for racial bias as a part of their racial and ethnic socialization (Hughes, Hagelskamp, Way, & Foust, 2009). This most likely reflects a more hostile environment for African American youth in the United States than for the Chinese Canadian youth.

The available research on cultural identity among ethnic minority youth indicates that most of these youth cope by becoming bicultural, developing skills to operate within at least two cultures. Research indicates that family conflict can arise when there are discrepancies in cultural identity between adolescents and their parents. One research team found that a sample of ethnic minority male and female adolescents had similar levels of disparity with their parents regarding ethnic identity. However, parent-adolescent discrepancies in ethnic identity were associated with elevated depression and social stress in female adolescents but not in male adolescents (Ansary, Scorpio, & Catanzariti, 2013). This research should alert social workers to tune in to the process of ethnic identity development when they work with ethnic minority youth. It appears that ethnic identity is a theme for both David Costa and Monica Golden. They both appear to be developing some comfort with being bicultural, but they are negotiating their bicultural status in different ways. Discussion about their ethnic identity might reveal more struggle than we expected. Some youth may be more likely to withdraw from the challenges of accessing mainstream culture rather than confronting these challenges and seeking workable solutions. We must be alert to this possibility.

> ### Critical Thinking Questions 6.2
>
> What do you recall about your own psychological reactions to your changing body during puberty? What factors do you think influenced your reactions? With which groups did you identify during adolescence? What were your multiple social identities? Which identities were most important to you during adolescence? Which identities are important to you now?

SOCIAL ASPECTS OF ADOLESCENCE

The social environment—family, peers, organizations, communities, institutions, and so on—is a significant element of adolescent life. For one thing, as already noted, identity develops through social transactions. For another, as adolescents become more independent and move into the world, they develop their own relationships with more elements of the social environment.

Relationships With Family

Answering the question "Who am I?" includes a consideration of the question "How am I different from my brothers and sisters, my parents, and other family members?" For many adolescents, this question begins the process of **individuation**—the development of a self or identity that is unique and separate. David Costa seems to have started the process of individuation; he recognizes that he may not want to be what his parents want him to be. He does not yet seem comfortable with this idea, however. Carl Fleischer is not sure how he is similar to and different from his absent father. Monica Golden has begun to recognize some ways that she is different from her siblings, and she is involved in her own personal exploration of career options that fit her disposition. It would appear that she is the furthest along in the individuation process.

The concept of independence is largely influenced by culture, and mainstream culture in the United States places a high value on independence. However, as social workers, we need to recognize that the notion of pushing the adolescent to develop an identity separate from family is not acceptable to all cultural groups in the United States or other places around the world (Gardiner & Kosmitzki, 2011). One research team found that African American adolescents have less decision making autonomy in middle adolescence than European American adolescents (Gutman & Eccles, 2007). Peter Nguyen (2008; Nguyen & Cheung, 2009) has studied the relationships between Vietnamese American adolescents and their parents and found that a majority of the adolescents perceived their fathers as using a traditional authoritarian parenting style and see this as posing problems for the adolescents' mental health in the context of the multicultural society in the

United States. Latino families in the United States have been found to keep very close boundaries around the family during adolescence (Garcia-Preto, 2011). Filial piety, respect for parents and ancestors, is a strong value in East Asian cultures (Schneider, Lee, & Alvarez-Valdivia, 2012). Our assessments of adolescent individuation should be culturally sensitive. Likewise, we must be realistic in our assessments of the ability of adolescents with cognitive, emotional, and physical disabilities to function independently.

Overall, families tend to respond to the adolescent desire for greater independence by renegotiating family roles and opening family boundaries to allow for the adolescent's greater participation in relationships outside the family (Garcia-Preto, 2011). The research literature on the relationships between parents and their adolescents indicates that, in general, these relationships are "close, supportive, and warm" (Galambos & Kotylak, 2012). However, many families with adolescents have a high level of conflict. Conflict is particularly evident in families experiencing additional stressors, such as divorce and economic difficulties (Fine et al., 2010). Conflict also plays out differently at different points in adolescence. Research suggests that conflicts with parents increase around the time of puberty but begin to decrease after that (Galambos & Kotylak, 2012). Both parents and adolescents need some time to adjust to this new life stage.

How can families stay connected to their adolescents while also honoring their struggle for independence and increased agency in making choices?

Adolescent struggles for independence can be especially potent in multigenerational contexts (Garcia-Preto, 2011). These struggles typically come at a time when parents are in midlife and grandparents are entering late adulthood and both are facing stressors of their own. Adolescent demands for independence may reignite unresolved conflicts between the parents and the grandparents and stir the pot of family discord. Sibling relationships may also change in adolescence. Longitudinal research indicates that, compared with middle childhood, adolescents report lower levels of positive sibling relationships during early adolescence, followed by increased intimacy in midadolescence (Shanahan, Waite, & Boyd, 2012).

The Society for Research on Adolescence prepared an international perspective on adolescence in the 21st century and reached three conclusions regarding adolescents and their relationships with their families:

• Families are and will remain a central source of support to adolescents in most parts of the world. Cultural traditions that support family cohesion, such as those in the Middle East, South Asia, and China, remain particularly strong, despite rapid change. A great majority of teenagers around the world experience close and functional relationships with their parents.

• Adolescents are living in a wider array of diverse and fluid family situations than was true a generation ago. These include divorced, single-parent, remarried, gay and lesbian, and multilocal families. More adolescents live in households without men. As a result of AIDS, regional conflicts, and migratory labor, many adolescents do not live with their parents.

• Many families are becoming better positioned to support their adolescents' preparation for adulthood. Smaller family sizes result in adults devoting more resources and attention to each child. Parents in many parts of the world are adopting a more responsive and communicative parenting style, which facilitates development of interpersonal skills and enhances mental health (Larson, Wilson, & Mortimer, 2002).

Relationships With Peers

In the quest for autonomy and identity, adolescents begin to differentiate themselves from their parents and associate with their peers. Peer influence is strongest in early adolescence (Hafen, Laursen, & DeLay, 2012). Early adolescents are

Photo 6.2 Peer relationships are a fertile testing ground for youth and their emerging identities.

© Jack Hollingsworth/Digital Vision/ThinkStock

likely to select friends that are similar to them in gender and interests, but by middle adolescence, the peer group often includes opposite-sex friends as well as same-sex friends (Seiffge-Krenge & Shulman, 2012). Most early adolescents have one close friend, but the stability of these friendships is not high. In early adolescence the peer group tends to be larger than in middle childhood; these larger peer groups are known as *cliques*. By midadolescence, the peer group is organized around common interests; these groups tend to be even larger than cliques and are generally known as *crowds* (Brown & Klute, 2003). David Costa hangs out with the athletic crowd but seeks support from gay peers. Carl Fleischer is making contact with the "heads" crowd. Monica Golden's crowds would include peer counselors and the

Young Republicans. Peer relationships contribute to adolescents' identities, behaviors, and personal and social competence.

Peer relationships are a fertile testing ground for youth and their emerging identities. Many adolescents seek out a peer group with compatible members, and inclusion or exclusion from certain groups can affect their identity and overall development. For some adolescents, participation in certain peer groups influences their behavior negatively. Peer influence may not be strong enough to undo protective factors, but if the youth is already at risk, the influence of peers becomes that much stronger. Sexual behaviors and pregnancy status are often the same for same-sex best friends. Substance use is also a behavior that most often occurs in groups of adolescents. The same is true for violent and delinquent behaviors. Researchers debate whether selection (choosing friends based on shared delinquent behaviors) or socialization (peer influence) plays a more important role here (Hafen et al., 2012).

Romantic Relationships

Until recently, adolescent romantic relationships received little or no attention from researchers. Since the beginning of the 21st century, theories of adolescent romantic relationships have been developed and a great number of studies have been conducted. Both the theories and the research have typically focused on heterosexual romantic relationships. The following discussion of heterosexual romantic relationships in adolescence is based on a recent review of the research on the topic by Seiffge-Krenge and Shulman (2012). Although same-sex romantic relationships are becoming more visible, there is very little research on same-sex romantic relationships in adolescence. What research there is has tended to focus on same-sex attractions in adolescence from a risk perspective. The following discussion of same-sex romantic relationships in adolescence is based on a recent review of research on the topic by Russell, Watson, and Muraco (2012).

With the hormonal changes of adolescence, youth begin to be interested in sexual gratification and emotional union with a partner. This typically begins with romantic fantasies in early adolescence, fantasies that are often shared in same-gender friendship groups. As they move into mixed-gender groups in midadolescence, heterosexual youth have an opportunity to meet potential romantic partners. Researchers in the United States have found that nearly all 13- and 14-year-old adolescents report romantic fantasies and a desire to date. By late adolescence, most youth in the United States have been involved in some kind of romantic relationship, and the rates are similar in other economically advanced countries. The duration of romantic relationships is about 3 months in early adolescence and from 1 to 2 years in middle

and late adolescence. Research indicates that most people have at least one romantic breakup during adolescence, and that a breakup is a highly stressful event. (See Seiffge-Krenge & Shulman, 2012, for a fuller discussion of the research on adolescent heterosexual romantic relationships.) It is important to remember that in the United States and many other societies, romantic relationships develop through a dance of flirtation and dating, but in some cultures, the romantic relationship develops in the context of an arranged marriage.

In contrast to the burgeoning research on adolescent heterosexual romantic relationships, there is very little research on adolescent same-sex romantic relationships. There are a number of reasons why that research is hard to do, but an important reason is that, because of stigma and internalized homophobia, many youth with same-sex attractions do not "come out." Most of the research on this topic is based on small samples. Research is indicating, however, that as society becomes more accepting, U.S. youth with same-sex attractions are becoming more likely to act on those attractions. One longitudinal study of a cohort born in the mid-1990s found that less than 10% of youth with same-sex attractions reported ever having a same-sex romantic relationship, and a majority of these youth reported ever having a heterosexual romantic relationship. Another study, conducted 10 years later, found that a majority of same-sex-attracted youth were currently or had recently been in a same-sex romantic relationship. Research finds that one issue for youth with same-sex attractions is the relatively small pool of potential romantic partners. One study found that gay male youth typically begin the romantic relationship with a sexual experience, and lesbian youth typically begin as close friends. Another study found that youth with same-sex attractions who reported heterosexual dating had higher levels of internalized homophobia than similar youth who did not engage in heterosexual dating. (See Russell et al., 2012, for a fuller discussion of the research on adolescent same-sex romantic relationships.)

Relationships With Organizations, Communities, and Institutions

As adolescents loosen their ties to parents, they develop more direct relationships in other arenas such as school, the broader community, employment, and social media/technology.

School

In the United States, as well as in other wealthy nations, youth are required to stay in school through a large portion of adolescence. The situation is quite different in many poor nations, however, where children may not even receive a primary school education. In their time spent at school, adolescents are gaining skills and knowledge for their next step in life, either moving into the workforce or continuing their education. In school, they also have the opportunity to evolve socially and emotionally; school is a fertile ground for practicing future orientation, role experimentation, exploration, and self-evaluation.

Middle schools in the United States usually have a structured format and environment; high schools are less structured in both format and environment, allowing a gradual transition to greater autonomy. The school experience changes radically, however, at the college level. Many college students are away from home for the first time and are in very unstructured environments. David Costa, Carl Fleischer, and Monica Golden have had different experiences with structure in their environments to date. David's environment has required him to move flexibly between two cultures. That experience may help to prepare him for the unstructured college environment. Carl has had the least structured home life. It remains to be seen whether that has helped him to develop skills in structuring his own environment or left him with insufficient models for doing so. Monica is accustomed to juggling multiple commitments and expectations. Time management skills will help with the transition to college, but she may struggle with having freedom from

Photo 6.3 Adolescents in many cultures become involved in romantic relationships during middle school and high school.

© iStockphoto.com

pressing family and community expectations for the first time.

School is also an institutional context in the United States where cultures intersect, which may create difficulties for students whose appearance or behavior is different from the Eurocentric, female-centered education model. You may not realize how biased the educational model in the United States is until you view it through a different cultural lens. We can use a Native American lens as an example. Michael Walkingstick Garrett (1995) uses the experiences of the boy Wind-Wolf as an example of the incongruence between Native American culture and the typical education model:

> Wind-Wolf is required by law to attend public school. . . . He speaks softly, does not maintain eye contact with the teacher as a sign of respect, and rarely responds immediately to questions, knowing that it is good to reflect on what has been said. He may be looking out the window during class, as if daydreaming, because he has been taught to always be aware of changes in the natural world. These behaviors are interpreted by his teacher as either lack of interest or dumbness. (p. 204)

What are some ways that different cultural expectations regarding education affect adolescent development?

Children in the United States spend less time in school-related activities than do German, Korean, and Japanese children and have been noted to put less emphasis on scholastic achievement. Some researchers attribute oft-noted cross-cultural differences in mathematics achievement to these national differences in emphasis on scholastics (D. Newman, 2012). For adolescents, scholastic interest, expectations, and achievements may also vary, based not only on nationality but also on gender, race, ethnicity, economic status, and expectations for the future.

Most youth who drop out in the United States do so in high school, but worldwide, the concern is for youth who leave school before completing primary school, or who fail to enroll in school at all. The United Nations Educational, Scientific, and Cultural Organization (UNESCO) compiles global education statistics. They report that in 2010, there were 31.2 million "early school leavers" in the world, a drop-out rate of 42% in Sub-Saharan Africa, 33% in South and West Asia, 17% in Latin America and the Caribbean, and 13% in Arab states (UNESCO, 2012). Worldwide, girls are less likely than boys to enter primary school, but boys are more likely to repeat grades or leave school early once enrolled. Also, compared with youth who attend the appropriate grade for their age, overage pupils are more likely to leave school early. Finally, children from poor and rural households are also at an increased risk of leaving school before completing primary education (UNESCO, 2012).

The Broader Community

Recent studies have considered the ways adolescents attempt to make a contribution to society and found that they are increasingly using technology to engage in such activities as signing petitions and expressing opinions about societal issues (van Goethem et al., 2012). Adolescents and young adults were on the forefront of social unrest across North Africa and the Middle East in 2010 and 2011 and were able to use communication technologies to organize protest activities. Although they experienced success in their activism, they also faced serious threats to their lives (Sawyer et al., 2012).

In the United States, the participation of high school students in volunteer work in the community is becoming common, much more so than in Europe. Indeed, community service is required in many U.S. high schools. Flanagan (2004) argues that community volunteer service provides structured outlets for adolescents to meet a wider circle of community people and to experiment with new roles. The community youth development movement is based on the belief that such community service provides an opportunity to focus on the strengths and competencies of youth rather than on youth problems (see Villarruel, Perkins, Borden, & Keith, 2003). One research team found that participation in community service and volunteerism assisted in identity clarification and in the development of political and moral interests (McIntosh, Metz, & Youniss, 2005).

Another way adolescents can have contact with the broader community is through a mentoring relationship with a community adult. The mentoring relationship may be either formal or informal. The mentor becomes a role model and trusted adviser. Mentors can be found in many places: in part-time work settings, in youth-serving organizations, in religious organizations, at school, in the neighborhood, and so on. There is unusually strong evidence for the positive value of mentoring for youth. Here are some examples of research in this area. Longitudinal research found that natural mentoring relationships with nonparental adults were associated with greater psychological well-being (DuBois & Silverhorn, 2005). Another study found that perceived mentoring from an unrelated adult in the work setting was associated with psychosocial competencies and adjustment in both U.S. and European samples (Vazsonyi & Snider, 2008). Longitudinal research with foster care youth has found that youth who had been mentored had better overall health, less suicidal ideation, fewer sexually transmitted infections (STIs), and less aggression in young adulthood than foster care youth who had not been mentored (Ahrens, DuBois, Richardson, Fan, & Lozano, 2008). Another study investigated the mentor relationship between an adolescent survivor of acquired brain injury and an adult mentor who was also a survivor of this injury. The researchers found that both the mentors and the adolescents derived benefit from the relationship, with the adolescents reporting gains in social and emotional well-being and identity development (Fraas & Bellerose, 2010). One last study of adolescents identified as "at risk" and involved in an 8-month mentoring program designed to prevent substance abuse found that the mentors helped the youth to improve relationships with family and at school and to increase their overall life skills (Zand et al., 2009).

Work

Like many adolescents, Carl Fleischer and Monica Golden also play the role of worker in the labor market. Limited employment, no more than 20 hours per week, can provide an opportunity for social interaction and greater financial independence. It may also lead to personal growth by promoting notions of contribution, responsibility, egalitarianism, and self-efficacy and by helping the adolescent to develop values and preferences for future jobs—answers to questions like "What kind of job would I like to have in the future?" and "What am I good at?" (Mortimer, 2004). For example, Monica tried many jobs before deciding that she loves working with children and wants to become a pediatrician. In addition, employment may also offer the opportunity to develop job skills, time management skills, customer relation skills, money management skills, market knowledge, and other skills of value to future employers.

In July 2013, 19.7 million U.S. youth ages 16 to 24 were employed, for an employment rate of 50.7% of the civilian noninstitutional population (U.S. Bureau of Labor Statistics, 2013a). For that same month, the employment-population ratios were 51.7% for young men and 49.6% for young women; 54.3% for White youth, 38.6% for Black youth, 39.2% for Asian youth, and 47.4% for Hispanic youth. Being in the labor force means the individual is working either full-time or part-time as a paid employee in an ongoing relationship with a particular employer, such as working in a supermarket. Individuals are not considered to be in the labor force if they work in certain "freelance jobs" that involve doing tasks without a specific employer, such as babysitting or mowing lawns.

The U.S. Department of Labor has launched an initiative called YouthRules! that seeks to promote positive and safe work experiences for young workers (www.youthrules.dol.gov). These guidelines are the social policy result of research that suggests that for youth, work, in spite of some positive benefits, may also detract from development by cutting into time needed for sleep, exercise, maintenance of overall health, school, family relations, and peer relations. Unfortunately, the types of work available to adolescents are usually low-skill jobs that offer little opportunity for skill development. Some researchers have found that working more than 10 hours per week puts adolescents at risk for a number of physical and mental health problems (see Entwisle, Alexander, & Olson, 2005; Marsh & Kleitman, 2005), but as noted, longitudinal research suggests that working less than 20 hours per week is not detrimental (Mortimer, 2004). Although we cannot draw causal conclusions, Carl Fleischer works more than 10 hours a week and also has declining grades and uses tobacco and marijuana.

Photo 6.4 In wealthy nations, a sizable portion of an adolescent's life is spent in leisure pursuits.

© Phillippe Lissac/Godong/Corbis

Information and Communication Technologies (ICTs)

According to *Teens and Technology 2013*, research produced by the Pew Research Center and the Berkman Center for Internet and Society at Harvard University, since 2006, over 95% of U.S. teens consistently report using the Internet and being "online" (Madden, Lenhart, Duggan, Cortesi, & Gasser, 2013). The mechanisms teens use to go online have changed over time, however. In the early 2000s, Internet usage was mostly obtained through desktop computers, and it is now through ICTs (information and communication technologies), primarily smartphones. In 2011, 23% of U.S.

youth owned smartphones as compared with 37% in 2013. Thirty-four percent of girls ages 14 to 17 report that they mostly go online using their cell phone as compared with 24% of boys the same age. This is a significant difference since girls and boys are equally likely to own smartphones (Madden et al., 2013). Overall, in 2011, 78% of adolescents ages 12 to 17 had cell phones and used them to text a median number of 60 times a day, an increase over the 50 times a day median in 2009 (Lenhart, 2012). Here are other findings about how adolescents, ages 12 to 17, use ICTs to communicate every day, compared with the 35% who engage in face-to-face socializing outside of school (Lenhart, 2012):

- 63% exchange text messages every day
- 39% make cell phone calls
- 29% engage in social network site messaging
- 22% engage in instant messaging
- 19% make landline calls
- 6% use e-mail

The 2011 YRBS reports that 32.8% of students had texted or e-mailed while driving a car or other vehicle on at least 1 day during the last 30 days. This rate was higher for boys (35%) than girls (30%), higher for White youth (36%) than Hispanic (30%) or Black youth (24%), and highest for 12th graders (58%), followed by 11th graders (43%), 10th graders (23%), and 9th graders (12%) (Eaton et al., 2012).

These technologies are bringing both benefit and risk to adolescent development. They offer another level of connectedness, with potential benefits such as maintaining distant relationships, keeping parents updated on their child's whereabouts or needs, and providing broader social networks. They also introduce potential risks, such as driving while texting, mental and physical (primarily thumbs) fatigue, social disconnectedness, and instant gratification. Sherry Turkle (2011), professor of social studies of science and technology at the Massachusetts Institute of Technology, has been studying the impact of ICTs on human behavior since the 1990s. She acknowledges that the Internet fosters social connections, identity development, and access to information of almost any kind. She also suggests that, like adults, today's adolescents are

Photo 6.5 Adolescents are prolific users of text messaging, bringing a high level of connectedness.

© Izabela Habur/iStockphoto.com

tethered to their technologies, living in a constant state of waiting for connection and endangering themselves by texting while walking or driving. Some adolescents complain that their technologies mean they are always "on call" to parents and friends alike. They work on identity development in an era when photos or messages can be sent to audiences they did not select. They are often physically present in one setting while mentally present in one or more other settings, and they interact with both parents and friends who are physically present while being mentally present elsewhere.

Parents, school officials, and legislators have become increasingly concerned that adolescents will see sexually explicit material on the Internet and be sexually exploited or otherwise harassed via the Internet. The Crimes Against Children Research Center reports that Internet sex crimes are more often cases of statutory rape where adult offenders meet, develop relationships with, and openly seduce teenagers (Wolak, Finkelhor, Mitchell, & Ybarra, 2008).

Critical Thinking Questions 6.3

Children and adolescents in the United States spend less time on school-related activities than students in most other industrialized countries. Do you think children and adolescents in the United States should spend more time in school? How would you support your argument on this issue? How could high schools in the United States do a better job of supporting the cognitive development of adolescents? Should the high school be concerned about supporting emotional and social development of adolescents? Why or why not?

ADOLESCENT SPIRITUALITY/ RELIGIOSITY

As adolescents develop greater capacity for abstract thinking, they often search for meaning in life experiences, and some researchers consider adolescence to be the most sensitive life stage for spiritual exploration (Kim & Esquivel, 2011; Magaldi-Dopman & Park-Taylor, 2010). In recent years, behavioral scientists and mental health professionals have developed an interest in spirituality/religiosity (S/R) as a source of resilience for adolescents (Kim & Esquivel, 2011). Spirituality is a personal search for meaning and relationship with the sacred, whether that is found in a deity or some other life force. Religiosity comprises beliefs and actions associated with an organized religious institution (Good, Willoughby, & Busseri, 2011). S/R includes both personal and institutional ways of connecting with the sacred.

Research on adolescent S/R is still in its infancy, and very little is known. In an attempt to fill this gap, a Canadian research team undertook a longitudinal study to explore multiple dimensions of S/R. They studied 756 students in Grade 11 and the same students again in Grade 12 and found that at both time periods, the youth fell into a five-cluster typology of S/R:

1. Neither spiritual nor religious (14.2% of 11th graders and 13.4% of 12th graders)

2. Disconnected wonderers (35.9% of 11th graders and 44.6% of 12th graders)

3. High spirituality/high religiosity (16.7% of 11th graders and 8.3% of 12th graders)

4. Primarily spiritual (24.3% of 11th graders and 25.8% of 12th graders)

5. Meditators (9.0% of 11th graders and 7.9% of 12th graders)

The largest cluster at both time periods was the disconnected wonderers, a group that was not involved in any form of spiritual or religious practices but reported often wondering about spiritual issues. The meditators may or may not have been meditating as a spiritual practice; meditating may have been related to a physical fitness or other type of physical and/or mental health regimen.

> How important is it for social workers to assess the spirituality of adolescents with whom they work?

The National Study of Youth and Religion (NSYR) is the most comprehensive longitudinal study of spirituality and religion among U.S. adolescents. Supported by the Lilly Endowment, this study began in August 2001 and was funded through December 2013. The NSYR's study found that the vast majority of U.S. teenagers (aged 13 to 17) identify themselves as Christian (56.4% Protestant [various denominations], 19.2% Catholic). Fifteen percent are not religious. In addition, 2.3% are Mormon/Latter-Day Saints, 1.5% are Jewish, and other minority faiths (Jehovah's Witness, Muslim, Eastern Orthodox, Buddhist, Pagan or Wiccan, Hindu, Christian Science, Native American, Unitarian Universalist, or two affiliations) each comprised less than 1% of the representative sample. Four out of 10 U.S. adolescents say they attend religious services once a week or more, pray daily or more, and are currently involved in a religious youth group. Eighty-four percent of the surveyed youth believe in God whereas 13% are unsure about belief in God, and 3% do not believe in God (Denton, Pearce, & Smith, 2008). The researchers found that the single most important social influence on the religious and spiritual lives of adolescents is their parents.

For many youth, spirituality may be closely connected to culture. Interventions with adolescents and their families should be consistent with their spirituality and religion, but knowing someone's cultural heritage will not always provide understanding of their religious or spiritual beliefs. For example, it is no longer safe to assume that all Latino Americans are Catholic. Today, there is much religious diversity among Latino Americans who increasingly have membership in Protestant denominations such as Methodist, Baptist, Presbyterian, and Lutheran, as well as in such religious groups as Mormons, Seventh-Day Adventists, and Jehovah's Witnesses. Moreover, the fastest growing religions among Latino Americans are the Pentecostal and evangelical denominations (Garcia, 2011). Many Latino Americans, particularly Puerto Ricans, combine traditional religious beliefs with a belief in spiritualism, which is a belief that the visible world is surrounded by an invisible world made up of good and evil spirits who influence human behavior. Some Latino Americans practice Indigenous healing rituals, such as *Santeria* (Cuban American) and *curanderismo* (Mexican American). In these latter situations, it is important to know whether adolescents and their families are working with an Indigenous folk healer (Ho, Rasheed, & Rasheed, 2004). Although adolescents may not seem to be guided by their spirituality or religiosity, they may have underlying spiritual factors at work. As with any biological, psychological, or social dimensions of the individual, the spiritual dimensions of youth must be considered to gain the best understanding of the whole person.

ADOLESCENT SEXUALITY _____

With the changes of puberty, adolescents begin to have sexual fantasies, sexual feelings, and sexual attractions. They will come to understand what it means to be a sexual being and, similar to other facets of their identity, will explore their sexual identity. They will consider the kinds of people they find sexually attractive. Some will make decisions about engaging in various sexual behaviors. In this experimentation, some adolescents will contract sexually transmitted infections (STIs) and some will become pregnant. Unfortunately, some will also experience unwanted sexual attention and become victims of sexual aggression.

Sexual Decision Making

Transition into sexual behavior is partly a result of biological changes. The amount of the sex hormone DHEA in the blood peaks between the ages of 10 and 12, a time when both boys and girls become aware of sexual feelings. The way that sexual feelings get expressed, however, can depend largely on sociocultural factors. Youth are influenced by the attitudes toward sexual activity that they encounter in their environment, at school; among peers, siblings, and family; in their clubs or organizations; in the media; and so on. When and how they begin to engage in sexual activity are closely linked to what they perceive to be the activities of their peers (Hafen et al., 2012). Research also suggests that youth who are not performing well in school are more likely to engage in sexual activity than are those who are doing well (Rew, 2005). Finally, beliefs and behaviors regarding sexuality are also shaped by one's culture, religion/spirituality, and value system. Ponton and Judice (2004) suggest that "a nation's attitude about adolescent sexuality plays an important role in the adolescent's sexual development and affects the laws, sexual media, sexual services, and the interaction of religion and state as well as the type of education that they receive in their schools" (p. 7). Adolescents report a variety of social motivations for engaging in sexual intercourse, including developing new levels of intimacy, pleasing a partner, impressing peers, and gaining sexual experience (Impett & Tolman, 2006).

As the pubertal hormones cause changes throughout the body, most adolescents spend time becoming familiar with those changes. For many, exploration includes **masturbation**, the self-stimulation of the genitals for sexual pleasure. In the most comprehensive U.S. sex study in decades, the National Survey of Sexual Health and Behavior conducted in 2009 included a nationally representative sample of 14- to 17-year-olds and questions about masturbation (Herbenick et al., 2010). Seventy-four percent of boys and 48% of girls reported ever masturbating, and 58% of boys had masturbated in the past 90 days (compared with 36% of girls). Older research indicates that boys tend to masturbate earlier and more often than girls (Leitenberg, Detzer, & Srebnik, 1993). The gender difference has been found to be even greater in Bangkok, Thailand, where 79% of male secondary students report masturbating, compared with 9% of females (O-Prasetsawat & Petchum, 2004). Masturbation has negative associations for some adolescents. Thus, masturbation may have psychological implications for adolescents, depending on the way they feel about it and how they think significant others feel about it. Female college students who are high in religiosity report more guilt about masturbation than female college students who are low in religiosity (J. Davidson, Moore, & Ullstrup, 2004).

The 2011 U.S. YRBS suggests that nationwide 47.4% of high school students reported having had sexual intercourse during their life, 6.2% had sexual intercourse for the first time before age 13, 15.3% have had sexual intercourse with four or more persons during their life, and 33.7% were sexually active during the last 3 months (Eaton et al., 2012). Of the 33.7% of high school students who indicated that they are currently sexually active, 60.2% report that either they or their partner used a condom during last sexual intercourse, 22.1% had drunk alcohol or used drugs before their last sexual intercourse, and 12.9% reported not using any method to prevent pregnancy during their last sexual intercourse (Eaton et al., 2012).

International data suggest that, on average, adolescents in the United States experience first sexual intercourse at about the same age as youth in other economically advanced countries. Data from 26 countries in 2007 indicate that the average age for first sexual intercourse was 18 years in the United States, compared with 17.9 years in Australia, 17.3 years in Austria, 18.5 years in France, 17.6 years in Germany, and 18.3 years in the United Kingdom (Durex Network, 2007). (It should be noted that Durex is a condom manufacturer that does annual surveys of adolescent sexuality in a number of countries.) The same data set indicates that females are more likely than males to feel pressured into having sex, with 27.2% of females and 15% of males reporting that they felt pressured into their sexual debut. Females were also more likely than males to have negative feelings about their first sexual experience, 42% versus 32%. U.S. data indicate that adolescents are slightly less likely than in the past to report that first sex is involuntary: 11% of females from 2006 to 2010, compared with 13% in 2002; and 5% of males from 2006 to 2010, compared with 10% in 2002 (Guttmacher Institute, 2013c). A study of first sexual experiences of youth ages 14 to 18 in

the Philippines, El Salvador, and Peru found that approximately one fifth of the sample of both male and female adolescents regretted the experience (Osorio et al., 2012).

Regardless of nation or milieu, there is most certainly a need for adolescents to develop skills for healthy management of sexual relationships. Early engagement in sexual intercourse has some negative consequences. One research team studied early adolescent sexual initiation in five countries, the United States, Finland, France, Poland, and Scotland, and found it to be a risk factor for substance abuse and poor school attachment (Madkour, Farhat, Halpern, Godeau, & Gabhainn, 2010). They also found that early sexual initiation was disruptive to the parent-adolescent relationship, particularly for female adolescents in the United States but not in the other countries.

Rates of sexual activity among teens in the United States are fairly comparable to those in western Europe, yet the incidence of adolescent pregnancy and childbearing in the United States exceeds that in other economically advanced countries (Martinez, Copen, & Abma, 2011). For instance, the teen birth rate in the United States in 2009 was almost 3 times the rate in Canada, 3 times the rate in Germany, and about 5.7 times the rate in Italy. This discrepancy is probably related to three factors: Teenagers in the United States make less use of contraception than teens in European countries, reproductive health services are more available in European countries, and sexuality education is more comprehensively integrated into all levels of education in most of Europe than in the United States (Durex Network, 2010; Guttmacher Institute, 2013c).

Sexual Orientation

As they develop as sexual beings, adolescents begin to consider sexual attraction. **Sexual orientation** refers to erotic, romantic, and affectionate attraction to people of the same sex (gay or lesbian), the opposite sex (heterosexual), or both sexes (bisexual). There are also questioning adolescents who are less certain of their sexual orientation than those who label themselves as heterosexual, bisexual, or gay/lesbian (Poteat, Aragon, Espelage, & Koenig, 2009). Research indicates that the current generation of lesbian, gay, bisexual, and questioning youth uses the Internet to get information about sexual orientation and to begin the coming-out process. This provides a safe and anonymous venue for exploration and questioning as well as for initiating the coming-out process; it can lead to greater self-acceptance before coming out to family and friends (Bond, Hefner, & Drogos, 2009). Researchers are currently focusing on three indicators of sexual orientation: same-sex attractions, same-sex sexual behaviors, and self-labels as gay, lesbian, or bisexual (see Russell et al., 2012; Saewyc, 2011). Glover, Galliher, and Lamere

---

How does sexual orientation affect development during adolescence?

(2009) suggest that sexual orientation should be conceptualized as a "complex configuration of identity, attractions, behaviors, disclosure, and interpersonal explorations" (pp. 92–93).

Theory and research about adolescent sexual orientation are not new, but there has been a very large increase in research on the topic in the past 15 years. The following discussion presents the major themes of Elizabeth Saewyc's (2011) comprehensive review of the research on adolescent sexual orientation published in the decade from 1998 to 2008. The research is still trying to untangle the multiple influences on sexual orientation, but there is general agreement that both genetic and environmental influences are involved. Researchers have struggled with how to define and measure sexual orientation, for example, whether to use measures of attraction, self-identity, or sexual behavior. Even though different measures are used across different studies, researchers consistently find that adolescents with a sexual orientation other than heterosexual report less supportive environments and less nurturing relationships with their parents than heterosexual youth. The research also consistently indicates that sexual minority youth have increased risk for developmental stressors and compromised health.

Research also suggests that sexual minority youth are coming out at earlier ages than in previous eras, but there is still much heterogeneity in the coming-out process. Those who come out earlier appear to be more comfortable with their sexual orientation status but also face increased rejection and harassment from family and peers. African American and Latino youth have a similar trajectory of sexual orientation development as White youth in most ways, but they are more delayed in making public disclosure, and they are less likely to be involved in gay-related social networks that tend to have mostly White membership.

Some evidence contends that most people remain consistent in their sexual attractions across the adolescent and young-adult periods, but youth with a sexual orientation other than heterosexual are much more likely than heterosexual youth to change their self-identification and sexual behavior over a 10-year period. Bisexuality has received much less research attention than homosexuality.

Research from a number of countries indicates that sexual minority youth have a higher prevalence of emotional distress, depression, self-harm, suicidal thinking, and suicidal attempts than heterosexual youth. They also have a higher prevalence of smoking and alcohol and other drug use, are likely to report an earlier sexual debut and to have more sexual partners, and have a higher prevalence of sexually transmitted infections. They are also more likely to be the targets of violence (Saewyc, 2011).

It is important to note that although sexual minority youth face increased risks to physical and mental health, most are successful in navigating the challenges they face and achieve similar levels of well-being as heterosexual youth. Several protective factors have been found to promote resilience in sexual minority youth, including supportive family relationships, supportive friends, supportive relationships with adults outside the family, positive connections with school, and spirituality/religiosity. These are the same protective factors that have been found to promote resilience in all youth, and, unfortunately, the research indicates that sexual minority youth, on average, receive less support in all of these areas than heterosexual youth. Research indicates, however, that many sexual minority youth have protective factors specific to their sexual orientation, including involvement in gay-related organizations and attending schools with gay-straight alliances or schools where the staff is trained to make the school a safe zone for sexual minority youth. Consider David Costa's conflict over his sexual orientation. What do you see as the risk and protective factors he faces as he struggles with this aspect of identity?

There is hope that the changing legal status of same-sex relationships and the increased visibility of positive sexual minority role models will lead to decreased risk and increased protection for sexual minority youth. There is some evidence that growing numbers of the current generation of adolescents do not consider sexual orientation as central an identity concept as earlier generations and are less prone to make negative judgments about sexual orientations other than heterosexual.

Saewyc's (2011) research review indicates the important influence of school climate on the well-being of sexual minority youth. For more than a decade, GLSEN (the Gay, Lesbian, and Straight Education Network) has conducted a National School Climate Survey (NSCS) to document the unique challenges that 6th- to 12th-grade LGBT students face and to identify interventions that can improve school climate. In the 2011 NSCS (Kosciw, Greytak, Bartkiewicz, Boesen, & Palmer, 2012), 84.9% of LGBT students reported hearing homophobic or negative remarks regarding sexual orientation or gender expression at school and 56.9% of students reported hearing these types of comments from their teachers or other school staff. Sexual orientation and gender expression can also compromise adolescents' safety at school. The 2011 NSCS found that 63.5% of the LGBT students surveyed felt unsafe because of their sexual orientation (43.9% because of their gender expression). Over 80% of these students were verbally harassed because of their sexual orientation, 38.3% were physically harassed (e.g., pushed, shoved), and 18.3% were physically assaulted (punched, kicked, injured with a weapon). Moreover, 60.4% of the students who were harassed or assaulted at school did not report the incident to school personnel because they believed little or no action would be taken or the situation would be exacerbated if reported. These data indicate the serious risk that the school climate imposes on sexual minority youth, but the 2011 survey also found some hopeful signs. This was the first school climate survey to show both a decrease in negative indicators of school climate and also a continued increase in school supports for sexual minority youth.

To forestall potential rejection from family and friends, and at school, Parents, Families and Friends of Lesbians and Gays (PFLAG), a support, education, and advocacy organization with the goal of promoting a more supportive environment for lesbian, gay, bisexual, and transgender people, was founded in 1972. The organization's website, http://community.pflag.org, contains information on frequently asked questions, facts, resources, and advocacy issues.

Pregnancy and Childbearing

In 2012, there were 305,420 babies born to adolescent girls aged 15 to 19 in the United States (Hamilton, Martin, & Ventura, 2013). This is a birth rate of 29.4 per 1,000 15- to 19-year-old girls. Of these births, approximately 89% occurred outside of marriage and 17% were to girls who already had a child. The teen pregnancy rate in the United States has declined relatively consistently since the early 1990s (the 1991 rate was 61.8/1,000), but it is still higher than the rate in many other economically advanced countries (Hamilton et al., 2013). Teenage pregnancy rates and birth rates vary considerably by race and ethnicity as well as by region of the country. In 2012, Hispanic/Latino girls had the highest birth rate (46.3 per 1,000) and Black girls had the second highest rate (43.9 per 1,000), followed by their White counterparts (20.5 per 1,000). The national Office of Adolescent Health (U.S. Department of Health and Human Services, Office of Adolescent Health [DHHS/OAH], 2013) reports that the lowest

> What factors might contribute to regional differences in U.S. pregnancy rates?

teen birth rates were reported in the Northeast and the highest teen birth rates were from the southern region of the U.S. (See how your state compares on pregnancy rates, birth rates, sexual activity, and contraceptive use at www.hhs.gov/ash/oah/resources-and-publications/facts.)

Adolescent pregnancies carry increased risks to the mother, including delayed prenatal care; higher rates of miscarriage, anemia, toxemia, and prolonged labor; and increased likelihood of being a victim of intimate partner violence (Pinzon & Jones, 2012). They also carry increased risks to the infant, including perinatal mortality, preterm birth, low birth weight, and developmental delays and disabilities (Pinzon & Jones, 2012). In many Asian, eastern Mediterranean, African, and Latin American countries, the physical risks of adolescent pregnancy are mitigated by social and economic support (Hao & Cherlin, 2004). In the United States, however, adolescent mothers are more likely than their counterparts elsewhere to drop out of school, be unemployed or underemployed, receive public assistance, have subsequent pregnancies, and have children with poorer educational, behavioral, and health outcomes (U.S. DHHS/OAH, 2013). Teenage fathers may also experience lower educational and financial attainment (Pinzon & Jones, 2012).

The developmental tasks of adolescence are typically accomplished in this culture by going to school, socializing with peers, and exploring various roles. For the teenage mother, these avenues to development may be radically curtailed. The result may be long-lasting disadvantage. Consider Monica Golden's path. She obviously loves children and would like to have her own someday, but she would also like to become a pediatrician. If Monica were to become pregnant unexpectedly, an abortion would challenge her religious values and a baby could affect her health, challenge her future goals, and impact her educational and financial potential.

Sexually Transmitted Infections

Youth have always faced pregnancy as a possible consequence of their sexual activity, but other consequences include infertility and death as a result of **sexually transmitted infections (STIs)**, also known as sexually transmitted diseases (STDs). Adolescents aged 15 to 24 comprise almost half of the 20 million new cases of STIs each year in the United States, and 4 out of every 10 sexually active teenaged girls have had an STI that can cause infertility or even death (Centers for Disease Control and Prevention, 2012e). For girls aged 15 to 19, the rate of chlamydia infection continued to increase to a 2011 rate of 3,416.5 cases per 100,000 (757 cases per 100,000 boys aged 15 to 19); gonorrhea infection rates stayed about the same for a 2011 rate of 556.5 per 100,000 (248.6/100,000 boys); and primary and secondary syphilis rates decreased in 2011 to 2.4 cases per 100,000 girls (5.4/100,000 boys) (Centers for Disease Control and Prevention, 2012e). Girls aged 15 to 19 have the highest rates of chlamydia and gonorrhoea of any age or gender group (Martinez et al., 2011).

Research has found several contextual and personal factors to be associated with STIs, including housing insecurity, exposure to crime, childhood sexual abuse, gang participation, frequent alcohol use, and depression (Buffardi, Thomas, Holmes, & Manhart, 2008). The Centers for Disease Control and Prevention (2012e) add that the "higher prevalence of STDs among adolescents also may reflect multiple barriers to accessing quality STD prevention services, including lack of health insurance or ability to pay, lack of transportation, discomfort with facilities and services designed for adults, and concerns about confidentiality" (para. 1).

Data collection on STIs is complicated for several reasons. State health departments have different requirements about which STIs must be reported. STIs are not always detected and reported. Some STIs, such as chlamydia and HPV (human papillomavirus), are often asymptomatic and go undetected. In addition, many surveys are not based on representative samples. The best estimates available indicate that adolescents and young adults ages 15 to 24 constitute 25% of the sexually active population but account for almost half of the STI diagnoses each year (Centers for Disease Control and Prevention, 2012e).

Unfortunately, HIV/AIDS is also a risk to adolescent health around the world. In 2012, there were 32.2 to 38.8 million people living with HIV worldwide, according to the Joint United Nations Programme on HIV/AIDS (UNAIDS, 2013). The rate of HIV diagnoses increased in youth ages 15 to 19 and 20 to 24 from 2006 to 2009. Despite only comprising about 20% of the 13- to 19-year-old U.S. population, 70% of the 13- to 19-year-olds diagnosed with HIV are Black teens. Almost 80% of the HIV+ adolescents are boys, and 90% of male HIV infections result from male-to-male sexual contact. See Exhibit 6.5 for the racial and ethnic distribution of HIV in adolescents aged 13 to 19. The highest concentrations of HIV diagnoses among adolescents were located in the southeastern United States—notably Florida, South Carolina, and Louisiana. Of the more than 1.2 million people living with HIV in the United States, approximately 1 in 5 (~220,000) doesn't know she or he is infected. The CDC estimates that half of all undiagnosed HIV infections are youth aged 13 to 24 (Torian, Chen, & Hall, 2011). Many of these individuals contract the disease in their teen years and don't learn they have the virus until they become adults. Fortunately, 84% of students responding to the YRBS reported that they received HIV/AIDS education in school, and 12.9% state that they have been tested for HIV (Eaton et al., 2012).

> ## Critical Thinking Questions 6.4
>
> What sources of information did you use to learn about human sexuality when you were an adolescent? Which sources were the most useful and accurate? Do you believe that public schools should be involved in sexuality education? Why or why not? If so, what topics should be covered in such education?

Exhibit 6.5   Diagnoses of HIV Infection and Population Among Adolescents Aged 13 to 19, by Race or Ethnicity, in the United States, 2011

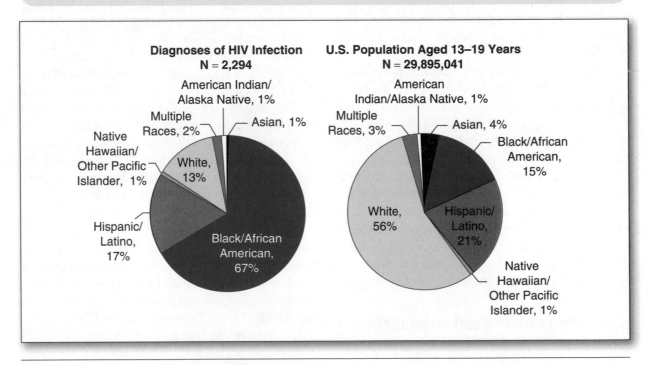

SOURCE: Centers for Disease Control and Prevention, 2012d

POTENTIAL CHALLENGES TO ADOLESCENT DEVELOPMENT___

Many adjustments have to be made during adolescence in all areas of life. Adjustments to biological changes are a major developmental task of adolescence, family relationships are continuously renegotiated across the adolescent phase, and career planning begins in earnest for most youth in mid- to late adolescence. Most adolescents have the resources to meet these new challenges and adapt. But many adolescents engage in risky behaviors or experience other threats to physical and mental health. We have already looked at risky sexual behavior. Nine other threats to physical and mental health are discussed briefly here: substance use and abuse, juvenile delinquency, bullying, school-to-prison pipeline, community violence, dating violence and statutory rape, poverty and low educational attainment, obesity and eating disorders, and depression and suicide.

Substance Use and Abuse

In adolescence, many youth experiment with nicotine, alcohol, and other psychoactive substances with the motivation to be accepted by peers or to cope with life stresses (Weichold, 2007). For example, Carl Fleischer's use of tobacco and marijuana has several likely effects on his general behavior. Tobacco may make him feel tense, excitable, or anxious, and these feelings may amplify his concern about his weight, his grades, and his family relationships. Conversely, the marijuana may make Carl feel relaxed, and he may use it to counteract or escape from his concerns.

The rate of illicit drug use declined among U.S. adolescents aged 12 to 17 from 2002 (11.6%) to 2008 (9.3%), then increased to 10.1% from 2009 to 2011, and in 2012 declined to 9.5%, according to the Substance Abuse and Mental Health Services Administration's *National Survey on Drug Abuse and Health* (Substance Abuse and Mental Health Services Administration [SAMHSA], 2013a). Earlier research suggested that high school students in the United States maintain a higher rate

of illicit drug use than youth in other economically developed countries (Johnston, O'Malley, Bachman, & Schulenberg, 2004, 2005). More recent research indicates that rates of adolescent use of illicit substances are lower in Latin America than in the United States (Torres, Peña, Westhoff, & Zayas, 2008). Overall, in 2012, SAMHSA reports that for those aged 12 to 17 in the United States, 7.2% used marijuana, 2.8% used prescription-type drugs for nonmedical purposes, 0.8% used inhalants, 0.6% used hallucinogens, and 0.1% used cocaine (SAMHSA, 2013a). Alcohol continues to be the most widely used of all substances for adolescents. An estimated 9.3 million (underage) people aged 12 to 20 report drinking currently (24.3% of this age group reported drinking alcohol in the past month), according to 2012 statistics (SAMHSA, 2013a). Furthermore, approximately 5.9 million (15.3%) considered themselves binge drinkers, and 1.7 million (4.3%) stated they were heavy drinkers. Meanwhile tobacco use has steadily but only slightly declined over time. In 2011, 18.1% of 9th- to 12th-grade students had smoked cigarettes on at least one day in the previous month, and 7.7% of students had used smokeless tobacco on at least one day in the previous month.

When asked why youth choose to use alcohol, adolescents cite the following reasons: to have a good time with friends, to appear adult-like, to relieve tension and anxiety, to deal with the opposite sex, to get high, to cheer up, and to alleviate boredom. When asked why youth use cocaine, the additional responses were to get more energy and to get away from problems. Drug use at a party is also cited quite often as a reason (Engels & Knibbe, 2000). The following factors appear to be involved in adolescents' choice of drugs: the individual characteristics of the drug, the individual characteristics of the user, the availability of the drug, the current popularity of the drug, and the sociocultural traditions and sanctions regarding the drug (Segal & Stewart, 1996).

> What are the risk factors for substance abuse in adolescence?

Some adolescents are clearly more at risk for substance abuse than others. National survey data indicate that Native American adolescents (47.5%) have the highest prevalence of past year alcohol and other drug use of U.S. youth ages 12 to 17, followed by White adolescents (39.2%), Hispanic adolescents (36.7%), adolescents of multiple race or ethnicity (36.4%), African American adolescents (32.2%), and Asian or Pacific Islander adolescents (23.7%) (Wu, Woody, Yang, Pan, & Blazer, 2011). The same survey found racial and ethnic disparities in the prevalence of youth meeting the diagnostic criteria for substance-related disorders: Native American youth had the highest prevalence (15.0%), followed by adolescents of multiple race or ethnicity (9.2%), White adolescents (9.0%), Hispanic adolescents (7.7%), African American adolescents (5.0%), and Asian or Pacific Islander adolescents (3.5%).

Although these data indicate that many adolescents use alcohol and other substances, not all of them get into trouble with their usage, except for the potential legal trouble related to the illegality of their use of these substances. Problematic alcohol and drug use, however, can have a negative influence on adolescents, their families, and their communities. Because alcohol and illicit drugs alter neurotransmission, regular use can have harmful effects on the developing brain and nervous system (Wu et al., 2011). Early substance use increases the risk for later addiction and depression (Esposito-Smythers, Kahler, Spirito, Hunt, & Monti, 2011). Use of alcohol and other drugs can also affect the immune system and emotional and cognitive functioning, including sexual decision making (Weichold, 2007).

Juvenile Delinquency

Almost every adolescent breaks the rules at some time—disobeying parents or teachers, lying, cheating, and perhaps even stealing or vandalizing. Many adolescents smoke cigarettes and drink alcohol and use other drugs; some skip school or stay out past curfew. For some adolescents, this behavior is a phase, passing as quickly as it appeared. Yet for others, it becomes a pattern and a probability game. Although most juvenile

delinquency never meets up with law enforcement, the more times young people offend, the more likely they are to come into contact with the juvenile justice system.

In the United States, persons older than 5 but younger than 18 can be arrested for anything for which an adult can be arrested. (Children younger than 6 are said not to possess mens rea, which means "guilty mind," and thus are not considered capable of criminal intent.) In addition, they can be arrested for what are called **status offenses**, such as running away from home, skipping school, violating curfew, and possessing tobacco or alcohol— behaviors not considered crimes when engaged in by adults. When adolescents are found guilty of committing either a crime (by adult standards) or a status offense, we refer to their behavior as **juvenile delinquency**.

The Office of Juvenile Justice and Delinquency Prevention (OJJDP) reports that the number of delinquency cases, at about 1.5 million, increased from 1985 through 1997 and declined from 1997 to 2009 (Knoll & Sickmund, 2012). Juveniles (persons younger than 18) accounted for 13.7% of all violent crime arrests and 22.5% of all property crime arrests in 2010. And in that same year, 784 juveniles were arrested for murder, 2,198 were arrested for forcible rape, and 35,001 were arrested for aggravated assault (Federal Bureau of Investigation, 2011). Although rate of delinquency among girls has increased (from 19% in 1985 to 28% in 2009), it is still a relatively small proportion of the overall delinquency caseload at 415,600 in 2009 (as compared with 1,088,600 for boys in that same year) (Knoll & Sickmund, 2012). And, of the total U.S. adolescent population in 2009, White youth comprised 78%, Black youth comprised 16%, Asian youth (including Native Hawaiian and other Pacific Islander) comprised 5%, and Native American (including Alaska Native) comprised 1%. However, 64% of the delinquency cases handled in 2009 were for White youth, 34% were for Black youth, 1% were for Asian American youth, and 1% were for Native American youth. Despite similar offending patterns and rates of self-reported crime, the rate at which Black youth were referred to juvenile court for a delinquency offense was more than 150% greater than the rate for White youth. The rate at which petitioned cases were waived to criminal court was 5% greater for Black youth than the rate for White youth, and the rate at which youth in adjudicated cases were ordered to residential placement was 23% greater for Black youth than for White youth in a phenomenon called disproportionate minority contact (Knoll & Sickmund, 2012; McCarter, 2011).

Since 1996, the National Gang Center has conducted the National Youth Gang Survey (NYGS) annually (Egley & Howell, 2013). Three indicators are typically used in the United States to measure gang magnitude: number of gangs, number of gang members, and number of gang-related homicides. In 2011, the NYGS estimated that 29,900 gangs with 782,500 gang members were active in 3,300 jurisdictions in the United States. The number of gang-related homicides was 1,824 in 2011 (Egley & Howell, 2013).

Bullying

Social workers are beginning to see the short- and long-term effects of bullying on children's physical and mental health. The U.S. Department of Education and other federal agencies have collaboratively developed an online bullying prevention website at www.stopbullying.gov. There, bullying is defined as "unwanted, aggressive behavior among school aged children that involves a real or perceived power imbalance," and three types of bullying are highlighted:

- *Verbal bullying*: saying or writing mean things (teasing, name-calling, inappropriate sexual comments, taunting, threatening to cause harm)
- *Social/relational bullying*: hurting a person's reputation (leaving someone out on purpose, telling others not to be friends with someone, spreading rumors about someone, publicly embarrassing someone)
- *Physical bullying*: hurting a person's body or possessions (hitting/kicking/pinching, spitting, tripping/pushing, taking or breaking someone's things, making mean or rude hand gestures)

Most adolescents who bully have also been victims of bullying, and both bullies and victims can have serious, lasting problems.

The 2011 YRBS found that 20.1% of high school students had been bullied on school property in the 12 months preceding the survey (Eaton et al., 2012). Prevalence rates were higher for girls (22%) than boys (18%); higher for White youth (23%) than Hispanic (18%) and Black youth (12%); and highest for younger youth, led by 9th graders (24%) and followed by 10th graders (22%), 11th graders (17%), and 12th graders (15%). Similarly, 16.2% of high school students had been cyber-bullied or electronically bullied (via e-mail, chat rooms, instant messaging, websites, or texting) during the 12 months before the YRBS, following the same prevalence trends as those bullied on school property with the exception of age. Tenth graders were the most bullied electronically (18.1%), followed by 11th graders (16.1%), 9th graders (15.5%), and 12th graders (15%). Finally, nationwide, 26.1% of high school students reported that they had property stolen or deliberately damaged on school property one or more times during the past year, and 5.9% of students had not gone to school at least once during the last 30 days because they felt unsafe at school or on their way to or from school (Eaton et al., 2012).

School-to-Prison Pipeline

The "school-to-prison pipeline" refers to policies and practices that "push" students, notably at-risk students, out of classrooms and into the juvenile and criminal justice systems (American Civil Liberties Union, 2013). Eight factors typically affect youth in the school-to-prison pipeline: "zero-tolerance" policies, high-stakes testing, exclusionary discipline, race/ethnicity, gender identity/sexual orientation, socioeconomic status, disability/mental health, and school climate (which includes the presence of school resource officers [SROs], school social workers, guidance counselors, and nurses). Students of color, with disabilities, or with nonheterosexual orientation are overrepresented in school disciplinary actions. The U.S. Department of Education's Office for Civil Rights (2013) reports that more than 3 million students are suspended at least once and more than 100,000 are expelled each year. Exhibit 6.6 lists the number of students suspended in 2006 by race or ethnicity. Given their proportion in the population, African American students are 3 times as likely to be suspended and 3.5 times as likely to be expelled, and Latino students are 1.5 times as likely to be suspended and 3.5 times as likely to be expelled, as compared with White students.

According to the Council of State Governments' study (Fabelo et al., 2011) of almost a million students in Texas, only 3% of the schools' disciplinary actions were for state-mandated suspensions and expulsions. In that study, approximately 83% of African American male students had at least one discretionary violation, meaning a violation of the school's code of conduct rather than a violation of state law. When the state researchers used multivariate analyses to control for 83 different variables and isolate the effects of race on disciplinary action, they found that African American students had a 31% higher likelihood of school discretionary action when compared with identical White or Hispanic youth.

When students are suspended or expelled, the likelihood that they will repeat a grade, drop out, or have contact with the juvenile or criminal justice system increases significantly. Fabelo et al. (2011) report that students who have been suspended or expelled at least once have a more than 1 in 7 chance of subsequent contact with the juvenile justice system. By race, this means that 1 in 5 Black students,

1 in 6 Hispanic students, and 1 in 10 White students who have school disciplinary action will become court-involved as compared with 1 in 50 students without school disciplinary action. Of David, Carl, and Monica, who do you think is most likely to face school disciplinary action and possible juvenile justice involvement? Why?

Community Violence

Juveniles are more likely than adults to be both victims and perpetrators of violence. Although National Crime Victimization Survey data found that victimization rates for boys and girls did not differ significantly (boys at 20.1/1,000; girls at 18.5/1,000), the national data do suggest that the risk for violence victimization is higher for those aged 14 to 18 (19.9/1,000) when compared with the risk of violence victimization for persons aged 25 to 34 (13.8/1,000) (Lauritsen & Rezey, 2013). Also, persons aged 12 to 17 were 4.7 times more likely to be victimized by friends or acquaintances than were persons aged 35 or older. These rates certainly reflect the different types of violence experienced by younger versus older persons.

Data collected in 2011 as part of the YRBS reveal that on at least 1 of the 30 days preceding the survey, 16.6% of high school students had carried a weapon and 5.1% had carried a gun. During the 12 months that preceded the survey, 3.9% had been in a physical fight for which they had to be treated by a doctor or nurse and 12% had been in a physical fight on school property one or more times in the

Exhibit 6.6 Students Suspended in 2006 by Race or Ethnicity

	Hispanic	Black (Non-Hispanic)	White (Non-Hispanic)	Total
Suspended	670,699	1,244,821	1,302,409	3,328,754
Expelled	22,144	38,642	32,028	102,077

SOURCE: U.S. Department of Education Office for Civil Rights, 2013

last 12 months (Eaton et al., 2012). Even if they are not perpetrators or direct victims of violence, many U.S. adolescents witness violence. One study of 935 urban and suburban youth found that more than 45% had witnessed a shooting or stabbing or other serious act of violence during the previous year (O'Keefe, 1997). Moreover, participating in violence and/or witnessing violence can be a significant predictor of aggressive acting-out behavior for both male and female adolescents (O'Keefe, 1997) as well as a significant source of depression, anger, anxiety, dissociation, post-traumatic stress, and total trauma symptoms (Fitzpatrick & Boldizar, 1993; Singer, Anglin, Song, & Lunghofer, 1995).

Homicide also disproportionately affects younger persons in the United States. In 2010, 4,828 youth aged 10 to 24 were the victims of homicide, representing 13 youth murders each day. Of those 4,828 homicide victims, 86% (4,171) were boys and 14% (657) were girls. Homicide was the second leading cause of death for all juveniles ages 10 to 24, and by race/ethnicity, it was the leading cause of death for African American youth, second leading cause of death for Hispanic youth, and third leading cause of death for American Indian/Alaska Native youth. Almost 83% of all youth homicides are conducted with firearms, but less than 2% occur at school (Centers for Disease Control and Prevention, 2013n).

Dating Violence and Statutory Rape

Dating violence is violence that occurs between two people in a close relationship; it includes physical violence, emotional violence, and sexual violence. **Acquaintance rape** can be defined as forced, manipulated, or coerced sexual contact by someone known to the victim. Women ages 16 to 24 are the primary victims of acquaintance rape, but junior high school girls are also at great risk (Lauritsen & Rezey, 2013). In the United States in 2011, 9.4% of high school students responded to the YRBS that they had been hit, slapped, or physically hurt on purpose by their boyfriend or girlfriend at least once over the course of the 12 months

that preceded the survey (Eaton et al., 2012). The YRBS data reveal that 8.0% of the students stated that they had been physically forced to have sexual intercourse against their will. This prevalence was higher for girls (11.8%) than boys (4.5%), and overall, the prevalence was higher among Black (10.5%) and Hispanic (8.8%) than White (7%) students. The prevalence of having been forced to have sexual intercourse was higher among 10th-grade (8.0%), 11th-grade (8.8%), and 12th-grade (9.5%) than among 9th-grade (5.8%) students (Eaton et al., 2012). Because they are underreported, dating violence and acquaintance rape may be even more prevalent among adolescents than we have data to suggest.

Unfortunately, researchers have found that adolescent girls who report a history of experiencing dating violence are more likely to exhibit other serious health outcomes. Longitudinal research has found that female young adults who were victims of adolescent dating violence are more likely than other female young adults to report heavy episodic drinking, depressive symptoms, suicidal ideation, smoking, and further interpersonal violence victimization in young adulthood. Males victimized as adolescents are more likely to report antisocial behaviors, suicidal ideation, marijuana use, and interpersonal violence victimization in young adulthood (Exner-Cortens, Eckenrode, & Rothman, 2013). One researcher found that the majority of high school counselors report that their school does not have a protocol for responding to incidents of dating violence (Khubchandani et al., 2012).

Statutory rape, a crime in every state in the United States, is having sex with someone younger than an age specified by law as being capable of making an informed, voluntary decision. Different states have established different ages of consent, usually from 16 to 18, and handle the offense in different ways. Throughout history, the age of consent has varied from 10 to 21 (Oudekerk, Farr, & Reppucci, 2013). The majority of victims of statutory rape are females ages 14 to 15, whereas 82% of the rape perpetrators of female victims are adults aged 18 and older (Snyder & Sickmund, 2006).

About half of the male offenders of female victims in statutory rapes reported to law enforcement are at least 6 years older than their victims. For male victims of female perpetrators, the difference was even greater; in these incidents, half of the female offenders were at least 9 years older than their victims (Snyder & Sickmund, 2006). Adolescent romantic relationships with older partners have been found to increase the likelihood of early sexual activity, pregnancy, STIs, school problems, and delinquency (Oudekerk et al., 2013). On the other hand, there is also some concern that late-adolescent and young-adult perpetrators may face long-lasting negative consequences from legal problems that come from engaging in relationships they think of as consensual. One research team found that a sample of young adults thought that a sexual relationship between a 15-year-old and a partner who is 2, 4, and 6 years older should not be treated as a crime, but there was greater disagreement among the research participants as the gap in age got larger. There were no significant differences between men's and women's attitudes (Oudekerk et al., 2013).

Poverty and Low Educational Attainment

Additional threats to physical and mental health may stem from poverty and low educational attainment, both of which are rampant in the non-industrialized world. Poverty is also a growing problem among U.S. adolescents aged 12 to 17. In 2000, 14% of adolescents lived in poverty (by the U.S. definition of poverty), and by 2009, the poverty rate among youth was 17%; the rate grew to 23% by 2012 (Annie E. Casey Foundation, 2013; Wight, 2011). When youth living in near poverty are added, 38% of adolescents live in low-income households, an increase from 33% in 2000 (Wight, 2011). Black (31%), Hispanic (28.6%), and Native American (23.7%) youth are more likely to live in poverty than White (10%) or Asian (16.6%) youth. Youth in immigrant families (24.1%) are more likely than youth with native-born parents (15.4%) to be poor. Living in poverty in adolescence increases the

likelihood of low academic achievement, dropping out of school, teen pregnancy and childbearing, engaging in delinquent behavior, and unemployment during adolescence and young adulthood (Wight, 2011).

Low school attainment has a negative effect on adult opportunities and health across the adult life course. In the United States, high school graduation rates are a key measure of whether schools are making adequate yearly progress (AYP) under the provisions of the No Child Left Behind (NCLB) legislation (see Chapter 5 for a fuller discussion of NCLB). For a number of years, educational experts were confident that high school graduation rates in the United States had risen from about 50% in the mid-20th century to almost 90% by the end of the century (Pharris-Ciurej, Hirschman, & Willhoft, 2012). Around 2004, researchers began to suggest that a more accurate picture was that 65% to 70% of high school students actually earned a high school diploma. Controversies developed about how to measure high school graduation. A number of researchers noted that surveys were picking up high school equivalency certification (e.g., GED) as equivalent to high school graduation, leading to an overestimation of high school graduation and an underestimation of high school dropout rates. The percentage of high school credentials awarded through equivalency certificate has risen from 2% to 15% in recent years (Pharris-Ciurej et al., 2012). Unfortunately, the employment patterns and earnings of GED recipients are more similar to high school dropouts than to those who receive a high school diploma. Students from low-income families are 25% less likely than students from nonpoor families to graduate from high school. Recent research indicates that transition to 9th grade is a particularly vulnerable time for students who will later drop out of school (Pharris-Ciurej et al., 2012). The Annie E. Casey Foundation's (2013) Kids Count Data Center reports that in 2012, 9% of U.S. students aged 6 to 17 (4,478,000) repeated a grade. Sixty-eight percent of 8th-grade students scored below proficient in reading, 66% scored below proficient in math, 69% scored below proficient in writing, and 70% scored below proficient in science (for the last year with available data). (Proficiencies determined by the National Assessment of Educational Progress [NAEP].) Twenty-two percent of students entering freshman classes did not graduate 4 years later (2009–2010).

Obesity and Eating Disorders

Weight concerns are so prevalent in adolescence that they are typically thought of as a normative part of this developmental period. Dissatisfaction with weight and attempts to control weight are widely reported by adolescents (Lam & McHale, 2012). As suggested earlier, the dietary practices of some adolescents put them at risk for overall health problems. These practices include skipping meals, usually breakfast or lunch; snacking, especially on high-calorie, high-fat, low-nutrition snacks; eating fast foods; and dieting. Poor nutrition can affect growth and development, sleep, weight, cognition, mental health, and overall physical health.

An increasing minority of adolescents in the United States is obese, and the risks and biopsychosocial consequences of this can be profound (Cromley, Neumark-Sztainer, Story, & Boutelle, 2010). The Centers for Disease Control and Prevention (2013o) estimate that the percentage of adolescents aged 12 to 19 who are obese increased from 5% to 18% from 1980 to 2010. (Obesity is defined as a BMI greater than or equal to the 95th percentile.)

It is important to note that this is a worldwide trend. According to one report (James, 2006), almost half of the children in North and South America, about 38% of children in the European Union, and about 20% of children in China were expected to be overweight by 2010. Significant increases were also expected in the Middle East and Southeast Asia. Mexico, Brazil, Chile, and Egypt have rates comparable to fully industrialized countries. Although nationally representative data on obesity are rare, the available data indicate that child and adolescent obesity continues to increase around the world (Harvard School of Public Health, 2012).

This chapter has emphasized how tenuous self-esteem can be during adolescence, but the challenges are even greater for profoundly overweight or underweight youth. Overweight adolescents may suffer exclusion from peer groups and discrimination in education, employment, marriage, housing, and health care (Cromley et al., 2010). Carl Fleischer has already begun to face some of these challenges. He thinks of himself as a "fat, slow geek" and assumes females would not be interested in him because of his weight.

Research is exposing the breadth of the problem. According to self-reports of weight and height, more than 15% of the high school students in the nationwide sample of the YRBS are overweight and 13.0% of the students are obese (Eaton et al., 2012). Twenty-nine percent of that same sample described themselves as slightly or very overweight, and 46.0% were trying to lose weight. Moreover, within the 30 days preceding the survey, 12.2% of the high school students had gone without eating for 24 hours or more; 5.1% had taken diet pills, powders, or liquids; and 4.3% had vomited or taken laxatives to lose weight or to keep from gaining weight (Eaton et al., 2012).

Adolescents' body dissatisfaction reflects the incongruence between the societal ideal of thinness and the beginning of normal fat deposits in pubescent young people. Body dissatisfaction is a significant factor in three feeding/eating disorders, **anorexia nervosa**, **bulimia nervosa**, and **binge eating disorder**, that often have their onset in adolescence. (See Exhibit 6.7 for a description of these disorders; American Psychiatric Association, 2013.) Epidemiological studies find that the overall incidence of anorexia nervosa has remained stable over the past decades, but there has been an increase among 15- to 19-year-old girls. It appears there might be a slight decrease of bulimia nervosa over the past two decades. Though anorexia and bulimia occur mainly in girls, binge eating, compared with these other disorders, is more common in boys (Smink, van Hoeken, & Hoek, 2012). All three eating disorders have elevated mortality risk, but the risk is greatest in anorexia nervosa.

> **Exhibit 6.7**   Feeding and Eating Disorders That Often Have Onset in Adolescence

Anorexia nervosa is characterized by a distorted body image and excessive dieting that results in severe weight loss. It involves a pathological fear of becoming fat.

Bulimia nervosa is characterized by episodes of binge eating followed by behaviors such as self-induced vomiting at least once a week to avoid weight gain.

Binge eating disorder is characterized by recurring episodes of eating significantly excessive amounts of food in a short period of time; the episodes are accompanied by feelings of lack of control.

SOURCE: Based on American Psychiatric Association, 2013

Depression and Suicide

Unipolar depression is common in adolescents worldwide, with an estimated 4% to 5% of mid- to late adolescents having the disorder in any given year. The probability of depression rises from 5% in early adolescence to as high as 20% by the end of adolescence (Thapar, Collishaw, Pine, & Thapar, 2012). Although there are no known gender differences in depression prior to adolescence, during adolescence, girls are about twice as likely as boys to have a major depressive disorder (Thapar et al., 2012).

Adolescent depression may also be underdiagnosed, among boys and girls alike, because it is difficult to detect. Many parents and professionals expect adolescence to be a time of ups and downs, moodiness, melodrama, anger, rebellion, and increased sensitivity. There are, however, some reliable outward signs of depression in adolescents: poor academic performance, truancy, social withdrawal, antisocial behavior, changes in eating or sleeping patterns, changes in physical appearance, excessive boredom or activity, low self-esteem, sexual promiscuity, substance use, propensity to run away from home, and excessive family conflict. Additional symptoms of depression not unique to adolescence include pervasive inability to experience pleasure, severe psychomotor retardation, delusions, and a sense of hopelessness (Sadock & Sadock, 2007). Depressed adolescents often present with irritable rather than depressed mood (Thapar et al., 2012).

The many challenges of adolescence sometimes prove overwhelming. We have already discussed the risk of suicide among gay male and lesbian adolescents. In the United States during the 12 months preceding the 2011 YRBS survey, 28.5% of high school students reported having felt so sad or hopeless almost every day for 2 weeks or more that they stopped doing some usual activities (Eaton et al., 2012). Furthermore, 15.8% had seriously considered attempting suicide; 12.8% had made a suicide plan; 7.8% had actually attempted suicide; and 2.4% had made a suicide attempt that resulted in an injury, poisoning, or overdose that had to be treated by a doctor or nurse (Eaton et al., 2012).

Overall, suicide is the third leading cause of death for adolescents in the United States. About 4,600 youth ages 15 to 24 take their own lives each year. The top three methods that youth use in suicide are firearm (45%), suffocation (40%), and poisoning (8%). Boys are about 4 times as likely as girls to die by suicide, but girls are more likely to attempt suicide. Native American/Aslaskan Native youth have the highest rates of suicide-related deaths, and Hispanic youth are more likely to report attempting suicide than Black and White non-Hispanic youth (Centers for Disease Control and Prevention, 2014). Cheryl King and Christopher Merchant (2008) have analyzed the research on factors associated with adolescent suicidal thinking and behavior and identified a number of risk factors: social isolation, low levels of perceived support, childhood abuse and neglect, and peer abuse.

RISK FACTORS AND PROTECTIVE FACTORS IN ADOLESCENCE

There are many pathways through adolescence; both individual and group-based differences result

What are the implications of research on risk and protection for social work program development?

in much variability. Some of the variability is related to the types of risk factors and protective factors that have accumulated prior to adolescence. In addition, as we have seen throughout this chapter, the journey through adolescence is impacted by the risk and protective factors encountered during this phase of life. Social disadvantage and negative experiences in infancy and early childhood put a child at risk of poor peer relationships and poor school performance during middle childhood, which increases the likelihood of risky behaviors in adolescence (Sawyer et al., 2012). Emmy Werner and associates (see Werner & Smith, 2001) have found, in their longitudinal research on risk and protection, that girls have a better balance of risk and protection in childhood, but the advantage goes to boys during adolescence. Their research indicates that the earlier risk factors that most predict poor adolescent adjustment are a childhood spent in chronic poverty, alcoholic and psychotic parents, moderate to severe physical disability, developmentally disabled siblings, school problems in middle childhood, conflicted relationships with peers, and family disruptions. The most important earlier protective factors are easy temperament, positive social orientation in early childhood, positive peer relationships in middle childhood, non-sex-typed extracurricular interests and hobbies in middle childhood, and nurturing from nonparental figures.

Much attention has also been paid to the increase in risk behaviors during adolescence (Silbereisen & Lerner, 2007b). Attention has been called to a set of factors that are risky to adolescent well-being and serve as risk factors for adjustment in adulthood as well. These factors include use and abuse of alcohol and other drugs; unsafe sex, teen pregnancy, and teen parenting; school underachievement, failure, and dropout; delinquency, crime, and violence; youth poverty and undernutrition; and marketing of unhealthy products and lifestyles (Sawyer et al., 2012). The risk and resilience research indicates, however, that many youth with several of these risk factors overcome the odds. Protective factors that have been found to contribute to resilience in adolescence include family creativity in coping with adversity, good family relationships, spirituality and religiosity, social support in the school setting, and school-based health services. Giving adolescents a voice in society has also been identified as a potential protective factor. As social workers, we will want to promote these protective factors while at the same time work to prevent or diminish risk factors.

Critical Thinking Questions 6.5

Adolescence is a time of rapid transition in all dimensions of life, physical, emotional, cognitive, social, and spiritual. What personal, family, cultural, and other social factors help adolescents cope with all of this change? What factors lead to dissatisfaction with body image and harmful or unhealthy behaviors? How well does contemporary society support adolescent development?

Implications for Social Work Practice

Adolescence is a vulnerable period. Adolescents' bodies and psyches are changing rapidly in transition from childhood to adulthood. Youth are making some very profound decisions during this life course period. Thus, the implications for social work practice are wide ranging.

- When working with adolescents, meet clients where they are physically, psychologically, and socially—don't assume that you can tell where they are, and be aware that that place may change frequently.
- Be familiar with typical adolescent development and with the possible consequences of deviations from developmental timelines.

- Be aware of, and respond to, the adolescent's level of cognition and comprehension. Assess the individual adolescent's ability to contemplate the future, to comprehend the nature of human relationships, to consolidate specific knowledge into a coherent system, and to envision possible consequences from a hypothetical list of actions.
- Recognize that the adolescent may see you as an authority figure who is not an ally. Develop skills in building rapport with adolescents. Avoid slang terms until you have immersed yourself in adolescent culture long enough to be certain of the meaning of the terms you use.
- Assess the positive and negative effects of the school climate on the adolescent in relation to such issues as early or late maturation, popularity/sociability, culture, and gender identity/sexual orientation.
- Consider how to advocate for change in maladaptive school settings, such as those with Eurocentric models or homophobic environments.
- Seek appropriate resources to provide information, support, or other interventions to assist adolescents in resolving questions of gender identity and sexual decision making.
- Link youth to existing suitable resources or programs, such as extracurricular activities, education on STIs, prenatal care, and LGBTQQ (lesbian/gay/bisexual/transgender, queer, and questioning) support groups.
- Provide information, support, or other interventions to assist adolescents in making decisions regarding use of alcohol, tobacco, or other drugs.
- Develop skills to assist adolescents with physical and mental health issues, such as nutritional problems, obesity, eating disorders, depression, and suicide.
- Participate in research, policy development, and advocacy on behalf of adolescents.
- Work at the community level to develop and sustain recreational and social programs and safe places for young people.

Key Terms

acquaintance rape
anorexia nervosa
binge eating disorder
bulimia nervosa
gender identity
generalized other
gonads
individuation
juvenile delinquency

masturbation
menarche
postconventional moral reasoning
primary sex characteristics
psychological identity
puberty
rites of passage
secondary sex characteristics
sex hormones

sexual orientation
sexually transmitted infections (STIs)
social identity
spermarche
status offenses
statutory rape

Active Learning

1. Recalling your own high school experiences, which case study individual do you most identify with—David, Carl, or Monica? For what reasons? How can you keep your personal experiences with adolescence from biasing your social work practice? How could a social worker have affected your experiences?

2. Visit a public library and check out some preteen and teen popular fiction or magazines. Which topics from this chapter are discussed and how?

3. Have lunch at a local high school cafeteria. Be sure to go through the line, eat the food, and enjoy conversation with some students. What are their concerns? What are their notions about social work?

ABA's Juvenile Justice Committee: apps.ameri canbar.org/dch/committee.cfm?com=CR200000

Site presented by the American Bar Association's Juvenile Justice Committee contains links to juvenile justice–related sites.

Add Health: www.cpc.unc.edu/projects/addhealth

Site presented by the Carolina Population Center contains a reference list of published reports of the National Longitudinal Study of Adolescent Health (Add Health), which includes measures of social, economic, psychological, and physical well-being.

Adolescent and School Health: www.cdc.gov/ healthyyouth

Site maintained by the Centers for Disease Control and Prevention contains links to a variety of health topics related to adolescents, including alcohol and drug use, sexual behavior, nutrition, youth suicide, and youth violence.

DukeLEARN: dukebrainworks.com

Site presented by DukeLEARN, an interdisciplinary team of neuroscientists, psychologists, physicians, and social scientists at Duke University, contains links to research and publications directed to public understanding of the brain.

Sexually Transmitted Infections Information: www.ashastd.org

Site maintained by the American Sexual Health Association, which is dedicated to improving sexual health, contains information about sexual health, STDs, and publications.

Youth Risk Behavior Surveillance System (YRBSS): www.cdc.gov/HealthyYouth/yrbs/index .htm

Site presented by the Centers for Disease Control and Prevention contains the latest research on adolescent risk behavior.

⑤SAGE edge™

Sharpen your skills with SAGE edge at **edge.sagepub.com/hutchisonclc5e**

SAGE edge for students provides a personalized approach to help you accomplish your coursework goals in an easy-to-use learning environment.

CHAPTER 7

Young Adulthood

Holly C. Matto

Chapter Outline

Opening Questions

- Why is it important for social workers to understand transitional markers associated with young adulthood from a multidimensional perspective, recognizing systemic-structural impacts on development as well as the psychosocial factors that are traditionally studied?

- How do social class, culture, and gender affect the transition to adulthood?

- Given that our educational institution serves as gatekeeper to economic opportunities, what are the ways in which our educational system identifies and responds to the changing labor market trends in order to create viable long-term opportunities for all of society's young adults?

Key Ideas

As you read this chapter, take note of these central ideas:

1. A new phase called "emerging adulthood" (ages 18 to 25) has been proposed as a time when individuals explore and experiment with different life roles, occupational interests, educational pursuits, religious beliefs, and relationships—with more focus than in adolescence but without the full commitment of young adulthood.

2. Traditional transitional markers associated with young adulthood have included obtaining independent housing, establishing a career, developing significant partnerships that lead to marriage, and becoming a parent; current research suggests that financial independence and authority in decision making are the markers considered important by emerging adults.

3. In young adulthood, cognitive capacities become more flexible; "moral conscience" expands in social awareness, responsibility, and obligation; and religious beliefs are often reexamined.

4. Identity development continues into adulthood and is not static but is dynamic and ever evolving through significant interpersonal relationships.

5. Young adults struggle with the Eriksonian psychosocial crisis of intimacy versus isolation—the challenge of finding meaningful connections to others without losing oneself in the process.

6. Labor force experience and connection in young adulthood is associated with psychological and social well-being; advanced education is increasingly important in attaining quality jobs.

7. Discrimination and multilevel racism-related stressors can directly and indirectly affect entry into young adulthood.

CASE STUDY 7.1

Dominique Castillo's Food Insecurity

Food insecurity and economic instability are not new to Dominique Castillo, although she prefers to let Congress use those more academic terms in their debate on the fate of the Supplemental Nutrition Assistance Program, which has already seen significant cutbacks in November 2013. To Dominque it's more simple than that to explain.

It's about extreme hunger and poor health—deep, entrenched, gut-wrenching hunger that she and her three brothers experience in their *colonia*, a border town in Hidalgo County, South Texas. Hidalgo County, Texas, is the poorest area in the United States, where diabetes and obesity exceed, by far, the national average, and where 40% of residents receive SNAP (food stamps) benefits. The colonias are mostly populated with first-generation immigrants. Dominique is 18 years old, living with her mother, grandmother, and three brothers in a windowless trailer with no electricity and makeshift furniture, and is one of the 47 million Americans who rely on SNAP to be able to support their family's nutritional needs. Dominique and her family struggle to keep fed and at the same time struggle to keep on top of the chronic health conditions they have inherited in part from their inability to meet their most basic nutritional needs. In fact, now that she thinks about it, Dominique explains that all of her relatives have some sort of health challenge: hyptertension, high cholesterol, obesity, or diabetes.

Amid the unpredictability in what and how much each member will have to eat each day, one thing is certain: Dominique knows how to stretch a dollar and is clever in being able to prepare meals from too scarce ingredients. Today she peers into her refrigerator and knows it is one of those days she will be called on to be most resourceful. Three more days until her food stamps come in, and all that's left are three eggs, a stick of butter, a few instant oatmeal packets, a white potato, and some chips. She knows where she can stand in line for charity food bags tomorrow, but she also knows her family is hungry today. And even when she has the money, the closest grocery store with fresh produce is 11 miles away. There are, however, 12 fast-food restaurants and several convenience stores that surround her small community. There is also a free health clinic where her family goes frequently to get their blood checked and to receive medications to control her mother's high cholesterol.

One day, Dominique knows, she would like to have a family of her own, but that's not on her mind at the moment. First, she has a responsibility to care for her younger siblings and to care for her mother and grandmother, and that means sacrificing her own goals right now. Dominique works unpredictable shifts, and only part-time, at the nearby Stop & Shop convenience store, but she needs a full-time and better-paying job with more predictable hours. She did manage to graduate from high school and knows her diploma will come in handy some day. She would love to go to college, but right now managing to survive day to day seems to take most all her energy.

SOURCE: This case study is based on the story by Eli Saslow in the *Washington Post* on November 9, 2013. The following link provides a short video on life in Hidalgo County, South Texas, presented in Saslow's article on the obesity and food insecurity challenges for the families that live in this part of the United States: www.washingtonpost.com/sf/national/2013/11/09/too-much-of-too-little.

CASE STUDY 7.2

Sheila Henderson's Long-Awaited Family Reunification

Sheila Henderson, 25 years old, her boyfriend, David, 27 years old, and her 4-year-old daughter, Johanna, from a previous relationship, all said goodbye at the Family Readiness Center at Fort Bragg, North Carolina, 18 months ago, as Sheila departed for her second tour to Afghanistan as a lieutenant in the infantry division of the United States Army. The family hasn't seen each other since, although they have participated in weekly family video calls. While Sheila was on tour, she sustained a minor closed-head injury when she was participating in a training exercise with her unit in Afghanistan. Her injury was deemed "minor" and not likely to cause significant

(Continued)

(Continued)

or long-term impairment, but Sheila can't help but notice a change in her ability to handle emotions. She notices new limitations in her ability to concentrate and says she becomes easily agitated or "set off" over minor inconveniences, which is "not like her." And she cries more than she used to. She is opposed to calling her injury a disability and can't help but think that maybe it's just all in her mind anyway. She regularly experiences a variety of emotions, from frustration, anger, and resentment at her time spent away from family and friends, to loyalty and pride in serving her country. She occasionally feels guilty for taking so much time to "dwell" on her own challenges when she knows so many others have died or have been more seriously incapacitated while serving their country in Afghanistan and Iraq.

Now that she is returning from tour, Sheila knows she will struggle with transitioning back into life with her family but is giddy with excitement to be reunited with her daughter, who will be turning 5 shortly and entering kindergarten in the fall, and to rejoin her boyfriend whom she says has had the most difficulty with her absence. Her boyfriend, though officially a civilian working as an accountant, considers the military community where they live to be family. There is an informal ethos in their community that military families care for each other's children when one or more parents are deployed, and David has benefited from this support while Sheila's been away. What concerns him most is Sheila's transition back into their family life. He can't help but wonder how she will respond to the year and a half of developmental changes Johanna has gone through and how she will jump back into the role of disciplining her behavior and facilitating the family routines and schedule that David has worked so hard to establish. In fact, of Johanna's 4½ years, Sheila has really only been physically present for about a year and a half of that time. David wonders how the routine will play itself out now and how the family will reunite together. There is also the lingering anticipation and unpredictability of the next possible deployment, and that keeps him up at night. He wonders why Sheila seems so at ease with the uncertainty, and he hopes he will be able to gain her strength in negotiating the ambiguity of their family's shared life space in the future. But for now, he's overjoyed that she's coming home. They have a lot of catching up to do.

CASE STUDY 7.3

Jonathan and Kai as Older Parents of Twins

Jonathan and Kai have a lot to celebrate in this new year. In mid-December 2013, Jonathan, 37, and Kai, 39, got married. The couple will tell you they have been committed to each other since 1999, but on December 2, 2013, when Hawaii became the 15th state to recognize same-sex marriage, they rushed to officially ring in their love for each other in Honolulu . . . legally, at long last. And their love for each other will extend even further into a family of their own; they are going to be parents for the first time this summer. Their surrogate, Renee, is 2 months pregnant with twins. After an unsuccessful initial attempt at reproduction, the couple found a new surrogate and separate egg donor from whom two embryos, one from Jonathan and one from Kai, were successfully implanted.

By their own account Jonathan and Kai are comfortable financially—they wanted to wait to become parents until they were—but mixed in with their heightened excitement about the impending due date, they collectively experience anxiety about what the future might be like when the twins arrive. They know they are considered "older parents" by the medical industry's account—they are both older than 35—but they grapple more with the big questions of parenthood: Will they be good fathers? What will it be like to be responsible for two new vulnerable and totally dependent infants? What kind of child care arrangements do they want for their newborn babies? Should one of them take a leave from his job to care for the twins in that critical first year? The recent ultrasound that showed the twin heartbeats reined in these big questions and brought them back to the present moment. Their long-time dream of some day becoming parents is finally coming true. And for now that eases the anxiety, and they know in their hearts that with their love for each other they can weather through the challenges of parenting twins—even if they are "older" fathers.

Kai and Jonathan met at the University of Hawaii. Kai, originally from rural Waimea in Kauai County, Hawaii, and Jonathan, originally from Portland, Oregon, both came from families who valued education. Kai is a first-generation college student, and Jonathan's parents both have graduate degrees. They both talk about how influential their parents were in supporting their transition from high school to college. For Kai it was the extreme financial sacrifices his parents made on his behalf, and for Jonathan it was the emotional support he experienced for his studies from his mother. After they graduated from the university, Jonathan and Kai worked hard to build their careers in software development and the hospitality industry.

A DEFINITION OF YOUNG ADULTHOOD

Defining young adulthood and the transitional markers that distinguish this period from adolescence and middle adulthood has been the challenge and life's work of a number of developmental scholars. A broad challenge has been to determine a framework for identifying the developmental characteristics of young adulthood. For example, is a young adult one who has reached a certain biological or legal age? One who has achieved specific physiological and psychological milestones? Or perhaps one who performs certain social roles? Research, theory, and scholarly thinking about young adulthood present a variety of perspectives related to each of these dimensions. Current research suggests that the transitional markers that have traditionally defined adulthood in decades past, such as marriage and childbearing, are no longer the most salient markers characterizing the young adult in today's society (e.g., see Settersten, Furstenberg, & Rumbaut, 2005). For

Is it biological age, psychological age, social age, or spiritual age that best defines young adulthood?

example, in 1960, three fourths (77%) of women and 65% of men left home, completed school, became financially independent, got married, and had at least one child by age 30. In 2000, not even half (46%) of women and 31% of men had done so by age 30 (Furstenberg, Kennedy, McCloyd, Rumbaut, & Settersten, 2003, cited in Draut, 2005, p. 6).

Typical chronological ages associated with young adulthood are 22 to 34 (Ashford & LeCroy, 2010) or 18 to 34 (Settersten et al., 2005), and the international chronological standard for defining adulthood is age 18 (Lloyd, Behrman, Stromquist, & Cohen, 2006). Some scholars define young adulthood even more broadly, from the age of 17 to about 40 (Levinson, 1978). Other scholars assert that such broad ranges encompass too much variety of experience:

If ages 18 [to] 25 are young adulthood, what would that make the thirties? Young adulthood is a term better applied to the thirties, which are still young but are definitely adult in a way that the years 18 [to] 25 are not. It makes little sense to lump late teens, twenties, and thirties together and call the entire period young adulthood. The period from ages 18 to 25 could hardly be more distinct from the thirties. (Arnett, 2000, p. 479)

Grossman (2005) calls those persons who are no longer adolescents and yet are not adults by conventional standards "twixters" and suggests that this period can extend to age 29; Gordon and Shaffer (2004) call this developmental transition "adultscence." Similarly, "freeters," in Japan, are those individuals aged 15 to 34 who are typically unattached to the full-time labor market and are not enrolled in higher education, often working in part-time, temporary positions (Newman, 2008).

In this book, however, we are using a broad range of approximately 18 to 40. Although a wide chronological age range can be useful in providing some chronological boundaries around this developmental period, from a life course perspective it is more useful to examine the social role transitions, important life events, and significant turning points associated with young adulthood. The major challenges facing young adults are attaining independent financial stability and establishing autonomy in decision making, although attaining financial independence is becoming more delayed as advanced educational credentials are increasingly necessary to secure quality employment (Arnett, 2004). Young adults ages 18 to 25 agree when asked about what they see as markers of entry into young adulthood (Arnett, 1998). Young persons who do not attend college are as likely as college students to say that making independent decisions based on their own values and belief systems is important for defining adult status (Arnett, 2000). And there are international differences in home-leaving timing. For example, in Japan 64% of unmarried emerging adult men aged 25 to 29 reside with their parents, and 80% of unmarried emerging adult women reside with their parents (Newman, 2008).

Some scholars also define young adulthood as the point at which young persons become functioning members of the community, demonstrated by obtaining gainful employment, developing their own social networks, and establishing independent housing (Halpern, 1996). More recently, Burstein (2013) notes that adulthood "sign posts" are changing, with more focus on the "social impact" young adults make in their communities as a marker of this transition. Young adults are increasingly seeking entrepreneurship opportunities with increased global social awareness and connection to issues that might lead to social action, all in a context of a "shared economy" (p. 107). From a psychosocial perspective, this period is seen as a time of progressive movement out of an individualized and egocentric sense of self and into greater connection with significant others.

From a cumulative advantage/disadvantage (CAD; Dannefer, 2003c) perspective, we need to be mindful of the systematic creation of inequity in the distribution of opportunity and burden through such institutions as our labor market and educational system. Scholars suggest that advantages and disadvantages begin through inequities present in early schooling, which are then replicated and immured throughout the life course (Dannefer, 2003c), but it is important to remember that advantages and disadvantages have already accrued before children enter school. Dominique Castillo's story helps us to understand the grip intergenerational poverty and limited material resources can have on later life course economic and social mobility. Dominique currently feels "stuck" educationally (can't pursue higher education) and economically (working at a low-wage part-time job) because of the material disadvantage she has experienced in her family's colonia community. She managed to graduate from high school, despite the financial instability of her childhood, and that opens up some labor market possibilities for her, while others remain closed. CAD theory asks us to reflect on the ways in which our educational system replicates social stratification (binding one to a set socioeconomic location) or, in turn, facilitates social and economic mobility. How do you think our educational system serves various communities? What about our labor market system? Which of our social institutions serve to preserve inequality and regulate opportunity, and which ones tend to facilitate social and economic mobility?

Exhibit 7.1 Social Role Transitions in Young Adulthood

- Leaving home
- Taking on work and/or education tasks
- Gaining financial independence
- Gaining independence in decision making
- Making a partnership commitment
- Becoming a parent
- Renegotiating relationships with parents
- Making time commitments to families of origin and to newly created families
- Starting a career
- Engaging with the community and the wider social world

Photo 7.1 Young adulthood is a challenging and exciting time in life, bringing new opportunities and new challenges.

© JupiterImages/liquidlibrary/ThinkStock

Typical social role transitions in young adulthood are summarized in Exhibit 7.1. Timing of these transitions and psychological readiness for adopting adult roles are important factors in the individual's life course trajectory. However, research indicates that individual variation in the timing and sequence of transitions—when and in what order the individual leaves home, starts a career, and forms a family, for example—does not have large-scale effects on the individual's eventual socioeconomic status (Marini, 1989). These findings contradict the popular notion that people who don't "grow up" on schedule will never "amount to much." However, the timing and sequencing of childbearing, entry into postsecondary educational institutions, and labor market attachment may have wide-ranging effects on economic viability and security over the long term. For example, very young single parents employed in full-time, low-wage work without adequate access to affordable quality child care or health care will be faced with difficulty in affording and finding time for the additional higher education necessary to obtain employment with better wages, better benefits, and better work schedules

(e.g., see Edin & Lein, 1997). However, it is important to consider that other macro-context variables may be interacting with individuals' planned sequences to influence life chances. Jonathan and Kai waited to become parents until their late 30s, waiting until they were financially stable. Now as impending parents they have little concern over how parenthood will affect their economic security but are more worried about how they will balance two careers and all of the family obligations that will come with having twins. They have demanding work schedules but also a great deal of support from colleagues in their workplaces and have formed a strong social support network in Honolulu.

Nevertheless, young adulthood is a challenging and exciting time in life. Young people are confronted with new opportunities and the accompanying stressors associated with finances, occupational planning, educational pursuits, development of significant relationships, and new family roles (Newman & Newman, 2012). Kenneth Keniston (1966), an eminent developmental scholar writing in the late 1960s, during an era of student activism and bold social expression, described young adulthood as a time of struggle and alienation between an individual and society. Young adulthood remains a period of intrapersonal and interpersonal questing as well as a period of critiquing and questioning of social norms. Young persons grapple with decisions across several polarities: independence versus relatedness, family versus work, care for self versus care for others, and individual pursuits versus social obligations.

THEORETICAL APPROACHES TO YOUNG ADULTHOOD_____

Two prominent developmental theories, promulgated by Erik Erikson and Daniel Levinson, specifically address this life course phase.

Erikson's Psychosocial Theory

Erik Erikson's psychosocial theoretical framework is probably one of the most universally known approaches to understanding life course development. Young adulthood is one of Erikson's original eight stages of psychosocial development (refer back to Exhibit 3.7). Erikson described it

> How is the capacity for intimacy affected by earlier social relationships?

as the time when individuals move from the identity fragmentation, confusion, and exploration of adolescence into more intimate engagement with significant others (Erikson, 1968, 1978). Individuals who successfully resolve the crisis of **intimacy versus isolation** are able to achieve the virtue of love. An unsuccessful effort at this stage may lead the young adult to feel alienated, disconnected, and alone. A fear at the core of this crisis is that giving of oneself through a significant, committed relationship will result in a loss of self and diminution of one's constructed identity. To

pass through this stage successfully, young adults must try out new relationships and attempt to find a way to connect with others in new ways while preserving their individuality (Erikson, 1978; Fowler, 1981).

For example, we might wonder about the relational context of Sheila's family of origin and how it might be influencing her current relationships. What were the relationship templates that were established in her years up to 5 years old? How are these relationships being replicated in her current family, particularly in her daughter? How are Sheila's own intimacy needs being addressed with so many geographic disruptions and work that is engaging but intense and at times unpredictable and physically and emotionally risky?

Levinson's Theory of Life Structure

Daniel Levinson (1978) describes adulthood as a period of undulating stability and stress, signified by transitions that occur at specific chronological times during the life course. He initially developed his theory based on interviews with men about their adult experiences; later he included women in the research (1996). From his research he developed the concept of **life structure**, which he described as the outcome resulting from specific decisions and choices made along the life course in such areas as relationships, occupation, and childbearing. He considered the ages of 17 to 33 to be the **novice phase** of adulthood. The transition into young adulthood, which occurs during the ages of 17 to 22, includes the tasks of leaving adolescence and making preliminary decisions about relationships, career, and belief systems; the transition out of this phase, which occurs about the age of 30, marks significant changes in life structure and life course trajectory.

During the novice phase, young persons' personalities continue to develop, and they prepare to differentiate (emotionally, geographically, financially) from their families of origin (Levinson, 1978). The transition to adulthood takes hold primarily in two domains: work and relationships.

Levinson suggested that it may take up to 15 years for some individuals to resolve the transition to adulthood and to construct a stable adult life structure.

Building on Levinson's concepts, others have noted that cultural and societal factors affect life structure choices during young adulthood by constraining or facilitating opportunities (Newman & Newman, 2012). For example, socioeconomic status, parental expectations, availability of and interactions with adult role models, neighborhood conditions, and community and peer group pressures may all contribute to a young person's decisions about whether to marry early, get a job or join the military before pursuing a college education or advanced training, or delay childbearing. Social and economic factors may directly or indirectly limit a young person's access to alternative choices, thereby rigidifying a young person's life structure. Along these lines, many researchers discuss the strong link between social capital and human capital, suggesting that a family's "wealth transfer" or extent of familial assets, such as the ability to pay for children's college education, is influential in opening up or limiting young adults' opportunities for advanced education and viable employment (Lui, Robles, Leondar-Wright, Brewer, & Adamson, 2006; Rank, 2005).

Jonathan and Kai reflect on how these early familial expectations and support might have contributed to their decision to delay parenting until their late 30s. And as they have begun telling family and friends that they are soon-to-be-parents of twins, they are curious about the varied responses they are getting to their pregnancy news—most have been congratulatory while some have expressed skepticism about how they will manage. Jonathan and Kai can't help but wonder whether such skepticism comes from the fact that they are perceived as older parents, or because they are a dual-income family with two successful careers who will be trying to raise newborn twins, or if it is because they are a gay couple.

Especially in young adulthood, life structures are in constant motion, changing with time and evolving as new life circumstances unfold.

Decisions made during the young adulthood transition, such as joining the military, forgoing postsecondary education, or delaying childbearing, may not accurately or completely represent a young person's desired life structure or goals. We can see this in the case of Dominique Castillo, who says she desires to start a family but could not imagine doing so when her family of origin is in such a struggle to even put food on the table each day. Social workers need to explore goal priorities and the resources and obstacles that will help or hinder the individual in achieving these goals. Social workers are also often called on to help young adults negotiate conflicting, incompatible, or competing life roles throughout this novice phase, such as renegotiating family and work responsibilities as parenthood approaches.

Arnett's "Emerging" Adulthood

A number of prominent developmental scholars who have written about the stages of adolescence and young adulthood

> What historical trends are producing "emerging adulthood"?

in advanced industrial countries have described phenomena called "prolonged adolescence," "youthhood," or "psychosocial moratorium," which represent an experimentation phase of young adulthood (Arnett, 2000; Erikson, 1968; Settersten et al., 2005; Sheehy, 1995). Jeffrey Jensen Arnett has gone one step further, defining a phase he terms **emerging adulthood** in some detail (Arnett, 2000, 2004; Arnett & Tanner, 2005). He describes emerging adulthood as a developmental phase distinct from both adolescence and young adulthood, occurring from ages 18 to 25 in industrialized societies (Arnett, 2000). There is considerable variation in personal journeys from emerging adulthood into young adulthood, but most individuals make the transition by age 30 (Arnett, 2000). Arnett conceptualized this new phase of life based on research showing that a majority of young persons ages 18 to 25 believe they have not yet reached adulthood and that a majority of people in their 30s do agree they have reached adulthood.

According to Arnett, identity exploration has become the central focus of emerging adulthood, not of adolescence (Arnett, 2006, 2007). Emerging adulthood is a period of prolonged exploration of social and economic roles where young people try out new experiences related to love, work, financial responsibilities, and educational interests without committing to any specific lasting plan. The social role experimentation of adolescence becomes further refined, more focused, and more intense, although commitment to adult roles is not yet solidified. Arnett explains this adulthood transition using an organizing framework that includes cognitive, emotional, behavioral, and role transition elements (Arnett & Taber, 1994).

Most young persons in emerging adulthood are in education, training, or apprenticeship programs working toward an occupation; most individuals in their 30s have established a more solid career path and are moving through occupational transitions (e.g., promotion to leadership positions and recognition for significant accomplishments). Studies do show more occupational instability during the ages 18 to 25 as compared with age 30 (Rindfuss, Cooksey, & Sutterlin, 1999). Indeed, Arnett (2007) suggests that emerging adulthood can be an "unstructured time" characterized by a lack of attachment to social institutions, where young people are moving out from their families of origin, have not yet formed new families of their own, and are moving out of prior educational systems and into new vocational, educational, or employment sectors (p. 25).

Although marriage has traditionally been cited as a salient marker in the adulthood transition, current research shows that marriage has not retained its high status as the critical benchmark of adulthood. Today, independent responsibility for decision making and finances seems to be more significant in marking this transition than marriage is (Arnett, 1998). Overall, the emphasis in emerging adulthood is on trying out new roles without the pressure of making any particular commitment (Schwartz, Cote, & Arnett, 2005). The transition, then, from *emerging* adulthood into *young* adulthood is marked by solidifying role

commitments. Newer research shows that, across race and ethnicity, the difference between those who follow a **default individualization** pathway (adulthood transitions defined by circumstance and situation, rather than individual agency) versus a **developmental individualization** pathway (adulthood transitions defined by personal agency and deliberately charted growth opportunities in intellectual, occupational, and psychosocial domains) is a firmer commitment to goals, values, and beliefs for those in the developmental individuation pathway (Schwartz et al., 2005). In addition, these researchers found that personal agency, across race and ethnicity, is associated with a more flexible and exploratory orientation to adulthood commitments and is less associated with premature closure and circumscribed commitment.

Residential stability and mobility is another theme of this transition. Emerging adults in their early 20s may find themselves at various times living with family, living on their own in independent housing arrangements yet relying on parents for instrumental support, and living with a significant partner or friends. Indeed, residential instability and mobility is typically at its height in the mid-20s (Rindfuss et al., 1999). In our case example, Sheila experiences residential instability and considers the military a primary residence when deployed for months at a time. Thus, a traditional definition of the separation-individuation process may not be appropriately applied to emerging adulthood. True "separation" from the family of origin may appear only toward the end of young adulthood or, perhaps for some, during the transition to middle adulthood.

Demographic changes over the past several decades, such as delayed marriage and childbearing, have made young adulthood a significant developmental period filled with complex changes and possibilities (Arnett, 2000; Sheehy, 1995). Current global demographic trends suggest a similar picture. Overall, globally, family size has decreased, the timing of first marriage is being delayed, including a decrease in teenage marriages, and there are overall decreases in adolescent labor accompanied by increases in educational attainment. However, in some countries, such as Pakistan, the delay in first marriage has been attributed to a rise in the rate of adolescent girls in the labor market (see Lloyd et al., 2006; White, 2003). In addition, there is similarity in adulthood transitioning trends between developing countries and more economically developed countries, with East Asian countries showing the most trend similarities and Sub-Saharan African countries showing the fewest similarities (Behrman & Sengupta, 2006). Specifically, there has been an increased reliance on finding employment outside the family, an emphasis on more formal schooling, rather than family-based learning, a decreased gender gap, and greater transiency in young adulthood (Behrman & Sengupta, 2006).

Trends in fertility data reported in *The Economist* ("Go Forth and Multiply a Lot Less," 2009) suggest a worldwide trend in declining fertility rates (the number of children a woman is projected to have during her lifetime), even in poor and developing countries, which have typically yielded larger fertility rates. Scholars believe that the disparity between women's desired and actual number of children has decreased in recent years in part because of increased access to family planning and literacy programs that have remarkably grown in countries such as Iran, where such education for women just decades ago was negligible (e.g., in 1976, 10% of rural Iranian women aged 20 to 24 were literate; today it is 91%) (p. 30). These changing demographic trends have other societal ramifications, one of which is the potential to make it easier for women across the globe to transition to the formal workplace. A chart in *The Economist* ("Go Forth and Multiply a Lot Less," 2009) based on data from 2007 shows a clear association between countries' fertility rates and the economy. Countries with fertility rates above the replacement rate of 2.1 (such as Ghana and India) have lower income per person, while countries that have maintained fertility rate stability at or below the replacement rate of 2.1 (such as China, Brazil, Iran, South Korea, and the United States) have higher income per person.

Cultural Variations

How do culture and socioeconomic status affect the transition to adulthood?

Another advantage of the theory of emerging adulthood is that it recognizes diversity. Individual routes of development (the timing and sequence of transitions) are contingent on socialization processes experienced within family, peer groups, school, and community. Specifically, environmental opportunities, expressed community attitudes, and family expectations may all influence the timing and sequencing of transitions during emerging adulthood. Socially constructed gauges of adulthood—such as stable and independent residence, completion of education, entry into a career path, and marriage or significant partnership—hold varying importance across families and cultures.

For some young persons, decisions may be heavily weighted toward maintaining family equilibrium. For example, some may choose not to move out of the family home and establish their own residence in order to honor the family's expectation that children will continue to live with their parents, perhaps even into their 30s. For others, successful adult development may be defined through the lens of pragmatism; a young person may be expected to make decisions based on immediate, short-term, utilitarian outcomes. For example, they may be expected to enter the labor force and establish a career in order to care for a new family and release the family of origin from burden.

One study examined the home-leaving behavior of poor and nonpoor emerging adults in the United States. Using a longitudinal data set and a family economic status measure that included a federal poverty line indicator and childhood public assistance receipt, the authors found significant home-leaving and returning differences between poor and nonpoor emerging adults (De Marco & Cosner Berzin, 2008). Specifically, having a family history of public welfare assistance, dropping out of high school, and becoming a teen parent were the characteristics most likely to predict leaving the family home before age 18. Repeated home leaving (leaving, returning, leaving again) was more frequent for nonpoor as compared with poor emerging adults. And when they left home, nonpoor emerging adults were more likely than poor emerging adults to transition to postsecondary educational opportunities (De Marco & Cosner Berzin, 2008).

International research that has focused specifically on foster youth aging out of care suggests that such youth face significant transitioning risks, such as homelessness, substance abuse, and involvement with the criminal justice system (Tweddle, 2007). More successful transitioning outcomes for former foster youth, such as finding stable housing and employment, are associated with having had a strong social support system and problem-solving skill development before leaving care (Stein, 2005; Tweddle, 2007).

Culture and gender also have significant influence on young adult roles and expectations (Arnett & Taber, 1994). Social norms may sanction the postponement of traditional adult roles (such as marriage) or may promote marriage and childbearing in adolescence. There may be different family expectations about what it means to be a "good daughter" or "good son," and these expectations may be consistent or inconsistent with socially prescribed gender roles, potentially creating competing role demands. For example, a young woman may internalize her family's expectations of going to college and having a career while at the same time being aware of her family's expectations that her brothers will go directly into a job to help support the family and her college expenses. In addition, this woman may internalize society's message that women can "do it all"—have a family and career—and yet see her friends putting priority on having a family and raising children. As a result, she may feel compelled to succeed in college and a career to make good on the privilege that her brothers did not have while at the same time feeling anxious about putting a career over creating a new family of her own. It is clear in Dominique Castillo's story that she feels a strong obligation to stay and help contribute to the economic well-being of her family of origin, rather than leaving her colonia community.

Here are a couple of examples of cultural variations in the young adult transition. One research team studied 450 college students in one southeastern U.S. state and found that African American, Latino, and Asian American students were more likely than White students to perceive themselves as adult, while the White students were more likely to perceive themselves as emerging adult. Likewise, low-income students were more likely than other students to perceive themselves as adults. The ethnic minority students were more likely than White students to put high value on family obligations. Students who perceived themselves as adults were less likely to binge drink, smoke cigarettes, and gamble than students who perceived themselves as emerging adults (Blinn-Pike, Worthy, Jonkman, & Smith, 2008). In another study examining the life course priorities of Appalachian emerging adults aged 19 to 24, Brown, Rehkopf, Copeland, Costello, and Worthman (2009) found that high family poverty, and particularly the combination of poverty and parental neglect, was associated with emerging adults' lower educational goals. In addition, the experience of traumatic stressors was associated with lowered economic attainment priorities among Appalachian emerging adults.

Some environments may offer limited education and occupational opportunities. Economic structures, environmental opportunities, family characteristics, and individual abilities also contribute to variations in transitioning during emerging adulthood. Young adults with developmental disabilities tend to remain in high school during the adulthood transitioning years of 18 to 21, as compared with their peers without such disabilities who are more likely to continue on to college or enter the workforce. Research suggests that more inclusive postsecondary environments that offer higher education opportunities for young adults with developmental disabilities, and the necessary accommodations for such adults to succeed, can increase their social and academic skills as well as facilitate productive interactions between young adults with and without disabilities (Casale-Giannola & Kamens, 2006). Some studies have shown that Latina mothers of young adults with developmental disabilities encourage family centered adulthood transitioning, with less emphasis on traditional markers of independence and more emphasis on the family's role in the young adults' ongoing decision making, with such mothers reporting that their young adults' social interactions were more important to them than traditional measures of productivity (Rueda, Monzo, Shapiro, Gomez, & Blacher, 2005).

Individuals who grow up in families with limited financial resources or who are making important transitions during an economic downturn have less time for lengthy exploration than others do and may be encouraged to make occupational commitments as soon as possible. Although Kai grew up in a rural area with limited financial means, his family's strong expectations and material sacrifices made to support his transition from high school to college, and then again from college to the work world, allowed him the opportunity for extended exploration of his career choices that others without such family support may not have. Indeed, research shows that childhood socioeconomic status is an important mediating factor in young adult transitions (Smyer, Gatz, Simi, & Pedersen, 1998). For example, Astone, Schoen, Ensminger, and Rothert (2000) examined the differences between "condensed" (or time-restricted) and "diffuse" (or time-open) human capital development, with findings suggesting that a diffuse educational system offers opportunities for school reentry across the life course, which may be beneficial to young people who do not immediately enter higher education because of family or economic reasons, such as going into the military or entering the labor force. And, more specifically, they found that military service after high school increased the probability of returning to higher education for men, but not for women.

A family's economic background and resources are strongly associated with the adult status of the family's children; high correlations exist between parents' income and occupational status and that of their children (Rank, 2005). For example, about one third (34%) of youth from low-income families go on to college compared with 83% of youth from high-income families (Hair, Ling, & Cochran, 2003). Individuals with greater financial stability

often have more paths to choose from and may have more resources to negotiate the stressors associated with this developmental period.

Multigenerational Concerns

In today's society, young persons are increasingly becoming primary caretakers for elderly family members. Such responsibilities can dramatically affect a young adult's developing life structure. Family life, relationships, and career may all be affected (Dellmann-Jenkins & Blankemeyer, 2009). The demographic trend of delaying childbearing, with an increase of first births for women in their 30s and 40s and a decrease of first births to women in their 20s (Ashford & LeCroy, 2010), suggests that young adults are also likely to face new and significant role challenges as primary caretakers for their own aging parents. This can result in young adults caring for the generation ahead of them as well as the generation behind them. An Associated Press article (Stobbe, 2009) cited a report from the U.S. Centers for Disease Control and Prevention on the link between premature births and infant mortality in the United States, with 1 in 8 premature births (defined as birth before 37 weeks' gestation) contributing to the United States' 30th ranking worldwide in infant death. Causes of premature birth are thought to be related to maternal risk factors, such as smoking, obesity, infection, and health care industry practices, such as early cesarean section delivery, induced labor, fertility treatments, and lack of access to prenatal care for some segments of the pregnant population (e.g., poor, low-income women). In addition to the special, intensive care premature babies need in the immediate year postbirth, such infants are also at risk for cognitive delays and vision, hearing, and learning disorders, which are often detected when children enter formal schooling. Therefore, for sandwich-generation families with children who have special physical, emotional, and/or learning needs, the challenge of providing the necessary care for their children while simultaneously providing care for their parents can be overwhelming. We can understand that Dominique may be experiencing role overload in contributing economic support for her younger siblings and mother and grandmother, and we might wonder what the future will be like for Dominique if family members' health worsens over time simultaneous to these economic stressors. As a social worker, what kinds of supports do you think Dominique might need now and in the future?

The concern is that young adults will face a substantial caregiving burden, trying to help their aging parents with later-in-life struggles while nurturing their own children. We might see a shorter period of "emerging adulthood" for many people, which would mean that they have less opportunity to explore, to gain a sense of independence, and to form new families themselves. There may be less support for the notion of giving young people time to get on their feet and establish a satisfactory independent adulthood. In addition, young adults may increasingly experience the emotional responsibilities of supporting late-in-life divorcing parents or parents deciding to go back to school at the same time these young adults may be considering advanced educational opportunities themselves. Although currently Kai and Jonathan's parents are in good health and seem to be aging well, there may be a time in the future when Kai and Jonathan will struggle with caregiving responsibilities for young twins and their aging parents, while also trying to manage two careers. Geographic distance may also pose a challenge given that Kai's parents still remain in the rural area where he grew up and Jonathan's parents are on the mainland in Oregon. Being in the IT field, Jonathan knows quite a bit about the telehealth trends and technological advances being used in health care, and so his career expertise may one day be very important to his own family's well-being.

Critical Thinking Questions 7.1

Which transitional markers do you see as the best indicators that one has become an adult? Why did you choose these particular markers? How do the stories of Dominique Castillo, Sheila Henderson, and Jonathan and Kai fit with the developmental markers you have chosen?

PHYSICAL FUNCTIONING IN YOUNG ADULTHOOD

Physical functioning is typically at its height during early adulthood. But as young adults enter their 30s, an increased awareness of physical changes—in vision, endurance, metabolism, and muscle strength—is common (e.g., Bjorklund, 2011). With new role responsibilities in family, parenting, and career, young adults may also spend less time in exercise and sports activities than during adolescence and pay less attention to their physical health. And at the same time, young adults ages 18 to 34 are the least insured when it comes to health care coverage as compared with any other age cohort (Draut, 2005). However, with the new Affordable Care Act young adults are able to stay on their parents' health insurance until age 26. It will be important to track how these changes in law affect young adult insurance coverage and health outcomes over time. As we prepare this book for press, a January 13, 2014, *Washington Post* article cites disappointing rates in young adult enrollment in health plans to date, an enrollment rate of 24% for persons aged 18 to 34 (Goldstein & Somashkehar, 2014). How the extended dependent coverage might influence this enrollment number will be of interest.

Many young adults make an effort to maintain or improve their physical health, committing to exercise regimens and participating in wellness classes (such as yoga or meditation). They may choose to get more actively involved in community recreational leagues in such sports as hockey, soccer, racquetball, and Ultimate Frisbee. Sometimes physical activities are combined with participation in social causes, such as Race for the Cure runs, AIDS walks, or organized bike rides.

Behavioral risks to health in emerging and young adulthood may include unprotected sex. The potential for sexually transmitted infections, including HIV, is related to frequent sexual experimentation, substance use (particularly binge drinking), and smoking or use of other tobacco products.

According to the Substance Abuse and Mental Health Administration's most recent data from the

Photo 7.2 Young adults may choose to get more actively involved in community recreational leagues.

© Tim Pannell/Corbis

National Survey on Drug Use and Health, one fifth (21.3%) of young adults aged 18 to 25 used illicit drugs in 2012, which was higher than the rate for youth aged 12 to 17 (9.5%) and for adults older than age 26 (7.0%). The nonmedical use of pain medications for this age group during 2012 was 5.3%, up from 4.1% in 2002. Illicit drug use for adults aged 18 years and older showed highest rates for the unemployed (18.1%) and lower rates for part-time (12.5%) and full-time (8.9%) employment status (Substance Abuse and Mental Health Services Administration, 2013a).

Data from the Drug Abuse Warning Network (DAWN) showed that 2.5 million illicit drug–related emergency department (ED) visits occurred in 2011. Cocaine, then marijuana, heroin, stimulants, and other drugs represent an ordered account of the illicit drugs linked to these ED visits (Substance Abuse and Mental Health Services Administration, 2013b). The National Hospital Ambulatory Medical Care Survey showed a 19% increase from 1993 to 2003 in ED visits by adults ages 22 to 49, with 11.4% of alcohol-related ED visits accounted for by adolescents and young adults younger than 21 and half (53.2%) by adults ages 21 to 44. Young adults ages 15 to 24 had the highest injury-related emergency ED visits, with two thirds (66.7%) of alcohol-related visits characterized by injury. In addition, African Americans, across age cohorts, had an 86% higher rate of ED use compared with that of Whites (McCaig & Burt, 2005). Combined, the data seem to indicate that young adults are at high risk for accidents and related health injuries associated with drug use.

Community and cultural affiliation may play a role in young adults' behavioral health decision making. Kei-ho Pih, Hirose, and Mao's (2012) study of low-wage Chinese immigrant communities found that families in these communities tended to rely on interpersonal relationships to provide important information and social connections to employment opportunities but that these intracommunity network connections were not as helpful for the dissemination of health care information. The authors identified limited English proficiency as a significant barrier that reduced the bridging social capital opportunities of key community members to be able to understand the majority community's health care system and its resources and, therefore, decreased the informational support they could provide to the community's residents. In addition, other studies have shown that socioeconomic (material) disadvantage and other environmental factors, such as neighborhood disorder, are significant risk factors for substance use in early adulthood (Kuipers, van Poppel, van den Brink, Wingen, & Kunst, 2012; Redonnet, Chollet, Fombonne, Bowes, & Melchior, 2012). Molina, Alegria, and Chen (2012) found that Latinos living in Latino immigrant-dense neighborhoods were at lower risk for an alcohol use disorder as compared with Whites, and foreign-born Latinos living in such Latino immigrant neighborhoods had less substance use risk compared with U.S.-born Latinos in the same neighborhoods. As acculturation increases, so does the risk for substance use and other health and mental health problems. Asian Americans, a rapidly growing minority group in the United States, have seen an increase in substance use among young adults aged 18 to 29 (Grant et al., 2004), with significant health and mental health consequences. Although African American youth and young adults tend to have lower substance use rates when in more racially homogeneous settings, substance use increases in frequency when Black youth reside in predominantly White communities (Stock et al., 2013). Strong racial identity tends to have a protective effect in decreasing substance use risk for African American young adults, especially for youth living in predominantly Caucasian communities (Stock et al., 2013).

Online social networks are also important communities that shape the social norms in emerging adulthood and influence substance-use behavioral decision making. The social influence of network ties is not a new phenomenon, but the influence of social networking affiliations, and their influence on the development and maintenance of social norms that influence behavioral decision making, is a relatively new and important area to examine for the emerging adulthood population for whom the vast majority of the demographic are engaged in some form of social networking. Cook, Bauermeister, Gordon-Messer, and Zimmerman's (2013) data analysis from the Virtual Networks Study of emerging adults' (ages 18 to 24) online relationships found that drug use was associated with frequency of network discussion around drug use and network acceptance of drug use, which was stronger in effect for males as compared with females. In addition, alcohol use was associated with greater density and emotional closeness to network ties (e.g., photos and discussions on such sites may create norms that encourage drinking within a network). In addition, Nitzburg and Farber (2013) found that emerging adults with anxious and disorganized, as compared with secure, adult attachment styles tended to use Facebook as a way of avoiding intimate face-to-face human interaction and as a way to gain emotional connection in a safe way. A study in Indonesia also found that young adults with anxious attachment style were more active in using Facebook than other young adults, but young adults with avoidant attachment style were reluctant to use Facebook (Andangsari, Gumilar, & Godwin, 2013).

Other health concerns include type 1 diabetes ("juvenile diabetes"), typically diagnosed in children and young adults. Although this type of diabetes is less prevalent than type 2 (diagnosed in older adults), young adults do have a risk of getting type 1 diabetes in their 20s. Adults diagnosed with diabetes will have to adjust to lifestyle changes, such as more consistent exercise, modified diets, and monitoring of blood sugar levels.

Research has shown physical and psychosocial interactions. For example, obesity in adolescence leads to depression and lower social attainment (i.e., educational, economic, work satisfaction) in young adulthood for females but not males (Merten, Wickrama, & Williams, 2008). Important associations exist between being overweight and having depression in adolescence and young adulthood for African American and White females (Franko, Streigel-Moore, Thompson, Schreiber, & Daniels, 2005). And Geronimus and colleagues' (2006) decades of research on the physical weathering hypothesis suggests that accelerated aging characterized by early onset of chronic disease may disproportionately affect African Americans as compared with Whites and may be linked to an environmental impact on the body, such as stress exposure, racial discrimination, and economic hardship. Newer research by Geronimus, Hicken, Keene, and Bound (2006) is examining biomarkers such as telomeres, indicators associated with the physical aging process, and their differential expression in African American and White populations.

The changing economic environment, particularly the recent economic volatility experienced nationally, has also been found to affect physical health. According to the 2008 National Study of the Changing Workplace (Aumann & Galinsky, 2011), workers' overall health has declined from 2002 levels, with an increase in frequency of minor health problems (such as headaches), rising obesity rates, and rising stress levels (41% reported significant stress). Of those workers who experience chronic health problems, most report high blood pressure (21%), high cholesterol (14%), diabetes (7%), heart condition (3%), or a mental health disorder (4%). Dominique Castillo and her family remind us of the lived experiences behind these statistics, where obesity and its relationship to other chronic diseases are disproportionately represented within the most economically distressed communities. Dominique and her family struggle to meet their most basic human needs in an environment that does not offer the economic or healthy food opportunities that research shows are necessary to support good health and prevent disease.

Research on teens and young adults has given rise to growing concern over post-concussive syndrome that may arise from repetitive concussions sustained from contact sports. Repetitive concussions may lead to increased risk of mild cognitive impairment and early dementia later in adulthood (Stern et al., 2011). Young adults who have played contact sports and sustained even mild repetitive concussions, and young adults who have served in the military, particularly those who have been deployed in the last decade's conflicts in Iraq and Afghanistan where there was heightened risk for traumatic brain injury, are particularly vulnerable to such long-term neurodegenerative concerns.

In working with young adults who have a health-related illness, social workers will want to assess the client's relationship to the illness and evaluate how the treatments are affecting the psychosocial developmental tasks of young adulthood (Dunbar, Mueller, Medina, & Wolf, 1998). For example, an illness may increase a young person's dependence on others at a time when independence from parents is valued and individuals may have concerns about finding a mate. Societal stigma associated with the illness may be intense at a time when the individual is seeking more meaningful community engagements, and adjustment to the possibilities of career or parenthood delays may be difficult. Increasingly, social networking sites such as Patients Like Me (www.patientslikeme .com) are being used by young adults with chronic health conditions to create online communities to promote social interaction and information exchange. Users can create a shared health profile and find other users who have the same health condition to share treatment experiences. Examples of current disease communities include HIV/AIDS, fibromyalgia, mood conditions, and multiple sclerosis. Currently, about one third (34%) of the Patients Like Me member base is younger than age 39, with the majority (72%) women.

> How does infertility alter the young adult phase of the life course?

In addition, young adult partners who struggle with infertility problems may have to confront disappointment from family members and adjust to feelings of unfulfilled social and family expectations. Costs of treatment may be prohibitive, and couples may experience a sense of alienation from peers who are moving rapidly into parenthood and child rearing. See Chapter 2 in this book for further discussion of infertility.

Critical Thinking Questions 7.2

Levinson talks about how culture and society affect young adults' life structure. How do you think our American society's growing attention to changing marriage laws, to make them inclusive of marriage for same-sex couples, will affect family formation and family health and well-being for such same-sex couple families? How does socioeconomic status affect life structure for gay couples, particularly in areas of access to reproductive technological advances?

THE PSYCHOLOGICAL SELF_____

Young adulthood is a time when an individual continues to explore personal identity and his or her relationship to the world. Cognition, spirituality, and identity are intertwined aspects of this process.

Cognitive Development

Psychosocial development will depend on cognitive and moral development, which are parallel processes (Fowler, 1981). Young adulthood is a time when individuals expand, refine, and challenge existing belief systems, and the college environment is especially fertile ground for such broadening experiences. Late adolescents and young adults are also entering Piaget's formal operations stage, during which they begin to develop the cognitive ability to apply abstract principles to enhance problem solving and to reflect on thought processes (refer back to Exhibit 3.5 for an overview of Piaget's stages of cognitive development). These more complex cognitive capabilities, combined with a greater awareness of personal feelings, characterize cognitive development in young adulthood (Gardiner & Kosmitzki, 2011).

The abstract reasoning capabilities of adulthood and the awareness of subjective feelings can be applied to life experiences in ways that help individuals negotiate life transitions, new roles, stressors, and challenges (Labouvie-Vief, 2005). You might think of the development in cognitive processing from adolescence to young adulthood as a gradual switch from obtaining information to using that information in more applied ways (Arnett & Taber, 1994). Young adults are better able to see things from multiple viewpoints and from various perspectives than adolescents are.

With increasing cognitive flexibility, young adults begin to solidify their own values and beliefs. They may opt to retain certain traditions and values from their family of origin while letting go of others in order to make room for new ones. During this sorting-out process, young adults are also defining what community means to them and what their place in the larger societal context might be like. Individuals begin establishing memberships in, and attachments to, selected social, service, recreational, and faith communities. Research indicates that religious beliefs, in particular, are reevaluated and critically examined in young adulthood, with individuals sorting out beliefs and values they desire to hold on to and those they choose to discard (Arnett & Jensen, 2002). However, there is a danger that discarded family beliefs may not be replaced with new meaningful beliefs (Arnett, 2000). Many emerging adults view the world as cold and disheartening and are somewhat cynical about the future. With this common pitfall in mind, we can take comfort from Arnett's finding that nearly all the 18- to 24-year-olds who participated in his study believed they would ultimately achieve their goals at some point in the future (Arnett, 2000).

In terms of moral development, Lawrence Kohlberg (1976) categorized individuals ages 16 and older as fitting into the postconventional

> How does continued moral development affect the capacity for human agency in making choices?

stage, which has these characteristics (refer back to Exhibit 4.2 for an overview of Kohlberg's stages of moral reasoning):

- Greater independence in moral decision making
- More complex contemplation of ethical principles
- Development of a "moral conscience"
- Move from seeking social approval through conformity to redefining and revising values and selecting behaviors that match those values
- Recognition of larger systems and appreciation for community
- Understanding that social rules are relativistic, rather than rigid and prescribed

Young adults begin to combine the principles of utility and production with the principle of equality, coming to the realization that individual or group gain should not be at the detriment of other individuals or social groups.

Kohlberg's research indicates that people do not progress in a straight line through the stages of moral development. Late adolescents and young adults may regress to conventional moral reasoning as they begin the process of critical reflection. In any case, successful resolution of the adolescent identity crisis, separation from home, and the willingness and ability to take responsibility for others are necessary, but not sufficient, conditions for postconventional moral development (Kohlberg, 1976).

Spiritual Development

As mentioned earlier, young adulthood is a time when individuals explore and refine their belief systems. Part of that process is development of **spirituality**, a focus on that which gives meaning, purpose, and direction to one's life. Spirituality manifests itself through one's ethical obligations and behavioral commitment to values and ideologies. It is a way of integrating values relating to self, other people, the community, and a "higher being" or "ultimate reality" (Hodge, 2001). Spirituality has been found to be associated with successful

marriage (Kaslow & Robison, 1996), considerate and responsible interpersonal relations (Ellison, 1992), positive self-esteem (Ellison, 1993), more adaptive approaches to coping with stress (Tartaro, Luecken, & Gunn, 2005), and general well-being (George, Larson, Koenig, & McCullough, 2000). Other studies have found that searching for and finding meaning after experiencing traumatic experiences reduces the presence of depressive symptoms in emerging adults, but only for those who experienced a moderate to high frequency of traumatic events (Woo & Brown, 2013).

Spirituality develops in three dimensions related to one's connection with a higher power (George et al., 2000; Hodge, 2001):

1. *Cognition*: beliefs, values, perceptions, and meaning related to work, love, and life
2. *Affect*: sense of connection and support; attachment and bonding experiences; psychological attachment to work, love, and life
3. *Behavior*: practices, rituals, and behavioral experiences

Generally, consistency across all three dimensions is necessary for a vigorous spiritual life. Research has shown that religious behavioral practices are correlated with life course stages. One study found that religiosity scores (reflecting beliefs, practices, and personal meaning) were higher for a group of young adults (ages 18 to 25) than for a group of adolescents (ages 14 to 17) (Glover, 1996), suggesting a growing spiritual belief system with age. Individuals making the transition from adolescence into young adulthood seem to place a particularly high value on spirituality. In addition, religious participation has been found to increase with age, even within the young adulthood stage (Gallup & Lindsay, 1999; Stolzenberg, Blair-Loy, & Waite, 1995; Wink & Dillon, 2002).

Etengoff and Daiute (2013) examined the small and large system influences on the religious development and cultural construction of self in emerging adulthood for Sunni-Muslim Americans.

Social, institutional, and community interactions offered emerging adults important opportunities to reflect on and practice their religious beliefs and, in many cases, initiated a new transition in understanding and religious orientation. Some study participants reported that such reflection led them to become more spiritual, while others reported that it was the conversations with new acquaintances who were spiritually curious and asked questions they could not answer about their own religion that prompted their greater involvement in Muslim study and practice. It was through these dynamic interactions within various sociocultural spaces that religious development occurred in these emerging adults, with the age of 18 being a particularly salient chronological marker for such pronounced deepening exploration.

In an attempt to understand the development of spirituality, James W. Fowler (1981) articulated a theory of six stages of faith development. Fowler's research suggested that two of these stages occur primarily in childhood and two others occur primarily during late adolescence and young adulthood. Fowler's stages are very closely linked with the cognitive and moral development paradigms of Piaget and Kohlberg. Adolescents are typically in a stage characterized by **synthetic-conventional faith**, during which faith is rooted in external authority. Individuals ages 17 to 22 usually begin the transition into **individuative-reflective faith**, a stage when the person begins to let go of the idea of external authority and looks for authority within the self (Fowler, 1981). During this time, young adults establish their own belief system and evaluate personal values, exploring how those values fit with the various social institutions, groups, and individuals with whom they interact.

The transition from synthetic-conventional faith to individuative-reflective faith usually occurs in the early to mid-20s, although it may occur in the 30s and 40s or may never occur at all (Fowler, 1981). An individual's faith development depends on his or her early attachments to other people, which serve as templates for understanding one's connection to more abstract relationships and which help shape these relationships. Faith growth, therefore, is heavily related to cognitive, interpersonal, and identity development.

The process also depends on crises confronted in the 20s and 30s; challenges and conflict are critical for change and growth in faith. In one study, young adult women who were HIV-positive were interviewed in order to explore coping strategies, women's experiences of living with the diagnosis, and life transformations or changes (Dunbar et al., 1998). The majority of women discussed the spiritual dimensions activated by their illness, such as renewing relationships, developing a new understanding of the self, experiencing heightened connections with nature and higher powers, and finding new meaning in the mundane. The interviews revealed several themes related to spiritual growth, including "reckoning with death," which led to the will to continue living and renewed "life affirmation"; finding new meaning in life; developing a positive sense of self; and achieving a "redefinition of relationships." These young women found new meaning and purpose in their lives, which gave them renewed opportunities for social connection (Dunbar et al., 1998).

Identity Development

Identity development is generally associated with adolescence and is often seen as a discrete developmental marker, rather than as a process spanning all stages of the life course. However, identity development—how one thinks about and relates to oneself in the realms of love, work, and ideologies—continues well into adulthood. Ongoing identity development is necessary to make adult commitments possible, to allow individuals to abandon the insular self, and to embrace connection with important others. In addition, continuing identity development is an important part of young adults' efforts to define their life's direction (Kroger, 2007; Kroger, Martinussen, & Marcia, 2010).

The classic work of James Marcia (1966) defined stages of identity formation in terms of level of exploration and commitment to life values, beliefs, and goals (as discussed in Chapter 6) as follows:

- Diffused (no exploration, no commitment)
- Foreclosed (no exploration, commitment)
- Moratorium (exploration, no commitment)
- Achievement (exploration, commitment)

Marcia (1993) has stated that people revisit and redefine their commitments as they age. As a result, identity is not static but dynamic, open, and flexible. More recently, he has suggested that during times of great upheaval and transition in young adulthood, people are likely to regress to earlier identity modes (Marcia, 2002). A recent meta-analysis of research on identity development in adolescence and young adulthood found that the proportions of people in foreclosed and diffused stages decreased over time while the proportions in the achievement stage increased over time. The analysis indicated that a relatively large proportion of individuals had not attained identity achievement by young adulthood (Kroger et al., 2010).

Research exploring this notion of identity formation as a process that continues deep into adulthood shows several interesting outcomes. In one study researchers interviewed women and men ages 27 to 36 to explore the process of commitment in five domains of identity: religious beliefs, political ideology, occupational career, intimate relationships, and lifestyle (Pulkkinen & Kokko, 2000). Results showed that men and women differed in their overall commitment to an identity at age 27. Women were more likely to be classified in Marcia's "foreclosed" identity status, and men were more likely to be classified in the "diffused" identity status. However, these gender differences diminished with age, and by age 36, foreclosed and achieved identity statuses were more prevalent than diffused or moratorium statuses for both men and women. This trend of increasing commitment with age held constant across all domains except political ideology, which showed increased diffusion with age. Also, across ages, women were more likely than men to be classified in the achieved identity status for intimate relationships; for men, the diffused identity status for intimate relationships was more prevalent at age 27 as compared with age 36.

The young adult who is exploring and expanding identity experiences tension between independence and self-sufficiency on one hand and a need for connection with others and reliance on a greater whole on the other. Young adults are often challenged to find comfort in connections that require a loosening of self-reliant tendencies. Some suggest that the transition into adulthood is signified by increased self-control while simultaneously submitting to the social conventions, structure, and order of the larger community. We can see that Jonathan and Kai are circling back through this identity construction space where they are considering how they will take on the new parent role, moving from a care-for-self focus that defined the early years of their young adult lives to an interdependent commitment to care for others.

Another study of the development of identity well into adulthood used a sample of women in their 20s (Elliott, 1996). Researchers found that the transition into young adulthood excites new definitions of identity and one's place in society, leading to potential changes in self-esteem and psychological self-evaluations. Although self-esteem tends to remain stable in young adulthood, several factors appeared to influence self-esteem in a positive or negative direction:

- Marriage may have a positive effect on self-esteem if it strengthens a young adult's economic stability and social connectedness.
- Parenthood is likely to have a negative effect if the role change associated with this life event significantly increases stresses and compromises financial stability.
- Receiving welfare is likely to decrease a young woman's self-esteem over time.
- Employment may mitigate the negative effects brought about by the transition into parenthood.

Employment tends to expand one's self-construct and identity and can offer a new parent additional social support as well as a supplemental source of validation. However, the extent to which employment will operate as a stress buffer is contingent on the occupational context and conditions. Certainly, good-quality jobs with benefits may enhance, and are unlikely to harm, a woman's psychological well-being (Elliott, 1996). However, dead-end, low-paying jobs do not help with the stresses of parenthood and have the potential to undermine a young woman's self-esteem.

Some scholars suggest that identity development for African American emerging adults may be significantly influenced by "stereotype threat" whereby there is a collective internalization that society expects African American emerging adults to fail. Identity development, then, for some emerging adults may require confrontation with held stereotypes at a collective level that serve to inform how they are expected to perform as a group (Arnett & Brody, 2008).

Research shows that social networking media sites, such as Facebook, that allow the development of and participation in Internet communities, have significant impact on emerging adults' identity and social development (Pempek, Yermolayeva, & Calvert, 2009). One study reported that college students' average use was 30 minutes per day with 80% using Facebook to communicate with existing friends. Such social networking technology offers young adults the opportunity to create personal identity profiles that can be shared and responded to in a public forum.

Social workers need to be aware of how people's work life impinges on their development of identity.

Critical Thinking Questions 7.3

Erik Erikson suggested that identity development occurred in adolescence, but recent theory and research suggest that identity is open and flexible and continues to develop across adulthood. What do you think about this recent suggestion that identity development is an ongoing process? What types of experiences in young adulthood might affect identity development? Do you think your identity has changed since late adolescence? If so, which aspects of your identity have changed? What role do you think new technologies, particularly smartphones and the Internet, have on young adult identity development?

SOCIAL DEVELOPMENT AND SOCIAL FUNCTIONING

There are, of course, many paths to early adulthood, and not all arrive at this phase of the life course with equal resources for further social role development. This section looks at some of the special challenges faced by young adults as they negotiate new social roles and the impact on social functioning in young adulthood—particularly in regard to interpersonal relationships and work attachment.

Katherine Newman, in *The Accordion Family* (2012), offers an international comparative analysis of the young adulthood transition, demonstrating that countries

> What factors put individuals at risk when making the transition to adulthood?

with weak welfare states tend to put families in the role of safety net provider, with adult children relying on their parents for support for longer periods of time, more than countries with more generous welfare states. The research presents a current demographic landscape that looks much different from a generation ago, where it takes longer to launch adult children due to extended educational requirements, credentials that often require unpaid internships, and the high cost of higher education and housing. Thus, currently more emerging adults are dependent on their families of origin and/or extended social networks, and for longer periods of time, than ever before. Given this situation, perhaps it is not surprising that one research team found that U.S. parents of emerging adults reported a higher desired age for marriage than was reported by the emerging adults themselves (Willoughby, Olson, Carroll, Nelson, & Miller, 2012).

Research has shown that problem behavior in young adults is linked to challenges experienced in negotiating new social roles (see Kroger, 2007). However, it is oftentimes difficult to definitively capture the direction of influence. For example, does prior "deviant" behavior create difficulties in committing to work, or does a failure in finding a good job lead to problematic behaviors?

The Child Trends study (Hair et al., 2003) on educationally disadvantaged youth identifies six categories of vulnerable youth making the transition to adulthood: out-of-school youth, youth with incarcerated parents, young welfare recipients, youth transitioning out of incarceration, runaway/homeless youth, and youth leaving foster care. The largest group was out-of-school youth, although there is considerable overlap among these vulnerable categories. Many of these educationally disadvantaged youth lack parental monitoring, supervision, and support that would help facilitate the transition into adulthood. Along these lines, poor social functioning in young adulthood appears to be linked to a variety of difficulties in making the transition to new roles (Ronka & Pulkkinen, 1995):

- Problems in school and family in adolescence lead to social functioning problems in young adulthood.
- Unstable employment for males is associated with strained relationships, criminality, and substance abuse.
- Men who have many behavioral problems in young adulthood can be differentiated from young adult males who do not exhibit behavioral problems by several childhood factors, such as aggressive history, problems in school and family, and lack of formal educational attainment.

It is estimated that approximately half of educationally disadvantaged 18- to 24-year-olds have not completed a high school education or have not moved on to college or more advanced vocational training (Hair et al., 2003). The transition to young adulthood from the secondary school environment can be challenging, particularly for students with learning disabilities. They drop out of high school at a higher rate than students without these challenges. Results from a qualitative study suggest some reasons why (Lichtenstein, 1993), one being that many students with learning disabilities worked while in high school, often because employment provided an environment where they could gain control over decision making, exercise authority, garner support, and increase self-esteem—outcomes that such students were not able to experience in the traditional educational system. In this study, working during the high school years was related to later employment but was also related to the risk of dropping out of high school altogether before graduation. These findings suggest a need for a well-tailored individual education plan (IEP) for each learning-disabled youth that outlines how that person can best make the transition out of high school and which postschool opportunities might be appropriate, as well as a need for better transitioning services and active follow-up. In addition, the parents of students with learning disabilities need to be educated on their rights, and parent advocacy efforts within the school need to be strengthened (Lichtenstein, 1993).

The Child Trends study of educationally disadvantaged youth (Hair et al., 2003) cites 12 empirically evaluated programs that operate to facilitate adulthood transitioning for youth: Alcohol Skills Training Program; Job Corps; JOBSTART; Job Training Partnership Act; New Chance; Nurse Home Visitation Program; Ohio Learning, Earning and Parenting Program; School Attendance Demonstration Project; Youth Corps; AmeriCorps; Skill-Based Intervention on Condom Use; and Teenage Parent Demonstration. These programs primarily focus on educational and employment gains, and most showed solid gains in employment and improvement in school attendance and completion of a general equivalency diploma or gaining of a high school diploma, but not definitive gains in increasing earnings or job retention. Specifically, the Youth Corps program showed the most significant outcomes for African American males, who earned higher incomes from their employment, had better employment relationships, and were more likely to have attained advanced education than those who did not participate in the program. Latino males who participated in the program also showed increased employment and work promotions as compared with those who did not participate, while White males actually showed negative effects from participation as they were less likely to be employed and received lower earnings from their work. African American, Latina, and

White females all benefited from participation, showing increased work hours and higher educational aspirations (Hair et al., 2003).

A summary of empirically tested programs that have been found to positively influence young adulthood transitioning include the following: Alcohol Skills Training geared to college students; AmeriCorps for youth ages 17 and older; Job Corps; JOBSTART for 16- to 24-year-old disadvantaged youth; and the Job Training Partnership Act, aimed at increasing educational and occupational advancement of adults and out-of-school youth (Bronte-Tinkew, Brown, Carrano, & Shwalb, 2005).

Connecting to mentors, particularly for high-risk populations, is critical to success. Paid community service opportunities that facilitate meaningful connections among different youth populations (e.g., those living in high-risk communities and those volunteering within such communities) can provide opportunities for young adults to develop skills and enhance social capital. For example, AmeriCorps deploys members throughout the United States to work in nonprofit and other public and community organizations. Such experiences promote members' connection to civic society, expand critical thinking about social problems, instill a sense of purpose and meaning, and facilitate a critical "insider" understanding of the social, economic, and political environment (Benner, 2007). In their review of service-learning experiences, Lemieux and Allen (2007) discuss the value of such programs in working with vulnerable populations, such as children with disabilities and older adults, and identify the enhanced problem-solving abilities, civic understanding, and enduring commitment to service that comes from such opportunities. Service learning experiences have been shown to change attitudes and perceptions toward vulnerable populations, such as substance-dependent mothers (Hogan & Bailey, 2010) and older adult populations (Singleton, 2009).

Another special population that is likely to face challenges in making the transition into young adulthood is young persons with more severe emotional difficulties. Approximately three quarters of adults with psychiatric diagnoses experienced symptoms before the age of 24, with symptom expression peaking in the early 20s (McGorry & Purcell, 2009). These young adults often have trouble forming meaningful interpersonal relationships, maintaining employment, managing physical health needs, and gaining financial independence. Recent research indicates that young adults living with mental illness are more likely than young adults who are not living with mental illness to use social networking sites to create a supportive community. They express an interest in using such sites to seek information about community integration, independent living, social skills, and overcoming isolation (Gowen, Deschaine, Gruttadara, & Markey, 2012).

Research shows that disability diagnosis and severity may influence social outcomes. For example, young adults with severe cognitive disability and coexisting impairments tend to show the most limited leisure involvement and date less frequently than those young adults with cerebral palsy, hearing loss, or epilepsy (Van Naarden Braun, Yeargin-Allsopp, & Lollar, 2006, 2009).

Many young adults with developmental and/or emotional disabilities may have tenuous experience with the labor market and weakened connections to work. Often their families do not have sufficient resources to help them make the transition from high school, potentially delaying the youth's opportunity to live independently. Many of these young persons do not have a stable support network, and as a result, they are at higher than usual risk for homelessness (Davis & Vander Stoep, 1997). In a 20-year longitudinal study following a cohort of individuals with developmental delays who were first diagnosed at age 3, both parents and their young adult children expressed concern about the young adults' social isolation and inability to find gainful employment. Many of the young adults were concerned about not having enough peer involvement and too much parental involvement in their lives. Three types of parent–young adult relationships tended to emerge: (1) *dependent* relationships, which were comfortable to the young adults in that parents responded to needs in appropriate quality and quantity; (2) *independent* relationships, which were comfortable to the young adults in that parents responded to young adult needs only in times of crisis; and (3) *interdependent* relationships, which were the most conflictual of the three types and were characterized by young adult resentment of parental involvement (Keogh, Bernheimer, & Guthrie, 2004).

Another group of youth at risk in the transition from late adolescence to early adulthood are those with poor relationships with their parents. Emotional intimacy in the parent-child relationship has been found to be important in the development of self-esteem, with the benefits lasting into adulthood. For example, Poon and Knight (2013) found in their longitudinal data analysis that parental emotional support in emerging adulthood served a buffering role in preserving health and well-being later in adulthood, contributing to enhanced midlife psychosocial outcomes. Specifically, maternal support was associated with emotional well-being, while paternal support was associated with improved health. However, engaging and satisfying employment seems to mediate a poor parent-child relationship, increasing the youth's well-being (Roberts & Bengston, 1993).

Youth with unstable attachments to adult caregivers, like many foster care youth who are transitioning out of the foster care system, have a great need for developmentally appropriate and culturally sensitive supportive services as they make the transition into young adulthood. Social workers should examine the ways in which formal services facilitate the transition to adulthood for youths who have no informal supports. Certainly, terminating services to these youths at the age of majority, without making arrangements for them to receive adult services, will undermine the efforts made during the youth's adolescence and put these individuals at a disadvantage as young adults (Davis & Vander Stoep, 1997). Particularly for individuals with developmental disabilities, there may be a strong need for services to continue on into young adulthood (Keogh et al., 2004).

Finally, the immigration experience for youth may pose a risk during the adulthood transition. Research shows that more than one third (38.2%) of young adult Latinos do not have a high school degree, and immigration transition and associated stressors as well as socioeconomic barriers may be contributing factors (U.S. Census Bureau, 2012a). As social workers, we must ask about the context of the immigration experience and examine how it influences young adult development. For example, was immigration a choice? Were there family separations along the way, and what was the nature of such separations? What motivated the immigration experience? Was there a change in the family's socioeconomic and/or role statuses? What are the hardships encountered in the new country? Are these hardships experienced differently by different members of the same family? What is the level of the family's and individual members' acculturation (Chapman & Perreira, 2005)? It is important to assess for the extent of intergenerational stress that may have developed from the immigration experience as studies show that both high and low levels of acculturation are associated with risk behaviors such as substance abuse and mental health problems (Chapman & Perreira, 2005).

Relationship Development in Young Adulthood

Erikson's concept of intimacy, which relies on connection with a significant partner, is at the core of relationship development during early adulthood. Typically, young adults develop sustained commitments to others and come to recognize a responsibility for others' well-being. This developmental process may manifest as thoughtful awareness in the early years, changing to more active behavioral commitment in later years—for example, caring for children or aging parents, getting involved in the community, and taking on social obligations.

Intimacy, which can be defined as a sense of warmth or closeness, has three components: interdependence with another person, self-disclosure, and affection (Perlman & Fehr, 1987). Intimacy may take the form of cognitive/intellectual intimacy, emotional intimacy, sexual intimacy, physical intimacy apart from a sexual relationship, and spiritual intimacy. When reflecting on intimate relations, some people talk about finding a "soul mate"; feeling intensely connected; sharing values, beliefs, and philosophical inquiries; and feeling as though the relationship has strong direction and purpose.

Establishing intimacy is a multifaceted process. Exhibit 7.2 lists some of the tasks involved in fostering an intimate relationship with someone. The ability to perform these tasks depends not only on personal abilities (see Busch & Hofer, 2012) but also on external factors, such as the individual's family background. Research has found two family factors in adolescence to be important in the ability to develop intimate relationships during young adulthood: (1) a positive relationship with the mother (e.g., effective, clear communication with her, as well as mutual respect and empathy) and (2) adaptability of the family unit (e.g., good habits of conflict resolution and appropriate discipline) (Robinson, 2000). The young adult's ability to develop intimate relationships also depends on favorable environmental conditions, such as having adequate resources to accommodate stressors, handle life responsibilities, and deal effectively with the multiple life transitions of this developmental stage.

An individual's family relationships and attachment to the family unit as a whole are transformed during young adulthood. The family's life course stage and the psychosocial development of individual members will influence the nature of family relationships in young adulthood. Generally, though, young adults may see parents, siblings, and relatives less frequently as work, romantic attachments, and new family responsibilities take precedence. With greater independence, geographic distance may also preclude more visits. Thus, time spent together may center on holiday celebrations. As traditional family roles evolve, young adults may take more active responsibility for holiday preparations. They may find themselves wanting to spend less time with old friends and more time with family. As young adults have children, holiday activities and family interactions may increasingly focus on the new generation.

Exhibit 7.2 Tasks in Fostering Intimacy

- Effectively negotiating expectations for the relationship
- Negotiating roles and responsibilities
- Making compromises
- Prioritizing and upholding values
- Deciding how much to share of oneself
- Identifying and meeting individual needs
- Identifying and meeting partnership needs
- Renegotiating identity
- Developing trust and security
- Allowing for reciprocal communication
- Making time commitments to partner
- Effectively resolving conflict and solving problems
- Demonstrating respect, support, and care

Romantic Relationships

Romantic relationships are a key element in the development of intimacy during early adulthood. **Romantic love** has been described as a relationship that is sexually oriented, is "spontaneous and voluntary," and occurs between equal partners (Solomon, 1988). Satisfaction in romantic partnerships depends on finding a delicate balance between positive and negative interactions across time (Gottman, 1994).

Anthropologist Helen Fisher (2004) suggests that the choice of romantic partners is based on three distinct emotional systems: lust, attraction, and attachment. *Lust* is sexual attraction and is associated with androgen hormones. *Attraction* involves feeling great pleasure in the presence of the romantic interest and thinking of the other person all the time. Fisher suggests that attraction is associated with increased levels of dopamine and norepinephrine and decreased levels of serotonin, which are neurotransmitters in the brain. Fisher's

Photo 7.3 The transition from emerging adulthood to young adulthood is marked by solidifying role commitments, such as marriage.

© Creatas/ThinkStock

description of *attachment* is similar to Bowlby's concept described in Chapter 3 of this book. It involves a sense of security when in the presence of the attachment figure, which is the romantic partner in this discussion. Attachment has been associated with the hormone oxytocin.

In the United States, heterosexual romantic love has traditionally been considered a precursor to marriage. However, a recent trend in romantic relationships is to have sex earlier but marry later. For the past two decades, more than half of all marriages occurred after a period of cohabitation (Heuveline & Timberlake, 2004). It is important to remember, however, that in many parts of the world and among many recent immigrant groups to the United States, marriage is arranged and not based on romantic

courtship. Many other variations in relationship development exist as well, represented by single-parent families, childless couples, gay and lesbian partnerships, couples who marry and choose to live apart to establish individual career tracks, and couples where partners are in different life stages (e.g., early adulthood and middle adulthood).

In the past, increasing education decreased women's likelihood of marrying, but recent data suggest a reversal of that trend. The cohort of women who recently graduated from college, both Black and White, are likely to marry later than women of their cohort without a college education, but their rate of eventual marriage will be higher (Goldstein & Kenney, 2001). The researchers interpret this trend to indicate that marriage is

How does sexual orientation affect young adult development?

increasingly becoming a choice only for the most educated members of society. Given the advantages of a two-earner family, this trend may contribute toward the widening economic gap in our society.

An increasing awareness of variation in relationships has prompted research into all sorts of romantic attachments. One focus is homosexual relationships. One study that identified three "scripts" (summarized in Exhibit 7.3) in lesbian relationships helps to differentiate romantic attachment from other kinds of intimacy (Rose & Zand, 2000):

1. The "romance" script combines emotional intimacy and sexual attraction. It is characterized by an attenuated dating period and quick commitment to a relationship.

2. "Friendship" is a script in which individuals fall in love and are emotionally committed, though sexual behaviors are not necessarily a part of the relationship. Research shows that this is the most common script among lesbians, emphasizing emotional intimacy over sexuality. Women have suggested that the ambiguity implicit in this script often makes defining the relationship difficult.

3. "Sexually explicit" focuses on sexual attraction and leaves emotional intimacy at the periphery. This script is void of any direct expression of future commitment.

Lesbian and gay partnering becomes more complex if the coming-out process begins in early adulthood. The individuals involved have to negotiate through their parents' emotional reactions and responses at the same time as the new relationship is developing. One study found that lesbian and gay partners are less likely to identify family as a significant social support as compared with heterosexual couples (Kurdek, 2004). One possible reason is that siblings and other relatives may be forced to confront their own comfort, biases, and values

Exhibit 7.3 Lesbian Relationship Development

Script	Descriptor
Romance	Emotional and sexual attraction; quick commitment
Friendship	Emotional commitment; sexual behavior may or may not be part of relationship
Sexually explicit	Sexual attraction is focal point; emotional intimacy secondary

SOURCE: Adapted from Rose & Zand, 2000

associated with the young adult's relationship. If gay and lesbian couples decide to have children, their own parents will inevitably be forced to confront the homosexual identity in order to develop their grandparent role with the new child.

Even in families where "acceptance" has taken root, people in the family's social network may have limited understanding that is difficult to work through. Family members who thought they had come to terms with the young adult's homosexual identity may find themselves harboring anger, hurt, disappointment, or confusion about how the young person's life trajectory is affecting their own life trajectories.

Other complicating factors related to gay and lesbian relationship development can be connections with the larger community and with the gay and lesbian community itself. Current legal inequities—such as the lack of legal sanction for marriage-like partnerships, the associated lack of benefits (e.g., survivorship and inheritance rights and housing loans), and the lack of authority in decision making for gay and lesbian partners (in such matters as child custody and health care/medical procedures)—can cause additional external strain on new couples.

There has been recent progress in state recognition of same-sex marriage. At the time this book went to press, same-sex couples were able to marry in 16 states and the District of Columbia (California, Connecticut, Delaware, Hawaii, Illinois, Iowa, Maine, Maryland, Massachusetts, Minnesota, New Hampshire, New Jersey, New York, Rhode Island, and Vermont). This is up from five states plus the District of Columbia at the previous edition of this book. In addition, in June 2013, the U. S. Supreme Court declared section 3 of the Defense of Marriage Act (DOMA) unconstitutional. Section 3 prevented the federal government from recognizing marriage between gay or lesbian couples for the purpose of federal law even if those couples are considered legally married in their home states. This court ruling set in place recognition of same-sex marriage by the federal government.

The legal impact of these political wranglings on gay and lesbian adults' rights has been described, but how a young adult's family status is defined in legal terms by society may also influence other decision-making processes, such as choice of community or residential neighborhood, childbearing decisions, employment choices, and options during times of unemployment (e.g., if one partner's benefits, such as health insurance, are not legally available to the other partner when one young adult loses a job). In addition, impact may be experienced via various systems' (e.g., school, health care, child care centers) interactions with same-sex parents if there is a lack of recognition of the rights of both parents in decision making for their child.

Regardless of the sexuality of young adult clients, social workers need to consider the client's partner when exploring intimacy issues (LaSala, 2001). These partners may be a valuable resource in matters relating to the partnership itself as well as relations with the family of origin. Social workers also need to assess the adequacy of a young adult's support system across multiple dimensions and to identify and respond to any perceived gaps. Although marriages and partnerships typically expand a young adult's social support network, this might not be the case for all individuals, and

social workers should be cautious about making such assumptions.

Parenthood

Parenting is an interactive process, with reciprocal parent-child and child-parent influences (Maccoby, 2002b). The multiple role transitions that mark entry into parenthood during young adulthood can be both exciting and challenging, as new familial interdependencies evolve. New social obligations and responsibilities associated with caregiving affect the relationship between the young adult partners and between the young adults and their parents.

Often, the nature of the partners' relationship before parenthood will determine how partners will manage the demands of these changing roles (Durkin, 1995). Adjustment to parenthood, and successful role reorganization, depends on five dimensions (Cowan, 1991):

1. Individual factors, such as how role changes affect one's sense of self

2. Quality of the partners' relationship (e.g., how the couple negotiates responsibilities and their decision-making capabilities)

3. Quality of the relationship between the young adults and their children

4. Quality of each partner's relationships with his or her family of origin

5. Quality of external relationships (e.g., school, work, community)

How partners negotiate the division of labor along gender lines also influences parenting and marital satisfaction. Much of the parenting literature has focused on the role strain mothers face in maintaining work commitments alongside new parenting responsibilities. Some new literature has focused on the more positive aspects of mothers' participation in the workforce (Gürsory & Bicakci, 2007; Losoncz & Bortolotto, 2009). However, fatherhood and the positive impact of paternal parenting on both child well-being and the father's own successful male adult development need further exploration.

There has been interest in recent years in the role of fathers in the lives of children, and father involvement has been shown to have a positive effect on children in such areas as academic success and reducing likelihood of delinquency and substance abuse (cited in Jones & Mosher, 2013). A recent National Survey of Family Growth examined U.S. fathers' (ages 15 to 44) involvement with their children from 2006 to 2010 (Jones & Mosher, 2013). This study included both biological and nonbiological fathers and co-residential fathers as well as nonresidential fathers. A larger percentage of non-Hispanic White fathers had co-residential children than either non-Hispanic Black or Hispanic fathers. As might be expected, a higher percentage of co-residential fathers (90%) were involved in bathing, diapering, or dressing their children than nonresidential fathers (31%). Among co-residential fathers, Black fathers (70%) were more likely than White (60%) or Hispanic (45%) fathers to bathe, dress, diaper, or help their children use the toilet. Likewise, Black nonresidential fathers (66%) were more likely than White nonresidential fathers (61%) and Hispanic nonresidential fathers (34%) to be involved in these activities with children in the past 4 weeks. On the other hand, co-residential Hispanic fathers (71%) were more likely than co-residential White fathers (64%) to eat daily meals with their children. Fathers who lived with their children were twice as likely as fathers who did not live with their children to perceive themselves as doing a very good job as a father. Other research has shown that very young fathers have significant mental health needs (Weinman, Buzi, & Smith, 2005).

Recently, Kathryn Edin and Timothy Nelson (2013) contributed an in-depth examination of fatherhood and the meaning it plays in low-income men's lives. Over 7 years, Edin and Nelson document the lived experiences of unmarried low-income fathers and their perceptions of parenting children in the urban environments of Philadelphia and Camden, New Jersey. When asked, "What would your life be like without your children?" fathers explained that they did not see their children "as millstones but as life preservers, saviors, redeemers" (p. 58). Children, the interviews showed, facilitated a connection to life and love, helped men stay out of institutions (jails, drug rehabs), and motivated in men a commitment to doing well by and for their children. The child was often at the core of the connection between the father and the child's mother. Babies often represent the symbolic opportunity to transition to a "fresh start" or a new life trajectory, regardless of the tenuous relationship a man might have with the baby's mother. When fathers have children as a result of many different relationships, they may selectively focus on one child with whom to devote time and resources, rather than trying to desperately make limited time and resources distribute equally across all children. Fathers discussed the increased difficulty they experienced in keeping up relationships with their sons and daughters as their children aged. Relational fathering, or the importance of spending quality time with their children, was emphasized over the financial role. "Why muster the effort to avoid pregnancy when being appropriately 'situated' is viewed as a contingency that may never occur?" (Edin & Nelson, 2013, p. 227). Think for a moment about how you think we do as a society in *valuing* and *supporting* the fathering role of men across socioeconomic strata.

Research on tasks associated with responsible fathering identify the provision of economic and emotional support to children, basic caregiving, offering guidance and control, and "being there" (or being present) as most important to the fathering role as defined by young fathers and linked to successful fathering (Peart, Pungello, Campbell, & Richey, 2006). Fathers who are highly involved with their children often describe their peers' parents as being influential in their own development as a father (Masciadrelli, Pleck, & Stueve, 2006). Further research needs to account for the presence of male **fictive kin** (nonrelatives that are considered family) and their role in helping young adults develop as fathers, and to document the strengths of special populations of fathers, such as young African American fathers (see Connor & White, 2006).

As for mothers, the evidence suggests that maternal employment may have a positive influence on her sense of self, leading to better outcomes for her children. However, Pamela Stone's book *Opting Out?* (2007) reminds us that the decision to opt out of careers, even after intensive postsecondary advanced education and career success, may be related to institutional barriers experienced in the employment sector rather than an indicator of personal choice or family preference. For example, workplace environments that require long work hours or that may have inflexible family policies that compete with family demands may pose barriers to choosing full-time work for some families.

With these findings in mind, it becomes necessary to identify groups for whom employment opportunities may be limited. Parents of children with disabilities fall into this category. Research shows that 12% of children in the United States have at least one developmentally related functional limitation that requires special attention and care (Hogan & Msall, 2002). Parenting a child with a functional disability demands extra care, which may decrease a parent's opportunity to enter or continue participation in the labor market. One study suggested that two thirds of families with a child who has a functional limitation will experience significant changes in labor force participation (Hogan & Msall, 2002).

Low-income mothers are another group for whom maternal employment is significantly related to child well-being (Zaslow & Emig, 1997). Employment often creates child care difficulties. However, characteristics associated with positive parenting (e.g., the mother's ability to express warmth to the child, her lack of depressive symptoms, and the quality of her verbal interaction with the child) have been found to mediate the ill effects on child well-being that may arise in welfare-to-work programs, which sometimes leave low-income mothers with poor child care options (McGroder, Zaslow, Moore, Hair, & Ahluwalia, 2002). Other studies have found that parents who have more social support are better at parenting (Marshall, Noonan, McCartney, Marx, & Keefe, 2001).

Given that the vast majority of women with children younger than age 6 are employed in the workforce, it is therefore important to understand how workplace policies and conditions support or undermine parenting, particularly for low-income workers for whom employment is often characterized by unpredictable schedules and who often have little control or input into their day-to-day work routine (Gassman-Pines, 2013). Research has found that, indeed, mothers who were in emerging adulthood and working in low-wage jobs experienced significant distress in mother-child interactions related to both high and low workload stressors, as compared with mothers in other socioeconomic classes and as compared with older mothers.

Helping young adults to develop parenting efficacy may help them overcome environmental conditions and improve their children's well-being. Unfortunately, research shows that one of the biggest gaps in independent living services for young adults transitioning out of foster care is in parenting skills development (the other was housing preparation) (Georgiades, 2005). Another study compared the effects of increasing the mother's parenting efficacy in White and Black families characterized by a weak marriage and living in economically disadvantaged neighborhoods (Ardelt & Eccles, 2001). The Black families showed greater benefits in the form of increased academic success for their children. Parenting efficacy also contributed more to positive child outcomes in Black families with a compromised marriage than in Black families where the marriage was strong and secure. Parenting-related protective factors in Latino families include respect, familism, and biculturalism (Chapman & Perreira, 2005).

Mentoring and Volunteering

Although young adults seek out older adult mentors in work as they begin establishing themselves in new careers, young persons also often serve as mentors themselves. Serving as a mentor can help young adults move through the adulthood transition by facilitating new experiences and helping them to develop new roles that require "taking care of others" as opposed to "being taken care of" themselves. As young adults refine their ideologies, beliefs, and values, they form group affiliations consistent with their emerging identity, career, relationships, community, and religious and political views.

With the Edward M. Kennedy Serve America Act (signed April 21, 2009), President Obama reauthorized and expanded the service opportunities funded by the Corporation for National and Community Service, such as initiating the Summer of Service programs aimed at engaging youth in tutoring, recreation, and service opportunities.

Some examples of current groups and mentoring programs young adults might get involved in include 20 Something, a gay/lesbian young adult social group; Young Democrats/Young Republicans political groups; YMCA/YWCA; and Big Brothers/Big Sisters youth mentoring programs. Service-related groups young adults may choose to become involved with include Junior Achievement, a nonprofit organization that brings young adults together with elementary school students to teach children economic principles, and Streetwise Partners, where young adults help low-income and unemployed persons with job skills training. College students may also get actively involved in Habitat for Humanity projects or student associations such as the College Hispanic American Society, Campus Crusaders for Christ, and Association of Black Students, which spearhead philanthropic and community-integration activities.

And more recently, a November, 25, 2013, article in the *Washington Post* by Sarah Halzack, "Luring Millennials With Good Deeds," highlighted the interface between the business community and community service whereby community pro bono work is increasing in corporations that seek to hire young adults in the millennial generation, who more than other generations desire employment environments that have a commitment to broader community impact. For example, Advisory Board Company allows employees 10 hours each month to devote to community-oriented service projects. Such projects have led to skill development and enhancement in opportunities that staying insular to the company's daily routine would not have afforded. In turn, such opportunities have also been shown to increase productivity and commitment among employees.

Critical Thinking Questions 7.4

What social roles are Dominique Castillo, Sheila Henderson, and Jonathan and Kai playing? What special challenges have each faced in social development during emerging and young adulthood? Community engagement and commitment to larger community roles is often heralded as a marker of adulthood. What are the specific ways in which each of the people in our case examples have engaged in meaningful ways in their communities?

Work and the Labor Market

The recent economic recession has produced significant stress on young adults and young families who may have lost jobs, are currently underemployed, or have had difficulties obtaining initial entry-level positions because of employers' cost-cutting measures. Research shows that 77% of employers surveyed had to implement cost-saving measures during 2008–2009, with 69% of those employers laying off employees (Galinsky & Bond, 2009).

According to Andrew Sum's Children's Defense Fund report (2011), young adults (16 to 29) were the most represented age demographic in the ranks of the unemployed during the decade of 2000 to 2010, with the youngest group, 16 to 19 years old, the least likely to be employed of all young adults. Sum (2011) reports that "in 2010, the employment rate of the nation's young adults (16–29 years old) was 55.3 percent, the lowest such employment rate for all youth in this age group combined since the end of World War II. In contrast, the employment rate of young adults stood at 67.3 percent at the height of the labor market boom in 2000" (para. 2). Although both men and women in this age group experienced a decline in labor attachment, men fared worse in comparison, and those with no postsecondary degree also showed greater decline in employment as compared with those with a bachelor's degree or higher. There was also an increase in young adult underemployment (reduced hours on the job) and malemployment (employed but not in a job consistent with skills or education level); underemployment increased by 150% for young adults during this decade. Lost economic opportunities in young adulthood can reduce the cumulative labor experience necessary for middle adulthood career trajectories. Recommendations include offering more paid internships to teens and young adults, work-based learning activities, and strengthening programs that help young adults transition from high school to work or college. As a social worker working with Dominique and her family in the colonia community, we might be concerned about how her part-time work experience might contribute to her long-term chances for job promotion, as we question whether it will leave her permanently underemployed or give her the experience she needs to get a better job in the future.

The transition into the world of work is an important element of social development during early adulthood. A young adult's opportunity for successful adulthood transitioning into the labor market depends on a variety of dimensions, to include **human capital** (talents, skills, intellectual capacity, social development, emotional regulatory capacity) as well as **community assets** such as public infrastructure (e.g., adequate transportation to get to work), community networks, and educational opportunities. In addition, family capital is important. "Transformative assets," or those family contributions that aid in deferring the immediate economic costs of long-term investments such as a college education or the down payment for a house, are differentially spread across race, with half of White families giving young adults this investment edge, while data show that only 20% of Black families are able to do so (Lui et al., 2006). This coupled with the fact that, in some states, children of undocumented immigrants do not receive in-state tuition for higher education, makes the prospects of getting into and affording a college education out of reach for many young

adults and erodes their longer-term access to asset growth and economic stability. One report (Draut & Silva, 2004) indicates that young adults face daunting economic challenges characterized by underemployment, the high cost of purchasing a first home, and rising debt from student loans and credit cards. According to another report, in 2004 adults aged 18 to 24 spent close to two times the amount on debt expenditures as they did in 1992, with approximately 30% of income going to paying off their debt (Mintel Report, 2004).

Given that our educational institution operates as society's gatekeeper to economic opportunities, we need to examine how our educational system is preparing our youth for future employment as well as how and to whom such opportunities are afforded. For example, what kind of jobs are our youth getting, and what educational and vocational paths lead to these jobs? Are we effectively and appropriately matching educational and vocational opportunities to the current economic landscape so that all youth transitioning into the adult world of work can benefit? Does our educational system effectively track and keep pulse on changing labor market trends, identify careers with long-term gains (e.g., with benefits and growth potential), and then create the appropriate education and training experiences necessary to be attractive in competing for these jobs? In other words, if education provides opportunities to gain assets such as jobs, promotions, credit, and safety-net benefits such as health care (Lui et al., 2006), and asset accumulation leads to prosperity and economic stability (Rank, 2005), we need to examine how differential education and training tracks might be influencing lifelong economic and labor market trajectories, keeping certain groups entrenched in poverty.

Indeed, as important as individual factors are in the transition to work, the changing labor market and structural shifts in the economy may have an even greater influence by shaping a young person's opportunities for finding and maintaining productive work. Work in industry and manufacturing has been diminishing for 4 decades now, and the number of jobs in the service sector has increased (Portes & Rumbaut, 2001). Manufacturing jobs once offered unskilled youth with relatively little education an opportunity for good wages, employment benefits, and job security. However, the service sector is divided between low-wage, temporary, or part-time service jobs and work opportunities that call for advanced, technical skills. Today there is a high labor market demand for low-wage, low-skill jobs as well as a high demand among employers for workers with more specialized and technical skills (Portes & Rumbaut, 2001).

> How do factors such as gender, race, ethnicity, and disability affect transitions into the labor market?

Data suggest that youth with disabilities are at higher risk for dropping out of high school compared with youth who do not have a disability. More specifically, African American and Latino youth with disabilities are at significantly higher risk than their White counterparts (Trainor, 2008). Although approximately three quarters of White youth with disabilities entered paid employment after high school, only 61.7% of African American and 65.4% of Latino youth with disabilities obtained employment after high school. Only one fifth of youth with disabilities go on to higher education opportunities (Wagner, Newman, Cameto, & Levine, 2005). Other vulnerable youth populations, such as youth transitioning out of state care, face challenges in moving to paid employment in young adulthood. Reid (2007) suggests that "seven pillars" serve as a foundation for success for youth transitioning out of state care at age of majority: relationships, education, housing, life skills, identity, youth engagement (ownership over the transitioning plan), and emotional healing (p. 35). A Child Trends report summarized specific empirically validated competencies that have been shown to increase high school students' success in the labor market: second language competency; ability to interact with others to problem-solve and work through conflict; critical thinking skills; planfulness; good judgment; strong work ethic such as reliability and professionalism in the work environment;

having had internship experience; and general self-management skills such as responsibility, initiative, and time management skills (Lippman & Keith, 2009). Policies and programs such as the Foster Care Independence Act (Pub. L. No. 106-169) and the John H. Chafee Foster Care Independence Program of 1999 provide additional support for postsecondary education, vocational training, housing, health care, and counseling until age 21 and are a good start in responding to these specific needs (U.S. Children's Bureau, 2012b).

Incarcerated youth who are discharged from the juvenile justice system as emerging adults also face significant labor attachment challenges. Many face uncertain outcomes upon discharge back into their preinstitutionalized communities that can include rearrest for new crimes (about one third will be rearrested) or violence from peers who vow revenge for wrongs committed before the youth were institutionalized (Inderbitzin, 2009). Difficulty in obtaining gainful employment upon release can be complicated because of deficient legitimate job skills, stigma of institutionalization, and lack of prosocial community and economic capital (Inderbitzin, 2009). Job training, transitioning to new neighborhoods, and engaging in a safety net of continuing care services are critical predictors for successful release back into the community.

The dilemma facing disadvantaged youth entering adulthood is vexing. Labor market attachment is not only the surest route to material well-being (for example, according to Shapiro [2004], once basic living expenses are accounted for, each additional dollar of annual income generates $3.26 in net worth over a person's lifetime), but labor market attachment also has been found to be significantly related to mental health and psychosocial well-being. One study looked at factors associated with well-being and adjustment from ages 16 to 21. The study found that experiences of unemployment were significantly associated with thoughts of suicide, substance abuse, and crime (Fergusson, Horwood, & Woodward, 2001). Benefits of work include increased self-esteem, increased social interaction, and external validation through social recognition. Increasingly, therefore, youths' life trajectories will be determined by access to advanced education and then good jobs.

Immigration and Work

Alejandro Portes and Ruben G. Rumbaut (2001), in their book *Legacies: The Story of the Immigrant Second Generation*, based on results from the Children of Immigrants Longitudinal Study (CILS), noted that the structural labor market change of the past few decades disproportionately affects immigrants, particularly youth in late adolescence who will be emerging into this new occupational landscape. "Increasing labor market inequality implies that to succeed socially and economically, children of immigrants today must cross, in the span of a few years, the educational gap that took descendents of Europeans several generations to bridge," the authors note (p. 58). An important finding from the CILS is the contrast in job selection between older and younger generations of immigrants. Today's young people are more likely to turn down "traditional immigrant jobs" that are seen as unfulfilling, in contrast to older immigrants who often felt compelled to take any job available in their youth without such questioning (Portes & Rumbaut, 2001).

Another study investigated how migration affects the earnings prospects of Latino men making the transition into young adulthood (Padilla & Jordan, 1997). Specifically, seeking work opportunities in more favorable socioeconomic environments during early adulthood was found to be associated with decreased likelihood of poverty in adulthood. Increased education and cognitive ability were also associated with a decreased likelihood of being in poverty during the transition into adulthood.

It is important for social workers to understand the social and economic conditions that immigrant youth face. This large and growing group, born from the surge in immigration of recent decades, faces special challenges as young adults under recent economic conditions.

Role Changes and Work

A number of other factors are related to the type of work young adults secure and thus their occupational prestige and income earned later in life. Across race and gender, educational attainment has a strong effect. Marriage itself is not a significant predictor of occupational prestige or earnings for males or females. Analysis of data from the National Survey of Families found that men were more likely to be employed if they were fathers and that their work hours increased as the number of children in the family increased. Conversely, women were less likely to work if they had children, and their work hours decreased as the number of children in the family increased (Kaufman & Uhlenberg, 2000).

For the social worker, it is important to examine to what extent culture affects educational and work-related opportunities and timing sequences. Social workers also need to explore with individuals the extent of role overload that may exist. For example, an additional effect of employment on low-income earners may be the added expense that occurs when work and family pressures collide. Jonathan and Kai have the protection of good-paying jobs and college degrees that will likely confer greater flexibility and employment prospects over their life course as compared with lower-income wage workers who may not have a college degree. This economic security may offer child care opportunities and other flexible arrangements that will help in their work-family planning in the future. Exploring the unique costs and benefits of employment decisions for each individual, recognizing the larger family context, can be helpful. Social workers should also assess clients' coping strategies and ask clients for their perceptions about how identified stressors are affecting the individual and family.

Race, Ethnicity, and Work

The associations among race, ethnicity, and work attachment have received some attention. Although first-generation Mexican immigrants earn incomes half that of White males, second-generation

Photo 7.4 A major challenge facing young adults is attaining independent financial stability and establishing autonomy and decision making.

© Patricia Nelson/iStockphoto.com

immigrants typically earn three quarters that of White men and more than Black men. About 40% of first-generation Mexican immigrants ages 16 to 20 are in high school or college as compared with two thirds of second-generation immigrants in this age cohort ("Of Meat, Mexicans and Social Mobility," 2006).

Unfortunately, the labor force participation among young Black men has declined since 1980. Labor force connection tends to be weakest for Black males who have little formal education and who lack work experience (Holzer, 2009). Of course, the economic restructuring of past decades

has made good-quality jobs for young adults without specialized skills hard to come by. Other barriers for young Black men include discrimination in hiring, absence of adult mentors in the community who might help socialize youth toward work roles, a disconnect from a good-paying job with benefits, diminished self-efficacy related to perceptions of constricted economic opportunities, hopelessness about finding quality jobs, and the presence of alternative informal and more prosperous economic options (e.g., drug dealing, gambling). All may decrease the youth's ability or motivation to pursue formal work opportunities. But that is not to say that young Black men do not want to succeed in the world of work:

> Young black men want jobs and wages comparable to white young men, and their reluctance to take inferior jobs, despite less experience, lengthens their period of unemployment. They share middle-class values and aspirations. The problem is how to achieve those aspirations. (Laseter, 1997, p. 74)

Racism may be a factor in job prospects for young Black males as well. Sociological studies have shown that White men with a prison record are more likely to be hired for a job than Black men without a prison record (Lui et al., 2006). Racism can directly tax individuals and families and can indirectly deplete their buffering resources and weaken solutions to managing direct stressors (Harrell, 2000). Stressors and resources change over the life course, however, and social workers need to be able to assess the ways in which individuals and families are able to adapt to such changes.

Although social workers need to understand the effects of oppressive living conditions and environmental stressors on all groups, they should be aware of the disproportionate number of African Americans living in such conditions. Regardless of socioeconomic status (SES), African American males have the lowest well-being scores of any group studied (White women and men, African American women and men) (Woody & Green, 2001). Their low scores are potentially explained by social conditions such as stigma, constrained economic opportunities, health-related discrepancies, and a perception of lack of control over their lives. It is dually important, however, for social workers to understand the range of diversity within the African American community along many social dimensions, including SES, in order to avoid perpetuating the stereotypes that further stigmatize this diverse group.

In addition, social workers should be aware of how social assistance is unequally distributed and should work toward eliminating such disparities. For example, of those exiting welfare, Whites are twice as likely as Blacks or Latinas to receive child care or transportation transitional assistance. In addition, the median wage for a White welfare exiter from 1997 to 1999 was $7.31/hour compared with $6.88 and $6.71 for African American and Latina exiters, respectively (Lui et al., 2006). Other research shows that when women who leave Temporary Assistance to Needy Families (TANF) are employed in steady jobs and remain employed over time, their wages increase with this longevity in the work world (Corcoran, Danziger, Kalil, & Seefeldt, 2000). However, the reality is that many young women leaving TANF do not enter long-term continuous employment because of a variety of barriers, such as maternal and filial physical and/or mental health problems; unaffordable, inaccessible, or poor-quality child care; or unreliable transportation (Corcoran et al., 2000). Without addressing these problems, the *long-term* wage stability and economic viability of these families remain in question. The living wage social movement that continues to gain momentum will ideally help bring more public awareness and policy change to these issues.

RISK FACTORS AND PROTECTIVE FACTORS IN YOUNG ADULTHOOD

A longitudinal study that followed a cohort of individuals born in 1955 from infancy to age 40 identified clusters of protective factors at significant points across the life course (see Exhibit 7.4) that are associated with successfully making the transition to adulthood (Werner & Smith, 2001). The researchers identified high-risk individuals and then determined the specific factors that influenced their positive adaptation to adulthood at age 32. The protective factors included successful early social, language, and physical development; good problem-solving skills in middle childhood; educational and work

> How can social workers help to provide protective factors for the adult transition?

expectations and plans by age 18; and social maturity and a sense of mastery and control in late adolescence. Family factors included stable maternal employment when the child was 2 to 10 years old, access to a variety of social support sources, and the child's sense of belonging within the family unit at age 18. Community factors included having access to nurturing, caring adults in one's community, including the presence of adult mentors, and having access to "enabling," as opposed to "entrapping," community niches (see Saleebey, 1996). It would be important to find out from Dominique where the community assets or resources are in her community and to help her identify how to connect to those existing sources of support. For example, she already has said she knows where to get charity food donations to extend the emergency gap between when her food stamps run out and when she receives renewed monthly assistance. Perhaps there are other community-based organizations, formal or informal, that she could meaningfully connect to in new ways, with your help.

Other researchers have identified similar protective factors associated with successful developmental transitions into emerging adulthood and young adulthood, including childhood IQ, parenting quality, and socioeconomic status. Adaptation in emerging adulthood, specifically, is associated with an individual's planning capacity, future motivation, autonomy, social support, and coping skills (Masten et al., 2004).

Risk factors that researchers found to be associated with the transition to adulthood included low family income during infancy, poor reading achievement by age 10, problematic school behavior during adolescence, and adolescent health problems (Werner & Smith, 2001). For men, an excessive number of stressful events, living with an alcoholic or mentally ill father, and substance abuse contributed to problematic coping in early adulthood. Other studies have found that adolescent fatherhood can be a risk factor for delinquency, which, in turn, can lead to problematic entry into adulthood (Stouthamer-Loeber & Wei, 1998).

Exhibit 7.4 Common Core Protective Factors Predicting Adult Adaptation

	Individual Characteristics	Caregiving Context
Infancy	Autonomy; social competence Health status	Maternal competence Emotional support Number of stressful events
Middle childhood	Academic proficiency Health status	Emotional support to child (extended family; mentor) Number of stressful events
Adolescence	Self-efficacy Health status	Emotional support to child (peer relations; feelings about family) Number of stressful events
Young adulthood	Temperament Health status	Emotional support (quality of partner, work, and community relationships) Number of stressful events

SOURCE: Adapted from Werner & Smith, 2001, pp. 161–163

For women, a sibling death in early childhood, living with an alcoholic or mentally ill father, and a conflicted relationship with the mother were significant risk factors for successful coping at age 32 (Werner & Smith, 2001).

One study (Ringeisen, Casaneuva, Urato, & Stambaugh, 2009) found that although about half (48%) of young adults with a maltreatment history had mental health problems, only 25% of these young adults received treatment services for their problems. In particular, there was a significant decline in those receiving services in adolescence (47.6%) to those continuing to receive such services in adulthood (14.3%). Data suggest that there is a significant risk of losing continuity of mental health services when making the move out of adolescence and into young adulthood, with data showing particularly high risk for non-Whites and those without Medicaid assistance (Ringeisen et al., 2009).

Other studies of youth aging out of the foster care system have found similar declining trends in mental health service use during the adolescent-adult transition. A study by McMillan and Raghavan (2009) found that 60% of 19-year-old foster youth dropped out of services during the transition from pediatric system care to the adult service system. This is significant given that 24,000 youth age out of foster care each year (National Association of Counties, 2008) and that former foster youth (ages 19 to 30) have twice the rate of post-traumatic stress disorder as U.S. war veterans (Pecora et al., 2005) and more severe mental health and behavioral problems than the general population and than children who have a maltreatment history but not foster care placement (Lawrence, Carlson, & Egeland, 2006).

A study of the effects of war on adult mental health reveals other risk factors that social workers should be aware of. Although some researchers have found that military service often provides youth a positive opportunity in transitioning into adulthood (Werner & Smith, 2001) and frequently leads to facilitating a young adult's return to higher education (Astone et al., 2000), the ravages of war experienced during military service can pose

significant mental health risk. For example, Hoge, Auchterlonie, and Milliken (2006) examined the prevalence of mental health problems and service use among military personnel who returned from service in Iraq and found that one fifth (19.1%) of those returning from Iraq had at least one mental health problem, with about one third (35%) of those adults accessing mental health services during their first year back home. In addition, those personnel who were assessed as having a mental health condition were more likely to subsequently leave the military as compared with those personnel who returned home without a mental health condition. Therefore, it appears that although military service can be a positive path for many transitioning youth, the nature and quality of a youth's military experience may influence later physical and mental health outcomes as well as work trajectory decisions (e.g., to leave the military early). It appears that military service in a time of war may be a risk factor rather than protective factor. In addition, the availability of, access to, and quality of mental health care for military personnel upon their return home may also contribute to the severity of wartime service as a risk factor. We see Sheila's struggle with her own military deployments—the time away from family, the physical risks, and the reliance on community to provide family support in her absence. Sheila's story helps us to see that it may be difficult to disentangle the emotional and physical sequelae related to a traumatic brain injury and illustrates the challenges in family reintegration.

Entering the military is a career choice for many young adults, but for others with limited formal education, it may be the only employment opportunity that comes with comprehensive benefits. Choosing military employment requires contracting into a work environment that can be unpredictable, dangerous, and relatively inflexible (i.e., high demand, low control, and variable deployments), which can all exacerbate work-family stress and impact family well-being (Wadsworth & Southwell, 2013). Studies have found that parental stress is the most important factor that affects children's behavioral and emotional functioning when a military parent is deployed. Family support programming that focuses on helping nondeployed parents strengthen their ability to provide care for their children during a military spouse's deployment is important for military families. Gewirtz, Erbes, Polusny, Forgatch, and DeGarmo (2011) offer specific strategy recommendations to support parenting in military families, including working from the family's strengths and recognizing the resilience that exists in military families, focusing on stressors affecting the family during deployment, and helping parents develop emotional regulation strategies as part of their parenting skills. Other strategies include helping parents set appropriate limits, keeping rituals and routines as usual during the time of deployment, and enhancing the problem-solving capacity of the family unit (Gewirtz et al., 2011).

Knowledge of risk and protective factors related to the adulthood transition can help social workers assess young adult clients' current challenges, vulnerabilities, strengths, and potentials. Gaining an accurate understanding of the client's developmental history provides guidance to the social worker in formulating appropriate goals and intervention strategies. It is important to remember to check out your own assumptions of "risk" with clients in order to clarify the unique impact such experiences have on individual clients.

Critical Thinking Questions 7.5

How do you think cumulative advantage and cumulative disadvantage affect human behavior during young adulthood? What personal, family, cultural, and other social factors during childhood and adolescence have an impact on the transition into young adulthood? What do you see as the risk and protective factors in the stories of Dominique Castillo, Sheila Henderson, and Jonathan and Kai?

Implications for Social Work Practice

This discussion of young adulthood suggests several practice principles for social workers:

- Recognize that social roles during emerging adulthood may be different from those later in young adulthood.
- Explore cultural values, family expectations, attitudes toward gender roles, and environmental constraints and resources that may influence life structure decisions and opportunities when working with young adult clients.
- Assess specific work, family, and community conditions as they pertain to young adult clients' psychological and social well-being; be aware of any caregiving roles young adults may be playing.
- Where appropriate, help young adults to master the tasks involved in developing intimate relationships.
- Where appropriate, assist young adults with concerns about differentiating from family of origin and do so in a culturally sensitive manner.
- Work with other professionals to advocate for policies that promote transitional planning and connect youth to the labor market, particularly for youth aging out of foster care placements, correction facilities, group home environments, or other formal residential mental health settings.
- Take the initiative to develop mentoring programs that build relations between young adults and younger or older generations.
- Take the initiative to develop parenting classes for first-time parents and recognize and develop the unique strengths of fathers, especially in mentoring teen fathers to increase parenting skills.
- Understand the ways that social systems promote or deter people from maintaining or achieving health and well-being.
- Discover, appraise, and attend to changing locales, populations, scientific and technological developments, and emerging societal trends.

community assets

human capital

novice phase

default individualization

individuative-reflective faith

romantic love

developmental individualization

intimacy

spirituality

emerging adulthood

intimacy versus isolation

synthetic-conventional faith

fictive kin

life structure

1. Identify one current social issue as portrayed in the media (e.g., housing, immigration policies, health care access or coverage or affordability, living wage) and explore how this social issue uniquely affects young adults.

2. Create your own theory of young adulthood. What are some of the important characteristics? What makes someone a young adult? What differentiates this stage from adolescence and middle adulthood? Start the process by answering the following question: "Do you consider yourself to be an adult?"

3. Choose one of the case studies at the beginning of the chapter (Dominique Castillo, Sheila Henderson, or Jonathan and Kai). Change the gender for that case without changing any other major demographic variable. Explore how your assumptions change about the individual's problems, challenges, and potential. Now choose a different case. Change the race or ethnicity for that case and again explore your assumptions. Finally, using the remaining case, change the SES and again explore how your assumptions change.

AmeriCorps NCCC (National Civilian Community Corps): www.nationalservice.gov/programs/americorps

Site details AmeriCorps' programs for young adults ages 18 to 24, offering full-time residential community service opportunities. Target goals include developing youths' leadership capacity through intensive and directed community service.

Child Trends: www.childtrends.org

Site of Child Trends, a nonprofit research organization located in Washington, DC, provides data and reports focused on child well-being and marriage and family, to include fatherhood and parenting.

National Fatherhood Initiative: www.fatherhood.org

Site of the National Fatherhood Initiative provides numerous resources and links to other fatherhood sites and discusses educational and outreach campaigns under way to promote involved fathering and family well-being.

National Gay and Lesbian Task Force: www.thetaskforce.org

Site presented by the National Gay and Lesbian Task Force contains information about the task force, news and views, special issues, state and local organizations, and special events.

National Guard Youth Challe*NG*e Program: www.ngyf.org

Site reports on success stories of a multistate program that targets youth who have dropped out of high school to provide them with a 5-month residential program and ongoing mentoring services to facilitate their entry into employment, higher education/training, or the military.

National Survey of Family Growth: www.cdc.gov/nchs/NSFG.htm

Site of the National Center for Health Statistics offers reports, other publications, and data from their CDC-sponsored survey documenting family formation issues in adulthood, such as fertility and family planning, sexual behavior, and health.

Network on Transitions to Adulthood: transitions2adulthood.com

Site presented by the Network on Transitions to Adulthood examines the policies, programs, and institutions influencing the adulthood transition; contains fast facts and information on research initiatives.

Work and Family Researchers Network: work-family.sas.upenn.edu

Site of the international membership organization of interdisciplinary work on the family and work (formerly the Sloan Work and Family Research Network) contains news, frequently asked questions, an online repository of research on work and the family, a literature database, a research newsletter, resources for teaching, research profiles, and work and family links. Part of the network's mission is to inform policymakers on key family-work issues.

Student Study Site

⑤SAGE edge™

Sharpen your skills with SAGE edge at **edge.sagepub.com/hutchisonclc5e**

SAGE edge for students provides a personalized approach to help you accomplish your coursework goals in an easy-to-use learning environment.

Middle Adulthood

Elizabeth D. Hutchison

Chapter Outline

CASE STUDY 8.1

Viktor Spiro, Finding Stability at 44

Viktor Spiro was born in a village outside of Tirana, Albania, and lived his early life, as did many Albanians in the Stalinist state, amid very impoverished conditions. He was the youngest of four children, with two sisters and a brother 12 years his senior. Viktor describes his childhood as "normal," until he sustained a serious head injury after falling from a tractor when he was 13. He experienced an increasing depression following his hospitalization; his school performance declined and he withdrew from his friends. When Viktor was 20, his older brother died from a rare gastrointestinal illness, another traumatic event that exacerbated Viktor's depression and substance abuse. He subsequently went absent without leave (AWOL) from his military post and fled to Greece, where he continued to drink heavily and was reportedly hospitalized at a psychiatric facility.

Because his father was a U.S. citizen, Viktor was able to immigrate to the United States in his late 20s after the dissolution of Albania's repressive communist regime. He secured a job as a painter, but the language barrier and fast-paced life left him feeling vulnerable. Struggling to cope, Viktor made a series of suicide attempts and was arrested after lunging for the gun of a police officer who was trying to help him. Viktor claims that he did not intend to harm the officer, but that he saw the gun as a quick means to end his own life. Viktor's suicide attempts and arrest led to the beginning of a long relationship with mental health services (MHS). He was diagnosed with bipolar I disorder with psychotic features, made more suicide attempts, was hospitalized, and lived in a group home.

After a few years, Viktor's father and mother, Petro and Adriana, moved to the United States to reunite with Viktor and his sister Maria. Viktor moved into an apartment with his parents and showed some signs of improved adjustment, including advances in his use of English and steady employment secured through the MHS job service program. However, his firsthand exposure to the worsening state of Petro's vascular dementia proved very traumatic, and he made another suicide attempt. Then, Petro broke his hip and was in a nursing home briefly. Viktor and his father were both referred to a residential program to obtain counseling and case management services. His social worker learned that Viktor had accrued more than $140,000 in hospital bills and was still on "medical leave" from his job. The family had no significant income other than Petro's monthly $400 social security check and Adriana's stipend from Social Services to "take care" of her husband. Viktor shared that he had deep regrets about his latest suicide attempt and could not put himself or his family through this again. He felt that he was at a turning point and needed to take on more responsibility as he approached 40, especially with caring for his ailing parents.

As Viktor and his social worker met regularly, Viktor became more aware of his mother's struggles to fulfill family needs and began to do more in the house. It became clear to the social worker that Adriana was the backbone of the family and that she found purpose and meaning in her role as keeper of the house. Adriana began to trust the social worker's commitment to her family, and with Viktor translating, the social worker learned that Adriana wears her black dress and gold crucifix on a daily basis in mourning for her deceased son. Adriana called her life "unlucky," as she recounted the death of her firstborn, the chronic depression and strokes that had afflicted her husband over the past 40 years, and Viktor's ongoing struggles with his mental illness. The social worker saw that although the Spiro family clearly had experienced much suffering and trauma, their incredible strength, resolve, and affection were impressive.

Viktor began to reveal a more reflective, insightful side during his recovery. He confided to his treatment team that he was hearing voices for nearly 6 months prior to his last suicide attempt but didn't tell anyone. He hoped the voices would just "go away." His social worker and job coach assisted him with transition back into the work force, and he eventually obtained the medical clearance to return to his dishwashing job, resuming the role as the primary breadwinner for the family. This was a real lift to Viktor's self-esteem. The Spiro family experienced another financial lift with the news of a total forgiveness of Viktor's outstanding hospital bills.

While the Spiro family was enjoying their improving situation, the treatment team worked with Viktor to expand his social network outside the family. Viktor had been spending all of his time with his parents in their apartment when he was not working. As his confidence grew with his psychiatric improvement, however, he became more receptive to suggestions about weekend social activities coordinated by the agency. He tried out a couple of the

(Continued)

groups and enjoyed the activities and chance to form new relationships. He quickly immersed himself in a variety of weekend activities that involved shopping, movies, athletics, and cultural events. The social worker assisted Viktor with the long process of reapplying for naturalization, after learning that he did not provide INS with the required documents on his previous application. With his improved mental state, Viktor was able to concentrate on studying for the citizenship test, which he passed. His citizenship ceremony was a wonderful day for Viktor and his family, and he made a poignant speech about dreaming of this day as a teenager watching *CHiPS* reruns in Albania.

The Spiro family clearly enjoyed the series of positive events for Viktor, but soon they faced another change of events. Petro had a series of strokes, was in and out of hospice several times, and ultimately died of heart failure in his home with his wife and son by his side. Viktor grieves for his father, but his handling of Petro's health crises and death is a remarkable change from the impulsive and often dangerous behavior he had previously exhibited when responding to stressful situations. Today, Viktor has balance in his life, working part-time in a grocery store, spending time with his mother, doing household chores, and attending church. Although he sees mental health workers less than he once did, he continues to attend a day program for people with serious mental illness, where he enjoys the social opportunities, friends, and varied community outings. He plays the guitar and sings American pop as well as traditional Greek and Albanian songs. Currently, his biggest struggles are medication side effects and trying to care for his mother, who is having a hard time with the loss of her caregiving role. The agency social worker is trying to help her get more connected to the church and the Albanian community, where her inability to speak English would not be a barrier.

—Derek Morch

CASE STUDY 8.2

Lisa Balinski, Trying to Balance It All at 50

Lisa Balinski grew up in a lower-middle-class neighborhood in a midsize city in Minnesota. Her parents were both brought to the United States from Poland as small children, during World War II. They grew up in a neighborhood where social life revolved around the Polish-speaking Catholic church, where they met and married. Lisa was an only child, and her parents worked hard in the small Polish restaurant they opened soon after marrying. She started helping out in the restaurant at an early age, with increasing responsibilities over time. Her parents were proud when she graduated from college and got a job teaching at the neighborhood high school.

The day after her college graduation, Lisa married Adam, her high school sweetheart. Adam had been working in the neighborhood hardware store since he graduated from high school and had been patiently waiting for Lisa to finish college. During their first year of marriage, Lisa was overwhelmed, trying to adapt to two new roles—wife and teacher—at the same time, and she and Adam were both thrilled when she learned that she was pregnant in the early spring of that year. Their plan was for Lisa to return to teaching in a few years, after getting a family started.

Adam's and Lisa's parents were thrilled about the baby girl, Rachel, but Lisa found the transition to motherhood more challenging than she had expected. Adam, on the other hand, seemed to be a natural and was an enormous help with the baby. They found, however, that they had underestimated the costs of a baby, and when Rachel was 6 months old, they decided to move in with Lisa's parents. The house was a bit crowded, but Lisa was happy to have her mother's help in the mornings before she went to the restaurant, and her mother loved having a chance to spend more time with Rachel.

When Rachel was 18 months old, Adam got a promotion at work, and with what they had saved over the past year, Lisa and Adam were able to move into an apartment of their own. When Rachel was 2½ years old, Lisa gave birth to another baby girl, Kristi. She was pleasantly surprised to find that she was more relaxed than she had been with Rachel, and for the first time since college, Lisa began to feel competent.

Finances were still tight, and when Kristi was 2 years old, Lisa began to do some substitute teaching. She hired her neighbor to watch the girls on the days that she was called in to teach. She really enjoyed being back in the classroom and took a full-time teaching position after a couple of years of subbing. After 2 years of full-time teaching, she began to take evening courses toward a master's degree. Adam supported her in this decision and stepped up to provide more help with household chores. He enjoyed the chance to grow even closer to his daughters.

With Adam and Lisa both working, they were able to buy a small house of their own in a more middle-class neighborhood. This was a good time in their lives. They were both enjoying their work, Lisa was becoming a respected teacher, and they enjoyed "fixing up" the house and participating in their daughters' varied activities. With two sets of grandparents close by, Rachel and Kristi reveled in having a loving multigenerational family.

When Lisa and Adam were 40 years old, Adam was seriously injured in an automobile accident. He was hospitalized for several weeks and spent 6 more weeks in a rehabilitation center. This was a very difficult time for the family. Lisa and her daughters realized how much they had depended on Adam to keep the family functioning, and Lisa worried that she was giving too much responsibility to Rachel and Kristi. She was happy to have an opportunity to talk with the rehabilitation social worker about these issues. And now, 10 years later, Lisa reports that although this was a stressful time for the family, good things came from it. Her family became much closer emotionally and she learned that she was stronger than she thought.

Adam recovered well from his accident and returned to work to find that Lisa and his daughters were not the only ones to develop new respect for him during his absence. His time away from work had also shown his boss what a valuable employee he was. He received another good promotion, which was welcomed at a time when the daughters were beginning college. Lisa was offered a vice principal position at school, but she turned it down, because she enjoyed being in the classroom—and she wanted to be free to challenge school district policies. She had become known as one of the best supervising teachers for education students from the local university.

Now, at age 50, Lisa says she has an overfull life. Last year, her father died suddenly of a heart attack, and her bereft mother has moved in with Lisa and Adam. They helped her to close the restaurant and sell the house. Lisa is growing increasingly concerned that her mother is immobilized with depression. Most afternoons when she arrives home from work, she finds that her mom is still in bed and has not eaten all day. Rachel recently became engaged and wants help with planning the wedding, and Kristi is struggling to find direction since leaving college in the midst of a severe recession. Adam continues to be a major support to Lisa, but he has needed to work longer hours in recent months. Lisa thinks she needs to talk with a mental health worker about her mother and how to be helpful to Kristi. Currently, she and Adam are helping Kristi pay her rent, but they are wondering if they should recommend that Kristi come home to live with them, instead.

Michael Bowling, Swallowing His Pride at 57

Michael Bowling always thought that if you are willing to work hard, you will never need public assistance. He realizes now that he made judgments about other people's lives without really knowing much about them. And he is convinced that his very life depends on getting some public assistance. Here is his story.

Michael grew up in a small town in Missouri, the oldest of five children. His parents were hard-working factory workers who had grown up in the midst of the Great Depression. His dad had to turn down a college scholarship to work odd jobs to help scrape together enough to feed the family. Michael's parents were determined to give their children an easier time, and though it was never easy, at least Michael and his siblings never went to bed hungry. They always felt loved, and their parents had high hopes for their children's futures.

Michael started working 20 hours a week when he was 16 to help his parents pay a hospital bill for one of his younger brothers. When he graduated from high school, he joined the U.S. Army, hoping that might provide some financial security for him and his family. He stayed in the U.S. Army for 4 years and then returned to his hometown. He soon found that there were no good jobs there for him, and he decided to move to a nearby college town to begin to study for a college degree. He found a low-paying job for 30 hours per week, so it took him 7 years to earn his engineering degree.

When he graduated from college, he married the woman he had been dating and found an engineering job in a larger city. The marriage lasted for 7 years, there were no children, and the divorce was friendly. The career went well and Michael moved up the ranks in small and moderate-size firms. He was able to buy a small house. He never married again, but he has been very close to a younger sister who lives in the same city, and he became a kind of substitute dad to her son and daughter after her husband left the family. His parents lived long enough to see him doing well and took pride in his success. Both parents died at a relatively young age, however, his dad of a stroke at age 55 and his mother of breast cancer at age 58, after moving in with Michael and using hospice care during her final 5 months.

In early 2007, at the age of 50, Michael got his dream job in a very large engineering firm. Life was good! And then, the deep recession of 2008 hit, and as one of the last hired, Michael was one of the first to be laid off. He had some savings, so he could make his mortgage payments and put food on the table. He cut where he could, things like his gym membership and cable television, but held on to the car and cell phone because he would need them for the job search. He put out 10 resumes a day and made two cold calls per day. He felt lucky when he found temporary jobs, but these projects never lasted long, and they never offered health insurance. For the first 2 years after he was laid off, he bought a very expensive individual health insurance policy, but as his savings diminished, he dropped the policy.

Then in October 2011, Michael awoke one morning with a severe headache, numbness in the right side of his face, and weakness in his right arm and leg. Because of his earlier experience with his father's stroke, Michael recognized these symptoms as warning signs of a stroke. He also knew that it was imperative that he get immediate medical care; he called 911 and was taken to the comprehensive hospital a few blocks from his home. Over the next 2 years, Michael used all of his savings and took a second mortgage on his house to pay his hospital and rehabilitation bills. He was lucky that his stroke was not as serious as the one that had killed his dad, and that he knew to get immediate help, and he has made a good recovery. The only remaining noticeable symptom is some left-sided weakness, particularly when he is tired. As he recovered from the stroke, he resumed the job search but, to date, has only found one very short-term project. His two brothers have helped him out a little, when they realized that he was choosing between buying food or his medication to prevent another stroke. But

Michael knows that his brothers struggle financially, and he finally realized that he had to swallow his pride and apply for SNAP (food stamps) and energy assistance, which he did after the New Year, 2014. At the same time, he signed up for health insurance through the Affordable Care Act's federal marketplace. He is sad that he is not able to help send his niece and nephew to college as he had expected to do, but he is still very involved in their lives. Michael is grateful to have survived his stroke, and he says that one bright spot is that he has begun a daily meditation practice, which he finds spiritually, emotionally, and physically beneficial. He credits this practice for helping him to stay calm in the midst of the stresses in his life, and he adds that it has helped him develop better understanding of himself and his life journey. It has also helped him to pay attention to what is happening in his body. He attends a stroke recovery support group at the rehabilitation center and has developed some close friendships in the group.

THE CHANGING SOCIAL CONSTRUCTION OF MIDDLE ADULTHOOD

Although their life paths have been very different, Viktor Spiro, Lisa Balinski, and Michael Bowling are all in the life course phase of middle adulthood. Not so long ago, middle adulthood was nearly an unstudied terrain. Recently, however, because of a confluence of demographic trends and research accomplishments, there has been intense interest in the middle adult years in affluent societies. Although we still have only a hazy picture of middle adulthood, that picture is coming into better focus.

Changing Age Demographics

Adults in the middle adult years currently constitute approximately one third of the U.S. population (Cohen, 2012), and so it is not surprising that researchers have been taking a serious interest in the middle adult phase of the life course for the past 2 decades. Beginning in the 1990s, an interdisciplinary group of researchers in North America and Europe launched several large research projects to move our understanding of middle adulthood from mythology to science (see Brim, Ryff, & Kessler, 2004; Willis & Martin, 2005). These researchers span the fields of anthropology, demography, epidemiology, health care policy, medicine, psychology, and sociology. From a life course perspective, it is

important to note that most of what we "know" about middle adulthood is based on research on the cohort known as the baby boom generation, a group born from 1946 to 1964 and spanning the ages of 50 to 68 in 2014. Therefore, it is important to remember that this cohort is the result of a "fifteen-year splurge of births" (Eggebeen & Sturgeon, 2006, p. 3) that occurred after World War II. This splurge of births was a departure from a long-term trend of declining births, a trend that was resumed in the 1960s when fertility began to decline again.

> How might these changing demographics affect the midlife phase of the life course?

The current large cohort of midlife adults, the largest middle-aged cohort ever alive (Cohen, 2012), was created by 15 years of high fertility, but increasing life expectancy is another contributing factor. In 1900, the median age of the U.S. population was 22.9 and the average life expectancy at birth was 47.3 years. By 1950, the median age was 30.2 years and average life expectancy was 68.2 years, and by 2000, the median age was 35.3 and the average life expectancy was 76.8 (Arias, 2012; Hobbs & Stoops, 2002). In 2013, the estimated median age was 37.2 years and the estimated average life expectancy at birth was 78.6 years (Central Intelligence Agency, 2013). These changing demographics are presented in Exhibit 8.1. These data do not mean that no one lived past what we now consider middle age in 1900. The average life

Exhibit 8.1   Changing Life Expectancy and Median Age

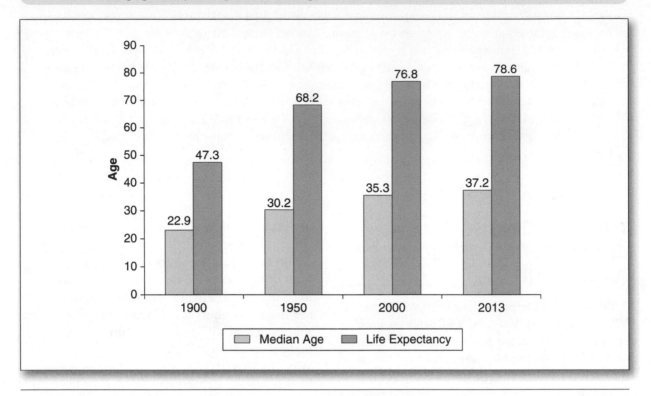

SOURCES: Based on Arias, 2012; Central Intelligence Agency, 2013; and Hobbs & Stoops, 2002

expectancy in 1900 was deflated by high rates of infant mortality. Indeed, in 1900, 18% of the population of the United States was 45 years old or older. This compares with 28% in 1950 and 34% in 2000. Living past age 45 is not new, but more people are doing it. This trend has an enormous impact on our understanding of the adult life course (Wahl & Kruse, 2005).

Longevity and birth rates vary across global populations. Mass longevity and declining birth rates hold true in advanced industrial societies, but in poor and less-developed societies, the trends are radically different. International data show a high life expectancy of 89.6 years in Monaco and a low of 49.1 years in Chad in 2013 estimates (Central Intelligence Agency, 2013). In that same year, the average life expectancy was less than 55 years in no fewer than 21 countries, including Afghanistan,

where the average life expectancy was 50.1 years. Social workers who work in the international arena or with immigrant families will need to develop appropriate understanding of how the life course varies across world populations.

A Definition of Middle Adulthood

Before we go further, we need to pause and consider *who* is included in middle adulthood. In the most general sense, we are talking about people who are in midlife, or the central part of the life course. Beyond that, we do not have generally agreed on ages to include in middle adulthood. The most frequently used definition of middle adulthood includes those persons ages 40 to 64 (Bjorklund,

Is biological age, psychological age, social age, or spiritual age the best marker for middle adulthood?

2011), and that is the definition I use in this chapter, but some scholars use a lower limit as young as age 30 and an upper limit as late as age 70 (Dittmann-Kohli, 2005). The U.S. Census Bureau uses the ages of 45 to 64, and the Pew Research Center uses 50 to 64 (Cohen, 2012; Taylor, Morin, Parker, Cohn, & Wang, 2010). In 2009, most respondents to a Pew Research Center poll said that midlife ended at 71, but those with more schooling and older respondents reported later ages than other respondents, and men reported earlier ages than women (Taylor et al., 2010). Dittmann-Kohli (2005) suggests that middle adulthood is "a friendly expression for not being young anymore but not really very old yet" (p. 323).

Some authors argue that middle adulthood should not be thought of in terms of chronological age, but instead in terms of achieving certain developmental tasks. Generally, midlife adults have established a family, settled into and peaked in a career, and taken responsibility for their children, their parents, and their community. The life course perspective would suggest that any definition of middle adulthood must include biological aging processes, subjective perceptions, and social roles as well as historical and generational contexts.

Some authors have been critical of any approach to defining middle adulthood that includes an age range as wide as 40 to 64. They suggest that the beginning of midlife is very different from the latter part of midlife and that lumping these parts of the life course together may lead to contradictory findings. They call for a division of middle adulthood into early midlife and late midlife (Kohli & Künemund, 2005; Lachman, 2004). You may recall a similar concern about the boundaries of young adulthood noted in Chapter 7. Late adulthood, which is divided into late adulthood and very late adulthood in this book, encompasses an even larger age span, potentially from 65 to 100-plus. As longevity increases, the adult portion of life is likely to be divided into finer and finer phases.

Culture and the Construction of Middle Adulthood

With the identification of a middlehood, societies must construct roles for, and make meaning of, middle adulthood. Wahl and Kruse (2005) argue that middle adulthood was created by the increase of life expectancy in modern society. Evidence indicates, however, that middle adulthood has been incorporated into views of the life course since at least the early Middle Ages (Dittmann-Kohli, 2005). In his book *Welcome to Middle Age! (And Other Cultural Fictions)*, Richard Shweder (1998) suggests that middle age is a "cultural fiction," and the fiction does not play out the same way in all cultures. He does not use "fiction" to mean false, but to mean, instead, that ideas about middle age are culturally created.

In some parts of the world today, middle adulthood is not defined as a separate stage of life, but to the extent it is recognized, it is thought of as "maturity" and seen in relation to transitions in family roles. In other cultures, aging is associated with power and creativity, and middle adulthood is seen as the "prime of life," a time of fullness, activity, and spiritual growth. In the United States, since middle adulthood was first identified as a separate life stage in the latter part of the 19th century, two cultural views of this life stage have competed. One view sees middle adulthood as a positive time of having accumulated resources for coping; the other view sees middle adulthood as a negative time of decline and loss (see Cohen, 2012). This latter view of decline and loss (of being "over the hill") often seems to permeate popular culture. However, much of the recent research on middle adulthood reveals an attempt to recast midlife as the "prime of life." What images come to mind when you think of middle adulthood? Do you think first of sagging chins, wrinkles, reading glasses, thinning or graying hair, hot flashes, loss of sex drive, and so on, or do you think first of emotional and spiritual maturity that gives power, creativity, and influence? What images do you think Viktor Spiro, Lisa Balinski, and Michael Bowling have of middle adulthood?

THEORIES OF MIDDLE ADULTHOOD

Few theories focus directly on middle adulthood, but a number of theories address middle adulthood as a part of a larger developmental framework. Themes from three of those theories are presented here.

Erikson's Theory of Generativity

According to Erik Erikson's (1950) life span theory, the psychosocial struggle of middle adulthood is *generativity versus stagnation* (refer back to Exhibit 3.7 for an overview of Erikson's psychosocial stage theory). **Generativity** is the ability to transcend personal interests to provide care and concern for younger and older generations; it encompasses "procreation, productivity, and creativity, and thus the generation of new beings, as well as of new products and new ideas, including a kind of self-generation concerned with further identity development" (Erikson, 1982, p. 67). Generative adults provide "care, guidance, inspiration, instruction, and leadership" (McAdams, 2001, p. 395) for future generations. Failure to find a way to contribute to future generations, or to make a contribution to the general well-being, results in self-absorption and a sense of stagnation. Erikson saw generativity as an instinct that works to perpetuate society. With some help, Viktor Spiro began to practice generativity in his relationship with his parents as he entered middle adulthood. Lisa Balinski expresses generativity in her teaching, mentoring of student teachers, and care of her mother and adult children. Michael Bowling found meaning in midlife in acting as a substitute dad for his sister's children, and he wants to be able to be more financially supportive to them now. He also found meaning in caring for his mother in her final months. As a social worker, however, you will most likely encounter people who struggle with a sense of stagnation in middle adulthood.

> How does generativity affect the capacity for being linked with others in interdependence?

Exhibit 8.2 McAdams and de St. Aubin's Seven Components of Generativity

1. Inner desire for immortality and to be needed
2. Cultural demand for productivity
3. Concern for the next generation
4. Belief in the species
5. Commitment
6. Action: creating, maintaining, or offering
7. Development of a generative life story

SOURCE: Adapted from McAdams, Hart, & Maruna, 1998

Dan McAdams and Ed de St. Aubin (de St. Aubin, McAdams, & Kim, 2004; McAdams, 2006; McAdams & de St. Aubin, 1992, 1998) have expanded on the work of Erikson and presented a model of generativity that includes the seven components found in Exhibit 8.2. McAdams and de St. Aubin (1992, 1998) see generativity coming from both the person (personal desire) and the social and cultural environment (social roles and cultural demand).

Even though Erikson outlined midlife generativity in 1950, generativity was not a subject of empirical investigation until the 1980s (Peterson & Duncan, 2007). There is limited longitudinal research to answer the question of whether midlife adults are more generative than people in other life course phases. Most of the cross-sectional research on generativity reports greater generativity during middle adulthood than in young adulthood or late adulthood (An & Cooney, 2006; McAdams, 2001; Zucker, Ostrove, & Stewart, 2002), but other researchers have found that generativity continues to grow past middle adulthood (Sheldon & Kasser, 2001), and there is growing interest in generativity in older adults (Bates & Goodsell, 2013; Ehlman & Ligon, 2012). Researchers have also found some evidence of generative concern and motivation in late adolescence and young adulthood, while also finding that middle-aged adults have a greater sense of capacity for generativity than these younger groups (Lawford, Pratt, Hunsberg, & Pancer, 2005; Matsuba et al., 2012).

Research also finds that generativity is associated with gender, class, and race. Several researchers (Marks, Bumpass, & Jun, 2004; McAdams & de St. Aubin, 1992; McKeering & Pakenham, 2000) have found that men who had never been fathers scored particularly low on measures of generativity, but not being a mother did not have the same effect for women. However, An and Cooney (2006) did not find parenting to be more associated with generativity for men than women but did find that midlife women are more involved in both private and public caring than midlife men. Another research project found that as generativity increases for adults ages 35 to 74, so does psychological well-being, and this association between generativity and well-being is equally strong for childless adults as for parents (Rothrauff & Cooney, 2008). Generativity has been found to increase with educational (Keyes & Ryff, 1998) and income levels (Jones & McAdams, 2013). Consistent with other research that found Black adults to score higher on some measures of generativity than White adults, Jones and McAdams (2013) found that African American late midlife adults reported higher levels of generativity, political and civic engagement, public service motivation, and religious engagement than White late midlife adults.

Jung's and Levinson's Theories of Finding Balance

Both Carl Jung and Daniel Levinson suggest that middle adulthood is a time when individuals attempt to find balance in their lives in several ways. Jung (1971) sees middle adulthood as a time when we discover and reclaim parts of the self that were repressed in the search for conformity in the first half of life. He emphasizes the importance of gender identity in middle adulthood. Adults begin to move from the stereotyped gender role behavior of young adulthood to a more androgynous

behavioral repertoire at this age. There is some evidence to support this idea. One research team found that scales measuring femininity and masculinity were among those that revealed the most change from the ages of 43 to 52 (Helson & Wink, 1992). Women were found by these and other researchers to increase in decisiveness, action orientation, and assertiveness during midlife (Roberts, Helson, & Klohnen, 2002). More recent research found that in late midlife, women's emotional satisfaction was correlated with bodily sexual practices, and men's physical pleasure was associated with relationship factors, a finding that contradicts gender stereotypes (Carpenter, Nathanson, & Kim, 2009). Joan Borysenko (1996), a cellular biologist, provides evidence for a gender crossover in personality in midlife that she attributes to changes in levels of sex hormones. Bjorklund (2011) suggest that it is more accurate to talk about "expansion of gender roles" rather than "gender role crossover."

Jung also suggested that **extroversion**, or orientation to the external world, and **introversion**, or orientation to the internal world, come into greater balance in middle adulthood. He suggested that the challenges of establishing family and work roles demand extroversion in young adulthood, but in middle adulthood individuals tend to turn inward and explore their own subjective experience. We will see later, in the discussion of the Big Five personality traits, that research supports this idea. Viktor Spiro began to show a more reflective side in therapy. Lisa Balinski seems to have been tuned in to her own subjective experience when she turned down the vice principal position. Michael Bowling is finding his meditation practice to be a source of greater personal awareness.

Daniel Levinson (Levinson, 1986, 1990; Levinson & Levinson, 1996; Levinson, Darrow, Klein, Levinson, & McKee, 1978) conceptualized the life course as a sequence of eras, each with its own biopsychosocial character (Levinson & Levinson, 1996) with major changes from one era to the next. Changes do occur within eras, but these changes are small and do not involve major revision of the life structure. Adult life is composed of alternating periods of relative stability and periods of transition. As mentioned in Chapter 7, a key concept of Levinson's theory is *life structure*, by which he means "the underlying pattern or design of a person's life at a given time" (Levinson & Levinson, 1996, p. 22). In most cases, family and occupation are the central components in the life structure, but people vary widely in how much weight they assign to each. During the transition to middle adulthood, individuals often try to give greater attention to previously neglected components. Levinson sees this transition in terms of balancing four opposing aspects of identity: young versus old, creation versus destruction, feminine versus masculine, and attachment versus separation (Levinson, 1977). Recent research has focused on how midlife adults attempt to balance the multiple roles of paid worker, parent, spouse, and caregiver of older adults (see Evandrou, Glaser, & Henz, 2002; Frisvold, Lindquist, & McAlpine, 2012; Gareis, Barnett, Ertel, & Berkman, 2009).

Life Span Theory and the Gain-Loss Balance

Life span theory has much in common with the life course perspective introduced in Chapter 1 of this book. It is more firmly rooted in psychology, however, whereas the life course perspective has more multidisciplinary roots and emphasizes the historical and cultural context of life course development. Life span theory is based in ongoing transactions between persons and environments and begins with the premise that development is lifelong. Six central propositions of the lifespan theory as they relate to middle adulthood are summarized in Exhibit 8.3.

We focus here particularly on the proposition that in midlife there is a tie in the balance of gains and losses (Staudinger & Bluck, 2001). Life span researchers have raised this question: What is the balance of gains and losses in midlife (Baltes, Lindenberger, & Staudinger, 1998)? For example, there is good evidence of gains in self-esteem and emotional maturity and of losses in biological functioning. Some researchers are finding that the balance shifts from a dominance of developmental gains in early midlife to a dominance of developmental losses in late midlife (e.g., Heckhausen, 2001; Staudinger & Bluck, 2001). It is important to note, however, that gains or losses are defined and given meaning in cultural contexts and are influenced by both group-based and individual-based

Exhibit 8.3   Central Propositions of Life Span Theory as They Relate to Middle Adulthood

- Human development is lifelong, and no age period is supreme in the developmental trajectory. Midlife cannot be studied in isolation; it must be studied in terms of both its antecedents and its consequences.
- Development involves both gains and losses. In midlife, there is a tie in the relationship between gains and losses.
- Biological influences on development become more negative, and cultural support becomes more important, with increasing age in adulthood. A distinction can be made between early and late midlife.
- With increasing age in adulthood, there is an overall reduction in resources. At midlife, adults must put a major effort into managing resources.
- Even though challenges increase and biological resources decrease in midlife, there is still possibility for change.
- The experience of midlife adults may depend on cultural and historical contexts.

SOURCE: Adapted from Staudinger & Bluck, 2001, pp. 17–18

attributes. For example, there is evidence that in Samoa, middle adulthood is associated with political power and physical activity, and "aging as a loss of youth is not given any importance" (p. 327) in the story told about midlife (Dittmann-Kohli, 2005). Partricia Cohen (2012) suggests that a singular focus on the physiological aspects of midlife, rather than a more multidimensional approach to this life stage, leads to a conclusion of greater loss than gain. One might wonder how Viktor Spiro, Lisa Balinski, and Michael Bowling see the gain-loss balance in their phase of middle adulthood.

With professional help, Viktor Spiro seems to be making some gains in emotion regulation, economic security, relationships, and comfort in his adopted country but has faced the loss of his father and increasingly concerns about his mother. For Lisa Balinski, midlife so far has been a time of professional competence, economic security, and deepening relationship with her husband but also a time of the loss of her father and incapacitation of her mother. For Michael Bowling, the early years of middle adulthood were marked by occupational and economic gain and the satisfaction of mentoring his niece and nephew, but his late midlife has been marred by a global economic crisis and personal health crisis. His balance of gain and loss, no doubt, would look very different in late midlife if he had not experienced these two crises. And his situation is an excellent illustration of the important role of historical events in life course trajectories.

As we review the research on changes in middle adulthood in the remaining sections of this chapter, it is important to note that it is hard to know whether what we are learning about midlife is tied to a specific cohort, the baby boomers. Research on middle adulthood is quite new, and there are no long-term longitudinal studies available of earlier cohorts of midlife adults. Among the factors to keep in mind as you read research results is that the baby boomers (born from 1946 to 1964) represent a very large cohort and have, throughout their adulthood, faced more competition for jobs and other resources than earlier cohorts.

Critical Thinking Questions 8.1

What do you think is the balance of gains and losses in Viktor Spiro's early phase of middle adulthood compared with his experience with young adulthood? What are the gains and what are the losses? What about Lisa Balinski; what was the balance of gains and losses for her in the early phase of middle adulthood compared with young adulthood? What were the gains and what were the losses? What do you see as the potential gains and losses as she enters the later phase of middle adulthood? And what about Michael Bowling in the late phase of middle adulthood; what is the balance of gains and losses for him in this phase of life compared with earlier phases? What are the gains and what are the losses?

BIOLOGICAL CHANGES AND PHYSICAL AND MENTAL HEALTH IN MIDDLE ADULTHOOD

There have been dramatic changes in the last few decades in the numbers of adults who enjoy healthy and active lives in the years from 45 to 65 and beyond. However, some physical and mental decline does begin to occur. Most biological systems reach their peak performance in the mid-20s. Age-related changes over the next 20 to 30 years are usually gradual, accumulating at different rates in different body systems. The changes are the result of interactions of biology with psychological, sociocultural, and spiritual factors, and individuals play a very active role in the aging process throughout adulthood, as we can see in the life trajectories of Viktor Spiro, Lisa Balinski, and Michael Bowling. However, by the age of 50, the accumulation of biological change becomes physically noticeable in most people. Amy Lodge and Debra Umberson (2013) suggest that because Western culture worships youthful bodies,

What factors have led to changes in biological age in middle adulthood?

we have developed an "ideology of midlife decline" (p. 225). In the chapter on adolescence, we emphasized the importance of psychological reactions to biological changes, and recent research indicates that late midlife is another period of the life course when this issue becomes important (see Lodge & Umberson, 2012; Perz & Ussher, 2008).

The biggest stories in biological functioning and physical and mental health in middle adulthood are changes in physical appearance; changes in mobility; changes in the reproductive system; and changes in health, more specifically the beginnings of chronic disease. Enormous individual differences exist in the timing and intensity of these changes, but some changes affect almost everyone, such as presbyopia for both men and women and menopause for women.

Changes in Physical Appearance

Probably the most visible signs of physiological changes in middle adulthood are changes in physical appearance (Bjorklund, 2011). The skin begins to sag and wrinkle as it loses its firmness and elasticity. Small, localized areas of brown pigmentation, often called aging spots, may appear in parts of the body exposed to sunlight. As the sebaceous glands that secrete oils become less active, the skin becomes drier. Hair on the head often becomes thinner and grayer, and hair may appear in places where it is not wanted, such as ears, thicker clumps around the eyebrows, and the chin on women. Many midlife adults wear glasses for the first time because of the decreased ability to focus on near objects (presbyopia) that occurs in most adults from ages 45 to 55.

There are significant changes in body build as midlife adults begin to lose height and gain weight. Beginning in their 40s, people lose about one half inch in height per decade as a result of loss of bone material in the vertebrae. Starting about age 20, there is a tendency to gain weight until about the mid-50s. Body fat begins to accumulate in the torso and accounts for a greater percentage of weight in middle adulthood than in adolescence and early adulthood. In the late 50s, people tend to begin to lose weight, but this weight loss comes from loss of lean body mass (bone and muscle) rather than from loss of fat.

Changes in skin can be minimized by using sunscreen, skin emollients, applications of vitamin E, and facial massages, and by smoking cessation. Patricia Cohen (2012) argues that although there are many psychological and spiritual gains in middle adulthood, in our current cultural focus on the physiological aspects of middle adulthood "a successful midlife has become equated with an imitation of youth" (p. 13). Increasingly, affluent baby boomers are using procedures such as plastic surgery and Botox to maintain a youthful appearance. Changes in body build can be minimized by involvement in aerobic exercise and resistance training to improve muscle tone, reduce fat, and offset bone loss. The American Heart Association (2013) recommends at least 30 minutes of moderate-intensity aerobic activity at least 5 days per week *or* at least 25 minutes of vigorous aerobic activity at least 3 days per week *and* moderate- to high-intensity muscle-strengthening activity at least 2 or more days per week.

Changes in Mobility

Beginning in the 40s, losses in muscles, bones, and joints start to have an impact on mobility. Some muscle loss begins in our 30s and 40s, and by about age 50, muscle mass loss averages about 1% to 2% per year. By age 60, muscle strength begins to decline at an average rate of 3% per year (Giancoli, 2012). Eating a protein-rich diet and engaging in strength training can minimize the loss of muscle mass in midlife.

A longitudinal population-based assessment of bone loss over the adult period found that loss begins at different times in different types of bones. Loss in trabecular (spongy) bones begins in young adulthood for both women and men. Loss in cortical (solid) bones begins in midlife for women but mainly after age 75 in men (Riggs et al., 2008). The rate of cortical bone loss accelerates for women in their 50s, associated with loss of estrogen after menopause. Microcracks begin to develop in the bones in response to stress, and bones also begin to lose their elasticity. By the end of middle adulthood, bones are less strong and more brittle. Bone loss tends to be greater in people with fair skin, and Black women have higher bone mineral than White women or Hispanic women. Bone loss is accelerated by smoking, alcohol use, and poor diet. It is slowed by aerobic activity, resistance training, increased calcium intake in young adulthood, and use of vitamin D (Bjorklund, 2011).

Changes in the joints begin to occur before skeletal maturity, but without injury, no obvious symptoms appear until the 40s. The joints become stiffer and less flexible, and fluid in the joints begins to decrease, causing the cartilage to rub together and erode. Minerals may deposit in and around the joints (Dugdale, 2012a). Unlike muscles, joints do not benefit from constant use. To prevent unnecessary wear and tear on joints, it is important to wear the proper footwear when engaging in exercise activities and to avoid repetitive movements of the wrists. Flexibility exercises help to expand the range of motion for stiff joints. Exercises to strengthen the muscles that support joints also help to minimize the mobility problems associated with changes in joints.

Changes in the Reproductive System and Sexuality

Perhaps the most often noted biological change in middle adulthood is the lost or diminished reproductive capacity. Although both men and women experience reproductive changes during adulthood, changes in women have received much more attention from researchers and the popular media than changes in men. For this reason, the following discussion begins with what is known about women's reproductive changes during middle adulthood.

In middle adulthood, women's capacity to conceive and bear children gradually declines until menopause, when the capacity for conceiving children ends (although reproductive technology to extend a woman's reproductive life may eventually become more generally available). **Menopause** is the permanent cessation of menstruation and for research purposes is usually defined as 12 consecutive months with absence of menstruation (Magon, Chauhan, Malik, & Shah, 2012). The average age of women having their last period is 51 years, but it can occur in the 40s or late 50s.

Although female menopause is often described as a less gradual process than occurs in men, it is a more gradual process than often recognized. The menopause process begins when the woman is in her 30s and begins to have occasional menstrual cycles without ovulation, or the production of eggs. By the mid- to late 40s, the supply of egg cells is depleted, ovarian production of hormones slows, and more and more menstrual cycles occur without ovulation. The menstrual cycle becomes irregular, some menstrual periods are skipped, and the production of estrogen drops. In this period, known as *perimenopause*, changes in the reproductive system begin to be noticed. **Perimenopause** is defined as the period of time that begins immediately prior to menopause, when there are biological and clinical indicators that reproductive capacity is reaching exhaustion, and continues through the first year after the last menstrual period (National Institute on Aging, 2013). Symptoms that are often proposed to be associated with perimenopause include hot flashes, night sweats, vaginal dryness, headaches, insomnia, fatigue, anxiety, depression, irritability, memory loss, difficulty concentrating, and weight gain.

Although perimenopause, and purported associated symptoms and discomforts, has received much attention in the popular media in recent years, intensive scientific study of the phenomenon is just beginning. This increased interest seems to come from a confluence of factors. Chief among those factors is that the current baby boom generation of women, who are now in midlife, have, as a cohort, asserted their control over their reproductive lives and challenged taboos about sexuality. Two other influential factors include epidemiological studies that identified estrogen decline in menopause as a risk factor for osteoporosis and cardiovascular disease and the development of medications for the "treatment" of menopause. To date, however, research on the connection between menopause and many of the symptoms believed to be a consequence is far from conclusive.

Decreased estrogen results in genital atrophy, including a decrease in uterus size. The blood supply to the vagina and surrounding nerves and glands is reduced. The tissues become thinner and drier and cannot produce sufficient lubrication for comfortable intercourse. There is also increased risk of infection unless estrogen replacement or an artificial lubricant is used. The breast nipples have reduced sensitivity (Magon et al., 2012).

Menopause is big business in the United States, but perhaps not as big as it once was. Starting in the 1940s, menopause was constructed as a deficiency disease, a disease that could be treated pharmaceutically with hormone replacement therapy (HRT). The purpose of the treatment was not to prolong reproductive capacity but rather to treat the symptoms thought to be associated with menopause. The popularity of HRT has waxed and waned since the 1970s as new research, often with contradictory findings, has indicated both benefits and risks associated with its use. At the time this chapter is being written, the current state of evidence suggests that a combination of estrogen and progestin therapy has beneficial effects on osteoporosis and on such menopausal symptoms as hot flashes, vaginal dryness, sleep disturbance, and depression and anxiety. Unfortunately, the research also indicates that HRT increases the risk for breast cancer and cardiovascular diseases. The National Institute on Aging (2013) captures the decision midlife women must make about HRT: "It's hard to know what to do" (para. 20). The concerns about the risks of HRT, now commonly known as menopausal hormone therapy, have led to recent efforts to find alternative, plant-derived treatments for menopausal symptoms that will not carry the risks of HRT; this research is in the early stages (Wuttke et al., 2014).

Unlike women, men do not experience a major rapid change in fertility as they age. Changes in the male reproductive system occur mostly in the testes,

What effect do these sex differences in changes in the reproductive system have on middle adulthood?

with testicular tissue decreasing. There is some disagreement about how much decline occurs in the hormone testosterone in aging men, but there is agreement that the decline is gradual, no greater than 1% per year (Mayo Clinic Staff, 2011). Problems with erectile function may develop. The tubes that carry sperm may harden and become less elastic. The quantity of viable sperm begins to decrease in the late 40s and 50s, but fairly old men have been known to father children (Dugdale, 2012b). Research has begun to show, however, that advanced paternal age may be associated with pregnancy complications and miscarriage (Strøm-Roum, Haavaldsen, Tanbo, & Eskild, 2013). Although little research has been done on the topic, there has been some speculation that, in some men, the decline in testosterone is associated with low energy, decreased sexual desire and performance, muscle and bone loss, sleep disturbance, hot flashes, decreased cognitive function, and depression (Mayo Clinic Staff, 2011). This condition is called male menopause, climacteric, or *andropause*.

Just as hormone replacement for women became a lucrative business for pharmaceutical companies in the last decades of the 20th century, testosterone replacement was an expanding business for them in the first decade of the 21st century. David Handelsman (2013) found a "large and progressive increase in testosterone prescribing across a wide range of countries" from 2000 to 2011 (p. 549). By far the largest increases occurred in Canada, whose Internet pharmacies are beyond the reach of national controls in other countries. You probably have noticed that a number of the suggested symptoms of testosterone deficiency are very similar to the symptoms often proposed for female menopause. The evidence for the association between these symptoms and testosterone deficiency is even sparser than the evidence for symptoms of female menopause, however. Given the still unfolding history of the benefits and risks of HRT for women, it seems wise to proceed with caution with testosterone therapy. The very limited research suggests that testosterone may increase the risk of prostate cancer and cardiovascular disease (Handelsman, 2013; Mayo Clinic Staff, 2011).

Researchers have begun to take interest in the sexual lives of midlife and older adults, but, to date, that research has focused on heterosexual couples. Much less is known about the sexual lives of midlife gay males and lesbians. Lindau and Gavrilova (2010) suggest that this recent interest in mid- and late life sexuality is driven by the availability of drugs to treat male erectile dysfunction. The research to date indicates that age is a major predictor of diminished sexual desire, decreased sexual frequency, and decreased intensity of the sexual response, particularly after age 45 (see Goberna, Francés, Paulí, Barluenga, & Gascón, 2009; Karraker, DeLamater, & Schwartz, 2011; Lodge & Umberson, 2012). Men and women with partners in midlife have been found to be equally likely to be sexually active, but the frequency of sexual activity declines for women more than men over middle and late adulthood (Lindau & Gavrilova, 2010). Researchers have found, however, that the increasing proportion of women who are widowed is the major explanation for this sex difference in the research findings (Karraker et al., 2011). One research team found that many midlife couples are distressed when they experience physical changes that affect their sex lives (Lodge & Umberson, 2012). One consistent finding is that vaginal dryness often causes painful intercourse for women, and this is a factor in the declining sexual frequency. Research also indicates that both men and women report men's physical health problems as the most common reason for sexual inactivity (Lindau & Gavrilova, 2010).

Changes in Health Status

As we can see in the stories of Viktor Spiro, Lisa Balinski, and Michael Bowling, health during middle adulthood is highly variable. In general, there are some positive changes: The frequency of accidents declines, as does susceptibility to colds and allergies. Conversely, although many people live through middle adulthood with little disease or disability,

What might be some reasons for these race and gender differences in health in middle adulthood?

the frequency of chronic illness, persistent symptoms, and functional disability begins to rise in midlife. And the death rate increases continuously over the adult years, as demonstrated by death rates in the United States reported in Exhibit 8.4. You will also note significant gender and race/ethnicity differences in the death rates in middle adulthood, with men having higher death rates than women in Black, Asian or Pacific Islander, and White populations, and Blacks of both genders having alarmingly higher death rates than their White and Asian counterparts. The exhibit also shows that Asians and Pacific Islanders have much lower death rates across middle adulthood than Whites. (Given their rising percentage of the U.S. population, it would be good to include death rates for Hispanic Americans in Exhibit 8.4, but this group was not included in the database used to construct the exhibit.)

In the past century, there has been a change in the types of diseases that are likely to affect health across the life course in affluent countries. In the early 1900s, when life expectancy was in the mid-40s, most deaths were caused by infectious diseases, such as pneumonia, tuberculosis, and influenza (Sapolsky, 2004). With the increase in life expectancy, chronic disease plays a more important role in the great stretch of middle adulthood and beyond. People are now living long enough to experience a chronic illness: "We are now living well enough and long enough to slowly fall apart. . . . [T]he diseases that plague us now are ones of slow accumulation of damage—heart disease, cancer, cerebrovascular disorders" (Sapolsky, 2004, p. 3).

The prevalence of chronic conditions increases with each decade from middle adulthood on. (Note: *Prevalence* measures the proportion of a population that has a disease at a point in time. *Incidence* measures the number of new cases of a disease or condition over a period of time, such as 1 year.) There is an increase in potentially fatal chronic conditions as well as nonfatal chronic conditions. The important role of chronic illness as cause of death is demonstrated in Exhibit 8.5, which reports the five leading causes of death for selected age groups in the United States. Except for accident, suicide, and homicide, all the leading

Age Group	Both Sexes All Origins	Male				Female			
		All Origins	Black	Asian or Pacific Islander	White	All Origins	Black	Asian or Pacific Islander	White
35–39 years	138.8	175.4	263.0	67.2	169.5	102.6	160.5	38.1	97.3
40–44 years	201.1	248.4	351.2	101.8	241.8	154.3	237.7	61.1	146.9
45–49 years	324.0	401.1	549.8	164.8	392.5	248.9	377.8	104.0	236.7
50–54 years	491.7	613.5	893.0	268.6	592.7	374.5	589.3	154.0	353.5
55–59 years	711.7	911.2	1,425.7	427.8	869.4	524.5	833.0	234.2	496.1
60–64 years	1,015.8	1,269.2	1,977.9	632.2	1,222.1	781.7	1,151.8	378.1	756.2
65–69 years	1,527.6	1,871.3	2,745.1	982.5	1,825.2	1,222.0	1,691.9	584.3	1,197.3

SOURCE: Based on National Center on Health Statistics, 2012

causes of death are chronic diseases: heart disease, cancer, chronic liver disease and cirrhosis, chronic obstructive pulmonary disease (COPD; includes chronic bronchitis and emphysema), cerebrovascular disease, and diabetes. With advancing age, chronic conditions replace accidents, suicide, and homicide as primary causes of death.

As you can see from Exhibit 8.5, accidents are a leading cause of death in the 40-to-44 age group. Lisa Balinski's husband, Adam, was lucky to recover from the serious injuries he sustained in an automobile accident at age 40. The period of his recovery and rehabilitation were a very stressful time for the family. If Adam had not had good health insurance, the costs of his rehabilitation program could have been a financial ruin for the family, and their life trajectories over the next decade might have been very different from what we read about.

Michael Bowling faced a health crisis in the midst of a global economic crisis, and it is possible that the stress of the economic crisis contributed to his health crisis. He was fortunate to know as much as he knew about stroke and to get immediate care.

Unlike his father who died from a stroke, Michael has made a good recovery with minimal residual disability. His treatment and rehabilitation have been costly, however, and have interfered with his ability to regain his career footing.

It is important to note that there are some global differences in causes of death. The World Health Organization (WHO, 2012d) reports on the leading causes of death in low-income, lower-middle-income, upper-middle-income, and high-income countries. In high-income and lower-middle-income countries, heart disease is the number one cause of death, and cerebrovascular disease (stroke) is the number two cause of death. In upper-middle-income countries, the situation is reversed, with stroke the number one cause and heart disease the number two cause. In low-income countries, however, lower respiratory infection (pneumonia) is the number one cause and HIV/AIDS is the number two cause. These data indicate that chronic illness is the major cause of death in high-income and middle-income countries, but infectious diseases continue to be a major challenge in less affluent nations.

Exhibit 8.5 Five Leading Causes of Death and Percentage of Total Deaths in Selected Age Groups in the United States, 2010

20–24 years	Accidents (41.8%) Suicide (15.8%) Homicide (15.2%) Cancer (5.4%) Heart disease (3.7%)	45–49 years	Cancer (23.9%) Heart disease (19.2%) Accidents (13.5%) Suicide (5.9%) Chronic liver disease and cirrhosis (4.9%)
25–29 years	Accidents (37.5%) Suicide (14.8%) Homicide (11.9%) Cancer (7.0%) Heart disease (1.2%)	50–54 years	Cancer (29.8%) Heart disease (20.6%) Accidents (8.9%) Chronic liver disease and cirrhosis (4.6%) Suicide (4.0%)
30–34 years	Accidents (31.7%) Suicide (12.4%) Cancer (10.0%) Heart disease (9.3%) Homicide (8.4%)	55–59 years	Cancer (33.5%) Heart disease (21.6%) Accidents (5.7%) Chronic liver disease and cirrhosis (3.8%) COPD (3.8%)
35–39 years	Accidents (24.8%) Cancer (14.2%) Heart disease (13.0%) Suicide (11.0%) Homicide (4.8%)	60–64 years	Cancer (36.6%) Heart disease (22.1%) COPD (5.2%) Diabetes mellitus (3.9%) Cerebrovascular diseases (3.6%)
40–44 years	Accidents (18.7%) Cancer (18.7%) Heart disease (16.6%) Suicide (8.3%) Chronic liver disease and cirrhosis (3.9%)	65–69 years	Cancer (37.1%) Heart disease (21.7%) COPD (7.2%) Cerebrovascular diseases (4.0%) Diabetes mellitus (3.7%)

SOURCE: Based on National Center on Health Statistics, 2012

COPD: chronic obstructive pulmonary disease (includes chronic bronchitis and emphysema)

The most common forms of cebrebrovascular disease are cerebral thrombosis, cerebral embolism, and cerebral hemorrhage.

Death is not the only outcome of chronic illness. As Sapolsky (2004) suggests, chronic disease often has a slow course and involves some level of disability over a number of years. The WHO uses the concept of disability adjusted life year (DALY) to measure the sum of the years lost because of premature death *plus* the number of years spent in states of poor health or disability. There is much international evidence that socioeconomic position is a powerful predictor of both mortality and poor health (morbidity). The WHO has calculated the worldwide causes of DALYs for low-income countries, lower-middle-income countries, upper-middle-income countries, and high-income countries. The leading worldwide causes are presented in Exhibit 8.6, which also shows how these causes are distributed across countries of different income levels. It is important to note that the WHO data include mental and behavioral health as well as physical health conditions, whereas health statistics in the United States do not. Therefore, the WHO data are useful because they give a better picture of the impact of mental and behavioral health conditions on global health.

Viktor Spiro's story demonstrates the important impact that mental health conditions can have on life trajectories, and Lisa Balinski is concerned about whether mental health issues will jeopardize the quality of her mother's late adulthood. It is important to note, however, that the data in Exhibit 8.6 are for all age groups and not just for middle adulthood. There is evidence that baby boomers in the United States and Europe have higher rates of depression and substance abuse than previous generations (Piazza & Charles, 2006). A longitudinal study in the Netherlands found that mental health tends to improve across the life course, but a minority of midlife adults shows persistently high levels of depressive symptoms and loneliness across the middle adult years (Deeg, 2005). These researchers, like many other researchers of middle adulthood, emphasize that reporting average results can mask the great variability in middle adult trajectories. Researchers have found that "midlife is a particularly high-risk period for either delayed onset or reactivated PTSD" (Solomon & Mikulincer, 2006,

p. 664). A recent longitudinal investigation of PTSD symptoms among combat veterans found that the symptoms decreased by the 3rd year following combat trauma but had been reactivated in many veterans in the 20-year follow-up (Solomon & Mikulincer, 2006). It is important for social workers to recognize the possibility of delayed and reactivated PTSD in their midlife clients. This will be particularly important in the years ahead as veterans of the Iraq and Afghanistan wars become clients in every social service sector.

Viktor Spiro struggled with depression and substance abuse before he immigrated to the United States, and, as happens with many immigrants, the multiple losses and demands associated with the immigration experience exacerbated his mental health problems. As Karen Aroian and Anne E. Norris (2003) note, "Depression significantly impairs immigrants' ability to adapt to the new country and has serious emotional and economic consequences for immigrants and their families" (p. 420). Aroian and Norris found high levels of depression in a sample of immigrants from the former Soviet Union; they also found that the severity and longevity of depressive symptoms were correlated with the level of immigration-related stressors. They concluded that mental health interventions with depressed immigrants should focus on relieving these stressors by focusing on such practical issues as learning English and obtaining employment as well as on emotional issues such as loss, trauma, and feeling at home in the new country. Viktor was lucky to find mental health professionals who did just this, assisting him to get debt forgiveness and attain citizenship while also working on issues of emotion regulation and expanding his social network.

Before we leave this discussion about changes in health in midlife, it is important to go back to the partial story told in Exhibit 8.4 about racial health disparities in middle adulthood. Life course scholars have theorized that inequalities in midlife health status are a result of developmental opportunities and vulnerabilities at each stage of the life course (Johnson, Schoeni, & Rogowski, 2012). They suggest two primary pathways for the effect of

Exhibit 8.6 Leading Causes of Disease Burden (DALYs) Worldwide and for Low-Income Countries, Lower-Middle-Income Countries, Upper-Middle-Income Countries, and High-Income Countries, 2011

Cause	World (%)	Low-Income Countries (% Total)	Lower-Middle-Income Countries (% Total)	Upper-Middle-Income Countries (% Total)	High-Income Countries (% Total)
Infectious and parasitic diseases	16.5	30.9	19.3	7.5	2.3
Cardiovascular disease	13.8	5.7	11.6	21.2	18.4
Injuries	10.8	9.1	10.7	12.6	10.0
Cancers	8.1	3.3	4.7	12.8	18.3
Neonatal conditions	8.4	12.9	11.3	3.8	1.1
Mental and behavioral disorders	7.2	4.2	5.8	9.6	12.1
Respiratory infections	6.3	10.0	7.8	2.0	1.8
Respiratory disease (COPD)	4.9	3.1	5.4	5.1	5.7
Musculoskeletal disease	4.0	1.9	2.7	5.4	8.6

SOURCE: Based on World Health Organization, 2012e

earlier life experiences on midlife health: (1) early adverse circumstances may fundamentally alter the body's basic physiology, with health consequences showing up at a later date; and (2) social disadvantage at one stage leads to social disadvantage at a later stage, resulting in a cumulative physiological toll. Life course researchers have been investigating the developmental factors that contribute to racial health disparities across adulthood and have found that disparities in health between Blacks and Whites exist at all life stages and grow across the adult life course. One research team found that, on average, Black adults reach a particular level of health deterioration about 30 years earlier than their White counterparts (Johnson et al., 2012). They further found that three quarters of the racial differences in health over the age of 55 are explained by childhood socioeconomic conditions and young adult family and neighborhood factors. Living in a neighborhood of concentrated poverty prior to middle adulthood significantly increases the likelihood of midlife health problems, whether or not the individual comes from an impoverished family. These kinds of research findings have great implications for social policy, not only because of equity issues but also because poor health of its population carries enormous economic costs for a society.

INTELLECTUAL CHANGES IN MIDDLE ADULTHOOD

Perhaps no domain of human behavior in middle adulthood arouses more concern about the balance of gains and losses than intellectual functioning. A trip to your local pharmacy will confront you with the variety of supplements and herbal remedies that are marketed to midlife adults with promises of maintaining mental alertness and mental acuity. And yet middle-aged adults are often at the peak of their careers and filling leadership roles. Most of the recent presidents of the United States were men older than 50. Most multinational corporations are run by midlife adults.

Research on cognitive changes in middle adulthood is recent, but there is growing and clear evidence that cognitive performance remains relatively stable for the majority of midlife adults (Martin & Zimprich, 2005; Willis & Schaie, 2005). However, a significant subset of midlife adults shows important gains in cognitive functioning, and another significant subset shows important decline (Willis & Schaie, 2005). The amount of gain and decline varies across different types of cognitive functioning. For example, one study found that depending on the specific cognitive skill, the proportion of midlife adults who were stable in performance ranged from 53% to 69%, the proportion who gained ranged from 6% to 16%, and the proportion who declined ranged from 15% to 31% (Willis & Schaie, 2005).

Researchers are finding that individual differences in intellectual performance increase throughout middle adulthood (Martin & Zimprich, 2005).

These increasing variations are related to both biological factors and environmental factors. Several biological risk factors have been identified for cognitive decline in midlife—including hypertension, diabetes, high cholesterol, and the APOE gene (a gene that has been associated with one type of Alzheimer's disease). Adverse circumstances early in life, including low socioeconomic position during childhood, have also been found to be a risk for midlife cognitive decline (Osler, Avlund, & Mortensen, 2012). Several protective factors have also been identified, including education; work or other environments that demand complex cognitive work; control beliefs; social support; cognitive exercise, including computer use; and physical exercise (Agrigoroaei & Lachman, 2011; Lachman, Agrigoroaei, Murphy, & Tun, 2010; Tun & Lachman, 2010; Willis & Schaie, 2005). These findings are consistent with the increasing evidence of brain plasticity throughout the life course and suggest that cognitive decline can be slowed by engaging in activities that train the brain. The news on this front keeps getting better. Lachman and colleagues (2010) have found that frequent cognitive activity, such as writing, reading, attending lectures, or playing word games, can compensate for lower education.

The Seattle Longitudinal Study (SLS) studied intellectual changes from the early 20s to very old age by following the same individuals over time as well as drawing new samples at each test cycle. Willis and Schaie (2006) summarized the findings about changes for selected mental abilities across the life course, paying attention to gender differences. By incorporating data on new participants as the survey progressed, they were also able to study generational (cohort) differences, addressing the question of whether the current baby boom midlife cohort is functioning at a higher intellectual level than their parents' generation.

Willis and Schaie (2005, 2006) summarize the findings for six mental abilities:

1. *Vocabulary*: ability to understand ideas expressed in words

2. *Verbal memory*: ability to encode and recall language units, such as word lists

3. *Number*: ability to perform simple mathematical computations quickly and accurately

4. *Spatial orientation*: ability to visualize stimuli in two- and three-dimensional space

5. *Inductive reasoning*: ability to recognize and understand patterns in and relationships among variables to analyze and solve logical problems

6. *Perceptual speed*: ability to quickly make discriminations in visual stimuli

The research showed that middle adulthood is the period of peak performance of four of the six mental abilities: inductive reasoning, spatial orientation, vocabulary, and verbal memory. Two of the six mental abilities, perceptual speed and numerical ability, showed decline in middle adulthood, but the decline in perceptual speed was much more dramatic than the decline in numerical ability. The question is how much the culture values speed. In the United States, speed is highly valued, and quick thinking is typically seen as an indication of high intelligence. In many non-Western countries, perceptual speed is not so highly valued (Gardiner & Kosmitzki, 2011). Willis and Schaie (2005) note that the mental abilities that improve in middle adulthood—inductive reasoning, spatial orientation, vocabulary, and verbal memory—are among the more complex, higher-order mental abilities.

Willis and Schaie (2005, 2006) found gender differences in the changes in mental abilities during middle adulthood. On average, men were found to reach peak performance somewhat earlier than women. Men reach peak performance on spatial orientation, vocabulary, and verbal memory in their 50s, and women reach peak performance on these same mental abilities in their early 60s. Conversely, on average, women begin to decline in perceptual speed somewhat earlier than men, in their 20s compared with the 30s for men. The improvement in mental abilities in middle adulthood is more dramatic for women than for men. Across the adult life course, women score higher than men on vocabulary, verbal memory, perceptual speed, and inductive reasoning. Men,

conversely, score higher than women across the adult life course on spatial orientation. Some evidence indicates that cognitive decline in middle adulthood is predictive of cognitive impairment in late adulthood (Willis & Schaie, 2005).

Willis and Schaie (2006) also report on cohort differences in the selected mental abilities. They found that the baby boom cohort scored higher on two of the abilities, verbal memory and inductive reasoning, than their parents' generation did at the same chronological age. The baby boomers also scored higher than their parents did on spatial orientation, but these differences were smaller than those for verbal memory and inductive reasoning. There were virtually no cohort differences on vocabulary and perceptual speed. The boomers did not score as well as their parents' generation on numerical ability, and the authors note that this is a continuation of a negative trend in numerical ability since the early 1900s found in other studies.

> What factors might be producing this historical trend toward declines in numerical ability?

Recent longitudinal research in Germany explored cognitive change during middle adulthood but used a different classification of dimensions of cognition than used in the SLS. Zimprich and Mascherek (2010) studied four dimensions of cognition: fluid intelligence (the ability to think quickly and think abstractly), crystallized intelligence (the ability to use knowledge from accumulated learning), processing speed, and memory. They found that over a 12-year period in middle adulthood, research participants showed significant declines in fluid intelligence, processing speed, and memory. In contrast, they showed gains in crystallized intelligence.

Currently, intense research efforts are exploring what is happening in the middle-aged brain (see Strauch, 2010, for a summary of the research). It is clear that some brains age better than others, resulting in much variability in middle-aged brains. Researchers are finding evidence of both loss and gain, but, on balance, the news is good. Parts of memory wane, most notably the part that remembers names. But the ability to make accurate judgments about people and situations gets stronger. In summarizing this situation, Barbara Strauch (2010) notes that "this middle-aged brain, which just as it's forgetting what it had for breakfast can still go to work and run a multinational bank or school or city . . . then return home to deal with . . . teenagers, neighbors, parents" (pp. xvi–xvii). Neuroscientists are suggesting that as we reach midlife, our brains begin to reorganize and behave in a different way. Most notably, people in middle age begin to use both sides of their brains to solve problems for which only one side was used in the past, a process called bilateralization. The two hemispheres of the brain become better integrated. Research also indicates that starting in middle age, the brain's ability to tune out irrelevant material wanes, leading to more time in daydream mode but also greater capacity to capture "the big picture." The growing evidence, noted earlier, that there are things we can do to enhance brain functioning in midlife and beyond hold implications for social work practice with midlife and late-life adults.

PERSONALITY CHANGES IN MIDDLE ADULTHOOD

Does it appear to you that Viktor Spiro, Lisa Balinski, and Michael Bowling have grown "more like themselves" over their life course trajectories, or do you see changes in their personalities as they travel the life course? Little attention has been paid to the issue of personality in middle adulthood until quite recently. The literature that does exist on the topic consists largely of an argument about whether personality is stable or dynamic during middle adulthood. Dan McAdams and Bradley Olson (2010) suggest that the theoretical attempts to address that question can be divided into three main categories, which I am calling the trait approach, the human agency approach, and the life narrative approach. The confluence of research based on these different approaches indicates that middle adulthood is a time of both continuity and change.

Trait Approach

According to the **trait approach**, personality traits are enduring characteristics rooted in early temperament and influenced by genetic and organic factors. A large and growing international research literature focuses on the degree to which individuals exhibit five broad personality traits, often referred to as the Big Five personality traits (see, for example, Hampson & Goldberg, 2006; Lucas & Donnellan, 2011; Pulkkinen, Kokko, & Rantanen, 2012):

> How might personality traits be related to developmental risk and protection?

1. *Neuroticism*: tendency to be moody, anxious, hostile, self-conscious, and vulnerable

2. *Extroversion*: tendency to be energetic, outgoing, friendly, lively, talkative, and active

3. *Conscientiousness*: tendency to be organized, reliable, responsible, hardworking, persistent, and careful

4. *Agreeableness*: tendency to be cooperative, generous, cheerful, warm, caring, trusting, and gentle

5. *Openness to experience*: tendency to be curious, imaginative, creative, intelligent, adventurous, and nonconforming

Research on the Big Five personality traits suggests long-term stability in terms of the ranking of the traits for a given individual. For example, a person who is high in agreeableness at one point in adulthood will continue to be high in agreeableness across the life course (Lucas & Donnellan, 2011). However, recent research suggests that there may be some gender differences in the stability of trait ranking, with men showing more consistency than women (Pulkkinen et al., 2012) and some traits (extroversion and conscientiousness) showing more consistency than others (Hampson & Goldberg, 2006). Studies of identical and fraternal twins suggest that adult personality traits have a large genetic base, with about a 50% heritability quotient (McAdams & Olson, 2010). That, of course, leaves a great deal of room for environmental influences, but scholars who favor the idea that personality is stable across adulthood argue that people with particular personality traits choose environments that reinforce those traits.

Another way to look at the question of stability or change in personality traits in adulthood is to look at mean levels of particular traits at different points in the adult life course. A number of both cross-sectional and longitudinal studies have done this and found that mean levels of extroversion (activity and thrill seeking) and openness to experience decline with age starting in middle adulthood. Conversely, the mean level of agreeableness has been found to increase with age, and mean levels of conscientiousness and emotional stability have been found to peak in middle adulthood (see Lucas & Donnellan, 2011). What's more, these patterns of age-related changes in personality have been found in cross-cultural research that included samples from Croatia, Germany, Italy, Portugal, South Korea, and the United States (Gardiner & Kosmitzki, 2011). These findings suggest that some personality change does occur in middle adulthood, but McAdams and Olson (2010) note that studies of mean changes are unable to tell the more complex story of middle adult personality. Some people change more than others and sometimes in ways that are not consistent with overall trends. Social workers should be aware of overall trends but pay close attention to the specific story lines of unique individuals.

It is also important to note that some researchers have found gender differences in personality traits to be greater than age-related differences (Lachman & Bertrand, 2001). Women score higher than men in agreeableness, conscientiousness, extroversion, and neuroticism. Men, conversely, score higher than women on openness to experience. These gender differences in personality have been found in 26 cultures, but the magnitude of differences varied across cultures. The researchers were surprised to find that the biggest gender differences occurred in European and North American cultures, where traditional gender roles are less pronounced than in many other countries (Costa, Terracciano, & McCrae, 2001).

Human Agency Approach

Other personality psychologists, consistent with life course scholars, have recently placed human agency at the center of adult personality development, focusing on how human agency facilitates change in midlife personality (McAdams & Pals, 2006). They are interested in motives, goals, plans, strategies, values, schemas, and choices and see these as important forces in adult personality. They recognize the ways that culture influences motives, goals, and the like (McAdams & Olson, 2010). Researchers in this vein of thought have found that middle-aged adults, on average, focus their goals on the future of their children and on prosocial societal engagement (Freund & Riediger, 2006). You probably recognize that this is the essence of generativity as presented by Erikson (1950). Researchers have also found that while young adults set goals to expand the self and change the environment to fit their goals, midlife adults are more likely to set goals that involve changing the self to adjust to the environment (Wrosch, Heckhausen, & Lachman, 2006).

The concept of human agency is consistent with humanistic models of personality that see middle adulthood as an opportunity for continued growth. It is also consistent with the work of neo-Freudians like Carl Jung, Erik Erikson, and George Vaillant who propose that middle adulthood is a time when the personality ripens and matures. Jung conceptualizes middle adulthood as a time of balance in the personality. Although Erikson sees early life as important, he suggests that societal and cultural influences call for different personal adaptations over the life course. Vaillant (1977, 2002, 2012) suggests that with age and experience, **coping mechanisms,** or the strategies we use to master the demands of life, mature. He divides coping mechanisms into *immature mechanisms* (denial,

> How does human agency contribute to diversity in life course trajectories?

projection, passive aggression, dissociation, acting out, and fantasy) and *mature mechanisms* (sublimation, humor, altruism, and suppression). He proposes that as we age across adulthood, we make more use of mature coping mechanisms such as altruism, sublimation, and humor and less use of immature coping mechanisms such as denial and projection. Definitions for both the immature and mature coping mechanisms are found in Exhibit 8.7. One research team found evidence of personality growth throughout middle adulthood, with slow and steady favorable resolution of earlier life tasks (suggested by Erikson) of industry, identity, and intimacy, suggesting that work on these tasks continues into middle adulthood (Whitbourne, Sneed, & Sayer, 2009). They also found that midlife change in regard to these life tasks was influenced by life history, a finding consistent with the life narrative approach.

Life Narrative Approach

Beginning in the 1980s, personality psychologists began to develop new theories of personality development that conceptualize the developing person as a storyteller who puts together characters, plots, and themes to develop an evolving story of the self, a life narrative (McAdams, 1985, 2006; McLean, Pasupathi, & Pals, 2007). These stories may include high points, low points, turning points, and intersecting plot lines. McAdams and Olson (2010) suggest that in modern societies, people begin to put together their life narratives, which can be thought of as narrative identities, in adolescence or young adulthood. They suggest that in the construction of the life narrative, adults draw on stories from childhood, stories rooted in culture.

In contrast to the trait approach, which has received considerable longitudinal research

Exhibit 8.7   Coping Mechanisms

Immature Coping Mechanisms
Acting out. Ideas and feelings are acted on impulsively rather than reflectively.
Denial. Awareness of painful aspects of reality are avoided by negating sensory information about them.
Dissociation. Painful emotions are handled by compartmentalizing perceptions and memories and detaching from the full impact.
Fantasy. Real human relationships are replaced with imaginary friends.
Passive-aggression. Anger toward others is turned inward against the self through passivity, failure, procrastination, or masochism.
Projection. Unacknowledged feelings are attributed to others.
Mature Coping Mechanisms
Altruism. Pleasure is attained by giving pleasure to others.
Mature humor. An emotion or thought is expressed through comedy, allowing a painful situation to be faced without individual pain or social discomfort.
Sublimation. An unacceptable impulse or unattainable aim is transformed into a more acceptable or attainable aim.
Suppression. Attention to a desire or impulse is postponed.

SOURCE: Vaillant, 1977, 2002, 2012

attention, there has been little longitudinal research to explore the changes in life narratives across adulthood. Cross-sectional research has suggested that midlife adults construct more complex and coherent life narratives than adolescents and young adults (Baddeley & Singer, 2007), with increased tendency to draw summary conclusions about the self from the narrative (McLean et al., 2007). One research team found that the life narratives of midlife adults older than age 50 used more positive and fewer negative emotional words than the life narratives of college students (Singer, Rexhaj, & Baddeley, 2007). McAdams and Olson (2010) note that culture provides the menu of stories from which individuals choose to develop their own life narratives. They further note that identity choices are shaped by the confluence of social locations—gender, race, ethnicity, social class, geographical location, and so on—in which a particular person exists.

Although there is evidence that midlife adults often engage in review and reappraisal, there is much disagreement about whether that review and reappraisal is serious enough to constitute the midlife crisis proposed by some theorists. Most researchers who have studied this issue take a middle ground, suggesting that some midlife adults do reach crisis level in midlife, but in general, the idea of a midlife crisis has been greatly overstated (see, e.g., Sterns & Huyck, 2001). One research team found that turning points are most likely to occur in young adulthood (Wethington, Kessler, & Pixley, 2004), but another research team found that when older adults were asked to identify turning points in their lives, there was some clustering of situations in their middle adulthood (Cappeliez et al., 2008).

Erikson suggested that the life task to be resolved in middle adulthood is generativity versus stagnation. Research on life narratives shows much diversity in midlife narrative identities. For many midlife adults, life narratives are full of themes of agency, relationships, generativity, and personal growth, of forgiveness and overcoming obstacles. For others, depression, depletion, stagnation, and life gone bad are the content of the life narrative

(McAdams & Olson, 2010). One research team examined the effect of major stressful life events on personality development in middle adulthood (Sustin, Costa, Wethington, & Eaton, 2010). They found that sometimes, major stressful events are viewed as lessons learned, and other times they are viewed as negative turning points. The interpretation of the event is what determines the impact on personality traits, if any. When the person sees the stressful event as a point when life changed direction for the worse, neuroticism increases. If, however, the person sees the stressful event as a life lesson, there is an increase in both extroversion and conscientiousness. Positive turning points, on the other hand, are not associated with change in personality traits.

Let's consider the situations of Viktor Spiro, Lisa Balinski, and Michael Bowling. For Viktor Spiro, the tractor accident at age 13 and the death of his brother when he was 20 appear to have been interpreted as negative turning points. (Of course, it is important to remember that the adolescent accident involved a head injury that may have influenced Viktor's storytelling.) These events appear to have contributed to growing neuroticism and deterioration in conscientiousness. It could be argued that his relocation to the United States was a mixed turning point, offering possibilities as well as great stress. It seems clear, however, that Viktor's immediate response was growing neuroticism. With the help of mental health professionals and psychotropic medications, Viktor appears to be developing more positive themes for his life narrative, and he has shown great growth in conscientiousness in recent years. Lisa Balinski talks of Adam's automobile accident as a time of great family stress, but, 10 years later, she speaks about it as a positive turning point in family cohesion and a time of personal growth when she recognized some of her own strengths. Michael Bowling faced a pileup of highly stressful events in his early 50s. We could understand if he interpreted this confluence of stressful events as a negative turning point, but the way he tells his story does not seem to indicate that it has resulted in any major personality change to date. He continues to demonstrate the high level of conscientiousness that has been evident in each stage of his life. It might be helpful to Michael to have an opportunity to talk with a professional mental health worker about what story he is telling himself about this unfortunate turn of events—and perhaps this has happened. A chance to engage in this kind of reflection can help him develop a survivor rather than victim narrative.

SPIRITUAL DEVELOPMENT IN MIDDLE ADULTHOOD

Institutional religion is a source of social belonging for Viktor Spiro. For Michael Bowling, a personal meditation practice has been a source of spiritual growth and emotional regulation. The major world religions associate spiritual growth with advancing age (see McCullough, Enders, Brion, & Jain, 2005; Wink & Dillon, 2002). And yet the burgeoning literature on middle adulthood pays little attention to the issue of spiritual development. The primary effort has been models of spiritual development proposing that humans have the potential for continuous spiritual growth across the life course.

For example, James Fowler's theory of faith development (1981) proposes six stages of faith. The first two stages occur primarily in childhood. These are the four stages that can occur in adulthood:

1. *Synthetic-conventional faith.* The basic worldview of this faith stage is that spiritual authority is found outside the individual. In this faith stage, the individual relies on a pastor or rabbi or other spiritual leader to define morality. Many people remain in this faith stage throughout their lives and never progress to the other stages.

2. *Individuative-reflective faith.* The adult no longer relies on outside authority and begins to look for authority within the self, based on moral reasoning. The individual also takes responsibility for examining the assumptions of his or her faith.

Photo 8.1 Religion and spiritual connectedness often play a major role in the lives of midlife adults.

© Lynn Johnson/National Geographic Society/Corbis

3. *Conjunctive faith.* In this stage, the individual looks for balance in such polarities as independence and connection, recognizes that there are many truths, and opens out beyond the self in service to others. Fowler proposes that many people never reach the stage of **conjunctive faith**, and if they do, they almost never reach it before middle adulthood.

4. *Universalizing faith.* In Fowler's final stage, **universalizing faith**, individuals lead selfless lives based on principles of absolute love and justice. Fowler notes that only rare individuals reach this stage.

Fowler's theory has received support in cross-sectional research but has not yet been put to the test in longitudinal research. Therefore, it should be applied with caution, recognizing that it may reflect the influences of culture and historical time on faith development.

Fowler's description of conjunctive faith overlaps with theories of middle adulthood previously discussed in this chapter. For example, the reference to balance calls to mind the theories of Jung and Levinson, who saw middle adulthood as a time of bringing balance to personality and life structure. In addition, the idea of opening oneself in service to others is consistent with Erikson's idea of generativity as the psychosocial struggle of middle adulthood. The emphasis is on spirituality as a state of "being connected." Using data from a national survey of midlife adults in the United States, one researcher has found a strong correlation between regular participation in religious activities and community volunteer service, particularly in terms of making financial contributions to community organizations and charities (Rossi, 2004).

Actually, there are two different models of spiritual development in adulthood (Wink & Dillon, 2002). Fowler's theory can be called a growth model, an approach that sees spiritual growth as a positive outcome of a maturation process. The other model sees increased spirituality across the adult life course as an outcome of adversity (Wink and Dillon call it an adversity model) rather than as a natural maturation process; in this view spirituality becomes a way to cope with losses, disappointments, and difficulties. One rare longitudinal study of spiritual development across the adult life course found evidence for both of these models (Wink & Dillon, 2002). The researchers found a strong tendency for increased spirituality beginning in late middle adulthood, something that occurred among all research participants but was more pronounced among women than men. They also found that experiencing negative life events in early adulthood was associated with higher levels of spirituality in middle and late adulthood. Perhaps Michael Bowling's motivation for a daily meditation practice includes both a drive for spiritual growth and a resource for coping with loss and difficulty.

Although Fowler's conceptualization of faith included both religious faith as well as the more personal, nonreligiously based search for purpose and meaning, commonly referred to as spirituality, most of the research on faith development

across the life course has focused on the concept of religiousness or religiosity. This research suggests that for most people, religiousness is quite stable across the life course, meaning that people who are highly religious relative to their peers at any given point in time are likely to be more highly religious than their peers at any other point in time (McCullough et al., 2005; Roberts & Yamane, 2012). Much of the existing longitudinal research indicates that, on average, adults in the United States become more religious over time, but for most people "religiosity does not proceed in a straight line" (Roberts & Yamane, 2012, p. 97) but is punctuated by temporary increases or reductions related to life events and life transitions (McCullough et al., 2005).

Some research suggests that it may be even more complex than this. Using longitudinal data over a 60-year time span for two cohorts, one born in the early 1920s and the other born in the late 1920s, Dillon and Wink (2007) found a U-curve of religiousness over the life course. Religiousness was high in adolescence and late adulthood but, on average, lower in middle adulthood. Another research team used longitudinal data from the Terman study, begun in 1921, of highly intelligent children and adolescents (McCullough et al., 2005). These researchers found three distinct trajectories of religious development during adulthood. A first group, making up 40% of the sample, entered adulthood as slightly religious but became more religious throughout midlife and declined in religiousness after that. A second group, 41% of the sample, had low levels of religiousness in young adulthood and became less religious over time. A third group, 19% of the sample, entered adulthood with relatively high levels of religiousness that increased throughout adulthood. The researchers note that their sample was less religious than the U.S. general population, and representative samples look more like the third group.

The two longitudinal studies noted in the previous paragraph indicate both cohort and other group-based differences in religiousness in middle adulthood. In the report of their findings, McCullough and colleagues (2005) note that the trend toward increasing religiousness across the life course is more pronounced in Japan than in the United States but does not show up at all in research on adults in the Netherlands. The Dillon and Wink (2007) study found that although both cohorts in their study showed a U-curve pattern in religiousness, the decline in religiousness began in the younger cohort while they were in their 30s, but the decline in the older cohort did not begin until the late 40s. They suggest that the different ages of these two cohorts during the Great Depression and World War II may have been an influential factor in this difference.

Wade Clark Roof has been interested in the question of cohort effects on spiritual journeys. His book *A Generation of Seekers* (1993) reported on the "spiritual journeys of the baby boom generation" in the United States. Drawing on survey data and interview responses, Roof suggested that the baby boom generation was "changing America's spiritual landscape" (p. 50). He reported that most baby boomers grew up in religious households, but 58% of his sample dropped their relationship with religious institutions for at least 2 years during their adolescence or young adulthood. Roof acknowledged that earlier generations had also dropped out of religion during early adulthood, but not in the numbers found in his sample of baby boomers. He suggests that the turmoil of the 1960s and 1970s, with a youth culture that questioned authority, was probably largely responsible for the high rate of dropout among baby boomers. Roof found that about one fourth of his sample that had dropped out had returned to religious activities by the end of the 1980s. For many of them, their return seemed to be related to having children at home. Roof found that religious affiliation and activity did not tell the whole story about the spiritual lives of baby boomers, however. Regardless of religious affiliation, baby boomers were involved in an intense search for personal meaning (Roof, 1993). But for many of Roof's sample, the current spiritual journey was a very personal, introspective quest—one that embraced a wide range of nontraditional as well as traditional beliefs.

In a follow-up study with the same sample from 1995 to 1997, Roof (1999) found that many boomers had shifted in their religious affiliation again. More than half of the earlier dropouts who had returned to religious activities by the late 1980s had dropped out again. But, conversely, one half of those who had dropped out in the 1980s had returned to religious activities by the mid-1990s. Presence of children in the home again seemed to be the factor that motivated a return to religion.

Roof suggested that the baby boomers are leading a shift in U.S. religious life away from an unquestioning belief to a questioning approach and toward a belief that no single religious institution has a monopoly on truth. That shift is certainly not total, however. Roof identifies five types of contemporary believers from his sample: 33% are born-again or evangelical Christians, 25% are old-line mainstream believers, 15% are dogmatists who see one truth in the doctrine and form of their religious tradition, 15% are metaphysical seekers, and 12% are nonreligious secularists. Thus, almost three quarters of his sample could be classified as more or less unquestioning adherents of a particular system of beliefs but with an increasing trend toward recognition of the legitimacy of multiple spiritual paths. It is important to note that religion plays a much more central role in the lives of adults in the United States than it does in European countries (Reid, 2004).

Unfortunately, Roof does not analyze racial and ethnic differences in religious and spiritual expression for his baby boom sample. Others have found evidence, however, that Black and Hispanic midlife adults have higher levels of religiousness than White midlife adults (Fitchett et al., 2007). Black and Hispanic baby boomers have been much more constant in their religious beliefs and participation than White baby boomers and are far more likely to consider religion very important in their lives.

> What does Roof's research suggest about spiritual age in middle adulthood?

RELATIONSHIPS IN MIDDLE ADULTHOOD

Social relationships play a major role in life satisfaction and physical well-being across the life course. In contemporary life, both women and men fulfill multiple social roles in midlife. The most central roles are related to family and paid work. Relationships with family, friends, and co-workers are an important part of life in middle adulthood, and some scholars argue that the current generation of midlife adults are experiencing unprecedented complexity in their configurations of relationships (Blieszner & Roberto, 2006). The life course perspective reminds us that relationships in middle adulthood have been shaped by relationships in earlier life phases, in the attachment process in infancy as well as in family and peer relationships in childhood, adolescence, and young adulthood. Although current relationships are shaped by our experiences with earlier relationships, longitudinal research indicates that it is never too late to develop new relationships that can become turning points in the life course (Vaillant, 2002; Werner & Smith, 2001).

Numerous studies have examined how social networks change over the life course. Researchers have been interested in different types of social networks and have used the term **global network** to indicate all existing social relationships that a person has with such people as family members, spouses and romantic partners, friends, co-workers, neighbors, religious congregations, and so forth. The **personal network** is a subnetwork of the closest relationships. Most of us are involved in other subnetworks, such as friendship networks, family networks, and work-related networks. Researchers have been interested in the changing size of social networks and the changing nature of specific subnetworks (Wrzus, Hänel, Wagner, & Neyer, 2013).

Two main theories have been used to think about how social networks change over the life course: socioemotional selectivity theory and social convoy theory. **Socioemotional selectivity theory** proposes that social goals change over the life course based on shifts in perspectives about how much time one has left to live, and changes in social goals result in changes in social networks (Carstensen, 1995). More specifically, this theory suggests that during adolescence and young adulthood, when life left to live seems unlimited, people focus on gathering information and resources from a large network of diverse relationships. Beginning with midlife, when life ahead begins to seem increasingly limited, people focus more on the emotional aspects of relationships and the social network decreases in size as peripheral relationships decrease but close relationships do not. **Social convoy theory** suggests that we each travel through life with a *convoy*, or a network of social relationships that protect, defend, aid, and socialize us (Antonucci & Akiyama, 1987, 1997; Antonucci, Akiyama, & Takahashi, 2004). Relationships in the convoy differ in level of closeness and are affected in different ways across the life course. The closest relationships are expected to be stable over time, but the more peripheral relationships are assumed to be less stable and prone to drop away over time with changing circumstances. Social convoy theory acknowledges that the convoy can have damaging effects on individuals, contributing more stress than support and creating problems rather than solving them.

Cornelia Wrzus and colleagues (2013) suggest that, even though they propose different reasons for the changes, both socioemotional selectivity theory and social convoy theory indicate that the global network becomes smaller across adulthood, with a continuous decrease in peripheral relationships, but close relationships with family and close friends remain. They conducted a meta-analysis of 277 studies, which included both Western and non-Western samples, of age-related changes in social networks to test these ideas. Both cross-sectional and longitudinal studies found that the global network size increased during adolescence and emerging adulthood, plateaued in the mid-20s and early 30s, and continuously decreased after that. The size of personal and friendship networks decreased across adulthood. The size of family networks was highly consistent across adulthood, however. In middle adulthood, new relationships are often added to the family network, with adult children marrying and having children of their own, but there are also losses of parents and other older relatives. The meta-analysis also revealed that personal and friendship networks were significantly smaller in more recent studies. It also indicated that there were no significant differences in family network size between countries with collectivist values and those with more individualistic values. The global and personal networks were larger, however, in more individualistically oriented countries. It is important to note that studies from non-Western countries were scarce in the database used for the meta-analysis.

Some research has found racial and ethnic differences as well as social class differences in reported convoys in the United States. Whites have been found to have larger convoys than African Americans, and the convoys of African American adults as well as adults with low incomes have a higher proportion of kin in them than the convoys of higher-income White adults (Ajrouch, Antonucci, & Janevic, 2001; Antonucci, Akiyama, & Merline, 2001; Montague, Magai, Consedine, & Gillespie, 2003). A study conducted in Taiwan suggests that in our very mobile times, when younger generations leave home to follow jobs in global cities, some people may have only one or two circles in their convoys, instead of the three proposed by social convoy theory (Chen, 2006). Certainly, it is important to understand the very dynamic nature of convoys in the lives of many people in a globalized world.

Most of the other research on midlife adult relationships is based on the premise that the marital or partner relationship is the focal relationship in middle adulthood. Consequently, too little is known about other familial and nonfamilial relationships. Recently, however, gerontologists have suggested that a variety of relationships are important to adults in late adulthood, and this hypothesis has led to preliminary investigations of a variety of relationships in middle adulthood. In the following sections, we look first at multigenerational family relationships and then review the limited research on friendship.

Middle Adulthood in the Context of the Multigenerational Family

The life circumstances of midlife adults are very much influenced by the number of living generations in the family. In 1990, Bengtson, Rosenthal, and Burton proposed that increased longevity was leading to an increase in the number of generations in the family, with fewer people in each generation, leading to what has been described as a beanpole-shaped family, tall and thin (Putney & Bengtson, 2003). Four- and even 5-generation families were expected to become the norm. This raised concern about the possibility that midlife adults would become stressed by the need to simultaneously provide care to both the oldest and the youngest family generations, a situation sometimes called "both-end carers" (Lundholm & Malmberg, 2009).

Other researchers argue that the trend toward greater longevity must be placed alongside two other trends, low fertility and delayed childbearing, when considering the generational structure of contemporary families. They suggest that these latter two trends may cancel out the effect of increased longevity. Matthews and Sun (2006) used data from two waves of the National Survey of Families and Household to investigate what percentage of U.S. families included four or more generations. They found that in the early 1990s the majority of their adult respondents, who were age 22 or older, reported 3-generation families, with 32% reporting at least 4-generation families. Adults ages 51 to 61 were slightly more likely than other adults to report at least 4-generation families (37%). They also found social class and racial differences in the likelihood of living in 4-generation families. As socioeconomic status increased, the likelihood of a 4-generation family decreased, and Blacks were more likely than Whites to live in 4-generation families. Matthews and Sun conclude that the timing of childbearing is playing a bigger role than longevity in the generational structure of families. Adults with higher levels of education and income begin childbearing at a later age than their peers with less education and income.

Lundholm and Malmberg (2009) used data from the Swedish registry to investigate what percentage of 55-year-old Swedish residents lived in families of 4 generations in 1990 and in 2005. They found a large decrease from 1990 to 2005 in 55-year-olds who had grandchildren, from 70% to 35%. They also found that the percentage of 55-year-olds who had living parents increased from 37% to 47% from 1990 to 2005, an increase that was not nearly as dramatic as the decrease in the percentage having grandchildren. They further found that after

Photo 8.2   Research finds a lot of intergenerational solidarity in contemporary families.

© Goodshoot/ThinkStock

the year 2000, the percentage of 55-year-olds who became grandparents while their own parents were still alive decreased from 28% to 18%. Lundholm and Malmberg (2009) conclude that in Sweden demographic trends are not resulting in more midlife adults becoming both-end carers. They found, however, that after 1996, 4-generation families became more common for adults with less education, similar to Matthews and Sun's findings with a U.S. sample. Other researchers have noted, however, that many midlife adults, like Lisa Balinski, are still providing simultaneous care to aging parents and their emerging adult offspring who are making a slow transition to adulthood because of the dual challenges of economic downturns and increasing demand for prolonged education.

There is much popular speculation that family ties are weakening as geographic mobility increases. Research suggests, however, that there is more intergenerational solidarity than we may think (Kohli & Künemund, 2005; Wrzus et al., 2013). Certainly, we see much intergenerational solidarity in the families of Viktor Spiro, Lisa Balinski, and Michael Bowling. Using a national representative sample in the United States, Putney and Bengtson (2003) identified five types of extended family relationships. About one quarter (25.5%) of the families were classified as *tightly knit*, and another quarter (25.5%) were classified as *sociable*, meaning that family members are engaged with each other but do not provide for, and receive concrete assistance from, each other. The remaining families were about evenly split among the *intimate-but-distant* (16%); *obligatory*, or those who have contact but no emotional closeness or shared belief system (16%); and *detached* (17%) classifications. It is important to note that no one type of extended family relationship was found to be dominant, suggesting much diversity in intergenerational relationships in the United States. Ethnicity is one source of that variation. For example, Black and Hispanic families report stronger maternal attachments than are reported in White families, and they are also more likely to reside in multigenerational households. One researcher has also found much diversity in intergenerational relationships in Taiwan (Chen, 2006).

Despite the evidence that intergenerational family relationships are alive and well, there is also evidence that many family relationships include some degree of conflict. One longitudinal study concluded that about 1 in 8 adult intergenerational relationships can be described as "long-term lousy relationships" (Bengtson, 1996).

Whether or not midlife adults become both-end carers, several researchers (see, e.g., Sotirin & Ellingson, 2006) have found that they are the kinkeepers in multigenerational families and that this holds true across cultures. **Kinkeepers** are family members who work at keeping family members across the generations in touch with one another and who make sure that both emotional and practical needs of family members are met. Historically, when nuclear families were larger, kinkeepers played an important role in working to maintain ties among large sibling groups. With increased longevity and multiple generations of families, kinkeepers play an important role in the multigenerational family, working to maintain ties across the generations, ties among grandparents, parents, children, grandchildren, siblings, aunts, uncles, nieces, nephews, and cousins.

Researchers have found that most kinkeepers are middle-aged women (Sotirin & Ellingson, 2006). Women help larger numbers of kin than men and spend three times as many hours helping kin. Because of this kinkeeping role, midlife women have been described as the "sandwich generation." This term was originally used to suggest that midlife women are simultaneously caring for their own children as well as their parents. Recent research suggests that with demographic changes, few women still have children at home when they begin to care for parents, but midlife women continue to be "sandwiched" with competing demands of paid work roles and intergenerational kinkeeping (Kohli & Künemund, 2005).

It appears that Lisa Balinski is playing an important kinkeeping role in her 3-generation family. Since her father's death, she has provided assistance of various kinds to her mother. She also continues to be very involved in providing emotional support and guidance to her young adult daughters. She seems to be indicating that she feels like she is engaged in both-end caring and trying to balance her family caring roles with her employee role. She describes her current life as overfull. It also appears that Michael Bowling has been something of a kinkeeper from a young age, assisting his parents financially as an adolescent, caring for his mother in her final months, and providing both emotional and practical assistance to his younger sister and her children. In late midlife, he has been faced with the need to learn to be the recipient as well as the giver of family assistance.

Relationships With Spouse or Partner

In recent decades, there has been an increased diversity of marital statuses at midlife. Some men and women have been married for some time, some are getting married for the first time, some are not yet married, some will never marry, some were once married but now are divorced, some are in a second or third marriage, and some are not married but are living in a long-term committed relationship with someone of the same or opposite sex. In recent years, many long-term same-sex couples have finally been able to form a legal marriage in middle adulthood in an increasing number of countries and U.S. states. Adults such as Viktor Spiro who have struggled with mental health issues are more likely than other adults to be single.

The number of couples who are cohabiting rather than marrying has been increasing for 2 decades. The 2000 U.S. census reported that 5.5 million couples were living together but not married, up from 3.2 million in 1990 (Simmons & O'Connell, 2003). The majority of these couples were opposite-sex partners, but 1 in 9 was a same-sex couple. In 2010, the U.S Census Bureau found that 7.5 million opposite-sex couples were living together but not married, a 13% increase in opposite-sex cohabiting couples from 2009 to 2010. This increase was thought to be related to economic circumstances, because newly formed cohabiting couples in 2010 had a lower percentage with both partners employed (39%) than couples who had been cohabiting before 2010 (50%) (Kreider, 2010). One research team found that midlife African American men with higher education and income were more likely to be married than cohabiting, while the opposite was true of midlife African American men with lower education and income. This finding is consistent with research that finds that African Americans place greater emphasis than European Americans on security and upward mobility as requirements for marriage (Cutrona, Russell, Burzette, Wesner, & Bryant, 2011). Of course, many cohabiting couples will marry each other at some point, but that option is still not available to same-sex couples in most states in the United States.

We know very little about the different midlife experiences of partners of different marital statuses, but there is evidence that each person brings prior relationship experiences to partner relationships of all types. Möller and Stattin (2001) reviewed the empirical literature on these relationships and identified a number of characteristics of prior relationships that have been found to influence partner relationships in adulthood. For example, affection and warmth in the household during the preschool years has been associated with long and happy partnerships in adulthood. Interactions with peers during adolescence help to build the social skills necessary to sustain partner relationships. Based on these findings, Möller and Stattin (2001) engaged in longitudinal research with a Swedish sample to investigate the links between early relationships and later partner relationships. They found that warm relationships with parents during adolescence are associated with later satisfaction in the partner relationship. Relationships with fathers were more strongly related to partner satisfaction for males than for females. Contrary to previous research, Möller and Stattin found that the quality of parents' marital relationship was not associated with the quality of later partner relationships. The parent-child relationship was a better predictor of later partner relationships than the quality of the parents' marital relationships.

For heterosexual marriages, a long line of research indicates a U-shaped curve in marital happiness, with high marital satisfaction in the early years of marriage, followed by a decline that hits bottom in early midlife but begins to rise again in the postparental years. However, one longitudinal research project, one of the few studies to use a national representative sample, found no upturn in marital satisfaction in later life. As found in other studies, satisfaction took a steep decline over the first 5 years of marriage. This was followed by a gradual decline during the next 20 years, after which marital satisfaction leveled off for a few years but declined again beginning at 40 years of marriage (VanLaningham, Johnson, & Amato, 2001). The researchers also found that for most marital cohorts, there was a steeper decline in marital satisfaction in the 1980s than in the 1990s, which seems to indicate an impact of some societal changes. There was also some indication that more recent cohorts have lower marital satisfaction than earlier cohorts.

Midlife adults are balancing a variety of roles: family roles, work roles, and community roles, and this requires partners to coordinate their role enactments. In one study of African American midlife baby boomers, couples described how they share responsibilities; stay engaged with work, family, and faith; and make time for each other to keep their relationship alive (Carolan & Allen, 1999). There is evidence that unmarried partners tend to be more egalitarian in the division of household activities than married couples (Simmons & O'Connell, 2003), and considerable evidence that African American married couples engage in more egalitarian role sharing than White married couples (Coltrane, 2000).

The 2010 U.S. census found 594,000 same-sex couple households in the United States, about 1% of all couple households (U.S. Census Bureau, 2011c). Of these same-sex couple households, 115,000, or about 19%, reported having children in the household. Midlife gay and lesbian partnerships have been found to be more egalitarian than married heterosexual couples. Kurdek (2004) compared gay, lesbian, and married heterosexual couples in long-term relationships. In this study, the gay and lesbian couples lived without children and the married heterosexual couples lived with children. For 50% of the comparisons, gay and lesbian couples did not differ from married heterosexual couples with children. Three major differences between gay and lesbian couples and married heterosexual couples were found: (1) gay and lesbian couples reported more autonomy and more equality; (2) gay and lesbian couples were better at conflict resolution; and (3) heterosexual married couples had more support from their families. In a later project, Kurdek (2008) followed four groups of couples—gay couples without children, lesbian couples without children, heterosexual married couples without children, and heterosexual married couples with children—for the first 10 years they cohabited. Lesbian partners reported the highest relationship quality at all points of assessment and showed no change in relationship quality over time. Gay partners reported the second highest relationship quality and also showed no change over time. Both groups of heterosexual couples reported lower levels of relationship quality than both gay and lesbian partners, and both groups also reported change over time. Heterosexual couples without children reported a steep decline in relationship quality in the early years followed by stability. In contrast, heterosexual couples with children reported a steep decline in the early years, followed by a gradual decline until year 8 when another period of steep decline began. This research begins to clarify some different experiences in partner relationships of various types but only covers relationships through the young adult period. One hopes further longitudinal research will continue into middle adulthood and will also investigate relationships of gay and lesbian couples with children.

Weinberg, Williams, and Pryor (2001) followed 56 people who identify as bisexual from young adulthood to middle adulthood. They found that the participants continue to report a bisexual identity and attraction to members of both sexes in middle adulthood. However, they also report less involvement in the bisexual community and more investment in work or a partner and a move toward activity with just one sex. In other words, there is no change in bisexual attraction but a growing commitment to work and partnerships.

The current generation of midlife adults has more complex marital biographies than earlier generations. The baby boomers were the first cohort to divorce and remarry in large numbers during young adulthood, and remarriages are 2.5 times as likely to end in divorce as first marriages. From 1980 to 2010, the percentage of midlife remarriages rose from 18% to 32%. One in four persons who divorced in 2010 was 50 years old or older, compared with 1 in 10 in 1990 (Brown & Lin, 2012). The overall divorce rate is higher for women than men, higher for Blacks than for Whites or Hispanics, and higher for those with a high school education compared with those with a college education. Men report more marital satisfaction than women in the United States and Chinese Malaysia (Mickelson, Claffey, & Williams, 2006; Ny, Loy, Gudmunson, & Cheong, 2009), and most divorces are initiated by women (McGoldrick, Carter, & Garcia-Preto, 2011b).

Although there is a period of adjustment to divorce, midlife adults cope better with divorce than young adults (Greene, Anderson, Forgatch, DeGarmo, & Hetherington, 2012). Some individuals actually report improved well-being after divorce. Women have been found to be more adversely affected by a distressed marriage and men more adversely affected by being divorced (Hetherington & Kelly, 2002). However, the financial consequences of divorce for women are negative. After divorce, men are more likely to remarry than women, and Whites are more likely to remarry than African Americans.

Relationships With Children

Although a growing number of midlife adults are parenting young or school-age children, most midlife adults are parents of adolescents or young adults. Delayed childbearing increases the likelihood that midlife adults will be stretched to provide care to their aging parents while also engaged in intense parenting to young children (Fingerman, Pillemer, Silverstein, & Suitor, 2012). Parenting adolescents can be a challenge if parent-child conflict escalates. Croatian mothers with high levels of conflict with their adolescent children have been found to feel a greater sense of isolation (Kereteš, Brković, & Jagodić, 2012). Launching young adult offspring from the nest is a happy experience for most families, but it is a family transition that has been undergoing changes in the past 20 years, coming at a later age for parents and becoming more fluid in its timing and progress (Newman, 2008).

> What factors are producing these trends in family life?

In the United States and the industrialized European countries, it became common for young adults to live outside the family prior to marriage in the 1960s. Then, in the United States, in the 1980s, two trends became evident: increased age at first leaving home and increased incidence of returning home. Data from 2012 indicate that 36% of U.S. young adults ages 18 to 31 lived in their parents' home, the highest percentage in at least 4 decades (Fry, 2012). A majority, 56%, of emerging adults ages 18 to 24 lived with their parents, a phenomenon more common among young men than young women. A very similar trend exists in northern Europe, and young adults are even more likely to live with their parents in Spain and Italy (Kohli & Künemund, 2005). In general, parents are more positive than their young adult children about living together (Blieszner & Roberto, 2006).

Blieszner and Roberto (2006) argue that "lifestyles of midlife baby-boom parents revolve around their children" (p. 270). Recent research bears that out. In a summary of findings of three studies, Fingerman and colleagues (2012) report that the current generation of midlife adults is much more involved in the lives of their adult children than their parents were with them, a trend that began when their offspring were young children. Contemporary young adults report more frequent contact with and more similar values to their parents than occurred in earlier decades; they also report receiving more support. Middle-aged parents report offering each adult child a listening ear and emotional support more than once per week, giving advice once a month, and providing practical and financial assistance at least several times per year. Providing support to children is associated with better psychological well-being in midlife adults, and receiving various kinds of support from their midlife parents is associated with better adjustment and well-being of young adults. In general, mothers have closer relationships with their young adult children than fathers, and divorced fathers have been found to have weaker emotional attachments with their adult children than either married fathers or divorced mothers. Midlife parents help their young adult children in different ways, depending on the resources they have to share.

It is important to note the common exchange of material resources between generations. Viktor Spiro and his mother are pooling resources to stay afloat economically. Lisa and Adam Balinski moved in with Lisa's parents after their baby was born, until they could afford a place of their own, and now they are providing a home for Lisa's mother and wondering if they should do the same for their young adult daughter, Kristi. Michael Bowling provided much material support to his niece and nephew until he was faced with both an employment crisis and a health crisis. He continues to be a source of social and emotional support for them. Research in Germany suggests that intergenerational financial transfers are common and often sizable, with midlife and late-life adults particularly providing financial assistance to adult children with poor economic position (Kohli & Künemund, 2005).

Research also indicates that midlife adults can be negatively affected by their relationships with their adult children. Greenfield and Marks (2006) found that midlife adults whose adult children have problems such as chronic disease or disability, emotional problems, problems with alcohol or other substances, financial problems, work-related problems, partner relationship problems, and so on report lower levels of well-being than midlife adults who do not report such problems in their adult children. Ha, Hong, Seltzer, and Greenberg (2008) found that midlife parents of adult children with developmental disabilities or mental health problems were more likely than parents of nondisabled children to report higher levels of negative emotions, decreased psychological well-being, and somatic symptoms. Seltzer et al. (2009) found that midlife adults had more negative emotions, more disruption in cortisol, and more physical symptoms on the days they spent more time with their disabled children. These findings suggest a need for social service support for midlife parents whose adult children are facing ongoing challenges.

Relationships With Parents

Most research shows that middle-aged adults are deeply involved with their aging parents (Fingerman et al., 2012). As suggested in the stories of Viktor Spiro, Lisa Balinski, and Michael Bowling, the nature of the relationship with aging parents changes over time. A cross-national study of adults in Norway, England, Germany, Spain, and Israel found that across countries, support was bidirectional, with aging parents providing emotional and financial support to their midlife adult children and also receiving support from them (Lowenstein & Daatland, 2006). As the parents' health begins to deteriorate, they turn more to their midlife children for help, as is currently the case for Viktor Spiro and Lisa Balinski and was earlier the case for Michael Bowling. A German study found that caring for elderly family members peaks between ages 50 and 54 (Kohli & Künemund, 2005).

Traditionally, and typically still, caregivers to aging parents are daughters or daughters-in-law (Fingerman, VanderDrift, Dotterer, Birditt, & Zarit, 2011). This continues to be the case, even though a great majority of midlife women are employed full-time. This does not tell the whole story, however. The baby boom cohort has more siblings than earlier and later cohorts, and there is some evidence that caregiving is often shared among siblings, with sisters serving as coordinators of the care (Hequembourg & Brallier, 2005). In spite of competing demands from spouses and children, providing limited care to aging parents seems to cause little psychological distress. Extended caregiving, conversely, has been found to have some negative effects as midlife adults try to balance a complex mix of roles (Savia, Almeida,

Davey, & Zant, 2008), but there is also some evidence of rewards of caregiving (Robertson, Zarit, Duncan, Rovine, & Femia, 2007).

Most of the research on caregiving focuses on *caregiver burden*, or the negative effects on mental and physical health caused by caregiver stress. Compared with matched comparison groups who do not have caregiving responsibilities, caregivers of elderly parents report more depressive symptoms, taking more antidepressant and antianxiety medication; poorer physical health; and lower marital satisfaction (Sherwood, Given, Given, & Von Eye, 2005). Savia et al. (2008) found that psychological distress was greater on days that adult children provided assistance to aging parents, but they also found more distressed mood among caregivers with higher caregiving demands and lower resources. Another research team studying caregiver burden in caregivers of individuals with dementia found that the number of hours devoted to caregiving was a significant predictor of caregiver burden. They also found that having multiple helpers did not relieve caregiver burden and that caregivers who lived with the care recipient had higher levels of caregiver burden (Kim, Chang, Rose, & Kim, 2012).

Although this research is not as prevalent, some researchers have been interested in a phenomenon they call *caregiver gain* or *caregiver reward*. One early proponent of this line of inquiry found that the majority of caregivers have something positive to say about their caregiving experiences (Kramer, 1997). One group of researchers was interested in the balance of positive and negative emotions in family caregivers of older adults with dementia (Robertson et al., 2007). They found considerable variation in the responses of caregivers in terms of the balance of stressful and positive experiences of caregiving. The stressful experiences included behavior problems of the care receiver; need to provide personal assistance with activities such as eating, dressing, grooming, bathing, toileting, and transferring into bed; role overload; and role captivity (feeling trapped in caregiver role). The positive experiences of caregiving included caregiving rewards such as growing personally, repaying care

receiver, fulfilling duty, and getting perspective on what is important in life; sense of competence; and positive behaviors in care receiver. The researchers identified different groups of caregivers in terms of their levels of distress. The most well-adjusted group had more resources in terms of health, education, and so on and reported fewer behavior problems and fewer needs for personal assistance of the care recipients.

Culture appears to play a role in whether providing care to aging parents is experienced as burden or gain. For example, Lowenstein and Daatland (2006) found a strong expectation of providing care for parents in Spain and Israel but a more negotiable obligation in northern Europe. In countries where caregiving is normalized, caregiving is often provided out of affection, not obligation, may be shared among family members, and may be less likely to be experienced as burden. This seems to have been the case for Michael Bowling when he cared for his mother. Evans and colleagues (Evans, Crogan, Belyea, & Coon, 2009) report that Hispanic caregivers have been found to have slightly less caregiver burden than Anglos. Fingerman et al. (2011) found that middle-aged Blacks, on average, give more support of all kinds to aging parents and are also more likely to report an expectation that one support one's parents and that personal rewards are found in providing such support. Very individualistic families value individual independence and may find elder care particularly troublesome to both caregiver and care recipient. However, there is evidence that both individualistically oriented families and collectivist-oriented families experience negative effects of long-term, intensive caregiving, especially those families with few economic and social resources (Robertson et al., 2007).

Other Family Relationships

Midlife is typically a time of launching children and a time when parents die. It is also a time when new family members get added by marriage and the birth of grandchildren. However, family relationships other than marital relationships and parent-child relationships have received little research attention. The grandparent-grandchild relationship has received the greatest amount of research attention, followed by a growing body of research on sibling relationships.

In the United States, about three fourths of adults become grandparents by the time they are 65 (Bjorklund, 2011). For those adults who become grandparents, the onset of the grandparent role typically occurs in their 40s or 50s, or increasingly in their 60s. Grandparenthood has been reported to be among the top three most important roles among middle-aged men and women in the United States (Reitzes & Mutran, 2002). Baby boom grandparents are likely to have fewer grandchildren than their parents had, spend more years in the grandparent role, and share that role with more people, including stepgrandparents (Blieszner & Roberto, 2006). Vern Bengtson (2001) asserts that grandparents play an important socializing role in families and that this role is likely to grow in importance in the near future.

There are many styles of grandparenting and many cultures of grandparenting. In cultures with large extended families and reverence for elders—such as in China, Mexico, and many Asian and African countries—grandparents often live with the family. In the United States, Asian American, African American, Hispanic American, and Italian American grandparents are more likely to play an active role in the lives of grandchildren than other ethnic groups (Gardiner & Kosmitzki, 2011). Research has indicated gender differences in enactment of the grandparent role as well, with most research suggesting that grandmothers, particularly maternal grandmothers, play more intimate roles in their grandchildren's lives than grandfathers (Bjorklund, 2011). However, Bates and Goodsell (2013) argue that grandfathers have been underrepresented in research on grandparenting and recommend a more focused research effort to examine these relationships. In their own exploratory research, they found a wide variation in the nature of grandfather-grandson relationships, but grandsons saw grandfathers involved in seven domains of grandfathering work: lineage work, mentoring work, spiritual work, character work, recreation work, family identity work, and investment work. They concluded that "generative grandfathers provided grandsons with meaningful interactive experiences that built developmental competencies, including those that potentially might lead to strong generativity" (p. 46).

Researchers have noted two potential problems for grandparents. First, if adult children divorce, custody agreements may fail to attend to the rights of grandparents for visitation (Blieszner & Roberto, 2006). And baby boom adults are often serving as stepgrandparents, a role that can be quite ambiguous. Second, if adult children become incapacitated by substance abuse, illness, disability, or incarceration, grandparents may be recruited to step in to raise the grandchildren. The number of children cared for by grandparents in the United States has risen dramatically in the past 30 years. About 2.4 million baby boom grandparents are serving as the primary caregiver to grandchildren. Racial and ethnic minority grandparents are two to three times more likely than European American grandparents to be serving in this role (Blieszner & Roberto, 2006). Unfortunately, grandparents with the fewest resources are often the ones called on to become primary caregivers to their grandchildren.

Baby boomers have more siblings than earlier and later cohorts, and most midlife adults today have at least one sibling. Sibling relationships have been found to be important for the well-being of both men and women in midlife. Siblings often drift apart in young adulthood, but contact between siblings increases in late midlife (McGoldrick & Watson, 2011). Midlife adults are often brought together around the care and death of aging parents, and recent research indicates that sibling contact decreases again after the death of the last parent (Khodyakov & Carr, 2009). Sibling collaboration in the care of aging parents may bring them closer together or may stir new as well as unresolved resentments. Pillemer and colleagues (Pillemer, Suitor, Pardo, & Henderson, 2010) found that midlife adults who recall their mothers playing favorites when they were children often have problematic relationships in midlife. Although step- and half siblings tend to stay connected to each other, their contact is less frequent than the contact between full siblings.

Research in the Netherlands found that brothers provide more practical support to siblings and sisters provide more emotional support (Voorpostel & van der Lippe, 2007). In Taiwan, however, brother-brother dyads were found to provide the most companionship and emotional support of any dyad type (Lu, 2007). In the Netherlands, siblings seemed to overcome geographic distance to provide emotional support more easily than friends, but relationship quality was an important predictor of which sibling groups would offer emotional support (Voorpostel & van der Lippe, 2007).

Viktor Spiro's sister was an important lifeline for him when he immigrated to the United States, but tensions developed during the time when Viktor was suicidal. Their mutual concern about their father's health drew them closer again. Michael Bowling has close relationships with his siblings, and the closest relationship he has is with his younger sister.

Relationships With Friends

Midlife adults have fewer friends in their social convoys than do adolescents and young adults, but they also continue to report at least a few important friendships (Wrzus et al., 2013). Baby boom midlife adults are good friends with about seven people on average; these friends are usually of the same age, sex, race or ethnicity, social class, education, and employment status (Blieszner & Roberto, 2006). Some boomers also maintain cross-sex friendships, and these are particularly valued by men who are more likely than women to see a sexual dimension to these relationships (Monsour, 2002). It has been suggested that midlife adults have less time than other adult age groups for friendships.

Friendships appear to have an impact on midlife well-being for both men and women, although they do not seem to be as important as close familial relationships. For instance, the adequacy of social support, particularly from friends, at age 50 predicts physical health for men at age 70 (Vaillant, 2002). Likewise, midlife women who have a confidant or a close group of female friends report greater well-being than midlife women without such interpersonal resources (McQuaide, 1998). Women who report positive feelings toward their women friends also have fewer depressive symptoms and higher morale than women who report less positive feelings toward female friends (Paul, 1997). Whether good feelings toward friends protect against depression or depression impairs the quality of friendships remains to be determined, however.

Given this research, we might want to know more about Lisa Balinksi's friendship network. Viktor Spiro's recent participation in social events is providing him an opportunity to expand his social convoy and appears to be adding an important dimension to his life circumstances. Michael Bowling has developed some close friendships in the stroke recovery support group, and given what we know about Michael, we can suspect that he is giving as well as receiving support from this group.

It appears that the importance of friends in the social convoy varies by sexual orientation, race, and marital status. Friends are important sources of support in the social convoys of gay and lesbian midlife adults, often serving as an accepting "chosen family" for those who have traveled the life course in a homophobic society (Croghan, Moone, & Olson, 2014). These chosen families provide much care and support to each other, as evidenced by the primary caregiving they have provided in times of serious illness such as AIDS and breast cancer (Muraco & Fredriksen-Goldsen, 2011). Taking care of friends is often seen as a responsibility in some LGBT friend networks, and one research team found that midlife individuals reported that helping friends in their LGBT network raises their esteem. On average, they also reported tenuous ties to the family networks (Muraco & Fredriksen-Goldsen, 2011). Friends also become family in many African American families. The literature on African American families often calls attention to the "nonblood" family members as a strength for these families (Boyd-Franklin & Karger, 2012). Friendships also serve an important role in the social convoys of single midlife adults, serving as a chosen family rather than a "poor substitute" for family (Berliner, Jacob, & Schwartzberg, 2011).

Critical Thinking Questions 8.4

The research indicates that family ties remain strong in societies around the world. What do you think about this? Do you think the family ties are strong in your multigenerational family? Are there kinkeepers in your multigenerational family? If so, who are they, and why do you think they play this role? What have you observed about your own friendship networks over time?

WORK IN MIDDLE ADULTHOOD

Like Viktor Spiro and Lisa Balinski, the majority of midlife adults engage in paid labor, but the first decade of the 21st century has been a precarious time for middle-aged workers, and Michael Bowling is a good example of that precariousness. In the deep economic recession of 2008, workers age 45 and older had a lower unemployment rate than younger workers, but they have been disproportionately represented among the long-term unemployed (Luo, 2009). In 2011, the median duration of unemployment for job seekers age 55 and older was 35 weeks, compared with 26 weeks for younger job seekers (U.S. Government Accountability Office, 2012). These midlife baby boomers are too young to draw a pension or social security (before the age of 62) or to have medical coverage through Medicare. Therefore, it is no surprise that in the first 3 months of the enrollment period for the Affordable Care Act's federal and state marketplaces, 55% of enrollees were ages 45 to 64 (Shear & Pear, 2014).

Work and retirement have different meanings for different people. Among the meanings work can have are the following (Friedmann & Havighurst, 1954):

- A source of income
- A life routine and way of structuring time
- A source of status and identity

- A context for social interaction
- A meaningful experience that provides a sense of accomplishment

Given these meanings, employment is an important role for midlife adults in many parts of the world, for men and women alike (Dittmann-Kohli, 2005). Involuntary unemployment can be a source of great stress.

In affluent societies, the last decades of the 20th century saw a continuing decline in the average age of retirement, particularly for men (Moen, 2003). This trend existed alongside trends of longer midlife and late adulthood periods and the fact that adults are entering midlife healthier and better educated than in previous eras. Improved pension plans were at least partially responsible for the trend of declining age of retirement. But, with the demise of defined-benefit pension plans, and particularly since the recession of 2008, retirement patterns have been changing again, with older adults remaining engaged in the workforce later in life (Carr & Kail, 2012).

Overall, the work patterns of middle-aged workers in the United States have changed considerably in the past 3 decades. Four trends stand out:

1. *Greater job mobility among middle-aged workers.* Changes in the global economy have produced job instability for middle-aged workers. In the late 20th century, corporate restructuring, mergers, and downsizing revolutionized the previous lockstep career trajectories and produced much instability in midcareer employment (Ritzer, 2013). Midlife white-collar workers who had attained midlevel management positions in organizations have been vulnerable to downsizing and reorganization efforts aimed at flattening organizational hierarchies. Midlife blue-collar workers have been vulnerable to changes in job skill requirements as the global economy shifts from an industrial base to a service base. Within these broad trends, gender, class, and race have all made a difference in the work patterns of midlife adults (D. Newman, 2012). Women are more likely than men to have job disruption throughout the adult life course,

Photo 8.3   Changes in the global economy have produced job instability for middle-aged workers, and job retraining often becomes essential.

© Bonnie Jacobs/iStockphoto.com

although those with higher education and higher income are less vulnerable to job disruption. In the recent recession, however, men were more vulnerable to job loss than women. Race is a factor in the midlife employment disruption for men but not for women. Although Black men have more job disruptions than White men, there are no race differences for women when other variables are controlled. Research indicates that loss of work in middle adulthood is a very critical life event that has negative consequences for emotional well-being (Dittmann-Kohli, 2005).

2.   *Greater variability in the timing of retirement.* Some midlife workers retire in their late 50s. Today, many other midlife adults anticipate working into their late 60s or early 70s. The decision to retire is driven by both health and financial

status (more particularly, the availability of pension benefits). The National Academy on an Aging Society (Sterns & Huyck, 2001) found that 55% of persons in the United States who retired at ages 51 to 59 reported a health condition as a major reason for retirement. Although availability of a pension serves as inducement for retirement, men and women who work in physically demanding jobs often seek early retirement whether or not they have access to a pension. Some leave the workforce as a result of disability and become eligible for Social Security disability benefits.

3.   *Blurring of the lines between working and retirement.* Many people now phase into retirement (Carr & Kail, 2012). Some middle-aged retirees return to work in different occupational fields than those from which they retired. Others leave

a career at some point in middle adulthood for a part-time or temporary job. Increasing numbers of middle-aged workers leave a career position because of downsizing and reorganization and find reemployment in a job with less financial reward, a "bridge job" that carries them into retirement.

4. *Increasing educational reentry of midlife workers.* This trend has received little research attention. However, workers with high levels of educational attainment prior to middle adulthood are more likely than their less-educated peers to retrain in middle adulthood (Luo, 2009). This difference is consistent with the theory of cumulative advantage; those who have accumulated resources over the life course are more likely to have the resources for retraining in middle adulthood. But in this era of high job obsolescence, relatively few middle-aged adults will have the luxury of choosing to do one thing at a time; to remain marketable, many middle-aged adults will have to combine work and school.

These trends aside, there is both good news and bad news for the middle-aged worker in the beginning of the 21st century. Research indicates that middle-aged workers have greater work satisfaction, organizational commitment, and self-esteem than younger workers (Dittmann-Kohli, 2005). Lisa Balinski appears to be a good example

Photo 8.4   Research indicates that middle-aged workers often have greater work satisfaction, organizational commitment, and self-esteem than younger workers.

© iStockphoto.com

of this finding. However, with the current changes in the labor market, employers are ambivalent about middle-aged employees. Employers may see middle-aged workers as "hard-working, reliable, and motivated" (Sterns & Huyck, 2001, p. 476). But they also often cut higher-wage older workers from the payroll as a short-range solution for reducing operating costs and staying competitive.

For some midlife adults, such as Viktor Spiro, the issue is not how they will cope with loss of a good job but rather how they can become established in the labor market. In the previous industrial phase, poverty was caused by unemployment. In the current era, the major issue is the growing proportion of low-wage, no-benefit jobs. Black men with a high school education or less have been particularly disadvantaged in the current phase of industrialization, largely because of the declining numbers of routine production jobs. Adults such as Viktor, with disabilities, have an even harder time finding work that can support them. In June 2013, the unemployment rate for persons with a disability was 13.4% compared with 7.9% for persons with no disability (U.S. Bureau of Labor Statistics, 2013b). Even with legislation of the past few decades, much remains to be done to open educational and work opportunities to persons with disabilities. In addition, Viktor has had to contend with language and cultural barriers.

Thus, middle-aged workers, like younger workers, are deeply affected by a changing labor market. Like younger workers, they must understand the patterns in those changes and be proactive in maintaining and updating their skills. However, that task is easier for middle-aged workers who arrive in middle adulthood with accumulated resources. Marginalization in the labor market in adulthood is the result of "cumulative disadvantage" over the life course. Unfortunately, adults such as Viktor Spiro who have employment disruptions early in the adult life course tend to have more job disruption in middle adulthood as well. But Michael Bowling's situation shows that even college-educated people with a strong work history can be vulnerable in times of economic downturn.

RISK FACTORS AND PROTECTIVE FACTORS IN MIDDLE ADULTHOOD

From a life course perspective, midlife behavior has both antecedents and consequences. Earlier life experiences can serve either as risk factors or as protective factors for health and well-being during middle adulthood. And midlife behaviors can serve either as risk factors or as protective factors for future health and well-being. The rapidly growing body of literature on risk, protection, and resilience based on longitudinal research has recently begun to add to our understanding of the antecedents of midlife behavior.

One of the best-known programs of research is a study begun by Emmy Werner and associates with a cohort born in 1955 on the island of Kauai, Hawaii. The research participants turned 40 in 1995, and Werner and Ruth Smith (2001) captured their risk factors, protective factors, and resilience in *Journeys From Childhood to Midlife*. They summarize their findings by suggesting that they "taught us a great deal of respect for the self-righting tendencies in human nature and for the capacity of *most* individuals who grew up in adverse circumstances to make a successful adaptation in adulthood" (p. 166). At age 40, compared with previous decades, the overwhelming majority of the participants reported "significant improvements" in work accomplishments, interpersonal relationships, contributions to community, and life satisfaction. Most adults who had a troubled adolescence had recovered by midlife. Many of these adults who had been troubled as youth reported that the "opening of opportunities" (p. 168) in their 20s and 30s had led to major *turning points*. Such turning points included continuing education at community college, military service, marriage to a stable partner, religious conversion, and survival

> Why is it important for social workers to understand both antecedents and consequences of midlife behavior?

despite a life-threatening illness or accident. At midlife, participants were still benefiting from the presence of a competent, nurturing caregiver in infancy, as well as from the emotional support along the way of extended family, peers, and caring adults outside the family.

Although this research is hopeful, Werner and Smith (2001) also found that 1 out of 6 of the study cohort was doing poorly at work and in relationships. The earlier risk factors associated with poor midlife adjustment include severe perinatal trauma, small-for-gestational-age birth weight, early childhood poverty, serious health problems in early childhood, problems in early schooling, parental alcoholism and/or serious mental illness, health problems in adolescence, and health problems in the 30s. Viktor Spiro's early life produced several of these risk factors: early childhood poverty, health problems in adolescence, and his father's chronic depression. For men, the most powerful risk factor was parental alcoholism from birth to age 18. Women were especially negatively affected by paternal alcoholism during their adolescence. It is interesting to note that the long-term negative effects of serious health problems in early childhood and adolescence were just beginning to show up at age 40. We are also learning that some negative effects of childhood and adolescent trauma may not present until early midlife.

Studies have also examined the effects of midlife behavior, specifically the effects on subsequent health (see Dioussé, Driver, & Gaziano, 2009). They have found a number of health behaviors that are risk factors for more severe and prolonged health and disability problems in late adulthood. These include smoking, heavy alcohol use, diet high in fats, overeating, and sedentary lifestyle. Economic deprivation and high levels of stress have also been found to be risk factors throughout the life course. Health behaviors that are receiving much research attention as protective factors for health and well-being in late adulthood are a healthy diet; a physical fitness program that includes stretching exercises, weight training, and aerobic exercise; meditation; and giving and receiving social support (Cohen, 2012; Davidson & Begley, 2012).

Critical Thinking Questions 8.5

What have you observed about the work life of the midlife adults in your family? How has the work life of the midlife adults in your family been affected by growing insecurity in the labor market, if at all? How are the midlife adults in your family working to balance family and work? How well are their efforts working? What evidence do you see of antecedent risk factors and protective factors that are affecting the midlife experiences of Viktor Spiro, Lisa Balinski, and Michael Bowling? What evidence do you see of current behaviors that might have consequences, either positive or negative, for their experiences with late adulthood?

Implications for Social Work Practice

This discussion has several implications for social work practice with midlife adults:

- Be familiar with the unique pathways your clients have traveled to reach middle adulthood.
- Recognize the role that culture plays in constructing beliefs about appropriate midlife roles and assist clients in exploring their beliefs.

- Help clients to think about their own involvement in generative activity and the meaning this involvement has for their lives.
- Become familiar with biological changes and special health issues in middle adulthood. Engage midlife clients in assessing their own health behaviors.
- Be aware of your own beliefs about intellectual changes in middle adulthood and evaluate those against the available research.
- Be aware of both stability and the capacity for change in personality in middle adulthood.
- Help clients assess the role that spirituality plays in their adjustments in middle adulthood and, where appropriate, to make use of their spiritual resources to solve current problems.
- Engage midlife clients in a mutual assessment of their involvement in a variety of relationships, including romantic relationships, relationships with parents, relationships with children, other family relationships, and relationships with friends.
- Collaborate with social workers and other disciplines to advocate for governmental and corporate solutions to work and family life conflicts.

Key Terms

conjunctive faith
coping mechanism
extroversion
generativity
global network
introversion

kinkeepers
life span theory
menopause
perimenopause
personal network
social convoy theory

socioemotional selectivity
 theory
trait approach
universalizing faith

Active Learning

1. Think about how you understand the balance of gains and losses in middle adulthood. Interview three midlife adults ranging in age from 40 to 65 and ask them whether they see the current phase of their lives as having more gains or more losses over the previous phase.

2. Draw your social convoy as it currently exists with three concentric circles:

   - Inner circle of people who are so close and important to you that you could not do without them
   - Middle circle of people who are not quite that close but are still very close and important to you
   - Outer circle of people who are not as close and important as those in the two inner circles but still close enough to be considered part of your support system

   What did you learn from engaging in this exercise? Do you see any changes you would like to make in your social convoy?

3. In groups of three or four, talk about the meanings of work for you and make a list of all of the meanings mentioned. How does your list compare with the list proposed by Friedmann and Havighurst (1954)? Talk about your expectations about how your work life trajectory will go over the next 10 years. What do you expect to be the special challenges of your work life, and what do you expect to be the special rewards?

Boomers International: boomersint.org

Site presented by Boomers International: World Wide Community for the Baby Boomer Generation contains information from the trivial to the serious on the popular culture of the baby boomer generation.

Families and Work Institute: www.familiesandwork.org

Site presented by the Families and Work Institute contains information on work-life research, community mobilization forums, information on the Fatherhood Project, and frequently asked questions.

Max Planck Institute for Human Development: www.mpib-berlin.mpg.de/index_js.en.htm

Site presented by the Max Planck Institute for Human Development, Berlin, Germany, contains news and research about life course development.

Midlife in the United States: www.midus.wisc.edu/index.php

Site presented by Midlife Development in the U.S. (MIDUS) contains an overview of recent research on midlife development, multimedia presentations, featured publications, and links to other human development research projects.

Student Study Site

$SAGE edge™

Sharpen your skills with SAGE edge at **edge.sagepub.com/hutchisonclc5e**

SAGE edge for students provides a personalized approach to help you accomplish your coursework goals in an easy-to-use learning environment.

Late Adulthood

Matthias J. Naleppa

Acknowledgment: The author wishes to thank Dr. Peter Maramaldi, Dr. Michael Melendez, and Rosa Schnitzenbaumer for contributions to this chapter.

Opening Questions

- How will the trend toward increased longevity affect family life and social work practice?

- What do social workers need to understand about the biological, psychological, social, and spiritual changes in late adulthood and the coping mechanisms used to adapt to these changes?

- What formal and informal resources are available for meeting the needs of elderly persons?

Key Ideas

As you read this chapter, take note of these central ideas:

1. Unlike in earlier historical eras, many people in the United States and other industrialized countries today reach the life phase of late adulthood, and the older population is a very heterogeneous group.

2. The cumulative effect of health disparities based on race, ethnicity, gender, and socioeconomic status impacts the quality of aging for significant subpopulations of older people in the United States and around the world.

3. The most commonly discussed psychosocial theories of social gerontology are disengagement, activity, continuity, social construction, feminist, social exchange, life course, age stratification, and productive aging theories; the most common theories of biological aging are the programmed aging theories and damage or error theories.

4. All systems of the body appear to be affected during the aging process.

5. It has been difficult to understand psychological changes in late adulthood without long-term longitudinal research, but recent longitudinal research suggests that with age and experience, individuals tend to use more adaptive coping mechanisms.

6. Families play an important role in late adulthood, and as a result of increased longevity, multigenerational families are more common than ever.

7. Although most persons enter retirement in late adulthood, some individuals continue to work even after they are eligible to retire, either out of financial necessity or by choice.

8. Older adults rely on a number of both informal and formal resources to meet their changing needs.

CASE STUDY 9.1

The Smiths in Early Retirement

The Smiths are a Caucasian couple in their early retirement years who have sought out couples counseling. Lois Smith is 66 and Gene Smith is 68 years of age. They have lived in the same quiet suburban neighborhood since they married 20 years ago. When they met, Gene was a widower and Lois had been divorced for 3 years. They have no children from this marriage but three children from Lois's first marriage. The Smiths are grandparents to the three children of their married daughter, who lives 4 hours away. Their two sons are both single and also live in a different city. The Smiths visit their children frequently, but family and holiday gatherings usually take place at the Smiths' house.

The Smiths live in a comfortable home, but their neighborhood has changed over the years. When they bought the house, many other families were in the same life stage, raising adolescent children and seeing them move out as young adults. Many of the neighbors from that time have since moved, and the neighborhood has undergone a change to young families with children. Although the Smiths feel connected to the community, they do not have much interaction with the people in their immediate neighborhood. Only one other neighbor, a woman in her mid-80s, is an older adult. This neighbor has difficulty walking and no longer drives a car. The Smiths help her with chores around the house and often take her shopping.

Until her divorce, Lois had focused primarily on raising her children. After the divorce at age 43, she needed to enter the job market. Without formal education beyond high school, she had difficulty finding employment. She worked in a number of low-paying short-term jobs before finding a permanent position as a secretary at a small local company. She has only a small retirement benefit from her 12 years on that job. Gene had worked as a bookkeeper and later assistant manager with a local hardware store for more than 30 years. Although their combined retirement benefits enable them to lead a comfortable retirement, Gene continues to work at the hardware store on a part-time basis.

The transition into retirement has not been easy for the Smiths. Both Gene and Lois retired last year, which required them to adjust all at once to a decrease in income. Much more difficult, however, has been the loss of status and feeling of void that they are experiencing. Both were accustomed to the structure provided by work. Gene gladly assists in his former company on a part-time basis, but he worries that his employer will think he's getting too old. Lois has no plans to reenter the workforce. She would like her daughter to live closer so she could spend more time with the grandchildren. Although the infrequency of the visits with the grandchildren has placed some strain on Lois's relationship with her daughter, especially in the period following her retirement, Lois has now begun to enjoy the trips to visit with her daughter as a welcome change in her daily routine. But those visits are relatively infrequent, and Lois often wishes she had more to do.

CASE STUDY 9.2

Ms. Ruby Johnson, Caretaker for Three Generations

Ms. Ruby Johnson is a handsome woman who describes herself as a "hard-boiled, 71-year-old African American" who spent the first 30 years of her life in Harlem, until she settled in the Bronx, New York. She married at 19 and lived with her husband until her 30th birthday. During her initial assessment for case management services, she explained her divorce with what appeared to be great pride. On her 29th birthday, Ruby told her husband that he had one more year to choose between "me and the bottle." She tolerated his daily drinking for another year,

(Continued)

(Continued)

but when he came home drunk on her 30th birthday, she took their 6-year-old daughter and left him and, she explained, "never looked back."

Ruby immediately got a relatively high-paying—albeit tedious—job working for the postal service. At the same time, she found the Bronx apartment, in which she has resided for the past 41 years. Ruby lived there with her daughter, Darlene, for 18 years until she "put that girl out" on what she describes as the saddest day of her life.

Darlene was 21 when she made Ruby the grandmother of Tiffany, a vivacious little girl in good health. A year later, Darlene began using drugs when Tiffany's father abandoned them. By the time Darlene was 24, she had a series of warnings and arrests for drug possession and prostitution. Ruby explained that it "broke my heart that my little girl was out there sellin' herself for drug money." Continuing the story in an unusually angry tone, she explained that "I wasn't gonna have no 'ho' live in my house."

During her initial interview, Ruby's anger was betrayed by a flicker of pride when she explained that Darlene, now 46, has been drug-free for more than 20 years. Tiffany is 25 and lives with her husband and two children. They have taken Darlene into their home to help Ruby. Ruby flashed a big smile when she shared that "Tiffany and Carl [her husband] made me a great-grandma twice, and they are taking care of Darlene for me now." Darlene also has a younger daughter—Rebecca—from what Ruby describes as another "bad" relationship with a "no-good man." Rebecca, age 16, has been living with Ruby for the past 2 years since she started having difficulty in school and needed more supervision than Darlene was able to provide.

In addition, about a year ago, Ruby became the care provider for her father, George. He is 89 and moved into Ruby's apartment because he was no longer able to live independently after his brother's death. On most weeknights, Ruby cooks for her father, her granddaughter, and everyone at Tiffany's house as well. Ruby says she loves having her family around, but she just doesn't have half the energy she used to have.

Ruby retired 5 years ago from the postal service, where she worked for 36 years. In addition to her pension and Social Security, she now earns a small amount for working part-time providing child care for a former co-worker's daughter. Ruby explains that she has to take the extra work in order to cover her father's prescription expenses not covered by his Medicare benefits and to help pay medical/prescription bills for Tiffany's household. Tiffany and Carl receive no medical benefits from their employers and have been considering lowering their income in order to qualify for Medicaid benefits. As this is being written in 2014, they are confused about whether the Affordable Care Act will allow them to continue to work and also have health insurance. Ruby wants them to keep working, so she has been trying to use her connections to get them jobs with the postal service. Ruby reports this to be her greatest frustration, because her best postal service contacts are "either retired or dead." Although Ruby's health is currently stable, she is particularly concerned that it may worsen. She is diabetic and insulin dependent and worries about all the family members for whom she feels responsible. During the initial interview, Ruby confided that she thinks her physical demise has begun. Her greatest fear is death; not for herself, she says, but for the effect it would have on her family. She then asked her social worker to help her find a way to ensure their well-being after her death.

—Peter Maramaldi

Joseph and Elizabeth Menzel, a German Couple

Christine, the 51-year-old daughter of Joseph and Elizabeth Menzel, came to the geriatric counseling center in a small town in Bavaria, Germany. She indicated that she could no longer provide adequate care to her parents and requested assistance from the geriatric social work team. Christine described the family situation as follows.

Her parents, Joseph and Elizabeth, live in a small house about 4 miles away from her apartment. Her brother Thomas also lives close by, but he can only provide help on the weekends because of his employment situation. The 79-year-old mother has been diagnosed with dementia of the Alzheimer's type. Her increasing forgetfulness is beginning to interfere with her mastery of the household and some other activities of daily living. Her 84-year-old father's behavior is also adding to the mother's difficulties. Joseph Menzel is described as an authoritarian and a very dominant person. For example, Christine says that he does not allow his wife to select which television shows she can watch or what music she can to listen to, even though she would like to make such choices by herself. According to the daughter, his behavior seems to add to Elizabeth Menzel's confusion and lack of personal confidence. At the same time, however, Joseph Menzel spends a lot of his time in bed. During those times he does not interact much with Elizabeth Menzel. Sometimes he does not get up all day and neglects his own personal care. It is not clear how much his staying in bed is related to his general health condition; he has silicosis and congestive heart failure.

The couple lives a fairly isolated life and has no friends. Family members, the son Thomas, the daughter Christine and her partner, four grandchildren, and a brother of Elizabeth Menzel, are the only occasional visitors. Christine's primary concern is with her mother's well-being. The mother needs assistance with the instrumental activities of daily living as well as with her health care. Having full-time employment, Christine indicates that she has a hard time providing the assistance and care she thinks is needed. Chores such as doctors' visits, shopping, cleaning, and regular checking in with the parents can be done by her and her brother. However, additional care responsibilities seem to be beyond Christine's capacity at this time. During the initial contact with Christine, the following services were discussed:

- An application for additional funding through the long-term care insurance (German Pflegeversicherung) will be completed. Because Elizabeth Menzel suffers from dementia, she would be eligible for higher levels of support.
- A local care provider will be hired to help with managing medications. It is expected that this may help the parents get used to receiving outside assistance, in case they require higher levels of support with physical care and hygiene down the road. Having someone stop by on a daily basis will also provide an added measure of security and social contact.
- The Menzels will apply for daily lunch delivery through the local Meals on Wheels service.
- A volunteer will be found through the local volunteer network. This person should stop by one to two times per week to engage the mother in activities such as music, walks, playing games, or memory training.
- Elizabeth Menzel will be asked whether she would like to attend the weekly Erzählcafé meetings, a local group for persons with dementia.

(Continued)

- Joseph Menzel will receive information from the geriatric counseling center regarding how to attend to his wife's dementia. Furthermore, an assessment will be completed to establish whether he has depression, and, if needed, he will be connected to relevant medical services.
- In addition to receiving assistance from the geriatric counseling center, Christine will be invited to participate in a support group for relatives and caregivers of persons with dementia.

All of the described services and programs were secured within a short succession. After three initial visits, Elizabeth Menzel has established a good relationship with the volunteer helper and indicates that she likes attending the Erzählcafé meetings. After the assistance for his wife started, Joseph Menzel opened up to having a conversation with the geriatric social worker. He indicated that he was thinking a lot lately about his own personal biography. He and his wife were displaced after the war. They grew up as neighbors in Silesia (today part of Poland). Both of their families had to leave everything behind and flee overnight in October 1946. After staying in various refugee camps, their families finally ended up in Bavaria. This is where they started dating and finally married. Having lost everything, they had to start all over again. They had to work hard for everything they have today. Joseph Menzel worked his entire life as a miner, supplementing his income through a second job painting houses. His wife was employed as a seamstress. Respected for their hard work and engagement, they were soon accepted as members of their new community. However, Joseph Menzel says that he has never come to terms with his postwar displacement and the loss of his homeland. He started a community group and organized regular meetings for displaced persons. Together with his daughter, he also wrote a book about his homeland. Now he feels too weak and ill to do anything. He just wants to stay at home and sit in his recliner all day. After talking with the geriatric social worker, Joseph Menzel overcame his initial reluctance and agreed to have additional contacts with the geriatric counseling center.

Soon after connecting with the geriatric counseling center, Christine unexpectedly died during a routine surgery. After the initial shock and grieving of the unexpected loss, the family began adjusting to the new situation. The brother assumed the overall coordination and management of his mother's care. Other family members took on more responsibilities and increased the frequency of visiting their grandmother. The contacts with the volunteer proved to be a valuable support for Elizabeth Menzel's work around the loss and grief issues. In spite of her dementia, she experienced her daughter's death intensively.

While this all was occurring, Joseph Menzel's health declined rapidly. He has been hospitalized twice for longer periods over the past few months. During this time, more intensive assistance had to be provided to his wife.

Students in the United States are probably not familiar with the Bavarian geriatric counseling centers. So some description is in order. The regional funding providers in Bavaria realized that older adults have a higher unmet need for social-psychiatric assistance than younger adults. In an effort to address this need, geriatric counseling centers were created. In urban settings, the work is accomplished through interdisciplinary teams consisting of social workers, psychiatric nurses, psychologists, and occupational therapists. The task of the counseling center is to coordinate and provide geriatric services to older adults in the community and to create service provider networks. In rural areas, such as the area in which the Menzels live, geriatric counseling centers assume additional provision-related tasks, including direct practice, home visiting, caregiver support and counseling, case management, developing senior groups (groups focusing on dementia, life review/biographical work, grief, or depression), creation of volunteer networks and training of volunteers, and psycho-educational work.

—Rosa Schnitzenbaumer

DEMOGRAPHICS OF THE OLDER POPULATION _____

As you can see from the stories of Gene and Lois Smith, Ruby Johnson, and Joseph and Elizabeth Menzel, older adults do not live primarily in the past. Like all other individuals, their day-to-day life incorporates past, present, and future orientations. In terms of their life span, they have more time past them and less time ahead, but research regularly shows that the overemphasis on the past is a myth (Mayer et al., 1999). Research from the longitudinal Berlin Aging Study has been able to dispel some of the commonly held beliefs about older adults. According to their research as well as findings from other studies, older adults

- are not preoccupied with death and dying,
- are able and willing to learn new things,
- still feel that they can and want to be in control of their life,
- still have life goals,
- do not live primarily in the past, and
- still live an active life, their health permitting.

Data collection for the Berlin Aging Study II began in 2009 and will provide new information about the aging process in the years to come.

The term *late adulthood* covers about one quarter to one third of a person's life and includes active and less active, healthy and less healthy, working and nonworking persons. Late adulthood encompasses a wide range of age-related life experiences. Someone reaching late adulthood today and having lived in the United States has experienced school segregation and busing for the purposes of school integration, Martin Luther King's "I Have a Dream" speech, but also the election of the first African American president and the appointment of the first Latina Supreme Court justice. He or she may have experienced the Dust Bowl and two world wars and would have grown up listening to radio shows before TV existed. The person may have been at Woodstock and could be the in the age cohort of Mick Jagger and Bob Dylan. Every client in the opening case studies could be considered old,

and yet, they are functioning in different ways and at different levels. In the context of U.S. society, the term *old* can have many meanings. These meanings reflect attitudes, assumptions, biases, and cultural interpretations of what it means to grow older. In discussing life course trajectories, we commonly use the terms *older population* or *elderly persons* to refer to those over 65 years of age. But an Olympic gymnast is "old" at age 25, a president of the United States is "young" at age 50, and a 70-year-old may not consider herself "old" at all.

Late adulthood is perhaps a more precise term than *old*, but it can still be confusing because of the 50-year range of ages it may include. Late adulthood is considered to start at 65 and continue through the 85-and-older range. Considering age 65 as the starting point for late adulthood is somewhat arbitrary, since there is no sudden change to our physiology, biology, or personality. Rather, it can be traced back to Bismarck's social insurance schemes in Germany more than 100 years ago and the introduction of the Social Security Act in the United States in 1935. In both cases, 65 years was selected for retirement based on population statistics and expected survival rates. Many people today reach the life stage of late adulthood. In 2013, there were approximately 579 million people 65 years or older in the world, and by 2050 this number is expected to increase to 1.6 billion (U.S. Census Bureau, 2014). In 2012, the World Health Organization (2012f) estimated that, worldwide, adults aged 65 and older will outnumber children younger than age 5 within 5 years, and by 2050, older adults will outnumber children younger than age 14. Globally, the United States is fairly young as wealthy nations go, with 41.1 million, or slightly more than 13% of its population, people 65 and older in 2011 (Administration on Aging, 2012). Most European countries average 15% of their population at 65 or older. Japan's and Italy's older populations stood at 20% of the total population in 2008 (Federal Interagency Forum on Aging-Related Statistics, 2008).

According to U.S. Census data, the 85-and-older population is the fastest growing segment of the aging population, projected to increase from

4.2 million in 2000 and 5.7 million in 2011 to 14.1 million in 2040 (Administration on Aging, 2012). There are increasing numbers of people 100 years and older, a staggering 117% increase from 1990 figures (Administration on Aging, 2008). As of 2011, persons reaching age 65 have an average life expectancy of an additional 19.2 years (20.4 years for females and 17.8 for males). A child born in 2011 could expect to live 78.7 years, about 30 years longer than a child born in 1900 (Administration on Aging, 2012).

> What factors are leading to this trend toward increased longevity?

Increased life expectancy is a product of a number of factors: decreased mortality of children and young adults, decreased mortality among the aging, improved health technology, and other factors. The enormous increase in life expectancy is not unique to the United States. Indeed, recent research found that the United States has the lowest average life expectancy of 17 high-income countries, including European countries, Canada, Australia, and Japan. The researchers speculated that these differences in life expectancy were related to differences in access to health care, health behaviors, income inequality, and physical environments (dependence on automobiles) (Woolf & Aron, 2013). But increasing life expectancy is not just happening in high-income countries. Currrently, 60% of the population older than 65 lives in low- and middle-income countries, and this may increase to 75% by 2020 (Hooyman & Kiyak, 2011). However, the average life expectancy at birth is 55 in the least economically advanced countries, compared with an average of 77 in the most economically advanced countries (Hooyman & Kiyak, 2011).

Life expectancy in the United States varies by race, sex, and socioeconomic status. In 2010, the overall life expectancy at birth in the United States was 78.7 years (Hoyert & Xu, 2012). It was 86.5 for Asian Americans, 82.8 for Latinos, 78.9 for Whites, 76.9 for Native Americans, and 74.6 for African Americans (Henry J. Kaiser Family Foundation, 2013). Females had an average life expectancy at birth of 81.0 years compared with an average of 76.2 years for males (Hoyert & Xu, 2012). Life expectancy increases with socioeconomic advantage, and recent research indicates that as income inequality grows, life expectancy is actually falling in some segments of the U.S. working class. In 2008, U.S. men and women with less than 12 years of education had life expectancies at the level experienced in the 1950s and 1960s (Olshansky et al., 2012). Researchers have noted the current health advantage of U.S. Latinos over other groups, except for Asian Americans, but predict that this advantage will disappear as second- and third-generation Latino immigrants reach late adulthood (Olshansky et al., 2012).

Age structure, the segmentation of society by age, will affect the economic and social condition of the nation, especially as it regards dependence. An interesting side effect of the growing elderly population is a shifting **dependency ratio**—a demographic indicator that expresses the degree of demand placed on society by the young and the aged combined, the ratio of dependent age groups to the working-age population. There are three dependency ratios: the old-age dependency ratio, the number of elders 65 and older per 100 people ages 20 to 64; the youth dependency ratio, the number of children younger than 20 per 100 persons ages 20 to 64; and the total dependency ratio, the combination of both of these categories (U.S. Census Bureau, 2010). The nature of the U.S. dependency ratio has changed gradually over the past century, as the percentage of children and adolescents in the population has decreased and the percentage of dependent older adults has increased. As Exhibit 9.1 demonstrates, the old-age dependency ratio is predicted to continue to increase at a fairly rapid pace in the near future. The overall dependency ratio is expected to stabilize to about 85 youth and older adults per 100 persons ages 20 to 64 between 2030 and 2050 (U.S. Census Bureau, 2010). The social and economic implications of this increase in the dependency ratio are the focus and concern of many scholars and policymakers.

The older population encompasses a broad age range and is often categorized into subgroups: the young-old (ages 65 to 74), the middle-old

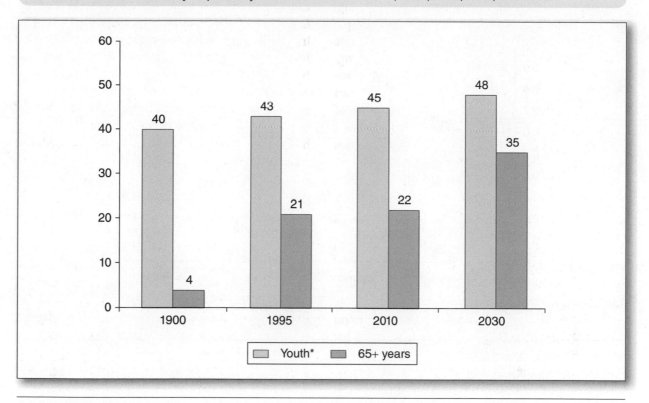

SOURCE: U.S. Census Bureau, 2010

*1900 and 1995 youth dependency based on newborns to 17-year-olds; 2010 and 2030 dependency based on newborns to 19-year-olds.

(ages 75 to 84), and the oldest-old (over 85). The Smiths and Ruby Johnson exemplify the young-old, the Menzels the middle-old. In this chapter, we discuss those persons in the young-old and middle-old categories, ages approximately 65 to 84. Very late adulthood is discussed in Chapter 10, covering ages 85 and older.

The United States is one of the most racially and ethnically diverse societies in the world and becoming more so every day. The aging population reflects the shifting racial and ethnic trends in the general population, with racial and ethnic minority persons projected to become 42% of the old-age population by 2050 (U.S. Census Bureau, 2010). Exhibit 9.2 demonstrates the profound shift in the racial and ethnic makeup of the older adult population projected to occur from 2010 to 2050. The share of the population 65 and older that is White is projected to decrease by 10%, the share that is Hispanic is projected to increase from 7% to 20%, the share that is Black is expected to increase from 9% to 12%, and the share that is Asian is projected to increase from 3% to 9%. Although their numbers will remain small, large growth is projected in the older adult population of American Indian and Alsaka Natives, Native Hawaiian and other Pacific Islanders, and individuals of two or more races.

> How are gender, race, ethnicity, and social class related in late adulthood?

Among the older population in the United States, women—especially those in very late adulthood (85 and older)—continue to outnumber

Exhibit 9.2   Racial or Ethnic Makeup of Elderly U.S. Population 2010–2050

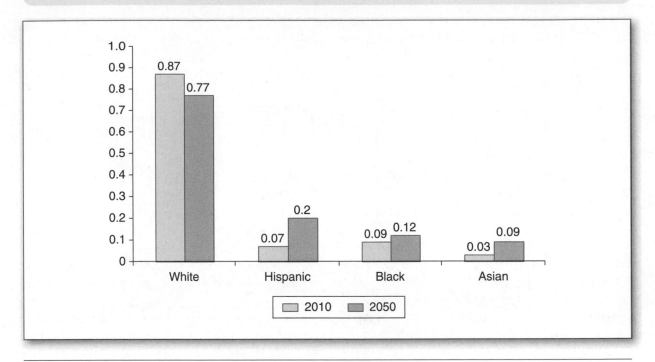

SOURCE: U.S. Census Bureau, 2010

men across all racial and ethnic groups. Census data analyzed in 2012 indicate that older women (23.4 million) outnumber older men (17.9 million) (Administration on Aging, 2012). In 2007, the sex ratio among older adults stood at 137 females per 100 males. The female-to-male ratio increases with age, ranging from 114 females per 100 males for the 65-to-69 age group to a high of 210 females per 100 males for those 85 and older (Administration on Aging, 2008). As long as men exceed women in mortality rates, women will outnumber men among the elderly, especially in the oldest-old group of 85 years or more.

One of the biggest gender differences in life circumstances of older adults relates to marital status. Older men are more likely to be married than older women. According to data from 2012, 72% of men 65 and older lived with a spouse compared with 45% of women in the same age group. The proportion of older adults living with a spouse decreased with age, more severely for women than for men;

only 32% of women over age 75 lived with a spouse. About 28% of noninstitutionalized older adults lived alone in 2012, 36% of older women and 19% of older men. The proportion living alone increases with age, and by age 75, 46% of older women live alone (Administration on Aging, 2012).

In 2012, 9.1% of the U.S. elderly population was living in poverty. Gender, race, and ethnicity have a significant effect on the economic status of elderly individuals. In 2010, the poverty rate for women age 65 and older was 60% higher than for older men, 10.7% compared with 6.7% (Women's Legal Defense and Education Fund, 2012). The rates of poverty were higher for older women and men living alone, 18.9% for women and 11.9% for men (Entmacher, Robbins, Vogtman, & Fohlich, 2013). There are also significant racial and ethnic differences in poverty rates among older adults. In 2012, 7.8% of White elderly lived in poverty, compared with 18.3% of African American, 12.4% of Asian, and 20.6% of Hispanic older adults (U.S. Census Bureau, 2013a).

The geographic distribution of the elderly population varies considerably across the United States. In 2011, about half (51%) of persons 65 and older lived in nine states: California, Florida, New York, Texas, Pennsylvania, Ohio, Illinois, Michigan, and North Carolina (Administration on Aging, 2012). A large majority, 81%, of persons 65 and older lived in metropolitan areas, with 77% of these living outside the principal city and 34% living inside the principal city. Older adults are less likely than other age groups to change residence; from 2011 to 2012, 3% of older adults moved compared with 14% of the younger-than-65 population. Residential mobility can lead to changing age structures within neighborhoods and thus affect the elderly person's life. One study noted that the role of neighborhood structural context, as measured by poverty, residential stability, and aged-based demographic concentration, was predictive of the health and well-being of elders (Subramanian, Kubzansky, Berman, Fay, & Kawachi, 2006). For example, the Smiths used to be a "typical" family in their neighborhood. Now, as one of only two households with elderly occupants, they are the exception.

CULTURAL CONSTRUCTION OF LATE ADULTHOOD

The ethnic and racial diversity of the older population in the United States underscores the complexity and importance of taking cultural differences in perceptions of aging into account. A salient example of cultural differences in approaches to aging is the contrasts between traditional Chinese and mainstream U.S. beliefs and values. China has been described in anthropological literature as a "gerontocracy," wherein older people are venerated, given deference, and valued in nearly every task. Benefiting from the Confucian value of filial piety, older people hold a revered position in the family and society.

> How important is social age in defining late adulthood?

By contrast, consider the traditional cultural influences in the United States, where individualism, independence, and self-reliance are core values that inherently conflict with the aging process. In the United States, older people have

Photos 9.1a & b The ethnic and racial diversity of the older population in the United States underscores the importance of taking cultural differences in perceptions of aging into account.

© Stockbyte/ThinkStock; © Creatas Images/ThinkStock

traditionally been collectively regarded as dependent, and cultural values dictate that older people living independently are given higher regard than those requiring assistance. As people age, they strive to maintain the independence and avoid—at all costs—becoming a burden to their family. Older people in the United States typically resort to intervention from private or social programs to maintain their independence rather than turning to family. By contrast, Chinese elders traditionally looked forward to the day when they would become part of their children's household, to live out their days being venerated by their families (Gardiner & Kosmitzki, 2011).

No discussion of comparisons between cultures would be complete without mention of differences that occur within groups. An individual Chinese person might value independence. And an individual in the United States might be closer to the Confucian value of filial piety than traditional U.S. values. Additionally, processes such as acculturation, assimilation, and bicultural socialization further influence the norms, values, expectations, and beliefs of all cultural groups, including that which is considered the dominant cultural norm. Globalization of economic and information exchange also impacts and changes the cultural norms of all countries so that culture must be construed as something that is dynamic, fluid, emergent, improvisational, and enacted (Gardiner & Kosmitzki, 2011). In fact, U.S. values of aging appear to be shifting, influenced in part by political and market forces. In the United States, we are now bombarded with contradictory information about aging—media presentations of long-lived, vibrant older adults are juxtaposed with media presentations of nursing home horror stories.

In his book *Aging Well*, George Vaillant (2002) raises the question "Will the longevity granted to us by modern medicine be a curse or a blessing?" (p. 3). The answer, he suggests, is influenced by individual, societal, and cultural values, but his research makes him optimistic. Vaillant (2002, 2012) reports on the most long-term longitudinal research available, the Study of Adult Development. The study includes three separate cohorts of 824 persons, all of whom have been studied since adolescence, covering almost 75 years:

1. *268 socially advantaged graduates of Harvard University born about 1920.* These research participants were selected for their physical and psychological health as they began college.

2. *456 socially disadvantaged inner-city men born in 1930.* These research participants were selected because they were nondelinquent at age 14. Half of their families were known to five or more social agencies, and more than two thirds of their families had been recent public welfare recipients.

3. *90 middle-class intellectually gifted women born about 1910.* These participants were selected for their high IQs when they were in California elementary schools.

A significant limitation of the study is the lack of racial and ethnic diversity among the participants, who are almost exclusively White. The great strength of the study is its ability to control cohort effects by following the same participants over such a long period of time.

Much of the news from the Study of Adult Development is good. Vaillant reminds us that Immanuel Kant wrote his first book of philosophy at 57, Titian created many artworks after 76, Ben Franklin invented bifocals at 78, and Will Durant won a Pulitzer Prize for history at 83. Unless they develop a brain disease, the majority of older adults maintain a "modest sense of well-being" (2002, p. 5) until a few months before they die. Older adults are also less depressed than the general population and have a tendency to remember pleasant more than unpleasant events (Vaillant, 2012). Many older adults acknowledge hardships of aging but also see a reason to continue to live. Vaillant (2002) concludes that "positive aging

> How much choice do we have over the six traits for "growing old with grace"?

Exhibit 9.3   Six Traits for Growing Old With Grace

1. Caring about others and remaining open to new ideas
2. Showing cheerful tolerance of the indignities of old age
3. Maintaining hope
4. Maintaining a sense of humor and capacity for play
5. Taking sustenance from past accomplishments while remaining curious and continuing to learn from the next generation
6. Maintaining contact and intimacy with old friends

SOURCE: Based on Vaillant, 2002, pp. 310–311

means to love, to work, to learn something we did not know yesterday, and to enjoy the remaining precious moments with loved ones" (p. 16). Although he found many paths to successful aging, Vaillant identifies six traits for "growing old with grace," found in Exhibit 9.3.

Another recent study using longitudinal data from the Americans' Changing Lives (ACL) study continues to examine the question of the impact of life expectancy and quality of life as a person ages. This is a nationally representative sample of adults age 25 and older, first interviewed in 1986 and reinterviewed in 1989, 1994, and 2001/2002 (House, Lantz, & Herd, 2005). A fifth wave of data collection was completed in May 2012, and data analysis is in the early stages as this chapter is being written (Americans' Changing Lives, 2013). The sample for this study has more racial diversity than the Study of Adult Development. The ACL was designed to address one central dilemma of research on aging and health: whether increased life expectancy in the United States and other economically advanced nations foreshadowed a scenario of longer life but worsening health with the result of increasing chronically ill and functionally limited and disabled people requiring expensive medical and long-term care—or whether, through increased understanding of psychosocial as well as biomedical risk factors, the onset of serious morbidity and attendant functional limitation and disability could be potentially postponed or "compressed."

These authors focused on socioeconomic disparities in health changes through the middle and later years. They represent a set of scholars who are examining a theoretical concept of cumulative advantage and disadvantage and its role in understanding differential aging among various populations (Schöllgen, Huxhold, & Tesch-Römer, 2010). (See Chapter 1 for a discussion of these concepts.) They argue that multiple interacting factors throughout the life course impact the quality of the health of older individuals. For example, early poverty, lifetime of poverty, poor environmental conditions, poor education, race, and gender have a direct impact on how a person will age. It is not a simple linear causal track but instead reflects the complexity of interacting risk and protective factors.

Reviewing research findings from the ACL study, House et al. (2005) examined the impact of two factors related to socioeconomic status (SES), education and income, on poor health. They found that overall socioeconomic disparities do impact health outcomes rather than the reverse. Additionally, they found that education has a greater impact than income on the onset of functional limitations or disabilities. Income, however, has a greater impact on the progression of functional limitations. Finally, the impact of educational disparities on the onset of functional limitations increased strikingly in later middle and early old age, with more highly educated individuals postponing limitations and thus compressing the number of years spent with limitations (House et al., 2005). Other authors (see George, 2005) raise the question as to whether race and gender are more fundamentally associated with illness and poor quality of aging than the more general category of SES.

PSYCHOSOCIAL THEORETICAL PERSPECTIVES ON SOCIAL GERONTOLOGY _____

How social workers see and interpret aging will inspire our interventions with older adults. **Social gerontology**—the social science that studies human aging—offers several theoretical perspectives that can explain the process of growing old. Nine predominant theories of social gerontology are introduced here. An overview of the primary concepts of each theory is presented in Exhibit 9.4.

    1. *Disengagement theory.* **Disengagement theory** suggests that as elderly individuals grow older, they gradually decrease their social interactions and ties and become increasingly self-preoccupied (Cumming & Henry, 1961). This is sometimes seen as a coping mechanism in the face of ongoing deterioration and loss (Tobin, 1988). In addition, society disengages itself from older adults. Although disengagement is seen as a normative and functional process of transferring

power within society, the theory does not explain, for example, the fact that a growing number of older persons, such as Gene and Lois Smith and Ruby Johnson, continue to assume active roles in society (Hendricks & Hatch, 2006). Although it was the first comprehensive theory trying to explain the aging process (Achenbaum & Bengston, 1994), disengagement theory has received much criticism and little research support. To the contrary, research conducted through the National Social Life Health and Aging Project shows that older Americans are generally well-connected and engaged in community life according to their abilities (Cornwell, Laumann, & Schumm, 2008). Disengagement theory is now widely discounted by gerontologists (Hooyman & Kiyak, 2011).

    2. *Activity theory.* **Activity theory** states that higher levels of activity and involvement are directly related to higher levels of life satisfaction in elderly people (Havighurst, 1968). If they can, individuals stay active and involved and carry on as many activities of middle adulthood as possible. There is growing evidence that examining

Exhibit 9.4   Psychosocial Theoretical Perspectives on Social Gerontology

Theory	Primary Theme
Disengagement theory	Elderly persons gradually disengage from society.
Activity theory	Level of life satisfaction is related to level of activity.
Continuity theory	Elderly persons continue to adapt and continue their interaction patterns.
Social construction theory	Self-concepts arise through interaction with the environment.
Feminist theories	Gender is an important organizing factor in the aging experience.
Social exchange theory	Resource exchanges in interpersonal interactions change with age.
Life course perspective/life course capital perspective	Aging is a dynamic, lifelong process characterized by many transitions. People accumulate human capital during the life course to address their needs.
Age stratification perspective	Society is stratified by age, which determines people's roles and rights.
Productive aging theory	A new generation of older adults is more physically active, mobile, healthy, and economically secure.

Photo 9.2 Variables that often predict healthy aging include practicing healthy habits such as exercising, eating well, maintaining a healthy weight, and not smoking or abusing alcohol.

© iStockphoto.com

and promoting physical activity is associated with postponing functional limitation and disability (Benjamin, Edwards, & Bharti, 2005). Activity theory has received some criticism for not addressing relatively high levels of satisfaction for individuals such as Ms. Johnson, whose level of activity is declining. It also does not address the choice made by many older individuals to adopt a more relaxed lifestyle. Some argue that the theory does not adequately address factors such as ethnicity, lifestyle, gender, and socioeconomic status (Eliopoulus, 2010; Moody & Sasser, 2012). Activity theory also does not sufficiently take into account individual life circumstances and loses sight of personhood in order to satisfy society's view of how people should age (Moody & Sasser, 2012).

3. *Continuity theory.* **Continuity theory** was developed in response to critiques of the disengagement and activity theories. According to continuity theory, individuals adapt to changes by using the same coping styles they have used throughout the life course, and they adopt new roles that substitute for roles lost because of age (Neugarten, Havighurst, & Tobin, 1968). Individual personality differences are seen as a major influence in adaptation to old age. Those individuals who were active earlier in life stay active in later life, whereas those who adopted a more passive lifestyle continue to do so in old age. Older adults also typically retain the same stance concerning religion and sex as they always did. Current scholarship considers the interaction between personal and contextual factors that promote or impede the accomplishment of desired goals and new roles, recognizing that individuals have control over some contextual factors but not others (Brandtstadter, 2006). Continuity theory might help counsel someone such as Lois Smith. Just as she adapted actively to her divorce by reentering the job market later in life, she might actively seek new roles in retirement. She might find great satisfaction in volunteering in her church and in being a grandmother. Continuity theory is difficult to empirically test (Hooyman & Kiyak, 2011). There is also criticism regarding the definition of "normal aging." The theory distinguishes normal aging from pathological aging and does not sufficiently address older persons with chronic health conditions (Quadagno, 2007).

4. *Social construction theory.* **Social construction theory** aims to understand and explain the influence of social definitions, social interactions, and social structures on the individual elderly person. This theoretical framework suggests that ways of understanding are shaped by the cultural, social, historical, political, and economic conditions in which knowledge is developed; thus, values are associated with various ways of understanding (Dean, 1993). Conceptions about aging arise through interactions of an individual with the social environment (Dannefer & Perlmutter, 1990). The recent conceptualization of "gerotranscendence" is an example of the application of social constructionist theory to aging. The idea of gerotranscendence holds that human development extends into old age and does not simply end or

diminish with aging (Hooyman & Kiyak, 2011; Tornstam, 2005). According to this theory, aging persons evaluate their lives in terms of the time they have ahead and try to derive a sense of identity, self, and place in the world and universe (Degges-White, 2005; Tornstam, 2005). Using focus group methodology, Wadensten (2005) found that participants identified the concept of gerotranscendence as salient and beneficial to them because it gave them a more positive view of aging, allowing them to affirm themselves as they are.

5. *Feminist theories.* Proponents of **feminist theories** of aging suggest that gender is a key factor in understanding a person's aging experience. They contend that because gender is a critical social stratification factor with attendant power, privilege, and status that produces inequalities and disparities throughout the life course, we can only understand aging by taking gender into account (Arber & Ginn, 1995). Gender is viewed as influencing the life course trajectory by impacting access and opportunity, health disparities, and disparities in socioeconomic opportunities and by creating a lifelong condition of "constrained choice" (Rieker & Bird, 2005). Gabriela Spector-Mersel (2006) argues that in Western societies, older persons have been portrayed as "ungendered." Older men are in a paradoxical position because the metaphors for old age are the opposite of the metaphors for masculinity in these societies. Think, for example, about Joseph Menzel's experience as a caregiver to his wife and how some of his role obligations differ from his lifelong role expectations as a man. Also, consider Ms. Johnson's experience as a single older woman. How might her personal situation differ if she were a man?

6. *Social exchange theory.* **Social exchange theory** is built on the notion that an exchange of resources takes place in all interpersonal interactions (Blau, 1964; Homans, 1961). This theory is rooted in an analysis of values developed from a market-driven capitalist society. Individuals will only engage in an exchange if they perceive a favorable cost/benefit ratio or if they see no better alternatives (Hendricks, 1987). As individuals

become older, the resources they are able to bring to the exchange begin to shift. Social exchange theory bases its explanation of the realignment of roles, values, and contributions of older adults on this assumption. For example, many older persons get involved in volunteer activities; this seemingly altruistic activity may also be seen as fulfilling an emotional need that provides a personal gain. Thus, they are able to adjust and adapt to the altered exchange equation. Older individuals who withdraw from social activities may perceive their personal resources as diminished to the point where they have little left to bring to an exchange, thus leading to their increasing seclusion from social interactions. As social workers, then, it is important to explore how older couples such as Joseph and Elizabeth Menzel are dealing with the shift in resources within their relationship. Several studies indicate that maintaining reciprocity is important for older individuals (Fiori, Consedine, & Magai, 2008). For example, one study of reciprocity among residents of assisted living looked at the positive contributions of aging care recipients to their social relationships, including their interactions with caregivers (Beel-Bates, Ingersoll-Dayton, & Nelson, 2007).

7. *Life course perspective.* From the life course perspective, the conceptual framework for this book, aging is a dynamic, lifelong process. Human development is characterized by multidirectionality, multifunctionality, plasticity, and continuity in the person's experiences of gains and losses over the life course (Greve & Staudinger, 2006). Individuals go through many transitions in the course of their life span. Human development continues through aging and involves the interaction of person-specific factors, social structures, and personal agency (Hendricks & Hatch, 2006). The era they live in, the cohort they belong to, and personal and environmental factors influence individuals during these transitions. "Life course capital" is a contemporary addition to the life course perspective. The theory states that people, over the course of their life, accumulate human capital, that is, resources, they can use to address their needs. This capital

can take on various forms; for example, it may be social, biological, psychological, or developmental human capital (Hooyman & Kiyak, 2011). This accumulation of life course capital has an impact on a person's aging, for example, on his or her health (e.g., morbidity, mortality) or wealth (e.g., standard of living in retirement).

8. *Age stratification perspective.* The **age stratification perspective** falls into the tradition of the life course perspective (Foner, 1995; Riley, 1971). Stratification is a sociological concept that describes a hierarchy in a given society. Social stratification is both multidimensional and interactive as individuals occupy multiple social locations with varying amounts of power, privilege, and status. The age stratification perspective suggests that, similar to the way society is structured by socioeconomic class, it is also stratified by age. Roles and rights of individuals are assigned based on their membership in an age group or cohort. Individuals proceed through their life course as part of that cohort. The experience of aging differs across cohorts because cohorts differ in size, composition, and experience with an ever-changing society. Current scholarship argues that social stratifications of gender, race or ethnicity, and socioeconomic status are pertinent stratifications to consider in aging, given the cumulative effect of disparities that are the result of such stratification (George, 2005).

9. *Productive aging.* **Productive aging theory** focuses on the positive changes that have occurred to the older adult population. A new generation of older adults is more independent and better off than previous cohorts in many areas, including health, economic status, mobility, and education (Kaye, 2005). Productive aging is not necessarily the continuation of an older person as contributor to the workforce but includes other behavior that is satisfying and meaningful to the older person. This approach maintains that the focus of aging theories has been too much on the losses, crises, and problems of aging, while neglecting the positive side of becoming older. The proponents of this perspective distinguish between three dimensions of productive aging: inner affective, inner utilitarian, and outer utilitarian (Kaye, 2005). The internal affective dimension focuses on personal growth and factors improving quality of life. The internal utilitarian dimension emphasizes functional growth, while the focus of the external utilitarian dimension is on societal contributions made by older adults to their communities, families, and friends (Kaye, 2005). Exhibit 9.5 provides an overview of these dimensions.

> ### Critical Thinking Questions 9.1
>
> At what age will you consider yourself old? What do you think your favorite activity will be when you are "old"? What do you think your biggest challenge will be when you are "old"? What do you think will be important to you when you are "old"? Where do you get your ideas about old age?

BIOLOGICAL CHANGES IN LATE ADULTHOOD

Every day, our bodies are changing. In a sense, then, our bodies are constantly aging. As social workers, however, we need not be concerned with the body's aging until it begins to affect the person's ability to function in her or his world, which typically begins to occur in late adulthood. There are more than a dozen biological theories of why our bodies age. In this discussion, I follow Kunlin Jin's (2010) lead and consider two categories of theories: programmed aging theories and damage or error theories. The following discussion of these theories is taken from a review article by Jin. I also discuss developmental biocultural co-constructivism, a newer theoretical approach to aging in the human environment.

Programmed aging theories suggest that aging follows a biological timetable. Jin (2010) identifies three subcategories of programmed aging

> How important is the impact of biological age on the experience of the late-adult phase of the life course?

Exhibit 9.5   Dimensions of Productive Aging

Dimension	Inner (Affective)	Inner (Utilitarian)	Outer (Utilitarian)
Focus and activity	Wellness promotion Life review Self-help Self-improvement Social interaction	Retirement planning Travel Recreation Physical exercise Education	Job training Employment Volunteer service Family support
Primary impact	Self	Self	Self and others
Specific outcomes	Increased personal growth Self-discovery Self-actualization Improved mental health Reduced isolation	Increased financial security Heightened intellectual stimulation Increased fitness and health Increased life security Increased knowledge and skills	Increased financial well-being Continued socialization Maintained identity and purpose Enhanced community well-being Heightened philanthropic expression
General outcomes (all three dimensions)	Enhanced self-esteem Heightened morale Higher quality of life Increased life satisfaction Heightened emotional and physical well-being	Enhanced self-esteem Heightened morale Higher quality of life Increased life satisfaction Heightened emotional and physical well-being	Enhanced self-esteem Heightened morale Higher quality of life Increased life satisfaction Heightened emotional and physical well-being

SOURCE: Adapted from Kaye, 2005, p. 13

theories. *Programmed longevity theory* proposes that biological aging occurs due to gene activity, but the genetic mechanisms of biological aging are not yet known. *Endocrine theory* proposes that biological clocks act through hormones to influence the pace of aging. Recent research indicates that hormones play an active role in regulating biological aging. *Immunological theory* proposes that the immune system is programmed to decline over time. There is strong evidence that the immune system peaks at puberty and gradually declines throughout adulthood.

Damage or error theories of aging emphasize the role of environmental assaults that cause cumulative damage to various biological systems. Jin (2010) identifies five subcategories of damage or error theories. *Wear and tear theory* proposes that parts of the body wear out from repeated use. *Rate of living theory* proposes that the rate of basal metabolism impacts the length of the life span. *Cross-linking theory* proposes that an accumulation of cross-linked proteins damages cells and tissues. *Free radicals theory* proposes that superoxide and other free radicals cause damage to cells, eventually

Photo 9.3 Social workers need to be concerned with aging if and when it affects a person's ability to function in his or her world.

© iStockphoto.com

resulting in cell and organ death. *Somatic DNA damage theory* proposes that aging results from accumulated damage to the genetic integrity of the body's cells. Jin (2010) reports some evidence for each of the damage or error theories, but no one theory is sufficient to explain biological aging.

Developmental biocultural co-constructivism is a recent theoretical orientation to human development (Li, 2009). Although not a theory of aging per se, it adds important concepts for understanding the process of human aging. Theorists following this perspective claim that "brain and culture are in a continuous, interdependent, co-productive transaction and reciprocal determination" (Baltes, Rösler, & Reuter-Lorenz, 2006, p. 3). With this definition, they go beyond the nature

and nurture debate, which focuses on whether nature or nurture makes the greater contribution to human behavior. In their view, this does not sufficiently address the *active* and *multidirectional* nature of this process. Developmental biocultural co-constructivism "gives equal standing to both the brain and the environment" (Baltes et al., 2006, p. 8). The perspective presumes dynamic reciprocal interactions of culture and human environment with the biology of a person. The brain is considered a dependent variable, that is, being coshaped by experiences and culture, and human behavior is "inherently the outcome of a 'dialogue' among and 'co-production' of genes, brain, and culture" (Baltes et al., 2006, p. 6). This is not a passive process. Rather, it can be described as a "shared and *collaborative production*, including *reciprocal modifications* and which under some conditions involves qualitatively new states whose emergence cannot be fully predicted from either of the two sources alone" (Baltes et al., 2006, p. 8, italics in original). Longitudinal research seems to provide support to this theory. For example, Schooler and Mulatu (2004) found reciprocal effects between the intellectual functioning and the complexity of tasks older adults had to fulfill during their employment years.

Health and Longevity

The **mortality rate**—the frequency at which death occurs within a population—has declined significantly for all segments of the population in the United States during the last century. From 1981 to 2009, the overall age-adjusted death rates for all causes of death for individuals 65 years and older declined by 25%. In this age bracket, death rates from heart disease and stroke declined by more than 50%. However, the death rates for some diseases increased; death rates from chronic lower respiratory diseases increased by 57% and death rates from diabetes mellitus were higher in 2009 than in 1981 but lower than in 2001. In 2009, the leading causes of death for people 65 and older were, in descending order, heart disease, cancer, chronic lower respiratory diseases, stroke, Alzheimer's disease, and influenza/pneumonia. Diabetes was the sixth leading cause of death among non-Hispanic Whites but the fourth leading cause of death among non-Hispanic Backs and Hispanics. Overall death rates in 2009 were higher for older men than for older women (Federal Interagency Forum on Aging-Related Statistics, 2012).

As mortality has decreased, **morbidity**—the incidence of disease—has increased. In other words, the proportion of the population suffering from age-related chronic conditions has increased in tandem with the population of elderly persons. In 2009–2010, for people 65 years or older, the most prevalent and debilitating chronic conditions in descending order were hypertension (54% of men, 57% of women), arthritis (45% of men, 56%

of women), heart disease (37% of men, 26% of women), cancer (28% of men, 21% of women), and diabetes (24% of men, 18% of women). Chronic illnesses are long-term, rarely cured, and costly (Federal Interagency Forum on Aging-Related Statistics, 2012).

The prevalence of chronic conditions varies significantly by gender, race, and ethnicity. For example, older women report higher levels of asthma, arthritis, and hypertension than do older men. Older men are more likely to identify heart disease, cancer, and diabetes. Racial and ethnic differences also exist. Non-Hispanic Blacks report higher levels of hypertension (69% compared with 54%) and diabetes (32% compared with 18%) than non-Hispanic Whites. Hispanics report higher levels of diabetes than Whites (33% compared with 18%). Physical decline is also associated with SES, but it is difficult to separate SES from race and ethnicity because minority groups tend to be overrepresented in lower SES groups (Wilmoth & Longino, 2006).

A chronic condition can have considerable impact on a family system. In Ms. Johnson's case, the seven people for whom she cares—including two toddlers, an adolescent, an adult daughter who is functionally impaired, a granddaughter and her husband who both are at risk of leaving the workforce, and an aging father—are all affected by her chronic diabetes. This case illustrates the untold impact of chronic conditions in aging populations that are rarely described by national trend reports.

For many people, illness and death can be postponed through lifestyle changes. In recent years, the importance of preventing illness by promoting good health has received considerable attention. The goals of health promotion for older adults include preventing or delaying the onset of chronic disease and disability; reducing the severity of chronic diseases; and maintaining mental health, physical health, and physical functioning as long as possible. Ways to promote health in old age include improving dietary habits, increasing activity levels and physical exercise, stopping smoking, and obtaining regular health screenings (blood sampling, blood pressure measurement, cancer screening, glaucoma screening) (Centers for Disease Control and Prevention, 2013p; Erickson, Gildengers, & Butters, 2013). An important finding has been the roles of self-efficacy, sense of mastery, positive attitude, and social supports in improving the quality of life and delaying functional limitation and disability (Meisner, 2012).

Age-Related Changes in Physiology

All systems of the body appear to be affected during the aging process. Consider the nervous system. In the brain, neurons and synapses are the transmitters of information throughout the nervous system. As noted in earlier chapters, the number of neurons decreases throughout the life span; the result is a slow decrease of brain mass after age 30. Because we are born with many more neurons and synapses than we need to function, problems usually do not arise, but nerve cells may begin to pass messages more slowly than in the past (Dugdale, 2012c). If the older adult develops brain deficits in one area of the brain, he or she may make up for these deficits by increasing activity in other brain regions (Whitbourne, 2001). However, a neurological injury or disease may result in more permanent and serious consequences for an older person. This is just one of the changes that may affect the brain, spinal cord, nerves, and mechanisms controlling other organs in the body. We look more closely at changes in the brain and neurodegenerative diseases in the next section.

Our cardiovascular system also changes in several ways as we become older. The cardiac output—the amount of blood pumped per minute—decreases throughout adult life, and the pulse slows with age. The arteries become less elastic and harden, which can result in arteriosclerosis. Fatty lipids accumulate in the walls of the blood vessels and make them narrower, which can cause atherosclerosis. As a result of these changes, less oxygen is available for muscular activities. With advancing age, it takes longer for the blood pressure and heart rate to return to normal resting levels after stressful events (Dugdale, 2012d).

The respiratory system too changes with age. Beginning at about 20 to 25 years of age, a person's lung capacity decreases throughout the life span. Breathing becomes a bit more labored. Respiratory muscle strength decreases with age and can interfere with effective coughing (Sharma & Goodwin, 2006). There is great variation in the effect of lung function, however; in healthy older adults who do not smoke, respiratory function is quite good enough for daily activities (Bjorklund, 2011; Sharma & Goodwin, 2006).

The most important age-related change in our skeletal system occurs after age 30, when the destruction of bones begins to outpace the reformation of bones. The gradual decrease in bone mass and bone density can cause osteoporosis, a condition in which the bones become brittle and fragile. Osteoporosis occurs in 20% of women older than 50 and half of women older than 80 (Bjorklund, 2011). It is estimated that bone mineral content decreases by 5% to 12% per decade from the 20s through the 90s. One result is that we get shorter as we age. As the cartilage between the joints wears thin, arthritis, a chronic inflammation of the joints, begins to develop. Although many individuals suffer from some form of arthritis in their 40s, the symptoms are often not painful until late adulthood. Some of these changes can be ameliorated by diet and exercise and by avoiding smoking and alcohol.

With increasing age, the muscular system declines in mass, strength, and endurance. As a consequence, an elderly person may become fatigued more easily. In addition, muscle contractions begin to slow down, which contributes to deteriorating reflexes and incontinence. However, the muscular system of older individuals can be successfully strengthened through weight training and changes in diet and lifestyle (Bjorklund, 2011).

Changes in the neurological, muscular, and skeletal systems have an impact on the sensory system and the sense of balance, which contributes to the increase in accidental falls and bone fractures in late adulthood. Vision decreases with age, and older persons need more light to reach the retina in order to see. The eye's adaptation to the dark slows with age, as does visual acuity, the ability to detect details. Age-related decreases in hearing are caused by degenerative changes in the spiral organ of the ear and the associated nerve cells. Many older adults have a reduced ability to hear high-pitched sounds. By age 65, about one third of adults have significant hearing loss, with men being more likely than women to suffer hearing loss (Federal Interagency Forum on Aging-Related Statistics, 2012). Age-related changes in taste appear to be minimal. Differences may reflect individual factors, such as exposure to environmental conditions like smoking, periodontal disease, or use of medications, rather than general processes of aging. The smell receptors in the nose can decrease with age, however, and become less sensitive (Hooyman & Kiyak, 2011).

The integumentary system includes the skin, hair, and nails. The skin comprises an outer layer (epidermis) and an inner layer (dermis). With age, the epidermis becomes thinner and pigment cells grow and cluster, creating age spots on the skin (Bjorklund, 2011). The sweat and oil-secreting glands decrease, leaving the skin drier and more vulnerable to injury. Much of the fat stored in the hypodermis, the tissue beneath the skin, is lost in age, causing wrinkles. The skin of an older person often feels cool because the blood flow to the skin is reduced (Bjorklund, 2011).

Sexual potency begins to decline at age 20, but without disease, sexual desire and capacity continue in late adulthood. Vaillant (2002) reports that *frequency* of sexual activity decreases, however. He found that partners in good health at 75 to 80 often continue to have sexual relations but that the average frequency is approximately once in every 10 weeks. Some illnesses and some medications can affect the ability of older adults to have and enjoy sex, as can problems in the relationship (National Institute on Aging, 2013a).

Contemporary views on the physiology of aging focus on longevity. For the past 2 decades, an anti-aging medicine movement has focused on developing biomedical interventions that will delay or reverse the biological changes of aging. Currently there are more than 26,000 members of the American Academy of Anti-Aging Medicine, and anti-aging medicine is a big business (Flatt, Settersen, Ponsaran, & Fishman, 2013). Science and technology are creating possibilities that show promise for the future, but there is no evidence that these gains have increased the maximum life span of humans. Some of the more promising possibilities in this area include the following:

• A calorie-restricted diet has the most robust empirical support of any of the anti-aging interventions; it has been shown to extend the maximum life span in laboratory organisms of various species. When caloric intake is reduced while maintaining the proper nutritional balance, age-related decline slows and age-related diseases are reduced (Barzilai & Bartke, 2009; Minor, Allard, Younts, Ward, & de Cabo, 2010). Increases in longevity do not occur because of a reduction in a particular part of the diet but because of caloric reduction in the whole. Some gerontologists believe that most humans will not choose to restrict their diet to the extent necessary to make a difference. Scientists are trying to develop compounds that can be consumed in food or water that will act in the same way as calorie restriction, but none of the compounds under investigation with animal research have been found to have that effect (Minor et al., 2010).

• Supernutrition involves properly dosed dietary supplements of multivitamins and multiminerals, along with restricted fats and fresh, whole, unprocessed foods. The convergence of nutritional sciences and the emphasis on preventive medicine could yield a new generation of supernutritional foods in the not-so-distant future. Reservatol, an ingredient in red wine and red grapes, has demonstrated antiplatelet, anti-inflammatory, anticancer, antimutagenic, and antifungal properties. It thus shows prospect in reducing many age-related diseases, including arthritis, cancer, cardiovascular disease, diabetes, pancreatitis, and kidney disease (Faloon, 2008; Olas & Wachowicz, 2005). Vitamin K keeps calcium in the bones and out of the arteries. New research shows that Vitamin K may reverse arterial calcification, protect against cancer, suppress chronic inflammatory disorders, and extend the human life span (Faloon, 2009). The pharmacy is full of items labeled "supernutrition," but many of the products being sold have no demonstrated effectiveness (Minor et al., 2010). Most nutritional supplements do not carry the same benefits as vitamins and minerals consumed through diet (Tosato, Zamboni, Ferrini, & Cesari, 2007).

- Hormone therapy is already used in some medical conditions today. Further breakthroughs with the use of estrogen, testosterone, melatonin, dehydroepiandrosterone (DHEA), and human growth hormone (HGH) are currently investigated but are wrought with potentially dangerous side effects (Cancer Research UK, 2013; Reed, Merriam, & Kargi, 2013). DHEA increases the production of immune cells and helps fight bacteria and viruses. It may enhance longevity as it increases strength and muscle mass, raises testosterone production, and increases sexual energy (Singh, 2009).

- Gene manipulation could potentially have the greatest impact of all interventions on human aging. The Human Genome Project (HGP), one of the greatest accomplishments in recent times, mapped the total human genetic content. Scientists are now at work trying to learn the function of each gene in the genome in order to find new therapeutic interventions that will target specific genes to prevent and cure diseases (Zhang et al., 2012).

- Bionics and organ or tissue cloning would have seemed like science fiction a generation ago, but the convergence of biological science and engineering may produce limbs and organs to replace those worn out or deteriorated with age. Currently, laboratories and biotechnology researchers can grow skin (used for burn victims) and cartilage (used for joint surgery). Bone substitutes are already being artificially produced. Drugs are being tested that stimulate nerve growth, and techniques may soon be available to implant cells that reverse damage to the central nervous system (Moody, 2010). Tissue and cell cloning have particular appeal for brain diseases such as Parkinson's or Alzheimer's, because they could provide patients with healthy neural tissue identical to their own. In each of these areas, significant research efforts are being conducted the world over. How many of these technologies will come into widespread use is uncertain. It is clear, however, that economic and ethical considerations and debates will be as unprecedented as the technologies themselves.

The Aging Brain and Neurodegenerative Diseases

Before discussing the most common neurodegenerative diseases, dementia, Alzheimer's, and Parkinson's disease, I would like to provide a brief overview of the brain and how it functions. The brain is probably the most complex and least well-understood part of the human body. It weighs about 3 pounds, or about 2% of a person's weight, and is made up of various types of cells. The most essential brain cells are the neurons. They are the "communicators," responsible for most of the information processing in our brain. Between the neurons are synaptic gaps. Our brain has more than 100 trillion of these so-called synapses (Alzheimer's Association, 2013). Information flows from a neuron through the synapses to neuroreceptors, which are the receiver of the next neuron. More than 50 types of such neurotransmitters exist, including dopamine, serotonin, acetylcholine, and norepinephrine. Glial cells are the second major type of brain cells. They are the "housekeepers," providing neurons with nutrition, insulating them, and helping transport damaged cells and debris (Alzheimer's Association, 2013). Capillaries are tiny blood vessels that provide the brain with oxygen, energy, nutrition, and hormones and transport waste. The brain has 400 billion such capillaries. Twenty percent of a person's blood flows through these capillaries to the brain (Alzheimer's Association, 2013).

The brain consists of two cerebral hemispheres. Current science believes that the difference is less in what information the two hemispheres process than in how they process it (Alzheimer's Association, 2013). It seems that the left hemisphere works on the details, while the right hemisphere processes the broader picture. Each brain hemisphere consists of four lobes.

The frontal lobe is the "organizer." This is where thinking, planning, memory, problem solving, and movement are processed. The parietal lobe deals with perceptions and inputs from our senses. It sits right behind the frontal lobe. The occipital lobe processes vision and sits at the back of the cerebral hemisphere. Finally, the temporal lobe focuses on taste, smell, sound, and memory storage. It sits at the side of the brain and below the frontal lobe. At the back bottom of the brain is the cerebellum. This is where balance, coordination, and motor coordination occur. Located below it is the brain stem, connecting the brain with the spinal cord. It manages the body functions that are immediately responsible for our survival such as breathing, heart rate, and blood pressure (Alzheimer's Association, 2013).

Several changes occur to the brain as we age. Between ages 20 and 90, the brain loses 5% to 10% of its weight (Palmer & Francis, 2006). The areas most affected by this decrease are the frontal lobe and the hippocampus. A general loss of neurons also occurs. At the same time, the normal aging brain does not appear to lose synapses (Palmer & Francis, 2006). The transmission of information between neurons through the neurotransmitters can also decrease in some brain regions as we age. Furthermore, there is less growth of new capillaries and a reduced blood flow caused by narrowing arteries in the brain. Plaques and tangles develop in and around the neurons (see discussion of Alzheimer's disease shortly) and inflammation and damage by free radicals increase (Alzheimer's Association, 2013). At the same time, the effects of these changes on performing tasks and memory are generally fairly small. Scores for task performance, for example, are similar for younger and older adults, when the older group is provided with additional time. Older adults can compensate and adapt well to many age-related brain changes. Part of this adaptation occurs through changes in the brain. Neuroimaging shows that some brain functions seem to get reorganized as the brain ages (Reuter-Lorenz, 2002). Imaging results point to a process in which the aging brain starts using areas of the two hemispheres that were previously not focusing on performing those tasks to compensate for age-related loss (Li, 2006). Negative changes can also be offset by age-related overall improvements in some cognitive areas such as verbal knowledge or vocabulary (Alzheimer's Association, 2013). Other brain changes, however, can become more challenging. We now turn to some of these neurodegenerative diseases.

Dementia

Dementia is the term for brain disease in which memory and cognitive abilities deteriorate over time. It may be significantly unrecognized and undiagnosed in many older adults. In 2005, it was estimated that 24.3 million people worldwide had dementia, and one new case is occurring every 7 seconds. A majority, 60%, of people with dementia live in low-income countries. It is forecasted that the numbers of people with dementia will increase by 100% between 2001 and 2040 in high-income countries and by more than 300% in India, China, and south Asia (Ferri et al., 2005). The first nationally representative population-based study of the prevalence of dementia in the United States, conducted in 2007, found the prevalence among persons aged 71 and older to be 13.9%. The prevalence increased with age; it was 5.0% for older adults aged 71 to 79 and 37.4% for those aged 90 or older (Plassman et al., 2007). Reversible dementia is caused by factors such as drug and alcohol use, a brain tumor, subdural hematomas, meningiomas, hypothyroid, syphilis or AIDS, or severe depression, and the cognitive decline is reversible if identified and treated early enough (Joshi & Morley, 2006; Yousuf et al., 2010). Irreversible dementia is not curable. In the advanced stages, the person may repeat the same words over and over again, may have problems using appropriate words, and may not recognize a spouse or other family members. At the same time, the person may still be able to recall and vividly describe events that happened many years ago. Epidemiological studies indicate that Alzheimer's disease is the most common form of dementia, responsible for about 70% of cases (Plassman et al., 2007).

The initial stage of cognitive dysfunction is called *age-associated memory impairment* (AAMI). It is followed by even greater memory loss and diagnosed as *mild cognitive impairment* (MCI), which may progress to dementia. The rate of decline in cognitive and functional skills is predictive of mortality among nondemented older adults (Schupf et al., 2005). AAMI and MCI involve primarily memory loss, whereas dementia results in disruption of daily living and difficulty or inability to function normally. MCIs have been thought not to constitute dementia but to be a transitional stage between normal cognitive functioning and Alzheimer's disease. Studies have identified one subtype of MCI, called nonamnestic, as evidence of early stage Alzheimer's disease (Petersen, 2011).

Risk factors for cognitive decline and dementia include age, family history, Down syndrome, alcohol use, atherosclerosis, high or low blood pressure, high levels of low-density liproprotein (LDL) cholesterol, depression, diabetes, high estrogen levels, elevated blood levels of homocysteine, obesity, and smoking (Mayo Clinic, 2013b). No positive answer has yet been found for how to prevent dementia. However, several studies suggest that social engagement as well as physical and intellectual activity may slow cognitive decline and the progression of dementia (Renaud, Bherer, & Maquestiaux, 2010; Savica & Petersen, 2011)

The case study of Elizabeth Menzel refers to her attendance at an Erzählcafé. We thought you might like to know more about the Erzählcafé. Exhibit 9.6 provides a description of the Erzählcafé and Mrs. Menzel's participation in it.

Alzheimer's Disease

Alzheimer's disease (AD) is the most common type of dementia, accounting for about 70% of cases. In 2013, care for people with AD in the United States was estimated to cost 203 billion dollars, and it is projected that the annual cost will rise to 142 trillion dollars by 2050 (Alzheimer's Association, 2013; Plassman et al., 2007). The number of deaths caused by heart disease, stroke, and many forms of cancer has seen significant reductions during the first half

decade of this century and has continued to decline. In contrast, deaths caused by AD increased 68% from 2000 to 2010 (Alzheimer's Association, 2013). As populations around the world age, this trend can be seen on a global level as well. AD is characterized by a progression of stages. A general distinction is made between mild, moderate, and severe stages of AD, although the description of the symptoms shows that the stages are not completely distinct. Exhibit 9.7 provides an overview of the three stages of Alzheimer's disease and the related symptoms.

Early detection and diagnosis of Alzheimer's disease is still difficult. The time period from the diagnosis of Alzheimer's disease to death ranges from 3 to 4 years up to 10 years, depending on the person's age. However, it is believed that the changes in the brain that cause Alzheimer's disease begin 10 or even 20 years before its onset. Consequently, there is a strong focus on trying to find biomarkers in cerebrospinal fluids, blood, or urine that may help to detect the presence of developing Alzheimer's disease.

In the mild or early stage, the first signs of the disease, such as forgetfulness, confusion, and mood and personality changes, appear. This stage may be the most stressful for many persons afflicted with Alzheimer's disease, since they often are very aware of the changes happening to their mind. Fluctuations in the severity of symptoms are common, both within a day and between days. Oftentimes the person will start to experience significant anxiety related to these changes.

Moderate-stage Alzheimer's disease is characterized by increased memory loss, problems organizing thoughts and language, difficulty recognizing friends and family members, and restlessness. As the disease progresses the person may exhibit reduced impulse control, repetitive behavior and speech, hallucinations, delusion, and suspiciousness.

In late-stage Alzheimer's disease, a person is often bedridden and has increasing health difficulties. The most common reason for death in the late stage is aspiration pneumonia, when the person can no longer swallow properly and fluids and food end up in the lungs (Alzheimer's Association, 2013). Mrs. Menzel would fall into the earlier phases of the

Erzählcafé (coffeehouse chat) is a group work concept for persons with dementia that takes into account the cultural tradition of going to social clubs to meet and chat with friends. The target group includes persons with mild to moderate dementia. Persons with dementia often retreat from social activities. By offering them an environment in which they can meet and interact with other persons in a safe small group setting, they receive the reassurance and appreciation that are important for persons with dementia. To provide continuity and structure, the meetings occur on a weekly basis. They are organized around the ritual of having coffee with friends. This is integrated with senior group work activities like mobility exercises and dance circles, reminiscing and life review, singing and listening to music, and celebrating holidays. The mix of activities and methods tries to help participants tap into their personal resources, including the hidden ones. Group leaders carefully plan the exercise to stimulate participants while not overwhelming them. For example, a clear separation exists between the physical activities, having coffee, and doing craft work. An intended corollary of the coffeehouse chat is to provide caregivers with respite and help them experience that it is O.K. to let someone else take care of their relative for a while. The latter can be difficult for caregivers and may contribute to burnout and failure to access available services in a timely manner. The interaction with group coordinators also is an opportunity to exchange information and reduce service barriers. German social work has a service concept called "niederschwellig" (the low doorstep when entering the house), meaning that the process of accessing service is particularly important, has to be carefully planned, and needs to be as easy as possible. Coffeehouse chats are coordinated by a geriatric social worker and led by trained volunteers from the local senior volunteer network.

Elizabeth Menzel in our case example is a regular visitor of an Erzählcafé. Her husband Joseph reminds her about the group in the morning, but usually she remembers herself, since it is listed on her weekly calendar and she looks forward to attending it. Before going to the Café, she changes and puts on nicer clothes. She still gets a little excited when the volunteer driver comes to pick her up. Her husband tells her to have a wonderful afternoon and gives her money for coffee and cake. Joseph also enjoys having some time to himself. In addition, it provides the couple an opportunity to share what each of them did that afternoon, which they like, since they otherwise do everything together. In the bus, the participants have a game: trying to remember who else will be picked up. At times they share with each other how it feels to forget things, for example when one of the participants checks for the fifth time whether she brought her keys. On sunny days, the van often gets stuck in traffic jams, caused by younger retirees flocking to the mountains.

Once the bus arrives, the participants greet each other and the group leader starts the afternoon with a sitting gymnastic and breathing exercise. Participants like doing the physical exercise. It loosens the entire body and deepens breathing, which helps their overall well-being. Over time, the group leaders see improvements in the lateral and cross-body coordination, which research shows can have a positive impact on the mental abilities of persons with dementia. Like most participants, Elizabeth Menzel enjoys the more playful activities, such as throwing a softball back and forth. All of these physical efforts have to be rewarded. After half an hour of exercising, it is time for coffee and cake and participants move to the already set tables. As a conversation piece and to get the chat going, tables are decorated in a different way each time. Today bouquets of herbal flowers are the centerpiece, since the church will have its annual blessing of the herbs the following Sunday. Elizabeth Menzel shares how it was celebrated where she grew up, and a woman from Romania notices parallels to her childhood memories. Together, participants start identifying the assortment of herbs and flowers and talk about the history of this religious tradition. Suddenly Elizabeth Menzel becomes very sad. For the past years, her daughter has taken care of the herbal bouquet, but now she is dead. Her neighbor spontaneously gives her a hug and after a while Elizabeth Menzel feels ready to continue. Today the third part of the group schedule, doing crafts or something creative, focuses on creating paper flowers. Everyone is cutting, gluing, and folding flowers. Participants help each other according to their skills. They just about get their craft work done, when it is time to leave again. After singing their farewell song, a ritual that the group has come up with, they are brought back home again. Elizabeth Menzel takes some of the leftover plum cake for her husband—his favorite cake. She also wants to give him the sunflower she crafted, so he has something to look at when he stays back home during the coffee chats. She already is looking forward to next week's Erzählcafé.

Exhibit 9.7 Stages and Symptoms of Alzheimer's Disease

Stage of Alzheimer's Disease	Typical Symptoms
Mild or early stage	• Memory loss • Confusion about location of familiar places • Taking longer for routine daily tasks • Trouble handling money and bills • Loss of spontaneity • Repeating questions • Losing things • Mood and personality changes • Increased anxiety and aggression
Moderate stage	• Increased memory loss and confusion • Problems recognizing friends and family members • Inability to learn new things • Inability to cope with new or unexpected situations • Hallucinations, delusions, suspiciousness, paranoia • Loss of impulse control • Inability to carry out complex tasks requiring multiple steps
Severe or late stage	• Weight loss • Seizures • Skin infections • Difficulty swallowing • Groaning, moaning, grunting • Increased sleeping • Lack of bladder and bowel control • Inability to communicate

SOURCE: Based on National Institute on Aging, 2013b

disease and would be considered to have mild- to moderate-stage dementia.

Despite significant progress in researching the disease and trying to find possible cures, much is still unknown. Current thinking is that multiple factors, not one single cause, are involved in the development of AD. Research shows that brains of persons with Alzheimer's disease have an unusual accumulation of two substances: neurofibrillary tangles and amyloidal plaques. Amyloidal plaques are a substance building up *outside* the neuron cells. The plaques develop when amyloidal peptides, proteins associated with the cell membrane of neurons, divide improperly and turn into beta amyloid, which in turn is toxic to neurons. The neurons die and together with the proteins create these lumps (Alzheimer's Association, 2013). Neurofibrillary tangles form inside the neurons. These tangles are caused by a protein (tau) breaking down and sticking together with other tau proteins to create tangled clumps *inside* the neuron cells. When these tangles develop, they reduce the neurons' ability to communicate with other neurons. The neuron cells eventually die, which over time leads to brain atrophy (Alzheimer's Association, 2013). The role of the plaques and tangles is still not well understood, but scans show that the brains of people with advanced AD have dramatic shrinkage from cell loss and widespread debris from dead and dying neurons.

Several medications are available for persons with AD, including donepezil (Aricept), galantamine (Razadyne), and rivastigmine (Exelon). All of these medications can slow the progression of the disease, but none can reverse or cure it. Data from the Cardiovascular Risk Factors, Aging and Dementia (CAIDE) study suggest that caffeine intake in midlife may reduce the risk of dementia. The authors of the study looked at a subset of study participants who were followed over a 21-year period and found that, adjusted for factors such as lifestyle and various health factors, drinking 3 to 5 cups of coffee on a daily basis reduced the risk of AD and other dementias by 65% (Eskelinen, Ngandu, Tuomilehto, Soininen, & Kivipelto, 2009). However, currently no cure for the disease is on the horizon.

Parkinson's Disease

Parkinson's disease (PD) is a chronic and progressive movement disorder that primarily affects older adults over the age of 70. However, as in the case of movie star Michael J. Fox, it can afflict persons earlier in life as well. It is estimated that 7 to 10 million people worldwide have PD and that about 1 million people in the United States live with the disease. Approximately 60,000 people in the United States are diagnosed with PD each year (Parkinson's Disease Foundation, 2010).

Symptoms of PD include tremors (arms, legs, head), rigidity (stiffness of limbs), bradykinesia (trouble with and slowness of movement), and postural instability (insecure gait and balance). It can also cause language problems and cognitive difficulties and in extreme cases lead to a complete loss of movement. The disease is difficult to accurately diagnose, because some features of the normal aging process can be mistaken for PD (Parkinson's Disease Foundation, 2014). Tremors, slower movements, or insecure walking all may be part of normal aging, symptoms of depression, or medication-induced side effects. Even though PD is a neurodegenerative movement disorder, it often has mental health consequences. For example, cognitive impairment, dementia, depression, and sleep disorders may be associated with or co-occur with PD.

PD is caused by a gradual loss of cells that produce dopamine in a part of the brain called the basal ganglia, which is located at the base of the frontal brain area and is involved in coordinating a body's movements. The chemical dopamine is a neurotransmitter that transmits information about movement in the brain. A decrease in neurons that transmit information with the help of dopamine alters the processing of information related to physical movement (Playfer, 2006). Losing neurons in the substantia nigra, which is a part of the basal ganglia, is part of normal aging. We are born with 400,000 neurons in this part of the brain; at age 60 we have about 250,000 neurons left. However, research indicates that persons afflicted with Parkinson's disease may have as little as 60,000 to 120,000 neurons present in this part of the brain (Palmer & Francis, 2006). Research has also found a decrease in the nerve endings that produce norepinephrine, a neurotransmitter responsible for some of the body's automatic functions like blood pressure and pulse (National Institute of Neurological Disorders and Stroke [NINDS], 2013). The brain cells of a person with PD also include abnormal clumps of a protein (synuclein) called Lewy bodies. It is not clear whether this contributes to the disease by preventing the cells from working correctly or whether it is an attempt of the body to bind these harmful proteins to keep other cells working (NINDS, 2013).

Several drugs are available to address PD. A combination of these drugs with physical rehabilitation has shown great success in reducing the symptoms of the disease (Playfer, 2006). One group of medications works on increasing the dopamine levels in the brain. Levodopa is an example of such a drug. It is the most common medication for treating Parkinson's disease and has been used with success for more than 40 years (Playfer, 2006). A second type of drug mimics dopamine (dopamine antagonists) or inhibits dopamine breakdown (NINDS, 2013). A more recent approach to treating the effects of PD is deep brain stimulation. Using this method, a tiny electrode is surgically implanted into the brain. Through a pulse generator this implant then stimulates the brain and stops many of the symptoms (NINDS, 2013). Results of deep brain simulation show a positive effect on cognitive functions (Zangaglia et al., 2009). Anticolinergics and MAO-B and COMT inhibitors are also used to treat the symptoms and slow progression of the disease (Parkinson's Disease Foundation, 2013).

Critical Thinking Questions 9.2

Would you like to know that your aging process could be reversed with anti-aging medicine? What are the reasons for your answer? How would society be affected if more of us could live to be well past 100 years of age? What social justice issues might arise about access to anti-aging medicine?

PSYCHOLOGICAL CHANGES IN LATE ADULTHOOD

Without good longitudinal research, it has been difficult to understand psychological changes in late adulthood. Because cross-sectional research cannot control for cohort effects, we need to exercise great caution in interpreting findings of age differences in human psychology. Three areas that have received a lot of attention are changes in personality, changes in intellectual functioning, and mental health and mental disorders in late adulthood. The Berlin Aging Study, one of the largest studies of older adults, included numerous measures of psychological aging. Findings suggest that one should not think about a uniform process of psychological aging (Baltes & Mayer, 1999). Rather, changes in areas such as cognition, social relationships, self, and personality occur to a large extent independent of each other.

Personality Changes

A couple of theorists have addressed the issue of how personality changes as individuals age. As noted in Chapter 8, Erik Erikson's (1950) life span theory proposes that the struggle of middle adulthood is generativity versus stagnation (refer back to Exhibit 3.7 for an overview of Erikson's stages of psychosocial development). You may recall that generativity is the ability to transcend personal interests to guide the next generation. The struggle of late adulthood, according to Erikson, is **ego integrity versus ego despair.** *Integrity* involves the ability to make peace with one's "one and only life cycle" and to find unity with the world. Erikson (1950) also noted that from middle adulthood on, adults participate in a "wider social radius," with an increasing sense of social responsibility and interconnectedness. Some support was found for this notion in a 50-year follow-up of adult personality development (Haan, Millsap, & Hartka, 1986). The researchers found that in late adulthood, three aspects of personality increased significantly: outgoingness, self-confidence, and warmth. A more recent study examining the association of chronological aging with positive psychological change supported the idea that some forms of positive psychological change are normative across the life span and that older people know clearly what values are most important and they pursue these objectives with a more mature sense of purpose and ownership (Sheldon, 2006).

Vaillant (2002, 2012) has also considered the personality changes of late adulthood. He found that for all three of the cohorts in the Study of Adult Development, mastery of generativity tripled the likelihood that men and women would find their 70s to be a time of joy instead of despair. He also proposed that another life task, guardianship, comes

Do you have any guardians in your multigenerational family?

between generativity and integrity. **Guardianship** involves taking on the task of passing on the traditions of the past to the next generation, and guardians extend their concern to concern for the culture as a whole. In addition, Vaillant suggests that humans have "elegant unconscious coping mechanisms that make lemonade out of lemons" (2002, p. 91). As discussed in Chapter 8, Vaillant (2012) reports that with age and experience, individuals tend to use more adaptive coping mechanisms. This idea is supported by Fiksenbaum et al. (2006), who see successful coping as an essential aspect of aging.

Vaillant finds support for the proposition that coping mechanisms mature with age. He found that over a 25-year period, the Harvard men made significant increases in their use of altruism and humor and significant decreases in their use of projection and passive aggression. Overall, he found that 19 of 67 Harvard men made significant gains in the use of mature coping mechanisms from ages 50 to 75, 28 men were already making strong use of mature mechanisms at age 50, use of mature mechanisms stayed the same for 17 men, and only 4 out of the 67 men used fewer mature coping mechanisms with advancing age. Vaillant (1993) in part attributed this maturation in coping to the presence of positive social support and the quality of their marriages. These findings are consistent with findings from another longitudinal study of aging that found that in late adulthood, participants became more forgiving, more able to meet adversity cheerfully, less prone to take offense, and less prone to venting frustrations on others (McCrae & Costa, 1990). Langle and Probst (2004) suggest that this might be the result of older adults being required to face fundamental questions of existence because coping with the vicissitudes of life looms ever larger during aging.

Despite a commonly held belief, one area of personality that seems to change little or even improve with becoming older is the level of happiness experienced by a person. Lacey, Smith, and Ubel (2006) found that on average, people's perceptions of their happiness increase with age. They manage stress better, have a more positive outlook, and set more achievable and realistic goals for themselves. Other research shows similar levels of happiness in older adults as in the general population (Pew Center for Social and Demographic Trends, 2009).

In Chapter 8, we read that there are controversies about whether personality changes or remains stable in middle adulthood. There are similar controversies in the literature on late adulthood. Findings from the large-scale Berlin Aging Study indicate that, on the whole, self and personality change only little with age (Staudinger, Freund, Linden, & Maas, 1999). Vaillant (2002, 2012), conversely, found evidence for both change and continuity. He suggests that personality has two components: temperament and character. Temperament, he concludes, does not change, and adaptation in adolescence is one of the best predictors of adaptation in late adulthood. Studies on depression, anxiety, and suicidal ideation in late adulthood support this idea that coping and adaptation in adolescence are a good predictor of later life temperament. Conversely, character, or adaptive style, does change, influenced by both experiences with the environment and the maturation process. Vaillant (2002) attributes this change in adaptive style over time to the fact that many genes are "programmed to promote plasticity," or the capacity to be shaped by experience. One personality change noted in Chapter 8 to occur in middle age is gender role reversal, with women becoming more dominant and men becoming more passive. This pattern has also been noted in late adulthood (Vaillant, 2012).

Intellectual Changes, Learning, and Memory

Answering the question about how our intellectual capabilities change in late adulthood is a complex and difficult task. One often-cited study on age-related intellectual changes found that fluid intelligence declines with age, but crystallized intelligence increases (Horn, 1982). **Fluid intelligence** is the capacity for abstract reasoning and involves such things as the ability to "respond quickly, to memorize quickly, to compute quickly with no error, and to draw rapid inferences from visual relationships" (Vaillant, 2002, p. 238). **Crystallized intelligence** is based on accumulated learning and includes the ability to reflect and recognize (e.g., similarities and differences, vocabulary) rather than to recall and remember. This theory has received much criticism, however, because it was based on a cross-sectional comparison of two different age groups. Researchers who followed a single cohort over time found no general decline of intellectual abilities in late adulthood (Schaie, 1984). Rather, they found considerable individual variation. Other longitudinal research has found that fluid intelligence declines earlier than crystallized intelligence, which has been found to remain the same at 80 as at 30 in most healthy older adults (Vaillant, 2002). Aspects of crystallized intelligence, such as world knowledge, continue to grow into the 60s and show only gradual declines in the 70s (Ornstein & Light, 2010).

Learning and memory are closely related; we must first learn before we can retain and recall. Memory performance, like the impact of aging on intelligence, demonstrates a wide degree of variability. One study suggests that the effects of aging on the underlying brain processes related to retention and recall are dependent on individual memory performance, and the researchers call for further investigation of performance variability in normal aging (Duarte, Ranganath, Trujillo, & Knight, 2006). When we process information, it moves through several stages of memory (Bjorklund, 2011; Hooyman & Kiyak, 2011):

- *Sensory memory.* New information is initially recorded in sensory memory. Unless the person deliberately pays attention to the information, it is lost within less than a second. There seems to be little age-related change in this type of memory.
- *Primary memory.* If the information is retained in sensory memory, it is passed on to the primary memory, also called recent or short-term memory. Primary memory has only limited capacity; it is used to organize and temporarily hold information.

- *Working memory.* This refers to the process of actively reorganizing and manipulating information that is still in primary memory. Although there are some age-related declines in working memory, there seems to be little age-related decline in primary memory.
- *Secondary memory.* Information is permanently stored in secondary memory. This is the memory we use daily when we remember an event or memorize facts for an exam. The ability to recall seems to decline with age, but recognition capabilities stay consistent.
- *Tertiary memory.* Information is stored for extended periods, several weeks or months, in tertiary memory, also called remote memory. This type of memory experiences little age-related change.

Another way to distinguish memory is between intentional and incidental memory. **Intentional memory** relates to events that you plan to remember. **Incidental memory** relates to facts you have learned without the intention to retain and recall. Research suggests that incidental memory declines with old age, but intentional memory does not (Direnfeld & Roberts, 2006).

Another element of intellectual functioning studied in relation to aging is *brain plasticity*, the ability of the brain to change in response to stimuli. Research indicates that even older people's brains can rewire themselves to compensate for lost functioning in particular regions and, in some instances, may even be able to generate new cells. As a result, people are capable of lifelong learning, despite myths to the contrary. Typically researchers have used years of education as the proxy and predictor of decline in cognitive ability, memory, and executive function. Manly, Schupf, Tang, and Stern (2005) found that literacy was a better predictor of learning, memory, retention, and cognitive decline than educational years. This is especially salient for minority ethnic groups whose access to formal education may be limited. However, adult education and intellectual stimulation in later life may actually help maintain cognitive health. Not only are humans capable of lifelong learning, but the stimulation associated with learning new things may reduce the risk of impairments (Willis, Schaie, & Martin, 2009).

Mental Health and Mental Disorders

A number of longitudinal studies indicate that, without brain disease, mental health improves with age (Vaillant, 2012). Older adults have a lower prevalence of mental disorders than young and middle-age adults. This finding is supported by virtually all epidemiological studies ever conducted (Bengtson, Gans, Putney, & Silverstein, 2009). Although older adults are at greater risk to certain brain diseases such as dementia, these disorders are not a part of the normal aging process. It is estimated that 15% to 25% of older adults living in the community have some type of mental health disorder, but higher rates are found among older adults living in long-term care facilities, where an estimated 10% to 40% have mild to moderate impairment and 5% to 10% have serious impairment (Hooyman & Kiyak, 2011). About 20% of first admissions to psychiatric hospitals are adults aged 65 and older. It is estimated that only about 25% of older adults who need mental health services ever receive them. However, many of the more common mental disorders associated with older age can be diagnosed and treated in elderly persons much as they would be in earlier adulthood (Rodda, Walker, & Carter, 2011). Given the aging of the population, the need for gero-psychiatric research and clinical practice is likely to increase.

Some of the more commonly diagnosed mental disorders in late adulthood include the following:

• *Depression.* The most common mental health problem in older adults is depression (Hooyman & Kiyak, 2011). Symptoms of depression include sadness and depressed mood, loss of interest, weight loss, insomnia, and fatigue. To be diagnosed, the depressive episode has to persist for at least 2 weeks. Many depressive episodes in older adults are associated with problems in coping with difficult life events, such as death of a loved person

or physical illness. Treatment with antidepressive medication, especially in combination with psychotherapy, significantly improves depressive symptoms in most older adults (Rodda et al., 2011). Comparison of White and Black older persons found that lower education and functional disability were common risk factors for severe depressive symptoms for both groups, and sense of mastery and satisfaction with support were common protective factors. Advanced age was a risk factor for Caucasians, but not for African American persons, and being female and being less religious were risk factors for African Americans but not for Caucasians (Jang, Borenstein, Chiriboga, & Mortimer, 2005). This is yet another reminder of the important role of religious coping among many African Americans. A comparison of older adults in the United States and Japan found that multiple roles were more detrimental to the mental health of the Japanese elders than to U.S. elders (Kikuzawa, 2006). A study of depression in older adults in Beijing found that economic hardship and poor physical health were the strongest risk factors. The researchers also found a risk factor that had not been identified in studies in other countries: lack of the expected filial piety in the older adults' offspring (Ning et al., 2011). It should be noted that depression is not a normal part of aging. Moreover, longitudinal research has found no increase in clinical levels of depression with age (Helmchen et al., 1999).

Depression is the leading cause of suicide in late adulthood, and older adults are at a higher risk of suicide than the general population. According to the National Institute of Mental Health (2011), older adults account for a disproportionately high number of suicides. Older men have a 7 times higher risk than older women. Moreover, men 85 and older have a 5 times higher risk than the general population to commit suicide (Administration on Aging, 2013). Among the most prevalent risk factors are depression, prior suicide attempts, pain and medical conditions that limit life expectancy, social isolation and declining role functioning, feeling hopeless, and abuse of medications and illicit substances (Conwell, Van Orden, & Caine, 2011).

- *Anxiety.* Anxiety in older adults is similar to that in the younger population, but anxiety has not received the same attention in geriatric practice and research as some of the other mental health problems such as depression. Diagnosis and treatment, however, are often more complex and difficult, because anxiety in older adults is often masked with physical health complaints but also may be an indication of an underlying mental or physical disorder (Grenier et al., 2012; Kasckow et al., 2013). Symptoms of anxiety include tension, worry, apprehension, and physiological symptoms such as dizziness, gastrointestinal distress, palpitations, urinary disturbance, sweating, and tremors. About 9% of the general older adult population experiences considerable anxiety levels (Bengtson et al., 2009). For older adults, anxiety is frequently connected with chronic conditions and co-occurs with neurodegenerative diseases such as Alzheimer's and Parkinson's disease. One study found that 5.2% of community-dwelling older adults with cardiovascular disease met the criteria for anxiety disorder, and 14.8% had anxiety symptoms that did not meet the threshold to be diagnosed as an anxiety disorder (Grenier et al., 2012). Anxiety symptoms often coexist with depressive symptoms in older adults, as they do with other adults, and the combination of the two, even when they do not meet the threshold for diagnosis for major depression or anxiety disorder, increases the risk for dementia and hospitalization for cardiovascular disease (Kasckow et al., 2013). Situational stressors that may trigger anxiety in older adults include financial concerns, physical stressors, and loss and loneliness. One study found that non-Hispanic Whites had twice the rate of anxiety symptoms as either non-Hispanic Blacks or Hispanics (Ostir & Goodwin, 2006). There is evidence that cognitive behavioral therapy is as effective with older adults as with younger adults, and one feasibility trial found that older adults with anxiety disorder showed significant improvement in symptoms after completion of an 8-week online cognitive behavioral treatment program. The participants reported a high level of satisfaction with the program, but their gains were not maintained at a 3-month follow-up (Zou et al., 2012).

- *Delirium.* One of the two most prevalent cognitive disorders in the elderly population, **delirium**, is characterized by an impairment of consciousness. Delirium has a sudden onset (a few hours or days), after which follows a brief and fluctuating course that includes impairment of consciousness, drowsiness, disorientation to time and place, inability to remember events before delirium began, problems concentrating, and incoherent thinking and speech. It has the potential for improvement when the causes are treated. Prevalent causative factors include alcohol or sedative drug withdrawal, drug abuse, body chemical disturbances, poisons, not only central nervous system disturbances but also outside factors such as toxicity from medications, low oxygen states, infections, retention of urine and feces, undernutrition and dehydration, surgery, and metabolic conditions (Jasmin, 2013; Joshi & Morley, 2006). The prevalence of delirium increases with age and is very common in acute care hospitals, particularly among postoperative patients and intensive care patients. Many older adults with delirium have an underlying dementia (Anand & MacLullich, 2013).

- *Dementia.* The other most prevalent cognitive disorder among older adults is dementia, which was discussed earlier in the context of neurodegenerative disease. Dementia has a slower onset than delirium and is not characterized by an impairment of consciousness. Rather, dementia is characterized by multiple impairments of the person's cognitive functioning.

- *Substance abuse.* Although it is hard to get good data, there is increasing evidence that a growing number of older adults are misusing and abusing alcohol and psychoactive prescription medications (Blow & Barry, 2012). Community surveys have reported prevalence rates from 1% to 16% of problem drinking for older adults. In 2002, 0.5% of adults 65 and older reported alcohol dependence. While light to moderate drinking typically causes no health concerns for younger adults, these amounts my cause a number of negative health effects in older adults. In addition, older adults take more prescription medications than young adults, and the research is suggesting that two types of prescription drug medications are abused by a small but significant group of older adults: opioid medications used for treatment of pain and benzodiazepines used for treatment of anxiety and insomnia. Benzodiazepines have been associated with cognitive losses, confusion, and depressed mood. The current generation of older adults rarely uses illicit drugs, but it is expected that the abuse of these substances will increase in older adults as the baby boomers reach late adulthood (Blow & Barry, 2012). When working with older adults, it is important to assess for levels of use of alcohol as well as psychoactive prescription medications.

Critical Thinking Questions 9.3

George Vaillant suggests that his longitudinal research indicates that humans have "elegant unconscious coping mechanisms that make lemonade out of lemons." Think of a late-life adult you know who has or is making lemonade out of lemons. What challenges has this person faced in earlier life or in late adulthood? What is it about this late-life adult that makes you think of her or him as making lemonade out of lemons? What types of coping mechanisms do you think this person uses to deal with adversities?

SOCIAL ROLE TRANSITIONS AND LIFE EVENTS OF LATE ADULTHOOD

Transitions are at the center of the life course perspective, and people experience many transitions, some of them very abrupt, in late adulthood. Retirement, death of a spouse or partner, institutionalization, and one's own death are among the most stressful events in human existence, and they are clustered in late adulthood. Several other events are more benign but may still enter into the social

worker's analysis of the changing configuration of person and environment represented by each of the case studies at the beginning of the chapter. Despite the concern of the impact of the loss of social roles, studies have demonstrated that older adults generally adapt to late-life role transitions and maintain emotional well-being (Hinrichsen & Clougherty, 2006).

Families in Later Life

As you saw with the Smiths, the Menzels, and Ms. Johnson, families continue to play an important role in the life of an older person. With increased longevity, however, the post–empty nest and postretirement period lengthens (Walsh, 2011). Thus, the significance of the marital or partner relationship increases in late adulthood. As older individuals are released from their responsibilities as parents and members of the workforce, they are able to spend more time together. Some studies have suggested a U-shaped curve of marital satisfaction, with the highest levels during the first period of the marital relationship and in late adulthood and lower levels during the childbearing years (Bjorklund, 2011). Moreover, overall satisfaction with the quality of life seems to be higher for married elderly individuals than for the widowed or never married. For married couples, the spouse is the most important source of emotional, social, and personal support in times of illness and need of care.

About 28% of noninstitutionalized U.S. older adults live alone. The most common living arrangement for men older than 65 is with their wife; in 2012, 72% of men older than 65 lived with their spouse (Administration on Aging, 2012). The picture is different for older women; only 45% of women age 65 and older live with a spouse, and by age 75, almost half (46%) of women live alone.

Living arrangements for older adults vary by race and ethnicity. In 2008, the proportion of White (41%) and Black (42%) women living alone was similar. Fewer older Hispanic women lived alone (27%), and even fewer Asian women lived alone (22%) (Jacobsen, Mather, Lee, & Kent, 2011). Older Black women (25%) are less likely than Asian

Photo 9.4 As older couples are released from responsibilities as parents and members of the workforce, they are able to spend more time together.

© Stephen Beaudet/zefa/Corbis

(45%), White (44%), and Hispanic (41%) women to live with a spouse (Jacobsen et al., 2011). White women (13%) are less likely than Black (32%), Asian (32%), or Hispanic (31%) women to live with relatives other than a spouse. Black men (30%) are more likely to live alone than White (18%), Hispanic (13%), or Asian (11%) men. Black men (54%) are also less likely than Asian (77%), White (74%), and Hispanic (67%) men to live with a spouse. Men of every race and ethnicity are less likely than women of the same race and ethnicity to live with a relative other than their spouse: 15% of Hispanic men, 10% of Asian men, 11% of Black men, and 6% of White men (Jacobsen et al., 2011). A complex relationship among culture, socioeconomic status, and individual personality has to be

considered in accounting for the ethnic and racial differences in living arrangements. Drawing inferences based solely on cultural differences is overly simplistic given the use of ethnic and racial categories devised by the U.S. Census Bureau as proxies for cultural identity.

Family relationships have been found to be closer and more central for older women than for older men. Mother-daughter relationships have been found to be particularly strong (Silverstein & Bengtson, 2001). Additionally, friendship appears to be a more important protective factor for older women than for older men. Friendships have been associated with lower levels of cognitive impairment and increased quality-of-life satisfaction (Beland, Zunzunegui, Alvardo, Otero, & del Ser, 2005).

The never married constitute a very small group of the current elderly population. It will further decrease for some time as the cohort of baby boomers, with its unusually high rate of marriage, enters late adulthood (Bjorklund, 2011). However, the proportion of elderly singles and never marrieds, will probably increase toward the middle of the next century, because the cohort that follows the baby boomers has had an increase in the number of individuals remaining single.

Singlehood caused by divorce in late adulthood is increasing, however, as divorce is becoming more socially accepted in all population groups. As in all stages of life, divorce in later life may entail financial problems, especially for older women, and it may be especially difficult to recuperate financially in postretirement. Divorce also results in a change of kinship ties and social networks, which are important sources of support in later life. The incidence of remarriage after divorce or widowhood is significantly higher for older men than for older women. The fact that there are more elderly women than men contributes to this trend. Even if older adults are not themselves divorced, they may need to adjust to the enlarged and complicated family networks that come from the divorces and remarriages of their children and grandchildren (Walsh, 2011).

Until very recently, very little research focused on aging among LGBT individuals; currently this is a small but growing area of research. The current generation of LGBT older adults in the United States and some other countries is experiencing rapid social change in their visibility and acceptance in society. Van Wagenen, Driskell, and Bradford (2013) summarize their unique historical perspective this way:

The oldest among them have lived through the emergence of the modern construction of "the homosexual," the concomitant social exclusion and medicalization of homosexuality as a mental disorder, the rise of the gay liberation and lesbian feminist movements, the emergence and devastating impact of HIV/AIDS, the proliferation of sexual and gender minority identities (including bisexual, transgender, and queer), the "normalization" of the movement and shift towards a politics of civil rights, and the increasing visibility and incorporation of LGBT issues into mainstream social and political discourse. (pp. 1–2)

In recent years, many older gay and lesbian couples have been able to marry, some after several decades of partnership.

The small research literature on LGBT older adults indicates that they have faced serious adversities throughout their lives, and this has resulted in compromised mental and physical health. They have faced barriers to receiving informal caregiving from loved ones and prejudice and discrimination from health and social service providers (Institute of Medicine, 2011). They also have demonstrated strength and resilience, building robust social networks of chosen families and developing skills for coping with disease (van Wagenen et al., 2013). During later life, many LGBT adults and their families have been able to find and model new ways of disclosure and living authentically (Ashton, 2011). Even though sexual minorities are facing less prejudice and discrimination in recent years, recent research indicates that they still face limited access to LGBT-sensitive social services and long-term care (Hughes, Harold, & Boyer, 2011; Jihanian, 2013).

Sibling relationships play a special role in the life of older adults. Siblings share childhood experiences and are often the personal tie with the longest duration. Siblings are typically not the primary source of personal care, but they often play a role in providing emotional support. Sibling relationships often change over the life course, with closer ties in pre-adulthood and later life and less involvement in early and middle adulthood. Women's ties with siblings have been found to be more involved than those of men (Bjorklund, 2011).

Co-residence of multiple generations of the family has been gradually decreasing in Western societies since the 19th century, but the multi-generational family household has been making a comeback in Europe and the United States in recent years (Albuquerque, 2011). While the percentage of persons living in multigenerational family households decreased in the United States from 24.7% in 1950 to 12.1% in 1980, it has since increased back up to 16.1% in 2010. This can be attributed to several factors, including demographic changes, the burst of the housing market and increase of foreclosures, higher unemployment rates since the onset of the last recession, and a high rate of immigration from Latin America and Asia (Pew Center for Social and Demographic Trends, 2013). The resurgence of multigenerational households has resulted in more interactions and exchanges across generations. Contrary to common belief, intergenerational exchanges between adult children and elderly parents are not one-directional. Children often take care of their elderly parents, but healthy elderly persons also provide significant assistance to their adult children, as is the case with Ms. Johnson. Research with multigenerational households in Portugal found that resources flowed both ways, particularly when the older generation was still young-old. Some contributions that the older generation provided to the household include income from employment, child care, and household chores (Albuquerque, 2011).

Grandparenthood

Gene and Lois Smith, Ruby Johnson, and Joseph and Elizabeth Menzel are grandparents, and Ruby Johnson is a great-grandmother. As people live longer, increasing numbers are becoming grandparents and great-grandparents. In addition, the current cohort of older adults is spending more years as grandparents than earlier cohorts did (Bjorklund, 2011). The transition to grandparenthood typically occurs in middle adulthood, and grandparents may be in their 30s or over 100 or anywhere in between (Hooyman & Kiyak, 2011). The grandchildren of older adults are more likely to be adolescents and young adults than to be young children. Great-grandchildren, however, are likely to be young.

In some cases, older people such as Ms. Johnson are assuming full responsibility for parenting their grandchildren, because their children have problems with drugs, HIV infection, or crime. Beginning in the early 1990s, the U.S. Census Bureau began to note an increasing number of children younger than 18 living with grandparents, rising from 3% in 1970 to 5.5% in 1997 (Bryson & Casper, 1999). Today, approximately 10% of children in the United States are living with a grandparent, and a grandparent is the primary caregiver for a large minority of these children. However, the majority of these grandparent co-residers are younger than age 60; 25% of grandparent caregivers are ages 60 to 69, and another 9% of grandparent caregivers are age 70 or older (Livingston, 2013). This has been viewed by some as a negative trend, but there is no inherent reason why grandchildren receiving care from grandparents is problematic, and, indeed, across time and place, grandparents have sometimes been seen as appropriate caregivers. Many cultural groups often have multigenerational households that are not predicated on dysfunction within the family. Recall that large percentages of Asian, Hispanic, and Black elders live with family members not their spouse. It does appear, however, that the current trend is influenced by the growth of drug use among parents, teen pregnancy, the rapid rise of single-parent families, and recent economic conditions (Hooyman & Kiyak, 2011; Livingston, 2013). As a result, new physical, emotional, and financial demands are placed on grandparents with already limited resources. Sometimes custodial grandparents are also caring for their own impaired adult child. Compared with their noncustodial counterparts, custodial grandparents have a higher rate of physical and mental health problems (Hayslip & Kaminski, 2005). However, many custodial grandparents and their grandchildren benefit or even thrive from the circumstance, and the parenting outcomes are often very positive. Parsons and Peluso (2013) compiled a list of famous custodial grandchildren that includes the likes of George Washington, Barack Obama, Bill Clinton, Clarence Thomas, Eric Clapton, Oprah Winfrey, Pierce Brosnan, Tammy Wynette, and Tipper Gore. They all have in common the fact that they were raised by their grandparents.

How do culture, social
class, and gender affect
grandparenting styles?

Grandparenthood is a normative part of the family life cycle, but the majority of grandparents do not co-reside with their grandchildren. In general, being a grandparent is a welcome and gratifying role for most individuals, but it may increase in significance and meaning for an older person. The Smiths, for example, both enjoy being grandparents, and Lois Smith especially gains pleasure and satisfaction from her role as grandmother to her daughter's children. Many grandparents today are maintaining relationships with grandchildren by means of various technologies, including texting, social networking sites, and webcam interactions.

Even when they do not co-reside with their grandchildren, grandparents can play an important role in their grandchildren's lives. Here are some examples from research. Candace Kemp (2005) found that both adult grandchildren and their grandparents see their relationship as a safety net that can be tapped when needed. Another research team found that emerging adults who had lived with a single parent or in a stepparent home had fewer depressive symptoms if they had a strong relationship with a grandparent (Ruiz & Silverstein, 2007). Another study found that the quality of the relationship with the maternal grandmother predicted the psychological adjustment of emerging adults after parental divorce (Henderson, Hayslip, Sanders, & Louden, 2009). And another study found that adolescents in single-parent homes had fewer difficulties with school conduct and peer relations if they had high levels of involvement with grandparents (Attar-Schwartz, Tan, Buchanan, Flouri, & Griggs, 2009). One last study found that grandparents play a critical role when a grandchild has a disability, and the grandparent derives much joy and satisfaction from the grandparent-grandchild relationship (Woodbridge, Buys, & Miller, 2011).

Family researchers have begun to take a strong interest in the grandparenting role, but little is actually known about grandparent-grandchild relationships. A classic study of middle-class grandparents in the early 1960s identified several styles of grandparents: formal grandparents, fun seekers, distant figures, surrogate parents, and mentors (Neugarten & Weinstein, 1964). A more recent study by Margaret Mueller and her associates focused particularly on the relationships between grandparents and adolescent grandchildren; the average age of grandparents in this study was 69 years old (Mueller, Wilhelm, & Elder, 2002). This study identified five dimensions of the grandparenting role in 451 families: face-to-face contact, activities done together, intimacy, assistance, and authority/discipline. Each of these grandparenting dimensions is defined in Exhibit 9.8. Using a statistical clustering method, the researchers identified five styles of grandparenting:

1. *Influential grandparents* are highly involved in all aspects of grandparenting, scoring high on all five dimensions. These grandparents constituted 17% of the sample. Ms. Johnson is grandparenting Rebecca in this manner.

2. *Supportive grandparents* are highly involved in the lives of their grandchildren but do not see themselves in a role of disciplinarian or authority figure. About a quarter of the sample fit this pattern.

3. *Passive grandparents* are moderately involved in their grandchildren's lives, but they do not provide instrumental assistance and do not see themselves as discipline/authority figures. About 19% of the sample fit this pattern. Lois and Gene Smith seem to be following this pattern of grandparenting.

4. *Authority-oriented grandparents* see their role as authority figures as the central component in their grandparenting, and they are relatively inactive in their grandchildren's lives compared with both influential and supportive grandparents. These grandparents constitute about 13% of the sample.

5. *Detached grandparents* are the least involved, scoring lowest on all the dimensions of grandparenting. This was the largest group, comprising about 28% of the sample.

Exhibit 9.8 Dimensions of Grandparenting Role

Dimension	Definition
Face-to-face contact	How often grandparents see their grandchildren
Activities done together	Participation in shared activities, such as shopping, working on projects together, attending grandchildren's events, teaching the grandchild a skill
Intimacy	Serving as confidant, companion, or friend; discussing grandparent's childhood
Assistance	Providing instrumental assistance, such as financial aid and/or interpersonal support
Discipline and authority	Disciplining the grandchild or otherwise serving as an authority figure

SOURCE: Based on Mueller et al., 2002

This research is helpful because it demonstrates that the grandparent role may be played in many different ways. A number of factors may influence the style of grandparenting, including geographic proximity, ages of grandparents and grandchildren, number of grandchildren, and family rituals. There is a major drawback to the sample, however; it is entirely White and midwestern. It does not, therefore, address the possibility of cultural variations in grandparenting roles. For example, one research team investigated Chinese American grandmothering and found that these grandmothers spent significant amounts of time with their grandchildren and considered their grandparenting style to be based on a sense of responsibility to teach their grandchildren to have good character and to honor filial piety. Their high involvement with their grandchildren was formal and hierarchical, unlike the friendly companionate style characterized by many European American grandparents (Nagata, Cheng, & Tsai, 2010). The researchers caution not to assume that formal and detached relationships necessarily result in low involvement. They also note language and acculturation issues that can interfere with grandparent-grandchild relationships in immigrant families.

A smaller-scale study of grandparenting in 17 Native American families, including Sioux, Creek, Seminole, Choctaw, and Chickasaw, also addresses the issue of cultural variation (Weibel-Orlando, 2001). Like the research of Mueller and her associates, this study identified five styles of grandparenting:

1. *The distanced grandparent* lives at considerable geographic distance from grandchildren but also has psychological and cultural distance. This type of grandparenting is not common among Native Americans. It is most likely to occur if the family has migrated to an urban area and the grandparents return to their ancestral homeland after retirement.

2. *The ceremonial grandparent* also lives at considerable geographic distance from grandchildren but visits regularly. Intergenerational visits are times for ethnic ceremonial gatherings, and grandparents model appropriate ceremonial behavior.

3. *The fictive grandparent* assumes the elder role with children who are not biologically related. These grandparents may have no grandchildren of their own or may live at a great distance from their biological grandchildren.

4. *The custodial grandparent* lives with the grandchildren and is responsible for their care. This style of grandparenting is usually the result of parental death, incapacitation, or abandonment and is based on necessity rather than choice.

5. *The cultural conservator grandparent* actively pursues the opportunity to have grandchildren live with her (all such grandparents were women in this study) so that she might teach them the Native American way of life.

Think about your relationships with your grandparents. How would you characterize their grandparenting styles? Did you have different types of relationships with different grandparents? Did your grandparents have different types of relationships with different grandchildren? What might explain any differences?

Work and Retirement

Until the 20th century, the average worker retired about 3 years before death. Increased worker productivity, mass longevity, and Social Security legislation changed that situation, however. The labor force participation of men aged 65 or older declined steadily from 1900, when it was about 66%, to 1985, when it was 15.8%. From 1986 to 2002, it stabilized at 16% to 18% but began to increase after 2002. The labor force participation of women aged 65 and older rose slightly from 1900 to 1956, from about 8% to 10.8%. It fell to 7.3% in 1985, remained at 7% to 9% from 1986 to 2002, and then began to rise. In 2012, 18.5% of adults aged 65 and older were in the labor force, including 23.6% of men and 14.4% of women (Administration on Aging, 2012). It is thought that this recent upward shift in the labor force participation of older adults is related to both financial considerations and improved health. Changes to Social Security policy allowed older adults to continue working and still receive partial Social Security benefits, but two other changes have increased the financial necessity for older adults to stay in the labor force: a reduction in pension plans and the scheduled increase in age for receiving full Social Security benefits. In addition, many older adults faced losses in savings, investments, and home equity during the economic recession that started in 2007 (Bjorklund, 2011).

Retirement patterns vary with social class. Vaillant found that only 20% of his sample of surviving inner-city men were still in the workforce at age 65, but half of the sample of Harvard men were still working full-time at 65. The inner-city men retired, on average, 5 years earlier than the Harvard men. Poor health often leads to earlier retirement among less advantaged adults (Hooyman & Kiyak,

> How do these social trends affect the late-adult phase of the life course?

2011). In addition, higher levels of education make workers eligible for more sedentary jobs, which are a better fit with the declining energy levels in late adulthood (Vaillant, 2002).

The "appropriate" age for retirement in the United States is currently understood to be 65. This cultural understanding has been shaped by Social Security legislation enacted in 1935. However, the 1983 Social Security Amendments included a provision for a gradual increase in the age at which a retired person could begin receiving Social Security retirement benefits. Exhibit 9.9 shows the schedule for increasing the age for receiving full benefits. In arguing for this legislative change, members of Congress noted increased longevity and improved health among older adults.

Older adults who continue to work fall into two groups: those who could afford to retire but choose to continue working and those who continue to work because of a financial need. Older adults of the first group usually receive great satisfaction in sharing their knowledge and expertise and gain a feeling of purpose from being productive. Members of the second group continue to work out of necessity. Because economic status in old age is influenced by past employment patterns and the resultant retirement benefits, this second group consists of individuals who had lower-paying employment throughout their lives. This group also includes elderly divorced or widowed women who depended on their husband's retirement income and are now faced with poverty or near poverty. Lifelong gender inequality in wages contributes to inequality in pension and retirement funds (Hooyman & Kiyak, 2011). Gene Smith falls into the first category, because he continued working even though he and his wife had sufficient combined benefits to retire. However, Lois Smith's own benefits would not have enabled her to lead a financially comfortable retirement if she were not married, and she would probably face some financial hardship if she were to become a widow. Ruby Johnson continues to be employed on a part-time basis out of financial necessity.

When we think about retirement, we often picture individuals cleaning up their desks to stop

Exhibit 9.9 Amended Age to Receive Full Social Security Benefits (1983)

Year of Birth	Full Retirement Age
1937 and earlier	65
1938	65 and 2 months
1939	65 and 4 months
1940	65 and 6 months
1941	65 and 8 months
1942	65 and 10 month
1943–1954	66
1955	66 and 2 months
1956	66 and 4 months
1957	66 and 6 months
1958	66 and 8 months
1959	66 and 10 month
1960 and later	67

SOURCE: Social Security Administration, 2013a

working completely and sit in a rocking chair on the front porch. Yet there are many ways of retiring from the workforce. Some individuals do cease work completely, but others continue with part-time or part-year employment. Others may retire for a period and then reenter the labor market, as Gene Smith did when his former employer offered him a part-time position. Retirement is a socially accepted way to end an active role in the workforce, but the transition to retirement is becoming much more blurred than we typically think (Hooyman & Kiyak, 2011). Most persons retire because of advancing age, health problems, a desire to pursue other interests, or simply a wish to relax and lead the life of a retiree.

Individuals vary in whether they view retirement as something to dread or something to look forward to. Most often, however, retirement is a positive experience. Vaillant (2002) found no evidence in his longitudinal research that retirement is bad for physical health. For every person who indicated that retirement was bad for her or his health, four retirees indicated that retirement had improved their health. Vaillant noted four conditions under which retirement is perceived as stressful (p. 221):

1. Retirement was involuntary or unplanned.

2. There are no other means of financial support besides salary.

3. Work provided an escape from an unhappy home life.

4. Retirement was precipitated by preexisting bad health.

These conditions are present among only a fraction of retirees, but those are the retirees with whom social workers are likely to come into contact.

Vaillant found that retirement has generally been rewarding for many of the participants of his study. Four basic activities appear to make retirement rewarding:

1. Replacing workmates with another social network

2. Rediscovering how to play

3. Engaging in creative endeavors

4. Continuing lifelong learning

Caregiving and Care Receiving

As retirement unfolds, declining health may usher in a period of intensive need for care. The majority of older adults with disabilities live in the community and receive predominately informal care from spouses, children, and extended family. Among older adults who need care and live in the community, about 9% rely exclusively on formal care, and about 70% rely exclusively on informal care. It is estimated that if informal care was unavailable, long-term care costs would double (Hooyman &

Kiyak, 2011). Women are the primary source of caregiving in old age. Daughters are more likely than sons to take care of elderly parents. Moreover, elderly men tend to be married and thus are more likely to have a wife available as caregiver (Walsh, 2011).

How can such programs buffer the stress of caregiving and care receiving?

Caregiving can be an around-the-clock task and often leaves caregivers overwhelmed and exhausted (see Chan, Malhotra, Malhotra, Rush, & Ostbye, 2013). Mr. Menzel is a good example of the burden that can be experienced by an elderly spouse. Programs that can assist caregivers such as him in reducing their exceptional levels of stress have received much attention. Many programs combine educational components—for example, information about and training in adaptive coping skills—with ongoing support through the opportunity to share personal feelings and experiences. In recent years, social workers have been using telephone and computer-mediated support groups to assist family caregivers and have found many benefits of these virtual groups (Jones & Meier, 2011; Toseland & Larkin, 2010). Respite programs for caregivers are also available. In-home respite programs provide assistance through a home health aide or a visiting nurse (Petrovic, 2013). Community-based respite is often provided through adult day care and similar programs.

Although there is much evidence that caregiving can be stressful, it is important to remember that not all caregivers have the same reactions to their caregiving responsibilities, and there are gains as well as losses associated with the caregiver role. Gains include pride and greater closeness with the care recipient. Some research indicates that African American caregivers provide a higher level of care than White caregivers but typically report less stress, anxiety, and feelings of burden related to caregiving. They are more likely than White caregivers to see caregiving as a spiritual experience (Dilworth-Andersen et al., 2005).

Based on their research on the topic, Rhonda Montgomery and Karl Kosloski (2000, 2009)

developed a caregiver identity theory. Their framework consists of seven "career markers," stages that individuals typically move through in their career as caregivers. The first marker signifies the time when the dependency situation begins. One person needs assistance with routine activities and another person starts performing caregiving tasks. The second marker is reached when the self-definition as a caregiver begins; that is, the person incorporates the role of caregiver into his or her personal and social identity. Marker 3 is characterized by the performance of personal care tasks. At this time, caregiving family members begin to evaluate whether to continue as caregivers or seek alternatives. Although spousal caregivers may already see themselves as such after reaching Marker 2, they now begin to unambiguously identify with their new role. The next marker is reached when outside assistance is sought and formal service use is considered. Whether outside help is requested depends on factors such as seeing one's personal situation as deficient, recognizing the potential service as addressing that deficiency, and the psychological and monetary cost-benefit of using the service (Montgomery & Kosloski, 1994). Considering nursing home placement is the fifth marker. Although the institutional placement is considered at earlier phases, the decision now is more imminent. Nursing home placement is the sixth marker. When caregiving becomes too overwhelming, a nursing home placement may be pursued. Caregiving often continues after a family member enters a nursing home. Although caregivers are relieved from direct care, they continue to be involved in the emotional and social aspects of care in the nursing home (Naleppa, 1996). Although many individuals will spend some time in a nursing home, others never enter such an institution and die at home. The final marker in Montgomery and Kosloski's caregiver identity theory is the termination of the caregiver role. This may occur because of recovery or death of the care recipient or through "quitting" as a caregiver.

Stress and burden are not experienced only by the caregiver. Although there has been very little research on the topic, it is suggested that the care recipient also experiences significant strain. Requiring care is a double loss: The person has lost the capability to perform the tasks for which he or she needs assistance and the person has also lost independence. Having to rely on others for activities that one has carried out independently throughout one's adult life can be the source of tremendous emotional and psychological stress. Some individuals respond by emotional withdrawal, whereas others become agitated and start blaming others for their situation. Still others make the best of the situation and even find benefits, such as being able to reside in the community, reducing the economic costs of care, and becoming closer to caregivers (Bjorklund, 2011).

Think of Joseph Menzel. His stress as a caregiver was probably amplified by culturally defined norms promoting independence, individuality, and pride. Helping someone like him to overcome his uneasiness about receiving assistance may include asking him to verbalize his worries, listening to him express his feelings, and looking together at ways that he could overcome his uneasiness in small steps.

Widowhood

A spouse's or partner's death may be the most stressful event in a person's life, but the existing research literature focuses on death of a heterosexual spouse. Widowhood within the context of a heterosexual spousal relationship is more common among women than men. In 2012, 37% of U.S. women aged 65 or older were widowed, compared with 12% of men (Administration on Aging, 2012). A similar pattern can be found in other economically advanced societies (see Fang et al., 2012; Schaan, 2013). Two factors drive this gender difference: women have tended to marry men who are a few years older than themselves, and women live longer than men. On average, women also have a longer duration of widowhood, and men are more likely than women to remarry after spousal death.

Considerable research across cultures has found that spousal death is associated with deteriorating health, increased depression, and even death,

but there are some inconsistencies in the research. Although this research has focused on heterosexual married couples, the findings are quite possibly applicable to other long-term partnered couples. Some studies have found that depressive symptoms are more pronounced for widowed men than for widowed women (Carr, 2004), others have found that widowed women suffer more from depressive symptoms (Lee & DeMaris, 2007), and still others have found no gender differences in the impact of spousal death on mental health (Schaan, 2013). A consistent finding in the research is that the negative effects of widowhood are particularly strong during the first years after spousal loss and then diminish over time.

One recent longitudinal study investigated depressive symptoms of widowed men and women older than age 50 in 11 European countries. Widowed persons were found to have more depressive symptoms than married persons; although women had more depressive symptoms than men, no gender differences in the effect of widowhood on depressive symptoms were found (Schaan, 2013). Consistent with earlier studies, this study found that loss of a spouse has more negative impact on mental health for widowed females and males who rated their marriage as positive and less negative impact on widowed females and males who had provided care to their spouses before their death. The study also found some cross-national differences in the negative impact of widowhood on mental health, and the researcher suggested that future research should investigate whether social welfare policies play a role in mitigating the negative effects of spousal death on mental health, noting a consistent finding of financial hardship as a risk factor for depression.

Researchers have also found that spousal death is not only linked to deteriorating health and increased depression but it is also associated with risk of death of the surviving partner. A recent research project examined data from a nationally representative sample of persons older than 60 in Taiwan, followed across five periods from 1989 to 2003, to study the impact of widowhood on mortality (Fang et al., 2012). The researchers found that spousal death was associated with a twofold risk of death in both men and women. They also found that the likelihood of death among widowed males was strongest for men who had been in poorer health prior to widowhood, but the same pattern was not found among widowed females. The researchers suggested that this finding might reflect the gender role division of labor that had been used by the couples. Loss, grief, and bereavement are discussed in greater detail in Chapter 10.

Adjustment to widowhood is facilitated by a person's own inner strength, family support, a strong network of friends and neighbors, and membership in a church or an active community. The family is the most important source of emotional, social, and financial support during this time (Walsh, 2011).

Institutionalization

Another myth of aging is that older individuals are being abandoned and neglected by their families and being pushed into nursing homes to get them out of the way. Fewer elderly persons are institutionalized than we generally assume, but the risk for entering a nursing home or similar institutional setting increases significantly with age. During the past decade, the percentage of older people living in nursing homes actually declined from 5.1% in 1990 to 3.6% in 2011 (Administration on Aging, 2012). However, the risk of entering a nursing home increases with age. Only 1% of older adults aged 65 to 74, compared with 11% of those 85 and older, lived in nursing homes. Additionally, 2.7% of older adults live in self-described senior housing with at least one supportive service (Administration on Aging, 2012). It is important to note that these data reflect the number of older adults living in institutional settings at a given point in time. The data do not reflect the movement in and out of such facilities, and it is estimated that 39% of people aged 65 and older will spend some time in a nursing home at some point; the percentage rises to 49% at age 85 (Hooyman & Kiyak, 2011). About three quarters of the residents of nursing homes are women, and about 86% are White (Hooyman & Kiyak, 2011). It remains to be seen whether Gene Smith, Lois Smith, Ms. Johnson, or Mr. or Mrs. Menzel will spend some time before death in a nursing home.

Most children and spouses do not use nursing homes as a dumping ground for their elderly relatives. They turn to nursing homes only after they have exhausted all other alternatives. Nor is institutionalization a single, sudden event. It is a process that starts with the need to make a decision, continues through the placement itself, and ends in the adjustment to the placement (Naleppa, 1996).

Researchers have taken a close look at the factors that predict a person's entry into a nursing home. Among the most important are the condition and needs of the elderly individual. Functional and behavioral deficits, declining health, previous institutionalization, and advanced age all contribute to the decision to enter a nursing home. Family characteristics that are good predictors of institutionalization include the need for 24-hour caregiving, caregiver feelings of distress, caregiver health and mental status, and caregiving environment (Naleppa, 1996). The placement decision itself is emotionally stressful for all involved and can be viewed as a family crisis (Chang & Schneider, 2010). Yet it can be considered a normative part of the family life cycle. The process of making a placement decision itself unfolds in stages. A grounded theory study of the nursing home placement decision among Chinese family caregivers in Taiwan identified four stages: initiating the placement decision, assessing and weighing the decision, finalizing the decision, and evaluating the decision (Chang & Schneider, 2010). Because many nursing home placements are arranged from the hospital for an elderly individual who entered the hospital expecting to return home, many older adults and their families may not have time to progress well through these stages. For those who unexpectedly enter a nursing home from the hospital, it may be advisable to arrange a brief visit home to say farewell to their familiar environment. Although society has developed rituals for many occasions, unfortunately no rituals exist for this difficult life transition.

Entering a nursing home means losing control and adjusting to a new environment, but the culture of nursing homes is changing. Increasingly, nursing homes focus on resident-centered care that offers more choices in such matters as waking and eating times. The new culture emphasizes a more home-like atmosphere, including companion animals; breaking large facilities into smaller communities; and humanizing staff-care recipient relationships. Evaluation of the impact of these changes on residents and staff indicate lower levels of boredom and helplessness among residents and less job turnover among staff (Hooyman & Kiyak, 2011). How well a person adjusts to moving to a nursing home depends on many factors. If the elderly individual sees entering the nursing home in a favorable light and feels in control, adjustment may proceed well. Frequent visits by relatives and friends also help in the adaptation to the new living arrangement.

Critical Thinking Questions 9.4

At what age do you expect to retire? If you were promised a full pension that would allow you to stop working now, would you want to continue to work? Why or why not? What does work mean to you? Do you work to live or live to work? What factors do you think a person should consider when making decisions about retirement?

THE SEARCH FOR PERSONAL MEANING

As adults become older, they spend more time reviewing their life achievements and searching for personal meaning. In gerontology, the concept of **life review** as a developmental task of late adulthood was introduced by Robert Butler (1963). He theorized that this self-reflective review of one's life is not a sign of losing short-term memory, as had been assumed. Rather, life review is a process of evaluating and making sense of one's life. It includes a reinterpretation of past experiences and unresolved conflicts. Newer forms of clinical interventions rooted in narrative

theory underscore the importance of providing structure, coherence, and opportunity for meaning making of one's experience that "storying" provides (Morgan, 2000). Social workers can influence a more positive outcome of a life review through relationship, empathic listening and reflection, witness to the story, and providing alternative reframes and interpretations of past events. For example, promoting a story of resiliency as a lifelong process helps to reframe stories that support successful mastery of challenges and compensatory recovery in the face of adversity (O'Leary & Bhaju, 2006; Wadensten, 2005).

The life review can lead to diverse outcomes, including depression, acceptance, or satisfaction (Butler, 1987). If the life review is successful, it leads the individual to personal wisdom and inner peace. But the reassessment of one's life may also lead to despair and depression. This idea that the process of life review may lead to either acceptance or depression is similar to the eighth stage of Erikson's theory of adult development; through the life review, the individual tries to work through the conflict between ego integrity (accepting oneself and seeing one's life as meaningful) and despair (rejecting oneself and one's life).

The ways in which individuals review their lives differ considerably. Some undertake a very conscious effort of assessing and reevaluating their achievements; for others, the effort may be subtle and not very conscious. Life review is believed to be a common activity for older adults, regardless of how they pursue it across cultures and time.

The concept of **reminiscence** is closely related to life review. Most older persons have a remarkable ability to recall past events. They reminisce about the past and tell their stories to anyone who is willing to listen, but they also reminisce when they are on their own. This reminiscing can serve several functions (Sherman, 1991):

- Reminiscing may be an enjoyable activity that can lift the spirits of the listener and of the person telling the story.
- Some forms of reminiscing are directed at enhancing a person's image of self, as when individuals focus on their accomplishments.

- Reminiscing may help the person cope with current or future problems, letting her or him retreat to the safe place of a comfortable memory or recall ways of coping with past stressors.
- Reminiscing can assist in the life review, as a way to achieve ego integrity.

Reminiscing combines past, present, and future orientations (Sherman, 1991). It includes the past, which is when the reviewed events occurred. However, the construction of personal meaning is an activity also oriented to the present and future, providing purpose and meaning to life. One study examined the association between reminiscence frequency, reminiscence enjoyment or regret, and psychological health outcomes. The study found that high frequency of reminiscence and having regret was associated with poor psychological health. Reminiscence enjoyment, conversely, was positively associated with psychological health outcomes (Mckee et al., 2005). The Erzählcafé that Elizabeth Menzel visits tries to incorporate this by regularly including group activities that foster reminiscing in a safe, positive, and fun environment.

Another factor in the search for personal meaning is religious or spiritual activity. Cross-sectional research has consistently found that humans become more religious or spiritual in late adulthood (Moody & Sasser, 2012). There seems to be consensus in the cross-sectional research from the United States that religiosity increases in late adulthood, with a short period of health-related drop-off in attendance at religious services at the end of life. Older adults are also more likely than other age groups to participate in private religious behaviors such as prayer, reading of sacred texts, or meditation (Bjorklund, 2011). One longitudinal study that followed a sample of men and women from age 31 to 78 found that women and men tend to increase in spirituality between the mid-50s and mid-70s (Wink & Dillon, 2002). Vaillant's (2012) longitudinal research did not find support for this idea among his sample of Harvard men, and he suggests that the nature of the sample may be an important factor in this finding.

RESOURCES FOR MEETING THE NEEDS OF ELDERLY PERSONS ____

The persons in the case studies at the beginning of this chapter needed several kinds of assistance. Lois and Gene Smith, for example, needed some counseling to help them settle comfortably into retirement together. Gene went back to work to fill some of his leisure hours, but Lois needed some suggestions about the volunteer opportunities that could give meaning to her life. Ms. Johnson requires a level of assistance most practically provided by effective and comprehensive case management. The Menzels' needs were quite different. Elizabeth Menzel is confronted with Alzheimer's-related care and assistance needs. Much of this assistance has been provided by her daughter Christine and her husband Joseph. Joseph Menzel, in turn, needs some respite services to prevent him from being overwhelmed by the demands of giving care. This respite is being provided by his wife's weekly attendance in an Alzheimer's social group meeting.

The types of support and assistance that elderly persons receive can be categorized as either formal or informal resources. Formal resources are those provided by formal service providers. They typically have eligibility requirements that a person has to meet in order to qualify. Some formal resources are free, but others are provided on a fee-for-service basis, meaning that anyone who is able to pay can request the service. Informal resources are those provided through families, friends, neighbors, churches, and so forth. Elderly persons receive a considerable amount of support through these informal support networks. As the society ages, more attention will need to be paid to the interaction between the informal and formal support systems (Wacker & Roberto, 2014).

Informal Resources

The family is the most important provider of informal resources for many older individuals. Usually family members can provide better emotional and social support than other providers of services. Family members know the person better

What types of social service programs can enhance informal supports for older adults?

and are more available for around-the-clock support. Different family members tend to provide different types of assistance. Daughters tend to provide most of the caregiving and are more involved in housekeeping and household chores. Sons are more likely to provide assistance with household repairs and financial matters (Hooyman & Kiyak, 2011).

However, the family should not be considered a uniformly available resource or support. Not all family networks are functional and able to provide needed support. As Ms. Johnson's story illustrates, even when family members are involved in the elderly person's life, they may place additional demands on the older person instead of relieving the burden. The increased presence of women in the labor market places them in a particularly difficult position—trying to balance the demands of raising children, taking care of their parents or partner, and being part of the workforce. Furthermore, the size of the family network available to support elderly persons is decreasing as a consequence of the decreasing average number of children in a family (Walsh, 2011).

A second source of informal resources is friends and neighbors, who often provide a significant amount of care and assistance. Although they may be less inclined than family members would be to provide personal care, friends and neighbors like Gene and Lois Smith often offer other forms of assistance, such as running errands or performing household chores. Sometimes a system of informal exchanges evolves—for example, an elderly woman invites her elderly neighbor over for meals while he mows her lawn and drives her to medical appointments.

Finally, informal resources are also provided by religious and community groups. Religious-related resources include social and emotional support through group activities and community events. It is this form of support that an active retired person such as Lois Smith finds most helpful. In addition, some religious groups are involved in providing more formal resources, such as transportation or meal services.

Formal Resources

The second type of support for older adults is the formal service delivery system, which offers a wide range of services. Four different Social Security trust funds are the backbone of formal resources to older people in the United States:

How do these federal programs serve as protective factors in late adulthood?

1. *Old-Age and Survivors Insurance (OASI).* The retirement and survivors' component of the U.S. Social Security system is a federally administered program that covers almost all workers. To qualify, a person must have worked at least 10 years in employment covered by the program. The benefit is based on the individual's earnings and is subject to a maximum benefit amount. Through cost-of-living adjustments, the amount is adjusted annually for inflation. Many older individuals are able to supplement this benefit with private pension benefits (Social Security Administration, 2013b).

2. *Hospital Insurance Trust Fund (Medicare Part A).* This fund covers a major part of the cost of hospitalization as well as a significant part of the costs of skilled nursing facility care, approved home health care, and under certain conditions, hospice care. Depending on the type of service needed, beneficiaries pay a one-time copayment or a percentage of the actual costs. Most beneficiaries do not need to pay a monthly premium (Medicare .gov, 2013a).

3. *Supplementary Medical Insurance. Medicare Part B* covers medical costs such as physicians' services, inpatient and outpatient surgery, and ambulance services, as well as laboratory services, medical equipment, outpatient mental health services, second opinions for surgery, and preventive services such as flu vaccinations. Under the Affordable Care Act, Part B also covers screening

mammograms, colorectal cancer screenings, and an annual wellness visit without a copayment charge (Medicare.gov, 2013b). Beneficiaries pay a monthly premium. Some services require a copayment or a deductible. *Medicare Part D*, a result of the Medication Prescription Drug Improvement and Modernization Act of 2003, became effective on January 1, 2006. It was designed to provide older adults and people with disabilities access to prescription drug coverage. Rather than being administered by the federal government, as in the case of Part A and Part B, Part D is administered by private insurance plans that are then reimbursed by the Centers for Medicare and Medicaid Services (CMS) (Medicare.gov, 2013c). Participants have choices of a number of private insurance plans, but the choices are not straightforward. Plans with the lowest premiums may not cover the drugs needed by a particular participant. In addition, plans may change their drug prices frequently. The initial coverage was limited to drug costs of $2,400, and catastrophic coverage did not pick up until drug costs reached $3,850, placing considerable financial burden on many older beneficiaries. This problem with Medicare Part D was termed the "doughnut hole." The health reform bill passed in March 2010 attempts to close the "doughnut hole" over time (Medicare.gov, 2013d).

4. *Disability insurance.* This component provides benefits for workers younger than 62 with a severe long-term disability. There is a 5-month waiting period, but the benefits continue as long as the disability exists.

In addition, Supplemental Social Security Income (SSI) is a financial need-based program that provides cash benefits to low-income, aged, blind, and disabled persons. It is not part of the Social Security trust funds but is a federal welfare program.

Other formal services are available regionally. Here is an overview of some of the most important ones (see Wacker & Roberto, 2014, for a fuller discussion of community resources for older adults):

- *Adult day care.* Some elderly individuals have conditions that prevent them from staying at home while their caregiver is at work, or the caregiver may benefit from respite. Two forms of adult day care exist for such situations. *The social adult day care model* provides meals, medication, and socialization but no personal care. *The medical adult day care model* is for individuals who need medical care, nursing services, physical or occupational therapy, and more intensive personal care.

- *Senior centers.* Community forums for social activities, educational programs, and resource information are available even in small communities.

- *Home health care services.* Several types of home health care are available, varying greatly in level of assistance and cost. They range from homemakers who assist with household chores, cleaning, and errands to registered nurses who provide skilled nursing service, use medical equipment, and provide intravenous therapy.

- *Hospice programs.* The purpose of a hospice program is to provide care to the terminally ill. Through inpatient or outpatient hospice, patients typically receive treatment by a team of doctors, nurses, social workers, and care staff.

- *Senior housing.* An elderly person may require a change in his or her living arrangement for a number of reasons, and several alternative living arrangements are available. Senior apartments and retirement communities are for persons who can live independently. They typically offer meals and housekeeping services but no direct care. Many offer transportation, community rooms, and senior programs.

- *Adult homes.* For seniors in need of more assistance, adult homes usually have rooms, rather than apartments, and provide meals, medication management, and supervision.

- *Health-related senior facilities.* For those in need of nursing care and intensive assistance with activities of daily living, residents live in private or semiprivate rooms and share living and dining rooms. Medications, meals, personal care, and some therapeutic services are provided. Included in this category is the growing number of *assisted living facilities*, which may provide small apartments as well as single rooms. The skilled nursing facility provides the highest level of care, including nursing and personal care and an array of therapeutic services. Several noninstitutional alternatives to the nursing home exist, including *adult foster care* programs that operate in a similar way to foster care programs for children and adolescents.

- *Nutrition programs.* Deficits in nutrition can affect a person's health and the aging process. Nutritional services are provided through a number of programs, the best known being Meals on Wheels.

- *Transportation services.* Public and private providers offer transportation for elderly persons with mobility problems.

- *Power of attorney.* Some elderly persons have difficulty managing their legal and financial affairs. A **power of attorney (POA)** is a legal arrangement by which a person appoints another individual to manage his or her financial and legal affairs. The person given the POA should be a person the client knows and trusts. Standard POA forms can usually be found at office supply stores or on websites for state bar associations, but legal advice is highly recommended for specific situations. The POA must be witnessed and notarized. A POA can be limited (in scope or for a certain time period), general (no restrictions), or durable (begins after the client reaches a specified level of disability).

With so many types of services available, the social worker's most daunting task is often assessing the elderly person's needs. It may also be a challenge, however, to find quality services that are affordable. Thus, advocacy on behalf of older adults remains a concern of the social work profession.

Naturally, the ways formal and informal resources are offered differ among countries and even regions of a country. As can be deduced from our discussion of the problems older adults face, many are neither unique to an individual nor country specific. Rather, they are occurring as part of the aging process for older adults around the globe. We already described some of the programs as they pertain to older adults in the United States. To illustrate different approaches taken to address similar problems, we include a brief comparison of the retirement benefits, health care, and long-term care in the United States, the environment of the Smiths and Ms. Johnson, and in Germany, the Menzels' home environment (see Exhibit 9.10). As you can see, there are similarities in some areas and significant differences in others. The United States often uses a more incremental approach to policy changes. In Germany, policy change usually takes a longer time, but when it occurs, the new policies are often very comprehensive and far-reaching in their application.

RISK FACTORS AND PROTECTIVE FACTORS IN LATE ADULTHOOD

Chapter 8 suggests that midlife behavior has both antecedents and consequences. The same can be said for late adulthood. Early life experiences can serve either as risk factors or as protective factors for health and well-being during late adulthood. And late-adult behaviors can serve either as risk factors or as protective factors for future health and well-being.

As the longest-term longitudinal research available on late-adult behavior, Vaillant's Study of Adult Development (2002, 2012) provides the clearest understanding of the antecedents of late-adult well-being. Like Emmy Werner, who has studied a cohort until midlife (see Chapter 8), Vaillant is impressed with the self-righting tendencies in human nature. He suggests that what goes right in childhood is more important

Exhibit 9.10   Some Comparisons of Aging Policy in Germany and the United States

Germany	United States
Retirement Benefits	**Retirement Benefits**
Current retirees receive a guaranteed income through a range of pension schemes. Social assistance kicks in if pensions are inadequate. Most retirement benefits are through the statutory pension system, which provides a monthly pension based on a formula that takes into consideration factors such as years of employment and income. Government employees and civil servants are part of a government retirement system, providing a slightly better level of benefits. Recent changes to statutory pension schemes require current members of the workforce to purchase additional private pension savings plans to supplement their future retirement benefits. In the future, statutory pensions will only provide basic financial security, not considered high enough to continue with a similar standard of living in retirement. The current retirement age of 65 is increasing incrementally to 67 years. Since the German job market discriminates against older workers, it is expected that this will cause problems for some retiring baby boomers.	Social Security is the foundation of the benefits for older individuals, including retirement benefits, disability benefits, and dependent's and survivor's benefits. Social Security provides a guaranteed retirement benefit to almost all citizens. The benefit level is based on a formula taking into consideration factors such as years of employment and income. Social Security is only considered to be a basic retirement benefit. Individuals are expected to supplement their Social Security income through private savings, individual retirement plans, or other retirement investments. Significant variation exists in retirement planning. Many in the current workforce are not able to contribute to private retirement savings, since their employment status does not come with retirement benefits. The current retirement age of 65 is increasing incrementally to 67 years. Aside from economic cycles and related unemployment, it can be expected that the job market in the United States will be able to adapt to this change.
Health Care	**Health Care**
Older adults continue to receive the same health care coverage and remain with their providers after reaching retirement age. No differences exist between pre- and postretirement health care coverage. Health care insurance is universal but not socialized. Almost all citizens are required to have health insurance. The premiums are shared with the employer. If someone is unemployed, the government covers costs. People select their own insurance plan from private insurance companies that are regulated by government. The system consists primarily of private players, i.e., health insurance companies, physicians, pharmacies, and many hospitals are for-profit businesses. In general, premiums for retirees remain at about the same levels; however, they have to pay the entire costs.	Health care for those over 65 years is provided almost exclusively through Medicare, making it a near universal health care plan for older adults. Eligibility includes U.S. citizens 65 years or older who have contributed Medicare taxes for at least 10 years. Medicare is considered a single-payer health care plan that covers most health care of older adults. It consists of four parts: Part A—hospital insurance, Part B—medical insurance, Part C—Medicare advantage plans, and Part D—drug prescription plans. Medicare is financed in part through a 2.9% payroll tax. Recipients may be required to pay additional fees; for example, Medicare Part B requires enrolees to pay a premium. "Medigap" insurances are available to purchase protection against costs that are not covered through Medicare.
Long-Term Care	**Long-Term Care**
Long-term care insurance (LTCI; Pflegeversicherung) is the youngest of the German social welfare programs. It was introduced in 1994 after 2 decades of political discussion (Scharf, 1998). The LTCI is formally attached	No comprehensive long-term care insurance exists. Recipients of Medicaid and VA benefits may receive some long-term care coverage. Individuals enrolled in Medicare Part A are covered for short-term stays in a

Germany	United States
to health insurance and is financed through a 1.7% payroll tax. LTCI is a needs-based program. In order to receive coverage, a person completes an application, a medical assessment is conducted, and the person is given a needs level score (Pflegestufe) of 1 to 3. The amount and type of caregiving services are based on this score. The care recipient is in control of the services, i.e., she decides which provider to hire from a menu of local for-profit and nonprofit service providers. Family members may be hired as well, but reimbursement rates are slightly lower. Recently an additional needs category has been added to include persons with dementia, who may not qualify in terms of their medical care needs but may require extensive other assistance by their caregivers.	skilled nursing facility (full coverage for the first 20 days, another 80 days with co-pay). Various options exist to purchase private long-term care insurance, albeit at rather high premiums. For example, federal employees can enroll in a federal long-term care insurance program.

for life in late adulthood than what goes wrong. A warm relationship with their mothers was a strong protective factor at age 80 for his sample of Harvard men (Vaillant, 2012). He also suggests that unhappy childhoods become less important over the stages of adulthood. Consequently, Vaillant suggests that it is more important to count up the protective factors than to count up the risk factors. Although he found childhood experiences to diminish in importance over time, Vaillant also found that much of the resilience, or lack thereof, in late adulthood is predicted by factors that were established by age 50. He suggests that risk factors and protective factors change over the life course. He emphasizes that longitudinal research demonstrates that "everything affects everything else" (2012, p. 258) and that the "etiology of successful aging is multifactorial" (2012, p. 259).

Exhibit 9.11 lists six variables that Vaillant (2002, 2012) was surprised to find did not predict healthy aging and seven factors that he did find to predict healthy aging. Some of the factors that did not predict healthy aging did predict good adjustment at earlier adult stages. In terms of stress, Vaillant found that if we wait a few decades, many people recover from psychosomatic illness. In terms of parental characteristics, he found that they are still important for predicting adaptation at age 40 but not by age 70. In terms of both childhood temperament and general ease in social relationships, he found that they are strong predictors of adjustment in young adulthood but no longer important at age 70.

Conversely, Vaillant found that the seven factors on the right side of Exhibit 9.11, collectively, are strong predictors of health 30 years in the future. He also found that each variable, individually, predicted healthy aging, even when the other six variables were statistically controlled. Vaillant has chosen to frame each of these predictive factors in terms of protection; he sees risk as the flip side of protection. He notes the danger of such a list of protective factors: that it is used to "blame the victim" rather than provide guidance for aging well. He sees the list of predictors as "good news," however, because they all represent something that can be controlled to some extent.

By following cohorts across the period of young-old and middle-old, Vaillant (2002) also has some suggestions about the consequences of late-adult behavior. We have already taken a look at his prescription for growing old gracefully. In addition, he notes the following personal qualities

Exhibit 9.11   Variables That Affect Healthy Aging

Variables That Do Not Predict Healthy Aging	Variables That Do Predict Healthy Aging
Ancestral longevity	Not smoking, or stopping young
Cholesterol	Using mature coping mechanisms
Stress	Not abusing alcohol
Parental characteristics	Healthy weight
Childhood temperament	Stable marriage
General ease in social relationships	Some exercise
	Years of education

SOURCE: Vaillant, 2002

in late adulthood to bode well for continued well-being:

- Good self-care
- Future orientation, ability to anticipate, plan, and hope
- Capacity for gratitude and forgiveness
- Capacity for empathy, to imagine the world as the other sees it
- Desire to do things with people rather than to them

Critical Thinking Questions 9.5

How do social welfare programs influence the experience of aging? How do they influence the caregiving experience of the multigenerational family? In the United States, do you think we have too many or too few formal resources for late-life adults and their families? Explain. What gaps, if any, do you see in formal services?

Implications for Social Work Practice

Several practice principles for social work with older adults can be recommended:

- When working with an older adult, take into account the person's life history.
- Develop self-awareness of your views on aging and how different theoretical perspectives may influence your practice.
- Be conscious that age-related social roles change over time and that they vary for different cohorts.
- Identify areas in which you can assist an elderly client in preventing future problems, such as health-related difficulties.
- Develop an understanding of and skills to assess the difference between the physical, biological, psychological, and socioemotional changes that are part of normal aging and those that are indicative of a problematic process. Develop an understanding of how such factors may affect the intervention process.

- Develop an understanding of the different types of families in later life. Because older adults continue to be part of their families, it may be beneficial to work with the entire family system.
- Develop an understanding of the retirement process and how individuals adjust differently to this new life stage.
- Carefully assess an elderly person's caregiving network. Be conscious of the difficulties that the caregiving situation poses for both the caregiver and the care recipient. Be conscious of the potential for caregiver burnout and familiarize yourself with local caregiver support options.
- Develop an understanding of the process of institutionalizing an older adult. Be careful not to label it as an act of abandonment. Rather, be aware that institutionalization is stressful for all involved and is typically done only as a last resort. Develop an understanding of the process of adaptation to nursing home placement and skills to assist an older adult and his or her family with that adaptation.
- When assessing the need for service, be conscious of the availability of formal and informal support systems. Develop an understanding and knowledge of the formal service delivery system.
- Avoid treating older persons as if they were incapable of making decisions simply because they may not be able to carry out the decision. Rather, involve them to the maximum extent possible in any decisions relating to their personal life and care, even if they are not able to carry out the related actions.

Key Terms

activity theory (of aging)
age stratification perspective
Alzheimer's disease
continuity theory (of aging)
crystallized intelligence
damage or error theories of aging
delirium
dementia
dependency ratio

developmental biocultural co-constructivism
disengagement theory (of aging)
ego integrity versus ego despair
feminist theories (of aging)
fluid intelligence
guardianship
incidental memory
intentional memory
life review

morbidity
mortality rate
power of attorney (POA)
productive aging theory
programmed aging theories
reminiscence
social construction theory (of aging)
social exchange theory (of aging)
social gerontology

Active Learning

1. Think about the three case studies presented at the outset of this chapter (Smith, Johnson, and Menzel). Which theory or theories of social gerontology seem to be the best fit with each of these individuals?

2. Think of examples of how older adults are presented in the media (TV, movies, advertisements). How are they typically characterized? What does this say about our society's views on aging? Think of examples of how older adults could be presented in an age-appropriate way in the media. Develop a short script for an advertisement that features older adults.

3. Think about your own extended family. What roles do the members of the oldest generation play in the family? How do the different generations interact, exchange resources, and influence each other? How do the different generations deal with their role changes and life transitions as they age? In what ways do the different generations support and hinder each other in life transitions?

Administration on Aging: www.aoa.gov

Site accesses information about the Older Americans Act, federal legislation, and range of programs and statistics.

Agency for Healthcare Research and Quality: www.ahrq.gov

Site provides consumer, patient, and clinical practice information focused on specific populations: aging, women, and rural.

American Association of Retired Persons: www .aarp.org

Organizational site provides a wide range of resources for health, technology, travel, law, and policy and advocacy.

Federal Interagency Forum on Aging-Related Statistics: www.agingstats.gov

Site covers 31 key indicators of the lives of older people in the United States and their families.

National Academy on an Aging Society: www .agingsociety.org

Organization provides clear, unbiased research and analysis focused on public policy issues arising from the aging of America's and the world's populations.

National Caucus and Center on Black Aging: www.ncba-aged.org

Site contains aging news for policymakers, legislators, advocacy groups, minority professionals, and consumers addressing finances, caregiving, intergenerational issues, and governmental programs.

National Council on Aging: www.ncoa.org

Site presented by the National Council on Aging (NCOA) contains information on advocacy, programs, publications, and a number of good links to other aging resources.

National Institute on Aging: www.nia.nih.gov

Site presented by the National Institute on Aging (NIA) contains information about the NIA, news and events, health information, research programs, funding and training, and the National Advisory Council on Aging.

Social Security Administration: www.ssa.gov

Site maintained by the U.S. Social Security Administration contains benefits information and online direct services.

Student Study Site

$SAGE edge™

Sharpen your skills with SAGE edge at **edge.sagepub.com/hutchisonclc5e**

SAGE edge for students provides a personalized approach to help you accomplish your coursework goals in an easy-to-use learning environment.

CHAPTER 10

Very Late Adulthood

Pamela J. Kovacs and Annemarie Conlon

Chapter Outline

CASE STUDY 10.1

Margaret Davis Stays at Home

Margaret Davis has lived in her small, rural community in southern West Virginia for all of her 85 years. It is in this Appalachian mountain town that she married her grade school sweetheart, packed his pail for long shifts in the mine, and raised their four children. It has been more than 30 years since she answered the door to receive the news that her husband had perished in an accident at the mine. She remains in that same house by herself, with her daughter living in a trailer on the same property and one of her sons living just down the road. Her other son recently moved to Cleveland to find work, and her other daughter lives in the same town but has been estranged from the family for several years.

Mrs. Davis has hypertension and was recently diagnosed with type 2 diabetes. The nurse from the home health agency is assisting her and her daughter with learning to give insulin injections. It is the nurse who asks for a social work consult for Mrs. Davis. The nurse and Mrs. Davis's daughter are concerned that she is becoming increasingly forgetful with her medications and often neglects her insulin regime. They also suspect that she is experiencing some incontinence, as her living room couch and carpet smell of urine. Mrs. Davis and her daughter Judy greet the social worker at her home. They have been baking this morning and offer a slice of peanut butter pie. Judy excuses herself to go to her trailer to make a phone call. The social worker asks Mrs. Davis about how her insulin regime has been going and if she feels that she could keep up with the injections. She responds that she has learned to give herself the shots and "feels pretty fair." The social worker conveys the concern that she may be missing some of the injections and other medications as well. To this she replies, "Oh, don't worry about me, I'm fine." The social worker proceeds to ask the sensitive question as to whether she has been having trouble with her bladder or getting to the bathroom. This causes Mrs. Davis to become very quiet. Looking up at the social worker she shares that witches have been visiting her house late at night and have been urinating in her living room. The witches are very "devious," but because she is a very religious person, she does not feel that they will harm her.

Judy returns to the home and joins her mother and the social worker. Judy voices her concern about her mother's safety, noting the problems with medications and with general forgetfulness. Judy is able to prepare meals, dispense the medications, and give insulin injections in the morning because she works evenings at a factory. Judy's daughter, Tiffany, has been staying overnight in the home but complains of her grandmother's wandering and confusion late at night. As a result, she is often exhausted during her day shifts at a nursing home in the next county and in caring for her small children. When asked about Mrs. Davis's son's involvement in her care, Judy responds, "He works and is in the Guard some weekends. He handles mom's money mostly, and his wife, well, she has her own problems." Judy also reported that her mother has Medicare, but she was not sure if that would be sufficient to pay for all her mother's care long-term. Judy is also worried because her old car has been giving her problems lately, and the repairs are becoming expensive. She concludes by stating, "We promised Mom that she would never go to a home . . . we take care of our own."

—Kristina Hash

—Meenakshi Venkataraman

CASE STUDY 10.2

Pete Mullin Loses His Sister's Support

Pete Mullin and Lucy Rauso, brother and sister, ages 96 and 92, have lived together since the death of Lucy's husband, Tony, 25 years ago. Pete and Lucy are second-generation Irish Catholic Americans, and Tony Rauso was Italian American. Pete was married in his 30s but had lived alone since his divorce at age 55. Pete and Lucy were both in their early 70s when they decided to pool their limited savings and retirement income to buy a small home in a rural retirement community in central Florida. The promise of a lower cost of living and milder winters, and the fact that many of their friends had moved or died, made it easier for Lucy and Pete to leave the community in Massachusetts where they had spent their entire lives.

Pete has been estranged from his one daughter since his divorce but is in touch with a granddaughter who "found" him when she moved to Florida a few years ago. Lucy has one surviving son in New Jersey and several grandchildren who provide limited financial support and some social support via phone calls and an occasional visit. Pete has enjoyed his life and, despite some difficulty with his vision and hearing, manages to get around well in his familiar surroundings. He is especially fond of tending his orchids in the back porch.

(Continued)

(Continued)

Lucy has just been hospitalized with chronic heart failure and is not expected to make it through the night. A neighbor has brought Pete to the intensive care unit to be with Lucy. Pete states that together he and Lucy managed to provide for each other and served as each other's durable power of attorney and health care surrogate and in general made it possible for each of them to remain in their home. He wonders what will happen to him after Lucy's death. He knows that many people his age live in nursing homes, but he prefers to stay in his own home. He wonders if the Meals on Wheels will still come to the home, because their eligibility was based on Lucy's diagnosis of chronic heart failure. He hopes he will die soon and quickly like Lucy.

The social worker employed for the Meals on Wheels program has been asked to make a home visit within the week following Lucy's death to reassess Pete's eligibility for services. The social worker had not realized how much her job would involve working with people who have experienced a major loss, whether death of a loved one as in Pete's case or the accompanying losses that come with illness, disability, and aging.

CASE STUDY 10.3

Marie Cipriani Is Losing Her Life Partner

Marie Cipriani was born in a small apartment house on the Lower East Side of Manhattan 86 years ago. Just one year before Marie's birth, her mother passed through Ellis Island with Marie's three older siblings. Her father and two brothers, already established in the states, eagerly awaited their arrival. Later, when Marie was an adolescent, the family moved to Long Island. Today Marie lives in a modest two-bedroom home that she shares with Irene Wright, her partner of 42 years. Irene, a petite 79-year-old African American woman, has recently been diagnosed with stage IV lung cancer. The disease has progressed rapidly, hastening Irene's decision to transition to hospice service.

Jessica, the hospice social worker, met with Irene and Marie at their home this Friday afternoon. Marie was making soup while Irene reclined in the warmth of the backyard sun when Jessica arrived. She immediately put the soup on simmer and accompanied Jessica out back to meet Irene. Marie was initially apprehensive as she was not sure how this stranger felt about two women sharing their lives together. However, when Jessica asked them how long they had lived in their home and complimented them on the length of their relationship, Marie began to feel at ease. Jessica worked from a family systems perspective and considered both Irene and Marie her clients. She discovered that Marie's siblings died years earlier. And, although Marie had one son from a previous marriage, he had died of congestive heart failure last June at age 64. Marie has no other close relatives. Irene, however, has two younger sisters who never understood Irene's relationship with Marie. "They generally do not visit when I am around," Marie said, hinting to Jessica that the relationship is rocky. "I don't know what they will do now because I am not leaving Irene's side."

Jessica was concerned about what would happen to Marie after Irene died. Although Marie appeared to be in good physical shape, going through the grieving process might impact Marie's mental and physical health. Should Marie decline, who will she rely on for help? Moreover, even though New York had marriage equality, they were not married. If they did not have all the proper paperwork in place, Marie could find herself at risk for eviction.

VERY LATE ADULTHOOD: CHARTING NEW TERRITORY _____

At 85, 86, 92, and 96, respectively, Margaret Davis, Marie Cipriani, Lucy Rauso, and Pete Mullin are charting new territory. They are a part of the rapidly growing population older than age 85, many of whom are surprised they are living so long.

> How does the fact that the current cohort of very-late-life adults are charting new territory affect their experience with this life course phase?

In the first edition of this book (1999), the chapter on late adulthood covered all persons 65 and older. The fact that subsequent editions present this content in two chapters ("Late Adulthood" and "Very Late Adulthood") indicates the scope and rapidity of the demographic changes taking place in the United States and other late-industrial societies. Within the past 20 to 25 years, some researchers have begun to more methodically consider age distinctions after age 65 or 75, given the population growth in this age group.

This chapter summarizes some of the emerging literature on very late adulthood, including those who reach 100—our **centenarians**. (Much of what appears in the previous chapter on late adulthood applies as well.) The current knowledge about very late adulthood is growing as the population and related interest increase each year. However, given the scarcity of longitudinal studies that have followed a cohort from early adulthood deep into very late adulthood, it is difficult to tease out the cohort effects in the available cross-sectional research.

One issue that comes up at all adult stages is the ages included in the stage. As you have seen throughout this book, chronological markers of age are arbitrary at best and influenced by biological age, psychological age, social age, and spiritual age. But it is fairly standard to think of 85 and older as old old, oldest old, or very late adulthood. The category of the very old, those older than 80, is also referred to by some as the "fourth age" (Hazan, 2011, p. 11). This is more about circumstances in one's life than about age; for example, the "third age" refers to being older and still remaining independent, and the "fourth age" refers to a time when people are more dependent and in need of care (MacKinlay, 2006). This is less a chronological distinction than a reflection of changes in life circumstances that often happen as one approaches age 80. For the most part, we use "very-late-life adults" to describe people in this life course phase, but we also use "old old" and "oldest old" when citing work where those terms are used. However, keep in mind that chronological age may not be the best marker for categorizing very-late-life adults (Agronin, 2011). Loss of health might be a better criterion for categorization as very late adulthood or old old. Nevertheless, in keeping with the other chapters in the book, this chapter uses a chronological distinction.

The drawback to using a chronological marker for entry into very late adulthood is that the path through very late adulthood is quite diverse, and for many people older than 85, ill health is not a central theme of their lives. In his book *Aging Well*, George Vaillant (2002) reminds us that

- Frank Lloyd Wright designed the Guggenheim Museum at age 90.
- Dr. Michael DeBakey obtained a patent for a surgical innovation when he was 90.
- Grandma Moses was still painting at 100.

In addition, we would add that

- Sarah and Elizabeth Delany (1993) published their book *Having Our Say: Our First 100 Years* when Sarah (Sadie) was 103 and Elizabeth (Bessie) was 101.
- Sadie Delany (1997) published *On My Own at 107: Reflections on Life Without Bessie* at the age of 107.
- Daniel Schorr was heard weekly on National Public Radio as the senior news analyst until the age of 93, having served as a news journalist for more than 60 years.
- Anna Halprin continues to teach and inspire at age 93. A pioneer in the experimental postmodern dance world and expressive arts healing movement, after a cancer diagnosis in 1972,

she continues to write and teach about dance/movement as an expressive therapy.

- Business owner Samuel Myers actively worked at his dry cleaning business until 3 months before he died at age 97.
- Golfer Pauline Whitacre, 85, of Canton, Ohio, not only continues to golf but shoots better than her age.
- Betty White, 92, hosts her own TV show while starring in another. Since turning 85, she has won a Grammy, an Emmy, and three SAG awards.
- Angie MacLean, 98, from Bridgeport, Connecticut, has been bartending for 81 years.

So, there is much variation in the age at which health issues take on great importance. Margaret Davis has reached this stage in her mid-80s. Marie Cipriani remains healthy at 86 while she cares for a younger life partner who is on hospice service at age 79. Lucy Rauso reached it in her early 90s, and it does not yet seem to have overtaken Pete Mullin in his mid-90s. But sooner or later in very late adulthood, health issues and impending death become paramount.

With our current ways of living, such as busy and pressured work schedules and families geographically scattered, late-industrial societies pose challenges as one ages. That portion of the physical environment attributable solely to human efforts was designed, in the main, by and for those in young and middle adulthood, not for children, persons with various types of physical disabilities, or older adults. However, increasingly, the current cohort of very-late-life adults is charting new territory, and some aspects of society are preparing for the growth in this age group. What can we learn from people who reach 85 and beyond, and what do social work practitioners need to know to provide meaningful and relevant interventions?

As Erik Erikson suggested, we have one and only one life cycle (at least in this incarnation). For some of us, death will come quickly, but for others, death will come after a protracted period of disease and disability. One of the life tasks we face in late adulthood is to come to terms with our one and only life cycle, and the evidence suggests that most very-late-life adults do that remarkably well. We began this book with a discussion of conception, pregnancy, and birth, the starting line of the life course, and in this chapter we end the book with a discussion of death and dying, the finish line of the life course. While this might sound linear, Erikson noted in relation to his life cycle chart that it "becomes really meaningful only when you have observed it as a weaving or, even better, have undertaken to weave it yourself" (Erikson & Erikson, 1997, p. 2). Our challenge as social workers is to be open to the uniqueness of each person's tapestry.

VERY LATE ADULTHOOD IN HISTORICAL AND CULTURAL PERSPECTIVE

There have always been those who outlive their cohort group, but greater numbers of people are surpassing the average life expectancy. Overall, the 85-and-older population is the fastest-growing segment of the population both in the United States and worldwide. This age group is projected to grow from 5.9 million in 2012 to nearly 18 million by 2050 in the United States (U.S. Census Bureau, 2012b, 2013b) and from 46.9 million to 224.1 million worldwide (U.S. Census Bureau, 2013c). This growth is due to advances in medical technology; the prevention and control of childhood diseases; improved nutrition, housing, and hygiene; and greater access to medical care (Crimmins, Preston, & Cohen, 2011).

The phenomenon of the baby boom generation helps explain the current growth in the midlife age groups as well as these projections for future growth in the older-than-85 population. But what else accounts for the fact that persons 85 and older are the fastest-growing segment of the older adult population? Several contributing factors include the following: better health care in early and middle years; earlier diagnosis and improved technology for treatment and overall health care;

improved health habits, including less smoking, less consumption of alcohol and saturated fats; and increased exercise in some groups. In addition, fewer people die of infectious diseases (Hooyman & Kiyak, 2011).

Because both group-based and individual differences within this age group are great, one is cautioned against stereotyping very-late-life adults in an attempt to describe them (Innes, 2009; Poon & Cohen-Mansfield, 2011). For instance, gender and racial or ethnic differences are embedded within these overall statistics. Life expectancy at birth in the United States in 2010 was about 81.1 years for non-Hispanic White females, 77.7 years for non-Hispanic Black females, 76.4 years for non-Hispanic White males, and 71.4 years for non-Hispanic Black males. Hispanic females born in that same period have an estimated life expectancy of 83.8 years and Hispanic males an estimated life expectancy of 78.5 years (National Center for Health Statistics, 2013). Life expectancy has not been uniformly calculated for other ethnic groups, but estimates do exist. Accordingly, an American Indian/Alaska Native (Census Bureau language) born in 2010 has a life expectancy of 75.1 years (no gender breakdown confirmed) (Lewis & Burd-Sharps, 2010). The estimated life expectancy of Asian females born in that period is 85.8 years, and for Asian males it is 84.5 years (Office of Minority Health, 2014). Among very-late-life adults, women outnumber men 2 to 1, and 4 out of 5 centenarians are women (U.S. Census Bureau, 2011a, 2012b). As the data show, very late adulthood is largely a woman's territory. Pete Mullin is an exception to this trend. Culturally, the most significant fact is that very-late-life adults, like other age groups, are becoming more diverse. It is projected that from 2012 to 2050, the racial and ethnic breakdown of the U.S. population of adults age 85 and older will change in the following way: the percentage of this population that is non-Hispanic White will decline from 84.5% to 67.5%; the percentage that is non-Hispanic Black will grow from 6.8% to 9.9%; the percentage that is Hispanic will grow from 5.8% to 15.1%; the percentage that is Asian will grow from 2.1% to 5.9%; and the percentage of all other racial and ethnic groups, including mixed race, will grow from 0.5% to 1.0% (U.S. Census Bureau, 2012b). These trends indicate an increased diversity among the old old.

Census data such as these are of interest to researchers studying *ethnogerontology*, the study of the causes, processes, and consequences of race, national origin, and culture on individual and population aging (Hooyman & Kiyak, 2011). Innes (2009) refers to the cross-cutting interplay of gender, class, and age on aging experiences. Poverty is another indicator of interest with the older population, given decreased earning power and increased health-related expenses. Older women (13%) were almost twice as likely to be poor as older men (7%) in 2010. Overall, the poverty rate increased with age, with 8.1% of people aged 65 to 74, 9.2% of people aged 75 to 84, and 12.3% of those 85 and older living in poverty. Race and ethnicity are also related to poverty among older adults, with older African Americans (20.7%), Hispanics (19%), Asian Americans (16.7%), and non-Hispanic Whites (7.9%) living in poverty (Tarver, 2013).

Chapter 1 suggests that one of the themes of the life course perspective is that individual and family development must be understood in historical context. It is particularly important when we interact with very-late-life adults to be aware of the historical worlds in which their life journeys have taken place. Inquiring about this will help social workers better understand a person's resilience, responses to life challenges, and personal goals. For example, one's experience with the Holocaust, the Depression, war, or other personal trauma may help contextualize current stressors, resilience, and other responses to life.

> What differences do you think this cohort effect makes for cognitive and social development?

Chapter 1 also discusses the concept of *cohort effects*, which suggests that a historical event affects one cohort differently than it affects subsequent cohorts because of the life phase in which it occurred. Let's look, for example, at the wide use of the computerized worldwide network (the Internet). It was experienced

- By the current cohort of 85-year-olds when they were in their 60s
- By the current cohort of 65-year-olds when they were in their 40s
- By the current cohort of 45-year-olds when they were in their 20s

For the current cohort of 25-year-olds and those younger, it may be hard to remember when social media and other aspects of the Internet were not part of their lives.

Individuals' cultural backgrounds also play a role in their perceptions of very late adulthood. Margaret Davis has spent her entire life in an impoverished small Appalachian town where families are expected to "take care of their own." In contrast, Pete Mullin and Lucy Rauso relocated from Massachusetts to Florida in their 70s, moving away from family and friends. Marie Cipriani grew up in New York in an Italian immigrant family. For the past 42 years, she has lived on Long Island with her female partner. Social workers need to try to understand clients' years in their previous homes and any important historical markers in those settings. They also need to know something about migration experiences as well.

WHAT WE CAN LEARN FROM CENTENARIANS

"Forget about Generation X and Generation Y. Today, the nation's most intriguing demographic is Generation Roman numeral C—folks age 100 and over" (Harvard Health Letter, 2002, p. 1). This seems to be a time of both resilience and ongoing development and vulnerability (Poon & Cohen-Mansfield, 2011).

How will this longevity trend alter our views on appropriate roles for other adult phases?

Although very few 100-year-old people were known to exist in the United States in 1900, there

Photo 10.1 Fred Hale Sr. smiles as his great-great-granddaughters arrive to celebrate his 113th birthday. In the United States, the number of centenarians totaled more than 53,000 in 2010.

© Chris Rank, Corbis

were 53,364 of them in 2010. The majority of these centenarians were women (82.8%) and were ages 100 to 104 (92%) (U.S. Census Bureau, 2012d). By 2050, it is estimated that more than 442,000 people in the United States will reach the century mark (U.S. Census Bureau, 2013a). Worldwide, more than 6 million are expected to reach age 100 by 2050 (U.S. Census Bureau, 2013b).

A small number of these centenarians, those aged 110 and older, are considered supercentenarians. As of January 2013, there were 63 validated supercentenarians throughout the United States, 58 women and 5 men (Coles, 2013). The Gerontology Research Group (2013) estimates that there are approximately 300 to 400 supercentenarians throughout the world. However, more than counting numbers, researchers want to know the answers to fundamental questions about human health and longevity, such as the following:

- What does it take to live a long life?
- How much do diet, exercise, and other lifestyle factors matter compared with "good" genes and other genetic factors?
- What is the quality of life among very-late-life adults?
- What role do individual characteristics such as gender, race or ethnicity, personality, and socioeconomic status play in longevity?
- What is the role of social support, religion and spirituality, and social environment in longevity?

Much of what is known about centenarians in the United States comes from the work of Leonard Poon and his colleagues (Poon et al., 2007; Poon & Cohen-Mansfield, 2011) in the Georgia Centenarian Study and from the New England Centenarian Study (Terry, Sebastiani, Andersen, & Perls, 2008). These and other centenarian studies are trying to understand the interrelationship between multiple variables such as family longevity, gender, personality, environmental support, adaptational skills, individual traits, life satisfaction, and health.

These studies reveal that because the more frail individuals die sooner, those remaining are a relatively robust group. Although these "extra" years are for the most part healthy years, several studies report high levels of dementia (66% in one study and 51% in another), cardiovascular disease (72%), urinary incontinence (60%), and osteoarthritis (54%) (Hall, 2008). What is more notable, however, is that the period of serious illness and disability for those who make it to 100 tends to be brief. Some factors thought to contribute to centenarians' robustness in U.S. studies are physical activity, such as walking, biking, golfing, and swimming, and mental exercise such as reading, painting, and playing a musical instrument. The Okinawa Centenarian Study notes the importance of the traditional lifestyle that includes high

physical activity, social integration at all ages, a deep spirituality, adaptability, and optimistic attitudes (cited in Hooyman & Kiyak, 2011). A cluster of personality traits—low neuroticism (reflecting emotional stability), high competence, and high extroversion—were found among centenarians in the Georgia study (Martin, da Rosa, & Poon, 2011).

However, 100 is still old, and life expectancy is short at 100, with most only living 1 to 2 more years. In the New England study, 75% of the people were still living at home and taking care of themselves at 95. By age 102, this number had dropped to 30%—which is still quite remarkable (Terry et al., 2008).

The gender gap in very late adulthood widens further past the age of 100, with female centenarians outnumbering males 4 to 1. However, men who reach their 100th birthday are, on the whole, more healthy than their female counterparts, reporting lower incidence of dementia and other serious medical problems. Estrogen may give women an edge in longevity. Another possibility is that there may be some protective genes in the X chromosome, of which women have two but men only one. Others theorize that menstruation and systems related to childbirth better equip women to eliminate toxins from the body. Another hypothesis is that genetics are relatively neutral, but women tend to be more social, and these connections are thought to be critical in weathering old age (Margrett et al., 2011).

> How does the gender gap affect the experience of very late adulthood?

In general, findings point to a life course of healthy lifestyles among centenarians: they didn't smoke, or if they did, not for long; didn't overeat, and their diet included many fruits and vegetables; didn't drink heavily; got regular physical exercise for as long as they were able; challenged their minds; had a positive outlook and were able to "shed stress easily"; and maintained close ties with family and friends (Harvard Health Letter, 2002). Future cross-cultural studies in which differences in diet, physical activity, and other lifestyle factors can be compared will be important in helping researchers better understand the influence of these multiple contributing variables. Overall, Poon and Cohen-Mansfield (2011) remind us it is important to focus on emotional as well as physical health and not to assume that physical decline necessarily means a decline in emotional well-being.

Critical Thinking Questions 10.1

Imagine that you are having lunch with Fred Hale Sr. (from Photo 10.1). How do you imagine the conversation going? What questions would you like to ask him? How do you think life will be different for centenarians in 2050?

FUNCTIONAL CAPACITY IN VERY LATE ADULTHOOD

Although persons who reach 85 years of age and older demonstrate resilience in the simple fact of their longevity, they continue to face an increased incidence of chronic illness and debilitation with age. Chapter 9 provides a good overview of changes in physiology and mental functioning that begin to occur in late adulthood and only become more prevalent with advancing age. Unfortunately, much of the available information does not distinguish the 85-and-older cohort group from the larger 65-and-older group. We do know that the likelihood of living in a nursing home increases with age. Among nursing home residents, about 14.6% are 65 to 74 years old, 27.5% are 75 to 84, and 42.9% are 85 and older (Centers for Medicare and Medicaid Services, 2012b). U.S. Census (2012a) data show that 37.5% of female centenarians and 23.3% of male centenarians were living in a nursing or group residence compared with 20.8% of females and 11.9% of males ages 90 to 94. Many late-life adults enter a nursing home for a period of convalescence after hospitalization and then return to home or another setting.

The prevalence of older adults with a disability and those needing assistance with **instrumental activities of daily living (IADLs)**, activities that are not necessary for fundamental functioning but do allow an individual to live independently, increases

Activities of Daily Living
Bathing
Dressing
Walking a short distance
Shifting from a bed to a chair
Eating
Instrumental Activities of Daily Living
Doing light housework
Doing the laundry
Using transportation
Handling finances
Using the telephone
Taking medications

steadily with age. Of those ages 65 to 69, 35% report a disability with 6.9% needing assistance; of those ages 70 to 74, 42.6% report a disability with 10.8% needing assistance; of those 75 to 79, 53.6% report a disability with 15.4% needing assistance; and of those age 80 and older, 70.5% report a disability with 30.2% needing assistance (Brault, 2012). Limitations in **activities of daily living (ADLs)**, basic care activities, also increase with age; 1.6% of those ages 65 to 74, 3.5% of those ages 75 to 84, and 9.7% of those age 85 and older need assistance with three or more activities (National Center for Health Statistics, 2009). (Exhibit 10.1 lists common ADLs and IADLs.)

In general, all persons experience **primary aging**, or changes that are a normal part of the aging process. There is a recognized slowing with age—slowing of motor responses, sensory responses, and intellectual functioning. For example, the percentage of older adults in the United

States with significant visual loss increases during late and very late adulthood: 12.2% among the 65- to 75-year-olds and 15.5% among those older than 75 (American Foundation for the Blind, 2013). Similarly, 37% of 61- to 70-year-olds, 60% of 71- to 80-year-olds, and 80% of persons 85 and older experience hearing loss of 25 dB (Walling & Dickson, 2012).

In addition, many experience **secondary aging** caused by health-compromising behaviors such as smoking or environmental factors such as pollution (Bjorklund, 2011). Access to health care, ample and nutritious food, safe and affordable housing, safe working conditions, and other factors that influence the quality of life also affect longevity.

How much control do we have over secondary aging?

Although late adulthood is a time of loss of efficiency in body systems and functioning, the body is an organism that repairs and restores itself as damage occurs. Those persons who live to be 85 and older may be fortunate enough to have a favorable genetic makeup. But they may also have found ways to compensate, to prevent, to restore, and to maintain other health-promoting behaviors. Most very-late-life adults come to think of themselves in ways that fit their circumstances. They narrow the scope of their activities to those that are most cherished, and they carefully schedule their activities to make the best use of their energy and talents.

Sooner or later, however, most very-late-life adults come to need some assistance with ADLs and IADLs. As a society, we must grapple with the question of who will provide that assistance. Currently, most of the assistance is provided by family members. But as families grow smaller, fewer adult children exist to provide such care. A number of family theorists have begun to wonder how multigenerational families might adjust their relationships and better meet long-distance caregiving needs (Cagle, 2008; Harrigan & Koerin, 2007).

Chapter 9 provides an overview of dementia and more specifically Alzheimer's disease (AD).

Additional content here emphasizes the importance of ongoing and longitudinal research and needs of families and other caregivers and also some interesting perspectives about the medicalization of dementia.

To better understand the progression of AD in the oldest old and compare it with the progression among younger older adults, functional ADLs and cognitive Mini Mental Status Evaluations, or MMSEs, were studied in a cohort of adults who were older than 85 and a cohort of adults who were younger than 85, all living in a community in France (Nourhashemi et al., 2009). The progression of cognitive impairment was the same across groups; however, after adjusting for age and dependency (help with ADLs), the progression of dependence occurred more quickly for the older group. In sum, even among the oldest old, dementia shortened life, especially among women. Studies such as this have important public health consequences, helping us better prepare for the type of care some of our oldest citizens, and our most rapidly growing age group, may need.

Innes (2009) summarizes some thought-provoking theories and commentaries about our current approach to understanding dementia, suggesting that we tend to medicalize dementia so as to then seek a cure for aging and death. Vincent (2006, cited in Innes, p. 22) writes of an anti-aging science that tends to perceive "old age as a problem to be resolved rather than a stage of life to be embraced and accepted." Gilleard and Higgs (2000, cited in Hazan, 2011, p. 18) warn against the "fear-riddled attitude" we have toward increasing dementia described as the "Alzheimerization of society." When aging and dementia become problems to fix or perhaps hide away, what are the implications for the persons living with this life challenge?

RELATIONSHIPS IN VERY LATE ADULTHOOD

Much of what is presented in Chapter 9 under the Families in Later Life section applies also to very late adulthood. Research that looks

How do current social arrangements threaten and/or support the desire for social connections among very-late-life adults?

specifically at relationship patterns among very-late-life adults notes the following themes (Litwin, 2011; Mayo Foundation for Medical Education and Research, 2012):

1. Individuals continue to desire and need connections to other people throughout life.

2. In very late adulthood, people interact with others less frequently, but old-old adults make thoughtful selections about the persons with whom they will interact.

3. Age per se doesn't account for diminishing social networks; rather it is the combination of older age and limitations related to increased disability.

Relationships With Family and Friends

Social isolation is considered to be a powerful risk factor not only for the development of cognitive and intellectual decline in very late adulthood but also for physical illness (McInnis-Dittrich, 2009; Steptoe, Shankar, Demakakos, & Wardle, 2013). A sense of connectedness with family and friends can be achieved in person, on the phone, and more recently via e-mail, Facebook, chat rooms, blogs, Skype, and other social networking technology. The focus in this section is on relationships with people; however, remember that pets, plants, and other connections with nature bring comfort to any age group, including older adults.

Pertinent to very-late-life adults is the increased likelihood that one will have lost a spouse or partner, friends, an adult child, or other family members to death, illness, debilitation, or relocation. Loss is more prevalent during this stage than at other times of life, but there is also greater opportunity for intergenerational family contact as 4-, 5-, and 6-generation families become more common.

Siblings often provide companionship and caregiving for each other, as Pete Mullin and Lucy Rauso did in the case study. Siblings are comforting because they are part of one's cohort and also have experienced many of the same family events. In addition, siblings tend to be the most long-standing relationships in a person's life (Hooyman & Kiyak, 2011). However, as we see with Marie Cipriani and Irene Wright, this is not always the case. Irene's relationship with her siblings is strained due to their nonacceptance of her life partner. Marie's siblings, who might have been able to provide support, have all died.

Obviously, sibling relationships may range from loving and close to ambivalent, distant, or even hostile. Sharing responsibility for aging parents may create greater closeness between siblings or increase tension. There is some evidence that sibling relationships are especially important sources of support among members of lower socioeconomic groups. Close relationships especially with sisters in very late adulthood have been found to be positively related to positive mental health (McGoldrick & Watson, 2011). Relationships with adult children are another important part of the social networks of very-late-life adults, as is the case with Margaret Davis. Very-late-life adults in the United States are in fact institutionalized more often for social reasons than for medical reasons (Hooyman & Kiyak, 2011). One reason for this is that approximately 1 in 5 women 80 and older has been childless throughout her life or, like Marie Cipriani, has outlived her children. In addition, baby boomers and their children tended to have more divorces and fewer children, decreasing the caregiving options for their parents and grandparents (Hooyman & Kiyak, 2011). Racial and ethnic variations exist, however. The proportion of multigenerational relationships that involve parents living with adult children tends to be higher among some families of color, especially African Americans (Hooyman & Kiyak, 2011), as well as there being more grandparents raising grandchildren, especially in African American and Latino families (Richardson & Barusch, 2006). Also, families with a collectivist heritage prefer to have elderly parents reside with their grown children. It is important to understand and honor historical and cultural expectations of each family when

Photo 10.2   Loss is more prevalent during this stage than at other times of life, but there is also greater opportunity for intergenerational family contact as 4-, 5-, and 6-generation families become more common.

© Rich Legg/iStockphoto.com

addressing the caregiving and health care needs of aging members. Geographic separation, most often because of the adult child's mobility, tends to interfere with intergenerational interaction among family members, although many manage "intimacy at a distance" (Hooyman & Kiyak, 2011, p. 359) or strong emotional ties despite the separation.

Agencies serving older adults and children often seek opportunities for contact across generations. Whether referred to as inter-, multi-, or cross-generational, many programs recognize the benefits of activities that bring older adults, young parents, teens, and/or children and infants together. Each has something to offer and something to receive. Some examples include elders providing tutoring, telephone support, or assistance in day care and school settings or serving as surrogate grandparents; adolescents providing assistance around the yards and homes of older adults, helping to write life reviews, or being pen or computer pals; and children and elders interacting around crafts, music, gardening, storytelling, or other activities that create ways of being together (Hooyman & Kiyak, 2011).

Relationships with friends remain important in very late adulthood. In general, women have fewer economic resources but more social resources and richer, more intimate relationships than do older men (Hooyman & Kiyak, 2011). But over time, women tend to outlive partners, friends, and other key members of their social support system, often being left to deal with end-of-life decisions at an advanced age, without the social and perhaps financial support of earlier life.

Relationships with a domestic partner become much less likely in very late adulthood than in earlier phases of life. Very-late-life adults have the potential to have shared 60 to 70 years with a spouse or partner. Such long-term relationships, where they do exist, present the risk of tremendous loss when one member of the relationship dies. (Widowhood is presented in more detail in Chapter 9.) Because women outnumber men 2 to 1 after the age of 85, heterosexual men stand a greater chance of starting a new relationship than heterosexual women. With women living longer than men, lesbian domestic partnerships may have the greatest opportunity for continued long-term relationships in very late adulthood. However, this is not the case for Marie Cipriani and Irene Wright.

Intimacy and Sexuality in Very Late Adulthood

Given the scarcity of men and the fact that many partners and friends have died, many persons 85 and older, especially women, are more alone in this life stage than at other times in their lives. The implications for intimacy and sexuality for heterosexual women are significant. Although limited research has been conducted specifically about intimacy and sexuality with this age group, some tentative conclusions can be drawn from literature on aging. In particular, a summer 2001 issue of *Generations* focused on "Intimacy and Aging," including the expressions of intimacy in a variety of relationships, challenges related to physical and mental illness, gay and lesbian relationships, and separation of couples because of institutionalization.

A greater understanding of intimacy may help people "navigate between current binary discourses of asexual old age and 'sexy seniors'" (Sandberg, 2013, p. 261). Intimacy can be seen as much broader than sexuality, which has been identified as only one of five major components of intimacy (Moss & Schwebel, 1993, cited in Blieszner & deVries, 2001). The five major components of intimacy in this view are the following:

1. *Commitment.* Feeling of cohesion and connection

2. *Affective intimacy.* A deep sense of caring, compassion, and positive regard and the opportunities to express the same

3. *Cognitive intimacy.* Thinking about and awareness of another, sharing values and goals

4. *Physical intimacy.* Sharing physical encounters ranging from proximity to sexuality

5. *Mutuality.* A process of exchange or interdependence

Closeness is inherent in cognitive, affective, and physical intimacy. Communication, or self-disclosure, facilitates intimacy. In sum, intimacy is about connection, closeness, and trust, whether it is physical, sexual, emotional, or spiritual intimacy (Mayo Foundation for Medical Education and Research, 2012). Guided by culturally informed practice and a belief that older adults are continuing to grow and develop, how might social workers work to help older adults minimize barriers to intimacy in their lives?

Although sexuality is only one aspect of intimacy, it deserves additional attention; it should not be neglected, as it often is in our interaction with older adults. A study aimed at preparing health care professionals to engage with older adults about emotional and physical intimacy concluded that "regular sexual activity is a normal finding in advanced age" (Lochlainn & Kenny, 2013). However, there may be barriers to meeting one's needs. The lack of a sexual partner because of divorce, death, or illness is one of the most common reasons for an older adult reporting low interest in sex and little sexual activity. However, there are other physical and psychosocial conditions that impact the level of sexual interest, satisfaction, and performance of older adults, and social workers need to be comfortable addressing this important aspect of quality of life. Medical conditions such as heart disease, diabetes, arthritis, chronic pain, depression, and medications prescribed to address these and other conditions may reduce or restrict movement or sexual function as well as impact pleasure (Hooyman & Kiyak, 2011). Some of the more common psychosocial factors associated with reduced sexual desire or sexual dysfunction include restrictive beliefs about sexuality and aging, role changes because of illness or disability in one or both of the partners, anxiety about sexual function, and psychological disorders (Lochlainn & Kenny, 2013). Depression and substance abuse are more prevalent in older adults with sexual dysfunction. Also, cultural ideals about body image, perceived sexual attractiveness, and expression of emotions that may influence capacity for intimacy make it more difficult for some older adults to embrace age-related changes (Mayo Foundation for Medical Education and Research, 2012).

Relationships With Organizations and Community

Relationships with the wider world peak in young and middle adulthood. They grow more constricted as access to social, occupational, recreational, and religious activities becomes more difficult due to decreased mobility and independence and as the physical and cognitive impairments associated with age increase. As mobility declines, community-based programs such as Meals on Wheels can become important resources to people like Pete Mullin and Lucy Rauso, not only providing them with essential resources such as food but serving also as a connection to the community.

One organizational relationship becomes more likely with advancing age, however. As people live longer and need greater assistance, many move into some form of institutional care. When reading the upcoming discussion about the housing continuum, consider the benefits and the challenges each option presents.

The Use of Technology

The use of computer technology and the Internet has steadily increased over the past 20 years. However, although adults age 85 and older access the Internet, the percentage of those who do is small (Choi & DiNitto, 2013a, 2013b). Those more likely to use the Internet generally have a higher socioeconomic status, are actively involved in the community, have a social network that encourages Internet usage, and are "computer ripened" (Choi & DiNitto, 2013a, 2013b; Richter, Bannier, Glott, Marquard, & Schwarze, 2013). Conversely, those less likely to use the Internet are less likely to have the resources to obtain computers or other devices for accessing the Internet and/or are more likely to have cognitive, perceptual, or motor skill deficits; vision impairment; or difficulty with ADLs and IADLs (Choi & DiNitto, 2013a).

Like any other age group, older adults have used the Internet for online banking and to pay bills, for shopping, to refill prescriptions, to contact medical providers, to participate in online forums and support groups, to communicate with family and friends, and to search for health-related and nonhealth-related information. However, those 85 and older most often use the Internet for e-mail or text messages (Choi & DiNitto, 2013b).

Internet usage does have its benefits for those age 85 and older. Although the findings are mixed, it has been suggested that Internet usage increases communication within social groups, allows the maintenance of long-distance relationships, increases access to health information and resources, allows those who are mobility challenged to participate in online health self-management programs and support groups, and enables access to community, church, and organization websites (Choi & DiNitto, 2013b).

In addition to the Internet, robots are being developed for improving the sociophysical environment for older adults (Kidd, Taggart, & Turkle, 2006; Kolling et al., 2013). Currently, robots can be used to assist with everyday tasks and activities as well as to increase social interactions for those who are mobility or cognitively challenged. The development of robotics is still in the early stages. Maintenance of the robots may require a team approach to turn the machine on and off and to keep it clean. Additionally, as this is a new field, ethical issues must be considered.

THE HOUSING CONTINUUM

As people live longer, the likelihood of illness and disability increases; spouses, partners, and friends die,

How do gender, race, ethnicity, and social class affect access to physical assistance in very late adulthood?

and the chance of needing more support than is available to the very-late-life adults in their own home increases. Review the section on informal and formal resources in Chapter 9 for a description of the variety of options along the continuum as need for assistance increases.

Other than skilled nursing care reimbursed by Medicare and other health insurance, the majority of assistance people need must be paid for privately. Financing is a major problem for low-income and even many middle-income people. Women, especially women of color, are overrepresented in lower socioeconomic categories, and in very-late adulthood, safe, affordable housing options are a serious concern. But even Pete Mullin and Lucy Rauso found housing a problem until they moved in together and pooled their resources. Margaret Davis's daughter, Judy, is determined that Margaret won't go "to a home," but she is also worried about how costly Margaret's care will become in the future. What if Marie Cipriani needs to leave her home? Will she find living arrangements that welcome a lesbian woman?

Current trends indicate that in the future, the following housing options will be in greater demand and hopefully more readily available (Hogstel, 2001; Office of Citizen Services and Innovative Technologies, 2013):

- Shared housing, shared expenses, and support by family members and friends
- Options for care and assistance in the home with education and support available to family and other informal caregivers, home health skilled services, reverse mortgages, home equity loans
- Independent living facilities, including retirement villages and naturally occurring retirement communities such as inner-city high-rise retirement communities close to medical, cultural, and recreational activities
- Assisted-living facilities that provide 24-hour assistance, continuing-care retirement communities that offer a range of services
- Nursing homes providing custodial care only (The number of skilled nursing facilities that also provide custodial care is likely to decrease, with their role taken over by assisted-living facilities)

Access and receptivity to this continuum of options are influenced by several factors: geographic location, including urban and rural location; socioeconomic status; race; ethnicity; gender; sexual orientation; family support; and health care status. Specifically, a substantial disparity in nursing home admissions of non-Hispanic White and minority late-life adults continues to exist, particularly among women (Mudrazija & Thomeer, 2012). Moreover, African American men and women more often report a need for help with their ADLs and are less likely to receive the appropriate level of care than White men and women (Hooyman & Kiyak, 2011). Obtaining assistance with ADLs and IADLs can be expensive. Some of the current cohort of very-late-life adults have arrived at that stage without any expectation that they would live so long or any preparation for such a prolonged life. And some arrive there after a full life course of limited resources, as is the situation with Margaret Davis.

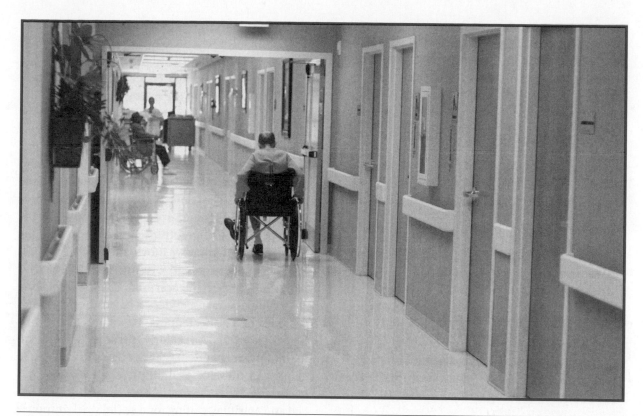

Photo 10.3 Although those who reach 85 and older demonstrate resilience by surviving, they continue to face increased incidence of chronic illness and debilitation with increased age.

© iStockphoto.com

SPIRITUALITY IN VERY LATE ADULTHOOD

When the first author, Pam, called her 85-year-old aunt to wish her a happy birthday, Pam's uncle said, "She has been thinking a lot more about the hereafter." Curious about what sounded like a connection to aging and spirituality, Pam asked her aunt to tell her more. Her aunt added with a chuckle, "Yes, I go into a room and I wonder 'What am I here after?'" On one hand, Pam's aunt was trying to make light of some short-term memory loss. But Pam also knew that increasingly her aunt had been questioning the meaning of her life and wondering about her own death, especially since the recent death of her 58-year-old son to cancer.

There is often a conceptual division when describing religion and spir,tualty, with religion connected to an institution and spirituality being a more personal experience. Bishop (2011) cautions against this binary conceptualization, suggesting that the two are more often related than independent of each other, and some longitudinal research indicates that the two are highly correlated in late-life adults (Vaillant, 2012). More simply, spirituality represents the way in which people seek meaning and purpose in their lives (Nelson-Becker & Canda, 2008; Sheridan, 2011). Our role as social workers is to understand what role, if any, religion and spirituality play in the unique lives of our clients. Given possible barriers related to mobility, vision, hearing, and other access issues, older adults may feel disenfranchised and less connected to religious institutions that had once been a meaningful source of social support (Bishop & Martin, 2011).

The following discussion about spirituality refers to aging in general, not specifically to very-late-life adults, but is included in this chapter because of the connection among aging, loss, spirituality, and meaning making. Often when faced with crises—particularly those of severe illness, disability, and/or loss—one tends to reexamine the meaning of life. And although illness, disability, and loss occur throughout life, these challenges tend to accumulate and come at a faster pace during very late adulthood. Dalby (2006) notes that some aspects of spirituality pertain across the life course; however, the following tasks, needs, or changes become more relevant with aging: integrity, humanistic concern, changing relationships with others and greater concern for younger generations, relationship with a transcendent being or power, self-transcendence, and coming to terms with death.

Spirituality late in life is often associated with loss (Armatowski, 2001). Over time, losses accumulate in the following areas:

- *Relationships:* to children, spouses and partners, friends, and others
- *Status and role:* in family, work, and society
- *Health:* stamina, mobility, hearing, vision, and other physical and cognitive functions
- *Control and independence:* finances, housing, health care, and other decision-making arenas

Whether incremental or sudden, these losses can be difficult for members of a society where personal autonomy, independence, and sense of control are highly valued. Ironically, this increased focus on spirituality often coincides with decreased mobility and independence and diminishing social contact, limiting access to religious services and other opportunities for spiritual fulfilment and social support (Watkins, 2001).

The search for meaning is a central element of Erik Erikson's (1963) eighth developmental task, referred to as maturity. It involves the challenge of *ego integrity versus ego despair* and centers on one's ability to process what has happened in life and accept these experiences as integral to the meaning of life. As Erik and Joan Erikson (1997) moved into their 8th decade, they began writing about a ninth stage. Joan published this previously unfinished work in 1997 following Erik's death in 1994 at the age of 92. She revisits the meaning of wisdom and integrity in light of the losses that occur with time and, despite the challenges, declares that "to grow is a great privilege" (p. 128). When describing this ninth stage, she refers to "gerotranscendence" and the work of Lars Torstam of Sweden, who coined the word as a possible path toward wisdom as we age. Joan Erikson, a dancer, played with the concept, calling it "gerotranscen*dance*" to note the room for creativity as we move though the "process towards maturation and wisdom" (p. 123).

Other important spiritual challenges facing elders include transcendence beyond oneself and a sense of connectedness to others (McInnis-Dittrich, 2009). An elderly person's struggle to maintain independence and the ability to make choices in the face of multiple challenges, versus becoming dependent on others, is both psychosocial and spiritual, calling for a social work response addressing both. It is important to remember that culture, race, religious upbringing, and other life experiences may influence each person's spiritual journey.

This is often a time for slowing down, looking back, and reaching out—steps that make sense developmentally as one nears the end of life. Over time, people tend to review their lives, some informally and others more formally. The more formal life review involves helping people shape their memories and experiences for others, usually family and loved ones, whether shared orally or in writing. Social workers, family members, or others who share a closeness with a person often help facilitate this process of reflection and meaning making (Hooyman & Kiyak, 2011).

The subject of spirituality is separated in this chapter from the subject of dying to emphasize the point that spirituality is not just about preparing for death. Rather, it is about making meaning of one's life (Bishop, 2011; Gordon, 2013; Jenkinson, 2013), transcending oneself, and remaining connected to others (McInnis-Dittrich, 2009).

Critical Thinking Questions 10.3

Why do you think it is important to people like Margaret Davis to stay in their own homes? The majority of very old adults today are women. What are the implications of this for housing policy and programs for this age group? How have you observed the very old adults in your family cope with the accumulation of loss? What role did religion and spirituality play in their coping?

THE DYING PROCESS

The topic of death and dying is almost always in the last chapter of a human behavior textbook, reflecting the hope that death will come as late as possible in life. Obviously, people die in all stages of life, but very late adulthood is the time when dying is considered "on time."

Despite our strong cultural predisposition toward denial of the topic, and perhaps in response to this, there have been a plethora of efforts to talk about death, starting most notably with Elisabeth Kübler-Ross's book *On Death and Dying* in 1969. Beginning in the late 1990s, initiatives such as the Project on Death in America (PDIA) funded by the Soros Foundation and end-of-life initiatives funded by the Robert Wood Johnson Foundation set out to change mainstream attitudes. The mission of PDIA was to understand and transform the culture and experience of dying and bereavement. It promoted initiatives in research, scholarship, the humanities, and the arts, and fostered innovations in the provision of care, education, and policy. Television programs such as the Public Broadcasting Service's *On Our Own Terms: Moyers on Dying* have facilitated public education and community dialogue (Moyers, Mannes, Pellet, O'Neill, & Moyers, 2000). Additionally, TV series, such as *Desperate Housewives*, have begun to integrate death and dying into a beloved character's storyline (Cherry, 2012).

On a more individual level, many factors influence the ways in which a person adjusts to death and dying, including one's religion and philosophy of life, personality, culture, and other personal traits. Adjustment may also be affected by the conditions of dying. A person with a prolonged terminal illness has more time and opportunity to accept and prepare for his or her own death, or that of a loved one, than someone with an acute and fatal illness or sudden death.

The following adjectives used to describe death are found in both the professional and popular literature: *good, meaningful, appropriate, timely, peaceful, sudden,* and *natural.* One can be said to die well, on time, before one's time, and in a variety of ways and places. This terminology reflects an attempt to embrace, acknowledge, tame, and integrate death into one's life. Other language is more indirect, using euphemisms, metaphors, medical terms, and slang, reflecting a need to avoid directly talking about death—suggesting that the person is "lost," has "passed away," or has "expired" (DeSpelder & Strickland, 2005). It is important for a social worker to be attentive to words that individuals and families choose because they often reflect one's culture and/or religious background and comfort level (Bullock, 2011).

As with life, the richness and complexity of death are best understood from a multidimensional framework involving the biological, psychological, social, and spiritual dimensions (Bern-Klug, 2004). The following conceptualizations of the dying process help capture the notion that dying and other losses, and the accompanying bereavement, are processes that differ for each unique situation, yet share some common aspects.

In *On Death and Dying*, Kübler-Ross (1969) described stages that people tend to go through in accepting their own inevitable death or that of others, summarized in Exhibit 10.2. Although these stages were written with death in mind, they have application to other loss-related experiences, including the aging process. Given time, most individuals experience these five reactions, although not necessarily in this order. People often shift back and forth between the reactions rather than experience them in a linear way, get stuck in a stage, and/or skip over others. Kübler-Ross suggests that,

Exhibit 10.2   Stages of Accepting Impending Death

Denial: The person denies that death will occur: "This is not true. It can't be me." This denial is succeeded by temporary isolation from social interactions.

Anger: The individual asks, "Why me?" The person projects his or her resentment and envy onto others and often directs the anger toward a supreme being, medical caregivers, family members, and friends. (Older adults may be less apt to raise this question and instead reflect on how fortunate they have been to live so long.)

Bargaining: The individual starts bargaining in an attempt to postpone death, proposing a series of deals with God, self, or others: "Yes, me, but I will do . . . in exchange for a few more months."

Depression: A sense of loss follows. Individuals grieve about their own end of life and about the ones that will be left behind. A frequent reaction is withdrawal from close and loved persons: "I just want to be left alone."

Acceptance: The person accepts that the end is near and the struggle is over: "It's okay. My life has been . . ."

SOURCE: Based on Kübler-Ross, 1969

on some level, hope of survival persists through all stages.

Although these reactions may fit people in general, very-late-life adults appear to experience far less denial about the reality of death than other age groups (McInnis-Dittrich, 2009). As they confront their limitations of physical health and become socialized to death with each passing friend and family member, most very-late-life adults become less fearful of death. Unfortunately, some professionals and family members may not be as comfortable expressing their feelings related to death and dying, which may leave the elder feeling isolated.

In addition to expressing feelings about death, some very-late-life adults have other needs related to dying. A fear of prolonged physical pain or discomfort, as well as fear of losing a sense of control and mastery, trouble very-late-life adults most. Some have suggested that older adults who are dying need a safe and accepting relationship in which to express the fear, sadness, anger, resentment, or other feelings related to the pending loss of life and opportunity, especially separation from loved ones (Agronin, 2011; Bowlby, 1980).

Advance Directives

On a more concrete level, social workers can help patients and families discuss, prepare, and enact health care **advance directives**, or documents

> How do advance directives promote a continued sense of human agency in making choices?

that give instructions about desired health care if, in the future, individuals cannot speak for themselves. Such discussions can provide an opportunity to clarify values and wishes regarding end-of-life treatment. Ideally, this conversation has been started prior to very late adulthood (see Chapter 9 regarding a power of attorney and other health care decision-making processes). If not, helping people to communicate their wishes regarding life-sustaining measures, who they want to act on their behalf when they are no longer competent to make these decisions, and other end-of-life concerns helps some people feel empowered.

Since the passage of the Patient Self-Determination Act in 1990, hospitals and other health care institutions receiving Medicare or Medical Assistance funds are required to inform patients that should their condition become

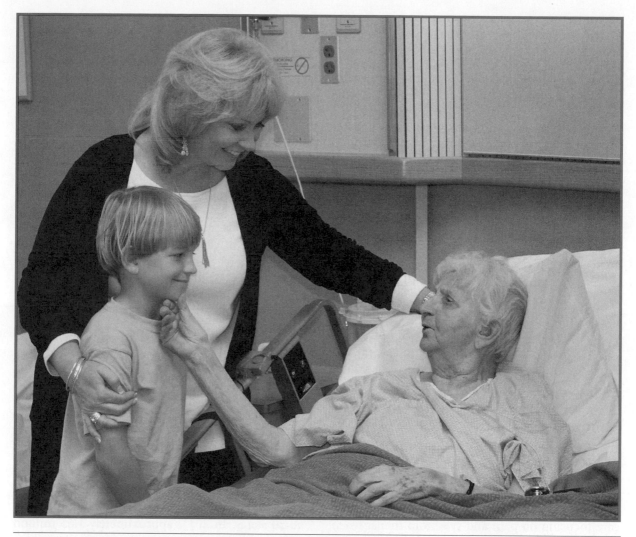

Photo 10.4 Palliative care focuses on providing pain and symptom management when cure of disease is no longer an option. The patient and the family together are the unit of care.

© iStockphoto.com

life-threatening, they have a right to make decisions about what medical care they wish to receive (McInnis-Dittrich, 2009). The two primary forms of advance directives are the living will and the durable power of attorney for health care.

A **living will** describes the medical procedures, drugs, and types of treatment that one would choose for oneself if able to do so in certain situations. It also describes the situations for which the patient would want treatment withheld. For example, one may instruct medical personnel not to use any artificial means or heroic measures to keep one alive if the condition is such that there is no hope for recovery. Although a living will allows an individual to speak for oneself in advance, a durable power of attorney designates someone else to speak for the individual.

The promotion of patient rights as just described has helped many patients feel empowered and comforted some family members, but this topic is not without controversy. Because the laws vary from state to state, laypersons and professionals must inquire about the process if one relocates. Also, rather than feeling comforted by knowing a dying person's wishes, some family members experience the burden of difficult decision making that once was handled by the physician. Advance directives are not accepted or considered moral by some ethnic, racial, and religious groups. Because of historical distrust of the White medical establishment, some African American and Hispanic families have preferred life-sustaining treatment to the refusal of treatment inherent in advance directives. Among some religious groups, the personal control represented in advance directives is seen to interfere with a divine plan and is considered a form of passive suicide. As discussed shortly, social workers must approach each patient and family with an openness to learn about their values and wishes. Volker (2005) cautions health care providers to consider the relevancy of Western values, such as personal control over one's future, in the lives of non-Western patient groups.

Care of People Who Are Dying

Although some associate hospice and palliative care with "giving up" and there being "nothing left to do," in fact hospices provide **palliative care**—a form of care focusing on pain and symptom management as opposed to curing disease. The focus is on "caring, not curing" (National Hospice and Palliative Care Organization [NHPCO], 2012), when curative focused treatment is no longer available or desired. Palliative care attends to the psychological, social, and spiritual issues in addition to the physical needs. The goal of palliative care is achievement of the best possible quality of life for patients and their families.

Hospice is one model of palliative care, borrowed from the British, that began in the United States in the mid-1970s to address the needs of dying persons and their loved ones. It is more a philosophy of care than a place, with the majority of persons receiving hospice services where they live, whether that is their private residence (41.6%), a nursing or residential facility (24.9%), or inpatient hospice facility (26.1%) (NHPCO, 2012). Marie Cipriani's partner, Irene Wright, receives hospice services in their home. Hospice services are typically available to persons who have received a prognosis of 6 months or less and who are no longer receiving care directed toward a cure. Exhibit 10.3 summarizes the key ideas that distinguish hospice care from more traditional care of the dying.

The National Hospice and Palliative Care Organization (2012) estimates that the United States had 5,300 hospice programs in 2011 serving most rural, suburban, and urban communities in all 50 states. In 2011, approximately 1.65 million

Exhibit 10.3   Key Ideas of Hospice Care

The patient and the family (as defined by the patient) are the unit of care.

Care is provided by an interdisciplinary team composed of physician, nurse, nurse's aide, social worker, clergy, volunteer, and other support staff who attend to the spectrum of biopsychosocial and spiritual needs of the patient and family.

The patient and family have chosen hospice services and are no longer pursuing aggressive, curative care but selecting palliative care for symptom management.

Bereavement follow-up is part of the continuum of care available to family members after the patient's death.

SOURCES: McInnis-Dittrich, 2009; NHPCO, 2012

patients, representing approximately 46.6% of all deaths in the United States, received hospice services. Four out of five hospice patients are 65 years of age or older, and about 39.3% are 85 and older. When hospice care was first established in the United States in the 1970s, cancer patients accounted for the majority of hospice admissions. Over time, hospices responded to the needs of others with end-stage disease (e.g., AIDS, dementia, heart disease, lung disease, and stroke as well as others), and in 2011, cancer accounted for less than half (37.7%) of all admissions (NHPCO, 2012).

Health disparities have been noted in hospice care, as in other health care settings, with persons of color historically being underserved. Initiatives through NHPCO, the Soros Foundation's Faculty Scholar program, and the Robert Wood Johnson Foundation's Promoting Excellence in End-of-Life Care have focused on program development specific to the needs of patients and families in African American, Hispanic, Native American, and other communities that have been underserved by more traditional hospice programs (Crawley et al., 2000; NHPCO, 2012).

Palliative care programs are emerging in hospital settings to address pain and symptom management in patients who might not fit the hospice criteria. Some hospitals have palliative care units specializing in management of short-term, acute symptoms; others have palliative care consultative services that bring their expertise to medical, oncology, pediatric, and other units throughout the hospital (Reith & Payne, 2009).

End-of-Life Signs and Symptoms

Family members and others caring for a person who is dying often experience a great deal of anxiety when they do not have adequate information about the dying process. Most families appreciate knowing what to expect, and honest, factual information can help allay their fears of the unknown (Cagle & Kovacs, 2009; Proot et al., 2004). Pete Mullin, for instance, might benefit by knowing what to expect as his sister is dying. Likewise for Marie Cipriani, who is caring for her dying partner. Many hospice services provide written information about symptoms of death for those families anticipating the death of a loved one at home. Exploring how much information people have and want is an important part of the social worker's assessment.

Obviously, each individual situation will differ, but the following general information about symptoms of impending death, summarized in Exhibit 10.4, helps people prepare (Lamers, 2013; Reith & Payne, 2009):

- *Temperature and circulation changes.* The patient's arms and legs may become cool to the touch, and the underside of the body may darken in color as peripheral circulation slows down. Despite feeling cool to touch, the patient is usually not aware of feeling cold, and light bed coverings usually provide sufficient warmth.

- *Sleeping.* The dying patient will gradually spend more time sleeping and at times may be difficult to arouse as metabolism decreases. The patient will gradually retreat from the surroundings. It is best to spend more time with the patient during the most alert times.

Exhibit 10.4   Signs and Symptoms of Impending Death

Lowered temperature and slowed circulation

Deeper and longer periods of sleep

Decreased acuity of vision and hearing

Increased secretions in the mouth and congestion

Incontinence

Restlessness and confusion

Reduced need for eating and drinking and difficulty swallowing

Irregular and interrupted breathing

Increased signs of pain

SOURCES: Lamers, 2013; Reith & Payne, 2009

- *Vision and hearing.* Clarity of vision and hearing may decrease. The patient may want the lights on as vision decreases. Hearing is the last of the five senses to be lost, so it should not be assumed that an unresponsive patient cannot hear. Speech should be soft and clear but not louder than necessary. Many patients talk until minutes before death and are reassured by the exchange of words between loved ones.

- *Secretions in the mouth and congestion.* Oral secretions may become more profuse and collect in the back of the throat. Most people are familiar with the term *death rattle*, a result of a decrease in the body's intake of fluids and inability to cough up normal saliva. Tilting the head to the side and elevating the head of the bed will ease breathing. Swabbing the mouth and lips also provides comfort.

- *Incontinence.* Loss of bowel and bladder function may occur around the time of death or as death is imminent, as the muscles begin to relax. The urine will become very dark in color. If needed, pads should be used to keep skin clean and dry.

- *Restlessness and confusion.* The patient may become restless or have visions of people or things that do not exist. These symptoms may be a result of a decrease in the oxygen circulation to the brain and a change in the body's metabolism. Someone should stay with the patient, reassuring the person in a calm voice, telling the person it is okay to let go, and using oxygen as instructed. Soft music, back rubs, and gentle touch may help soothe the patient. The patient should not be interfered with or restrained, yet should be prevented from falling.

- *Eating, drinking, and swallowing.* Patients will have decreased need for food and drink. It may be helpful to explain that feeding will not improve the condition and in fact may exacerbate symptoms. Slight dehydration may be beneficial in reducing pulmonary secretions and easing breathing. Dehydration also generally results in mild renal insufficiency that is mildly sedating. To withhold food and water feels counterintuitive, however, because food and water are usually equated with comfort and sustaining life. Ice chips, small sips of water, and small amounts of food that have meaning to the patient and family are more helpful than forcing food or liquids.

- *Breathing changes.* Breathing may become irregular, with periods of 10 to 30 seconds of no breathing. This symptom is very common and indicates a decrease in circulation and buildup of body waste products. Elevating the head of the bed and turning the patient on his or her side often helps relieve irregular breathing patterns.

- *Pain.* Frequent observation will help determine if the patient is experiencing pain. Signs of discomfort include moaning, restlessness, and a furrowed brow. Medication should be given as instructed, or the nurse or physician should be contacted if pain persists.

Dying may take hours or days; no one can predict the time of death even when the person is exhibiting signs and symptoms of dying. The following are signs that death has occurred:

- Breathing stops
- Heart stops beating
- Bowel or bladder control is lost
- No response to verbal commands or shaking
- Eyelids may be slightly open with eyes fixed on a certain spot
- Mouth may fall open slightly as the jaw relaxes

Such explicit discussion of death with those attending a dying family member or close friend may seem upsetting, but this knowledge is also comforting and can help ease the anxiety related to the fear of the unknown. Dying persons are also comforted knowing that their family members have the informational, medical, and social support they need to help them in their caregiving role. It is also helpful to have funeral plans in place so that one phone call to the mortuary facilitates the process, rather than facing difficult and emotional decision making at the time of death.

LOSS, GRIEF, AND BEREAVEMENT

Loss is a common human experience. There is a great deal of evidence that people of all cultures have strong, painful reactions to the death of the people to whom they are emotionally attached (Doka & Tucci, 2009). Sadness, loneliness, disbelief, and anxiety are only a few of the feelings a person may experience in times of bereavement. The challenge is to refrain from making grief the problem, thereby pathologizing someone's experience, and to understand the complexities related to death in a society that has grown increasingly old-age and death avoidant (Jenkinson, 2012). So we offer the following, cautioning against turning someone's grief into a problem and encouraging readers to help others understand grief as a normal part of life, perhaps even a skill that we need to learn (Jenkinson, 2012).

Grief, bereavement, and *mourning* are words that are often used interchangeably, perhaps because no one word "reflects the fullness of what a death introduces into the life of an individual, family or community" (Silverman, 2004, p. 226). The following definitions help distinguish the various aspects of this process:

- **Loss.** The severing of an attachment an individual has with a loved one, a loved object (such as a pet, home, or country), or an aspect of one's self or identity (such as a body part or function, physical or mental capacity, or role or position in family, society, or other context) (Stroebe, Stroebe, & Hansson, 1993). Silverman (2004) suggests that loss doesn't happen to us; rather it is "something we must make sense out of, give meaning to, and respond to" (p. 226).
- **Bereavement.** The state of having suffered a loss.
- **Grief.** The normal internal reaction of an individual experiencing a loss. Grief is a complex coping process, is highly individualized (Stroebe et al., 1993), and is an expected period of transition (Silverman, 2004).
- **Mourning.** The external expression of grief (Stroebe et al., 1993); the "mental work following the loss of a loved one . . . social process including the cultural traditions and rituals that guide behavior after a death" (Silverman, 2004, p. 226).

Photo 10.5   Many factors influence the way in which a person adjusts to death and dying, including one's religion and philosophy of life, personality, and other traits.

© iStockphoto.com

The rituals associated with death vary in historical and cross-cultural context (Bullock, 2011; Doka & Tucci, 2009). In some cultures, the dead are buried; in other cultures, the dead are burned and the ashes are spread. In some places and times, a surviving wife might have been burned together with her husband. In the United States, death rituals can be as different as a traditional New Orleans funeral, with street music and mourners dressed in white, or a somber and serene funeral with hushed mourners dressed in black. Some cultures prescribe more emotional expression than others. Some cultures build ritual for the expression of anger, and some do not.

Throughout life, we are faced with many losses, some that occur by death but many that occur in other ways as well. For example, Margaret

Did these earlier experiences with loss serve as either risk factors or protective factors for coping with current losses?

Davis lost her husband to death, but she has also lost a daughter through estrangement and faced much loss of independence and privacy as she increasingly needed assistance from her children and grandchildren. Pete Mullin lived through the losses related to divorce and retirement. Marie Cipriani has experienced similar losses, as well as the loss of her siblings and her adult child. Recently, the burgeoning literature on loss, grief, and bereavement has recognized that there may be similar processes for grieving all losses, including those that occur for reasons other than death. Loss is one of the most important themes in our work as social workers. For example, we encounter loss caused by foster care placement, divorce, disease and disability, migration and immigration, forced retirement, and so on. Disenfranchised grief occurs when a loss is not honored or recognized by individuals and/or society because of the nature of one's relationship, such as often occurs with same-sex couples, like Marie Cipriani and Irene Wright.

Critical Thinking Questions 10.4

What does death mean to you? Is it the final process of life, the beginning of life after death, a joining of the spirit with a cosmic consciousness, rest and peace, a continuation of the spirit? How has culture influenced your understanding of the meaning of death? How has religion influenced your understanding of the meaning of death? How might your understanding of the meaning of death affect your work with someone who is dying? What does it mean to live a good life?

Theories and Models of Loss

A variety of theorists have sought to make sense of the complex experience of loss. Much of the literature on grief and bereavement for the past century has been influenced by Sigmund Freud's (1917/1957) classic article "Mourning and Melancholia." Freud described the "work of mourning" as a process of severing a relationship with a lost person, object, or ideal. He suggested that this happens over time as the bereaved person is repeatedly faced with situations that remind him or her that the loved person (object or ideal) has, indeed, been lost. From this classic work came the idea of a necessary period of **grief work** to sever the attachment bond, an idea that has been the cornerstone of a number of stage models of the grief process.

In the United States, Erich Lindemann (1944) was a pioneer in grief research. Through his classic study of survivors of a fire at the Cocoanut Grove Lounge in Boston, he conceptualized grief work as both a biological and a psychological necessity. The common reactions to loss that he identified included the following:

- Somatic distress, occurring in waves lasting from 20 minutes to an hour, including tightness in throat, choking and shortness of breath, need for sighing, empty feeling in abdomen, lack of muscular power, and intense subjective distress
- Preoccupation with image of deceased, yearning for the lost one to return, wanting to see pictures of the deceased or touch items associated with the deceased
- Guilt
- Hostile reactions, toward the deceased as well as toward others
- Loss of patterns of conduct, where the ability to carry out routine behaviors is lost

Lindemann proposed that grief work occurs in stages, an idea that has been popular with other theorists and researchers since the 1960s. A number of stage models of grief have been proposed, and four are presented in Exhibit 10.5. As you can see, although the number and names of stages vary somewhat among theorists and researchers, in general the stage models all agree that grief work progresses from disbelief and feelings of unreality, to painful and disorganizing reactions, to a kind of "coming to terms" with the loss. Stages or phases run the risk of being misused when taken too literally; however, they have served to remind us that grief is a process with different parts that

Exhibit 10.5   Four Stage Models of Grief

Typical Stages	Erich Lindemann (1944)	Elisabeth Kübler-Ross (1969)	John Bowlby (1980)	Therese Rando (1993)
Disbelief and feelings of unreality	Shock and disbelief	Denial and isolation	Numbness	Avoidance
Painful and disorganizing reactions	Acute mourning	Anger Bargaining Depression	Yearning Disorganization Despair	Confrontation
A kind of "getting over" the loss	Resolution	Acceptance	Reorganization	Accommodation

people experience in their own time (Winokuer & Harris, 2012).

J. William Worden (2009) took a somewhat different approach, writing about the "tasks of mourning" rather than stages of mourning. He considered *task* to be more consistent with Freud's concept of grief work given that the mourner needs to take action and do something rather than passively move through grief. Worden suggests that the following four tasks of mourning are important when a person is adapting to a loss:

Task I: to accept the reality of the loss. Working through denial takes time, because this involves both an intellectual and an emotional acceptance. Some people have traditional rituals that help with this process.

Task II: to work through the pain of grief. Because people are often uncomfortable with the outward displays of grief, our society often interferes with this task. People often seek a geographic cure or quickly replace the lost person in a new relationship but often still have this task to complete.

Task III: to adjust to an environment in which the deceased is missing. This includes filling roles previously filled by the deceased and making appropriate adjustments in daily activities. In terms of roles, many widows report being thrown the first time they have to cope with a major home repair. Regarding adjustments in daily activities, many

bereaved persons report that they find themselves automatically putting the favorite foods of the deceased in their grocery carts.

Task IV: to emotionally relocate the deceased and move on with life. This task was best described by Sadie Delany after the loss of her beloved sister, Bessie: "I don't want to get over you. I just want to find a way to live without you" (Delany, 1997).

In the past few decades, there has been a critique of the idea of grief work. A highly influential article, "The Myths of Coping With Loss" (Wortman & Silver, 1989), disputed two major themes of the traditional view of grief work: distress is an inevitable response to loss, and the failure to experience distress is a sign of improper grieving. In fact, a number of researchers have found that those who show the highest levels of distress immediately following a loss are more likely than those who show little distress to be depressed several years later. In another vein, Silverman (2004) challenges the notion of "tasks," which suggests something can be completed, recommending that we focus instead on "issues and processes" (p. 237).

Given the tremendous diversity among individuals based on gender, culture, personality style, and life experience, as well as the various circumstances surrounding a loss, the grieving process is not easily defined, but theorists and practitioners continue to try to provide some framework for understanding the process. Camille Wortman and Roxanne Silver (1990) proposed that at least four patterns of grieving are possible: normal, chronic, delayed, and absent. Worden (2009) elaborated on these patterns:

1. *Normal or uncomplicated grief.* Relatively high level of distress soon after the loss encompassing a broad range of feelings and behaviors, followed by a relatively rapid recovery.

2. *Chronic or prolonged grief.* High level of distress continuing over a number of years without coming to a satisfactory conclusion.

3. *Delayed grief (or inhibited, suppressed, or postponed grief).* Little distress in the first few months after the loss, but high levels of distress at some later point.

4. *Absent grief.* No notable level of distress either soon after the loss or at some later time. Some question this notion and wonder if it is not absent, but masked or delayed; observation over time is important.

In their research, Wortman and Silver (1990) found absent grief in 26% of their bereaved participants, as well as a high rate (more than 30%) of chronic grief.

Given these critiques of traditional models of grief, theorists and researchers have looked for other ways to understand the complex reactions to loss. The study of bereavement has been influenced by developments in the study of stress and trauma reactions. Research on loss and grief has produced the following findings (Bonanno & Kaltman, 1999):

- It is the evaluation of the nature of the loss by the bereaved survivor that determines how stressful the loss is.
- How well a coping strategy works for dealing with loss depends on the context and the nature of the person-environment encounter.
- Maintaining some type of continued bond with the deceased, a strong sense of the continued presence of the deceased, may be adaptive.
- The capacity to minimize negative emotions after a loss allows the bereaved to continue to function in areas of personal importance.

- Humor can aid in the grief process by allowing the bereaved to approach the enormity of the loss without maximizing psychic pain or alienating social support.
- In situations of traumatic loss, there is a need to talk about the loss, but not all interpersonal relationships can tolerate such talk.

Martin and Doka (2000) propose an approach to adult bereavement that explores the role of gender, culture, and other characteristics that influence a person's grieving style. This approach includes two aspects of adaptive grieving: the internal experience of loss and the outward expression relating to the loss. Martin and Doka (2000) suggest that adaptive grieving styles exist on a continuum with intuitive grievers at one end and instrumental grievers at the other end. Intuitive grievers experience and express their grief primarily through emotion, and instrumental grievers experience and express their grief primarily through a cognitive, behavioral, problem-solving approach. They suggest that few people tend to be at either extreme of the continuum, but rather most tend to have a blended style of grieving, using both intuitive and instrumental strategies (Doughty, 2009). They assert that the difficulty may arise when an individual for whatever reason uses a grieving style that is in conflict with their more natural adaptive style. Doughty (2009) sought more empirical feedback about this model, in addition to the strong anecdotal evidence from practitioners. She surveyed 20 experts in the field of thanatology to examine their opinions about this model. Consensus was found on the following items: the uniqueness of the griever; recognition of multiple factors influencing the grief process; the use of both cognitive and affective strategies in adapting to bereavement; and both internal and external pressures to grieve in certain ways.

In summary, grief is a multidimensional process—a normal life experience—that theorists and practitioners continue to try to understand (Gordon, 2013). There seems to be general agreement that culture, past experience, gender, age, and other personal characteristics influence how one copes with loss.

Culture and Bereavement

Some suggest that all people feel the same pain with grief but that cultural differences shape our mourning rituals, traditions, and behavioral expressions of grief (Walsh, 2012). While there are good sources for exploring ethnic variations related to death and grief (see Irish, Lundquist, & Nelson, 1993), we hesitate to provide overviews of various cultural groups,

> Why is it important for social workers to learn about cultural variations in grief and bereavement?

because of the diversity within groups, as well an increasing cultural diversity in most communities. So instead we suggest you come to each encounter with an openness and curiosity, acknowledging people as the experts about what has been helpful in the past and inquiring about what you need to know to best work with them now. Hooyman and Kramer (2006) provide detailed suggestions for conducting a good cross-cultural assessment and communication (see pp. 174–178), some of which include the following:

- Do your homework before talking to members of the group.
- Begin by listening to their story using open-ended questions.
- Approach them with humility and caution, recognizing them as "insiders" who have the more immediate and critical knowledge of their experience.
- Never judge or have predetermined ideas of what they should feel or do.
- Recognize potential cultural conflicts and respect their decisions and choices.
- Use and train qualified interpreters, understanding the benefits and limitations of doing so.

Important components of an assessment include reactions to loss; mourning style; level of acculturation; cultural history; the role and presence of religion and/or spirituality; grieving rituals; family dynamics, including intergenerational relationships; and other components of any good multidimensional assessment such as social support, financial resources, strengths, and personality. Inquire more specifically about the following:

- Their interpretation of the illness and/or death (asking what they call it, think caused it, think will help, fear most)
- Questions relevant to the care of the body after the death and related beliefs and rituals
- How people in their family and culture commonly express grief (i.e., who, when, how long)

Knowledge about beliefs, values, and customs puts certain behaviors in a context that will help guide you in your work.

A few examples of important components of some cultural norms that may be helpful to consider include the following:

- In the United States, the dominant culture tends to psychologize grief, understanding it in terms of sadness, depression, anger, and other emotions.
- In China and other Eastern societies, grief is often somatized, or expressed in terms of physical pain, weakness, and other physical discomfort (Walsh, 2012).
- Gender differences exist in many cultures, including the dominant U.S. culture, where men have learned to be less demonstrative with emotions of grief and sadness than women (Walsh, 2012).

Mourning and funeral customs also differ a great deal even within groups. For example, among African Americans, customs vary depending on whether the family is Southern Baptist, Catholic, Unitarian Universalist, Muslim, or Pentecostal; in fact "religion may be a stronger determining factor than race alone" (Barrett, 2009, p. 85). Perhaps because of some vestiges of traditional African culture and slavery and a strong desire to celebrate the person's life and build up a sense of community, funerals are important external expressions of mourning in many Black communities.

Tremendous diversity exists within the Latino cultures in the United States, depending on country of origin and degree of acculturation; however, for the most part these subgroups share Latino values, language, religion, and traditional family structure. Some Latino cultural themes that can influence care at the end of life include *familismo* (emphasis of family over individual), *personalismo* (trust building over time based on mutual respect), *jerarquismo* (respect for authority and hierarchy), *presentismo* (focus on present more than past or future), *espiritismo* (belief that good and evil spirits can impact health), and *fatalism* (fate determines life outcomes) (Sandoval-Cros, 2009).

Given approximately 350 distinct Native American tribes in the United States and more than 596 bands among the First Nations in Canada, and because of the differing degrees of acculturation and religious practices from one group to another, it is difficult to provide useful generalizations about this cultural group (Brokenleg & Middleton, 1993). Most understand death as a natural end of life, not fearing it, and although it may be a painful separation for the living who are left behind, rituals exist to help with the transition (Cox, 2009).

A good source of more specific information about rituals and practices is websites on particular cultural/ethnic groups such as Hmong Americans: Dying and Death Rituals (http://sfsuyellowjournal .wordpress.com/2011/11/17/hmong-americans-dying-and-death-ritual). Sites such as these are often written by members of the respective community, and they too remind you of the great diversity among their members. The complex and at times impersonal health care system in the United States can be inadvertently insensitive to important cultural traditions. For example, in some cultures, proper handling of the body, time to sit with the deceased, and other traditions are valued. For one specific example, the Hmong believe that proper burial and worship of ancestors directly influence the safety and health of the surviving family members. They believe that the spiritual world coexists with the physical world and that each person has several souls that must be appropriately sent back to the spiritual world.

These are only a few examples of the rich diversity and complexity you will face in working in our increasingly multiethnic society. You cannot possibly know all the specific traditions, so start by knowing you do not know, and do your homework on their world, including being open to their story and teachings. It is exciting to think of how much there is to learn about how others make sense of these mysterious times of life.

Critical Thinking Questions 10.5

Think of your first experience of a human loss due to death. What do you remember observing the adults in your life do? How did the adults explain what was happening to you? What do you recall thinking and feeling at the time? What death rituals were used to acknowledge the loss? How do you think your current attitudes and beliefs about loss and grief are influenced by this early experience?

THE LIFE COURSE COMPLETED

In this book, we have explored the seasons of the life course. These seasons have been and will be altered by changing demographics. Current demographic trends have led to the following predictions about the future of the life course (Hogstel, 2001):

- The size and inevitable aging of the baby boom generation will continue to drive public policy debate and improve services for very-late-life adults.
- Women will continue to live longer than men.
- Educational attainment levels of the very-late-life adult will increase, with more women having been in the labor force long enough to have their own retirement income.
- Six-generation families will be common, although the generations will live in geographically dispersed settings, making care for very-late-life adults difficult.
- Fewer family caregivers will be available for very-late-life adults because the baby boomers and their children tended to marry later and have fewer children. At the same time, the need for informal or family caregiving to supplement formal care will increase.
- Assessment and management of health care, as well as health care education, will increasingly be available via telephone, the Internet, and television, providing greater access in remote areas but running the risk of rendering the service more impersonal.

As a society, we have a challenge ahead of us to see that newborns begin the life course on a positive foot and that everyone reaches the end of life with the opportunity to see his or her life course as a meaningful whole. As social workers, we have a responsibility to take a look at our social institutions and evaluate how well they guarantee the opportunity for each individual to meet basic needs during each season of life, as well as whether they guarantee the opportunity for interdependence and connectedness appropriate to the season of life. We close this section with a quote by Socrates about how we would do well to learn from our elders (Agronin, 2011, p. 279): "I enjoy talking with very old people. They have gone before us on a road by which we, too, may have to travel, and I think we do well to learn from them what it is like."

Implications for Social Work Practice

All the implications for practice listed in Chapter 9 on late adulthood apply in very late adulthood as well. See the following resources for additional information about social work practice and end-of-life-related patient and family care: Csikai and Jones (2007); Hooyman and Kramer (2006); Kashushin and Egan (2008); Kovacs, Bellin, and Fauri (2006); and Walsh (2012). In addition, the following practice principles focus on the topics of spirituality, relationships, the dying process, and loss, grief, and bereavement.

- Given the links among aging, disability, loss, and spirituality, consider doing a spiritual assessment to find ways to help very-late-life adults address increasing spiritual concerns.
- Assess the impact of loss in the lives of your very-late-life clients—loss of partners, friends, children, and other relationships but also loss of role, status, and physical and mental capacities.
- Recognize and be delighted when very-late-life adults are grateful for their "extra time."
- Assess the loneliness and isolation that may result from cumulative loss.
- Be informed about available formal and informal resources to help minimize isolation for older adults.
- Be aware of your own feelings about death and dying so that you may become more comfortable being physically and emotionally present with clients and their loved ones.
- Identify literature, websites, cultural experiences, key informants, and other vehicles for ongoing education about your clients' cultural, ethnic, and religious and spiritual practices that are different from your own. Remember, the client may be your best teacher.
- Assume that the very-late-life adult continues to have needs for intimacy. Stretch your conceptualization of intimacy to include any relationship the person might have, wish for, or grieve, including a spouse or partner, friends, children, self, and community.

Key Terms

activities of daily living (ADLs)	grief work	loss
advance directives	hospice	mourning
bereavement	instrumental activities of daily	palliative care
centenarian	living (IADLs)	primary aging
grief	living will	secondary aging

1. Take an inventory of your assumptions about what it is like to be 85 and older. What are your biggest fears? What do you think would be the best part of reaching that age? Think about how these assumptions might influence your feelings about working with clients in very late adulthood.

2. You have recently been hired as the social worker at an assisted-living facility, and Margaret Davis, Pete Mullin, and Marie Cipriani have all recently moved in. All three are unhappy to be there, preferring their prior living arrangements. Pete's sister and Marie's partner recently died. You want to help them share some of their recent experiences related to loss but want to be sensitive to the diversity in life experience that they bring with them. What barriers might you face in accomplishing your goal? What are some ways you might begin to help them?

3. Think about possible relationships among poverty, gender, sexual orientation, and race as one ages in the United States today. Identify ways that social workers can influence policies that affect housing, health care, and other essential services directly related to quality of life in very-late-life adulthood.

Web Resources

Administration for Community Living: www.acl.gov

Site of U.S. Department of Health and Human Services Administration for Community Living contains help and resources, information about programs and activities, a newsroom, and funding opportunities.

American Society on Aging: www.asaging.org

Site provides general information about aging-related services, including a link to LGBT Aging Issues Network (LAIN) and LGBT Aging Resources Clearinghouse (LARC) and information on older adults, alcohol, medication, and other drugs.

Generations United: www.gu.org

Site maintained by Generations United (GU), the national membership organization focused solely on improving the lives of children, youth, and older people through intergenerational strategies, programs, and public policies. See site for links to resources, bibliographies, and so on.

Hospice Foundation of America: www.hospice-foundation.org

Site contains information for locating hospice programs, a newsletter, and links to resources.

National Association of Social Workers: www.naswdc.org/aging.asp

Site provides access to resources related to aging and social work practice, including some online courses.

National Caregivers Library: www.caregiverslibrary.org

Site created and maintained by FamilyCare America contains information and tools for caregivers, seniors, and employers.

National Center for Gerontological Social Work Education: www.cswe.org/CenterInitiatives/GeroEdCenter.aspx

Site maintained by the Council on Social Work Education Gero-Ed Center (National Center for

Gerontological Social Work Education) provides resources for aging and end-of-life care.

National Hospice and Palliative Care Organization: www.nhpco.org

Site maintained by the National Hospice and Palliative Care Organization contains information on the history and current development of hospice and palliative care programs, advance directives, grief and bereavement, caregiving, and other related topics.

National Resource Center on LGBT Aging: www.lgbtagingcenter.org

Site of the National Resource Center on LGBT Aging formed in 2010 provides education, training, and critical resources to providers, organizations, and consumers.

Office on Aging: www.apa.org/pi/aging

Site presented by the Office on Aging of the American Psychological Association contains news briefs, publications, and links to aging organizations.

The Retirement Research Foundation: www.rrf.org/aging-related-websites

Site provides links to many age-related websites.

Student Study Site

SAGE edge™

Sharpen your skills with SAGE edge at edge.sagepub.com/hutchisonclc5e

SAGE edge for students provides a personalized approach to help you accomplish your coursework goals in an easy-to-use learning environment.

REFERENCES

Abrams, K., Rifkin, A., & Hesse, E. (2006). Examining the role of parental frightened/frightening subtypes in predicting a disorganized attachment within a brief observational procedure. *Development and Psychopathology, 18*(2), 345–361.

Achenbaum, W. A., & Bengtson, V. C. (1994). Re-engaging the disengagement theory of aging: Or the history and assessment of theory development in gerontology. *The Gerontologist, 34,* 756–763.

Addy, S., Engelhardt, W., & Skinner, C. (2013). *Basic facts about low income children: Children under 18 years, 2011.* National Center for Children in Poverty. Retrieved from www.nccp.org/publications/pdf/text_1074.pdf.

Addy, S., & Wight, V. (2012). *Basic facts about low-income children, 2010: Children under age 3.* New York: National Center for Children in Poverty. Retrieved from http://www.nccp.org/publications/pdf/text_1056.pdf.

Adler-Tapia, R. (2012). *Child psychotherapy: Integrating developmental theory into clinical practice.* New York: Springer.

Administration on Aging. (2008). *A profile of older Americans: 2008.* Retrieved from www.nowaa.org/Document.Doc?id=69.

Administration on Aging. (2012). *A profile of older Americans: 2012.* Retrieved from http://www.aoa.gov/Aging_statistics/Profile/2012/docs/2012profile.pdf.

Administration on Aging. (2013). *Older Americans behavioral health: Preventing suicide in older adults.* Retrieved from http://www.aoa.gov/AoARoot/AoA_Programs/HPW/Behavioral/docs/Older%20Americans%20Issue%20Brief%204_Preventing%20Suicide_508.pdf.

Advanced Fertility Center of Chicago. (2014). *Single cycle IVF cost details—Advanced Fertility Center of Chicago.* Retrieved from http://www.advancedfertility.com/ivfprice.htm.

Affordable Care Act Maternal, Infant, and Early Childhood Home Visiting Program. (2010, September 20). Retrieved from http://www.hrsa.gov/grants/apply/assistance/home visiting/homevisitingsupplemental.pdf.

Agrigoroaei, S., & Lachman, M. (2011). Cognitive functioning in midlife and old age: Combined effects of psychosocial and behavioral factors. *The Journals of Gerontology, Series B: Psychological Sciences and Social Sciences, 66B*(S1), i130–i140.

Agronin, M. E. (2011). *How we age: A doctor's journey into the heart of growing old.* Philadelphia: Da Capo Press.

Ahmann, E. (2013). Making meaning when a child has mental illness: Four mothers share their experiences. *Pediatric Nursing, 39*(4), 202–205.

Ahrens, K., DuBois, D., Richardson, L., Fan, M., & Lozano, P. (2008). Youth in foster care with adult mentors during adolescence have improved adult outcomes. *Pediatrics, 121*(2), 246–252.

Ahrons, C. R. (2011). Divorce: An unscheduled family transition. In M. McGoldrick, B. Carter, & N. Garcia-Preto (Eds.), *The expanded family life cycle: Individual, family, and social perspectives* (4th ed., pp. 292–316). Boston: Allyn & Bacon.

Aibar, L., Puertas, A., Valverde, M., Carrilo, M. P., & Montoya, F. (2012). Fetal sex and perinatal outcomes. *Journal of Perinatal Medicine, 40*(3), 271–276.

Ainsworth, M., Blehar, M., Waters, E., & Wall, S. (1978). *Patterns of attachment: A psychological study of the strange situation.* Hillsdale, NJ: Lawrence Erlbaum.

Aitken, R. J., Baker, M. A., Doncel, G. F., Matzuk, M. M., Mauck, C. K., & Harper, M. J. K. (2008). As the world grows: Contraception in the 21st century. *Journal of Clinical Investigation, 118*(4), 1330–1343.

Ajrouch, K., Antonucci, T., & Janevic, M. (2001). Social networks among blacks and whites: The interaction between race and age. *Journal of Gerontology: Social Sciences, 56,* S112–S118.

Albuquerque, P. (2011). Grandparents in multigenerational households: The case of Portugal. *European Journal of Ageing, 8*(3), 189–198.

Aleccia, J. (2013, November 4). *Obesity linked to early puberty in girls, study finds.* Retrieved from http://www.nbcnews.com/health/obesity-linked-early-puberty-us-girls-study-finds-8C11514727.

Alink, L., Mesmon, J., & van Zeijl, J. (2006). The early childhood aggression curve: Development of physical aggression in 10- to 50-month-old children. *Child Development, 77*(4), 954–966.

Alio, A. P., Lewis, C. A., Scarborough, K., Harris, K., & Fiscella, K. (2013). A community perspective on the role of fathers during pregnancy: A qualitative study. *British Medical Journal: Pregnancy and Childbirth, 12*(1), 1–11.

Als, H., Heidelise, A., & Butler, S. (2008). Newborn individualized developmental care assessment program: Changing the future for infants and families in intensive care and special care nurseries. *Early Childhood Services: An Interdisciplinary Journal of Effectiveness, 2*(1), 1–19.

Alwin, D. (2012). Integrating varieties of life course concepts. *The Journals of Gerontology, Series B: Psychological Sciences and Social Sciences, 67*(2), 206–220.

Alwin, D., & McCammon, R. (2003). Generations, cohorts, and social change. In J. Mortimer & M. Shanahan (Eds.), *Handbook of the life course* (pp. 23–49). New York: Kluwer Academic/Plenum.

Alwin, D., McCammon, R., & Hofer, S. (2006). Studying baby boom cohorts within a demographic and developmental context: Conceptual and methodological issues. In S. Whitbourne & S. Willis (Eds.), *The baby boomers grow up: Contemporary perspectives on midlife* (pp. 45–71). Mahwah, NJ: Lawrence Erlbaum.

Aly, H., Hammad, T., Nada, A., Mohamed, M., Bathgate, S., & El-Mohandes, A. (2010). Maternal obesity, associated complications and risk of prematurity. *Journal of Perinatology, 30*(7), 447–451.

Alzheimer's Association. (2013). *2013 Alzheimer's Disease facts and figures.* Chicago: Author.

Amato, P. (2003). Family functioning and child development: The case of divorce. In R. M. Lerner, F. Jacobs, & D. Wertlieb (Eds.), *Handbook of applied developmental science* (Vol. 1, pp. 319–333). Thousand Oaks, CA: Sage.

American Academy of Child & Adolescent Psychiatry. (2013). *Facts for families: Children & divorce.* Retrieved from www.aaccap.org/APP_Themes/AACAP/docs/facts_for_families/01_children_and_divorce.pdf.

American Academy of Pediatrics. (2012). *American Academy of Pediatrics study documents early puberty onset in boys.* Retrieved from http://www.aap.org/en-us/about-the-aap/aap-press-room/pages/AAP-Study-Documents-Early-Puberty-Onset-In-Boys.aspx.

American Alliance for Health, Physical Education, Recreation and Dance. (2013). *Maximizing the benefits of youth sport* (position statement). Retrieved from http://www.aahperd.org/naspe/publications/teachingTools/coaching/upload/Maximizing-the-Benefit-of-Youth-Sport-ADA-Approved.pdf.

American Civil Liberties Union. (2013). *What is the school-to-prison pipeline?* Retrieved from http://www.aclu.org/racial-justice/what-school-prison-pipeline.

American College of Medical Genetics. (2013). *ACMG releases policy statement on noninvasive prenatal screen (NIPS).* Retrieved from www.acmg.net/docs/NIPS_Release.pdf.

American College of Nurse-Midwives. (2013). Miscarriage. *Journal of Midwifery & Women's Health, 58*(4), 479–480.

American Congress of Obstetricians and Gynecologists (ACOG). (2012). *Human immunodeficiency virus and acquired immunodeficiency syndrome and women of color.* Retrieved from http://www.acog.org/About_ACOG/ACOG_Departments/HIV/~/media/Committee%20Opinions/Committee%20on%20Health%20Care%20for%20Underserved%20Women/co536.pdf.

American Congress of Obstetricians and Gynecologists (ACOG). (2013). *Genetic disorders.* Retrieved from http://www.acog.org/~/media/For%20Patients/faq094.pdf?dmc=1&ts=20131228T1710532555.

American Foundation for the Blind. (2013). *Special report on aging.* Retrieved from http://www.afb.org/section.aspx?SectionID=15&DocumentID=4423.

American Heart Association. (2013). *American Heart Association recommendations for physical activity in adults.* Retrieved from http://www.heart.org/HEARTORG/GettingHealthy/PhysicalActivity/StartWalking/Wmerican-Heart-Association-Guidelines_UCM_307976_Article.jsp.

American Pregnancy Association. (2012). *Preimplantation genetic diagnosis: PGD.* Retrieved from http://americanpregnancy.org/infertility/preimplantiongeneticdiagnosis.html.

American Psychiatric Association. (2013). *Diagnostic and statistical manual of mental disorders: DSM-5.* Washington, DC: American Psychiatric Association.

American Society for Reproductive Medicine. (2013). Consideration of the gestational carrier: A committee opinion. *Fertility and Sterility, 99*(7), 1838–1841.

Americans' Changing Lives. (2013). *Understanding social disparities in health and aging: The Americans' changing lives study.* Retrieved from http://www.isr.umich.edu/acl.

amfAR The Foundation for AIDS Research. (2013). *Statistics: Women and HIV/AIDS.* Retrieved from http://www.amfar.org/about-hiv-and-aids/facts-and-stats-statistics–women-and-hiv-aids.

Amudha, M., Rani, S., Kannan, K., & Manavalan, R. (2013). An updated overview of causes, diagnosis, and management of infertility. *International Journal of Pharmaceutical Sciences Review & Research, 18*(1), 155–164.

An, J., & Cooney, T. (2006). Psychological well-being in mid to late life: The roles of generativity development and parent-child relationships across the lifespan. *International Journal of Behavioral Development, 30*(5), 410–421.

Anand, A., & MacLullich, A. (2013). Delirium in hospitalized older adults. *Medicine, 41*(1), 39–42.

Andangsari, E., Gumilar, I., & Godwin, R. (2013). Social networking sites use and psychological attachment need among Indonesian young adults population. *International Journal of Social Science Studies, 1*(2), 133–138.

Anderson, C. (2005). Single-parent families: Strengths, vulnerabilities, and interventions. In B. Carter & M. McGoldrick (Eds.), *The expanded family life cycle: Individual, family, and social perspectives* (3rd ed., pp. 399–416). Boston: Allyn & Bacon.

Anderson, C. (2010). *The importance of nutrition in pregnancy for lifelong health.* United States Department of Agriculture: Agricultural Research Service. Retrieved from http://www.ars.usda.gov/News/docs.htm?docid=20977&pf=1&cg_id=0.

Anderson, C., & Anderson, M. (2011). Single-parent families: Strengths, vulnerabilities, and interventions. In M. McGoldrick, B. Carter, & N. Garcia-Preto (Eds.), *The expanded family life cycle: Individual, family, and social perspectives* (4th ed., pp. 307–316). Boston: Allyn & Bacon.

Andrew, M., & Ruel, E. (2010). Intergenerational health selection in wealth: A first look at parents' health events and *inter vivos* financial transfers. *Social Science & Research, 39,* 1126–1136.

Annie E. Casey Foundation. (2013). *The 2013 kids count data book.* Retrieved from http://datacenter.kidscount.org/publications/databook/2013.

Ansary, N., Scorpio, E., & Catanzariti, D. (2013). Parent-adolescent ethnic identity discrepancies and adolescent psychosocial maladjustment: A study of gender differences. *Child and Adolescent Social Work Journal, 30,* 275–291.

Antonucci, T., & Akiyama, H. (1987). Social networks in adult life and a preliminary examination of the convoy model. *Journal of Gerontology: Social Sciences, 42,* S519–S527.

Antonucci, T., & Akiyama, H. (1997). Concern with others at midlife: Care, comfort, or compromise? In M. Lachman & J. James (Eds.), *Multiple paths of midlife development* (pp. 145–169). Chicago: University of Chicago Press.

Antonucci, T., Akiyama, H., & Merline, A. (2001). Dynamics of social relationships in midlife. In M. Lachman (Ed.), *Handbook of midlife development* (pp. 571–598). New York: Wiley.

Antonucci, T., Akiyama, H., & Takahashi, K. (2004). Attachment and close relationships across the life span. *Attachment & Human Development, 6*(4), 353–370.

Applegate, J., & Shapiro, J. (2005). *Neurobiology for clinical social work: Theory and practice.* New York: W. W. Norton.

Arber, S., & Ginn, J. (1995). *Connecting gender and aging: A sociological approach.* Philadelphia: Open University Press.

Ardelt, M., & Eccles, J. S. (2001). Effects of mothers' parental efficacy beliefs and promotive parenting strategies on inner-city youth. *Journal of Family Issues, 22*(8), 944.

Arias, E. (2012). United States life tables, 2008. *National Vital Statistics Report, 61*(3), 1–64.

Armatowski, J. (2001). Attitudes toward death and dying among persons in the fourth quarter of life. In D. O. Moberg (Ed.), *Aging and spirituality: Spiritual dimensions of aging theory, research, practice, and policy* (pp. 71–83). New York: Haworth Pastoral Press.

Armstrong, S., & Akande, V. (2013). What is the best treatment option for infertile women aged 40 and over? *Journal of Assisted Reproduction and Genetics, 30*(5), 667–671.

Arnett, J. J. (1998). Learning to stand alone: The contemporary American transition to adulthood in cultural and historical context. *Human Development, 41*(5), 295–297.

Arnett, J. J. (2000). Emerging adulthood: A theory of development from the late teens through the twenties. *American Psychologist, 55*(5), 469–480.

Arnett, J. J. (2004). *Emerging adulthood: The winding road from the late teens through the twenties.* New York: Oxford University Press.

Arnett, J. J. (2006). G. Stanley Hall's adolescence: Brilliance and nonsense. *History of Psychology, 9,* 186–197.

Arnett, J. J. (2007). Suffering, selfish, slackers? Myths and reality about emerging adults. *Journal of Youth and Adolescence, 36,* 23–29.

Arnett, J. J., & Brody, G. H. (2008). A fraught passage: The identity challenges of African-American emerging adults. *Human Development, 51,* 291–293.

Arnett, J. J., & Jensen, L. (2002). A congregation of one. *Journal of Adolescent Research, 17*(5), 451–467.

Arnett, J. J., & Taber, S. (1994). Adolescence terminable and interminable: When does adolescence end? *Journal of Youth & Adolescence, 23*(5), 517–538.

Arnett, J. J., & Tanner, J. L. (2005). *Emerging adults in America: Coming of age in the 21st century.* Washington, DC: American Psychological Association.

Aroian, K., & Norris, A. (2003). Depression trajectories in relatively recent immigrants. *Comprehensive Psychiatry, 44*(5), 420–427.

Aron, L., & Loprest, P. (2012). Disability and the education system. *Future of Children, 22*(1), 97–122.

Arsenio, W., & Gold, J. (2006). The effects of social injustice and inequality on children's moral judgments and behavior: Towards a theoretical model. *Cognitive Development, 21,* 388–400.

Ashford, J., & LeCroy, C. (2010). *Human behavior in the social environment: A multidimensional perspective* (4th ed.). Belmont, CA: Cengage Learning.

Ashton, D. (2011). Lesbian, gay, bisexual, and transgender individuals and the family life cycle. In M. McGoldrick, B. Carter, & N. Garcia-Preto (Eds.), *The expanded family life cycle: Individual, family, and social perspectives* (4th ed., pp. 115–132). Boston: Allyn & Bacon.

Association of Reproductive Health Professionals. (2009). *Health matters facts sheet.* Retrieved from http://www.arhp.org/Publications-and-Resources/Patient-Resources/Fact-Sheets/Breastfeeding.

Association of Women's Health, Obstetric and Neonatal Nurses. (2011). Shackling incarcerated pregnant women. *Journal of Obstetric, Gynecologic, and Neonatal Nurses, 40*(6), 817–818.

Astone, N. M., Schoen, R., Ensminger, M., & Rothert, K. (2000). School reentry in early adulthood: The case of inner-city African Americans. *Sociology of Education, 73,* 133–154.

Attar-Schwartz, S., Tan, J., Buchanan, A., Flouri, E., & Griggs, J. (2009). Grandparenting and adolescent adjustment in two-parent biological, lone parent, and step-families. *Journal of Family Psychology, 23,* 67–75.

Auerbach, S., & Collier, S. (2012). Bringing high stakes from the classroom to the parent center: Lessons from an intervention program for immigrant families. *Teachers College Record, 114*(3), 1–40.

Aumann, K., & Galinsky, E. (2011). *The state of health in the American workforce: Does having an effective workplace matter?* New York: Families and Work Institute. Retrieved from http://www.familiesandwork.org/down loads/StateofHealthinAmericanWorkforce.pdf.

Azrin, N., & Foxx, R. (1989). *Toilet training in less than a day.* New York: Simon & Schuster.

Azzi, A. E. (2011). *Identity and participation in culturally diverse societies: A multidisciplinary perspective.* Malden, MA: Wiley-Blackwell.

Bäckström, C., & Hertfelt Wahn, E. (2011). Support during labour: First-time fathers' descriptions of requested and received support during the birth of their child. *Midwifery, 27,* 67–73.

Baddeley, J., & Singer, J. (2007). Charting the life story's path: Narrative identity across the life span. In J. Clandinin (Ed.), *Handbook of narrative research methods* (pp. 177–202). Thousand Oaks, CA: Sage.

Bahrick, L., Lickliter, R., & Flom, R. (2006). Up versus down: The role of intersensory redundancy in the development of infants' sensitivity to the orientation of moving objects. *Infancy, 9,* 73–96.

Bailey, M., & Danziger, S. (Eds.). (2013). *Legacies of the war on poverty.* New York: Russell Sage.

Baillargeon, R. (2004). Infants' physical world. *Current Directions in Psychological Science, 13,* 89–94.

Baker, L. (2006). Are we transferring women into the community too quickly? *British Journal of Midwifery, 14*(3), 148–149.

Bakhru, A., & Stanwood, N. (2006). Performance of contraceptive patch compared with oral contraceptive pill in a high-risk population. *Obstetrics and Gynecology, 108*(2), 378–386.

Balasch, J., & Gratacos, E. (2011). Delayed childbearing: Effects on fertility and the outcome of pregnancy. *Current Opinion in Obstetric Gynecology, 24*(3), 187–193.

Baldacchino, D. (2011). Myocardial infarction: A turning point in meaning in life over time. *Cardiovascular Nursing, 20*(2), 107–114.

Baldry, A. (2003). Bullying in schools and exposure to domestic violence. *Journal of Child Abuse & Neglect, 27* (7), 713–732.

Baldur-Felskov, B., Kjaer, S., Albieri, V., Steding-Jessen, M., Kjaer, T., Johansen, C., et al. (2013). Psychiatric disorder in women with fertility problems: Results from a large Danish register-based cohort study. *Human Reproduction, 28*(3), 683–690.

Ballantine, J., & Roberts, K. (2014). *Our social world: Introduction to sociology* (4th ed.). Thousand Oaks, CA: Pine Forge.

Baltes, P. B., Lindenberger, U., & Staudinger, U. (1998). Life-span theory in developmental psychology. In R. Lerner (Ed.), *Handbook of child psychology* (5th ed., pp. 1029–1143). New York: Wiley.

Baltes, P. B., & Mayer, K. U. (Eds.). (1999). *The Berlin Aging Study: Aging from 70 to 100.* Cambridge, UK: Cambridge University Press.

Baltes, P. B., Rösler, F., & Reuter-Lorenz, P. A. (2006). Prologue: Biocultural co-constructivism as a theoretical metascript. In P. B. Baltes, P. A. Reuter-Lorenz, & F. Rössler, (Eds.), *Life span development and the brain: The perspective of biocultural co-constructivism* (pp. 3–39). Cambridge, UK: Cambridge University Press.

Bandura, A. (1977). *Social learning theory.* Englewood Cliffs, NJ: Prentice Hall.

Bandura, A. (2002). Social cognitive theory in cultural context. *Applied Psychology: An International Review, 51*(2), 269–290.

Bandura, A. (2006). Toward a psychology of human agency. *Perspectives on Psychological Science, 1*(2), 164–180.

Banks, J. A., & Banks, C. A. M. G. (2010). *Multicultural education: Issues and perspectives.* Hoboken, NJ: Wiley.

Barajas, R., Philipsen, N., & Brooks-Gunn, J. (2008). Cognitive and emotional outcomes for children in poverty. In D. Crane & T. Heaton (Eds.), *Handbook of families & poverty* (pp. 311–333). Thousand Oaks, CA: Sage.

Barbaro, J., & Dissanayake, C. (2012). Early markers of autism spectrum disorders in infants and toddlers prospectively identified in the Social Attention and Communication Study. *Autism, 17*(1), 64–86.

Barber, B., & Demo, D. (2006). The kids are alright (at least, most of them): Links between divorce and dissolution and child well-being. In M. Fine & J. Harvey (Eds.), *Handbook of divorce and relationship dissolution* (pp. 289–311). Mahwah, NJ: Lawrence Erlbaum.

Barbu, S., Le Maner-Idrissi, G., & Jouanjean, A. (2000). The emergence of gender segregation: Towards an integrative perspective. *Current Psychology of Letters: Behavior, Brain, and Cognition, 3,* 7–18.

Barclay, L. (2009). ACOG issues guidelines for stillbirth management. *Obstetrics & Gynecology, 113,* 748–761.

Barker, D., & Thornburg, K. (2013). The obstetric origins of health for a lifetime. *Clinical Obstetrics and Gynecology, 56*(3), 511–519.

Barker, K. K. (1998). "A ship upon a stormy sea": The medicalization of pregnancy. *Social Science & Medicine, 47*(8), 1067–1076.

Barrett, R. (2009). Sociocultural considerations: African Americans, grief, and loss. In D. J. Doka & A. S. Tucci (Eds.), *Living with grief: Diversity and end-of-life care* (pp. 79–91). Washington, DC: Hospice Foundation of America.

Barros, A., Matijasevich, A., Santos, I., & Halpern, R. (2010). Child development in a birth cohort: Effect of child stimulation is stronger in less educated mothers. *International Journal of Epidemiology, 39*, 285–294.

Bartholomae, S., & Fox, J. (2010). Economic stress and families. In S. Price, C. Price, & P. McKenry (Eds.), *Families & change: Coping with stressful events and transitions* (pp. 185–209). Thousand Oaks, CA: Sage.

Barzilai, N., & Bartke, A. (2009). Biological approaches to mechanistically understand the healthy life span extension achieved by calorie restriction and modulation of hormones. *The Journals of Gerontology, Series A: Biological Sciences & Medical Sciences, 64A*(2), 187–191.

Bates, J., & Goodsell, T. (2013). Male kin relationships: Grandfathers, grandsons, and generativity. *Marriage & Family Review, 49*, 26–50.

Bauldry, S., Shanahan, M., Boardman, J., Miech, R., & Macmillan, R. (2012). A life course model of self-rated health through adolescence and young adulthood. *Social Science & Medicine, 75*, 1311–1320.

Baumrind, D. (1971). Current patterns of parental authority. *Developmental Psychology Monographs, 41*(1, Pt. 2), 1–103.

Baumrind, D. (1991). The influence of parenting style on adolescent competence and substance use. *Journal of Early Adolescence, 11*(1), 56–95.

Bayer, J., Ukoumunne, O., Lucas, N., Wake, M., Scalzo, K., & Nicholson, J. (2011). Risk factors for childhood mental health symptoms: National Longitudinal Study of Australian Children. *Pediatrics, 128*(4), 1–15.

Beck, S., Wojdyla, D., Say, L., Betran, A., Merialdi, M., Requejo, J., et al. (2010). The worldwide incidence of preterm birth: A systematic review of maternal mortality and morbidity. *Bulletin of World Health Organization, 88*, 31–38.

Beel-Bates, C. A., Ingersoll-Dayton, B., & Nelson, E. (2007). Deference as a form of reciprocity on aging. *Research on Aging, 29*, 626–643.

Behrens, K., Hesse, E., & Main, M. (2007). Mothers' attachment status as determined by the Adult Attachment Interview predicts their 6-year-olds' reunion responses: A study conducted in Japan. *Developmental Psychology, 43*(6), 1553–1567.

Behrman, J., & Sengupta, P. (2006). Documenting the changing contexts within which young people are transitioning to adulthood in developing countries: Convergence toward developed economies? In C. B. Lloyd, J. R. Behrman, N. Stromquist, & B. Cohen (Eds.), *The changing transitions to adulthood in developing countries: Selected studies* (pp. 13–55). Washington, DC: National Research Council.

Beland, F., Zunzunegui, M., Alvardo, B., Otero, A., & del Ser, T. (2005). Trajectories of cognitive decline and social relations. *The Journals of Gerontology, Series B: Psychological Sciences and Social Sciences, 60*(6), 320–330.

Belden, A., Thompson, N., & Luby, J. (2008). Temper tantrums in healthy versus DSM-IV depressed and disruptive preschoolers: Defining tantrum behaviors associated with clinical problems. *Journal of Pedatrics, 152*, 117–122.

Bellenir, K. (2012). *Mental health disorders sourcebook: Basic consumer health information about healthy brain functioning and mental illnesses, including depression, bipolar disorder, anxiety disorders, posttraumatic stress disorder, obsessive-compulsive disorder, psychotic and personality disorders, eating disorders, impulse control disorders* (5th ed.). Detroit, MI: Omnigraphics.

Belsky, J. (1987). Infant day care and socioemotional development: The United States. *Journal of Child Psychology and Psychiatry, 29*, 397–406.

Belsky, J., & Braungart, J. M. (1991). Are insecure-avoidant infants with extensive day care experience less stressed by and more independent in the strange situation? *Child Development, 62*, 567–571.

Belsky, J., Campbell, S., Cohn, J., & Moore, G. (1996). Instability of infant-parent attachment security. *Developmental Psychology, 32*, 921–924.

Bem, S. L. (1993). *The lenses of gender: Transforming the debate on sexual inequality.* New Haven, CT: Yale University Press.

Bem, S. L. (1998). Gender schema theory and its implications for child development: Raising gender-aschematic children in a gender-schematic society. In D. L. Anselmi & A. L. Law (Eds.), *Questions of gender: Perspectives and paradoxes.* Boston: McGraw Hill.

Benasich, A., & Leevers, H. (2003). Processing of rapidly presented auditory cues in infancy: Implications for later language development. In H. Hayne & J. Fagen (Eds.), *Progress in infancy research* (Vol. 3, pp. 245–288). Mahwah, NJ: Lawrence Erlbaum.

Benenson, J. (1993). Greater preference among females than males for dyadic interaction in early childhood. *Child Development, 64*, 544–555.

Bener, A., Salameh, K. M. K., Yousafzal, M. T., & Saleh, N. M. (2012). Pattern of maternal complications and low birth weight: Associated risk factors among highly endogamous women. *ISRN Obstetrics and Gynecology.* Article ID 540495/dpo:10.54021/2012/54049.

Bengtson, V. L. (1996). Continuities and discontinuities in intergenerational relationships over time. In V. Bengtson & K. Schaie (Eds.), *Adulthood and aging* (pp. 246–268). New York: Springer.

Bengtson, V. L. (2001). Beyond the nuclear family: The increasing importance of multigenerational bonds. *Journal of Marriage and Family, 63*, 1–16.

Bengtson, V. L., Gans, D., Putney, N. M., & Silverstein, M. (2009). *Handbook of theories of aging* (2nd ed.). New York: Springer.

Bengtson, V. L., Rosenthal, C., & Burton, L. (1990). Families and aging: Diversity and heterogeneity. In R. Binstock & L. George (Eds.), *Handbook of aging and the social sciences* (3rd ed., pp. 263–287). New York: Academic Press.

Benjamin, K., Edwards, N. C., & Bharti, V. K. (2005). Attitudinal, perceptual, and normative beliefs influencing the exercise decisions of community-dwelling physically frail seniors. *Journal of Aging and Physical Activity, 13*(3), 276–293.

Benner, A. (2011). The transition to high school: Current knowledge, future directions. *Educational Psychology Review, 23*, 299–328.

Benner, M. A. (2007). AmeriCorps: Idaho community HealthCorps. *Journal of Rural Mental Health, 31*(3), 29–34.

Benson, P. L., Scales, P. C., & Roehlkepartain, E. C. (2011). *A fragile foundation: The state of developmental assets among American youth* (2nd ed.). Minneapolis, MN: Search Institute.

Benson, P. L., Scales, P. C., Syvertsen, A. K., & Roehlkepartain, E. C. (2012). Is youth spiritual development a universal developmental process? An international exploration. *Journal of Positive Psychology, 7*(6), 453–470.

Bergen, D., & Davis, D. (2011). Influences of technology-related playful activity and thought on moral development. *American Journal of Play, 4*(1), 80–99.

Berger, L. (2005). Income, family characteristics, and physical violence toward children. *Child Abuse & Neglect, 29*(2), 107–133.

Berk, L. E. (2005). *Infants, children, and adolescents* (5th ed.). Boston: Pearson.

Berk, L. E. (2012). *Infants, children, and adolescents* (7th ed.). Boston: Pearson/Allyn & Bacon.

Berliner, K., Jacob, D., & Schwartzberg, N. (2011). Single adults and the life cycle. In M. McGoldrick, B. Carter, & N. Garcia-Preto (Eds.), *The expanded family life cycle: Individual, family, and social persepctives* (4th ed., pp. 163–175). Boston: Allyn & Bacon.

Bern-Klug, M. (2004). The ambiguous dying syndrome. *Health and Social Work, 29*(1), 55–65.

Bertrand, J., Floyd, R. L., & Weber, M. K. (2005, October 28). Guidelines for identifying and referring persons with fetal alcohol syndrome. *Centers for Disease Control, 54*(RR11), 1–10.

Bhathena, R. K., & Guillebaud, J. (2006). Contraception for the older woman: An update. *Climacteric: The Journal of the International Menopause Society, 9*(4), 264–276.

Billingsley, A. (1999). *Mighty like a river: The black church and social reform*. New York: Oxford University Press.

Birknerová, Z. (2011). Social and emotional intelligence in school environment. *Asian Social Science, 7*(10), 241–248.

Bisagni, F. (2012). Shrapnel: Latency, mourning and the suicide of a parent. *Journal of Child Psychotherapy, 38*(1), 22–31.

Bishop, A. J. (2011). Spirituality and religiosity connections to mental and physical health among the oldest old. In L. W. Poon & J. Cohen-Mansfield (Eds.), *Understanding well-being in the oldest old* (pp. 227–239). New York: Cambridge University Press.

Bishop, A. J., & Martin, P. (2011). The measurement of life satisfaction and happiness in old-old age. In L. W. Poon & J. Cohen-Mansfield (Eds.), *Understanding well-being in the oldest old* (pp. 290–331). New York: Cambridge University Press.

Bitler, M., & Schmidt, L. (2012). Utilization of fertility treatments: The effects of insurance mandates. *Demography, 49*(1), 125–149.

Bjorklund, B. (2011). *The journey of adulthood* (7th ed.). Boston: Prentice Hall.

Black, B., Holditch-Davis, D., & Miles, M. (2009). Life course theory as a framework to examine becoming a mother of a medically fragile preterm infant. *Research in Nursing & Health, 32*, 38–39.

Black, M. C., Basile, K. C., Breiding, M. J., Smith, S. G., Walters, M. L., Merrick, M. T., et al. (2011). *The National Intimate Partner and Sexual Violence Survey (NISVS): 2010 Summary Report*. Atlanta: GA: National Center for Injury Prevention and Control, Centers for Disease Control and Prevention. Retrieved from http://www.cdc.gov/violenceprevention/pdf/nisvs_report2010-a.pdf.

Blackmon, S., & Vera, E. (2008). Ethnic and racial identity development in children of color. In J. Asamen, M. Ellis, & G. Berry (Eds.), *The Sage handbook of child development, multiculturalism, and the media* (pp. 47–61). Thousand Oaks, CA: Sage.

Blakemore, S. (2012). Imaging brain development: The adolescent brain. *Neuroimaging, 61*, 397–406.

Blakemore, S., & Robbins, T. (2012). Decision-making in the adolescent brain. *Nature Neuroscience, 15*(9), 1184–1191.

Blasco-Fontecilla, H., Delgado-Gomez, D., Legido-Gil, T., Leon, J., Perez-Rodriguez, M., & Baca-Garcia, E. (2012). Can the Holmes-Rahe Social Readjustment Rating Scale (SRRS) be used as a suicide risk scale? An exploratory study. *Archives of Suicide Research, 16*, 13–28.

Blau, P. M. (1964). *Exchange and power in social life*. New York: Wiley.

Blieszner, R., & deVries, B. (2001). Perspectives on intimacy. *Generations, 25*(2), 7–8.

Blieszner, R., & Roberto, K. (2006). Perspectives on close relationships among the baby boomers. In S. Whitbourne & S. Willis (Eds.), *The baby boomers grow up: Contemporary perspectives on midlife* (pp. 261–281). Mahwah, NJ: Lawrence Erlbaum.

Blinn-Pike, L., Worthy, S., Jonkman, J., & Smith, G. R. (2008). Emerging adult versus adult status among college students: Examination of explanatory variables. *Adolescence, 43*(171), 577–591.

Blow, F., & Barry, K. (2012). Alcohol and substance misuse in older adults. *Current Psychiatry Reports, 14,* 310–319.

Blumenthal, P. D., Voedisch, A., & Gemzell-Danielsson, K. (2011). Strategies to prevent unwanted pregnancy: Increasing use of long-acting reversible contraceptives. *Human Reproduction Update, 17*(1), 121–137.

Blunden, S., Thompson, K., & Dawson, D. (2011). Behavioural sleep treatments and night time crying in infants: Challenging the status quo. *Sleep Medicine Reviews, 15,* 327–334.

Boat, A. C., Sadhasivam, S., Loepke, A. W., & Kurth, C. D. (2011). Outcome for the extremely premature neonate: How far do we push the edge? *Pediatric Anesthesia, 21*(7), 765–770.

Boivin, A., Zhong-Cheng, L., Audibert, F., Masse, B., Lefebvre, F., Tessier, R., & Nuyt, A. M. (2012). Pregnancy complications among women born preterm. *Canadian Medical Association Journal, 184*(16), 1777–1784.

Boldizar, J. (1991). Assessing sex typing and androgyny in children: The children's sex role inventory. *Developmental Psychology, 27,* 505–515.

Bolin, M., Akerud, H., Cnattingius, S., Stephansson, O., & Wikstrom, A. K. (2013). Hyperemesis gravidarum and risks of placental dysfunction disorders: A population-based cohort study. *BJOG: An International Journal of Obstetrics and Gynaecology, 120*(5), 541–547.

Bonanno, G., & Kaltman, S. (1999). Toward an integrative perspective on bereavement. *Psychological Bulletin, 125*(6), 760–776.

Bond, B., Hefner, V., & Drogos, K. (2009). Information-seeking practices during the sexual development of lesbian, gay, and bisexual individuals: The influence and effects of coming out in a mediated environment. *Sexuality & Culture, 13,* 32–50.

Borges-Costa, J., Matos, C., & Pereira, F. (2012). Sexually transmitted infections in pregnant adolescents: Prevalence and association with maternal and foetal morbidity. *Journal of the European Academy of Dermatology & Venerology, 26*(8), 972–975.

Borysenko, J. (1996). *A woman's book of life: The biology, psychology, and spirituality of the feminine life cycle.* New York: Riverhead Books.

Boulet, S., Schieve, L., & Boyle, C. (2011). Birth weight and health and developmental outcomes in US children, 1997–2005. *Maternal and Child Health Journal, 15*(7), 836–844.

Bowlby, J. (1969). *Attachment and loss.* New York: Basic Books.

Bowlby, J. (1980). *Attachment and loss: Loss, sadness, and depression* (Vol. 3). New York: Basic Books.

Bowlby, J. (1982). *Attachment and loss* (Vol. 1). New York: Basic Books.

Boyd-Franklin, B., & Karger, M. (2012). Intersections of race, class, and poverty: Challenges and resilience. In F. Walsh (Ed.), *Normal family processes* (4th ed., pp. 273–296). New York: Guilford.

Boyle, C. A., Boulet, S., Schieve, L., Cohen, R. A., Blumberg, S. J., Yeargin-Allsopp, M., et al. (2011). Trends in the prevalence of developmental disabilities in US children, 1997–2008. *Pediatrics, 127*(6), 1034–1042. doi:10.1542/peds.2010-2989

Boyle, M. H., Miskovic, V., Van Lieshout, R., Duncan, L., Schmidt, L. A., Hoult, L., et al. (2011). Psychopathology in young adults born at extremely low birth weight. *Psychological Medicine, 41*(8), 1763–1774.

Boyle, M. H., Racine, Y., Georgiades, K., Snelling, D., Hong, S., Omariba, W., et al. (2006). The influence of economic development level, household wealth and maternal education on child health in the developing world. *Social Science & Medicine, 63,* 2242–2254.

Brache, V., Payan, L. J., & Faundes, A. (2013). Current status of contraceptive vaginal rings. *Contraception, 87*(3), 264–272.

Bradley, S. E. K. (2000). *Affect regulation and the development of psychopathology.* New York: Guilford Press.

Bradley, S. E. K., Croft, T. N., & Rutstein, S. O. (2011). The impact of contraceptive failure on unintended births and induced abortions: Estimates and strategies for reduction. *U.S. Aid for American People, DHS Analytical Studies 22.* Retrieved from http://www.measuredhs.com/pubs/pdf/AS22/AS22.pdf.

Branch, C., Tayal, P., & Triplett, C. (2000). The relationship of ethnic identity and ego identity status among adolescents and young adults. *International Journal of Intercultural Relations, 23,* 777–790.

Brandtstadter, J. (2006). Adaptive resources in later life: Tenacious goal pursuits and flexible role adjustment. In M. Csikszentmihalyi & I. Csikszentmihalyi (Eds.), *A life worth living: Contributions to positive psychology* (pp. 143–164). New York: Oxford Press.

Brault, M. W. (2012). *Americans with disabilities 2010: Household economic studies: Current population report.* Washington, DC: United States Census Bureau. Retrieved from http://www.census.gov/prod/2012pubs/p70-131.pdf.

Brennan, D., & Spencer, A. (2009). Life events and oral-health-related quality of life among young adults. *Quality of Life Research, 18*(5), 557–565.

Brewer, M. (1999). The psychology of prejudice: Ingroup love or outgroup hate? *Journal of Social Issues, 55,* 429–444.

Brezina, P. R., & Zhao, Y. (2012). The ethical, legal, and social issues impacted by modern assisted reproductive technology. *Obstetrics and Gynecology International.* Article ID 686253. doi:10:1155/2-12/686253

Bridgett, D., Gartstein, M., Putnam, S., McKay, T., Iddins, E., Robertson, C., et al. (2009). Maternal and contextual influences and the effect of temperament development during infancy on parenting in toddlerhood. *Infant Behavior & Development, 32*, 103–116.

Briggs, L. (2011). Demoralization and psychological distress in refugees: From research to practice. *Social Work in Mental Health, 9*(5), 336–345. doi:10.1080/15332985.2011.569444

Brim, O., Ryff, C., & Kessler, R. (Eds.). (2004). *How healthy are we? A national study of well-being at midlife.* Chicago: University of Chicago Press.

Brinkman, B. G., Jedinak, A., Rosen, L. A., & Zimmerman, T. S. (2011). Teaching children fairness: Decreasing gender prejudice among children. *Analyses of Social Issues & Public Policy, 11*(1), 61–81.

Brockington, I. F., Aucamp, H. M., & Fraser, C. (2006). Severe disorders of the mother-infant relationship: Definitions and frequency. *Archives of Women's Mental Health, 9*(5), 243–251.

Brokenleg, M., & Middleton, D. (1993). Native Americans: Adapting, yet retaining. In D. Irish, K. Lundquist, & V. Nelsen (Eds.), *Ethnic variations in dying, death, and grief: Diversity in universality* (pp. 101–112). Washington, DC: Taylor & Francis.

Bromberg, D. S., & O'Donohue, W. T. (2013). *Handbook of child and adolescent sexuality: Developmental and forensic psychology.* Boston: Elsevier Science.

Bronfenbrenner, U. (1993). The ecology of cognitive development: Research models and fugitive findings. In R. Wozniak & K. Fischer (Eds.), *Development in context: Acting and thinking in specific environments* (pp. 3–44). Hillsdale, NJ: Lawrence Erlbaum.

Bronfenbrenner, U. (1996). *The ecology of human development: Experiments by nature and design.* Cambridge, MA: Harvard University Press.

Bronfenbrenner, U., & Morris, P. (1998). The ecology of developmental processes. In W. Damon (Series Ed.) & R. M. Lerner (Vol. Ed.), *Handbook of child psychology: Vol 1. Theoretical models of human development* (5th ed., pp. 993–1028). New York: Wiley.

Bronte-Tinkew, J., Brown, B., Carrano, J., & Shwalb, R. (2005). *Logic models and outcomes for youth in the transition to adulthood.* Washington, DC: Child Trends. Retrieved from http://www.childtrends.org/Files/Child_Trends-2005_04_19_FR_logicModel.pdf.

Broussard, B. (2012). Psychological and behavioral traits associated with eating disorders and pregnancy: A pilot study. *Journal of Midwifery & Women's Health, 57*(1), 61–66.

Brown, B., & Klute, C. (2003). Friendships, cliques, and crowds. In G. Adams & M. Berzonsky (Eds.), *Blackwell handbook of adolescence* (pp. 330–345). Oxford, UK: Blackwell.

Brown, J. (2003). The self-enhancement motive in collectivistic cultures: The rumors of my death have been greatly exaggerated. *Journal of Cross-Cultural Psychology, 34*, 603–605.

Brown, J., Dutton, K., & Cook, K. (2001). From the top down: Self-esteem and self-evaluation. *Cognition and Emotion, 15*, 615–631.

Brown, R. A., Rehkopf, D. H., Copeland, W. E., Costello, E. J., & Worthman, C. M. (2009). Lifecourse priorities among Appalachian emerging adults: Revisiting Wallace's organization of diversity. *ETHOS, 37*(2), 225–242.

Brown, S., & Lin, I-F. (2012). The gray divorce revolution: Rising divorce among middle-aged and older adults, 1990–2010. *The Journals of Gerontology, Series B: Psychological Sciences and Social Sciences, 67*(6), 731–741.

Bruce, S., & Muhammad, Z. (2009). The development of object permanence in children with intellectual diability, physical disability, autism, and blindness. *International Journal of Disability, Development & Education, 56*(3), 229–246.

Bruce, S., & Vargas, C. (2013). Teaching object permanence: An action research study. *Journal of Impairment & Blindness, 107*(1), 60–64.

Brückner, H., & Mayer, K. (2005). De-standardization of the life course: What it might mean? And if it means anything, whether it actually took place? In R. MacMillan (Ed.), *The structure of the life course: Standardized? Individualized? Differentiated?* (pp. 27–53). New York: Elsevier.

Brunner, H., Larissa, R., & Huber, K. R. (2009). Contraceptive choices of women 35–44 years of age: Findings from the behavioral risk factor surveillance system. *Annals of Epidemiology, 19*(11), 823–831.

Bryson, K., & Casper, L. (1999). *Coresident grandparents and grandchildren.* Washington, DC: U.S. Census Bureau.

Buchwald, D., Delmar, C., & Schantz-Laursen, B. (2012). How children handle life when their mother or father is seriously ill and dying. *Scandinavian Journal of Caring Sciences, 26*(2), 228–235. doi:10.1111/j.1471-6712.2011.00922.x

Buffardi, A., Thomas, K., Holmes, K., & Manhart, L. (2008). Moving upstream: Ecosocial and psychosocial correlates of sexually transmitted infections among young adults in the United States. *American Journal of Public Health, 98*(6), 1128–1136.

Bullock, K. (2011). The influence of culture on end-of-life decision making. *Journal of Social Work in End-of-Life & Palliative Care, 7*, 83–98.

Bullough, V. L. (2005). Artificial insemination. In C. Summers (Ed.), *GLBTQ Social Sciences.* Retrieved from www.glbtq.com.

Bureau of Labor Statistics. (2013). *Employment characteristics of families summary.* Retrieved from http://www.bls.gov/news.release/famee.nr0.htm.

Burgess, W. C. (2009). Internal and external stress factors associated with the identity development of transgender and gender variant youth. In G. P. Mallon (Ed.), *Social work practice with transgender and gender variant youth* (pp. 53–62). London: Routledge.

Burns, L., Mattick, R. P., & Wallace, C. (2007). Smoking patterns and outcomes in a population of pregnant women and other substance use disorders. *Tobacco Research, 10*(6), 969–974.

Burstein, D. (2013). *Fast future: How the millennial generation is shaping our world.* Boston: Beacon Press.

Busch, H., & Hofer, J. (2012). Self-regulation and milestones of adult development: Intimacy and generativity. *Developmental Psychology, 48*(1), 282–293.

Butler, R. N. (1963). The life review: An interpretation of reminiscence in the aged. *Psychiatry, 26,* 65–70.

Butler, R. N. (1987). Life review. In G. L. Maddox (Ed.), *The encyclopedia of aging: A comprehensive resource in gerontology and geriatrics* (2nd ed., pp. 397–398). New York: Springer.

Butler-Sweet, C. (2011). "Race isn't what defines me": Exploring identity choices in transracial, biracial, and monoracial families. *Social Identities: Journal for the Study of Race, Nation and Culture, 17*(6), 747–769. doi:10.1080/13504630.2011.60667

Cagle, J. G. (2008). *Informal caregivers of advanced cancer patients: The impact of geographic proximity on social support and bereavement adjustment.* Unpublished doctoral dissertation, Virginia Commonwealth University. Retrieved from https://digarchive.library.vcu.edu/handle/1-156/1974.

Cagle, J. G., & Kovacs, P. J. (2009). Education: A complex and empowering social work intervention at the end of life. *Health & Social Work, 34*(1), 17–27.

Caillet, M., Vandromme, J., Rozenberg, S., Paesmans, M., Germay, O., & Degueldre, M. (2010). Robotically assisted laparopscopic microsurgical tubal reanastomosis. *Fertility and Sterility, 94*(5), 1844–1847.

Calkins, S., & Hill, A. (2007). Caregiver influences on emerging emotion regulation: Biological and environmental transactions in early development. In J. Gross (Ed.), *Handbook of emotion regulation* (pp. 229–248). New York: Guilford.

Calman, L., & Tarr-Whelan, L. (2005). *Early childhood education for all: A wise investment.* Retrieved from web.mit.edu/workplacecenter/docs/Full%20Report.pdf.

Cameron, J., Alvarez, J., Ruble, D., & Fuligni, A. (2001). Children's lay theories about ingroups and outgroups: Reconceptualizing research on prejudice. *Personality and Social Psychology Review, 5,* 118–128.

Cameron, S. T., Glasier, A., & Johnstone, A. (2012). Pilot study of home self administration of depo-medroxy-progesterone acetate for contraception. *Contraception, 85*(5), 458–464.

Campbell, L., Campbell, B., & Dickinson, D. (2004). *Teaching & learning through multiple intelligences.* Boston: Allyn & Bacon.

Campbell, S. (2002). *Behavioral problems in preschool children* (2nd ed.). New York: Guilford Press.

Cancer Research UK. (2013). *General side effects of hormone therapy.* Retrieved from www.cancerresearchuk.org/cancer-help/about-cancer/treatment/hormone/general-side-effects-of-hormone-therapy.

Cao, C., & O'Brien, K. O. (2013). Pregnancy and iron homeostatis: An update. *Nutrition Reviews, 71*(1), 35–51.

Cappeliez, P., Beaupré, M., & Robitaille, A. (2008). Characteristics and impact of life turning points for older adults. *Ageing International, 32,* 54–64.

Carey, T. A. (1994). "Spare the rod and spoil the child": Is this a sensible justification for the use of punishment in child rearing? *Child Abuse and Neglect, 18,* 1005–1010.

Carlson, E. (2009). 20th-century U.S. generations. *Population Bulletin, 64,* 1–17.

Carolan, M., & Allen, K. (1999). Commitments and constraints to intimacy for African American couples at midlife. *Journal of Family Issues, 20,* 3–4.

Carpenter, L., Nathanson, C., & Kim, Y. (2009). Physical women, emotional men: Gender and sexual satisfaction in midlife. *Archives of Sexual Behavior, 38*(1), 21–26.

Carpentier, N., Bernard, P., Grenier, A., & Guberman, N. (2010). Using the life course perspective to study the entry into the illness trajectory: The perspective of caregivers of people with Alzheimer's disease. *Social Science & Medicine, 70,* 1501–1508.

Carr, D. (2004). Gender, preloss marital dependence, and older adults' adjustment to widowhood. *Journal of Marriage and the Family, 66,* 220–235.

Carr, D., & Kail, B. (2012). The influence of unpaid work on the transition out of full-time paid work. *The Gerontologist, 53*(1), 92–101.

Carstensen, L. (1995). Evidence for a life-span theory of socioemotional selectivity. *Current Directions in Psychological Science, 4,* 151–156.

Carter, B., McGoldrick, M., & Petkov, B. (2011). In M. McGoldrick, B. Carter, & N. Garcia-Preto (Eds.), *The expanded family life cycle: Individual, family, and social perspectives* (4th ed., pp. 211–231). Boston: Allyn & Bacon.

Casale-Giannola, D., & Kamens, M. W. (2006). Inclusion at a university: Experiences of a young woman with Down syndrome. *Mental Retardation, 44*(5), 344–352.

Catsanos, R., Rogers, W., & Lotz, M. (2013). The ethics of uterine transplantation. *Bioethics, 27*(2), 65–73.

Ceelen, M., van Weissenbruch, M. M., Vermeiden, J. P. W., van Leeuwen, F. E., & Delemarre-van de Waal, H. A. (2008). Growth and development of children born after in vitro fertilization. *Fertility and Sterility, 90*(5), 1662–1673.

Center for Economic and Policy Research. (2009). *Parental leave policies in 21 countries*. Washington, DC: Author.

Center for Human Reproduction. (2013a). *Male infertility*. Retrieved from http://www.centerforhumanreprod.com/male_infertility.html.

Center for Human Reproduction. (2013b). *IVF success rates*. Retrieved from https://www.centerforhumanreprod.com/ivf-success-rates.html.

Center for Research on Women With Disabilities (CROWD). (2013). *Sexuality and reproductive health—Pregnancy and delivery*. Retrieved from https://www.bcm.edu/research/centers/research-on-women-with-disabilities/?pmid=1448.

Centers for Disease Control and Prevention. (2011). Diagnosis during pregnancy: Prenatal testing. Retrieved from http://www.cdc.gov/ncbddd/birthdefects/diagnosis.html.

Centers for Disease Control and Prevention. (2012a). Abortion surveillance—United States, 2009. *Morbidity and Mortality Weekly Report (MMWR), 61*(SS-8), 1–44.

Centers for Disease Control and Prevention. (2012b). *Women with disabilities*. Retrieved from http://www.cdc.gov/ncbddd/disabilityandhealth/women.html.

Centers for Disease Control and Prevention. (2012c). *Sexually transmitted diseases*. Retrieved from http://www.cdc.gov/std/infertility.

Centers for Disease Control and Prevention. (2012d). *Developmental monitoring and screening*. Retrieved from http://www.cdc.gov/ncbddd/childdevelopment/screening.html.

Centers for Disease Control and Prevention. (2012e). *Sexually transmitted disease surveillance 2011*. Retrieved from http://www.cdc.gov/std/stats11/surv2011.pdf.

Centers for Disease Control and Prevention. (2013a). *Genomic testing*. Retrieved from http://www.cdc.gov/genomics/gtesting/index.htm.

Centers for Disease Control and Prevention. (2013b). *Contraception: How effective are birth control methods?* Retrieved from http://www.cdc.gov/reproductivehealth/unintendedpregnancy/Contraception.htm.

Centers for Disease Control and Prevention. (2013c). *Infertility FAQ's*. Retrieved from http://www.cdc.gov/reproductivehealth/Infertility/index.htm.

Centers for Disease Control and Prevention. (2013d). *FastStats: Infertility*. Retrieved from http://www.cdc.gov/nchs/fastats/fertile.htm.

Centers for Disease Control and Prevention. (2013e). *What is ART?* Retrieved from http://www.cdc.gov/art.

Centers for Disease Control and Prevention. (2013f). *Sexually transmitted diseases: Chlamydia profiles 2011*. Retrieved from http://www.cdc.gov/std/chlamydia2011/default.htm.

Centers for Disease Control and Prevention. (2013g). *Prematurity campaign*. Retrieved from http://www.marchofdimes.com/mission/the-economic-and-societal-costs.aspx.

Centers for Disease Control and Prevention. (2013h). *Preterm birth*. Retrieved from http://www.cdc.gov/reproductive-health/MaternalInfantHealth/PretermBirth.htm.

Centers for Disease Control and Prevention. (2013i). *Using science to save lives: CDC and the fight against global HIV/Aids*. Retrieved from http://www.cdc.gov/globalaids/publications/cdc-global-hiv-update-2013.pdf.

Centers for Disease Control and Prevention. (2013j). *QuickStats: Infant mortality rates, by race and Hispanic ethnicity of mother—United States, 2000, 2005, and 2009*. Retrieved from http://www.cdc.gov/mmwr/preview/mmwrhtml/mm6205a6.htm.

Centers for Disease Control and Prevention. (2013k). *Child maltreatment: Consequences*. Retrieved from http://www.cdc.gov/violenceprevention/childmaltreatment/consequences.html.

Centers for Disease Control and Prevention. (2013l). *Attention deficit hyperactivity disorder: Data and statistics*. Retrieved from http://www.cdc.gov/ncbddd/adhd/data.html.

Centers for Disease Control and Prevention. (2013m). *Autism spectrum disorders: Data and statistics*. Retrieved from http://www.cdc.gov/ncbddd/autism/data.html.

Centers for Disease Control and Prevention. (2013n). Homicide rates among persons aged 10–24 years—United States 1981–2010. *Morbidity and Mortality Weekly Report (MMWR), 62*(27), 545–548.

Centers for Disease Control and Prevention. (2013o). *Childhood obesity facts*. Retrieved from http://www.cdc.gov/healthyyouth/obesity/facts.htm.

Centers for Disease Control and Prevention. (2013p). *The state of aging and health in America 2013*. Atlanta, GA: Centers for Disease Control and Prevention, U.S. Department of Health and Human Services.

Centers for Disease Control and Prevention. (2014). *Youth suicide*. Retrieved from http://www.cdc.gov/violenceprevention/pub/youth_suicide.html.

Centers for Medicare and Medicaid Services. (2012a). *Strong start for mothers and newborns*. Retrieved from http://innovations.cms.gov/initiatives/strong-start/index.html.

Centers for Medicare and Medicaid Services. (2012b). *Nursing home data compendium: 2012 edition*. Baltimore: Department of Health & Human Services.

Central Intelligence Agency. (2012). *The world factbook*. Retrieved from http://www.cia.gov/library/publications/the-world-factbook.

Central Intelligence Agency. (2013). *The world factbook*. Retrieved from https://www.cia.govlibrary/publications/the-world-factbook/fields/2177.html.

Chan, A., Malhotra, C., Malhotra, R., Rush, A., & Ostbye, T. (2013). Health impacts of caregiving for older adults with functional limitations: Results from Singapore Survey on Informal Caregiving. *Journal of Aging and Health, 25*(6), 998–1012.

Chang, G., McNamara, T., Orav, E., & Wilkins-Haug, L. (2006). Alcohol use by pregnant women: Partners, knowledge and other predictors. *Journal of Studies of Alcoholism, 67*(20), 245–251.

Chang, L. (2001). The development of racial attitudes and self concepts of Taiwanese preschoolers (China). *Dissertation Abstracts International: Section A: Humanities & Social Sciences, 61*(8-A), 3045.

Chang, W. H., Liu, J. Y., Wu, G. J., Chiang, Y. J., Yu, J. H., & Chen, C. H. (2011). Tubal ligation via colpotomy or laparoscopy: A retrospective comparative study. *Archives of Gynecology and Obstetrics, 283*(4), 805–808.

Chang, Y., & Schneider, J. (2010). Decision-making process of nursing home placement among Chinese family caregivers. *Perspectives in Psychiatric Care, 46*(2), 108–118.

Chao, S. M., Donatoni, G., Bemis, C., Donovan, K., Harding, C., Davenport, D., et al. (2010). Integrated approaches to improve birth outcomes: Perinatal periods of risk, infant mortality review, and the Los Angeles mommy and baby project. *Maternal and Child Health Journal, 14*(6), 827–837.

Chapin, L., & Altenhofen, S. (2010). Neurocognitive perspectives in language outcomes of Early Head Start: Language and cognitive stimulation and maternal depression. *Infant Mental Health Journal, 31*(5), 486–498.

Chapman, M. V., & Perreira, K. M. (2005). The well-being of immigrant Latino youth: A framework to inform practice. *Families in Society, 86,* 104–111.

Charles, P., & Perreira, K. (2007). Intimate partner violence during pregnancy and 1-year post-partum. *Journal of Family Violence, 22*(7), 609–619.

Charlesworth, L. (2007). Child maltreatment. In E. Hutchison, H. Matto, M. Harrigan, L. Charlesworth, & P. Viggiani (Eds.), *Challenges of living: A multidimensional working model for social workers* (pp. 105–139). Thousand Oaks, CA: Sage.

Chen, C. (2006). A household-based convoy and the reciprocity of support exchange between adult children and noncoresiding parents. *Journal of Family Issues, 27*(8), 1100–1136.

Chen, X. (2009). The linkage between deviant lifestyles and victimization: An examination from a life course perspective. *Journal of Interpersonal Violence, 24*(7), 1083–1110.

Cherry, M. (Writer), & Grossman, D. (Director). (2012). Finishing the hat [Television series episode]. In M. Berry et al. (Producers), *Desperate Housewives.* NBC Studios: Burbank, CA.

Chervenak, F., McCullough, L., Brent, R., Levene, M., & Arabin, B. (2013). Planned home birth: The professional responsibility response. *American Journal of Obstetrics and Gynecology, 208*(1), 31–38.

Chesney-Lind, M., & Jones, N. (2010). *Fighting for girls: New perspectives on gender and violence.* Albany: State University of New York Press.

Chethik, M. (2000). *Techniques of child therapy: Psychodynamic approaches* (2nd ed.). New York: Guilford Press.

Child Trends. (2013a). *Food insecurity.* Retrieved from http://www.childtrends.org?indicators=food-insecurity.

Child Trends. (2013b). *Family structure: Indicators on children and youth.* Retrieved from www.childtrends.org/?indicators=family-structure.

Child Trends Data Bank. (2013). *Low and very low birth weight infants: Indicators on children and youth.* Retrieved from http://www.childtrends.org/wp-content/uploads/2012/11/57_Low_Birth_Weight.pdf.

Child Welfare Information Gateway. (2011). *How many children were adopted in 2007 and 2008?* Washington, DC: U.S. Department of Health and Human Services. Retrieved from https://www.childwelfare.gov/pubs/adopted0708.pdf.

Child Welfare Information Gateway. (2013a). *Foster care statistics 2012.* Washington, DC: U.S. Department of Health and Human Services, Children's Bureau. Retrieved from https://www.childwelfare.gov/pubs/factsheets/foster.pdf.

Child Welfare Information Gateway. (2013b). *Child Maltreatment 2011: Summary of key findings.* Washington, DC: U.S. Department of Health and Human Services, Children's Bureau. Retrieved from https://www.childwelfare.gov/pubs/factsheets/canstats.pdf.

Children's Defense Fund. (2012). *The state of America's children handbook of 2012.* Retrieved from http://www.childrensdefense.org/child-research-data-publications/data/soac-2012-handbook.html.

Childrens Defense Fund. (2013). *Children in the United States.* Retrieved from www.childrensdefense.org/child-research-data-publications/data/state-data-repository/cits/2013/2013-united-states-children-in-the-states/pdf.

Chodorow, N. (1991). *Feminism and psychoanalytic theory.* New Haven, CT: Yale University Press.

Chodorow, N. (1999). *The reproduction of mothering: Psychoanalysis and the sociology of gender.* Berkeley: University of California Press.

Choi, N. G., & DiNitto, D. M. (2013a). The digital divide among low-income homebound older adults: Internet use patterns, eHealth literacy, and attitudes toward computer/Internet use. *Journal of Medical Internet Research, 15*(5), e97.

Choi, N. G., & DiNitto, D. M. (2013b). Internet use among older adults: Association with health needs, psychological capital, and social capital. *Journal of Medical Internet Research, 15*(5), e93.

Chomsky, N. (1968). *Language and mind.* New York: Harcourt Brace Jovanovich.

Choudhury, S. (2010). Culturing the adolescent brain: What can neuroscience learn from anthropology? *SCAN, 5,* 159–167.

Chowdhury, F. (2004). The socio-cultural context of child marriage in a Bangladeshi village. *International Journal of Social Welfare, 13,* 244–253.

Christen, M., & Narvaez, D. (2012). Moral development in early childhood is key for moral enhancement. *AJOB Neuroscience, 3*(4), 25–26.

Chugani, H., Behen, M., Muzik, O., Juhasz, C., Nagy, F., & Chugani, D. (2001). Local brain functional activity following early deprivation: A study of post-institutional Romanian orphans. *Neuroimage, 14,* 1290–1301.

Chumlea, W. C., Schubert, C. M., Roche, A. F., Kulin, H. E., Lee, P. A., Himes, J. H. J., et al. (2003). Age at menarche and racial comparisons in US girls. *Pediatrics, 111*(1), 110–113.

Chung, R., Bemak, F., & Grabosky, T. (2011). Multicultural-social justice leadership strategies: Counseling and advocacy with immigrants. *Journal for Social Action in Counseling & Psychology, 3*(1), 86–102.

Cicchetti, D. (2013). Annual research review: Resilient functioning in maltreated children—past, present, and future perspectives. *Journal of Child Psychology & Psychiatry, 54*(4), 402–422. doi:10.1111/j.1469-7610.2012.02608.x

Claas, M. J., de Vries, L. S., & Bruinse, H. W. (2011). Maternal characteristics of a cohort of preterm infants with a birth weight <750 g without major structural anomalies and chromosomal abnormalities. *American Journal of Perinatology, 28*(5), 367–375.

Clare, R., Mazzucchelli, T., Studman, L., & Sanders, M. (2006). Behavioral family intervention for children with developmental disabilities and behavioral problems. *Journal of Clinical Child and Adolescent Psychology, 35*(2), 180–193.

Clark, K., & Clark, M. (1939). The development of consciousness of self and the emergence of racial identification in Negro preschool children. *Journal of Social Psychology, 10,* 591–599.

Clark, M. K., Dillon, J., Sowers, M., & Nichols, S. (2005). Weight, fat mass, and central distribution of fat increase when women use depotmedroxprogesterone acetate for contraception. *International Journal of Obesity, 29*(10), 1252–1258.

Clark, P. A. (2009). Embryo donation/adoption: Medical, legal, and ethical perspectives. *The Internet Journal of Law, Healthcare, and Ethics, 5*(2), 1–12.

Clark, R., Glick, J., & Bures, R. (2009). Immigrant families over the life course. *Journal of Family Issues, 30*(6), 852–872.

Clarke, J., & Adashi, E. (2011). Perinatal care for incarcerated patients: A 25-year-old woman pregnant in jail. *Journal of the American Medical Association, 305*(9), 923–929.

Clarke, L. (2008). Grandparents: A family resource? In D. R. Crane & T. Heaton (Eds.), *Handbook of families & poverty* (pp. 365–380). Thousand Oaks, CA: Sage.

Clarke, M., Tanskanen, A., Huttunen, M., Leon, D., Murray, R., Jones, P., et al. (2011). Increased risk for schizophrenia from additive interaction between infant motor developmental delay and obstetric complications: Evidence from a population-based longitudinal study. *American Journal of Psychiatry, 168*(12), 1295–1302.

Clearfield, M., & Nelson, N. (2006). Sex differences in mothers' speech and play behavior with 6-, 9-, and 14-month-old infants. *Sex Roles, 54*(1/2), 127–137.

Cleland, K., Zhu, H., Goldstuck, N., Cheng, L., & Trussell, J. (2012). The efficacy of intrauterine devices for emergency contraception: A systematic review of 35 years of experience. *Human Reproduction, 27*(7), 1994–2000.

Clinton, J. (2008). Resilience and recovery. *International Journal of Children's Spirituality, 13*(3), 213–222. doi:10.1080/13644360802236474

Cohen, A. A., McEvoy, C., & Castile, R. C. (2010). Respiratory morbidity and lung function in preterm infants of 32 to 36 weeks' gestational age. *Pediatrics, 126*(1), 115–128.

Cohen, J., & Sandy, S. (2007). The social, emotional and academic education of children: Theories, goals, methods and assessments. In R. Bar-On, J. Maree, & M. Elias (Eds.), *Educating people to be emotionally intelligent* (pp. 63–77). Wesport, CT: Praeger.

Cohen, P. (2012). *In our prime: The invention of middle age.* New York: Scribner.

Coie, J. D., Dodge, K. A., & Coppotelli, H. (1982). Dimensions and types of social status: A cross age perspective. *Developmental Psychology, 18,* 557–570.

Cole, J., & Durham, D. L. (2008). *Figuring the future: Globalization and the temporalities of children and youth.* Santa Fe, NM: School for Advanced Research Press.

Cole, P., Luby, J., & Sullivan, M. (2008). Emotions and the development of childhood depression: Bridging the gap. *Child Development Perspectives, 2*(3), 141–148.

Coles, L. S. (2013). Validated worldwide supercentenarians, living and recently deceased. *Rejuvenation Research, 16*(1), 82–84.

Coles, R. (1987). *The moral life of children.* Boston: Houghton Mifflin.

Coles, R. (1990). *The spiritual life of children.* Boston: Houghton Mifflin.

Coles, R. (1997). *The moral intelligence of children.* New York: Random House.

Colle, L., & Del Giudice, M. (2011). Patterns of attachment and emotional competence in middle childhood. *Social Development, 20*(1), 51–72

Collins, P. H. (2012). Looking back, moving ahead: Scholarship in service to social justice. *Gender & Society, 26,* 14–22.

Coltrane, S. (2000). Research on household labor: Modeling and measuring the social embeddedness of routine family work. *Journal of Marriage and the Family, 62,* 1208–1233.

Colver, A., & Longwell, S. (2013). New understanding of adolescent brain development: Relevance to transitional healthcare for young people with long term conditions. *Archives of Disease in Childhood, 98,* 902–907.

Combs-Orme, T. (2013). Epigenetics and the social work imperative. *Social Work, 58*(1), 23–30.

Condon, J. (2006). What about dad? Psychosocial and mental health issues for new fathers. *Australian Family Physician, 35*(9), 690–692.

Conger, R., & Conger, K. (2008). Understanding the processes through which economic hardship influences families and children. In D. Crane & T. Heaton (Eds.), *Handbook of families & poverty* (pp. 64–81). Thousand Oaks, CA: Sage.

Congress.gov. (2013). *S.252. PREEMIE Reauthorization Act.* Retrieved from http://beta.congress.gov/bill/113th-congress/senate-bill/252.

Connor, M. E., & White, J. L. (2006). *Black fathers: An invisible presence in America.* Mahwah, NJ: Lawrence Erlbaum.

Constable, R. T. (2006). *School social work: Practice, policy, and research.* Chicago: Lyceum Books.

Conwell, Y., Van Orden, K., & Caine, E. D. (2011). Suicide in older adults. *The Psychiatric Clinics of North America, 34*(2), 451–468.

Cook, S. H., Bauermeister, J. A., Gordon-Messer, D., & Zimmerman, M. A. (2013). Online network influences on emerging adults' alcohol and drug use. *Journal of Youth and Adolescence, 42,* 1674–1686.

Cooper, S., Bandelow, S., & Nevill, M. (2011). Breakfast consumption and cognitive function in adolescent school children. *Physiology and Behavior, 103*(5), 431–439.

Corcoran, M., Danziger, S. K., Kalil, A., & Seefeldt, K. S. (2000). How welfare reform is affecting women's work. *Annual Review of Sociology, 26,* 241–269.

Cornish, J. A., Tan, E., Simillis, C., Clark, S. K., Teare, J., & Tekkis, P. P. (2008). The risk of oral contraceptives in the etiology of inflammatory bowel disease: A meta analysis. *American Journal of Gastroenterology, 103*(9), 2394–2400.

Cornwell, B., Laumann, E. O., & Schumm, L. P. (2008). The social connectedness of older adults: A national profile. *American Sociological Review, 73*(2), 185–203.

Corsaro, W. (2011). *The sociology of childhood* (3rd ed.). Los Angeles: Sage.

Costa, P., Terracciano, A., & McCrae, R. (2001). Gender differences in personality traits across cultures: Robust and surprising findings. *Journal of Personality and Social Psychology, 81*(2), 322.

Costantino, A., Cerpolini, S., Perrone, A., Ghi, T., Pelusi, C., Pelusi, G., et al. (2007). Current status and future perspectives in male contraception. *Minerva Ginecologica, 59*(3), 299–310.

Costigan, C., & Dokis, D. (2006). Similarities and differences in acculturation among mothers, fathers, and children in immigrant Chinese families. *Journal of Cross-Cultural Psychology, 37,* 723–741.

Costigan, C., Su, T., & Hua, J. (2009). Ethnic identity among Chinese Canadian youth: A review of the Canadian literature. *Canadian Psychology, 50*(4), 261–272.

Council on Social Work Education. (2008). *Educational policy and accreditation standards.* Alexandria, VA: Author.

Courage, M., & Howe, M. (2010). To watch or not to watch: Infants and toddlers in a brave new electronic world. *Developmental Review, 30,* 101–115.

Courage, M., & Setliff, A. (2009). Debating the impact of television and video material on very young children: Attention, learning, and the developing brain. *Child Development Perspectives, 3*(1), 72–78.

Cowan, P. A. (1991). Individual and family life transitions: A proposal for a new definition. In P. A. Cowan & M. Hetherington (Eds.), *Family transitions* (pp. 3–30). Hillsdale, NJ: Lawrence Erlbaum.

Cox, G. R. (2009). Death, dying, and end of life in American-Indian communities. In D. J. Doka & A. S. Tucci (Eds.), *Living with grief: Diversity and end-of-life care* (pp. 107–115). Washington, DC: Hospice Foundation of America.

Crain, R. (1996). The influences of age, race, and gender on child and adolescent multidimensional self-concept. In B. Bracken (Ed.), *Handbook of self-concept* (pp. 395–420). New York: Wiley.

Crawley, L., Payne, R., Bolden, J., Payne, T., Washington, P., & Williams, S. (2000). Palliative and end-of-life care in the African American community. *Journal of the American Medical Association, 284*(19), 2518–2521.

Creanga, A. A., Shapiro-Mendoza, C. K., Bish, C. L., Zane, S., Berg, C. J., & Callaghan, W. M. (2011). Trends in ectopic pregnancy mortality in the United States 1980–2007. *Obstetrics and Gynecology, 117*(4), 837–843.

Crimmins, E. M., Preston, S. H., & Cohen, B. (2011). Difference between life expectancy in the United States and other high-income countries. In E. Crimmins, S. Preston, & B. Cohen (Eds.), *Explaining divergent trends in longevity in high-income countries* (pp. 7–25). Washington, DC: The National Academies Press.

Croghan, C., Moone, R., & Olson, A. (2014). Friends, family, and caregiving among midlife and older lesbian, gay, bisexual, and transgender adults. *Journal of Homosexuality, 61,* 79–102.

Cromley, T., Neumark-Sztainer, D., Story, M., & Boutelle, K. (2010). Parent and family associations with weight-related behaviors and cognitions among overweight adolescents. *Journal of Adolescent Health, 47*(3), 263–269.

Crouse, J. S. (2010). *Children at risk: The precarious state of children's well-being in America.* New Brunswick, NJ: Transaction.

Csikai, E. L., & Jones, B. (2007). *Teaching resources for end of life and palliative care courses.* Chicago: Lyceum Books.

CTParenting.com. (2014). *Toddler cognitive development—thinking and problem-solving.* Retrieved from http://www.ctparenting.com/toddlercognitivedevelopment thinking.php.

Culp, R., McDonald Culp, A., Dengler, B., & Maisano, P. (1999). First-time young mothers living in rural communities use of corporal punishment with their toddlers. *Journal of Community Psychology, 27*(4), 503–509.

Cumming, E., & Henry, W. (1961). *Growing old.* New York: Basic Books.

Cutrona, C., Russell, D., Burzette, R., Wesner, K., & Bryant, C. (2011). Predicting relationship stability among midlife African American couples. *Journal of Consulting and Clinical Psychology, 79*(6), 814–825.

Dahlberg, G., Moss, P., & Pence, A. (2007). *Beyond quality in early childhood education and care: Postmodern perspectives* (2nd ed.). New York: Routledge Falmer.

Dalby, P. (2006). Is there a process of spiritual change or development associated with ageing? A critical review of research. *Aging and Mental Health, 10*(1), 4–12.

Dannefer, D. (2003a). Whose life course is it, anyway? Diversity and "linked lives" in global perspective. In R. Settersten Jr. (Ed.), *Invitation to the life course: Toward new understandings of later life* (pp. 259–268). Amityville, NY: Baywood.

Dannefer, D. (2003b). Toward a global geography of the life course: Challenges of late modernity for life course theory. In J. Mortimer & M. Shanahan (Eds.), *Handbook of the life course* (pp. 647–659). New York: Kluwer Academic/Plenum.

Dannefer, D. (2003c). Cumulative advantage/disadvantage and the life course: Cross-fertilizing age and social science theory. *Journal of Gerontology: Social Sciences, 58B,* S327–S337.

Dannefer, D., & Perlmutter, M. (1990). Development as a multidimensional process: Individuals and social constituents. *Human Development, 33,* 108–137.

Darling-Hammond, L. (2010). *The flat world and education: How America's commitment to equity will determine our future.* New York: Teachers College Press.

Davidson, J., Moore, N., & Ullstrup, L. (2004). Religiosity and sexual responsibilities: Relationships of choice. *Journal of Health Behavior, 28*(4), 335–346.

Davidson, R. J., & Begley, S. (2012). *The emotional life of your brain: How its unique patterns affect the way you think, feel, and live—and how you can change them.* New York: Penguin Books.

Davies, D. (2011). *Child development: A practitioner's guide* (3rd ed.). New York: Guilford.

Davis, J., & Bauman, K. (2013). *School enrollment in the United States: 2011.* U.S. Census Bureau. Retrieved from www.census.gov/prod/2013pubs/p20-571.pdf.

Davis, M., & Vander Stoep, A. (1997). The transition to adulthood for youth who have serious emotional disturbance: Developmental transition and young adult outcomes. *Journal of Mental Health Administration, 24*(4), 400–427.

Dean, R. G. (1993). Teaching a constructivist approach to clinical practice. In J. Laird (Ed.), *Revisioning social work education: A social constructionist approach* (pp. 55–75). New York: Haworth Press.

De Brucker, M., Haentjens, P., Evenepoel, J., Devroey, P., Collins, J., & Tournaye, H. (2009). Cumulative delivery rates in different age groups after artificial insemination with donor sperm. *Human Reproduction, 24*(8), 1891–1899.

De Marco, A. C., & Cosner Berzin, S. (2008). The influence of family economic status on home-leaving patterns during emerging adulthood. *Families in Society, 89*(2), 208–218.

De Schipper, J., Tavecchio, L., & Van IJzendoorn, M. (2008). Children's attachment relationship with day care caregivers: Associations with positive caregiving and the child's temperament. *Social Development, 17*(3), 454–470.

de St. Aubin, E., McAdams, D., & Kim, T. (2004). *The generative society: Caring for future generations.* Washington, DC: American Psychological Association.

Declercq, E. (2012). Trends in midwife attended births in the United States, 1989–2009. *Journal of Midwifery and Women's Health, 57*(4), 321–326.

Declercq, E., Sakala, C., Corry, M., Applebaum, S., & Herrlich, A. (2013). *Listening to mothers III: Pregnancy and birth.* New York: Childbirth Connection.

Deeg, D. (2005). The development of physical and mental health from late midlife to early old age. In S. Willis & M. Martin (Eds.), *Middle adulthood: A lifespan perspective* (pp. 209–241). Thousand Oaks, CA: Sage.

Degges-White, S. (2005). Understanding gerotranscendence in older adults: A new perspective for counselors. *Adultspan Journal, 4*(1), 36–48.

Degner, J., & Wentura, D. (2010). Automatic prejudice in childhood and early adolescence. *Journal of Personality and Social Psychology, 98*(3), 356–374.

Delany, S., & Delany, E., with Hearth, A. (1993). *Having our say: The Delany sisters' first 100 years.* New York: Kodansha International.

Delany, S., with Hearth, A. (1997). *On my own at 107: Reflections on life without Bessie.* New York: HarperCollins.

Delaunay-El Allam, M., Marlier, L., & Schaal, B. (2006). Learning at the breast: Preference formation for the artificial scent and its attraction against the odor of maternal milk. *Infant Behavior and Development, 29*(3), 308–321.

Della Porta, D., & Diani, M. (2006). *Social movements: An introduction* (2nd ed.). Malden, MA: Blackwell.

DelliFraine, J., Langabeer, J., Williams, J. F., Gong, A. K., Delgavori, R. I., & Gill, S. L. (2011). Cost comparisons of baby-friendly and nonbaby-friendly hospitals in the United States. *Pediatrics, 127*(4), 989–994.

Dellmann-Jenkins, M., & Blankemeyer, M. (2009). Emerging and young adulthood and caregiving. In K. Shifren (Ed.), *How caregiving affects development: Psychological implications for child, adolescent, and adult caregivers* (pp. 93–117). Washington, DC: American Psychological Association.

Deng, J., Lian, Y., Shen, C., Zhang, M., Wang, Y., & Zhou, H. (2012). Adverse life event and risk of cognitive impairment: A 5-year prospective longitudinal study in Chongqing, China. *European Journal of Neurology, 19*(4), 631–637.

Denner, J., & Dunbar, N. (2004). Negotiating femininity: Power and strategies of Mexican American girls. *Sex Roles, 50,* 301–314.

Dennis, C., & Chung-Lee, L. (2006). Postpartum depression help-seeking barriers and maternal treatment preferences: A qualitative systematic review. *Birth, 33*(4), 323–331.

Dennison, B., Edmunds, J., & Stratton, H. (2006). Rapid infant weight gain predicts childhood overweight. *Obesity, 14*(3), 491–499.

Denton, M. L., Pearce, L. D., & Smith, C. (2008). *Religion and spirituality on the path through adolescence* (Research report No. 8). National Study of Youth and Religion, University of North Carolina at Chapel Hill. Retrieved from www.youothandreligion.org/sites/youthandreligion .org/files/imported/publication/docs/w2_pub_report_ final.pdf.

Derauf, C., LaGasse, L., Smith, L., Newman, E., Shah, R., Arria, A., et al. (2011). Infant temperament and high-risk environment relate to behavior problems and language in toddlers. *Journal of Developmental & Behavioral Pediatrics, 32*(2), 125–135.

Derezotes, D., Testa, M., & Poertner, J. (2005). *Race matters in child welfare: The overrepresentation of African American children in the system.* Washington, DC: CWLA Press.

DeSpelder, L. A., & Strickland, A. L. (2005). *The last dance: Encountering death and dying* (7th ed.). Boston: McGraw-Hill.

Destefanis, J., & Firchow, N. (2013). *Developmental milestones: Ages 3 through 5.* Retrieved from http://www .greatschools.org/special-education/health/724-devel opmental-milestones-ages-3-through-5.gs?page=all.

DeVries, C., & De Vries, R. (2007). Childbirth education in the 21st century: An immodest proposal. *Journal of Perinatal Education, 16*(4), 38–48.

Dewey, D., Creighton, D., Heath, J. A., Wilson, B. N., Anseeuw-Deks, D., Crawford, S. G., et al. (2011). Assessment of developmental coordination in children born with extremely low birth weights. *Developmental Neuropsychology, 36*(1), 42–56.

Diamond, L. M., & Savin-Williams, R. C. (2003). Gender and sexual identity. In R. M. Lerner, F. Jacobs, & D. Wertlieb (Eds.), *Handbook of applied developmental science* (Vol. 1, pp. 101–121). Thousand Oaks, CA: Sage.

Dick-Read, G. (1944). *Childbirth without fear: Principles and practices of natural childbirth.* New York: Harper & Row.

Dillon, M., & Wink, P. (2007). *In the course of a lifetime: Tracing religious belief, practice, and change.* Berkeley: University of California Press.

Dilworth-Andersen, P., Brummett, B., Goowdwin, P., Williams, S., Williams, R., & Siegler, I. (2005). Effects of race on cultural justification for caregiving. *Journal of Gerontology: Social Sciences, 60B,* S257–S262.

DiNitto, D. M. (2011). *Social welfare: Politics and public policy.* Boston: Allyn & Bacon.

Dioussé, L., Driver, J., & Gaziano, J. (2009). Relation between modifiable lifestyle factors and lifetime risk of heart failure. *Journal of American Medical Association, 302*(4), 394–400.

Direnfeld, D., & Roberts, J. (2006). Mood congruent memory in dysphoria: The roles of state affect and cognitive style. *Behavior Research and Therapy, 44*(9), 1275–1285.

Dittmann-Kohli, F. (2005). Middle age and identity in a cultural and lifespan perspective. In S. Willis & M. Martin (Eds.), *Middle adulthood: A lifespan perspective* (pp. 319–353). Thousand Oaks, CA: Sage.

Dohetry, I. A., & Stuart, G. S. (2011). Coitus interruptus is not contraception. *Sexually Transmitted Diseases, 38*(4), 356.

Doka, K. J., & Tucci, A. S. (2009). *Living with grief: Diversity and end-of-life care.* Washington, DC: Hospice Foundation of America.

Domenech Rodriguez, M., Donovick, M., & Crowley, S. (2009). Parenting styles in a cultural context: Observations of "protective parenting" in first-generation Latinos. *Family Process, 48*(2), 195–210.

Donleavy, G. (2008). No man's land: Exploring the space between Gilligan and Kohlberg. *Journal of Business Ethics, 80,* 807–822.

Doughty, E. A. (2009). Investigating adaptive grieving styles: A delphi study. *Death Studies, 33,* 462–480.

Downs, S., Moore, E., & McFadden, E. J. (2010). *Child welfare and family services: Policies and practice.* Boston: Pearson.

Draut, T. (2005). *Strapped: Why America's 20- and 30-somethings can't get ahead.* New York: Doubleday.

Draut, T., & Silva, J. (2004).*Generation broke: The growth of debt among young Americans. Borrowing to make ends meet series.* Retrieved from www.aecf.org/upload/publi cations.files/fe3679k542.pdf.

Drehmer, M., Duncan, B. B., Kac, G., & Schmidt, A. I. (2013). Association of second and third trimester weight gain in pregnancy with maternal and fetal outcomes [Special section]. *PLoS One, 8*(1), 1–8.

Duarte, A., Ranganath, C., Trujillo, C., & Knight, R. T. (2006). Intact recollection memory in high-performing older-adults: RP and behavioral evidence. *Journal of Cognitive Neuroscience, 18*(1), 33–47.

DuBois, D., & Silverthorn, N. (2005). Characteristics of natural mentoring relationships and adolescent adjustment: Evidence from a national study. *Journal of Primary Prevention, 26,* 69–92.

Dubrow, N., & Garbarino, J. (1989). Living in the war zone: Mothers and young children in a public housing development. *Child Welfare, 68,* 3–20.

Ducanto, J. N. (2010). Divorce and poverty are often synonymous. *American Journal of Family Law, 24*(2), 87–94.

Dugdale, D. (2012a). Aging changes in the bones—muscles—joints. *MedlinePlus.* U.S. National Library of Medicine. Retrieved from http://nlm.nih.gov/medlineplus/ency/article/004015.htm.

Dugdale, D. (2012b). Aging changes in the male reproductive system. *MedlinePlus.* U.S. National Library of Medicine. Retrieved from http://www.nlm.nih.gov/medlineplus/ency/article/004017.htm.

Dugdale, D. (2012c). Aging changes in the nervous system. *MedlinePlus.* U.S. National Library of Medicine/National Institutes of Health. Retrieved from www.nlm.nih.gov/medlineplus/ency/article/004023.htm.

Dugdale, D. (2012d). Aging changes in the heart and blood vessels. *MedlinePlus.* U.S. National Library of Medicine/National Institutes of Health. Retrieved from http://www.nm.nih.gov/medlineplus/ency/article/004006.htm.

Duke Eye Center. (2009). *Genetic counseling and social work: A multidisciplinary approach to caring for hereditary eye conditions.* Retrieved from http://www.dukehealth.org/eye_center/specialties/genetic_counseling/care_guides/genetic_counseling_and_social_work_a_multidisciplinary_approach_to_caring_for_hereditary_eye_conditions.

Dulin-Keita, A., Hannon, L., III, Fernandez, J. R., & Cockerham, W. C. (2011). The defining moment: Children's conceptualization of race and experiences with racial discrimination. *Ethnic & Racial Studies, 34*(4), 662–682.

Dunbar, H. T., Mueller, C. W., Medina, C., & Wolf, T. (1998). Psychological and spiritual growth in women living with HIV. *Social Work, 43,* 144–154.

Duncan, G. J., & Magnuson, K. (2011, Winter). The long reach of early childhood poverty. *The Stanford Center on Poverty and Inequality Pathways Magazine,* 22–27.

Duncan, G. J., & Murnane, R. J. (2011). *Whither opportunity? Rising inequality, schools, and children's life chances.* New York: Russell Sage Foundation.

Dupre, M. (2008). Educational differences in health risks and illness over the life course: A test of cumulative disadvantage theory. *Social Science Research, 37,* 1253–1266.

Durex Network. (2007). *The face of global sex 2007: First sex: An opportunity of a lifetime.* Retrieved from http://www.durexnetwork.org/SiteCollectionDocuments/Research%20-%Face%20of%20Global%20sex%202007.pdf.

Durex Network. (2010). *The face of global sex 2010: They won't know unless we tell them.* Retrieved from http://www.durexnetwork.org/SiteCollectionDocuments/The%20Face%20of%20Global20%20sex%202010.pdf.

Durkin, K. (1995). *Developmental social psychology.* Malden, MA: Blackwell.

Dyson, A. (2011). Full service and extended schools, disadvantage, and social justice. *Cambridge Journal of Education, 41*(2), 177–193. doi:10.1080/0305764X.2011.572864

Early Intervention Support. (2013). *How children develop.* Retrieved from http://www.earlyinterventionsupport.com/how-children-develop.

Easton, S., Coohey, C., Rhodes, A., & Moorthy, M. (2013). Posttraumatic growth among men with histories of child sexual abuse. *Child Maltreatment, 18*(4), 211–220.

Eaton, D., Kann, L., Kinchen, S., Shanklin, S., Flint, K., Hawkins, J., et al. (2012). Youth risk behavior surveillance—United States 2011. *Morbidity and Mortality Weekly Report (MMWR), 61*(4), 1–168.

Economist Intelligence Unit. (2012). *Starting well: Benchmarking early education across the world.* Retrieved from www.lienfoundaton.org/pdf/publications/sw_report.pdf.

Edin, K., & Lein, L. (1997). *Making ends meet.* New York: Russell Sage Foundation.

Edin, K., & Nelson, T. J. (2013). *Doing the best I can: Fatherhood in the inner city.* Berkeley: University of California Press.

Edmiston, B. (2010). Playing with children, answering with our lives: A Bakhtinian approach to coauthoring ethical identities in early childhood. *British Journal of Educational Studies, 58*(2), 197–211.

Edwards, C. (1992). Normal development in the preschool years. In E. V. Nuttall, I. Romero, & J. Kalesnik (Eds.), *Assessing and screening preschoolers* (pp. 9–22). Boston: Allyn & Bacon.

Edwards, E., Eiden, R., & Leonard, K. (2006). Behavior problems in 18–36-month-old children of alcoholic fathers: Secure mother-father attachment as a protective factor. *Developmental and Psychopathology, 18*(2), 395–407.

Eggebeen, D., & Sturgeon, S. (2006). Demography of the baby boomers. In S. Whitbourne & S. Willis (Eds.), *The baby boomers grow up: Contemporary perspectives on midlife* (pp. 3–21). Mahwah, NJ: Lawrence Erlbaum.

Egley, A., Jr., & Howell, J. C. (2013, September). *Highlights of the 2011 National Youth Gang Survey.* Washington, DC: U.S. Department of Justice, Office of Justice Programs,

Office of Juvenile Justice and Delinquency Prevention. Retrieved from http://www.ojjdp.gov/pubs/242884.pdf.

Ehlman, K., & Ligon, M. (2012). The application of a generativity model for older adults. *International Journal of Aging and Human Development, 74*(4), 331–344.

Ehrenberg-Buchner, S., Sandadi, S., Moawad, N. S., Pinkerton, J. S., & Hurd, W. W. (2009). Ectopic pregnancy: Role of laparoscopic treatment. *Clinical Obstetrics & Gynecology, 52*(3), 372–379.

Eidelman, A., & Schanler, R. (2012). Breastfeeding and the use of human milk. *Pediatrics, 129*(5), 827–841.

Eisenberg, N. (2000). Emotion, regulation, and moral development. *Annual Review of Psychology, 51,* 665–697.

Eisenberg, N., Guthrie, I., Murphy, B., Shepard, S., Cumberland, A., & Carlo, G. (1999). Consistency and development of prosocial dispositions: A longitudinal study. *Child Development, 70,* 1360–1372.

Eisenhauer, E., Uddin, D., Albert, P., Paton, S., & Stoughton, R. (2011). Establishment of a low birth weight registry and initial outcomes. *Maternal and Child Health Journal, 15*(7), 921–930.

Elder, G., & Giele, J. (2009). Life course studies: An evolving field. In G. Edler & J. Giele (Eds.), *The craft of life course research* (pp. 1–24). New York: Guilford.

Elder, G., Jr. (1974). *Children of the Great Depression.* Chicago: University of Chicago Press.

Elder, G., Jr. (1994). Time, human agency, and social change: Perspectives on the life course. *Social Psychology Quarterly, 57*(1), 4–15.

Elder, G., Jr. (1998). The life course as developmental theory. *Child Development, 69*(1), 1–12.

Eliopoulus, C. (2010). *Gerontological nursing* (7th ed.). Philadelphia: Lippincott, Williams & Wilkins.

Elliott, M. (1996). Impact of work, family, and welfare receipt on women's self-esteem in young adulthood. *Social Psychology Quarterly, 59*(1), 80–95.

Ellison, C. G. (1992). Are religious people nice? Evidence from a national survey of Black Americans. *Social Forces, 71*(2), 411–430.

Ellison, C. G. (1993). Religious involvement and self-perception among Black Americans. *Social Forces, 71*(4), 1027–1055.

Emergency Contraception Website. (2013). *Plan B.* Retrieved from http://ec.princeton.edu/pills/plan-b.html.

Emery, R. (1999). *Marriage, divorce, and children's adjustment* (2nd ed.). Thousand Oaks, CA: Sage.

Emmett, T., & Alant, E. (2006). Women and disability: Exploring the interface of multiple disadvantage. *Development of Southern Africa, 23*(4), 455–460.

Engel, S. (2005). *Real kids: Creating meaning in everyday life.* Cambridge, MA: Harvard University Press.

Engels, R., & Knibbe, R. (2000). Alcohol use and intimate relationships in adolescence: When love comes to town. *Addictive Behavior, 25,* 435–439.

Englander, E. K. (2013). *Bullying and cyberbullying: What every educator needs to know.* Cambridge, MA: Harvard University Press.

Entmacher, J., Robbins, K., Vogtman, J., & Fohlich, L. (2013). *Insecure & unequal: Poverty and income among women and families 2000–2012.* Washington, DC: National Women's Law Center. Retrieved from http://www.nwlc.org/sites/default/files/pdfs/fina_2013_nwlc_poverty report.pdf.

Entwisle, D., Alexander, K., & Olson, L. (2005). Urban teenagers: Work and dropout. *Youth and Society, 37,* 3–32.

Epstein, S. (1973). The self-concept revisited: Or, a theory of a theory. *American Psychologist, 28,* 404–416.

Epstein, S. (1991). Cognitive-experiential self-theory: An integrative theory of personality. In R. Cutis (Ed.), *The self with others: Convergences in psychoanalytic, social, and personality psychology* (pp. 111–137). New York: Guilford.

Epstein, S. (1998). Cognitive-experiential self-theory. In D. Barone & M. Hersen (Eds.), *Advanced personality* (pp. 211–238). New York: Plenum Press.

Erickson, K., Gildengers, A., & Butters, M. (2013). Physical activity and brain plasticity in late adulthood. *Dialogues in Clinical Neuroscience, 15*(1), 99–108.

Erikson, E. H. (1950). *Childhood and society.* New York: Norton.

Erikson, E. H. (1959). The problem of ego identity. *Psychological Issues, 1,* 101–164.

Erikson, E. H. (1963). *Childhood and society* (2nd ed.). New York: Norton.

Erikson, E. H. (1968). *Identity: Youth and crisis.* New York: Norton.

Erikson, E. H. (Ed.). (1978). *Adulthood.* New York: Norton.

Erikson, E. H. (1982). *The life cycle completed.* New York: Norton.

Erikson, E. H., & Erikson, J. M. (1997). *The life cycle completed: Extended version with new chapters on the ninth stage of development.* New York: W. W. Norton.

Eskelinen, M., Ngandu, T., Tuomilehto, J., Soininen, H., & Kivipelto, M. (2009). Midlife coffe and tea drinking and the risk of late-life dementia: A population-based CAIDE study. *Journal of Alzheimer's Disease, 16,* 85–91.

Espelage, D. L., & Swearer, S. M. (2011). *Bullying in North American schools.* New York: Routledge.

Esposito-Smythers, C., Kahler, C., Spirito, A., Hunt, J., & Monti, P. (2011). Treatment of co-occuring substance abuse and suicidality among adolescents: A randomized trial. *Journal of Consulting and Clinical Psychology, 79*(6), 728–739.

Etengoff, C., & Daiute, C. (2013). Sunni-Muslim American religious development during emerging adulthood. *Journal of Adolescent Research, 28*(6), 690–714.

Evandrou, M., Glaser, K., & Henz, U. (2002). Multiple role occupancy in midlife: Balancing working and family life in Britain. *The Gerontologist, 42*(6), 781–789.

Evans, B., Crogan, N., Belyea, M., & Coon, D. (2009). Utility of the life course perspective in research with Mexican American caregivers of older adults. *Journal of Transcultural Nursing, 20*(1), 5–14.

Exner-Cortens, D., Eckenrode, J., & Rothman, E. (2013). Longitudinal associations between teen dating violence victimization and adverse health outcomes. *Pediatrics, 131*(1), 71–78.

Fabelo, T., Thompson, M. D., Plotkin, M., Carmichael, D., Marchbanks, M. P., & Booth, E. A. (2011). *Breaking Schools' rules: A statewide study of how school discipline relates to students' success and juvenile justice involvement.* New York: Council of State Governments Justice Center. Retrieved from http://csgjusticecenter.org/wpcontent/uploads/2012/08/Breaking_Schools_Rules_Report_Final.pdf.

Falicov, C. (2005). The Latino family life cycle. In B. Carter & M. McGoldrick (Eds.), *The expanded family life cycle: Individual, family, and social perspectives* (3rd ed., pp. 141–152). Boston: Allyn & Bacon.

Falicov, C. (2011). Migration and the life cycle. In M. McGoldrick, B. Carter, & N. Garcia-Preto (Eds.), *The expanded family life cycle: Individual, family, and social perspectives* (4th ed., pp. 336–347). Boston: Allyn & Bacon.

Faloon, W. (2008). Extreme life extension. *Life Extension, 14*(2), 9–18.

Faloon, W. (2009). Protection against arterial calcification, bone loss, cancer and aging. *Life Extension, 15*(1), 62–75.

Fan, F., Zou, Y., Ma, A., Yue, Y., Mao, W., & Ma, X. (2009). Hormonal changes and somatopsychologic manifestations in the first trimester of pregnancy and post partum. *International Journal of Gynecology and Obstetrics, 105*(1), 46–49.

Fan, W., Williams, C. M., & Wolters, C. A. (2012). Parental involvement in predicting school motivation: Similar and differential effects across ethnic groups. *Journal of Educational Research, 105*(1), 21–35.

Fang, S., Huang, N., Chen, K., Yeh, H., Lin, K., & Chen, C. (2012). Gender differences in widowhood effects among community-dwelling elders by causes of death in Taiwan. *Annals of Epidemiology, 22*(7), 457–465.

Farmer, R. (2009). *Neuroscience and social work practice: The missing link.* Thousand Oaks, CA: Sage.

Farroni, T., Menon, E., Rigato, S., & Johnson, M. H. (2007). The perception of facial expressions in newborns. *European Journal of Developmental Psychology, 4*(1), 2–13.

Farver, J., Xu, Y., Eppe, S., Fernandez, A., & Schwartz, D. (2005). Community violence, family conflict and preschoolers' socioemotional functioning. *Developmental Psychology, 41*(1), 160–170.

Fass, P., & Mason, M. (Eds.). (2000). *Childhood in America.* New York: New York University Press.

Fawley-King, K., & Merz, E. (2014). Effects of child maltreatment on brain development. In H. Matto, J. Strolin-Goltzman, & M. Ballan (Eds.), *Neuroscience for social work: Current research and practice* (pp. 111–139). New York: Springer.

Federal Bureau of Investigation. (2011). *Crime in the United States 2010.* Uniform Crime Reports. Washington, DC: U.S. Department of Justice. Retrieved from www.fbi.gov/about-us/cjis/ucr/crime-in-the-u.s/2010/crime-in-the-u.s.-2010/index-page.

Federal Interagency Forum on Aging-Related Statistics. (2008). *Older Americans 2008: Key indicators of well-being: Health status.* Retrieved from http://www.agingstats.gov/agingstatsdotnet/Main_Site/Data/2008_Documents/OA_2008.pdf.

Federal Interagency Forum on Aging-Related Statistics. (2012). *Older Americans 2012: Key indicators of well-being: Health status.* Retrieved from www.agingstats.govMain_Site/Data/2012_Documents/Health_Status.Aspx.

Federal Interagency Forum on Child and Family Statistics. (2013). *America's children: Key national indicators of well-being.* Washington, DC: U.S. Government Printing Office. Retrieved from http://www.childstats.gov/pdf/ac2013/ac_13.pdf.

Feldman, R. (2004). Mother infant skin-to-skin contact and the development of emotion regulation. In S. Shohov (Ed.), *Advances in psychology research* (Vol. 27, pp. 113–131). Hauppauge, NY: Nova Science.

Feldman, R., & Masalha, S. (2007). The role of culture in moderating the links between early ecological risk and young children's adaptation. *Development & Psychopathology, 19*, 1–21.

Felitti, V., Anda, R., Nordenburg, D., Williamson, D., Spitz, A., Edwards, V., et al. (1998). Relationship of childhood abuse and household dysfunction to many of the leading causes of death in adults: The Adverse Childhood Experiences (ACE) Study. *American Journal of Preventive Medicine, 14*(4), 245–258.

Fergusson, D. M., Horwood, L. J., & Boden, J. (2009). Reactions to abortion and subsequent mental health. *The British Journal of Psychiatry, 195*, 420–426.

Fergusson, D. M., Horwood, L. J., & Woodward, L. J. (2001). Unemployment and psychosocial adjustment in young adults: Causation or selection? *Social Science & Medicine, 53*(3), 305.

Ferraro, K., & Shippee, T. (2009). Aging and cumulative inequality: How does inequality get under the skin? *The Gerontologist, 49*(3), 333–343.

Ferri, C., Prince, M., Brayne, C., Brodaty, H., Fratiglioni, L., Ganguli, M., et al. (2005). Global prevalence of dementia: A Delphi consensus study. *The Lancet, 366*, 2112–2117.

Figueiredo, B., & Conde, A. (2011). Anxiety and depression in women and men from early pregnancy to 3-months postpartum. *Archives of Women's Mental Health, (14)*3, 247–255.

Figueiredo, B., Pacheco, A., Costa, R., Conde, A., & Teixeira, C. (2010). Mother's anxiety and depression during the third pregnancy trimester and neonate's mother versus stranger's face/voice visual preference. *Early Human Development, 86,* 479–485.

Fiksenbaum, L. M., Greenglass, E. R., & Eaton, J. (2006). Perceived social support, hassles, and coping among the elderly. *Journal of Applied Gerontology, 25*(1), 17–30.

Findlay, L., Girardi, A., & Coplan, R. (2006). Links between empathy, social behavior, and social understanding in early childhood. *Early Childhood Research Quarterly, 21*(3), 347–359.

Fine, M., Ganong, L., & Demo, D. (2010). Divorce: A risk and resilience perspective. In S. Price, C. Price, & P. McKenry (Eds.), *Families & change: Coping with stressful events and transitions* (4th ed., pp. 211–233). Thousand Oaks, CA: Sage.

Fingerman, K., Cheng, Y. P., Wesselmann, E., Zarit, S., Furstenberg, F., & Birditt, K. (2013). Helicopter parents and landing pad kids: Intense parental support of grown children. *Journal of Marriage and Family, 74,* 880–896.

Fingerman, K., Pillemer, K., Silverstein, M., & Suitor, J. (2012). The baby boomers' intergenerational relationships. *The Gerontologist, 52*(2), 199–209.

Fingerman, K., VanderDrift, L., Dotterer, A., Birditt, D., & Zarit, S. (2011). Support to aging parents and grown children in Black and White families. *The Gerontologist, 51*(4), 441–452.

Finkelhor, D., Turner, H., Hamby, S., & Ormrod, R. (2011, October). Polyvictimization: Children's exposure to multiple types of violence, crime and abuse. *Juvenile Justice Bulletin.* Retrieved from https://www.ncjrs.gov/pdffiles1/ojjdp/235504.pdf.

Finkelhor, D., Turner, H., Ormrod, R., Hamby, S., & Kracke, K. (2009, October). Children's exposure to violence: A comprehensive national survey. *Juvenile Justice Bulletin.* Retrieved from https://www.ncjrs.gov/pdffiles1/ojjdp/227744.pdf.

Finn, J. (2009). Making trouble. In L. Nybell, J. Shook, & J. Finn (Eds.), *Childhood, youth, & social work in transformation: Implications for policy & practice* (pp. 37–66). New York: Columbia University Press.

Fiori, J. L., Consedine, N. S., & Magai, C. (2008). Ethnic differences in patterns of social exchange among older adults: The role of resource context. *Ageing & Society, 28,* 495–524.

First Ladies Community Initiative. (2013). *Birth shelter.* Retrieved from www.1stladies.org/programs/birthing-shelter.

Fisher, C., Hauck, Y., Bayes, S., & Byme, J. (2012). Participants experience of mindfulness-based childbirth education: A qualitative study. *British Medical Journal, 12*(1), 126–135.

Fisher, H. (2004). *Why we love: The nature and chemistry of romantic love.* New York: Holt.

Fitchett, G., Murphy, P., Kravitz, H., Everson-Rose, S., Krause, N., & Powell, L. (2007). Racial/ethnic differences in religious involvement in a multi-ethnic cohort of midlife women. *Journal for the Scientific Study of Religion, 46*(1), 119–132.

Fitzpatrick, K. M., & Boldizar, J. P. (1993). The prevalence and consequences of exposure to violence among African American youth. *Journal of the American Academy of Child and Adolescent Psychiatry, 56,* 22–34.

Fjerstad, M., Truissell, J., Sivin, I., Lichtenberg, S., & Cullins, V. (2009). Rates of serious infection after changes in regimens for medical abortion. *New England Journal of Medicine, 361*(2), 145–151.

Flanagan, C. (2004). Institutional support for morality: Community-based and neighborhood organizations. In T. A. Thorkildsen & H. Walberg (Eds.), *Nurturing morality* (pp. 173–183). New York: Kluwer Academic/Plenum.

Flatt, M., Settersten, R., Ponsaran, R., & Fishman, J. (2013). Are "anti-aging medicine" and "successful aging" two sides of the same coin? Views of anti-aging practitioners. *The Journals of Gerontology, Series B: Psychological Sciences and Social Sciences, 68*(6), 944–955.

Foa, E. B., Keane, T. M., Friedman, M. J., & Cohen, J. A. (2010). *Effective treatments for PTSD: Practice guidelines from the international society for traumatic stress studies.* New York: Guilford.

Fogarty, R. (2009). *Brain compatible classrooms* (3rd ed.). Thousand Oaks, CA: Corwin.

Foley, M. (2011). A comparison of family adversity and family dysfunction in families of children with attention deficit hyperactivity disorder (ADHD) and families of children without ADHD. *Journal for Specialists in Pediatric Nursing, 16*(1), 39–49. doi:10.1111/j.1744-6155.2010.00269.x

Foner, A. (1995). Social stratification. In G. L. Maddox (Ed.), *The encyclopedia of aging: A comprehensive resource in gerontology and geriatrics* (2nd ed., pp. 887–890). New York: Springer.

Fowler, J. (1981). *Stages of faith: The psychology of human development and the quest for meaning.* San Francisco: Harper.

Fraas, M., & Bellerose, A. (2010). Mentoring programme for adolescent survivors of acquired brain injury. *Brain Injury, 24*(1), 50–61.

Frankenberg, E., & Debray, E. H. (2011). *Integrating schools in a changing society: New policies and legal options for a* multiracial generation. Chapel Hill: University of North Carolina Press.

Franko, D. L., & Striegel-Moore, R. H. (2002). The role of body dissatisfaction as a risk factor for depression in adolescent girls: Are the differences Black and White? *Journal of Psychosomatic Research, 53,* 975–983.

Franko, D. L., Striegel-Moore, R. H., Thompson, D., Schreiber, G. B., & Daniels, S. R. (2005). Does adolescent depression predict obesity in black and white young adult women? *Psychological Medicine, 35,* 1505–1513.

Fraser, M., Kirby, L., & Smokowski, P. (2004). Risk and resilience in childhood. In M. Fraser (Ed.), *Risk and resilience in childhood: An ecological perspective* (2nd ed., pp. 13–66). Washington, DC: NASW Press.

Freeman, L., Shaffer, D., & Smith, H. (1996). Neglected victims of homicide: The needs of young siblings of murder victims. *American Journal of Orthopsychiatry, 66,* 337–345.

French, S., Seidman, E., Allen, L., & Aber, J. (2006). The development of ethnic identity during adolescence. *Developmental Psychology, 42,* 1–10.

Freud, S. (1905/1953). Three essays on the theory of sexuality. In J. Strachey (Ed. & Trans.), *The standard edition of the complete works of Sigmund Freud* (Vol. 7, pp. 135–245). London: Hogarth.

Freud, S. (1917/1957). Mourning and melancholia. In J. Strachey (Ed. & Trans.), *The standard edition of the complete psychological works of Sigmund Freud* (Vol. 14, pp. 237–258). London: Hogarth.

Freud, S. (1927). Some psychological consequences of the anatomical distinction between the sexes. *International Journal of Psycho-analysis, 8,* 133–142.

Freund, A. M., & Riediger, M. (2006). Goals as building blocks of personality and development in adulthood. In D. K. Mroczek & T. Little (Eds.), *Handbook of personality development* (pp. 353–372). Mahwah, NJ: Lawrence Erlbaum.

Freundl, G., Sivin, I., & Batár, I. (2010). State of the art of nonhormonal methods of contraception: IV. Natural family planning. *European Journal of Contraceptive and Reproductive Health Care, 15*(2), 113–123.

Friedman, S. H., & Boyle, D. E. (2008). Attachment in US children experiencing nonmaternal care in the early 1990s. *Attachment & Human Development, 10*(3), 225–261.

Friedman, S. H., Kessler, A. R., & Martin, R. (2009). Psychiatric help for caregivers of infants in neonatal intensive care. *Psychiatric Services, 60*(4), 554.

Friedmann, E., & Havighurst, R. (1954). *The meaning of work and retirement.* Chicago: University of Chicago Press.

Frisvold, M., Lindquist, R., & McAlpine, C. (2012). Living life in the balance at midlife: Lessons learned from mindfulness. *Western Journal of Nursing Research, 34*(2), 265–278.

Frith, L., & Blyth, E. (2013). They can't have my embryo: The ethics of conditional embryo donation. *Bioethics, 27*(6), 317–324.

Fry, R. (2012). *A rising share of young adults live in their parents' home.* Pew Social Trends. Retrieved from http://www.pewsocialtrends.org/2013/08/01/a-rising-share-of-young-aduls-live-in-their-parents-home.

Fulmer, R. (2011). Becoming an adult: Finding ways to love and work. In M. McGoldrick, B. Carter, & N. Garcia-Preto (Eds.), *The expanded family life cycle: Individual, family, and social perspectives* (4th ed., pp. 176–192). Boston: Allyn & Bacon.

Gable, I., Gostin, L., & Hodge, J. (2008). HIV/AIDS, reproductive and sexual health, and the law. *American Journal of Public Health, 98*(10), 1779–1786.

Galambos, N., & Kotylak, L. (2012). Transformations in parent-child relationships from adolescence to adulthood. In B. Laursen & W. A. Collins (Eds.), *Relationship pathways from adolescence to young adulthood* (pp. 23–42). Los Angeles: Sage.

Galinsky, E., & Bond, J. T. (2009). *The impact of the recession on employers.* New York: Families and Work Institute. Retrieved from http://www.familiesandwork.org/downloads/ImpactoftheRecession.pdf.

Gallup, G., Jr., & Lindsay, D. M. (1999). *Surveying the religious landscape: Trends in U.S. beliefs.* Harrisburg, PA: Morehouse.

Gallup.com. (2013). *Abortion. Gallop historical trends.* Retrieved from http://www.gallup.com/poll/1576/abortion.aspx.

Garbarino, J. (1995). *Raising children in a socially toxic environment.* San Francisco: Jossey-Bass.

Garbarino, J. (2007). *See Jane hit: Why girls are growing more violent and what we can do about it.* New York: Penguin Books.

Garcia, B. (2011). Cultural competence with Latino Americans. In D. Lum (Ed.), *Culturally competent practice* (4th ed., pp. 302–332). Belmont, CA: Brooks/Cole.

Garcia, D., & Siddiqui, A. (2009). Adolescents' psychological well-being and memory for life events: Influences on life satisfaction with respect of temperamental dispositions. *Journal of Happiness Studies, 10*(4), 407–419.

Garcia, E. (2001). Parenting in Mexican American families. In N. Boyd Webb (Ed.), *Culturally diverse parent-child and family relationships: A guide for social workers and other practitioners* (pp. 157–179). New York: Columbia University Press.

Garcia-Preto, N. (2011). Transformation of the family system during adolescence. In M. McGoldrick, B. Carter, & N. Garcia-Preto (Eds.), *The expanded family life cycle: Individual, family, and social perspectives* (4th ed., pp. 232–246). Boston: Allyn & Bacon.

Gardiner, H., & Kosmitzki, C. (2011). *Lives across cultures: Cross-cultural human development* (5th ed.). Boston: Allyn & Bacon.

Gardner, H. (1993). *Multiple intelligences: The theory in practice.* New York: Basic Books.

Gareis, K., Barnett, R., Ertel, K., & Berkman, L. (2009). Work-family enrichment and conflict: Additive effects, buffering, or balance? *Journal of Marriage and the Family, 71,* 696–707.

Gargiulo, R. M., & Kilgo, J. L. (2011). *An introduction to young children with special needs: Birth through age 8.* Belmont, CA: Wadsworth/Cengage Learning.

Garralda, M. E., & Raynaud, J.-P. (2010). *Increasing awareness of child and adolescent mental health.* Lanham, MD: Jason Aronson.

Garrett, B. (2009). *Brain & behavior: An introduction to biological psychology* (2nd ed.). Thousand Oaks, CA: Sage.

Garrett, M. W. (1995). Between two worlds: Cultural discontinuity in the dropout of Native American youth. *The School Counselor, 10,* 199–208.

Gartstein, M., Gonzales, C., Carranza, J., Adaho, S., Rothbart, M., & Yang, S. (2006). Studying cross-cultural differences in the development of infant temperament: People's Republic of China, the United States of America, and Spain. *Child Psychiatry and Human Development, 37,* 145–161.

Gartstein, M., Knyazev, G., & Slobodskaya, H. (2005). Cross-cultural differences in the structure of temperament: United States of America (U.S.) and Russia. *Infant Behavior and Development, 28,* 54–61.

Gartstein, M., Peleg, Y., Young, B., & Slobodskaya, H. (2009). Infant temperament in Russia, United States of America, and Israel: Differences and similarities between Russian-speaking families. *Child Psychiatry and Human Development, 40,* 241–256.

Garvey, C. (1984). *Children's talk.* Cambridge, MA: Harvard University Press.

Garvin, V., Kalter, N., & Hansell, J. (1993). Divorced women: Factors contributing to resiliency and vulnerability. *Journal of Divorce and Remarriage, 21*(1/2), 21–39.

Gassman-Pines, A. (2013). Daily spillover of low-income mothers' perceived workload to mood and mother-child interactions. *Journal of Marriage and Family, 75,* 1304–1318.

Gawande, S., Vaidya, M., Tadke, R., Kirpekar, V., & Bhave, S. (2011). Progressive muscle relaxation in hyperemesis gravidarum. *Journal of South Asia Federation of Obstetrics and Gynecology, 3*(1), 28–32.

Geary, S., & Moon, Y. S. (2006). The human embryo in vitro: Recent progress. *Journal of Reproductive Medicine, 51*(4), 293–302.

Gee, J. P. (2012). *Social linguistics and literacies: Ideology in discourse* (4th ed.). New York: Routledge.

Gehlbach, H. (2006). How changes in students' goal orientations relate to outcomes in social studies. *Journal of Education Research, 99,* 358–370.

Geiger, B. (1996). *Fathers as primary caregivers.* Westport, CT: Greenwood.

Gelles, R. (2010). Violence, abuse, and neglect in families and intimate relationships. In S. Price, C. Price, & P. McKenry (Eds.), *Families & change: Coping with stressful events and transitions* (4th ed., pp. 119–139). Thousand Oaks, CA: Sage.

Generations. (2001, Summer), *25*(2).

Genetics Home Reference. (2013). *Genetic disorders A to Z.* Retrieved from http://ghr.nlm.nih.gov.

George, L. K. (2005). Socioeconomic status and health across the life course: Progress and prospects. *The Journals of Gerontology, Series B: Psychological Sciences and Social Sciences, 60B,* 135–139.

George, L. K. (2009). Conceptualizing and measuring trajectories. In G. Elder Jr. & J. Giele (Eds.), *The craft of life course resource* (pp. 163–186). New York: Guilford.

George, L. K., Larson, D. B., Koenig, H. G., & McCullough, M. E. (2000). Spirituality and health: What we know, what we need to know. *Journal of Social & Clinical Psychology, 19,* 102–116.

Georgiades, S. D. (2005). Emancipated young adults' perspectives on independent living programs. *Families in Society, 86*(4), 503–510.

Gerhardt, S. (2004). *Why love matters: How affection shapes a baby's brain.* New York: Brunner-Routledge.

Geronimus, A. T., Hicken, M., Keene, D., & Bound, J. (2006). "Weathering" and age patterns of allostatic load scores among blacks and whites in the United States. *American Journal of Public Health, 96,* 826–833.

Gerontology Research Group. (2013). *Current validated living supercentenarians.* Retrieved from http://www.grg.org/Adams/E.HTM.

Gerouki, M. (2010). The boy who was drawing princesses: Primary teachers' accounts of children's non-conforming behaviours. *Sex Education, 10*(4), 335–348. doi:10.1080/14681811.2010.51.5092

Gewirtz, A. H., Erbes, C. R., Polusny, M. A., Forgatch, M. S., & DeGarmo, D. S. (2011). Helping military families through the deployment process: Strategies to support parenting. *Professional Psychology: Research and Practice, 42,* 56–62.

Ghazi, S., Shahzada, G., Gilani, U., Shabbir, M., & Rashid, M. (2011). Relationship between students' self perceived multiple intelligences and their academic achievement. *International Journal of Academic Research, 3*(2), 619–623.

Giancoli, A. (2012, November 28). Protein key to preventing age-related muscle loss. *Chicago Tribune.* Retrieved from http://articles.chicagotribune.com/2012-11-28/features/sns-2012111281830-tms-foodstylts-v-f2021128-20121128_1_muscle-loss-protein-declines.

Gielen, U., & Markoulis, D. (2001). Preference for principled moral reasoning: A developmental and cross-cultural perspective. In L. Adler & U. Gielen (Eds.), *Cross-cultural topics in psychology* (2nd ed., pp. 81–101). Westport, CT: Praeger/Greenwood.

Gilchrist, J. (2012). Trends in child injury deaths United States, 2000–2009. *Morbidity and Mortality Weekly Report*. Retrieved from http://www.cdc.gov/stltpubli chealth/townhall/presentations/2012/04_2012_Child_ Injury.pdf.

Gilligan, C. (1982). *In a different voice: Psychological theory and women's development*. Cambridge, MA: Harvard University Press.

Gilman, S. (2012). The successes and challenges of life course epidemiology: A commentary on Gibb, Fergusson and Horwood. *Social Science & Medicine, 75*, 2124–2128.

Ginath, S., Lerman-Sagle, T., Haratz Krajden, K., Lev, D., Cohen-Sacher, B., Bar, J., et al. (2013). The fetal vermis, pons and brainstem: Normal longitudinal development as shown by dedicated neurosonography. *Journal of Maternal-Fetal and Neonatal Medicine, 26*(8), 757–762.

Glascoe, F. (2005). Screening for developmental and behavioral problems. *Mental Retardation and Developmental Disabilities Research Reviews, 11*(3), 173–179.

Glaser, D. (2000). Child abuse and neglect and the brain—A review. *Journal of Child Psychology and Psychiatry, 41*(1), 97–116.

Global Issues. (2013). *Poverty facts and stats*. Retrieved from http://www.globalissues.org/article/26/poverty-facts-and-stats.

Glover, J., Galliher, R., & Lamere, T. (2009). Identity development and exploration among sexual minority adolescents: Examination of a multidimensional model. *Journal of Homosexuality, 56*, 77–101.

Glover, R. (1996). Religiosity in adolescence and young adulthood: Implications for identity formation. *Psychological Reports, 78*, 427–431.

Goberna, J., Francés, L., Paulí, A., Barluenga, A., & Gascón, E. (2009). Sexual experiences during the climacteric years: What do women think about it? *Maturitas, 62*, 47–52.

Go Forth and Multiply a Lot Less. (2009, October 29). *The Economist*. Retrieved from http://www.economist.com/ node/14743589.

Goldberg, W., Clarke-Stewart, K., Rice, J., & Dellis, E. (2002). Emotional energy as an explanatory construct for fathers' engagement with their infants. *Parenting: Science & Practice, 2*, 379–408.

Goldenring, J. (2011). *Infant reflexes*. MedlinePlus medical encyclopedia. Retrieved from http://www.nlm.nih.gov/ medlineplus/ency/article/oo3292.htm.

Goldstein, A., & Somashkehar, S. (2014, January 13). Health-insurance sign-ups by young adults are off pace seen as key to new law's success. *Washington Post*. Retrieved from www.washingtonpost.com/national/ heal-science/young-adults-make-up-almost-one-quar ter-of-aca-signups/2014/01/13/ed5846d0-7c73-11e3cl-0e888170b723_story_html?wprss=rss_health_science.

Goldstein, J., & Kenney, C. (2001). Marriage delayed or marriage forgone? New cohort forecasts of first marriage for U.S. women. *American Sociological Review, 66*(4), 506–519.

Goldstein, S., & Brooks, R. B. (2013). *Handbook of resilience in children*. New York: Springer.

Goleman, D. (2006). *Social intelligence: The new science of human relationships*. New York: Bantam.

Gong, F., Xu, J., Fujishiro, K., & Takeuchi, D. (2011). A life course perspective on migration and mental health among Asian immigrants: The role of human agency. *Social Science & Medicine, 73*, 1618–1626.

Good, M., Willoughby, T., & Busseri, M. (2011). Stability and change in adolescent spirituality/religiosity: A person-centered approach. *Developmental Psychology, 47*(2), 538–550.

Goodfellow, A. (2012). Looking through the learning disability lens: Inclusive education and the learning disability embodiment. *Children's Geographies, 10*(1), 67–81. doi:1 0.1080/14733285.2011.638179

Goodman, S., & Brand, S. (2009). Infants of depressed mothers: Vulnerabilities, risk factors, and protective factors for the later development of psychopathology. In C. H. Zeanah, Jr. (Ed.), *Handbook of infant mental health* (3rd ed., pp. 153–170). New York: Guilford Press.

Gopaul-McNicol, S. (1988). Racial identification and racial preference of Black preschool children in New York and Trinidad. *Journal of Black Psychology, 14*(2), 65–68.

Gordon, J. D., DiMattina, M., Reh, A., Botes, A., Celia, G., & Payson, M. (2013). Utilization and success rates of unstimulated in vitro fertilization in the United States: An analysis of the society for reproductive technology database. *Fertility and Sterility, 100*(2), 392–395.

Gordon, L., & Shaffer, S. (2004). *Mom, can I move back in with you? A survival guide for parents of twentysomethings*. New York: Tarcher.

Gordon, T. A. (2013). Good grief: Exploring the dimensionality of grief experiences and social work support. *Journal of Social Work in End-of-Life & Palliative Care, 9*, 27–42.

Gottman, J. M. (1994, May/June). Why marriages fail. *Family Therapy Networker*, 41–48.

Govande, V. P., Brase, K. J., Das, U. G., Koop, J. I., Lagatta, J., & Basir, M. A. (2013). Prenatal counseling beyond the threshold of viability. *Journal of Perinatology, 33*(5), 358–362.

Gowen, K., Deschaine, M., Gruttadara, D., & Markey, D. (2012). Young adults with mental health conditions and social networking websites: Seeking tools to build community. *Psychiatric Rehabilitation Journal, 35*(3), 245–250.

Grandin, T., & Panek, R. (2013). *The autistic brain: Thinking across the spectrum*. Boston: Houghton Mifflin Harcourt.

Granger, A. (2013, April 26). What the Affordable Care Act says about fertility and pregnancy. *ConceiveEasy*. Retrieved from http://www.conceiveeasy.com/get-preg nant/what-the-affordable-care-act-says-about-fertility-and-pregnancy.

Grant, B. F., Dawson, D. A., Stinson, F. S., Chou, S. P., Dufour, M. C., & Pickering, R. P. (2004). The 12-month prevalence and trends in DSM-IV alcohol abuse and dependence: United States, 1991–1992 and 2001–2002. *Drug and Alcohol Dependence, 74,* 223–234.

Greenberg, J. (2010). Assessing policy effects on enrollment in early childhood education and care. *Social Service Review, 84*(3), 461–490.

Greene, S., Anderson, E., Forgatch, M., DeGarmo, D., & Hetherington, E. M. (2012). Risk and resilience after divorce. In F. Walsh (Ed.), *Normal family processes* (4th ed., pp. 102–127). New York: Guilford.

Greenfield, E., & Marks, N. (2006). Linked lives: Adult children's problems and their parents' psychological and relational well-being. *Journal of Marriage and Family, 68,* 442–454.

Greenspan, S. (2006). Rethinking "harmonious parenting" using a three-factor discipline model. *Child Care in Practice, 12*(1), 5–12.

Gregory, S. T. (2000). *The academic achievement of minority students: Perspectives, practices, and prescriptions.* Lanham, MD: University Press of America.

Greil, A. L., McQuillan, J., Lowry, M., & Shreffler, K. M. (2011). Infertility treatment and fertility-specific distress: A longitudinal analysis of a population-based sample of U.S. women. *Social Science and Medicine, 73*(1), 87–94.

Greil, A. L., McQuillan, J., Shreffler, K. M., Johnson, K. M., & Slauson-Blevins, K. S. (2011). Race-ethnicity and medical services for infertility: Stratified reproduction in a population-based sample of U.S. women. *Journal of Health and Social Behavior, 52*(4), 493–509.

Grenier, S., Potvin, O., Hudon, C., Boyer, R., Préville, M., & Desjardins, L. (2012). Twelve-month prevalence and correlates of subthreshold and threshold anxiety in community-dwelling older adults with cardiovascular diseases. *Journal of Affective Disorders, 136,* 724–732.

Greve, W., & Staudinger, U. M. (2006). Resilience in later adulthood and old age: Resources and potentials for successful aging. In D. Cicchetti & D. J. Cohen (Eds.), *Developmental psychopathology: Risk, disorder and adaptation* (Vol. 3, pp. 796–840). Hoboken, NJ: John Wiley & Sons.

Grogan-Kaylor, A., & Otis, M. (2007). Predictors of parental use of corporal punishment. *Family Relations, 56,* 80–91.

Gromley, W., Gayer, T., Phillips, D., & Dawson, B. (2005). The effects of universal pre-K on cognitive development. *Developmental Psychology, 41*(6), 872–884.

Grossman, L. (2005, January 24). Grow up? Not so fast. *Time, 165*(4), 42–48, 50, 52.

Guernsey, L., Bornfreund, L., McCann, C., & Williams, C. (2014). *Subprime learning: Early education in America since the great recession.* New American Education Policy Program. Retrieved from newamerica.net/sites/newamerica.net/files/policydocs/NewAmerica_SuprimeLearning_Release.pdf.

Guest, Y. (2012). Reflections on resilience: A psycho-social exploration of the life long impact of having been in care during childhood. *Journal of Social Work Practice, 26*(1), 109–124.

Gunnar, M., & Quevedo, K. (2007). The neurobiology of stress and development. *Annual Review of Psychology, 58,* 145–173.

Gupta, N., Gupta, A., Onyema, G., Pantofel, Y., Ying, S. C., Garon, J. E., et al. (2012). Accurate preoperative diagnosis of ovarian pregnancy with transvaginal scan. *Obstetrics and Gynecology.* Article ID 934571. Retrieved from http://dx.doi.org/10.155/2012/934571.

Guralnick, M., Neville, B., Hammond, M., & Connor, R. (2008). Continuity and change from full-inclusion early childhood programs through the early elementary period. *Journal of Early Intervention, 30*(3), 237–250.

Gurevich, R. (2011). *How much does IVF cost?* Retrieved from http://infertility.about.com/od/ivf/f/ivf_cost.htm.

Gurian, M. (2011). *Boys and girls learn differently! A guide for teachers and parents.* San Francisco: Jossey-Bass.

Gürsory, F., & Bicakci, M. (2007). A comparison of parental attitude perceptions in children of working and nonworking mothers. *Social Behavior & Personality: An International Journal, 35*(5), 693–706.

Guterman, N., & Embry, R. (2004). Prevention and treatment strategies targeting physical child abuse and neglect. In P. Allen-Meares & M. Fraser (Eds.), *Intervention with children and adolescents: An interdisciplinary perspective* (pp. 130–158). Boston: Allyn & Bacon.

Gutman, H. (1976). *The Black family in slavery and freedom, 1750–1925.* New York: Pantheon.

Gutman, L., & Eccles, J. (2007). Stage-environment fit during adolescence: Trajectories of family relations and adolescent outcomes. *Developmental Psychology, 43,* 522–537.

Guttmacher Institute. (2013a). *Facts on unintended pregnancy in the United States.* Retrieved from http://www.guttmacher.org/pubs/FB-Unintended-Pregnancy-US.html.

Guttmacher Institute. (2013b). *Facts on induced abortion in the United States.* Retrieved from http://www.guttmacher.org/pubs/fb_induced_abortion.html.

Guttmacher Institute. (2013c). *Facts on American teens' sexual and reproductive health.* Retrieved from http://www.gutmmacher.org/pub/FB-ATSRh.html.

Gutzwiller-Helfenfinger, E., Gasser, L., & Malti, T. (2010). Moral emotions and moral judgments in children's narratives: Comparing real-life and hypothetical transgressions. *New Directions for Child & Adolescent Development, 129,* 11–31.

Ha, J., Hong, J., Seltzer, M., & Greenberg, J. (2008). Age and gender differences in the well-being of midlife and aging parents with children with mental health or developmental problems: Report of a national study. *Journal of Health and Social Behavior, 49,* 3010–3016.

Haan, N., Millsap, R., & Hartka, E. (1986). As time goes by: Change and stability in personality over fifty years. *Psychology and Aging, 1,* 220–232.

Haddad, L., Yanow, S., Delli-Bovi, L., Cosby, K., & Weitz, T. (2009). Changes in abortion provider practices in response to the Partial-Birth Abortion Ban Act of 2003. *Contraception, 79,* 379–384.

Hafen, C., Laursen, B., & DeLay, B. (2012). Transformations in friends' relationships across the transition into adolescence. In B. Laursen & W. A. Collins (Eds.), *Relationship pathways from adolescence to young adulthood* (pp. 69–89). Los Angeles: Sage.

Hagelskamp, C., Suárez-Orozco, C., & Hughes, D. (2010). Migrating to opportunities: How family migration motivations shape academic trajectories among newcomer immigrant youth. *Journal of Social Issues, 66*(4), 717–739. doi:10.1111/j.1540-4560.2010.01672.x

Haider, A. (2006). Roper v. Simmons: The role of the science brief. *Ohio State Journal of Criminal Law, 375,* 369–377.

Haider, S., & Darney, P. D. (2007). Injectable contraception. *Clinical Obstetrics and Gynecology, 50*(4), 898–906.

Haidt, J. (2013). Moral psychology for the twenty-first century. *Journal of Moral Education, 42*(3), 281–297.

Hair, E., Ling, T., & Cochran, S. W. (2003). *Youth development programs and educationally disadvantaged older youths: A synthesis.* Washington, DC: Child Trends.

Hale, B., & Worden, T. (2009). World's oldest mother dies of cancer just three years after giving birth to twin boys, sparking new ethical debate. Retrieved from http://www.dailymail.co.uk/femail/article-1199866/Worlds-oldest-mother-dies-cancer-just-years-giving-birth-twin-boys.html.

Hale, R. (2007). Choices in contraception. *British Journal of Midwifery, 15*(5), 305–309.

Hall, G. (1904). *Adolescence: Its psychology and its relations to physiology, anthropology, sociology, sex, crime, religion, and education.* New York: Appleton.

Hall, J., Jaekel, J., & Wolke, D. (2012). Gender distinctive impacts on prematurity and small for gestational age (SGA) on age-6 attention problems. *Child and Adolescent Mental Health, 17*(4), 238–245.

Hall, W. J. (2008). Centenarians: Metaphor becomes reality. *Archives of Internal Medicine, 168*(3), 262–263.

Halpern, A. (1996). Transition: A look at foundations. *Exceptional Children, 51,* 479–486.

Halzack, S. (2013, November 25). Luring millennials with good deeds. *Washington Post.* Retrieved from www.highbeam.com/doc/1P2-35409369.html.

Hamada, A., Esteves, S. C., & Agarwai, A. (2011). The role of contemporary andrology in unraveling the mystery of unexplained male infertility. *Oral Reproductive Science Journal, 3,* 27–41.

Hamilton, B. E., Martin, J. A., & Ventura, S. J. (2013). Births: Preliminary data for 2012. *National Vital Statistics Reports, 62*(3). Retrieved from http://www.cdc.gov/nchs/data/nvsr/nvsr62/nvsr62_03.pdf.

Hampson, S., & Goldberg, L. (2006). A first large cohort study of personality trait stability over the 40 years between elementary school and midlife. *Journal of Personality and Social Psychology, 91*(4), 763–779.

Handelsman, D. (2013). Global trends in testosterone prescribing, 2000–2011: Expanding the spectrum of prescription drug misuse. *Medical Journal of Australia, 199*(8), 548–551.

Hane, A., Cheah, C., Rubin, K., & Fox, N. (2008). The role of maternal behavior in the relation between shyness and social reticence in early childhood and social withdrawal in middle childhood. *Social Development, 17*(4), 795–811.

Hankivsky, O. (2012). Women's health, men's health, and gender and health: Implications of intersectionality. *Social Science & Medicine, 74,* 1712–1720.

Hansen, C., & Zambo, D. (2007). Loving and learning with Wemberly and David: Fostering emotional development in early childhood education. *Early Childhood Education Journal, 34*(4), 273–278.

Hao, L., & Cherlin, A. J. (2004). Welfare reform and teenage pregnancy, childbirth, and school dropout. *Journal of Marriage and Family, 66,* 179–184.

Hareven, T. (Ed.). (1978). *Transitions: The family and the life course in historical perspective.* New York: Academic Press.

Hareven, T. (1982a). *Family time and industrial time: The relationship between the family and work in a New England industrial community.* New York: Cambridge University Press.

Hareven, T. (1982b). American families in transition: Historical perspectives on change. In F. Walsh (Ed.), *Normal family processes* (pp. 446–466). New York: Guilford.

Hareven, T. (Ed.). (1996). *Aging and generation relations over the life course: A historical and cross-cultural perspective.* New York: Walter de Gruyter.

Hareven, T. (2000). *Families, history, and social change.* Boulder, CO: Westview.

Harkness, S., & Super, C. (2003). Culture and parenting. In M. Bornstein (Ed.), *Handbook of parenting* (2nd ed., Vol. 2, pp. 253–280). Mahwah, NJ: Lawrence Erlbaum.

Harkness, S., & Super, C. (2006). Themes and variations: Parental ethnotheories in Western cultures. In K. Rubin (Ed.), *Parental beliefs, parenting, and child development in cross-cultural perspectives* (pp. 61–80). New York: Psychology Press.

Harrell, S. P. (2000). A multidimensional conceptualization of racism-related stress: Implications for the well-being of people of color. *American Journal of Orthopsychiatry, 70*(1), 42–57.

Harrigan, M. P., & Koerin, B. B. (2007). Long distance caregiving: Personal realities and practice implications. *Reflections, 13*(2), 5–16.

Harris, J. (1998). *The nurture assumption: Why children turn out the way they do.* New York: Touchstone.

Harry, B., & Klingner, J. K. (2006). *Why are so many minority students in special education? Understanding race & disability in schools.* New York: Teachers College Press.

Hartny, C. (2006). *US rates of incarceration: A global perspective.* National Council on Crime and Delinquency. Retrieved from http://www.nccdglobal.org/sites/default/files/publication_pdf/factsheet-us-incarceration.pdf.

Harvard Health Letter. (2002). Aging—living to 100: What's the secret? *Harvard Health Letter, 27*(3), 1–3.

Harvard School of Public Health. (2012). *Child obesity.* Retrieved from http://www.hsph.harvard.edu/obesity-prevention-source/obesity-trends/global-obesity-trends-in-children.

Harwood, R. (1992). The influence of culturally derived values on Anglo and Puerto Rican mothers' perceptions of attachment behavior. *Child Development, 63,* 822–839.

Hattier, M., Matson, J., Sipes, M., & Turygin, N. (2011). Communication deficits in infants and toddlers with development disabilities. *Research in Developmental Disabilities, 32,* 2108–2113.

Havighurst, R. J. (1968). Personality and patterns of aging. *The Gerontologist, 8,* 20–23.

Hayes, D. (2011). Predicting parental home and school involvement in high school African American adolescents. *High School Journal, 94*(4), 154–166.

Hayslip, B., & Kaminski, P. L. (2005). Grandparents raising their grandchildren: A review of the literature and suggestions for practice. *The Gerontologist, 45,* 262–269.

Hazan, H. (2011). From ageless self to selfless age: Toward a theoretical turn in gerontological understanding. In L. W. Poon & J. Cohen-Mansfield (Eds.), *Understanding well-being in the oldest old* (pp. 11–26). New York: Cambridge University Press.

Healthy People. (2014). *Access to health services.* Retrieved from http://www.healthypeople.gov/2020/topicsobjectives2020/overview.aspx?topicid=1.

Healthychildren.org. (2013). *Newborn reflexes.* Retrieved from http://www.healthychildren.org/English/ages-stages/baby/pages/Newborn-Reflexes.asps.

Heckhausen, J. (2001). Adaptation and resilience in midlife. In M. Lachman (Ed.), *Handbook of midlife development* (pp. 345–394). New York: Wiley.

Heckman, J. (2006). Skill formation and the economics of investing in disadvantaged children. *Science, 312*(5782), 1900–1902.

Heckman, J. (2008). *Schools, skills, and synapses.* National Bureau of Economic Research. Retrieved from www.nber.org/papers/w14064.pdf?new_windows=1.

Heckman, J., Moon, S., Pinto, R., Savelyev, P., & Yavitz, A. (2010). The rate of return to the HighScope Perry Preschool Program. *Journal of Public Economics, 94,* 114–128.

Heimpel, S., Wood, J., Marshall, J., & Brown, J. (2002). Do people with low self-esteem really feel better? Self-esteem differences in motivation to repair negative moods. *Journal of Personality and Social Psychology, 82,* 128–147.

Heisler, E. J. (2012). *The United States infant mortality rate: International comparisons, underlying factors, and federal programs.* Congressional Research Service. Retrieved from http://www.fas.org/sgp/crs/misc/R41378.pdf.

Helbig, A., Kaasen, A., Mait, U. F., & Haugen, G. (2013). Does antenatal maternal psychological distress affect placental circulation in the third trimester? *PLoS One, 8*(2), 1–7.

Helmchen, H., Baltes, M., Geiselmann, S., Kanowski, S., Linden, M., Reischies, F., et al. (1999). Psychiatric illness in old age. In P. Baltes & K. Mayer (Eds.), *The Berlin Aging Study: Aging from 70 to 100* (pp. 67–196). Cambridge, UK: Cambridge University Press.

Helson, R., & Wink, P. (1992). Personality change in women from the early 40s to the early 50s. *Psychology and Aging, 7,* 46–55.

Henderson, C., Hayslip, B., Sanders, L., & Louden, L. (2009). Grandmother-grandchild relationship quality predicts psychological adjustment among youth from divorced families. *Journal of Family Issues, 30*(9), 1245–1264.

Henderson, S. W. (2008). *Refugee mental health.* Philadelphia: Saunders.

Hendricks, J. (1987). Exchange theory in aging. In G. L. Maddox (Ed.), *The encyclopedia of aging* (pp. 238–239). New York: Springer.

Hendricks, J., & Hatch, L. R. (2006). Lifestyle and aging. In R. H. Binstock & L. K. George (Eds.), *Handbook of aging and the social sciences* (pp. 301–319). Amsterdam: Elsevier.

Henrich, J., Heine, S., & Norenzayan, A. (2010). The weirdest people in the world? *Behavioral and Brain Sciences, 33*(2–3), 61–83.

Henry J. Kaiser Family Foundation. (2013). *Life expectancy at birth (in years) by race/ethnicity.* Retrieved from kff.org/other/state-indicator/life-expectancy-by-re.

Hequembourg, A., & Brallier, S. (2005). Gendered stories of parental caregiving among siblings. *Journal of Aging Studies, 19,* 53–71.

Herbenick, D., Reece, M., Schick, V., Sanders, S., Dodge, B., & Fortenberry, J. D. (2010). Sexual behavior in the United States: Results from a national probability sample of men and women ages 14–94. *Journal of Sexual Medicine* (Suppl. 5), 255–265.

Herbert, M. R., & Weintraub, K. (2012). *The autism revolution: Whole-body strategies for making life all it can be.* New York: Ballantine Books.

Herberth, G., Weber, A., Röder, S., Elvers, H. E., Krämer, U., Schins, R., et al. (2008). Relation between stressful life events, neuropeptides and cytokines: Results from the LISA birth cohort study. *Pediatric Allergy & Immunology, 19*(8), 722–729.

Herron, J. (2013, January 31). Bundle of joy: The costs of adoption vs. surrogacy. *Fox Business*. Retrieved from http://www.foxbusiness.com/personal-finance/2013/01/29/bundle-joy-costs-adoption-vs-surrogacy.

Hetherington, E. M., & Kelly, J. (2002). *For better or for worse: Divorce reconsidered.* New York: W. W. Norton.

Hetherington, T., & Boddy, J. (2013). Ecosocial work with marginalized populations: Time for action on climate change. In M. Gray, J. Coates, & T. Hetherington (Eds.), *Environmental social work* (pp. 46–61). New York: Routledge.

Heuveline, P., & Timberlake, J. (2004). The role of cohabitation in family formation: The United States in comparative perspective. *Journal of Marriage and Family, 66,* 1214–1230.

Hinrichsen, G. A., & Clougherty, K. F. (2006). Role transitions. In G. Henrichsen & K. Clougherty (Eds.), *Interpersonal psychotherapy for depressed older adults* (pp. 133–152). Washington, DC: American Psychological Association.

Hinton, L., Kurinczuk, J., & Ziebland, S. (2010). Infertility, isolation and the internet: A qualitative interview study. *Parent Education and Counseling, 81,* 436–441.

Hinz, S., Rais-Bahramik, S., Weiske, W. H., Kempkensteffen, C., Schrader, M., Miller, K., et al. (2009). Prognostic value of intraoperative parameters observed during vasectomy reversal for predicting postoperative vas patency and fertility. *World Journal of Urology, 27*(6), 781–785.

Hitlin, S., & Elder, G., Jr. (2007). Time, self, and the curiously abstract concept of agency. *Sociological Theory, 25*(2), 170–191.

Ho, M., Rasheed, J., & Rasheed, M. (2004). *Family therapy with ethnic minorities* (2nd ed.). Thousand Oaks, CA: Sage.

Hobbs, F., & Stoops, N. (2002). *Demographic trends in the 20th century.* Census 2000 Special Reports, Series CENSR-4. Washington, DC: U.S. Government Printing Office.

Hodge, D. R. (2001). Spiritual assessment: A review of major qualitative methods and a new framework for assessing spirituality. *Social Work, 46*(3), 203–214.

Hodnett, E., Downe, S., & Walsh, D. (2012). Alternative versus conventional institutional settings for birth. *Cochrane Database System Review.* doi:10.1002/14651858.CD000012.pub4

Hodnett, E., Gates, S., Hofmeyr, J., Sakala, C., & Weston, J. (2012). Continuous support for women during childbirth. *Cochrane Database System Review.* doi:10:CD003766. Retrieved from http://www.ncbi.nlm.nih.gov/pubmed/21328263.

Hoff, E. (2003). The specificity of environmental influence: Socioeconomic status affects early vocabulary development via maternal speech. *Child Development, 74,* 1368–1378.

Hoff, E. (2005). *Language development.* Belmont, CA: Wadsworth/Thomson Learning.

Hoff, E. (2006). How social contexts support and shape language development. *Developmental Review, 26,* 55–88.

Hoff, E. (2009). *Language development* (4th ed.). Pacific Grove, CA: Cengage.

Hoffman, A., Rüttler, V., & Nieder, A. (2011). Ontogeny of object permanence and object tracking in the carrion crow. *Animal Behavior, 82,* 359–367.

Hogan, D. P., & Msall, M. E. (2002). Family structure and resources and the parenting of children with disabilities and functional limitations. In J. G. Borkowski, S. Landesman Ramey, & M. Bristol-Power (Eds.), *Parenting and the child's world* (pp. 311–344). Mahwah, NJ: Lawrence Erlbaum.

Hogan, S. R., & Bailey, C. E. (2010). Service learning as a mechanism for change in attitudes and perceptions of human services students toward substance-dependent mothers. *Journal of Teaching in Social Work, 30*(4), 420–434.

Hoge, C. W., Auchterlonie, J. L., & Milliken, C. S. (2006). Mental health problems, use of mental health services, and attrition from military service after returning from deployment to Iraq or Afghanistan. *Journal of the American Medical Association, 295*(9), 1023–1032.

Hogstel, M. (2001). *Gerontology: Nursing care of the older adult.* Albany, NY: Delmar-Thompson Learning.

Holder, M. D., Coleman, B., & Wallace, J. M. (2010). Spirituality, religiousness, and happiness in children aged 8–12 years. *Journal of Happiness Studies, 11*(2), 131–150.

Holmes, T. (1978). Life situations, emotions, and disease. *Psychosomatic Medicine, 19,* 747–754.

Holmes, T., & Rahe, R. (1967). The social readjustment rating scale. *Journal of Psychosomatic Research, 11,* 213–218.

Holtgrave, D. R., Maulsby, C., Kharfen, M., Jia, Y., Wu, C., Opoku, J., et al. (2012). Cost-utility analysis of a female condom promotion program in Washington, D.C. *Aids and Behavior, 16*(5), 1115–1120.

Holzer, H. (2009). The labor market and young black men: Updating Moynihan's perspective. *Annals of the American Academy of Political and Social Science, 621,* 47–69.

Homans, G. C. (1961). *Social behavior: Its elementary forms.* New York: Harcourt Brace Jovanovich.

Hooyman, N. R., & Kiyak, H. A. (2011). *Social gerontology: A multidisciplinary perspective* (9th ed.). Boston: Allyn & Bacon.

Hooyman, N. R., & Kramer, B. J. (2006). *Living through loss: Interventions across the life span.* New York: Columbia University Press.

Horn, A. W., & Alexander, C. I. (2005). Recurrent miscarriage. *Journal of Family Planning and Reproductive Health Care, 31*(2), 103–107.

Horn, J. L. (1982). The theory of fluid and crystallized intelligence in relation to concepts of cognitive psychology and aging in adulthood. In F. I. M. Craik & S. Trehub (Eds.), *Aging and cognitive processes* (pp. 237–278). New York: Plenum.

House, J. S., Lantz, P. M., & Herd, P. (2005). Continuity and change in the social stratification of aging and health over the life course: Evidence from a nationally representative longitudinal study from 1986 to 2001/2002 (Americans' Changing Lives Study). *The Journals of Gerontology, Series B: Psychological Sciences and Social Sciences, 60B*, 15–26.

Howard, T. C. (2010). *Why race and culture matter in schools: Closing the achievement gap in America's classrooms.* New York: Teachers College Press.

Howell, D., Wysocki, K., & Steiner, M. (2010). Toilet training. *Pediatrics in Review, 31*(6), 262–263.

Hoyert, D., & Xu, J. (2012). Deaths: Preliminary data for 2011. *National Vital Statistics Reports, 61*(6), 1–51. Retrieved from http://www.cdc/gov/nchs/data/nvsr/nvsr61/nvsr61_06.pdf.

Hser, Y., Longshore, D., & Anglin, M. (2007). The life course perspective on drug use. *Evaluation Review, 31*(6), 515–547.

Huebner, A., & Garrod, A. (1993). Moral reasoning among Tibetan monks: A study of Buddhist adolescents and young adults in Nepal. *Journal of Cross-Cultural Psychology, 24*, 167–185.

Hughes, A., Harold, R., & Boyer, J. (2011). Awareness of LGBT aging issues among aging services network providers. *Journal of Gerontological Social Work, 54*(7), 650–677.

Hughes, D., Hagelskamp, C., Way, N., & Foust, M. (2009). The role of mothers' and adolescents' perceptions of ethnic-racial socialization in shaping ethnic-racial identity among early adolescent boys and girls. *Journal of Youth and Adolescence, 38*, 605–626.

Hughes, F. (2010). *Children, play, and development* (4th ed.). Thousand Oaks, CA: Sage.

Huinink, J., & Feldhaus, M. (2009). Family research from the life course perspective. *International Sociology, 24*(3), 299–324.

Human Genome Project. (2010). *Gene testing.* Retrieved from http://www.ornl.gov/sci/techresources/Human_Genome/medicine/genetest.shtml.

Human Reproduction Update. (2008). Intrauterine devices and intrauterine systems. *Human Reproduction Update, 14*(3), 197–208.

Human Rights Campaign. (2013). *Adoption options overview.* Retrieved from http://www.hrc.org/resources/entry/adoption-options-overview.

Human Rights Watch. (2013). *Child labor.* Retrieved from http://www.hrw.org/topic/childrens-rights/child-labor.

Hutchison, E. (2007). Community violence. In E. Hutchison, H. Matto, M. Harrigan, L. Charlesworth, & P. Viggiani (Eds.), *Challenges of living: A multidimensional working model for social workers* (pp. 71–104). Thousand Oaks, CA: Sage.

Hutchison, E., Matto, H., Harrigan, M., Charlesworth, L., & Viggiani, P. (2007). *Challenges of living: A multidimensional working model for social workers.* Thousand Oaks, CA: Sage.

Hyde, J. (2005). The gender similarities hypothesis. *American Psychologist, 60*, 581–592.

Imdad, A., & Bhutta, Z. A. (2012). Maternal nutrition and birth outcomes: Effect of balanced protein-energy supplementation. *Paediatric and Perinatal Epidemiology, 26*(Suppl.), 178–190.

Impett, E., & Tolman, D. (2006). Late adolescent girls' sexual experiences and sexual satisfaction. *Journal of Adolescent Research, 21*, 628–646.

Inderbitzin, M. (2009). Reentry of emerging adults: Adolescent inmates' transition back into the community. *Journal of Adolescent Research, 24*, 453–476.

Infertility & Reproduction Health Center. (2010). *Gamete and zygote intrafallopian transfer (GIFT and ZIFT) for infertility.* Retrieved from http://www.webmd.com/infertility-and-reproduction/gamete-and-zygote-intra-fallopian-transfer-gift-and-zift-for-infertility.

Innes, A. (2009). *Dementia studies.* Los Angeles: Sage.

Insel, T. (2013). *Director's blog: The four kingdoms of autism.* National Institute of Mental Health. Retrieved from http://www.nimh.nih.gov/about/director/2013/the-four-kingdoms-of-autism.shtml.

Institute of Medicine. (2006). *Preterm birth: Causes, consequences and prevention.* Washington, DC: National Academies Press.

Institute of Medicine. (2011). *The health of lesbian, gay, bisexual, and transgender people: Building a foundation for better understanding.* Washington, DC: National Academies Press.

Institute of Medicine and National Research Council. (2012). *Child maltreatment research, policy, and practice for the next decade: Workshop summary.* Washington, DC: National Academies Press.

International Federation of Persons With Physical Disability. (2011). *Violence against women: Forced sterilization of women with disabilities is a reality in Europe.* Retrieved from http://www.fimitic.org/content/vioence-against-women-forced-sterilization-women-disabilities-reality-europe.

Irish, D., Lundquist, K., & Nelsen, V. (1993). *Ethnic variations in dying, death, and grief: Diversity in universality.* Washington, DC: Taylor & Francis.

Isenberg, J. P., & Jolongo, M. (2003). *Major trends and issues in early childhood education: Challenges, controversies, and insights* (2nd ed.). New York: Teachers College Press.

IVF Informant. (2012). *IUI costs 2012.* Retrieved from http://ivf-info.org/iui-cost-2012.

Iwata, S., Iwata, O., & Matsuishi, T. (2013). Sleep patterns of Japanese preschool children and their parents: Implications of co-sleeping. *Acta Paediatrica, 102,* 257–262.

Jackson, A., & Mott, P. (2007). Reproductive health care for women with spinal bifida. *Scientific World Journal, 7,* 1875–1883.

Jacobsen, L., Mather, M., Lee, M., & Kent, M. (2011). America's aging population. *Population Bulletin, 66*(1), 1–18. Retrieved from www.prb.org.

Jahromi, L., Putnam, S., & Stifter, C. (2004). Maternal regulation of infant reactivity from 2 to 6 months. *Developmental Psychology, 40,* 477–487.

Jain, R. B. (2013). Effect of pregnancy on the levels of blood cadmium, lead, and mercury for females 17–39 years old: Data from National Health and Nutrition Survey 2003–2010. *Journal of Toxicology and Environmental Health, Part A, 76*(1), 58–59.

James, K., & Bose, P. (2011). Self-generated actions during learning objects and sounds create sensori-motor systems in the developing brain. *Cognition, Brain, Behavior, 15*(4), 485–503.

James, S., Chilvers, R., Havermann, D., & Phelps, J. Y. (2010). Avoiding legal pitfalls in surrogacy arrangements. *Reproductive BioMedicine Online, 21*(7), 862–867.

James, W. P. T. (2006). The challenge of childhood obesity. *The International Journal of Pediatric Obesity, 1*(1), 7–10.

Jang, Y., Borenstein, A. R., Chiriboga, D. A., & Mortimer, J. A. (2005). Depressive symptoms among African American and white older adults. *The Journals of Gerontology, Series B: Psychological Sciences and Social Sciences, 6*(6), 313–319.

Jansen, P., Raat, H., Mackenbach, J., Jaddoe, V., Hofman, A., Verhulst, F., et al. (2009). Socioeconomic inequalities in infant temperament. *Social Psychiatry and Psychiatric Epidemiology, 44,* 87–95.

Jasmin, L. (2013). Delirium. *MedlinePlus.* U.S. National Library of Medicine/National Institutes of Health. Retreived from http://www.nlm.nih.gov/medlineplus/ency/article/000740.htm.

Jean, A., & Stack, D. (2012). Full-term and very-low-birthweight preterm infants' self-regulating behaviors during a still-face interaction: Influences of maternal touch. *Infant Behavior and Development, 35,* 779–791.

Jenkinson, S. (2012). *The skill of brokenheartedness: Euthanasia, palliative care and power.* Retrieved from http://www.youtube.com/watch?v=6dbmXWLCaRg.

Jenkinson, S. (2013). *The meaning of death.* Retrieved from http://www.youtube.com/watch?v=Zjm8gWY3etg.

Jensen, J. (2013). Vaginal ring delivery of selected progesterone receptor modulators for contraception. *Contraception, 87*(3), 314–318.

Jensen, L. A. (2003). Coming of age in a multicultural world: Globalization and adolescent cultural identity formation. *Applied Developmental Science, 7,* 188–195.

Jenson, J., & Fraser, M. (2011). *Social policy and children and families: A risk and resilience perspective* (2nd ed.). Los Angeles: Sage.

Jihanian, L. (2013). Specifying long-term care provider responsiveness to LGBT older adults. *Journal of Gay & Lesbian Social Services, 25*(2), 210–231.

Jin, K. (2010). Modern biological theories of aging. *Aging and Disease, 1*(2), 72–74.

Jobe-Shields, L., Cohen, R., & Parra, G. R. (2011). Patterns of change in children's loneliness: Trajectories from third through fifth grades. *Merrill-Palmer Quarterly, 57*(1), 25–47.

Johnson, A. G. (2006). *Privilege, power, and difference.* Boston: McGraw-Hill.

Johnson, A. N. (2008). Engaging fathers in the NICU: Taking down the barriers to the baby. *The Journal of Perinatal and Neonatal Nursing, 22*(4), 302–306.

Johnson, R., Browne, K., & Hamilton-Giachritis, C. (2006). Young children in institutional care at risk of harm. *Trauma, Violence & Abuse, 7*(1), 34–60.

Johnson, R., Schoeni, R., & Rogowski, J. (2012). Health disparities in mid-to-late life: The role of earlier life family and neighborhood socioeconomic conditions. *Social Science & Medicine, 74,* 625–636.

Johnson, S., Blum, R., & Giedd, J. (2009). Adolescent maturity and the brain: The promise and pitfalls of neuroscience research in adolescent health policy. *Journal of Adolescent Health, 45,* 216–221.

Johnston, L., O'Malley, P., Bachman, J., & Schulenberg, J. (2004). *Monitoring the future national results on adolescent drug use: Overview of key findings, 2003* (NIH Publication No. 04-5506). Bethesda, MD: National Institute of Drug Abuse.

Johnston, L., O'Malley, P., Bachman, J., & Schulenberg, J. (2005). *Monitoring the future national results on adolescent drug use: Overview of key findings, 2004* (NIH Publication No. 06-5882). Bethesda, MD: National Institute of Drug Abuse.

Jones, A., & Meier, A. (2011). Growing www.parentsofsuicide: A case study of an online support community. *Social Work with Groups, 34,* 101–120.

Jones, B., & McAdams, D. (2013). Becoming generative: Socializing influences recalled in late stories in late midlife. *Journal of Adult Development, 20,* 158–172.

Jones, J., & Mosher, W. (2013). Fathers' involvement with their children: United States, 2006–2010. *National Health Statistics Reports No. 71.* Hyattsville, MD: National Center for Health Statistics.

Jones, J., Mosher, W., & Daniels, K. (2012, May 18). Current contraceptive use in the United States, 2006–2010 and changes in patterns of use since 1995. *National Health*

Statistics Report, 60. Retrieved from http://www.cdc.gov/nchs/data/nhsr/nhsr060.pdf.

Jordan, J. (2005). Relational resilience in girls. In S. Goldstein & R. Brooks (Eds.), *Handbook of resilience in children* (pp. 79–90). New York: Kluwer Academic/Plenum Publishers.

Joseph, K. S., Allen, A. C., Dodd, S. C., Turner, L. A., Scott, H., & Liston, R. (2005). The perinatal effects of delayed childbearing. *Obstetrics and Gynecology, 105*(6), 1410–1418.

Joshi, S., & Morley, J. (2006). Cognitive impairment. *Medical Clinics of North America, 90*(5), 769–787.

Joss-Moore, L., & Lane, R. (2009). The developmental origins of adult diseases. *Current Opinions in Pediatrics, 21*(2), 230–234.

Jung, C. (1971). *The portable Jung.* New York: Viking Press.

Jurimae, J. (2013). *Growth, physical activity, and motor development in prepubertal children.* Ipswich, MA: Ebsco.

Kahneman, D. (2011). *Thinking fast and slow.* New York: Farrar, Straus and Giroux.

Kahraman, P., & Başal, H. (2012). Sex stereotypes of seven-eight year old girls and boys living in urban and rural areas. *International Journal of Human Sciences, 9*(1), 46–60.

Kamerman, S. (1996). Child and family policies: An international overview. In E. Zigler, S. Kagan, & N. Hall (Eds.), *Children, families, & government: Preparing for the twenty-first century* (pp. 31–48). New York: Cambridge University Press.

Kaneshiro, N. (2011). *Failure to thrive.* U.S. National Library of Medicine. Retrieved from http://www.nlm.nih.gov/medlineplus/ency/article/0000991.htm.

Kansas Statutes, § 21-3502 and § 21-3504; 2009 Kansas Statutes Annotated (KSA). Retrieved from kansasstatutes.lesterama.org/Chapter_21/Article_35.

Kaplan, J., Aziz-Zadeh, L., Uddin, L., & Iacoboni, M. (2008). The self across the senses: An fMRI study of self-face and self-voice recognition. *Social Cognitive & Affective Neuroscience, 3,* 218–223.

Kaplowitz, P. (2006). Pubertal development in girls: Secular trends. *Current Opinions in Obstetrics and Gynecology, 18,* 487–491.

Karjane, N. W., Stovall, D. W., Berger, N. G., & Svikis, D. S. (2008). Alcohol abuse risk factors and psychiatric disorders in pregnant women with a history of infertility. *Journal of Women's Health, 17*(10), 1623–1627.

Karraker, A., DeLamater, J., & Schwartz, C. (2011). Sexual frequency decline from midlife to later life. *The Journals of Gerontology, Series B: Psychological Sciences and Social Sciences, 66*(4), 502–512.

Karraker, M. W. (2013). *Global families.* Los Angeles: Sage.

Kasckow, J., Karp, J., Whyte, E., Butters, M., Brown, C., Begley, A., et al. (2013). Subsyndromal depression and anxiety in older adults: Health related, function, cognitive and diagnostic implications. *Journal of Psychiatric Research, 47,* 599–603.

Kashushin, G., & Egan, M. (2008). *Gerontological home health care: A guide for the social work practitioner.* New York: Columbia University Press.

Kaslow, F., & Robison, J. A. (1996). Long-term satisfying marriages: Perceptions of contributing factors. *The American Journal of Family Therapy, 24*(2), 153–170.

Kaufman, G., & Uhlenberg, P. (2000). The influence of parenthood on the work effort of married men and women. *Social Forces, 78,* 931–949.

Kaur, P., Shorey, L., Ho, E., Dashwood, R., & Williams D. E. (2013). The epigenome as a potential of cancer and disease prevention in prenatal development. *Nutritional Reviews, 71*(7), 441–457.

Kaye, L. W. (2005). The emergence of the new aged and the productive aging perspective. In L. W. Kaye (Ed.), *Perspectives on productive aging: Social work with the new aged* (pp. 3–18). Washington, DC: NASW.

Keenan, T., & Evans, S. (2009). *An introduction to child development* (2nd ed.). Thousand Oaks, CA: Sage.

Kegan, R. (1982). *The evolving self: Problem and process in human development.* Cambridge, MA: Harvard University Press.

Kegan, R. (1994). *In over our heads: The mental demands of modern life.* Cambridge, MA: Harvard University Press.

Kei-ho Pih, K., Hirose, A., & Mao, K. R. (2012). The invisible unattended: Low-wage Chinese immigrant workers, health care, and social capital in Southern California's San Gabriel Valley. *Sociological Inquiry, 82*(2), 236–256.

Kelly, Y., Sacker, A., Schoon, I., & Nazroo, J. (2006). Ethnic differences in achievement of developmental milestones by 9 months of age: The Millenium Cohort Study. *Developmental Medicine & Child Neurology, 48,* 825–830.

Kemp, C. (2005). Dimenions of grandparent-adult grandchild relationships: From family ties to intergenerational friends. *Canadian Journal on Aging, 24*(2), 161–177.

Keniston, K. (1966). *The uncommitted: Alienated youth in American society.* New York: Harcourt, Brace, & World.

Keogh, B. K., Bernheimer, L. P., & Guthrie, D. (2004). Children with developmental delays twenty years later: Where are they? How are they? *American Journal on Mental Retardation, 109*(3), 219–230.

Keresteš, G., Broković, I., & Jagodić, G. (2012). Predictors of psychological well-being of adolescents' parents. *Journal of Happiness Studies, 13,* 1073–1089.

Keyes, C., & Ryff, C. (1998). Generativity in adult lives: Social structural contours and quality of life consequences. In D. McAdams & E. de St. Aubin (Eds.), *Generativity and adult development: How and why we care for the next generation* (pp. 227–263). Washington, DC: American Psychological Association.

Khandaker, G. M., Dibben, C. R. M., & Jones, P. B. (2012). Does maternal body mass index during pregnancy influence risk of schizophrenia in the adult offspring? *Obesity Reviews, 13*(6), 518–527.

Khaw, L., & Hardesty, J. (2007). Theorizing the process of leaving: Turning points and trajectories in the stages of change. *Family Relations, 56,* 413–425.

Khodyakov, D., & Carr, D. (2009). The impact of late-life parental death on adult sibling relationships. *Research on Aging, 31*(5), 495–519.

Khubchandani, J., Price, J., Thompson, A., Dake, J., Wiblishauser, M., & Telljohann, S. (2012). Adolescent dating violence: A national assessment of school counselors' perceptions and practices. *Pediatrics, 130*(2), 202–210.

Kidd, C. D., Taggart, W., & Turkle, S. (2006). *A sociable robot to encourage social interaction among the elderly.* Paper presented at the Robotics and Automation, 2006 ICRA. Retrieved from web.mit.edu/sturkle/ICRA_Para.pdf.

Kikuzawa, S. (2006). Multiple roles and mental health in cross-cultural perspective: The elderly in the United States and Japan. *Journal of Health and Social Behavior, 47*(1), 62–76.

Kim, H., Chang, M., Rose, K., & Kim, S. (2012). Predictors of caregiver burden in caregivers of individuals with dementia. *Journal of Advanced Nursing, 68*(4), 846–855.

Kim, S., & Esquivel, G. (2011). Adolescent spirituality and resilience: Theory, research, and educational practices. *Psychology in the Schools, 48*(7), 755–765.

King, C., & Merchant, C. (2008). Social and interpersonal factors relating to adolescent suicidality: A review of the literature. *Archives of Suicide Research, 12,* 181–196.

King, W. (2009). Toward a life-course perspective of police organizations. *Journal of Research in Crime and Delinquency, 46*(2), 213–244.

Kissil, K., & Davey, M. (2012). Health disparities in procreation: Unequal access to assisted reproductive technologies. *Journal of Feminist Family Therapy, 24*(3), 197–212.

Kitayama, S., Karasawa, M., & Mesquita, B. (2004). Collective and personal processes in regulating emotions: Emotion and self in Japan and the United States. In P. Philippot & R. Feldman (Eds.), *The regulation of emotion* (pp. 251–276). Mahwah, NJ: Lawrence Erlbaum.

Klein, D., Mok, D., Chen, J., & Watkins, K. (2013). Age of language learning shapes brain structure: A cortical thickness study of bilingual and monolingual individuals. *Brain & Language.* Retrieved from http://dx.doi.org/10.1016/j.bandl.2013.05.014.

Klein, J. (2012). *The bully society: School shootings and the crisis of bullying in America's schools.* New York: New York University Press.

Kneas, D., & Perry, B. (2011). *Using technology in the early childhood classroom.* Retrieved from http://teacher.scholastic.com/professional/bruceperry/using_technology.htm.

Knitzer, J. (2007). Putting knowledge into policy: Toward an infant-toddler policy agenda. *Infant Mental Health Journal, 28*(2), 237–245.

Knoll, C., & Sickmund, M. (2012). *Delinquency cases in juvenile court, 2009.* Washington, DC: U.S. Department of Justice, Office of Justice Programs, Office of Juvenile Justice and Delinquency Prevention. Retrieved from http://www.ojjdp.gov/pubs/239081.pdf.

Kochanska, G. (1997). Multiple pathways to conscience for children with different temperaments: From toddlerhood to age 5. *Developmental Psychology, 33,* 228–240.

Kochanska, G., Aksan, N., & Joy, M. (2007). Children's fearfulness as a moderator of parenting in early socialization: Two longitudinal studies. *Developmental Psychology, 43,* 222–237.

Kochanska, G., Forman, D., Aksan, N., & Dunbar, S. (2005). Pathways to conscience: Early mother-child mutually responsive orientation and children's moral emotion, conduct, and cognition. *Journal of Child Psychology and Psychiatry, 46,* 19–34.

Koehn, M. (2008). Contemporary women's perceptions of childbirth education. *Journal of Perinatal Education, 17*(1), 11–18.

Kohlberg, L. (1969). Stage and sequence: The cognitive developmental approach to socialization. In D. A. Goslin (Ed.), *Handbook of socialization theory and research* (pp. 347–480). Chicago: Rand McNally.

Kohlberg, L. (1976). Moral stages and moralization: The cognitive-developmental approach. In T. Lickona (Ed.), *Moral development and behavior: Theory, research, and social issues* (pp. 31–53). New York: Holt.

Kohlberg, L. (1984). *Essays on moral development: Vol. 2. The psychology of moral development.* San Francisco: Harper & Row.

Kohli, M., & Künemund, H. (2005). The midlife generation in the family: Patterns of exchange and support. In S. Willis & M. Martin (Eds.), *Middle adulthood: A lifespan perspective* (pp. 35–61). Thousand Oaks, CA: Sage.

Kohut, H. (1971). *The analysis of the self.* New York: International Universities Press.

Kolling, T., Haberstroh, J., Kaspar, R., Pantel, J., Oswald, F., & Knopf, M. (2013). Evidence and deployment-based research into care for the elderly using emotional robots. *GeroPsych: The Journal of Gerontopsychology and Geriatric Psychiatry, 26*(2), 83–88.

Kominski, R., Shin, H., & Marotz, K. (2008, April 16–19). *Language needs of school-age children.* Paper presented at the Annual Meeting of the Population Association of America, New Orleans, LA. Retrieved from paa2008 princeton.edu/papers/80706.

Korkman, M., Stenroos, M., Mickos, A., Westman, M., Ekholm, P., & Byring, R. (2012). Does simultaneous bilingualism aggravate children's specific language problems? *Acta Paediatrica, 101*(9), 946–952. doi:10.1111/j.1651-2227.2012.02733.x

Kosciw, J., Greytak, E., Bartkiewicz, M., Boesen, M., & Palmer, N. M. (2012). *The 2011 National School Climate*

Survey: The experiences of lesbian, gay, bisexual and transgender youth in our nation's schools. New York: GLSEN. Retreived from http://glsen.org/research.

Kotch, J., Browne, D., Ringwalt, C., Dufort, V., Ruina, E., Stewart, P., et al. (1997). Stress, social support, and substantiated maltreatment in the second and third years of life. *Child Abuse and Neglect, 21*(11), 1026–1037.

Kovács, Á., & Mehler, J. (2009). Flexible learning of multiple speech structures in bilingual infants. *Science, 325,* 611–612.

Kovacs, P. J., Bellin, M. H., & Fauri, D. F. (2006). Family-centered care: A resource for social work in end-of-life and palliative care. *Journal of Social Work in End-of-Life & Palliative Care, 2*(1), 13–27.

Kowalski, K. (2003). The emergence of ethnic and racial attitudes in preschool-aged children. *Journal of Social Psychology, 143,* 677–690.

Kozhimannil, K. B., Hardeman, R., Attanasio, L., Blauer-Peterson, C., & O'Brien, M. (2013). Doula care, birth outcomes, and costs among Medicaid beneficiaries. *American Journal of Public Health, 103*(4), 113–121.

Kozhimannil, K. B., Law, M. R., & Virniq, B. A. (2013). Cesarean delivery rates vary tenfold among U.S. hospitals; reducing variation may reduce quality and cost issues. *Health Affiliates, 32*(3), 527–535.

Kozol, J. (2005). *The shame of the nation: The restoration of apartheid schooling in America.* New York: Crown.

Kramer, B. (1997). Gain in the caregiving experience: Where are we? What next? *The Gerontologist, 37,* 218–232.

Krayer, A., Ingledew, D., & Iphofen, R. (2008). Social comparison and body image in adolescence: A grounded theory approach. *Health Education Research, 23*(5), 892–903.

Kreider, R. (2010). *Increase in opposite-sex cohabiting couples from 2009 to 2010 in the Annual Social and Economic Supplement (ASEC) to the Current Population Survey (CPS).* Retrieved from www.census.gov/population/www/socdemo/Inc-opp-sex-2009-2010.pdf.

Kremer, H., Ironson, G., & Kaplan, L. (2009). The fork in the road: HIV as a potential positive turning point and the role of spirituality. *AIDS Care, 21*(3), 368–377.

Kristof, N., & WuDunn, S. (2009). *Half the sky: Turning oppression into opportunity for women worldwide.* New York: Vintage.

Kroger, J. (2007). *Identity development: Adolescence through adulthood* (2nd ed.). Thousand Oaks, CA: Sage.

Kroger, J., Martinussen, M., & Marcia, J. (2010). Identity status change during adolescence and young adulthood: A meta-analysis. *Journal of Adolescence, 33,* 683–698.

Krueger, A. K., Reither, E., Peppard, P. E., Krueger, P. M., & Hale, L. (2013). Do sleep-deprived adolescents make less healthy food choices? *Proceedings of the annual SLEEP Conference,* Baltimore.

Krug, E., Dahlberg, L., Mercy, J., Zwi, A., & Lozano, R. (2002). *World report on violence and health.* Geneva, Switzerland: World Health Organization.

Krupitzki, H. B., Gadow, E. C., Gili, J. A., Comas, B., Cosentino, V. R., Saleme, C., et al. (2013). Environmental risk factors and perinatal outcomes in preterm newborns, according to family reoccurrence of prematurity. *American Journal of Perinatology, 30*(6), 451–461.

Kübler-Ross, E. (1969). *On death and dying.* New York: Macmillan.

Kubota, T., & Hata, L. (2013). Epigenomics comes of age with expanding roles in biological understanding and clinical application. *Journal of Human Genetics, 59,* 395.

Kuipers, M. A. G., van Poppel, M. N. M., van den Brink, W., Wingen, M., & Kunst, A. E. (2012). The association between neighborhood disorder, social cohesion and hazardous alcohol use: A national multilevel study. *Drug and Alcohol Dependence, 126,* 27–34.

Kupersmidt, J. B., & Dodge, K. A. (2004). *Children's peer relations: From development to intervention.* Washington, DC: American Psychological Association.

Kurcinka, M. S. (2006). *Sleepless in America: Practical strategies to help your family get the sleep it deserves.* New York: HarperCollins.

Kurdek, L. (2004). Are gay and lesbian cohabiting couples *really* different from heterosexual married couples? *Journal of Marriage and the Family, 66,* 880–900.

Kurdek, L. (2008). Change in relationship quality for partners from lesbian, gay male, and heterosexual couples. *Journal of Family Psychology, 22*(5), 701–711.

Kurtz, L. (2012). *Gods in the global village: The world's religions in sociological perspective* (3rd ed.). Los Angeles: Sage.

Labouvie-Vief, G. (2005). Self-with-other representations and the organization of the self. *Journal of Research in Personality, 39,* 185–205.

Lacey, H. P., Smith, D. M., & Ubel, P. A. (2006). I hope I die before I get old: Mispredicting happiness across the adult life span. *Journal of Happiness Studies, 7,* 162–182.

Lachman, M. (2004). Development in midlife. *Annual Review of Psychology, 55,* 305–331.

Lachman, M., Agrigoroaei, S., Murphy, C., & Tun, P. (2010). Frequent cognitive activity compensates for education differences in episodic memory. *American Journal of Geriatric Psychiatry, 18*(1), 4–10.

Lachman, M., & Bertrand, R. (2001). Personality and the self in midlife. In M. Lachman (Ed.), *Handbook of midlife development* (pp. 279–309). New York: Wiley.

Laflamme, D., Pomerleau, A., & Malcuit, G. (2002). A comparison of fathers' and mothers' involvement in childcare and stimulation behaviors during free play with their infants at 9 and 15 months. *Sex Roles, 47,* 507–518.

Lagan, B., Sinclair, M., & Kernohan, W. (2010). Internet use in pregnancy informs women's decision-making: A web-based survey. *Birth, 37*(2), 106–115.

Lake, A. (2013). *Growing gulf between rich and poor reproach to the promise of the United Nations*. United Nations General Assembly GA11391. Retrieved from http://www.un.org/News/Press/docs/2013/ga11391.doc.htm.

Lam, C., & McHale, S. (2012). Developmental patterns and family predictors of adolescent weight concerns: A replication and extension. *International Journal of Eating Disorders, 45*(4), 524–530.

Lam, V., & Smith, G. (2009). African and Caribbean adolescents in Britain: Ethnic identity and Britishness. *Ethnic and Racial Studies, 32*(7), 1248–1270.

Lamaze, F. (1958). *Painless childbirth: Psychoprophylactic method* (L. R. Celestin, Trans.). London: Burke.

Lamers, W. (2013). *Signs of approaching death*. Washington, DC: Hospice Foundation of America. Retrieved from http://www.hospicefoundation.org/dyingsigns.

Lancet, The. (2013*). Maternal and child nutrition*. Retrieved from http://www.thelancet.com/series/maternal-and-child-nutrition.

Lane, J., Wellman, H., Olson, S., LaBounty, J., & Kerr, D. (2010). Theory of mind and emotion understanding predict moral development in early childhood. *British Journal of Development Psychology, 28*, 871–889.

Lang, A. J., Aarons, G. A., Gearity, J., Laffaye, C., Satz, L., Dresselhaus, T. R., & Stein, M. B. (2008). Direct and indirect links between childhood maltreatment, posttraumatic stress disorder, and women's health. *Behavioral Medicine, 33*(4), 125–135.

Langle, A., & Probst, C. (2004). Existential questions of the elderly. *Archives of Psychiatry and Psychotherapy, 6*(2), 15–20.

Lansford, J., Deater-Deckard, K., Dodge, K., Bates, J., & Pettit, G. (2004). Ethnic differences in the link between physical discipline and later adolescent externalizing behaviors. *Journal of Child Psychology and Psychiatry, 45*, 801–812.

Larson, R. W., Wilson, S., & Mortimer, J. T. (2002). Adolescence in the 21st century: An international perspective—Adolescents' preparation for the future. *Journal of Research on Adolescence, 12*(1), 159–166.

LaSala, M. C. (2001). The importance of partners to lesbians' intergenerational relationships. *Social Work Research, 25*(1), 27–40.

Laseter, R. (1997). The labor force participation of young Black men: A qualitative examination. *Social Service Review, 71*, 72–88.

Laskov, I., Birnbaum, R., Maslovitz, S., Kupferminc, M., Lessing, J., & Mony, A. (2012). Outcome of singleton pregnancy in women ≥ 45 years old: A retrospective cohort study. *Journal of Maternal-Fetal & Neonatal Medicine, 25*(11), 2190–2193.

Latva, R., Lehtonen, L., Salmelin, R. K., & Tamminen, T. (2007). Visits by the family to the neonatal intensive care unit. *Acta Paediatricia, 96*(2), 215–220.

Lau, A., Litrownik, A., Newton, R., Black, M., & Everson, M. (2006). Factors affecting the link between physical discipline and child externalizing problems in Black and White families. *Journal of Community Psychology, 34*(1), 89–103.

Lau, C., Ambalavanan, N., Chakraborty, H., Wingate, M. S., & Carlo, W. A. (2013). Extremely low birth weight and infant mortality rates in the United States. *Pediatrics, 131*(5), 855–860.

Lauritsen, J., & Rezey, M. (2013). *Measuring the prevalence of crime with the National Crime Victimization Survey*. Washington, DC: U.S. Department of Justice, Office of Justice Programs, Bureau of Justice Statistics. Retrieved from http://www.bjs.gov/content/pub/pdf/mpcncvs.pdf.

Lawford, H., Pratt, M., Hunsberg, B., & Pancer, S. M. (2005). Adolescent generativity: A longitudinal study of two possible contexts for learning concern for future generations. *Journal of Research on Adolescence, 15*(3), 261–273.

Lawrence, C. R., Carlson, E. A., & Egeland, B. (2006). The impact of foster care on development. *Development and Psychopathology, 18*(1), 57–76.

Lederberg, A., Schick, B., & Spencer, P. (2013). Language and literacy development of deaf and hard-of-hearing children: Successes and challenges. *Developmental Psychology, 49*(1), 15–30.

Lee, C., & Beckert, T. (2012). Taiwanese adolescent cognitive autonomy and identity development: The relationship of situational and agential factors. *International Journal of Psychology, 47*(1), 39–50.

Lee, G., & DeMaris, A. (2007). Widowhood, gender, and depression: A longitudinal analysis. *Research on Aging, 29*, 56–72.

Leeder, E. (2004). *The family in global perspective: A gendered journey*. Thousand Oaks, CA: Sage.

Leisering, L. (2003). Government and the life course. In J. Mortimer & M. Shanahan (Eds.), *Handbook of the life course* (pp. 205–225). New York: Kluwer Academic/Plenum.

Leitenberg, H., Detzer, M. J., & Srebnik, D. (1993). Gender differences in masturbation and the relationship of masturbation experience in preadolescence and/or early adolescence and sexual behavior and sexual adjustment in young adulthood. *Archives of Sexual Behavior, 22*, 299–313.

Lemieux, C. M., & Allen, P. D. (2007). Service learning in social work education: The state of knowledge, pedagogical practicalities, and practice conundrums. *Journal of Social Work Education, 43*(2), 309–325.

Lenhart, A. (2012, March). *Teens, smartphones & texting*. PewResearch Internet Project. Retrieved from www.pewinternet.org/2012/03/19/teens-smartphones-texting.

Leonard, R. (2006). Turning points in the lives of midlife and older women: Five-year follow-up. *Australian Psychologist, 41*(1), 28–36.

Levanon, G., Cheng, B., & Goldman, J. (2011). *U.S. workers delaying retirement.* Retrieved from www.financial finesse.com/wp-content/uploads/2012/01/us_workers_delay_retirement/pdf.

Levine, L. E., & Munsch, J. (2011). *Child development: An active learning approach.* Thousand Oaks, CA: Sage.

Levinson, D. (1977). The mid-life transition. *Psychiatry, 40,* 99–112.

Levinson, D. (1978). *The seasons of a man's life.* New York: Knopf.

Levinson, D. (1986). A conception of adult development. *American Psychologist, 41*(1), 3–13.

Levinson, D. (1990). A theory of life structure development in adulthood. In C. N. Alexander & E. J. Langer (Eds.), *Higher stages of human development* (pp. 35–54). New York: Oxford University Press.

Levinson, D., & Levinson, J. (1996). *The seasons of a woman's life.* New York: Ballantine Books.

Levinson, D., Darrow, C., Klein, E., Levinson, M., & McKee, B. (1978). *The seasons of a man's life.* New York: Knopf.

Lev-Wiesel, R., Sarid, M., & Sternberg, R. (2013). Measuring social peer rejection during childhood: Development and validation. *Journal of Aggression, Maltreatment & Trauma, 22*(5), 482–492.

Lewis, K., & Burd-Sharps, S. (2010). *The measure of America 2010–2011: Mapping risks and resilience.* New York: New York University Press.

Lewis, M. (2005). The child and its family: The social network model. *Human Development, 48,* 8–27.

Lewis, T. (1994). A comparative analysis of the effects of social skills training and teacher directed contingencies on social behavior of preschool children with disabilities. *Journal of Behavioral Education, 4,* 267–281.

Li, C. I., Beaber, E. F., Tang, M. C., Porter, P., Daling, J. R., & Malone, K. E. (2012). The effects of depo medroxyprogesterone acetate on breast cancer risk among women 20–44 years of age. *Cancer Research, 72*(8), 2028–2035.

Li, S.-C. (2006). Biocultural co-construction of life span development. In P. B. Baltes, P. A. Reuter-Lorenz, & F. Rössler (Eds.), *Life span development and the brain: The perspective of biocultural co-constructivism* (pp. 40–60). Cambridge, UK: Cambridge University Press.

Li, S.-C. (2009). Brain in macro experiential context: Biocultural co-construction of life span neurocognitive development. *Progress in Brain Research, 178,* 17–29.

Liang, K. (2014). The cross-domain correlates of subjective age in Chinese oldest-old. *Aging & Mental Health, 18*(2), 217–224.

Lichtenstein, S. (1993). Transition from school to adulthood: Case studies of adults with learning disabilities who dropped out of school. *Exceptional Children, 59*(4), 336–347.

Lie, K. K., Groholt, E. K., & Eskild, A. (2010). Association of cerebral palsy with apgar score in low and normal birth-weight infants: Population based cohort study. *British Medical Journal, 341.* Retrieved from http://www.bmj.com/content/341/bmj.c4990.

Lima-Pereira, P., Bermudez-Tamayo, C., & Jasienska, G. (2012). Use of the internet as a source of health information amongst participants of antenatal classes. *Journal of Clinical Nursing, 21*(3/4), 322–330.

Lindau, S. T., & Gavrilova, N. (2010). Sex, health, and years of sexually active life gained due to good health: Evidence from two US population based cross sectional surveys of ageing. *British Medical Journal.* 340:c810. doi:10.1136/bmj.c810

Lindell, G., Marsal, K., & Kallen, K. (2012). Impact of maternal characteristics on fetal growth in the third trimester: A population-based study. *Ultrasound in Obstetrics and Gynecology, 40*(6), 680–687.

Lindemann, E. (1944). Symptomatology and management of acute grief. *American Journal of Psychiatry, 101,* 141–148.

Lippman, L., & Keith, J. (2009). *A developmental perspective on workplace readiness: Preparing high school students for success.* Washington, DC: Child Trends. Retrieved from http://www.childtrends.org/wp-content/uploads/2009/04/Child_Trends-2009_04_28_RB_WorkReady.pdf.

Lippman, L., Vandivere, S., Keith, J., & Atienza, A. (2008). Child care use by low income families: Variations across states. *Child Trends Research Brief #2008-23.* Retrieved from www.childtrends.org/wp-content/uploads/2013/07/2008-23ChildcareLow-Income.pdf.

Lipscomb, A., & Gersch, I. (2012). Using "spiritual listening tools" to investigate how children describe spiritual and philosophical meaning in their lives. *International Journal of Children's Spirituality, 17*(1), 5–23.

Litty, C., & Hatch, J. A. (2006). Hurry up and wait: Rethinking special education identification in kindergarten. *Early Childhood Education Journal, 33*(4), 203–208.

Litwin, H. (2011). Social relationships and well-being in very late life. In L. W. Poon & J. Cohen-Mansfield (Eds.), *Understanding well-being in the oldest old* (pp. 213–226). New York: Cambridge University Press.

Livingston, G. (2013). *At grandmother's house we stay.* PewResearchCenter. Retrieved from www.pewsocialtrends.org/files/2013/09/grandparents_report_final_2013.pdf.

Lloyd, C. B., Behrman, J. R., Stromquist, N. P., & Cohen, B. (2006). *The changing transitions to adulthood in developing countries: Selected studies.* Washington, DC: National Research Council.

Lochlainn, M., & Kenny, R. (2013). Sexual activity and aging. *Journal of the American Medical Directors Association, 14*(8), 565–572.

Locke, A., Ginsborg, J., & Peers, I. (2002). Development and disadvantage: Implications for the early years and beyond. *International Journal of Language & Communication Disorders, 37*(1), 3–15.

Lodge, A., & Umberson, D. (2012). All shook up: Sexuality of mid- to later life married couples. *Journal of Marriage and Family, 74*, 428–443.

Lodge, A., & Umberson, D. (2013). Age and embodied masculinities: Midlife gay and heterosexual men talk about their bodies. *Journal of Aging Studies, 27*, 225–232.

Loftin, R. W., Habli, M., & DeFranco, E. A. (2010). Late preterm births. *Review in Obstetrics and Gynecology, 3*(1), 10–19.

Lombardi, J. (2012). The federal policy environment. In Institute of Medicine and National Research Council, *From neurons to neighborhoods: An update: Workshop summary* (pp. 26–30). Paper presented at Committee on From Neurons to Neighborhoods: Anniversary Workshop, Washington, DC. Washington, DC: The National Academies Press.

Losoncz, I., & Bortolotto, N. (2009). Work-life balance: The experience of Australian working mothers. *Journal of Family Studies, 15*(2), 122–138.

Lothian, J. A. (2008). Choice, autonomy, and childbirth education. *Journal of Perinatal Education, 17*(1), 35–38.

Loureiro, T., Ferreira, A. F. A., Ushokov, F., Montenegro, N., & Nicolaides, K. H. (2012). Dilated fourth ventricle in fetuses with trisomy 18, trisomy 13 and triploidy at 11–13 weeks' gestation. *Fetal Diagnosis and Therapy, 32*(3), 186–189.

Lowe, J., Erickson, S., MacLean, P., & Duvall, S. (2009). Early working memory and maternal communication in toddlers born very low birth weight. *Acta Paediatrica, 98*, 660–663.

Lowe, J., MacLean, P., Duncan, A., Aragón, C., Schrader, R., Caprihan, A., et al. (2012). Association of maternal interaction with emotional regulation in 4- and 9-month infants during the Still Face Pardigm. *Infant Behavior and Development, 35*, 295–302.

Lowenstein, A., & Daatland, S. (2006). Filial norms and family support in a comparative cross-national context: Evidence from the OASIS study. *Ageing and Society, 26*, 203–223.

Lu, P. (2007). Sibling relationships in adulthood and old age: A case study in Taiwan. *Current Sociology, 55*(4), 621–637.

Lucas, R., & Donnellan, M. B. (2011). Personality development across the life span: Longitudinal analyses with a national sample from Germany. *Journal of Personality and Social Psychology, 101*(4), 847–861.

Lui, M., Robles, B., Leondar-Wright, B., Brewer, R., & Adamson, R. (2006). *The color of wealth.* New York: The New Press.

Lum, D. (2011). *Culturally competent practice: A framework for understanding diverse groups and justice issues* (4th ed.). Belmont, CA: Brooks/Cole, Cengage Learning.

Lund, L. K., Vik, T., Skranes, J., Brubakk, A. M., & Indredavik, M. S. (2011). Psychiatric morbidity in two low birth weight groups assessed by diagnostic interview in young adulthood. *Acta Paediatricia, 100*(4), 598–604.

Lundholm, D., & Malmberg, G. (2009). Between elderly parents and grandchildren—Geographic proximity and trends in four-generation families. *Population Ageing, 2*, 121–137.

Lunkett, S., Behnke, A., Sands, T., & Choi, B. (2009). Adolescents' reports of parental engagement and academic achievement in immigrant families. *Journal of Youth & Adolescence, 38*(2), 257–268. doi:10.1007/s10964-008-9325-4

Luo, M. (2009, April 12). Longer unemployment for those 45 and older. *New York Times.* Retrieved from http://www.nytimes.com/2009/04/13/us/13age.html?pagewanted=all&_r=0.

Luthar, S. (Ed.). (2003). *Resilience and vulnerability: Adaptation in the context of childhood adversities.* New York: Cambridge University Press.

Lyn, A. (2009). *Middle childhood matters: An inventory of full-week after school programs for children 6–12 years old in Toronto.* Toronto: Community Social Planning Council of Toronto.

Lyons-Ruth, K., & Jacobvitz, D. (2008). Attachment disorganization: Genetic factors, parenting contents, and developmental transformation from infancy to adulthood. In J. Cassidy & P. R. Shaver (Eds.), *Handbook of attachment: Theory, research, and clinical applications* (2nd ed., pp. 666–697). New York: Guilford Press.

Maccoby, E. E. (2002a). Gender and group processes: A developmental perspective. *Current Directions in Psychological Science, 11*, 55–58.

Maccoby, E. E. (2002b). Parenting effects: Issues and controversies. In J. G. Borkowski, S. Landesman Ramey, & M. Bristol-Power (Eds.), *Parenting and the child's world* (pp. 35–45). Mahwah, NJ: Lawrence Erlbaum.

Maccoby, E. E., & Jacklin, C. (1974). *The psychology of sex differences.* Stanford, CA: Stanford University Press.

MacDorman, M., Mathews, M., & Declercq, E. (2012). Home births in the United States, 1990–2009. *NCHS Data Brief*, No. 84. Hyattsville, MD: National Center for Health Statistics. Retrieved from www.cdc.gov/nchs/data/databriefs/db84.htm.

Mackey, W. C. (2001). Support for the existence of an independent man-(to)-child afiiliative bond. *Psychology of Men and Masculinity, 2*, 51–66.

MacKinlay, E. (2006). *Spiritual growth and care in the fourth age of life*. London: Jessica Kingsley.

Madden, M., Lenhart, A., Duggan, M., Cortesi, S., & Gasser, U. (2013, March). *Teens and technology 2013*. Pew Research Center and Berkman Center for Internet & Society at Harvard University. Retrieved from http://www.pewinternet.org/Reports/2013/Teens-and-Tech.aspx.

Madkour, A., Farhat, T., Halpern, C., Godeau, E., & Gabhainn, S. (2010). Early adolescent sexual initiation as a problem behavior: A comparative study of five nations. *Journal of Adolescent Health, 47*, 389–398.

Magaldi-Dopman, D., & Park-Taylor, J. (2010). Sacred adolescence: Practical suggestions for psychologists working with adolescents' religious and spiritual identity. *Professional Psychology: Research and Practice, 41*(5), 382–390.

Magon, N., Chauhan, M., Malik, S., & Shah, D. (2012). Sexuality in midlife: Where the passion goes? *Journal of Mid-life Health, 3*(2), 61–65.

Mah, V., & Ford-Jones, E. (2012). Spotlight on middle childhood: Rejuvenating the "forgotten years." *Paediatrics & Child Health, 17*(2), 81–83.

Mahendru, A., Putran, J., & Khaled, M. A. (2009). Contraceptive methods. *Foundation Years Journal, 3*(3), 9–13.

Maier, M. F., Vitiello, V. E., & Greenfield, D. B. (2012). A multilevel model of child- and classroom-level psychosocial factors that support language and literacy resilience of children in Head Start. *Early Childhood Research Quarterly, 27*(1), 104–114.

Main, M., & Hesse, E. (1990). Parents' unresolved traumatic experiences are related to infant disorganized attachment status: Is frightened and/or frightening parental behavior the linking mechanism? In M. Greenberg, D. Cicchetti, & E. M. Cumming (Eds.), *Attachment in the preschool years: Theory, research and intervention* (pp. 161–182). Chicago: University of Chicago Press.

Mäkinen, T. E., Borodulin, K., Tammelin, T., Rahkonen, O., Laatikainen, T., & Prättälä, R. (2010). The effects of adolescence sports and exercise on adulthood leisure-time physical activity in educational groups. *International Journal of Behavioral Nutrition & Physical Activity*. Retrieved from link.springer.com/article/10.1186%2F1479-5868-7-27#page-1.

Mallon, G. P., & Hess, P. M. C. (2014). *Child welfare for the twenty-first century: A handbook of practices, policies, and programs*. New York: Columbia University Press.

Malmqvist, E., Rignell-Hydbom, A., Tinnerberg, H., Bjrk, J., Stroh, E., Jakobsson, K., et al. (2011). Maternal exposure to air pollution and Birth outcomes. *Environmental Health Perspectives, 119*(4), 553–558.

Mandy, G. T. (2013). Small for gestational age infant. *UpToDate*. Retrieved from http://www.uptodate.com/contents/small-for-gestational-age-infant.

Manly, J. J., Schupf, N., Tang, M., & Stern, Y. (2005). Cognitive decline and literacy among ethnically diverse elders. *Journal of Geriatric Psychiatry and Neurology, 18*(4), 213–217.

March of Dimes. (2010). *Pregnancy loss: Stillbirth*. Retrieved from www.marchofdimes.com/loss/stillbirth.aspx.

March of Dimes. (2012a). *Born too soon: The global action report of preterm birth*. Retrieved from http://www.marchofdimes.com/glue/files/BornToSoonGARonPretermBirth_05212012.pdf.

March of Dimes. (2012b). *March of Dimes 2012 Premature birth report card*. Retrieved from http://www.marchofdimes.com/peristats/pdflib/998/US.pdf.

March of Dimes. (2012c). *Prematurity campaign*. Retrieved from http://www.marchofdimes.com/mission/march-of-dimes-prematurity-campaign.aspx.

Marcia, J. E. (1966). Development and validation of ego-identity status. *Journal of Personality and Social Psychology, 3*, 551–558.

Marcia, J. E. (1980). Identity in adolescence. In J. Adelson (Ed.), *Handbook of adolescent psychology* (pp. 159–187). New York: Wiley.

Marcia, J. E. (1993). The ego identity status approach to ego identity. In J. E. Marcia, A. S. Waterman, D. R. Mattesson, S. L. Arcjer, & J. L. Orlofksy (Eds.), *Ego identity: A handbook for psychosocial research*. New York: Springer.

Marcia, J. E. (2002). Identity and psychosocial development in adulthood. *Identity: An International Journal of Theory and Research, 2*, 7–28.

Margrett, J. A., Daugherty, K., Martin, P., MacDonald, M., Davey, A., Woodard, J. L., et al. (2011). Affect and loneliness among centenarians and the oldest old: The role of individual and social resources. *Aging & Mental Health, 15*(3), 385–396.

Marini, M. (1989). Socioeconomic consequences of the process of transition to adulthood. *Social Science Research, 18*, 89–135.

Marks, N., Bumpass, L., & Jun, H. (2004). Family roles and well-being during the middle life course. In O. Brim, C. Ryff, & R. Kessler (Eds.), *How healthy are we? A national study of well-being at midlife* (pp. 514–549). Chicago: University of Chicago Press.

Markus, H., & Kitayama, S. (2003). Models of agency: Sociocultural diversity in the construction of action. In G. Berman & J. Berman (Eds.), *Cross-cultural differences in perspectives on the self* (pp. 2–57). Lincoln: University of Nebraska Press.

Marotz, L. R., & Allen, K. E. (2013). *Developmental profiles: Pre-birth through adolescence*. Belmont, CA: Wadsworth/Cengage Learning.

Marra, J., McCarthy, E., Lin, H. J., Ford, J., Rodis, E., & Frisman, L. (2009). Effects of social support and conflict on parenting among homeless mothers. *American Journal of Orthopsychiatry, 79*(3), 348–356.

Marsh, H., & Kleitman, S. (2005). Consequences of employment during high school: Character building, subversion of academic goals, or a threshold? *American Educational Research Journal, 42,* 331–370.

Marshall, N. L., Noonan, A. E., McCartney, K., Marx, F., & Keefe, N. (2001). It takes an urban village: Parenting networks of urban families. *Journal of Family Issues, 22*(2), 163.

Marshall, V., & Mueller, M. (2003). Theoretical roots of the life-course perspective. In W. Heinz & V. Marshall (Eds.), *Social dynamics of the life course: Transitions, institutions, and interrelations* (pp. 3–32). New York: Aldine de Gruyter.

Martin, J. A., Hamilton, B. E., Osterman, M. J. K., Curtin, S., & Mathews, T. J. (2013). Births: Final data for 2012. *National Vital Statistics Reports, 62*(9). Retrieved from http://www.cdc.gov/nchs/data/nvsr62/nvsr62_09.pdf.

Martin, J. A., Hamilton, B. E., Ventura, S. J., Osterman, M. J. K., Wilson, E., & Mathews, T. J. (2012). Births: Final data for 2010. *National Vital Statistics Reports, 61*(1). Retrieved from http://www.midwife.org/CNM/CM-attended-Birth-Statistics.

Martin, M., & Zimprich, D. (2005). Cognitive development in midlife. In S. Willis & M. Martin (Eds.), *Middle adulthood: A lifespan perspective* (pp. 179–206). Thousand Oaks, CA: Sage.

Martin, P., da Rosa, G., & Poon, L. W. (2011). The impact of life events on the oldest old. In L. W. Poon & J. Cohen-Mansfield (Eds.), *Understanding well-being in the oldest old* (pp. 96–110). New York: Cambridge University Press.

Martin, T. L., & Doka, K. J. (2000). *Men don't cry . . . women do: Transcending gender stereotypes of grief.* Philadelphia: Brunner/Mazel.

Martinez, G., Copen, C., & Abma, J. (2011). Teenagers in the United States: Sexual activity, contraceptive use, and childbearing, 2006–2010 National Survey of Family Growth. National Center for Health Statistics. *Vital Health Statistics, 23*(31). Retrieved from www.cdc.gov/nchs/data/series/sr_23_031.pdf.

Martinez, J. I., Gudiño, O. G., & Lau, A. S. (2013). Problem-specific racial/ethnic disparities in pathways from maltreatment exposure to specialty mental health service use for youth in child welfare. *Child Maltreatment, 18*(2), 98–107.

Martinez-Torteya, C., Bogat, G. A., von Eye, A., & Levendosky, A. (2009). Resilience among children exposed to domestic violence: The role of risk and protective factors. *Child Development, 80*(2), 562–577.

Martins, M. V., Peterson, B. D., Almeida, V. M., & Costa, M. E. (2011). Direct and indirect effects of perceived social support on women's infertility-related stress. *Human Reproduction, 26*(8), 2113–2121.

Martins, M. V., Peterson, B. D., Costa, P., Costa, M. E., Lund, R., & Schmidt, L. (2013). Interactive effects of social support and disclosure on fertility-related stress. *Journal of Social and Personal Relationships, 30*(4), 371–388.

Mascarenhas, M. N., Flaxman, S. R., Boerma, T., Vanderpoel, S., & Stevens, G. A. (2012). National, regional, and global trends in infertility prevalence since 1990: A systematic analysis of 277 health surveys. *PLOS.* Retrieved from http://www.plosmedicine.org/article/info%3Adoi%2F10.1371%2Fjournal.pmed.1001356.

Masciadrelli, B. P., Pleck, J. H., & Stueve, J. L. (2006). Fathers' role model perceptions: Themes and linkages with involvement. *Men and Masculinities, 9*(1), 23–34.

Masse, L., & Barnett, W. S. (2002). *A benefit cost analysis of the Abecedarian Early Childhood Intervention.* Retrieved from http://niecr.org/resources/research/AbecedarianStudy.pdf.

Masten, A. S., Burt, K. B., Roisman, G. I., Obradovic, J., Long, J. D., & Tellegen, A. (2004). Resources and resilience in the transition to adulthood: Continuity and change. *Development and Psychopathology, 16,* 1071–1094.

Matone, M., O'Reilly, A. L. R., Xianquin, L., Localio, R., & Rubin, D. (2012). Home visitation program effectiveness and the influence of community behavioral norms: A propensity score matched analysis of prenatal smoking cessation. *BMC Public Health, 12*(1), 1016–1021.

Matson, J., Fodstad, J., & Dempsey, T. (2009). What symptoms predict the diagnosis of autism or PDD-NOS in infants and toddlers with developmental delays using the baby and infant screen for autism traits. *Developmental Neurorehabilitation, 12*(6), 381–388.

Matsuba, M. K., Pratt, M., Norris, J., Mohle, E., Alisat, S., & McAdams, D. (2012). Environmentalism as a context for expressing identity and generativity: Patterns among activists and uninvolved youth and midlife adults. *Journal of Personality, 80*(4), 1091–1115.

Matthews, S., & Sun, R. (2006). Incidence of four-generation family lineages: Is timing of fertility or mortality a better explanation? *The Journals of Gerontology, Series B: Psychological Sciences and Social Sciences, 61B*(2), S99–S106.

Mathews, T. J., & MacDorman, M. F. (2013). Infant mortality statistics from the 2009 period linked birth/infant death data set. *National Vital Statistics Reports, 61*(8). Retrieved from http://www.cdc.gov/nchs/data/nvsr/nvsr61/nvsr61_08.pdf.

Matto, H., Strolin-Goltzman, J., & Ballan, M. (Eds.). (2014). *Neuroscience for social work: Current research and practice.* New York: Springer.

Mayer, K. U., Baltes, P. B., Baltes, M., Borchelt, M., Delius, J., Helmchen, H., et al. (1999). What do we know about old age and aging? Conclusions from the Berlin Aging Study. In P. B. Baltes & K. U. Mayer (Eds.), *The Berlin Aging Study: Aging from 70 to 100* (pp. 475–519). Cambridge, UK: Cambridge University Press.

Mayo Clinic Staff. (2011). *Male menopause: Myth or reality?* Retrieved from http://www.mayoclinic.org/male-menopause/art-20048056.

Mayo Clinic. (2013a). *Infertility: Treatment and drugs.* Retrieved from http://www.mayoclinic.com/health/infertility/DS00310/DSECTION=treatments-and-drugs.

Mayo Clinic. (2013b). *Dementia: Risk factors.* Retrieved from www.mayoclinc.com/health/dementia/DS01131/DSECTION=risk-factors.

Mayo Foundation for Medical Education and Research. (August, 2012). The power of connection: Physical, emotional and spiritual intimacy. *Mayo Clinic Health Letter* (Supplement, Special Report), *30*, 1–8. Rochester, MN: Author. Retrieved from http://web.ebscohost.com.proxy.library.vcu.edu/ehost/pdfviewer/pdfviewer?sid=3959452c-3aa2-422d-ac7d-c0d92582024d%40sessionmgr10&vid=4&hid=19.

McAdams, D. (1985). *Power, intimacy, and the life story: Personological inquries into identity.* New York: Guilford.

McAdams, D. (2001). Generativity in midlife. In M. Lachman (Ed.), *Handbook of midlife development* (pp. 395–443). New York: Wiley.

McAdams, D. (2006). *The redemptive self: Stories Americans live by.* New York: Oxford University Press.

McAdams, D., & de St. Aubin, E. (1992). A theory of generativity and its assessment through self-report, behavioral acts, and narrative themes in autobiography. *Journal of Personality and Social Psychology, 62,* 1003–1015.

McAdams, D., & de St. Aubin, E. (Eds.). (1998). *Generativity and adult development: How and why we care for the next generation.* Washington, DC: American Psychological Association.

McAdams, D., Hart, H., & Maruna, S. (1998). The anatomy of generativity. In D. McAdams & E. de St. Aubin (Eds.), *Generativity and adult development: How and why we care for the next generation* (pp. 7–43). Washington, DC: American Psychological Association.

McAdams, D., & Olson, B. (2010). Personality development: Continuity and change over the life course. *Annual Review of Psychology, 61,* 517–542.

McAdams, D., & Pals, J. (2006). A new big five: Fundamental principles for an integrative science of personality. *American Psychologist, 61,* 204–217.

McAdoo, H. P. (2001). Parent and child relationships in African American families. In N. B. Webb (Ed.), *Culturally diverse parent-child and family relationships:* *A guide for social workers and other practitioners* (pp. 89–106). New York: Columbia University Press.

McCaig, L. F., & Burt, C. W. (2005). *National Hospital Ambulatory Medical Care Survey: 2003 Emergency Department Summary* (Advance data from the vital and health statistics, No. 358). Hyattsville, MD: National Center for Health Statistics.

McCarter, S. A. (2011). Disproportionate minority contact in the American juvenile justice system: Where are we after 20 years, a philosophy shift, and three amendments? *Journal of Forensic Social Work, 1*(1), 96–107.

McCarter, S. A., & Bridges, J. B. (2011). Determining the age of jurisdiction for adolescents: The policy debate. *Journal of Policy Practice, 10*(3), 168–184.

McClure, E. (2000). A meta-analytic review of sex differences in facial expression processing and their development in infants, children and adolescents. *Psychological Bulletin, 126,* 424–453.

McCormack, D., Scott-Hayes, G., & McCusker, C. G. (2011). The impact of hyperemesis gravidaurm on maternal mental health and maternal-fetal attachment. *Journal of Psychosomatic Obstetrics and Gynecology, 32*(2), 79–87.

McCormick, M. S., Litt, J. S., Smith, V. C., & Zupancic, A. F. (2011). Prematurity: An overview and public health implications. *Annual Review of Public Health, 32,* 367–379.

McCrae, R., & Costa, P., Jr. (1990). *Personality in adulthood.* New York: Guilford Press.

McCullough, M., Enders, C., Brion, S., & Jain, A. (2005). The varieties of religious development in adulthood: A longitudinal investigation of religion and rational choice. *Journal of Personality and Social Psychology, 89*(1), 78–89.

McFarland, M., Pudrovska, T., Schieman, S., Ellison, C., & Bierman, A. (2013). Does a cancer diagnosis influence religiosity? Integrating a life course perspective. *Social Science Research, 42,* 311–320.

McFarlin, B. L. (2009). Solving the puzzle of prematurity. *American Journal of Nursing, 109*(1), 60–63.

McGoldrick, M., Carter, B., & Garcia-Preto, N. (2011a). Overview: The family life cycle in its changing context: Individual, family, and social perspectives. In M. McGoldrick, B. Carter, & N. Garcia-Preto (Eds.), *The expanded family life cycle: Individual, family, and social perspectives* (4th ed., pp. 1–19). Boston: Allyn & Bacon.

McGoldrick, M., Carter, B., & Garcia-Preto, N. (2011b). *The expanded family life cycle: Individual, family, and social perspectives* (4th ed.). Boston: Allyn & Bacon.

McGoldrick, M., & Watson, M. (2011). Siblings and the life cycle. In M. McGoldrick, B. Carter, & N. Garcia-Preto (Eds.), *The expanded family life cycle: Individual, family, and social perspectives* (4th ed., pp. 149–162). Boston: Allyn & Bacon.

McGorry, P., & Purcell, R. (2009). Youth mental health reform and early intervention: Encouraging early signs. *Early Intervention in Psychiatry, 3*(3), 161–162.

McGroder, S. M., Zaslow, M. J., Moore, K. A., Hair, E. C., & Ahluwalia, S. K. (2002). The role of parenting in shaping the impacts of welfare-to-work programs on children. In J. G. Borkowski, S. Landesman Ramey, & M. Bristol-Power (Eds.), *Parenting and the child's world* (pp. 383–410). Mahwah, NJ: Lawrence Erlbaum.

McHale, S., Crouter, A., & Whiteman, S. (2003). The family contexts of gender development in childhood and adolescence. *Social Development, 12,* 125–148.

McInnis-Dittrich, K. (2009). *Social work with elders: A biopsychosocial approach to assessment and intervention* (2nd ed.). Boston: Allyn & Bacon.

McIntosh, H., Metz, E., & Youniss, J. (2005). Community service and identity formation in adolescence. In J. Mahoney, R. Larson, & J. Eccles (Eds.), *Organized activities as contexts of development: Extracurricular activities, after-school and community programs* (pp. 331–351). Mahwah, NJ: Lawrence Erlbaum.

McIntosh, P. (1988). *White privilege: Unpacking the invisible knapsack.* (Available from Peggy McIntosh, Wellesley College Center for Research on Women, Wellesley, MA 02181.)

Mckee, K. J., Wilson, F., Chung, C. M., Hinchliff, S., Goudie, F., Elford, H., et al. (2005). Reminiscence, regrets and activity in older people in residential care: Associations with psychological health. *British Journal of Clinical Psychology, 44*(4), 543–561.

McKeering, H., & Pakenham, K. (2000). Gender and generativity issues in parenting: Do fathers benefit more than mothers from involvement in child care activities? *Sex Roles, 43*(7–8), 459–480.

McKenna, J. (2002). Breastfeeding and bedsharing: Still useful (and important) after all these years. *Mothering, 114,* 28–37.

McLean, K., & Mansfield, C. (2012). The co-construction of adolescent narrative identity: Narrative processing as a function of adolescent age, gender, and maternal scaffolding. *Developmental Psychology, 48*(2), 436–447.

McLean, K., Pasupathi, M., & Pals, J. (2007). Selves creating stories creating selves: A process model of self-development. *Personality and Social Psychology Review, 11,* 262–278.

McMahon, S. (2013). Enhancing motor development in infants and toddlers: A multidisciplinary process for creating parent education materials. *Newborn & Infant Nursing Reviews, 13,* 35–41.

McMichael, P. (2012). *Development and social change: A global perspective* (5th ed.). Los Angeles: Sage.

McMillan, D. (2011). *Challenge and resiliency: The stories of primary caregivers of people with Asperger's syndrome.* Auckland, New Zealand: University of Auckland.

McMillan, J. C., & Raghavan, R. (2009). Pediatric to adult mental health service use of young people leaving the foster care system. *Journal of Adolescent Health, 44,* 7–13.

McNeal, R. B. (2012). Checking in or checking out? Investigating the parent involvement reactive hypothesis. *Journal of Educational Research, 105*(2), 79–89.

McQuaide, S. (1998). Women at midlife. *Social Work, 43*(1), 21–31.

Mead, G. H. (1934). *Mind, self and society.* Chicago: University of Chicago Press.

Medical News Today. (2013). *What is a miscarriage? What causes a miscarriage?* Retrieved from http://www.medicalnewstoday.com/articles/262941.php.

Medicare.gov. (2013a). *What does Medicare Part A cover?* Retrieved from www.medicare.gov/what-medicare-cvoers/part-a/what-part-a-covers.html.

Medicare.gov. (2013b). *What does Medicare Part B cover?* Retrieved from www.medicare.gov/what-medicare-covers/part-b/what-medicare-part-b-covers.html.

Medicare.gov. (2013c). *Drug coverage (Part D).* Retrieved from www.medicare.gov/part-d.

Medicare.gov. (2013d). *The Affordable Care Act & Medicare.* Retrieved from www.medicare.gov/about-us/affordable-care-act/affordable-care-act.html.

MedLinePlus. (2011). *Small for gestational age.* U.S. National Library of Medicine. Retrieved from http://www.nlm.nih.gov/medlineplus/ency/article/002302.htm.

MedlinePlus. (2012a). *Female condoms.* Retrieved from http://www.nlm.nih.gov/medilineplus/ency/article/oo4002.htm.

MedLinePlus. (2012b). *Estrogen and progestin (oral contraceptives).* Retrieved from http://www.nlm.nih.gov/medlineplus/druginfo/meds/a601050.html.

Meek, M. (2000). Foreword. In K. Roskos & J. Christie (Eds.), *Play and literacy in early childhood: Research from multiple perspectives* (pp. vii–xiii). Mahwah, NJ: Lawrence Erlbaum.

Mehall, K., Spinrad, T., Eisenberg, N., & Gaertner, B. (2009). Examining the relations of infant temperament and couples' marital satisfaction to mother and father involvement: A longitudinal study. *Fathering, 7*(1), 23–48.

Meisner, B. (2012). A meta-analysis of positive and negative age stereotype priming effects on behavior among older adults. *The Journals of Gerontology, Series B: Psychological Sciences and Social Sciences, 67*(1), 13–17.

Meltzoff, A. (2002). Imitation as a mechanism of social cognition: Origins of empathy theory of mind, and the representation of action. In U. Goswami (Ed.), *Blackwell handbook of childhood cognitive development* (pp. 6–25). Malden, MA: Blackwell.

Mendle, J., Turkheimer, E., & Emery, R. (2007). Detrimental psychological outcomes associated with early pubertal timing in adolescent girls. *Developmental Review, 27*(2), 151–171.

Mensah, F., Bayer, J., Wake, M., Carlin, J., Allen, N., & Patton, G. (2013). Early puberty and childhood social and behavioral adjustment. *Journal of Adolescent Health, 53,* 118–124.

Merce, L. T., Barco, M. J., Alcazar, J. L., Sabatel, R., & Trojano, J. (2009). Intervillous and uteroplacental circulation in normal early pregnancy and early pregnancy loss assessed by 3-dimensional power Doppler angiography. *Journal of Obstetrics and Gynecology, 200*(3), 315.e1–8.

Mercer, J. (2013). *Child development: Myths and misunderstandings* (2nd ed.). Los Angeles: Sage.

Merten, J., Wickrama, K. A. S., & Williams, A. L. (2008). Adolescent obesity and young adult psychosocial outcomes: Gender and racial differences. *Journal of Youth & Adolescence, 37,* 1111–1122.

Merton, R. (1968). The Matthew Effect in science: The reward and communications systems of science. *Science, 199,* 55–63.

Michalsen, V. (2011). Mothering as a life course transition: Do women go straight for their children? *Journal of Offender Rehabilitation, 50,* 349–366.

Mickelson, K., Claffey, S., & Williams, S. (2006). The moderating role of gender and gender role attitudes on the link between spousal support and marital quality. *Sex Roles, 55,* 73–82.

Mikami, A., Griggs, M., Lerner, M. D., Emeh, C. C., Reuland, M. M., Jack, A., et al. (2013). A randomized trial of a classroom intervention to increase peers' social inclusion of children with attention-deficit/hyperactivity disorder. *Journal of Consulting & Clinical Psychology, 81*(1), 100–112.

Mikami, A., Lerner, M. D., & Lun, J. (2010). Social context influences on children's rejection by their peers. *Child Development Perspectives, 4*(2) 123–130.

Miklowitz, D., & Johnson, B. (2009). Social and familial factors in the course of bipolar disorder: Basic processes and relevant interventions. *Clinical Psychology: Science & Practice, 16*(2), 281–296.

Miller, A. K. (2010). Young adult daughters' accounts of relationships with nonresidential fathers: Relational damage, repair, and maintenance. *Journal of Divorce & Remarriage, 51*(5), 293–309.

Miller, D., Warren, L., & Owen, E. (2011). *Comparative indicators of education in the United States and other G-8 countries: 2011.* National Center for Education Statistics, U.S. Department of Education. Retrieved from nces.ed.gov/pubs2012/2012007.pdf.

Miller, J., & Garran, A. M. (2008). *Racism in the United States: Implications for the helping professions.* Belmont, CA: Thomson Brooks/Cole.

Miller, J., & Holman, J. (2006). Contraception: The state of the art. *Consultant, 46*(4), 28.

Min, J., Silverstein, M., & Lendon, J. (2012). Intergenerational transmission of values over the family life course. *Advances in Life Course Research, 17*(3), 112–120.

Minor, R., Allard, J., Younts, C., Ward, T., & de Cabo, R. (2010). Dietary interventions to extend life span and health span based on calorie restriction. *The Journals of Gerontology: Biological Sciences, 65*(7), 695–703.

Mintel Report. (2004). *Lifestyles of young adults.* Chicago: Mintel International Group.

Mishra, G., Cooper, R., & Kuh, D. (2010). A life course approach to reproductive health: Theory and methods. *Maturita, 65,* 92–97.

Misra, A. (2008). Impact of the HealthChoice program on cesarean section and vaginal birth after C-section deliveries: A retrospective analysis. *Maternal and Child Health Journal, 12*(2), 266–274.

Misra, D. P., Caldwell, C., Young, A. R., & Abelson, S. (2010). Do fathers matter? Paternal contributions to birth outcomes and racial disparities. *American Journal of Gynecology, 202*(2), 99–100.

Miyamoto, T., Tsujimura, A., Miyagawa, Y., Koh, E., Namiki, M., & Sengoku, K. (2012). Male infertility and its causes in humans. *Advances in Urology.* doi:10.1155/2012/38420. Retrieved from www.ncbi.nlm.nih.gov/pubmed/22046184.

Moen, P. (2003). Midcourse: Navigating retirement and a new life stage. In J. Mortimer & M. Shanahan (Eds.), *Handbook of the life course* (pp. 269–291). New York: Kluwer Academic/Plenum.

Mokrova, I., O'Brien, M., Calkins, S., Leerkes, E., & Marcovitch, S. (2012). Maternal expressive style and children's emotional development. *Infant and Child Development, 21,* 617–633.

Molina, K. M., Alegria, M., & Chen, C.-N. (2012). Neighborhood context and substance use disorders: A comparative analysis of racial and ethnic groups in the United States. *Drug and Alcohol Dependence, 125S,* S35–S43.

Möller, K., & Stattin, H. (2001). Are close relationships in adolescence linked with partner relationships in midlife? A longitudinal prospective study. *International Journal of Behavioral Development, 25*(1), 69–77.

Mongillo, E., Briggs-Gowan, M., Ford, J., & Carter, A. (2009). Impact of traumatic life events in a community sample of toddlers. *Journal of Abnormal Child Psychology, 37*(4), 455–468.

Monsour, M. (2002). *Women and men as friends: Relationships across the life span in the 21st century.* Mahwah, NJ: Lawrence Erlbaum.

Montague, D., Magai, C., Consedine, N., & Gillespie, M. (2003). Attachment in African American and European American older adults: The roles of early life socialization and religiosity. *Attachment and Human Development, 5,* 188–214.

Montgomery, R. J. V., & Kosloski, K. D. (1994). A longitudinal analysis of nursing home placement for dependent elders cared for by spouses vs. adult children. *The Journals of Gerontology: Social Sciences, 49,* S62–S74.

Montgomery, R. J. V., & Kosloski, K. D. (2000). Family caregiving: Change, continuity and diversity. In P. Lawton & R. Rubenstein (Eds.), *Alzheimer's disease and related dementias: Strategies in care and research*. New York: Springer.

Montgomery, R. J. V., & Kosloski, K. D. (2009). Caregiving as a process of changing identity: Implications for caregiver support. *Generations, 33*, 47–52.

Montirosso, R., Fedeli, C., Murray, L., Morandi, F., Brusati, R., Perego, G., et al. (2012). The role of negative maternal affective states and infant temperament in early interactions between infants with cleft lip and their mothers. *Journal of Pediatric Psychology, 37*(2), 241–250.

Moody, H. R. (2010). *Aging: Concepts and controversies* (6th ed.). Thousand Oaks, CA: Pine Forge Press.

Moody, H. R., & Sasser, J. (2012). *Aging: Concepts and controversies* (7th ed.). Los Angeles: Sage.

Moore, K. L., Persaud, T. V. N., & Torchia, M. G. (2013). *Before we are born: Essentials of embryology and birth defects* (8th ed.). Philadelphia: Saunders/Elsevier.

Moore, K. L., Redd, Z., Burkhauser, M., Mbwana, K., & Collins, A. (2009). *Children in poverty: Trends, consequences, and policy options*. Washington, DC: Child Trends. Retrieved from www.childtrends.org/wp-content/uploads/2013/11/2009-11ChildreninPoverty.pdf.

Moraru, L., Sameni, R., Schneider, U., Haueisen, J., Schleußner, E., & Hoyer, D. (2011). Validation of fetal auditory evoked cortical responses to enhance the assessment of early brain development using fetal MEG measurements. *Physiological Measurement, 32*(11), 1847–1868.

Moreau, C., Cleland, K., & Trussell, J. (2007). Contraceptive discontinuation attributed to method dissatisfaction in the United States. *Contraception, 76*(4), 267–272.

Moreno, M., Furtner, F., & Rivara, F. (2010). Information about adolescent sleep. *Archives of Pediatric and Adolescent Medicine, 164*(7), 684–687.

Morgan, A. (2000). *What is narrative therapy?* Adelaide, South Australia: Dulwich Centre.

Morris, T., & McInerney, K. (2010). Media representations of pregnancy and childbirth: An analysis of reality television programs in the United States. *Birth, 37*(2), 134–140.

Mortimer, J. (2004). *Working and growing up in America*. Boston: Harvard University Press.

Morton, C., & Hsu, C. (2007). Contemporary dilemmas in American childbirth education: Findings from a comparative ethnographic study. *Journal of Perinatal Education, 16*(4), 25–37.

Mosher, W. D., Jones, J., & Abma, J. C. (2012). *Intended and unintended births in the United States: 1982–2010*. Retrieved from http://www.cdc.gov/nchs/data/nhsr/nhsr055.pdf.

Moyer, K. (1974). Discipline. In K. Moyer, *You and your child: A primer for parents* (pp. 40–61). Chicago: Nelson Hall.

Moyers, B. D., Mannes, E., Pellet, G., O'Neill, J. D., & Moyers, J. D. (2000). *On our own terms: Moyers on dying*. New York: Films for the Humanities & Sciences.

Mudrazija, S., & Thomeer, M. B. (2012, August 16). *Race and gender differences in nursing home admissions and discharges*. Paper presented at the American Sociological Association Annual Meeting. Denver, Colorado. Retrieved from http://citation.allacademic.com/meta/p562808_index.html.

Mueller, M., Wilhelm, B., & Elder, G. (2002). Variations in grandparenting. *Research on Aging, 24*(3), 360–388.

Muir, D., & Lee, K. (2003). The still face effect: Methodological issues and new applications. *Infancy, 4*, 483–491.

Munakata, Y., McClelland, J., Johnson, M., & Siegler, R. (1997). Rethinking infant knowledge: Toward an adaptive process account of successes and failures in object permanence tasks. *Psychological Review, 104*(4), 618–713.

Muraco, A., & Fredriksen-Goldsen, K. (2011). "That's what friends do": Informal caregiving for chronically ill midlife and older lesbian, gay, and bisexual adults. *Journal of Social and Personal Relationships, 28*(8), 1073–1092.

Murano, T., & Cocuzza, T. (2009). Ectopic pregnancy. *Emergency Medicine Reports: The Practical Journal for Emergency Physicians, 30*(23), 281–287.

Murillo, E. G. (2010). *Handbook of Latinos and education: Theory, research and practice*. New York: Routledge.

Murphey, D. (2013). Home front alert: The risks facing young children in military families. *Child Trends Research Brief*. Retrieved from http://www.childtrends.org/wp-content/uploads/2013/07/2013-31MilitaryFamilies.pdf.

Nagata, D., Cheng, W., & Tsai, A. (2010). Chinese-American grandmothering: A qualitative exploration. *Asian American Journal of Psychology, 1*(2), 151–161.

Naleppa, M. J. (1996). Families and the institutionalized elderly: A review. *Journal of Gerontological Social Work, 27*, 87–111.

Nangia, A. K., Likosky, D. S., & Wang, D. (2010). Access to assisted reproductive technology centers in the United States. *Fertility and Sterility, 93*(3), 745–761.

National Association of Child Care Resources and Referral Agencies. (2012). *Child care in America: 2012 state fact sheets*. Retrieved from www.naccrra.org/sites/default/files/default_site_pages/2012/full2012cca_state_factsheetbook.pdf.

National Association of Counties. (2008). *Youth aging out of foster care*. Retrieved from www.dshs.wa.gov/pdf/ca/YouthAgingoutoffoster.pdf.

National Association of Social Workers. (2003). *NASW standards for integrating genetics into social work practice* (Item # S03). Washington, DC: Author.

National Association of Social Workers. (2008). *Code of ethics* (Rev. ed.). Washington, DC: Author.

National Business Group on Health. (2009). *Preventing prematurity and adverse birth outcomes: What employers should know*. Center for Prevention and Health Services. Retrieved from http://www.businessgrouphealth.org/pub/f314b76e-2354-d714-5142-0b6fe2192d60.

National Center for Biotechnology Information. (2013). *NCBI map viewer*. Retrieved from http://www.ncbi.nlm.nih.gov/mapview/maps.cgi?TAXID=9606&chr=Y&maps=ideogr%2CugHs%2Cgenes.

National Center for Clinical Infant Programs. (1992). How community violence affects children, parents, and practitioners. *Public Welfare, 50*(4), 25–35.

National Center for Health Statistics. (2009). *Limitations in activities of daily living and instrumental activities of daily living, 2003–2007*. Retrieved from http://www.cdc.gov/nchs/health_policy/ADL_tables.htm.

National Center for Health Statistics. (2012). *LCWK1. Deaths, percent of total deaths, and death rates for the leading causes of death in 5-year age groups, by race and sex: United States, 2010*. Retrieved from www.cdc.gov.nchs/data/dvs/LCWK1_2010.pdf.

National Center for Health Statistics. (2013). *Health, United States, 2012: With special feature on emergency care*. Hyattsville, MD: CDC.

National Down Syndrome Society (NDSS). (2013). *Down syndrome facts*. Retrieved from http://www.ndss.org/Down-Syndrome/Down-Syndrome-Facts.

National Eating Disorders Association. (n.d.). *Pregnancy and eating disorders*. Retrieved from www.nationaleatingdisorders.org/pregnancy-and-eating-disorders.

National Hospice and Palliative Care Organization. (2012). *NHPCO facts and figures: Hospice care in America 2011*. Alexandria, VA: National Hospice and Palliative Care Organization.

National Human Genome Research Institute (NHGRI). National Institutes of Health. (2012). *Genetic Information Nondiscrimination Act (GINA) of 2008*. Retrieved from http://www.genome.gov.

National Human Genome Research Institute (NHGRI). National Institutes of Health. (2013a). *Intellectual property and genomics*. Retrieved from https://www.genome.gov/19016590.

National Human Genome Research Institute (NHGRI). National Institutes of Health. (2013b). *FAQ about genetic disorders*. Retrieved from www.geome.gov/19016930.

National Institute of Health. (2013). *Puberty and precocious puberty: Overview*. Retrieved from http://nichd.nih.gov/health/topics/puberty/Pages/default.aspx.

National Institute of Mental Health. (2011). *Older adults: Depression and suicide facts*. Washington, DC: Author.

National Institute of Neurological Disorders and Stroke (NINDS). (2013). *Parkinson's disease: Hope through research*. Retrieved from www.ninds.nih.gov/disorders/parkinson_disease/detail_parkinsons_disease_htm.

National Institute on Aging. (2013a). *Health & aging: Menopause*. Retrieved from http://www.nia.nih.gov/health/publication/menopause.

National Institute on Aging. (2013b). *About Alzheimer's disease: Symptoms*. Retrieved from http://www.nia.nih.gov/alzheimers/topics/symptoms?utm_source=ad_fact_sheet&utm_medium=web&utm_content=symptoms&utm_campaign=top_promo_box#very.

National Newborn Screening and Global Resource Center (NNSGRC). (2013). *Newborn screening*. Retrieved from http://genes-r-us.uthscsa.edu/sites/genes-r-us/files/nbs-disorders.pdf.

National Research Council. (2012). *From neurons to neighborhoods: An update: Workshop summary*. Washington, DC: National Academies Press.

National School Board Association. (2013). *Issue brief. Individuals with Disabilities Education Act (IDEA): Early preparation for reauthorization*. Retrieved from http://www.nsba.org/Advocacy/Key-Issues/SpecialEducation/NSBA-Issue-Brief-Individuals-with-Disabilities-Education-Act-IDEA.pdf.

National Sleep Foundation. (2013). *Teens and sleep*. Retrieved from http://www.sleepfoundation.org/article/sleep-topics/teens-and-sleep.

National Women's Health Network. (2011). *Depo provera and bone mineral density: Fact sheets*. Retrieved from http://nwhn.org/depo-provera-and-bone-mineral-density.

National Women's Law Center. (2011). *Mothers behind bars: States are failing*. Retrieved from http://www.nwlc.org/resource/mothers-behind-bars-states-are-failing.

Natsuaki, M., Leve, L., Shaw, D., Scaramella, L., Ge, X., Neiderhiser, J., et al. (2010). Genetic libability, environment, and the development of fussiness in toddlers: The roles of maternal depression and parental responsiveness. *Developmental Psychology, 46*(5), 1147–1158.

Nazzi, T., & Gopnik, A. (2001). Linguistic cognitive abilities in infancy: When does language become a tool for categorization? *Cognition, 80*, B11–B20.

Needham, A. (2001). Object recognition and object segregation in 4-5-month-old infants. *Journal of Experimental Child Psychology, 78*, 3–24.

Nelson, C. (2001). The development and neural bases of face recognition. *Infant and Child Development, 10*, 3–18.

Nelson-Becker, H., & Canda, E. R. (2008). Spirituality, religion, and aging research in social work: State of the art and future possibilities. *Journal of Religion, Spirituality and Aging, 20*(3), 177–193.

Neto, R., Leite, M., Reis, A., Olavo, A., de Abreu, L., de Alencar, M., et al. (2012). Combined oral contraceptives and increased cardiovascular risk: Thromboembolism and hypertension. *HealthMed, 6*(9), 3004–3007.

Nettles, S., Mucherah, W., & Jones, D. (2000). Understanding resilience: The role of social resources. *Journal of Education for Students Placed at Risk, 5*(1 & 2), 47–60.

Neugarten, B. L., Havighurst, R. J., & Tobin, S. S. (1968). Personality and patterns of aging. In B. L. Neugarten (Ed.), *Middle age and aging*. Chicago: University of Chicago Press.

Neugarten, B. L., & Weinstein, K. K. (1964). The changing American grandparent. *Journal of Marriage and the Family, 26*, 199–204.

Newcomb, N., & Dubas, J. (1992). A longitudinal study of predictors of spatial ability in adolescent females. *Child Development, 63*, 37–46.

Newman, B., & Newman, P. (2012). *Development through life: A psychosocial approach* (11th ed.). Belmont, CA: Wadsworth/Cengage Learning.

Newman, D. (2012). *Sociology: Exploring the architecture of everyday life* (9th ed.). Thousand Oaks, CA: Sage.

Newman, K. S. (2008). Ties that bind: Cultural interpretations of delayed adulthood in Western Europe and Japan. *Sociological Forum, 23*(4), 645–669.

Newman, K. S. (2012). *The accordion family: Boomerang kids, anxious parents and the private toll of global competition*. Boston: Beacon Press.

Nguyen, P. (2008). Perceptions of Vietnamese fathers' acculturation levels, parenting styles, and mental health outcome in Vietnamese American adolescent immigrants. *Social Work, 53*(4), 337–346.

Nguyen, P., & Cheung, M. (2009). Parenting styles as perceived by Vietnamese American adolescents. *Child and Adolescent Social Work Journal, 26*, 505–581.

Ning, L. Pang, L., Chen, G., Song, X., Zhang, J., & Zheng, X. (2011). Risk factors for depression in older adults in Beijing. *The Canadian Journal of Psychiatry, 56*(8), 466–473.

Nishitani, S., Miyamura, T., Tagawa, M., Sumi, M., Takase, R., Doi, H., et al. (2009). The calming effect of a maternal breast milk odor on the human newborn infant. *Neuroscience Research, 63*(1), 66–71.

Nitzburg, G. C., & Farber, B. A. (2013). Putting up emotional (Facebook) walls? Attachment status and emerging adults' experiences of social networking sites. *Journal of Clinical Psychology: In Session, 69*(11), 1183–1190.

Noddings, N. (2013). *Caring: A relational approach to ethics and moral education*. Berkeley: University of California Press.

Nourhashemi, F., Gilletee-Guyonnet, S., Rolland, Y., Cante, C., Hein, C., & Vellas, B. (2009). Alzheimer's disease progression in the oldest old compared to younger elderly patients: Data from the REAL, FR study. *International Journal of Geriatric Psychiatry, 24*, 149–155.

Nuttgens, S. (2010). Biracial identity theory and research juxtaposed with narrative accounts of a biracial individual. *Child & Adolescent Social Work Journal, 27*(5), 355–364.

Ny, K., Loy, J., Gudmunson, C., & Cheong, W. (2009). Gender differences in marital and life satisfaction among Chinese Malaysians. *Sex Roles, 60*, 33–43.

Nybell, L., Shook, J., & Finn, J. (Eds.). (2009). *Childhood, youth, & social work in transformation: Implications for policy & practice*. New York: Columbia University Press.

Obama, B. (2014, January 28). *State of the union address*. Retrieved from www.whitehouse.gov/the-press-office/2014/28/president-barack-obama-state-union-address.

Office of Citizen Services and Innovative Technologies. (2013). *Housing for seniors*. Published by USA.gov. Retrieved from http://www.usa.gov/Topics/Seniors/Housing.shtml.

Office of Minority Health. (2014). *Asian American profile*. Retrieved from http://minorityhealth.hhs.gov/templates/browse.aspx?lvl=2&lvlID=53.

Of meat, Mexicans and social mobility. (2006, June 17). *The Economist, 379*(8482), 31–32.

Ogden, J., Stavrinaki, M., & Stubbs, J. (2009). Understanding the role of life events in weight loss and weight gain. *Psychology, Health, & Medicine, 14*(2), 239–249.

O'Keefe, M. (1994). Adjustment of children from maritally violent homes. *Families in Society, 75*, 403–415.

O'Keefe, M. (1997). Adolescents' exposure to community and school violence: Prevalence and behavioral correlates. *Journal of Adolescent Health, 20*, 368–376.

Olas, B., & Wachowicz, B. (2005). Resveratrol: A phenotic antioxidant with effects on blood platelet functions. *Platelets, 16*(5), 251–260.

O'Leary, V., & Bhaju, J. (2006). Resilience and empowerment. In J. Worrel & C. Goodheart (Eds.), *Handbook of girls' and women's psychological health: Gender and well-being across the life span* (pp. 157–165). New York: Oxford Press.

Olshansky, S. J., Antonucci, T., Berkman, L., Binstock, R., Boersch-Supan, A., Cacioppo, J., et al. (2012). Differnces in life expectancy due to race and educational differences are widening, and many may not catch up. *Health Affairs, 31*(8), 1803–1810.

Olusanya, B. (2010). Is undernutrition a risk factor for sensorineural hearing loss in early infancy? *British Journal of Nutrition, 103*, 1296–1301.

O-Prasetsawat, P., & Petchum, S. (2004). Sexual behavior of secondary school students in Bangkok metropolis. *Journal of the Medical Association of Thailand, 87*(7), 755–759.

O'Rand, A. (2009). Cumulative processes in the life course. In G. Elder & J. Giele (Eds.), *The craft of life course research* (pp. 121–140). New York: Guilford.

Orfield, G., Kucsev, J., & Siegal-Harvey, G. (2012). *E Pluribus . . . separation: Deepening double segregation for more students*. The Civil Rights Project. Retrieved from http://civilrightsproject.ucla.edu/research/k-12-education/integration-and-diversity/mlk-national/e-pluribus. . . separation-deepening-double-segregation-for-more-students.

Ornstein, P., & Light, L. (2010). Memory development across the life span. In R. Lerner (Series Ed.) & W. Overton (Vol. Ed.), *Handbook of life-span development: Vol. 1. Biology, cognition, and methods across the life span.* Hoboken, NJ: Wiley.

Orr, S. T., James, S. A., & Reiter, J. P. (2008). Unintended pregnancy and prenatal behaviors among urban, black women in Baltimore, Maryland: The Baltimore preterm birth study. *Annals of Epidemiology, 18*(7), 545–551.

Ortega, F. B., Konstabel, K., Pasquali, E., Ruiz, J. R., Hurtig-Wennlöf, A., Mäestu, J., et al. (2013). Objectively measured physical activity and sedentary time during childhood, adolescence and young adulthood: A cohort study. *Plos ONE, 8*(4), 1–8.

Ortega, F. B., Ruiz, J., Castillo, R., Chillón, P., Labayen, I., Martínez-Gómez, D., et al. (2010). Sleep duration and cognitive performance in adolescents: The AVENA study. *ACTA Paediatrica, 99,* 454–456.

Ortiz, I., Daniels, L. M., & Engilbertsdóttir, S. (Eds.). (2012). *Child poverty and inequality: New perspectives.* New York: United Nation's Children's Fund.

Osler, M., Avlund, K., & Mortensen, E. (2012). Socioeconomic position early in life, cognitive development and cognitive change from young adulthood to middle age. *European Journal of Public Health, 23*(6), 974–980.

Osorio, A., Burgo, C., Carlos, S., Ruiz-Canela, M., Delgado, M., & Irala, J. (2012). First sexual intercourse and subsequent regret in three developing countries. *Journal of Adolescent Health, 50,* 271–278.

Osterweil, N. (2013, November 6). Genetic anomalies account for majority of miscarriages. *Ob.Gyn News.* Retrieved from http://www.obgynnews.com/single-view/genetic-anomalies-account-for-majority-of-miscarriages/64d9325e6b83614b2d1aca488b2fd98.html.

Ostir, G., & Goodwin, J. (2006). High anxiety is associated with an increased risk of death in an older tri-ethnic population. *Journal of Clinical Epidemiology, 59*(5), 534–540.

Ostrov, J., Crick, N., & Stauffacher, K. (2006). Relational aggression in sibling and peer relationships during early childhood. *Journal of Developmental Psychology, 27*(3), 241–253.

Oudekerk, B., Farr, R., & Reppucci, N. D. (2013). Is it love or sexual abuse? Young adults' perceptions of statutory rape. *Journal of Child Sexual Abuse, 22*(7), 858–877.

Oyserman, D., Bybee, D., Mowbray, C., & MacFarlane, P. (2002). Positive parenting among African American mothers with a serious mental illness. *Journal of Marriage and Family, 65,* 65–77.

Ozgoli, G., Goli, M., & Simbar, M. (2009). Effects of ginger capsules on pregnancy, nausea, and vomiting. *Journal of Alternative and Complementary Medicine, 15*(3), 243–246.

Padilla, Y. C., & Jordan, M. W. (1997). Determinants of Hispanic poverty in the course of the transition to adulthood. *Hispanic Journal of Behavioral Sciences, 19*(4), 416–433.

Page, A., Milner, A., Morrell, S., & Taylor, R. (2013). The role of under-employment and unemployment in recent birth cohort effects in Australian suicide. *Social Science & Medicine, 93,* 155–162.

Painter, K. (2012). Outcomes for youth with severe emotional disturbance: A repeated measures longitudinal study of a wraparound approach of service delivery in systems of care. *Child & Youth Care Forum, 41*(4), 407–425.

Palmer, A. M., & Francis, P. T. (2006). Neurochemistry of aging. In J. Pathy, A. J. Sinclair, & E. J. Morley (Eds.), *Principles and practice of geriatric medicine* (4th ed., pp. 59–67). Chichester, England: John Wiley & Sons.

Palomba, S., Falbo, A., Dicelio, A., Materozzo, C., & Zullo, F. (2012). Nexplanon: A new implant for long-term contraception: A comprehensive descriptive review. *Gynecological Endocrinology, 28*(9), 710–721.

Paquette, K., & Bassuk, E. (2009). Parenting and homelessness: Overview and introduction to the special edition. *American Journal of Orthopsychiatry, 79*(3), 292–298.

Parham, L., Quadagno, J., & Brown, J. (2009). Race, politics and social policy. In J. Midley & M. Livermore (Eds.), *The handbook of social policy* (2nd ed., pp. 263–279). Thousand Oaks, CA: Sage.

Parish, S., Saville, A., & Swaine, J. (2011). Policies and programs for children and youth with disabilities. In J. Jenson & M. Fraser (Eds.), *Social policy for children and families: A risk and resilience perspective* (2nd ed., pp. 236–269). Los Angeles: Sage.

Parkinson's Disease Foundation. (2010). *Understanding Parkinson's: Parkinson's FAQ.* Retrieved from http://www.pdf.org/pdf/fs_frequently_asked_questions_10.pdf.

Parkinson's Disease Foundation. (2013). *Prescription medications.* Retrieved from http://www.pdf.org/parkinson_prescription_meds.

Parkinson's Disease Foundation. (2014). *Diagnosis.* Retrieved from http://www.pdf.org/en/diagnosis.

Parkland Memorial Hospital. (2000). *Parkland School of Nurse Midwifery: History of midwifery in the U.S.* Retrieved from http://www.swmed.edu/home_pages/parkland/midwifery/txt/mdwfhsustxt.html.

Parra-Cordeno, M., Rodrigo, R., Barja, P., Bosco, C., Rencoret, G., & Sepulveda Martinez, A. (2013). Prediction of early and late pre-eclampsia from maternal characteristics, uterine artery Doppler and markers of vasculogenesis during first trimester of pregnancy. *Ultrasound in Obstetrics and Gynecology, 41*(5), 538–544.

Parsons, M., & Peluso, P. R. (2013). Grandfamilies and their grand challenges. In P. R. Peluso, R. E. Watts, & M. Parsons (Eds.), *Changing aging, changing family therapy* (pp. 45–61). New York: Routledge.

Passel, J., & Cohn, D. (2008). *Immigration to play lead role in future U.S. growth.* Retrieved from www.pewhispanic.org/2008/02/11/us-population-projections-2005-2050.

Patil, C. L., Abrams, E. T., Steinmetz, A., & Young, S. L. (2012). Appetite sensations and nausea and vomiting in pregnancy: An overview of explanations. *Ecology of Food and Nutrition, 51*(5), 394–417.

Paul, E. (1997). A longitudinal analysis of midlife interpersonal relationships and well-being. In M. Lachman & J. James (Eds.), *Multiple paths of midlife development* (pp. 171–206). Chicago: University of Chicago Press.

Payne, R. K. (2013). *A framework for understanding poverty: A cognitive approach* (5th ed.). Highlands, TX: Aha! Process.

Pearlin, L., & Skaff, M. (1996). Stress and the life course: A paradigmatic alliance. *The Gerontologist, 36*(2), 239–247.

Pearlstein, T., Howard, M., Salisbury, A., & Zlotnick, C. (2009). Postpartum depression. *American Journal of Obstetrics & Gynecology, 200*(4), 357–364.

Peart, N. A., Pungello, E. P., Campbell, F. A., & Richey, T. G. (2006). Faces of fatherhood: African-American young adults view the paternal role. *Families in Society, 87*(1), 71–83.

Pecora, P. J., & Harrison-Jackson, M. (2011). Child welfare policies and programs. In J. Jenson & M. Fraser (Eds.), *Social policy for children and families: A risk and resilience perspective* (2nd ed., pp. 57–112). Thousand Oaks, CA: Sage.

Pecora, P. J., Kessler, R. C., Williams, J., O'Brien, K., Downs, A. C., English, D., et al. (2005). *Improving family foster care: Findings from the Northwest Foster Care Alumni Study.* Seattle, WA: Casey Family Programs.

Pempek, T. A., Yermolayeva, Y. A., & Calvert, S. L. (2009). College students' social networking experiences on Facebook. *Journal of Applied Developmental Psychology, 30*, 227–238.

Peng, G., & Wang, W. (2011). Hemisphere lateralization is influenced by bilingual status and composition of words. *Neuropsychologia, 49*, 1981–1986.

Pennings, G., & Mertes, H. (2012). Ethical issues in infertility treatment. *Best Practice & Research Clinical Obstetrics and Gynaecology, 26*, 853–863.

Pepino, M. Y., & Mennella, J. A. (2006). Children's liking of sweet tastes: A reflection of our basic biology. In W. Spillane (Ed.), *Optimising sweet taste in foods* (pp. 54–65). Cambridge, UK: Woodhead.

Pepler, D. J. (2012). *The development and treatment of girlhood aggression.* New York: Psychology Press.

Perlman, D., & Fehr, B. (1987). The development of intimate relationships. In D. Perlman & S. Duck (Eds.), *Intimate relationships: Development, dynamics, & deterioration* (pp. 13–42). Newbury Park, CA: Sage.

Perrig-Chiello, P., & Perren, S. (2005). Impact of past transitions on well-being in middle age. In S. Willis &

M. Martin (Eds.), *Middle adulthood: A lifespan perspective* (pp. 143–178). Thousand Oaks, CA: Sage.

Perry, B. (2002). Childhood experience and the expression of genetic potential: What childhood neglect tells us about nature and nurture. *Brain & Mind, 3*(1), 79–100.

Perry-Parrish, C., & Zeman, J. (2011). Relations among sadness regulation, peer acceptance, and social functioning in early adolescence: The role of gender. *Social Development, 20*(1), 135–153. doi:10.1111/j.1467-9507.2009.00568.x

Perz, J., & Ussher, J. (2008). "The horror of this living decay": Women's negotiation and resistance of medical discourses around menopause and midlife. *Women's Studies International Forum, 31*, 293–299.

Petersen, R. (2011). Mild cognitive impairment. *The New England Journal of Medicine, 364*(23), 2227–2234.

Peterson, B., & Duncan, L. (2007). Midlife women's generativity and authoritarianism: Marriage, motherhood, and 10 years of aging. *Psychology and Aging, 22*(3), 411–419.

Petrovic, K. (2013). Respite and the internet: Accessing care for older adults in the 21st century. *Computers in Human Behavior, 29*, 2448–2452.

Petty, T. C. (n.d.). *The second breath of life.* Retrieved from http://www.nlhep.org/Documents/SecondBreath.pdf.

Pew Center for Social and Demographic Trends. (2009). *Growing old in America: Expectations vs. reality.* Retrieved from http://www.pewsocialtrends.org/2009/06/29/growing-old-in-america-expectations-vs-reality.

Pew Center for Social and Demographic Trends. (2013). *The return of the multi-generational family household.* Retrieved from http://www.pewsocialtrends.org/2010/03/18/the-return-of-the-multi-generational-family-household.

Pew Research Center. (2010). *Millennials: A portrait of generation next. Confident. Connected. Open to change.* Retrieved from http://pewresearch.org/millennials.

Pharris-Ciurej, N., Hirschman, C., & Willhoft, J. (2012). The 9th grade shock and the high school dropout crisis. *Social Science Research, 41*, 709–730.

Phinney, J. (2006). Ethnic identity exploration in emerging adulthood. In J. Arnett & J. Tanner (Eds.), *Emerging adults in America: Coming of age in the 21st century* (pp. 117–134). Washington, DC: American Psychological Association.

Piacenti, R. (2011). Toward meaningful response to the problem of anti-gay bullying in American public schools. *Virginia Journal of Social Policy & the Law, 19*(1), 58–108.

Piaget, J. (1936/1952). *The origins of intelligence in children.* New York: International Universities Press.

Piaget, J. (1972). Intellectual evolution from adolescence to adulthood. *Human Development, 15*, 1–12.

Piazza, J., & Charles, S. (2006). Mental health among baby boomers. In S. Whitbourne & S. Willis (Eds.), *The baby boomers grow up: Contemporary perspectives on midlife (pp. 111–146). Mahwah, NJ: Lawrence Erlbaum.

Pierce, B. (2012). Genetics: A conceptual approach. New York: W. H. Freeman.

Pierce, K. (2011). Early functional brain development in autism and the promise of sleep fMRI. Brain Research, 1380, 162–174.

Pillemer, K., Suitor, J., Pardo, S., & Henderson, C. (2010). Mothers' differentiation and depressive symptoms among adult children. Journal of Marriage and the Family, 72, 333–345.

Pinker, S. (2002). The blank slate: The modern denial of human nature. New York: Penguin.

Pinzon, J., & Jones, V. (2012). Care of adolescent parents and their children. Pediatrics, 130(6), 1743–1756.

Plassman, B., Langa, K., Fisher, G., Heeringa, S., Weir, D., Ofstedal, M., et al. (2007). Prevalence of dementia in the United States: The aging, demographics, and memory study. Neuroepidemiology, 29, 125–132.

Playfer, J. R. (2006). Parkinson's disease and Parkinsonism in the elderly. In J. Pathy, A. J. Sinclair, & E. J. Morley (Eds.), Principles and practice of geriatric medicine (4th ed., pp. 765–776). Chichester, England: John Wiley & Sons.

Podulka, J., Stranges, E., & Steiner, C. (2011). Hospitalizations related to childbirth, 2008: Statistical brief 110. Healthcare Costs and Utilization Project. Rockville, MD: Agency for Health Care Policy and Research. Retrieved from http://www.hcup-us.ahrq.gov/reports/statbriefs/sb110.jsp.

Ponterotto, J. G. (2010). Handbook of multicultural counseling. Thousand Oaks, CA: Sage.

Ponton, L., & Judice, S. (2004). Typical adolescent sexual development. Child and Adolescent Psychiatric Clinics of North America, 13(3), 497–511.

Poon, C. Y. M., & Knight, B. G. (2013). Parental emotional support during emerging adulthood and baby boomers' well-being in midlife. International Journal of Behavioral Development, 37, 498–504.

Poon, L. W., & Cohen-Mansfield, J. (2011). Understanding well-being in the oldest old. New York: Cambridge University Press.

Poon, L. W., Jazwinski, M., Green, R. C., Woodard, J. L., Martin, P., Rodgers, W. L., et al. (2007). Methodological considerations in studying centenarians: Lessons learned from the Georgia Centenarian Studies. Annual Review of Gerontology & Geriatrics, 27, 231–264.

Portes, A., & Rumbaut, R. G. (2001). Legacies. Berkeley: University of California Press.

Posmontier, B., & Horowitz, J. (2004). Postpartum practices and depression prevalences: Technocentric and ethnokinship cultural perspectives. Journal of Transcultural Nursing, 15, 34–43.

Poteat, V. P., Aragon, S., Espelage, D., & Koenig, B. (2009). Psychosocial concerns of sexual minority youth: Complexity and caution in group differences. Journal of Consulting and Clinical Psychology, 77(1), 196–201.

Potter, C. (2004). Gender differences in childhood and adolescence. In P. Allen-Meares & M. Fraser (Eds.), Intervention with children and adolescents: An interdisciplinary perspective (pp. 54–79). Boston: Allyn & Bacon.

Prasad, B. (2001). Maternal employment and child abuse. The Indian Journal of Social Work, 62(3), 328–346.

Premberg, A. (2006). Fathers' experience of childbirth education. Journal of Perinatal Education, 15(2), 21–28.

Premberg, A., Carlsson, G., Hellström, A., & Berg, M. (2011). First-time fathers' experiences of childbirth: A phenomenological study. Midwifery, 27, 848–853.

Premberg, A., Hellström, A.-L., & Berg, M. (2008). Experiences of the first year as father. Scandinavian Journal of Caring Sciences, 22(1), 56–63.

Price, B. (2009). Body image in adolescents: Insights and implications. Paediatric Nursing, 21 (5), 38–43.

Price, S. K. (2008a). Stepping back to gain perspective: Pregnancy loss history, depression, and parenting capacity in the Early Childhood Longitudinal Study, Birth Cohort (ECLS-B). Death Studies, 32(2), 97–122.

Price, S. K. (2008b). Women and reproductive loss: Client-worker dialogues designed to break the silence. Social Work, 53(4), 367–376.

Proot, I. M., Abu-Saad, H. H., ter Meulen, R. H. J., Goldsteen, M., Spreeuwenberg, C., & Widdershoven, G. A. M. (2004). The needs of terminally ill patients at home: Directing one's life, health and things related to beloved others. Palliative Medicine, 18, 53–61.

PubMed Health. (2011). Premature infant. Retrieved from http://www.ncbi.nlm.nih.gov/pubmedhealth/PMH0002529.

Pulkkinen, L., & Kokko, K. (2000). Identity development in adulthood: A longitudinal study. Journal of Research in Personality, 34, 445–470.

Pulkkinen, L., Kokko, K., & Rantanen, J. (2012). Paths from socioemotional behavior in middle childhood to personality in middle adulthood. Developmental Psychology, 48(5), 1283–1291.

Putney, N., & Bengtson, V. (2003). Intergenerational relations in changing times. In J. Mortimer & M. Shanahan (Eds.), Handbook of the life course (pp. 149–164). New York: Kluwer Academic/Plenum.

Qouta, S., Punamaki, R., & El-Sarraj, E. (2003). Prevalence and determinants of PTSD among Palestinian children exposed to military violence. European Psychiatry and Adolescent Psychiatry, 12(6), 265–272.

Quadagno, J. (2007). Aging and the life course: An introduction to social gerontology (4th ed.). Hightstown, NJ: McGraw-Hill.

Raatikainen, K., Huurinainen, P., & Heinonen, S. (2007). Smoking in early gestation or through pregnancy: A decision crucial to pregnancy outcome. *Preventative Medicine, 44*(1), 59–63.

Rabkin, J., Balassone, M., & Bell, M. (1995). The role of social workers in providing comprehensive health care to pregnant women. *Social Work in Health Care, 20*(3), 83–97.

Rakison, D., & Poulin-Dubois, D. (2001). Developmental origin of the animate-inanimate distinction. *Psychological Bulletin, 127,* 209–228.

Ramsey, J., Langlois, J., Hoss, R., Rubenstein, A., & Griffin, A. (2004). Origins of a stereotype: Categorization of facial attractiveness by 6-month-old infants. *Developmental Science, 7,* 201–211.

Rando, T. (1993). *Treatment of complicated mourning.* Champaign, IL: Research Press.

Rank, M. R. (2005). *One nation, underprivileged: Why American poverty affects us all.* New York: Oxford University Press.

Ravitch, D. (2013). *Reign of error: The hoax of the privatization movement and the danger to America's public schools.* New York: Alfred A. Knopf.

Redonnet, B., Chollet, A., Fombonne, E., Bowes, L., & Melchior, M. (2012). Tobacco, alcohol, cannabis and other illegal drug use among young adults: The socio-economic context. *Drug and Alcohol Dependence, 121,* 231–239.

Reece, M., Herbenick, D., Schick, V., Sanders, S. A., Dodge, B., & Fortenbery, J. D. (2010). Condom use rates in national probability sample of males and females ages 14 to 94 in the United States. *Journal of Sexual Medicine,* (Suppl. 5), 266–276.

Reed, M., Merriam, G., & Kargi, A. (2013). Adult growth hormone deficiency: Benefits, side effects, and risks of growth hormone. *Frontiers of Epidemiology, 4.* doi:10.3389/fendo.2013.00064. Retrieved from www.ncbi.nlm.nih.gov/pmc/articles/PMC2671347.

Reichman, N. E., & Teitler, J. O. (2006). Paternal age as a risk factor for low birthweight. *American Journal of Public Health, 96*(5), 862–866.

Reid, C. (2007). The transition from state care to adulthood: International examples of best practices. *New Directions for Youth Development, 113,* 33–49.

Reid, T. R. (2004). *The United States of Europe: The new superpower and the end of American supremacy.* New York: Penguin.

Reith, M., & Payne, M. (2009). *Social work in end-of-life and palliative care.* Chicago: Lyceum Books.

Reitzes, D., & Mutran, E. (2002). Grandparenthood: Factors influencing frequency of grandparent-grandchildren contact and grandparent role satisfaction. *The Journals of Gerontology, Series B: Psychological Sciences and Social Sciences, 59B,* S9–S16.

Renaud, M., Bherer, L., & Maquestiaux, F. (2010). A high level of physical fitness is associated with more efficient response preparation in older adults. *The Journals of Gerontology: Psychological Sciences, 65B,* 756–766.

Repetti, R., Taylor, S., & Seeman, T. (2002). Risky families: Family social environments and the mental and physical health of offspring. *Psychological Bulletin, 18,* 330–366.

Reuter-Lorenz, P. A. (2002). New visions of the aging mind and brain. *Trends in Cognitive Sciences, 6,* 394–400.

Rew, L. (2005). *Adolescent health: A multidisciplinary approach to theory, research, and intervention.* Thousand Oaks, CA: Sage.

Reynolds, B., & Juvonen, J. (2012). Pubertal timing fluctuations across middle school: Implications for girls' psychological health. *Journal of Youth & Adolescence, 41*(6), 677–690.

Rich, M. (2013, August 15). School standards' debut is rocky, and critics pounce. *New York Times.* Retrieved from http://www.nytimes.com/2013/08/16/education/new-education-standards-face-growing-opposition.html?_r=0.

Richardson, M., Cobham, V., McDermott, B., & Murray, J. (2013). Youth mental illness and the family: Parents' loss and grief. *Journal of Child & Family Studies, 22*(5), 719–736.

Richardson, V. E., & Barusch, A. S. (2006). *Gerontological practice for the twenty-first century: A social work perspective.* New York: Columbia University Press.

Richmond, M. (1917). *Social diagnosis.* New York: Russell Sage.

Richter, D., Bannier, S., Glott, R., Marquard, M., & Schwarze, T. (2013). Are internet and social network usage associated with wellbeing and social inclusion of seniors? In C. Stephanidis & M. Antona (Eds.), *Universal access in human-computer interaction* (pp. 211–220). Berlin: Springer-Verlag.

Ridenour, A., Yorgason, J., & Peterson, B. (2009). The infertility resilience model: Assessing individual, couple, and external predictive factors. *Contemporary Family Therapy: An International Journal, 31*(1), 34–51.

Rieker, P. R., & Bird, C. E. (2005). Rethinking gender differences in health: Why we need to integrate social and biological perspectives. *The Journals of Gerontology, Series B: Psychological Sciences and Social Sciences, 60B,* 40–47.

Rieser-Danner, L. (2003). Individual differences in infant fearfulness and cognitive performance: A testing, performance, or competence effect? *Genetic, Social, and General Psychology Monographs, 129*(1), 41–71.

Rietz, C., Hasselhorn, M., & Labuhn, A. (2012). Are externalizing and internalizing difficulties of young children with spelling impairment related to their ADHD symptoms? *Dyslexia (10769242), 18*(3), 174–185.

Riggs, B., Melton, L., Robb, R., Camp, J., Atkinson, E., McDaniel, L., et al. (2008). A population-based assessment of rates of bone loss at multiple skeletal sites:

Evidence for substantial trabecular bone loss in young adult women and men. *Journal of Bone and Mineral Research, 23*(2), 205–214.

Riley, M. W. (1971). Social gerontology and the age stratification of society. *The Gerontologist, 11*, 79–87.

Rindfuss, R. R., Cooksey, E. C., & Sutterlin, R. L. (1999). Young adult occupational achievement: Early expectations versus behavioral reality. *Work & Occupations, 26*(2), 220–263.

Ringeisen, H., Casanueva, C. E., Urato, M., & Stambaugh, L. F. (2009). Mental health service use during the transition to adulthood for adolescents reported to the child welfare system. *Psychiatric Services, 60*(8), 1084–1091.

Riordan, J., & Auerbach, K. (1999). *Breastfeeding and human lactation* (2nd ed.). Sudbury, MA: Jones & Bartlett.

Ritzer, G. (2013). *Introduction to sociology.* Los Angeles: Sage.

Rivas-Drake, D. (2008). Perceived opportunity, ethnic identity, and achievement motivation among Latinos at a selective public university. *Journal of Latinos and Education, 7*(2), 113–128.

Robbins, T., Stagman, S., & Smith, S. (2012). *Young children at risk: National and state prevalence of risk factors.* New York: Columbia University National Center on Children in Poverty.

Robboy, J., & Anderson, K. G. (2011). Intergenerational child abuse and coping. *Journal of Interpersonal Violence, 26*(17), 3526–3541.

Roberts, B., Helson, R., & Klohnen, E. (2002). Personality development and growth in women across 30 years: Three perspectives. *Journal of Personality, 70*, 79–102.

Roberts, E., Burchinal, M., & Bailey, D. (1994). Communication among preschoolers with and without disabilities in same-age and mixed-age classes. *American Journal on Mental Retardation, 99*, 231–249.

Roberts, K., & Yamane, D. (2012). *Religion in sociological perspective* (5th ed.). Los Angeles: Sage.

Roberts, R. E. L., & Bengston, V. L. (1993). Relationship with parents, self-esteem, & psychological well-being in young adulthood. *Social Psychology Quarterly, 56*(4), 263–278.

Robertson, S., Zarit, S., Duncan, L., Rovine, M., & Femia, E. (2007). Family caregivers' patterns of positive and negative affect. *Family Relations, 56*, 12–23.

Robinson, L. C. (2000). Interpersonal relationship quality in young adulthood: A gender analysis. *Adolescence, 35*(140), 775–785.

Rodda, J., Walker, Z., & Carter, J. (2011). Depression in older adults. *British Medical Journal, 343*, 683–687.

Rogoff, B., & Chavajay, P. (1995). What's become of research on the cultural basis of cognitive development? *American Psychologist, 50*, 859–873.

Roggman, L. (2004). Do fathers just want to have fun? *Human Development, 47*, 228–236.

Roggman, L., Boyce, L., Cook, G., Christiansen, K., & Jones, D. (2004). Playing with daddy: Social toy play, early head start, and developmental outcomes. *Fathering, 2*, 83–108.

Rohde, L., Szobot, C., Polanczyk, G., Schmitz, M., Martins, S., & Tramontina, S. (2005). Attention-deficit/hyperactivity disorder in a diverse culture: Do research and clinical findings support the notion of a cultural construct for the disorder? *Biological Psychiatry, 57*, 1436–1441.

Roksa, J., & Velez, M. (2012). A late start: Delayed entry, life course transitions and bachelor's degree completion. *Social Forces, 90*(3), 769–794.

Rollins, A., & Hunter, A. G. (2013). Racial socialization of biracial youth: Maternal messages and approaches to address discrimination. *Family Relations, 62*(1), 140–153.

Roma, L., Mireles-Rios, R., & Lopez-Tello, G. (2014). Latina mothers' and daughters' expectations for autonomy at age 15 (la quinceañera). *Journal of Adolescent Research, 29*(2), 271–294.

Rönkä, A., Oravala, S., & Pulkkinen, L. (2003). Turning points in adults' lives: The effects of gender and amount of choice. *Journal of Adult Development, 10*(3), 203–215.

Ronka, A., & Pulkkinen, L. (1995). Accumulation of problems in social functioning in young adulthood: A developmental approach. *Journal of Personality and Social Psychology, 69*(2), 381–391.

Roof, W. (1993). *A generation of seekers: The spiritual journeys of the baby boom generation.* San Francisco: HarperCollins.

Roof, W. (1999). *Spiritual marketplace: Baby boomers and the remaking of American religion.* Princeton, NJ: Princeton University Press.

Rooij, S., Wouters, H., Yonker, J., Painter, R., & Roseboom, T. (2010). Prenatal undernutrition and cognitive function in late adulthood. *Proceedings of the National Academy of Sciences, 107*(9), 16681–16886.

Roopnarine, J., Shin, M., Donovan, B., & Suppal, P. (2000). Sociocultural contexts of dramatic play: Implications for early education. In K. Roskos & J. Christie (Eds.), *Play and literacy in early childhood: Research from multiple perspectives* (pp. 205–220). Mahwah, NJ: Lawrence Erlbaum.

Roper v. Simmons, 543 U.S. 551 (2005).

Rose, S., & Zand, D. (2000). Lesbian dating and courtship from young adulthood to midlife. *Journal of Gay & Lesbian Social Services, 11*(2/3), 77–104.

Roseboom, T., Painter, R. C., van Abeelen, A. F. M., Veenendall, M. V. F., & de Rooij, S. R. (2011). Hungry in the womb: What are the consequences? Lessons from the Dutch famine. *Maturitas, 70*(2), 141–145.

Roseboom, T., Ravelli, A., van der Post, J., & Painter, R. (2011). Maternal characteristics largely explain poor pregnancy outcome after hyperemesis gravidarum.

European Journal of Obstetrics and Gyncology and Reproductive Biology, 156(1), 56–59.

Rosenberg, M. (1986). *Conceiving the self.* Malabar, FL: Robert E. Krieger.

Rosenberg, S., Ellison, M., Fast, B., Robinson, C., & Lazar, R. (2013). Computing theoretical rates of Part C eligibility based on developmental delays. *Maternal and Child Health Journal, 17,* 384–390.

Roskos, K., & Christie, J. (2000). *Play and literacy in early childhood: Research from multiple perspectives.* Mahwah, NJ: Lawrence Erlbaum.

Ross, M., & Holmberg, D. (1992). Are wives' memories for events in relationships more vivid than their husbands' memories? *Journal of Social and Personal Relationships, 9,* 585–604.

Rossi, A. (2004). Social responsibility to family and community. In O. Brim, C. Ryff, & R. Kessler (Eds.), *How healthy are we? A national study of well-being at midlife* (pp. 550–585). Chicago: University of Chicago Press.

Rotenberg, K. J., McDougall, P., Boulton, M. J., Vaillancourt, T., Fox, C., & Hymel, S. (2004). Cross-sectional and longitudinal relations among peer-reported trustworthiness, social relationships, and psychological adjustment in children and early adolescents from the United Kingdom and Canada. *Journal of Experimental Child Psychology, 88*(1), 46–67.

Rothrauff, T., & Cooney, T. (2008). The role of generativity in psychological well-being: Does it differ for childless adults and parents? *Journal of Adult Development, 15*(3/4), 148–159.

Rowlands, S. (2009). New technologies in contraception. *BJOG: An International Journal of Obstetrics & Gynaecology, 116*(2), 230–239.

Rueda, R., Monzo, L., Shapiro, J., Gomez, J., & Blacher, J. (2005). Cultural models of transition: Latina mothers of young adults with developmental disabilities. *Exceptional Children, 71*(4), 401–414.

Ruffman, T., Slade, L., & Redman, J. (2005). Young infants' expectations about hidden objects. *Cognitive, 97,* B35–B43.

Ruiz, S., & Silverstein, M. (2007). Relationships with grandparents and the emotional well-being of late adolescent and young adult grandchildren. *Journal of Social Issues, 63,* 793–808.

Russell, S., Watson, R., & Muraco, J. (2012). The development of same-sex intimate relationships during adolescence. In B. Laursen & W. A. Collins (Eds.), *Relationship pathways from adolescence to young adulthood* (pp. 215–233). Los Angeles: Sage.

Rutter, M. (1996). Transitions and turning points in developmental psychopathology: As applied to the age span between childhood and mid-adulthood. *International Journal of Behavioral Development, 19*(3), 603–636.

Sabbagh, M., & Baldwin, D. (2001). Learning words from knowledgeable versus ignorant speakers: Links between preschoolers' theory of mind and semantic development. *Child Development, 72,* 1054–1070.

Sadock, B., & Sadock, V. (2007). *Kaplan & Sadock's synopsis of psychiatry: Behavioral sciences/clinical psychiatry* (10th ed.). Baltimore: Wolters Kluwer.

Saewyc, E. (2011). Research on adolescent sexual orientation: Development, health disparities, stigma, and resilience. *Journal of Research on Adolescence, 21*(1), 256–272.

Sagi, A., Koren-Karie, N., Gini, M., Ziv, Y., & Joels, T. (2002). Shedding further light on the effects of various types and quality of early child care on infant-mother attachment relationships: The Haifa study of early child care. *Child Development, 73,* 1166–1186.

Saleebey, D. (2012). *The strengths perspective in social work practice* (6th ed.). Upper Saddle River, NJ: Pearson.

Salihu, H. M., Myers, J., & August, E. M. (2012). Pregnancy in the workplace. *Occupational Medicine, 62*(2), 88–97.

Sandberg, L. (2013). Just feeling a naked body next to you: Men, sexuality and intimacy in later life. *Sexualities, 16,* 261–282.

Sanders, R. (2013). Adolescent psychosocial, social, and cognitive development. *Pediatrics in Review, 34,* 354–359.

Sandoval-Cros, C. (2009). Hispanic cultural issues in end-of-life care. In D. J. Doka & A. S. Tucci (Eds.), *Living with grief: Diversity and end-of-life care* (pp. 117–126). Washington, DC: Hospice Foundation of America.

Sands, R., & Goldberg, G. (2000). Factors associated with stress among grandparents raising their grandchildren. *Family Relations, 49*(1), 97–105.

Sang-Ho, Y. (2010). Hair nicotine levels in non-smoking pregnant women whose spouses smoke outside of the home. *Tobacco Control, 19*(4), 318–324.

Santrock, J. W. (2009). *Child development.* Boston: McGraw Hill.

Sapolsky, R. (2004). *Why zebras don't get ulcers* (3rd ed.). New York: Henry Holt.

Saslow, E. (2013, November 9). Too much of too little: A diet fueled by food stamps is making South Texas obese but leaving them hungry. *Washington Post.* Retrieved from http://www.washingtonpost.com/com/sf/national/2013/11/09/too-much-of-too-little

Savia, J., Almeida, D., Davey, A., & Zant, S. (2008). Routine assistance to parents: Effects on daily mood and other stressors. *The Journals of Gerontology, Series B: Psychological Sciences & Social Sciences, 36B*(3), S154–S161.

Savica, R., & Petersen, L. C. (2011). Prevention of dementia. *Psychiatric Clinics of North America, 34,* 127–145.

Sawin, K. S. (1998). Health care concerns for women with physical disability and chronic illness. In E. Q. Youngkin & M. S. Davis (Eds.), *Women's health: A primary care clinical guide* (2nd ed., pp. 905–941). Stamford, CT: Appleton & Lange.

Sawyer, S., Afifi, R., Bearinger, L., Blakermore, S., Dick, B., Ezeh, A., et al. (2012). Adolescence: A foundation for future health. *The Lancet, 379,* 1630–1641.

Scarlett, A. G., Naudeau, S., Salonius-Pasternak, D., & Ponte, I. (2005). *Children's play.* Thousand Oaks, CA: Sage.

Schaan, B. (2013). Widowhood and depression among older Europeans: The role of gender, caregiving, marital quality, and regional context. *The Journals of Gerontology, Series B: Psychological Science and Social Sciences, 68*(3), 431–442.

Schady, N. (2011). Parents' education, mothers' vocabulary, and cognitive development in early childhood: Longitudinal evidence from Ecuador. *American Journal of Public Health, 101*(12), 2299–2307.

Schaie, K. W. (1984). The Seattle Longitudinal Study: A 21-year exploration of psychometric intelligence in adulthood. In K. W. Schaie (Ed.), *Longitudinal studies of adult psychological development* (pp. 64–135). New York: Guilford.

Scharf, T. (1998). *Ageing and ageing policy in Germany.* Oxford, UK: Berg.

Schepens, J., Moi, B., Wiegerinck, M., Houterman, S., & Koks, C. (2011). Pregnancy outcomes and prognostic factors from tubal sterilization reversal by sutureless laparoscopical re-anastomosis: A retrospective cohort study. *Human Reproduction, 26*(2), 354–359.

Scherger, S. (2009). Social change and the timing of family transitions in West Germany: Evidence from cohort comparisons. *Time & Society, 18*(1), 106–129.

Schmitz, C., & Hilton, A. (1996). Combining mental health treatment with education for preschool children with severe emotional and behavioral problems. *Social Work in Education, 18,* 237–249.

Schneider, B., Lee, M., & Alvarez-Valdivia, I. (2012). Adolescent friendship bonds in cultures of connectedness. In B. Laursen & W. A. Collins (Eds.), *Relationship pathways from adolescence to young adulthood* (pp. 113–134). Los Angeles: Sage.

Schneir, A. (2009). *Psychological first aid for youth experiencing homelessness.* The National Child Traumatic Stress Network. Retrieved from www.hhyp.org/downloads/HHYP_PFA_youth.pdf.

Schöllgen, I., Huxhold, O., & Tesch-Römer, C. (2010). Socioeconomic status and health in the second half of life: Findings from the German Ageing Survey. *European Journal of Ageing, 7,* 17–28.

Schooler, C., & Mulatu, M. S. (2004). Occupational self-direction, intellectual functioning, and self-directed orientation in older workers: Findings and implications for individuals and societies. *American Journal of Sociology, 110,* 161–197.

Schore, A. N. (2002). Dysregulation of the right brain: A fundamental mechanism of traumatic attachment and the psychopathogenesis of post-traumatic stress disorder. *Australian and New Zealand Journal of Psychiatry, 36,* 9–30.

Schroeder, R., Giordano, P., & Cernkovitch, S. (2010). Adult child-parent bonds and life course criminality. *Journal of Criminal Justice, 38,* 562–571.

Schupf, N., Tang, M., Albert, S., Costa, A. R., Andrews, H., Lee, J., et al. (2005). Decline in cognitive and functional skills increases mortality risk in nondemented elderly. *Neurology, 65*(8), 1218–1226.

Schwartz, S., Cote, J., & Arnett, J. (2005). Identity and agency in emerging adulthood: Two developmental routes in the individualization process. *Youth and Society, 37*(2), 201–229.

Schweinhart, L., Montie, J., Xiang, Z., Barnett, W., Belfield, C., & Nores, M. (2005). *Lifetime effects: The High/Scope Perry preschool study through age 40.* Ypsilanti, MI: High/Scope Educational Research Foundation.

Seabrook, J., & Avison, W. (2012). Socioeconomic status and cumulative disadvantage processes across the life course: Implications for health outcomes. *Canadian Review of Sociology, 49*(1), 50–68.

Sedgh, G., Singh, S., Shah, I. H., Ahman, E., Henshaw, S. K., & Bankole, A. (2012). Induced abortion: Incidence and trends worldwide from 1995 to 2008. *The Lancet, 379*(9816), 625–632.

Segal, B. M., & Stewart, J. C. (1996). Substance use and abuse in adolescence: An overview. *Child Psychiatry and Human Development, 26*(4), 193–210.

Segall, M., Dasen, P., Berry, J., & Poortinga, Y. (1999). *Human behavior in global perspective* (2nd ed.). Boston: Allyn & Bacon.

Segev, Y., Riskin-Mashiah, S., Lavie, O., & Auslender, R. (2011). Assisted reproductive technologies: Medical safety issues in the older woman. *Journal of Women's Health, 20*(6), 853–861.

Seiffge-Krenge, I., & Shulman, S. (2012). Transformations in heterosexual romantic relationships across the transition into adolescence. In B. Laursen & W. A. Collins (Eds.), *Relationship pathways from adolescence to young adulthood* (pp. 157–189). Los Angeles: Sage.

Seligman, M. E. P., Reivich, K., Jaycox, L., & Gillham, J. (2007). *The optimistic child: A proven program to safeguard children against depression and build lifelong resilience.* Boston: Houghton Mifflin.

Seltzer, M., Almeida, D., Greenberg, J., Savla, J., Stawski, R., Hong, J., et al. (2009). Psychosocial and biological markers of daily lives of midlife parents of children with disabilities. *Journal of Health and Social Behavior, 50,* 1–15.

Seng, J., Lopez, W., Sperlich, M., Hamam, L., & Meldrum, C. (2012). Marginalized identities, discrimination, burden, and mental health: Empirical exploration of an interpersonal-level approach to modeling intersectionality. *Social Science & Medicine, 75,* 2437–2445.

Sengane, M. (2009). The experience of Black fathers concerning support for their wives/partners during labour. *Curationis, 32,* 67–73.

Sepilian, V. B. (2013, May 6). Ectopic pregnancy. *Medscape Reference, Drugs, Diseases and Procedures.* Retrieved from http://emedicine.medscape.com/article/2041923-overview#aw2aab6b2b5.

Settersten, R. A. (2003a). Introduction: Invitation to the life course: The promise. In R. Settersten Jr. (Ed.), *Invitation to the life course: Toward new understandings of later life* (pp. 1–12). Amityville, NY: Baywood.

Settersten, R. A. (2003b). Age structuring and the rhythm of the life course. In J. Mortimer & M. Shanhan (Eds.), *Handbook of the life course* (pp. 81–98). New York: Kluwer Academic/Plenum.

Settersten, R. A., Furstenberg, F. F., & Rumbaut, R. G. (2005). *On the frontier of adulthood: Theory, research, & public policy.* Chicago: University of Chicago Press.

Settersten, R. A., & Mayer, L. U. (1997). The measurement of age, age structuring, and the life course. *Annual Review of Sociology, 23,* 233–261.

Shade, K., Kools, S., Weiss, S., & Pinderhughes, H. (2011). A conceptual model of incarcerated adolescent fatherhood: Adolescent identity development and the concept of intersectionality. *Journal of Child and Adolescent Psychiatric Nursing, 24,* 98–104.

Shanahan, L., Waite, E., & Boyd, T. (2012). Transformations in sibling relationships from adolescence to adulthood. In B. Laursen & W. A. Collins (Eds.), *Relationship pathways from adolescence to young adulthood* (pp. 43–66). Los Angeles: Sage.

Shanahan, M. (2000). Pathways to adulthood in changing societies: Variability and mechanisms in life course perspective. *Annual Review of Sociology, 27,* 667–692.

Shannon, J. B. (2011). *Autism and pervasive developmental disorders sourcebook.* Detroit, MI: Omnigraphics.

Shapiro, T. (2004). *The hidden cost of being African-American: How wealth perpetuates inequality.* New York: Oxford University Press.

Sharma, G., & Goodwin, J. (2006). Effect of aging on respiratory system physiology and immunology. *Clinical Interventions in Aging, 1*(3), 253–260.

Sharma, V., Le, B., Sheth, K. R., Zargoroff, S., Dupree, J. M., Cashy, J., et al. (2013). Vasectomy demographics and postvasectomy desire for future children: Results from a contemporary national study. *Fertility and Sterility, 99*(7), 1880–1885.

Shear, M., & Pear, R. (2014, January 13). Older pool of health care enrollees stirs fears on costs. *New York Times.* Retrieved from http://www.nytimes.ocm/2014/01/14/us/health-care-plans-attracting-more-older-less-healthy-people.html?_r=0.

Sheehan, M., & Sheehan, M. (2013). Management of the pregnant substance abusing woman. *Clinical Obstetrics and Gynecology, 56*(1), 97–106.

Sheehy, G. (1995). *New passages.* New York: Random House.

Sheldon, K. (2006). Getting older, getting better? Recent psychological evidence. In M. Csikszentmihalyi & I. Csiksezentmihali (Eds.), *A life worth living: Contributions to positive psychology* (pp. 215–229). New York: Oxford University Press.

Sheldon, K., & Kasser, T. (2001). Getting older, getting better? Personal striving and psychological maturity aross the life span. *Developmental Psychology, 37,* 491–501.

Sherblom, S. (2008). The legacy of the "care challenge": Re-envisioning the outcome of the justice-care debate. *Journal of Moral Education, 37*(1), 81–98.

Sherer, M. (2009). *Challenging the whole child: Reflections on best practices in learning, teaching and leadership.* Alexandria, VA: Association for Supervision & Curriculum Development.

Sheridan, M. (2011). The spiritual person. In E. Hutchison (Ed.), *Dimensions of human behavior: Person and environment* (4th ed., pp. 163–208). Thousand Oaks, CA: Sage.

Sherman, E. (1991). *Reminiscence and the self in old age.* New York: Springer.

Sherwood, P., Given, C., Given, B., & Von Eye, A. (2005). Caregiver burden and depressive symptoms: Analysis of common outcomes in caregivers of elderly patients. *Journal of Aging Health, 17,* 125–147.

Shields, N., Nadasen, K., & Pierce, L. (2008). The effects of community violence on children in Cape Town South Africa. *Child Abuse & Neglect, 32*(5), 589–601.

Shonkoff, J., & Phillips, D. (Eds.). (2000). *From neurons to neighborhoods: The science of early childhood development.* Washington, DC: National Academy Press.

Shreffler, K. M., Greil, A. L., & McQuillan, J. (2011). Pregnancy loss and distress among U.S. women. *Family Relations, 60*(3), 343–355.

Shuey, K., & Willson, A. (2008). Cumulative disadvantage and Black-White disparities in life-course health trajectories. *Research on Aging, 30*(2), 200–225.

Shweder, R. (Ed.). (1998). *Welcome to middle age! (and other cultural fictions).* Chicago: University of Chicago Press.

Silbereisen, R., & Lerner, R. (2007a). *Approaches to positive youth development.* Thousand Oaks, CA: Sage.

Silbereisen, R., & Lerner, R. (2007b). Approaches to positive youth development: A view of the issues. In R. Silbereisen & R. Lerner (Eds.), *Approaches to positive youth development* (pp. 3–30). Thousand Oaks, CA: Sage.

Silverman, P. R. (2004). Bereavement: A time of transition and changing relationships. In J. Berzoff & P. R. Silverman (Eds.), *Living with dying: A handbook for end-of-life healthcare practitioners* (pp. 226–241). New York: Columbia University Press.

Silvers, J., Gabrieli, J., McRae, K., Gross, J., Remy, K., & Ochsner, D. (2012). Age-related differences in emotional reactivity, regulation, and rejection sensitivity in adolescence. *Emotion, 12*(6), 1235–1247.

Silverstein, M., & Bengtson, V. (2001). Intergenerational solidarity and the structure of adult child-parent relationships in American families. In A. Walker, M. Manoogian-O'Dell, L. McGraw, & D. L. White (Eds.), *Families in later life: Connections and transitions* (pp. 53–61). Thousand Oaks, CA: Pine Forge Press.

Simeoni, U., Ligi, I., Buffat, C., & Boubred, F. (2011). Adverse consequences of accelerated neonatal growth: Cardiovascular and renal issues. *Pediatric Nephrology, 26*(4), 493–508.

Simmons, R. (2011). *Odd girl out: The hidden culture of aggression in girls.* Boston: Mariner Books/Houghton Mifflin Harcourt.

Simmons, T., & O'Connell, M. (2003). *Married-couple and unmarried-partner households: 2000.* Washington, DC: U.S. Census Bureau.

Simonsen, S., Baksh, L., & Stanford, J. (2012). Infertility treatment in a population-based sample: 2004–2005. *Maternal and Child Health Journal, 16*(4), 877–886.

Simpson, G. A., Cohen, R. A., Pastor, P. N., & Reuben, C. A. (2008). Use of mental health services in the past 12 months by children aged 4–17 years: United States, 2005–2006. *NCHS Data Brief, 8,* 1–8.

Singer, D., & Singer, J. (2011). *Handbook of children and the media* (2nd ed.). Thousand Oaks, CA: Sage.

Singer, J., Rexhaj, B., & Baddeley, J. (2007). Older, wiser, and happier? Comparing older adults' and college students' self-defining memories. *Memory, 15,* 886–898.

Singer, M., Anglin, T., Song, L., & Lunghofer, L. (1995). Adolescents' exposure to violence and associated symptoms of psychological trauma. *Journal of American Medical Association, 273*(6), 477–482.

Singh, B. (2009). Clinical studies demonstrate benefits of life extension DHEA formulation. *Life Extension, 15*(6), 18.

Singh, L., Morgan, J., & Best, C. (2002). Infants' listening preferences: Baby talk or happy talk? *Infancy, 3,* 365–394.

Singleton, J. L. (2009). Service learning: The effect on BSW student interest in aging. *The Journal of Baccalaureate Social Work, 14,* 31–43.

Sisson, G. (2012). Finding a way to offer something more: Reframing teen pregnancy prevention. *Sexuality Research and Social Policy, 9,* 57–69.

Sitruk-Ware, R., Nath, A., & Mishell, D. R. (2013). Contraception technology: Past, present, and future. *Contraception, 87*(3), 319–330.

Sivin, I., & Batar, I. (2010). State-of-the-art of non-hormonal methods of contraception: III: Intrauterine devices. *European Journal of Contraception and Reproductive Health Care, 15*(2), 96–112.

Skinner, C., Wight, V. R., Aratani, Y., Cooper, J. L., & Thampi, K. (2010). *English language proficiency, family economic security, and child development.* National Center for Children in Poverty. Retrieved from http://www.nccp .org/publications/pub_948.html.

Slatcher, R., & Trentacosta, C. (2012). Influences of parent and child negative emotionality on young children's everyday behaviors. *Emotion, 12*(5), 932–942.

Smink, E., van Hoeken, D., & Hoek, H. (2012). Epidemiology of eating disorders: Incidence, prevalence and mortality. *Current Psychiatry Reports, 14*(4), 406–414.

Smith, A., Dannison, L., & Vach-Hasse, T. (1998). When grandma is mom. *Childhood Education, 75*(1), 12–16.

Smith, J. F., Eisenberg, M. L., Glidden, D., Millstein, S. G., Cedars, M., Walsh, T. J., et al. (2011). Socioeconomic disparities in the use and success of fertility treatments: Analysis of data from a prospective cohort in the United States. *Fertility and Sterility, 96*(1), 95–101.

Smith, J., O'Connor, I., & Berthelsen, D. (1996). The effects of witnessing domestic violence on young children's psychosocial adjustment. *Australian Social Work, 49*(4), 3–10.

Smith, Y., van Goozen, S., & Cohen-Kettenis, P. (2001). Adolescents with gender identity disorder who were accepted or rejected for sex assignment surgery: A prospective follow-up study. *Journal of the American Academy of Child and Adolescent Psychiatry, 40,* 472–481.

Smyer, M. A., Gatz, M., Simi, N. L., & Pedersen, N. L. (1998). Childhood adoption: Long-term effects in adulthood. *Psychiatry: Interpersonal and Biological Processes, 61*(3), 191.

Snyder, F. J., Acock, A. C., Vuchinich, S., Beets, M. W., Washburn, I. I., & Flay, B. R. (2013). Preventing negative behaviors among elementary-school students through enhancing students' social-emotional and character development. *American Journal of Health Promotion, 28*(1), 50–58.

Snyder, H., & Sickmund, M. (2006). *Juvenile offenders and victims: 2006 national report.* Washington, DC: U.S. Department of Justice, Office of Justice Programs, Office of Juvenile Justice and Delinquency Prevention.

Social Security Administration. (2013a). *Retirement planner: Full retirement age.* Retrieved from www.ssa.gov/retire2/ retirechart.htm.

Social Security Administration. (2013b). *Old-age and survivors insurance trust fund.* Retrieved from www.ssa.gov/ progdata/describeoasi.html.

Solmeyer, A., & Feinberg, M. (2011). Mother and father adjustment during early parenthood: The roles of infant temperament and coparenting relationship quality. *Infant Behvior and Development, 34,* 504–514.

Solomon, R. C. (1988). *About love: Reinventing romance for modern times.* New York: Simon & Schuster.

Solomon, Z., Helvitz, H., & Zerach, G. (2009). Subjective age, PTSD and physical health among war veterans. *Aging & Mental Health, 13*(3), 405–413.

Solomon, Z., & Mikulincer, M. (2006). Trajectories of PTSD: A 20-year longitudinal study. *American Journal of Psychiatry, 163*(4), 659–666.

Sonfield, A. (2010). The potential of health care reform to improve pregnancy-related services and outcomes. *Guttmacher Policy Review, 13*(3), 13–17.

Sotirin, P., & Ellingson, L. (2006). The "other" women in family life. In K. Floyd & M. Morman (Eds.), *Widening the family circle: New research on family communication* (pp. 81–99). Thousand Oaks, CA: Sage.

Southern California Center for Reproductive Medicine. (2013). *Age and fertility infographic.* Retrieved from http://www.socalfertility.com/age-and-fertility-infographic.

Spear, L. P. (2010). *The behavioral neuroscience of adolescence.* New York: W. W. Norton.

Spector-Mersel, G. (2006). Never-aging stories: Western hegemonic masculinity scripts. *Journal of Gender Studies, 15*(1), 67–82.

Spence, K., Henderson-Smart, D., New, K., Evans, C., Whitelaw, J., Woolnough, R., et al. (2010). Evidence-based clinical practice guideline for management of newborn pain. *Journal of Paediatrics and Child Health, 46,* 184–192.

Spencer, M. (1984). Black children's race awareness, racial attitudes and self concept: A reinterpretation. *Journal of Child Psychology and Psychiatry, 25*(3), 433–441.

Spencer, M. B., Harpalani, V., Fegley, S., Dell'Angelo, T., & Seaton, G. (2003). Identity, self, and peers in context: A culturally sensitive, developmental framework for analysis. In R. M. Lerner, E. Jacobs, & D. Wertlieb (Eds.), *Handbook of applied developmental science* (Vol. 1, pp. 123–142). Thousand Oaks, CA: Sage.

Spieker, S., Nelson, D., & Petras, A. (2003). Joint influence of child care and infant attachment security for cognitive and language outcomes of low-income toddlers. *Infant Behavior & Development, 26*(3), 326–344.

Spielman, V., & Taubman-Ben-Ari, O. (2009). Parental self-efficacy and personal growth in the transition to parenthood: A comparison between parents of premature and of full-term babies. *Health and Social Work, 34,* 201–222.

Spilsbury, J., Kahana, S., Drotar, D., Creeden, R., Flannery, D., & Friedman, S. (2008). Profiles of behavioral problems in children who witness domestic violence. *Violence and Victims, 23*(1), 3–17.

Spinrad, T., Eisenberg, N., Gaertner, B., Popp, T., Smith, C., Kupfer, A., et al. (2007). Relations of maternal socialization and toddlers' effortful control to children's adjustment and social competence. *Developmental Psychology, 43*(5), 1170–1186.

Sroufe, L. A., Egeland, B., Carlson, E., & Collins, W. A. (2005). *The development of the person: The Minnesota study of risk and adaptation from birth to adulthood.* New York: Guilford.

Stadelmann, S., Perren, S., Groeben, M., & von Klitzing, K. (2010). Parental separation and children's behavioral/emotional problems: The impact of parental representations and family conflict. *Family Process, 49*(1), 92–108.

Stapleton, S. R., Osborne, C., & Illuzzi, J. (2013). Outcomes of care in birth centers: Demonstration of a durable model. *Journal of Midwifery and Women's Health, 58*(1), 3–14.

Stark, M. D., Keathley, R. S., & Nelson, J. A. (2011). A developmental model for counseling infertile couples. *Family Journal, 19*(2), 225–230.

Staudinger, U. M., & Bluck, S. (2001). A view on midlife development from life-span theory. In M. Lachman (Ed.), *Handbook of midlife development* (pp. 3–39). New York: Wiley.

Staudinger, U. M., Freund, A. M., Linden, M., & Maas, I. (1999). Self, personality, and life regulation: Facets of psychological resilience in old age. In P. B. Baltes & K. U. Mayer (Eds.), *The Berlin Aging Study: Aging from 70 to 100* (pp. 302–328). Cambridge, UK: Cambridge University Press.

Steen, M., Downe, S., Bamford, N., & Edozien, L. (2012). Not-patient and not-visitor: A metasynthesis fathers' encounters with pregnancy, birth and maternity care. *Midwifery, 28,* 422–431.

Steensma, T., Kreukels, B., de Vries, A., & Cohen-Kettenis, P. (2013). Gender identity development in adolescence. *Hormones and Behavior, 64,* 288–297.

Stein, M. (2005). Resilience and young people leaving care: Implications for child welfare policy and practice in the UK. In R. J. Flynn, P. M. Dudding, & J. G. Barber (Eds.), *Promoting resilience in child welfare* (pp. 264–278). Ottawa: University of Ottawa Press.

Steinberg, J., & Finer, L. (2011). Examining the association of abortion history and current mental health: A reanalysis of the National Comorbidity Survey using a common-risk-factors model. *Social Science & Medicine, 72,* 72–82.

Steinberg, L. (2009). Should the science of adolescent brain development inform public policy? *American Psychologist, 64*(8), 739–750.

Stephan, Y., Chalabaev, A., Kotter-Grühn, D., & Jaconelli, A. (2013). "Feeling younger, being stronger": An experimental study of subjective age and physical functioning among older adults. *The Journals of Gerontology, Series B: Psychological Sciences and Social Sciences, 68*(1), 1–7.

Stephan, Y., Demulier, V., & Terracciano, A. (2012). Personality, self-rated health, and subjective age in a life-span sample: The moderating role of chronological age. *Psychology and Aging, 27*(4), 875–880.

Stephens, N., Hamedani, M., Markus, H., Bergsieker, H., & Eloul, L. (2009). Why did they "choose" to stay?

Perspectives of Hurricane Katrina observers and survivors. *Psychological Science, 20*(7), 878–886.

Steptoe, A., Shankar, A., Demakakos, P., & Wardle, J. (2013). Social isolation, loneliness, and all-cause mortality in older men and women. *Proceedings of the National Academy of Sciences, 110*(15), 5797–5801.

Stern, R. A., Riley, D. O., Daneshvar, D. H., Nowinski, C. J., Cantu, R. C., & McKee, A. C. (2011). Long-term consequences of repetitive brain trauma: Chronic traumatic encephalopathy. *PM&R, 3*(10), S460–S467.

Sterns, H., & Huyck, M. (2001). The role of work in midlife. In M. Lachman (Ed.), *Handbook of midlife development* (pp. 447–486). New York: Wiley.

Stillbirth Collaborative Research Network Writing Group. (2011). Causes of death among stillbirths. *Journal of the American Medical Association, 306*(22), 2459–2468.

Stobbe, M. (2009, November 3). *Premature births worsen U.S. infant death rates.* Associated Press. Retrieved from www.desertnews.com/article/70534177/Premature-births-worsen-US-infant-death-rate.html.

Stock, M. L., Gibbons, F. X., Gerrard, M., Houlihan, A. E., Weng, C.-Y., Lorenz, F. O., et al. (2013). Racial identification, racial composition, and substance use vulnerability among African American adolescents and young adults. *Health Psychology, 32*(3), 237–247.

Stockard, J., & O'Brien, R. (2002). Cohort effects on suicide rates: International variation. *American Sociological Review, 67,* 854–872.

Stolzenberg, R. M., Blair-Loy, M., & Waite, L. J. (1995). Religious participation in early adulthood: Age and family life cycle effects on church membership. *American Sociological Review, 60*(1), 84–104.

Stone, P. (2007). *Opting out? Why women really quit careers and head home.* Berkeley: University of California Press.

Stouthamer-Loeber, M., & Wei, E. H. (1998). The precursors of young fatherhood and its effect on delinquency of teenage males. *Journal of Adolescent Health, 22,* 56–65.

Stovall, K., & Dozier, M. (1998). Infants in foster care: An attachment theory perspective. *Adoption Quarterly, 2*(1), 55–88.

Strauch, B. (2010). *The secret life of the grown-up brain: The surprising talents of the middle-aged mind.* London: Viking.

Street, J., Harris-Britt, A., & Walker-Barnes, C. (2009). Examining relationships between ethnic identity, family environment, and psychological outcomes for African American adolescents. *Journal of Child and Family Studies, 18,* 412–420.

Street, K., Whitlingum, G., Gibson, P., Cairns, P., & Ellis, M. (2008). Is adequate parenting compatible with maternal drug use? A 5-year follow-up. *Child: Care, Health, and Development, 34,* 204–206.

Streri, A. (2005). Touching for knowing in infancy: The development of manual abilities in very young infants.

European Journal of Developmental Psychology, 2, 325–343.

Stroebe, M., Stroebe, W., & Hansson, R. (1993). *Handbook on bereavement: Theory, research and intervention.* New York: Cambridge University Press.

Strøm-Roum, E. M., Haavaldsen, C., Tanbo, T. G., & Eskild, A. (2013). Paternal age, placental weight and placental to birthweight ratio: A population-based study of 590,835 pregnancies. *Human Reproduction, 28*(1), 3126–3133.

Struge-Apple, M., Davies, P., & Cummings, E. (2006). Impact of hostility and withdrawal in interparental conflict on parental emotional unavailability and children's adjustment difficulties. *Child Development, 77,* 1623–1641.

Subramanian, S. V., Kubzansky, L., Berman, L., Fay, M., & Kawachi, I. (2006) Neighborhood effects on the self-rated health of elders: Uncovering the relative importance of structural and service-related neighborhood environments. *The Journals of Gerontology, Series B: Psychological Sciences and Social Sciences, 61B*(3), 153–161.

Substance Abuse and Mental Health Services Administration. (2013a). *Results from the 2012 National Survey on Drug Use and Health: Summary of national findings.* NSDUH Series H-46, HHS Publication No. (SMA) 13-4795. Rockville, MD: Substance Abuse and Mental Health Services.

Substance Abuse and Mental Health Services Administration. (2013b). *Highlights of the 2011 Drug Abuse Warning Network (DAWN) findings on drug-related emergency department visits.* Retrieved from http://www.samhsa.gov/data/2k13DAWN127/sr127-DAWN-highlights.htm.

Sullivan, M. C., Msall, M. E., & Miller, R. J. (2012). 17-year outcome of preterm infants with diverse neonatal morbidities: Part I. Impact on physical, neurological, and psychological health. *Journal for Specialists in Pediatric Nursing, 17*(3), 226–241.

Sum, A. M. (2011). *The deterioration in the labor market fortunes of America's young adults during the lost decade of 2000–2010.* Washington, DC: Children's Defense Fund.

Sunderam, S., Kissin, D. M., Flowers, L., Anderson, J. E., Folger, S. G., Jamieson, D. J., et al. (2012). Assisted reproductive technology surveillance—United States, 2009. *Centers for Disease Control and Prevention, 61*(SS7), 1–23.

Sustin, A., Costa, P., Wethington, E., & Eaton, W. (2010). Turning points and lessons learned: Stressful life events and personality trait development across middle adulthood. *Psychology and Aging, 25*(3), 524–533.

Sweet, S., & Meiksins, P. (2013). *Changing contours of work: Jobs and opportunities in the new economy* (2nd ed.). Los Angeles: Sage.

Sword, W., Watt, S., & Krueger, P. (2006). Postpartum health, service needs, and access to care experiences of immigrant and Canadian-born women. *Journal of Obstetric Gynecological and Neonatal Nurses, 35*(6), 717–727.

Szydlik, M. (2012). Generations: Connections across the life course. *Advances in Life Course Research, 17,* 100–111.

Taddio, A., Shah, V., Gilbert-Macleod, C., & Katz, J. (2002). Conditioning and hyperalgesia in newborns exposed to repeated heel lances. *Journal of American Medical Association, 288*(7), 857–861.

Takahashi, K. (1990). Are the key assumptions of the "strange situation" procedure universal? A view from Japanese research. *Human Development, 33,* 23–30.

Tam, E., Rosenbluth, G., Rogers, E., Ferriero, D., Glidden, D., Goldstein, R., et al. (2011). Cerebellar hemorrhage on magnetic resonance imaging in preterm newborns associated with abnormal neurologic outcome. *The Journal of Pediatrics, 158*(2), 245–250.

Tamaru, S., Kikuchi, A., Takagi, K., Wakamatsu, M., Ono, K., Horikoshi, T., et al. (2011). Neurodevelopmental outcomes of very low birth weight and extremely low birth weight infants at 18 months corrected age associated with prenatal factors. *Early Human Development, 87*(1), 55–59.

Tan, H., & Loth, S. (2010). Microsurgical reversal of sterilization—is this still clinically relevant today? *Annals: Academy of Medicine Singapore, 39*(1), 22–26.

Tang, C., Yeung, D., & Lee, A. (2003). Psychosocial correlates of emotional responses to meanarche among Chinese adolescent girls. *Journal of Adolescent Health, 33,* 193–201.

Tartaro, J., Luecken, L., & Gunn, H. (2005). Exploring heart and soul: Effects of religiosity/spirituality and gender on blood pressure and cortisol stress response. *Journal of Health Psychology, 10,* 753–766.

Tarver, T. (2013). *Older Americans 2012: Key indicators of wellbeing.* Washington, DC: U.S. Federal Interagency Forum on Aging Related Statistics (FIFARS) with the U.S. National Center for Health Statistics (NCHS). Retrieved from http://www.agingstats.gov/aging-statsdotnet/Main_Site/Data/2012_Documents/Docs/EntireChartbook.pdf.

Tate, A., Dezateux, C., Cole, T., & the Millennium Cohort Study Child Health Group. (2006). Is infant growth changing? *International Journal of Obesity, 30,* 1094–1096.

Tatum, B. D. (2003). *"Why are all the black kids sitting together in the cafeteria?" And other conversations about race.* New York: Basic Books.

Tatum, B. D. (2007). *Can we talk about race? And other conversations in an era of school resegregation.* Boston: Beacon Press.

Taylor, J. M., Gilligan, C., & Sullivan, A. M. (1995). *Between voice and silence: Women and girls, race and relationship.* Cambridge, MA: Harvard University Press.

Taylor, P., Morin, R., Parker, K., Cohn, E., & Wang, W. (2010). *Growing old in America: Expectations vs. reality.* Retrieved from www.pewsocialtrends.org/files/2010/10/Getting-Old-in-America.pdf.

Termini, R. B., & Lee, M. (2011). Sex, politics, and lessons learned from Plan B: A review of the FDA's actions and future direction. *Oklahoma City University Law Review, 36*(2), 351–373.

Terry, D. F., Sebastiani, P., Andersen, S. L., & Perls, T. T. (2008). Disentangling the roles of disability and morbidity in survival to exceptional old age. *Archives of Internal Medicine, 168*(3), 277–283.

Thapar, A., Collishaw, S., Pine, D., & Thapar, A. (2012). Depression in adolescence. *The Lancet, 379,* 1056–1067.

Thomas, A., Chess, S., & Birch, H. G. (1968). *Temperament and behavior disorders in children.* New York: New York University Press.

Thomas, A., Chess, S., & Birch, H. G. (1970). The origin of personality. *Scientific American, 223,* 102–109.

Tiet, A., Bird, H., Hoven, C., Wu, P., Moore, R., & Davies, M. (2001). Resilience in the face of maternal psychopathology and adverse life events. *Journal of Child and Family Studies, 10*(3), 347–365.

Tobin, S. (1988). Preservation of the self in old age. *Social Casework: The Journal of Contemporary Social Work, 66* (9), 550–555.

Tomoda, A., Polcari, A., Anderson, C. M., & Teicher, M. H. (2012). Reduced visual cortex gray matter volume and thickness in young adults who witnessed domestic violence during childhood. *Plos ONE, 7*(12), 1–11. doi:10.1371/journal.pone.0052528

Torian, L., Chen, M., & Hall, H. (2011). HIV Surveillance—United States—1981–2008. *Morbidity and Mortality Weekly Report, 60*(21), 689–693. Retrieved from www.cdc.gov/mmwr/preview/mmwrhtml/mm6021a2.htm.

Tornstam, L. (2005). *Gerotranscendence: A developmental theory of positive aging.* New York: Springer.

Torres, L., Peña, J., Westhoff, W., & Zayas, L. (2008). A cross-national comparison of adolescent alcohol and drug use behaviors: U.S. Hispanics and youth in the Dominican Republic. *Journal of Drug Issues, 38*(1), 149–170.

Tosato, M., Zamboni, V., Ferrini, A., & Cesari, M. (2007). The aging process and potential interventions to extend life expectancy. *Clinical Interventions in Aging, 2*(3), 401–412.

Toseland, R., & Larkin, H. (2010). Developing and leading telephone groups. *Social Work With Groups, 34*(1), 21–34.

Trainor, A. A. (2008). Using cultural and social capital to improve postsecondary outcomes and expand transition models for youth with disabilities. *Journal of Special Education, 42*(3), 148–162.

Trattner, W. (1998). *From poor law to welfare state: A history of social welfare in America* (6th ed.). New York: Free Press.

Treyvaud, K., Doyle, L. W., Lee, K. J., Roberts, G., Cheong, J. L. Y., Inder, T. E., et al. (2011). Family functioning, burden, and parenting stress 2 years after very preterm birth. *Early Human Development, 87*(60), 427–431.

Tun, P., & Lachman, M. (2010). The association between computer use and cognition across adulthood: Use it so you won't lose it? *Psychology and Aging, 25*(3), 560–568.

Turati, C., Montirosso, R., Brenna, V., Ferrara, V., & Borgatti, R. (2011). A smile enhances 3-month-olds' recognition of an individual face. *International Society on Infant Studies, 16*(3), 306–317.

Turiel, E. (2004). Commentary: Beyond individualism and collectivism: A problem or progress? *New Directions in Child and Adolescent Development, 104,* 91–100.

Turkle, S. (2011). *Alone together: Why we expect more from technology and less from each other.* New York: Basic Books.

Turner, H., Finkelhor, D., & Ormrod, R. (2006). The effect of lifetime victimization on the mental health of children and adolescents. *Social Science & Medicine, 62*(1), 13–27.

Tweddle, A. (2007). Youth leaving care: How do they fare? *New Directions for Youth Development, 113,* 15–31.

Uddin, L., Iacoboni, M., Lange, C., & Keenan, J. (2007). The self and social cognition: The role of cortical midline structures and mirror neurons. *Trends in Cognitive Sciences, 11*(4), 153–157.

Uhlenberg, P. (1996). Mutual attraction: Demography and life-course analysis. *The Gerontologist, 36*(2), 226–229.

UNAIDS. (2013). *Global report: UNAIDS reports on the global AIDS epidemic 2013.* Retrieved from www.unaids .org/en/resources/campaigns/globalreport2013/global report.

UNICEF. (2006). *Behind closed doors: The impact of domestic violence on children.* New York: Author.

UNICEF. (2012a). *Report Card 10. Measuring child poverty: New league tables of child poverty in the world's rich countries.* Florence, Italy: UNICEF Innocenti Research Centre.

UNICEF. (2012b). *The state of the world's children 2012: Children in an urban world.* New York: Author. Retrieved from www.unicef.org/protection/files/ BehindClosedDoors.pdf.

UNICEF. (2013a). *Levels & trends in child mortality.* New York: Author.

UNICEF. (2013b). *Child info: Monitoring the situation of children and women. Malnutrition.* Retrieved from http:// www.childinfo.org/malnutriton_status.html.

United Nations. (2011). *Children and armed conflict.* Retrieved from http://childrenandarmedconflict.un.org/publica tions/StrategicFramework2011–2013.pdf.

United Nations Educational, Scientific, and Cultural Organization, Institute for Statistics. (2012). *Opportunities lost: The impact of grade repetition and early school leaving.* Retrieved from http://www.uis.unesco.org/ Education/GED%20Documents%20C/GED-2012- Complete-Web3.pdf.

Urban Child Institute. (2013). *Baby's brain begins now: Conception to age 3.* Retrieved from http://www.urban childinstitute.org/why-0-3/baby-and-brain.

Ursache, A., Blair, C., Stifter, C., & Voegtline, K. (2013). Emotional reactivity and regulation in infancy interact to predict executive functioning in early childhood. *Developmental Psychology, 49*(1), 127–137.

U.S. Bureau of Labor Statistics. (2013a). *Employment and unemployment among youth summary.* Retrieved from http://www.bls.gov/news.release/youth.nr0.htm.

U.S. Bureau of Labor Statistics. (2013b). *Persons with a disability: Labor force characteristics summary.* Retrieved from http://www.bls.gov/news.release/disabl.nr0 .htm.

U.S. Census Bureau. (2008). *Women more likely to work during pregnancy.* Retrieved from www.census.gov/ newsroom/releases/archives/employment_occupations/ cb08-33.html.

U.S. Census Bureau. (2010). *The next four decades: The older population in the United States: 2010 to 2050: Population estimates and projections.* Washington, DC: U.S. Department of Commerce, Economics and Statistics Administration, U.S. Census Bureau.

U.S. Census Bureau. (2011a). *Negative population growth: Facts and figures.* Retrieved from http://www.npg.org/ facts/world_pop_year.htm.

U.S. Census Bureau. (2011b). *Who's minding the kids? Child care arrangements: Spring 2010, detailed tables.* Retrieved from http://www.census.gov/hhes/childcare/ data/sipp/2010/tables.html.

U.S. Census Bureau. (2011c). *Same-sex couple households.* Retrieved from www.census.gov/prod/1011pubs/ acsbr10-03.pdf.

U.S. Census Bureau. (2012a). *Statistical abstracts of the United States: 2012.* Washington, DC.

U.S. Census Bureau. (2012b). *Percent distribution of the projected population by selected age groups and sex for the United States: 2015 to 2060* (NP2012-T3). Retrieved from https://www.census.gov/population/projections/ data/national/2012/summarytables.html.

U.S. Census Bureau. (2012c). *2012 National population projections: Downloadable files.* Washington, DC: U.S. Census Bureau. Retrieved from http://www.census.gov/ population/projections/data/national/2012/download ablefiles.html.

U.S. Census Bureau. (2012d). *2010 Census Special Reports, Centenarians: 2010,* C2010SR-03. Washington, DC: U.S. Government Printing Office. Retrieved from http://www.census.gov/prod/cen2010/reports/c2010sr-03.pdf.

U.S. Census Bureau. (2013a). *Current population survey, annual social and economic supplements*. Retrieved from http://www.census.gov/prod/techdoc/cps/cpsmart13.pdf.

U.S. Census Bureau. (2013b). *Annual estimates of the resident population by single year of age and sex for the United States: April 1, 2010 to July 1, 2012*. Retrieved from http://factfinder2.census.gov/faces/tableservices/jsf/pages/productview.xhtml?src=bkmk.

U.S. Census Bureau. (2013c). *International data base*. Retrieved from http://www.census.gov/population/international/data/idb/informationGateway.php.

U.S. Census Bureau. (2014). *International data base: World population by age and sex for 2013*. Retrieved from https://www.census.gov/population/international/data/idb/worldpopu.php.

U.S. Children's Bureau. (2012a). *Child maltreatment 2011*. Retrieved from https://www.acf.hhs.gov/sites/defaults/files/cb/cm11.pdf.

U.S. Children's Bureau. (2012b). *John H. Chafee Foster Care Independence Program*. Retrieved from http://www.acf.hhs.gov/programs/cb/resource/chafee-foster-care-program.

U.S. Children's Bureau. (2013). How many children are in foster care in in the U.S.? In my state? In *Frequently asked questions*. Retrieved from http://www.acf.hhs.gov/programs/cb/faq/foster-care4.

U.S. Department of Agriculture and U.S. Department of Human Services. (2010). *Dietary guidelines for Americans 2010* (7th ed.). Washington, DC: U.S. Government Printing Office. Retrieved from http://www.health.gov/dietaryguidelines/dga/2010/DietaryGuidelines.2010/pdf.

U.S. Department of Education. (2010). *Blueprint for reform of the Elementary and Secondary Education Act*. Retrieved from http://www2.ed.gov/policy/elsec/leg/blueprint/index.html.

U.S. Department of Education. (2013). *Race to the top fund: Executive summary*. Retrieved from http://www2.ed.gov/programs/racetothetop/executive-summary.pdf.

U.S. Department of Education Office for Civil Rights. (2013). *2006 civil rights data collection: Projects values for the nation*. Retrieved from http://ocrdata.ed.gov/downloads/projections/2006/2006-nation-projection.xls.

U.S. Department of Health and Human Services, Administration on Children, Youth, and Families. (2012). *Child maltreatment 2011*. Retrieved from http://www.acf.hhs.gov/programs/cb/resource/child-maltreatment-2011.

U.S. Department of Health and Human Services. Maternal and Child Health Bureau. (2011). *Child Health USA, 2011*. Rockville, MD: U.S. Department of Health and Human Services.

U. S. Department of Health and Human Services. Office of Adolescent Health. (2013). *State facts*. Retrieved from http://www.hhs.gov/ash/oah/resources-and-publications/facts.

U.S. Food and Drug Administration. (2013). *FDA approves Plan B One-Step Emergency Contraceptive without a prescription for women 15 years of age and older*. Retrieved from http://www.fda.gov/NewsEvents/Newsroom/PressAnnouncements/ucm350230.htm.

U.S. Government Accountability Office. (2012). *Unemployed older workers: Many experience challenges regaining employment and face reduced retirement security*. Washington, DC: Author. Retrieved from www.gao.gov/assets/600/590408.pdf.

Uskul, A. (2004). Women's menarche stories from a multicultural sample. *Social Science & Medicine, 59*, 667–679.

Vaillant, G. (1977). *Adaptation to life*. Boston: Little, Brown.

Vaillant, G. (1993). *The wisdom of the ego*. Cambridge, MA: Harvard University Press.

Vaillant, G. (2002). *Aging well: Surprising guideposts to a happier life from the Landmark Harvard Study of Adult Development*. Boston: Little, Brown.

Vaillant, G. (2012). *Triumphs of experience: The men of the Harvard Grant Study*. Cambridge, MA: Belknap Press.

Valsiner, J. (2000). *Culture and human development*. Thousand Oaks, CA: Sage.

van de Beek, C., Thijssen, J. H., Cohen-Kettenis, P. T., van Goozen, S. H., & Buitelaar, J. K. (2004). Relationships between sex hormones assessed in amniotic fluid, and maternal and umbilical cord serum: What is the best source of information to investigate the effects of fetal hormonal exposure? *Hormones and Behavior, 46*(5), 663–669.

Van Dongen, J., Tekle, F. B., & van Roijen, J. H. (2012). Pregnancy rates after vasectomy reversal in a contemporary series: Influence of smoking, semen quality, and post-surgical use of assisted reproductive techniques. *BJU International, 110*(4), 562–567.

Van Goethem, A., van Hoof, A., van Aken, M., Raajmakers, Q., Boom, J., & de Castro, B. (2012). The role of adolescents' morality and identity in volunteering: Age and gender differences in a process model. *Journal of Adolescence, 35*, 509–520.

Van Naarden Braun, K., Yeargin-Allsopp, M., & Lollar, D. (2006). Factors associated with leisure activity among young adults with developmental disabilities. *Research in Developmental Disabilities, 27*, 567–583.

Van Naarden Braun, K., Yeargin-Allsopp, M., & Lollar, D. (2009). Activity limitations among young adults with developmental disabilities: A population-based follow-up study. *Research in Developmental Disabilities, 30*, 179–191.

Van Wagenen, A., Driskell, J., & Bradford, J. (2013). "I'm still raring to go": Successful aging among lesbian, gay, bisexual, and transgender older adults. *Journal of Aging Studies, 27*, 1–14.

VanLaningham, J., Johnson, D., & Amato, P. (2001). Marital happiness, marital duration, and the U-shaped curve: Evidence from a five-wave panel study. *Social Forces, 78*(4), 1313–1341.

Varma, R., Sinha, D., & Gupta, J. K. (2006). Non-contraceptive uses of levonorgestrel-releasing hormone system (LNG-IUS): A systematic enquiry and overview. *European Journal of Obstetric and Gynecological Reproductive Biology, 125*(1), 9–28.

Vazsonyi, S., & Snider, J. B. (2008). Mentoring, competencies, and adjustment in adolescents: American part-time employment and European apprenticeships. *International Journal of Behavioral Development, 32*(1), 46–55.

Vennemann, M., Hense, H., Bajanowski, T., Blair, P., Complojer, C., Moone, R., et al. (2012). Bed sharing and the risk of sudden infant death syndrome: Can we resolve the debate? *The Journal of Pediatrics, 160*(1), 44–50.

Vera, E. M., Vacek, K., Coyle, L. D., Stinson, J., Mull, M., Doud, K., et al. (2011). An examination of culturally relevant stressors, coping, ethnic identity, and subjective well-being in urban, ethnic minority adolescents. *Professional School Counseling, 15*(2), 55–66.

Vespa, J., Lewis, J., & Kreider, R. (2013). *America's families and living arrangements: 2012, current population reports.* Retrieved from http://www.census.gov/prod/2013pubs/p20-570.pdf.

Vikat, A., Speder, Z., Beets, G., Billari, F., & Buhler, C. (2007). Generations and Gender Survey (GGS): Towards a better understanding of relationships and processes in the life course. *Demographic Research Online, 17*, 389–440.

Villarruel, F., Perkins, D., Borden, L., & Keith, J. (2003). *Community youth development: Programs, policies, and practice.* Thousand Oaks, CA: Sage.

Volker, D. L. (2005). Control and end-of-life care: Does ethnicity matter? *American Journal of Hospice & Palliative Care, 22*(6), 442–446.

Volling, B., Blandon, A., & Kolak, A. (2006). Marriage, parenting, and the emergence of early self-regulation in the family system. *Journal of Child and Family Studies, 15*(4), 493–506.

Von Salisch, M., Haenel, M., & Freund, P. (2013). Emotion understanding and cognitive abilities in young children. *Learning & Individual Differences, 26*, 15–19.

Voorpostel, M., & van der Lippe, T. (2007). Support between siblings and between friends: Two worlds apart? *Journal of Marriage and Family, 69*, 1271–1282.

Vygotskii, L. S., Hanfmann, E., Vakar, G., & Kozulin, A. (2012). *Thought and language.* Cambridge, MA: MIT Press.

Wacker, R., & Roberto, K. (2014). *Community resources for older adults: Programs and services in an era of change* (4th ed.). Thousand Oaks, CA: Sage.

Wadensten, B. (2005). Introducing older people to the theory of gerotranscendence. *Journal of Advanced Nursing, 52*(4), 381–388.

Wadsworth, S. M., & Southwell, K. (2013). Military families: Extreme work and extreme "work-family." *The ANNALS of the American Academy of Political and Social Science, 638*, 163–183.

Wagmiller, R. L., & Adelman, R. M. (2009). *Childhood and intergenerational poverty: The long-term consequences of growing up poor.* New York: Columbia University National Center on Children in Poverty.

Wagner, M., Newman, L., Cameto, R., & Levine, P. (2005). *Changes over time in the early postschool outcomes of youth with disabilities.* Menlo Park, CA: SRI International.

Wahl, H., & Kruse, A. (2005). Historical perspectives of middle age within the life span. In S. Willis & M. Martin (Eds.), *Middle adulthood: A lifespan perspective* (pp. 3–34). Thousand Oaks, CA: Sage.

Walker, D., & Worrell, R. (2008). Promoting healthy pregnancies through perinatal groups: A comparison of Centering Pregnancy group prenatal care and childbirth education classes. *Journal of Perinatal Education, 17*(1), 27–34.

Walker, J., & Melvin, J. (2010). Emotional disorders in children and adolescents. In J. H. Stone & M. Blouin (Eds.), *International Encyclopedia of Rehabilitation.* Retrieved from http://cirrie.buffalo.edu/encyclopedia/en/article/7.

Walker, L. (1989). A longitudinal study of moral reasoning. *Child Development, 5*, 33–78.

Waller, T. (2009). Modern childhood: Contemporary theories and children's lives. In T. Waller (Ed.), *An introduction to early childhood* (2nd ed., pp. 2–15). Thousand Oaks, CA: Sage.

Wallerstein, I. (1974). *The modern world system: Capitalist agriculture and the origins of the European world economy in the 16th century.* New York: Academic Press.

Wallerstein, I. (1979). *The capitalist world economy.* London: Cambridge University Press.

Wallerstein, J., & Blakeslee, S. (1989). *Second chances: Men, women and children a decade after divorce.* New York: Ticknor & Fields.

Wallerstein, J., & Corgin, S. (1991). The child and the vicissitudes of divorce. In M. Lewis (Ed.), *Child and adolescent psychiatry: A comprehensive textbook* (pp. 1108–1118). Baltimore: Williams & Wilkins.

Wallien, M. S., & Cohen-Kettenis, P. T. (2008). Psychosocial outcome of gender dysphoric children. *Journal of the American Academy of Child and Adolescent Psychiatry, 47*(12), 1413–1423.

Walling, A. D., & Dickson, G. M. (2012). Hearing loss in older adults. *American Family Physician, 85*(12), 1150.

Walsh, F. (2011). Families in later life: Challenges, opportunities, and resilience. In M. McGoldrick, B. Carter, & N. Garcia-Preto (Eds.), *The expanded family life cycle: Individual, family, and social perspectives* (4th ed., pp. 261–277). Boston: Allyn & Bacon.

Walsh, K. (2012). *Grief and loss: Theories and skills for the helping professions* (2nd ed.). New York: Pearson.

Wang, L., Wang, S., & Huang, C. (2008). Preterm infants of educated mothers have better outcome. *Acta Paediatrica, 97*, 568–573.

Wang, R., Needham, L., & Barr, D. (2005). Effects of environmental agents on attainment of puberty: Considerations when assessing exposure to environmental chemicals in the National Children's Study. *Environmental Health Perspectives, 113*(8), 1100–1107.

Wang, Y., & Zhang, Q. (2006). Are American children and adolescents of low socioeconomic status at increased risk of obesity? Changes in the association between overweight and family income between 1971 and 2002. *American Journal of Clinical Nutrition, 84*(4), 707–716.

Warner, D., & Brown, T. (2011). Understanding how race/ethnicity and gender define age-trajectories of disability: An intersectionality approach. *Social Science & Medicine, 72*, 1236–1248.

Wasserman, G. A., & McReynolds, L. S. (2011). Contributors to traumatic exposure and posttraumatic stress disorder in juvenile justice youths. *Journal of Traumatic Stress, 24*(4), 422–429. doi:10.1002/jts.20664

Watkins, D. R. (2001). Spirituality in social work practice with older persons. In D. O. Moberg (Ed.), *Aging and spirituality: Spiritual dimensions of aging theory, research, practice, and policy* (pp. 133–146). New York: Haworth Pastoral.

Watson, J., & Crick, F. (1953). Molecular structure of nucleic acids. *Nature, 171*, 737–738.

Watson, M., Mann, M., Lloyd-Puryear, M., Rinaldo, P., & Howell, R. (2006). Newborn screening: Toward a uniform screening panel and system. *Genetics in Medicine, 8*(Suppl. 5), 1s–11s.

Weaver-Hightower, M. B. (2008). *The politics of policy in boys' education: Getting boys "right."* New York: Palgrave Macmillan.

Webb, N., & Dumpson, J. (2006). *Working with traumatized youth in child welfare.* New York: Guilford.

WebMD. (2010). *In vitro fertilization for infertility.* Retrieved from http://www.webmd.com/infertility-and-reproduction/in-vitro-fertilization-for-infertility.

Weibel-Orlando, J. (2001). Grandparenting styles: Native American perspectives. In A. Walker, M. Manoogian-O'Dell, L. McGraw, & D. White (Eds.), *Families in later life: Connections and transitions* (pp. 139–145). Thousand Oaks, CA: Pine Forge Press.

Weichold, K. (2007). Prevention against substance misuse: Life skills and positive youth development. In R. Silbereisen & R. Lerner (Eds.), *Approaches to positive youth development* (pp. 293–310). Thousand Oaks, CA: Sage.

Weigert, S. C. (2012). Aligning and inventing practices to achieve inclusive assessment policies: A decade of work toward optimal access for US students with disabilities 2001–2011. *International Journal of Disability, Development & Education, 59*(1), 21–36. doi:10.1080/1034912X.2012.654935

Weinberg, M., Williams, C., & Pryor, D. (2001). Bisexuals at midlife. *Journal of Contemporary Ethnography, 30*(2), 180–208.

Weingartner, N. (2008). Ohio woman, 56, gives birth to her own granddaughters. Retrieved from http://digitaljournal.com/article/261656.

Weininger, E., & Lareau, A. (2009). Paradoxical pathways: An ethnographic extension of Kohn's findings on class and childrearing. *Journal of Marriage and Family, 71*, 680–695.

Weinman, M. L., Buzi, R. S., & Smith, P. B. (2005). Addressing risk behaviors, service needs, and mental health issues in programs for young fathers. *Families in Society, 86*(2), 261–266.

Weisman, C. S., Hillemeier, M. M., Chase, G. A., Dyere, A. M., Baker, S. A., Feinberg, M., et al. (2006). Preconceptual health: Risks of adverse pregnancy outcomes by reproductive life stages in central Pennsylvania. *Women's Health Issues, 16*(4), 216–224.

Weisner, T. (2005). Attachment as cultural and ecological problem with pluralistic solutions. *Human Development, 48*, 89–94.

Weiss, D., & Lang, F. (2012). The two faces of age identity. *GeroPsych, 25*(1), 5–14.

Wendell, A. (2013). Overview and epidemiology of substance abuse in pregnancy. *Clinical Obstetrics and Gynecology, 56*(1), 91–96.

Werner, E., & Brendtro, L. (2012). Risk, resilience, and recovery. *Reclaiming Children and Youth, 21*(1), 18–23.

Werner, E. E., & Smith, R. S. (2001). *Journeys from childhood to midlife.* Ithaca, NY: Cornell University Press.

Wethington, E., Kessler, R., & Pixley, J. (2004). Turning points in adulthood. In O. Brim, C. Ryff, & R. Kessler (Eds.), *How healthy are we? A national study of well-being at midlife* (pp. 586–613). Chicago: University of Chicago Press.

Whitbourne, S. (2001). The physical aging process in midlife: Interactions with psychological and sociocultural factors. In M. Lachman (Ed.), *Handbook of midlife development* (pp. 109–155). New York: Wiley.

Whitbourne, S., Sneed, J., & Sayer, A. (2009). Psychosocial development from college through midlife: A 34-year sequential study. *Developmental Psychology, 45*(5), 1328–1340.

White, N. R. (2003). Changing conceptions: Young people's views of partnering and parenting. *Journal of Sociology, 39*(2), 149–164.

Whiting, E., & Ward, C. (2008). Food insecurity and provisioning. In D. R. Crane & T. Heaton (Eds.), *Handbook of families & poverty* (pp. 198–219). Thousand Oaks, CA: Sage.

Wigert, H., Johannson, R., Berg, M., & Hellstrom, A. L. (2006). Mothers' experiences of having their children in a neonatal intensive care unit. *Scandinavian Journal of Caring Sciences, 20*(10), 35–41.

Wight, V. (2011). Adolescents and poverty. *The Prevention Researcher, 18*(4), 3–6.

Wight, V., Chau, M., & Aratani, Y. (2011). *Who are America's poor children? The official story.* National Center for Children in Poverty. Retrieved from http://www.nccp.org/publications/pub_1001.html.

Wilber, K. (2000). *Integral psychology: Consciousness, spirit, psychology, therapy.* Boston: Shambhala.

Wilber, K. (2001). *A theory of everything: An integral vision for business, politics, science, and spirituality.* Boston: Shambhala.

Wilemon, T. (2013, March 5). Insurance plans give infertility treatments short shifts. *USA Today.* Retrieved from: http://www.usatoday.com/story/news/nation/2013/03/05/health-insurance-fertility/1964341.

Willis, S., & Martin, M. (Eds.). (2005). *Middle adulthood: A lifespan perspective.* Thousand Oaks, CA: Sage.

Willis, S., & Schaie, K. W. (2005). Cognitive trajectories in midlife and cognitive functioning in old age. In S. Willis & M. Martin (Eds.), *Middle adulthood: A lifespan perspective* (pp. 243–275). Thousand Oaks, CA: Sage.

Willis, S., & Schaie, K. W. (2006). Cognitive functioning in the baby boomers: Longitudinal and cohort effects. In S. Whitbourne & S. Willis (Eds.), *The baby boomers grow up: Contemporary perspectives on midlife* (pp. 205–234). Mahwah, NJ: Lawrence Erlbaum.

Willis, S., Schaie, K., & Martin, M. (2009). Cognitive plasticity. In V. Bengtson, D. Gans, N. Putney, & M. Silverstein (Eds.), *Handbook of theories of aging* (2nd ed.). New York: Springer.

Willoughby, B., Olson, C., Carroll, J., Nelson, L., & Miller, R. (2012). Sooner or later? The marital horizons of parents and their emerging adult children. *Journal of Social and Personal Relationships, 29*(7), 967–981.

Wilmoth, J. M., & Longino, C. F. (2006). Demographic trends that will shape U.S. policy in the twenty-first century. *Research on Aging, 28*(3), 269–288.

Wink, P., & Dillon, M. (2002). Spiritual development across the adult life course: Findings from a longitudinal study. *Journal of Adult Development, 9*(1), 79–94.

Winokuer, H. R., & Harris, D. L. (2012). *Principles and practice of grief counseling.* New York: Springer.

Wisner, K., Chambers, C., & Sit, D. (2006). Postpartum depression: A major public health problem. *Journal of American Medical Association, 296*(21), 2616–2618.

Witt, W., Wisk, L., Cheng, E., Hampton, J., & Hagen, E. (2012). Preconception mental health predicts pregnancy complications and adverse birth outcomes: A national population-based study. *Maternal and Child Health Journal, 16*(7), 1525–1541.

Wolak, J., Finkelhor, D., Mitchell, K., & Ybarra, M. (2008). Online "predators" and their victims: Myths, realities and implications for prevention and treatment. *American Psychologist, 63*(2), 111–128.

Women's Legal Defense and Education Fund. (2012). *Reading between the lines: Women's poverty in the United States, 2010.* Retrieved from http://www.legamomentum.org/sites/default/files/reports/reading-between-the-lines.pdf.

Wong, M., Lau, E., Wan, J., Cheung, S., Hui, C. H., & Mok, D. (2013). The interplay between sleep and mood in predicting academic functioning, physical health and psychological health: A longitudinal study. *Journal of Psychosomatic Research, 74,* 271–277.

Woo, C. R. S., & Brown, E. J. (2013). Role of meaning in the prediction of depressive symptoms among trauma-exposed and nontrauma-exposed emerging adults. *Journal of Clinical Psychology, 69*(12), 1269–1283.

Woodbridge, S., Buys, L., & Miller, E. (2011). "My grandchild has a disability": Impact on grandparenting identity, roles and relationships. *Journal of Aging Studies, 25,* 355–363.

Woods, R. (2013). *Children's moral lives: An ethnographic and psychological approach.* Hoboken, NJ: Wiley.

Woody, D. J., & Green, R. (2001). The influence of race/ethnicity and gender on psychological and social well-being. *Journal of Ethnic & Cultural Diversity in Social Work, 9*(3/4), 151–166.

Woolf, S., & Aron, L. (Eds.). (2013). *U.S. health in international perspective: Shorter lives, poorer health.* Washington, DC: Institute of Medicine.

Woolridge, M., & Shapka, J. (2012). Playing with technology: Mother-toddler interaction scores lower during play with electronic toys. *Journal of Applied Developmental Psychology, 33,* 211–218.

Worden, J. W. (2009). *Grief counseling and grief therapy: A handbook for the mental health practitioner* (4th ed.). New York: Springer.

World Bank. (2013a). *Mortality rate, infant (per 1,000 live births).* Retrieved from http://data.worldbank.org/indicator/SP.DYN.IMRT.IN.

World Bank. (2013b). *Monitoring the MDG's. World Bank Global Monitoring Report 2013.* Retrieved from http://econ.worldbank.org/WBSITE/EXTERNAL/EXTDEC/EXTDECPROSPECTS/0,,contentMDK:23391146~pagePK:64165401~piPK:64165026~theSitePK:476883,00.html.

World Health Organization. (2012a). *Hormonal contraception and HIV*. Retrieved from http://www.who.int/reproductivehealth/topics/family_planning/hc_hiv/en/-34k.

World Health Organization. (2012b). *Emergency contraception*. Retrieved from http://www.who.int/mediacentre/factsheets/fs244/en.

World Health Organization. (2012c). *Mother to child transfer of HIV data and statistics: Graphs and tables*. Retrieved from http://www.who.int/hiv/topics/mtct/data/en/index3.html.

World Health Organization. (2012d). *The 10 leading causes of death by income group (2011)*. Retrieved from http://www.who.int/mediacentre/factsheets/fs310/index1.html.

World Health Organization. (2012e). *Summary: DALYs (thousands) by cause and by World Bank income group*. Retrieved from www.who.int/healthinfo/global_burden/disease/estimates_regional/en/index. html.

World Health Organization. (2012f). *Are you ready? What you need to know about ageing*. Retrieved from www.who.int/world-health-day/2012/toolkit/bacground/en.

World Health Organization. (2013a). *Family planning*. Retrieved from http://www.who.int/mediacentre/factsheets/fs351/en/index.htm.

World Health Organization. (2013b). *Stillbirths*. Retrieved from http://www.who.int/maternal_child_adolescent/epidemiology/stillbirth/en.

World Health Organization. (2013c). *Preterm birth*. Retrieved from http://www.who.int/mediacentre/factsheets/fs363/en.

World Health Organization. (2013d). *WHO welcomes news that a child born with HIV now appears "functionally cured" through early antiretroviral treatment*. Retrieved from http://www.who.int/hiv/mediacentre/hiv_child_20130305/en/index.html.

World Health Organization. (2013e). *Antiretroviral therapy*. Retrieved from www.who.int/hiv/topics/treatment/en.

World Health Organization Multicentre Growth Reference Study Group. (2006a). Assessment of differences in linear growth among populations in the WHO Multicentre Growth Reference Study. *Acta Paediatrica (Suppl.), 450,* 56–65.

World Health Organization Multicentre Growth Reference Study Group. (2006b). WHO motor development study: Windows of achievement for six gross motor developmental milestones. *Acta Paediatrica (Suppl.), 450,* 86–95.

World Health Organization Multicentre Growth Reference Study Group. (2006c). Assessment of sex differences and heterogeneity in motor milestone attainment among populations in the WHO Multicentre Growth Reference Study. *Acta Paediatrica (Suppl.), 450,* 66–75.

Wortman, C., & Silver, R. (1989). The myths of coping with loss. *Journal of Consulting and Clinical Psychology, 57,* 349–357.

Wortman, C., & Silver, R. (1990). Successful mastery of bereavement and widowhood: A life course perspective. In P. Baltes & M. Baltes (Eds.), *Successful aging: Perspectives from the behavioral sciences* (pp. 225–264). Cambridge, UK: Cambridge University Press.

Wright, C., Cox, K., & Couteur, A. (2011). Symposium II. Infant and childhood nutrition and disease: How does infant behavior relate to weight gain and adiposity? *Proceedings of the Nutrition Society, 70,* 485–493.

Wright, P. M. (2011). Barriers to a comprehensive understanding of pregnancy loss. *Journal of Loss and Trauma, 16*(1), 1–12.

Wrigley, E. (1966). Family limitation in pre-industrial England. *Economic History Review, 19,* 82–109.

Wrosch, C., Heckhausen, J., & Lachman, M. (2006). Goal management across adulthood and old age: The adaptive value of primary and secondary control. In D. K. Mroczek & T. Little (Eds.), *Handbook of personality development* (pp. 399–421). Mahwah, NJ: Lawrence Erlbaum.

Wrzus, C., Hänel, M., Wagner, J., & Neyer, F. (2013). Social network changes and life events across the life span: A meta-analysis. *Psychological Bulletin, 139*(1), 53–80.

Wu, L., Woody, G., Yang, C., Pan, J., & Blazer, D. (2011). Racial/ethnic variations in substance-related disorders among adolescents in the United States. *Archives of General Psychiatry, 68*(11), 1176–1185.

Wuttke, W., Jarry, H., Haunschild, J., Stecher, G., Schuh, M., & Seidlova-Wuttke, D. (2014). The non-estrogenic alternative for the treatment of climacteric complaints: Black cohosh (*Cimicifuga* or *Actae racemosa*). *Journal of Steroid Biochemistry and Molecular Biology, 139,* 302–310.

Wyckoff, A. (2013). AAP: Babies born at home must receive same standard of care as in medical facility. *American Academy of Pediatrics News, 34*(5), 29.

Xiong, F., & Zhang, L. (2013). Role of hypothalamic pituitary-adrenal axis in developmental programming of health and disease. *Frontiers in Neuroendocrinology, 34*(1), 27–46.

Young, K. R., Merchant, M., & Wilder, L. K. (2004). School-based interventions for students with emotional and behavioral disorders. In P. Allen-Meares & M. Fraser (Eds.), *Intervention with children and adolescents: An interdisciplinary perspective* (pp. 175–204). Boston: Allyn & Bacon.

Yousuf, R., Fauzi, A., Wai, K., Amran, M., Akter, S., & Ramli, M. (2010). Potentially reversible causes of dementia. *International Journal of Collaborative Research on Internal Medicine & Public Health, 2*(8), 258–265.

Yow, W., & Markman, E. M. (2011). Young bilingual children's heightened sensitivity to referential cues. *Journal of Cognition & Development, 12*(1), 12–31. doi:10.1080/15248372.2011.539524

Zand, D., Thomson, N., Cervantes, R., Espiritu, R., Klagholz, D., Lablanc, L., et al. (2009). The mentor-youth alliance:

The role of mentoring relationships in promoting youth competence. *Journal of Adolescence, 32,* 1–17.

Zangaglia, R., Pacchetti, C., Pasotti, C., Mancini, F., Servello, D., Sinforiani, E., et al. (2009). Deep brain stimulation and cognitive functions in Parkinson's disease: A three year controlled study. *Movement Disorder, 11,* 1621–1628.

Zaslow, M. J., & Emig, C. A. (1997). When low-income mothers go to work: Implications for children. *Future of Children, 7*(1), 110–115.

Zeidner, M., Matthews, G., & Roberts, R. D. (2012). *What we know about emotional intelligence: How it affects learning, work, relationships, and our mental health.* Cambridge, MA: MIT Press.

Zeilmaker, M. J., Hoekstra, J., von Eijkeren, J. C. H., de Jong, N., Hart, A., Kennedy, M., et al. (2013). Fish consumption during child bearing age: A quantitative risk-benefit analysis on neurodevelopment. *Food and Chemical Toxology, 54,* 30–34.

Zeisel, J. (2006). *Inquiry by design: Environment/behavior/ neuroscience in architecture, interiors, landscape, and planning* (Rev. ed.). New York: W. W. Norton.

Zelazo, P. D., Chandler, M. J., & Crone, E. (2010). *Developmental social cognitive neuroscience.* New York: Psychology Press.

Zerfu, T. A., & Ayele, H. T. (2013). Micronutrients and pregnancy: Effects of supplementation on pregnancy and pregnancy outcomes: A systematic review. *Nutrition Journal, 12*(1), 1–5.

Zero to Three. (2013). *Baby matters: A gateway to state policies and initiatives.* Retrieved from http://policy.db/ zerotothree.org/policyp/home.aspx.

Zhang, J., Zhao, J., Jiang, W., Shan, X., Yang, X., & Gao, J. (2012). Conditional gene manipulation: Creating a new biological era. *Journal of Zhejiang Univesity Science B, 13*(7), 511–524.

Zhang, Y., Jin, X., Shen, X., Zhang, J., & Hoff, E. (2008). Correlates of early language development in Chinese children. *International Journal of Behavioral Development, 32*(2), 145–151.

Zigler, E., Finn-Stevenson, M., & Hall, N. (2002). *The first three years and beyond: Brain development and social policy.* Chicago: R. R. Donnelly & Sons.

Zimprich, D., & Mascherek, A. (2010). Five views of a secret: Does cognition change during middle adulthood? *European Journal of Ageing, 7,* 135–146.

Ziv, M., & Frye, D. (2003). The relation between desire and false belief in children's theory of mind: No satisfaction? *Developmental Psychology, 39,* 859–876.

Zou, J., Dear, B., Titov, N., Lorian, C., Johnston, L., Spence, J., et al. (2012). Brief internet-delivered cognitive behavioral therapy for anxiety in older adults: A feasibility trial. *Journal of Anxiety Disorder, 26,* 650–655.

Zucker, A., Ostrove, J., & Stewart, A. (2002). College-educated women's personality development in adulthood: Perceptions and age differences. *Psychology and Aging, 17*(2), 236–244.

GLOSSARY

Acquaintance rape Forced, manipulated, or coerced sexual contact by someone you know.

Activities of daily living (ADLs) Basic self-care activities, such as bathing, dressing, walking a short distance, shifting from a bed to a chair, using the toilet, and eating.

Activity theory (of aging) A theory of aging that proposes that higher levels of activity and involvement are directly related to higher levels of satisfaction in older adults.

Advance directives Documents that give instructions about desired health care if, in the future, an individual cannot speak for herself or himself.

Age norm The behaviors expected of people of a specific age in a given society at a particular point in time.

Age stratification perspective Theory of social gerontology proposed by Riley (1971) and Foner (1995). Similar to the way society is structured by socioeconomic class, it is also stratified by age. Roles and rights of individuals are assigned based on their membership in an age group or cohort. Individuals proceed through their life course as part of that cohort. Theory falls into the tradition of the life course perspective.

Age structuring The standardizing of the ages at which social role transitions occur, by developing policies and laws that regulate the timing of these transitions.

Alzheimer's disease The most common type of dementia, a progressive and incurable deterioration of key areas of the brain.

Anorexia nervosa An eating disorder characterized by a dysfunctional body image and voluntary starvation in the pursuit of weight loss.

Assisted reproductive technologies (ART) A range of techniques to help women who are infertile to conceive and give birth.

Attachment An enduring emotional bond between two people who are important to each other. Provides affection and a sense of security.

Authoritarian parenting A parenting style, identified by Baumrind, that involves unresponsive, inflexible, harsh, and controlling interactions with the child.

Authoritative parenting A parenting style, identified by Baumrind, that involves responsive and supportive interactions with the child while also setting firm limits. Thought to be the most effective parenting style.

Bereavement The state of having suffered a loss.

Binge eating disorder Characterized by recurring episodes of eating significantly excessive amounts of food in a short period of time, accompanied by feelings of lack of control.

Biological age A person's level of biological development and physical health, as measured by the functioning of the various organ systems.

Blooming A period of overproduction of brain synapses during infancy, followed by a period of synapse pruning.

Brain plasticity The ability of the brain to change in response to stimuli.

Bulimia nervosa An eating disorder characterized by a cycle of binge eating; feelings of guilt, depression, or self-disgust; and purging.

Capital A term used in different ways by different disciplines, but generally refers to having the potential, capacity, and resources to function, produce, or succeed; in the social sciences, refers to possession of attributes associated with civic engagement and economic success.

Centenarian A person who is 100 years old or older.

Cerebral cortex The outer layer of gray matter in the human brain thought to be responsible for complex, high-level intellectual functions such as memory, language, and reasoning.

Character education The direct teaching and curriculum inclusions of mainstream values thought to be universal by a community (e.g., kindness, respect, tolerance, and honesty).

Child maltreatment Physical, emotional, and sexual abuse and neglect of children, most often by adult caregivers. Definitions vary by culture and professional discipline but typically entail harm, or threatened harm, to the child.

Chromosomes Threadlike structures composed of DNA and proteins that carry genes and that are found within each body cell nucleus.

Cognition Ability to process and store information and solve problems. Commonly called thinking.

Cohort Group of persons who are born in the same time period and who are of the same age group at the time of specific historical events and social changes.

Cohort effects The effects of social change on a specific cohort.

Community assets Community resources such as public infrastructure (e.g., adequate transportation to get to work), community networks, and educational opportunities.

Concrete operations stage The third stage in Piaget's theory of cognitive development. School-age children (ages 7 to 11) begin to use logical reasoning, but their thinking is not yet abstract.

Conjunctive faith The fifth faith stage in James Fowler's theory of faith development, a stage when individuals look for balance among competing moral systems, recognize that there are many truths, and open themselves in service to others.

Continuity theory (of aging) Theory of social gerontology initially proposed by Neugarten, Havighurst, and Tobin (1968) in response to critiques of the disengagement and activity theories. Individuals adapt to changes by using the same coping styles they have used throughout the life course, with new roles serving as substitutes for roles lost because of age.

Coping mechanism Strategy used to master the demands of life.

Crystallized intelligence The ability to use knowledge from accumulated learning.

Cumulative advantage The accumulation of increasing advantage as early advantage positions an individual for later advantage.

Cumulative disadvantage The accumulation of increasing disadvantage as early disadvantage positions an individual for later disadvantage.

Damage or error theories of aging Theories of biological aging that emphasize the role of environmental assaults that cause cumulative damage to various biological systems.

Default individualization One possible pathway in young adulthood, which involves making transitions defined by circumstance and situation.

Delirium Syndrome characterized by an impairment of consciousness. It has a sudden onset (a few hours or days), follows a brief and fluctuating course that includes impairment of consciousness, and has the potential for improvement when causes are treated. Prevalence of delirium is high among hospitalized elderly persons; toxicity from prescribed medications is a common cause.

Dementia Impairment or loss of cognitive functioning caused by damage in the brain tissue. Dementia is not part of the brain's normal aging process, but its prevalence increases with age.

Dependency ratio A demographic indicator expressing the degree of demand placed on society by the dependent young and the dependent elderly combined.

Developmental biocultural co-constructivism A theory of human development that postulates dynamic reciprocal interactions between the human environment and the biology of the person.

Developmental delay Delay in developing skills and abilities in infants and preschoolers.

Developmental disability Name given when a child has a lifelong impairment that results in functional limitations in some dimension or dimensions.

Developmental individualization One possible pathway in young adulthood, which involves making transitions defined by personal agency and deliberately charted growth opportunities in intellectual, occupational, and psychosocial domains.

Developmental niche The cultural context into which a particular child is born, which guides every aspect of the developmental process.

Direct bullying Intentionally inflicting emotional or physical harm on another person through fairly explicit physical or verbal harassment, assault, or injury.

Discipline Action taken by a child's caretaker to help the child correct behavioral problems.

Disengaged parenting Aloof, withdrawn, and unresponsive parenting.

Disengagement theory (of aging) Theory of social gerontology that suggests that as elderly individuals grow older, they gradually decrease their social interactions and ties and become increasingly self-preoccupied.

Dominant genes Genes that express themselves if present on one or both chromosomes in a pair.

Ego integrity versus ego despair The psychosocial crisis of Erik Erikson's eighth stage of development, which centers on one's ability to process what has happened in life and accept these experiences as integral to the meaning of life.

Egocentrism The assumption by children in the preoperational stage of cognitive development that others perceive, think, and feel just the way they do. Inability to recognize the possibility of other perspectives.

Embryo The stage of prenatal development beginning in the 2nd week and lasting through the 8th week.

Emerging adulthood A developmental phase distinct from both adolescence and young adulthood, occurring from ages 18 to 25 in industrialized societies.

Emotional intelligence The ability to motivate oneself to persist in the face of frustration, to control impulses, to delay gratification, to regulate one's moods, and to empathize with others; theory proposed by Daniel Goleman.

Empathy Ability to understand another person's emotional condition.

Event history The sequence of significant events, experiences, and transitions in a person's life from birth to death.

Extremely low birth weight (ELBW) A newborn weight of less than 1,000 grams (2.2 pounds).

Extroversion Orientation to the external world, in contrast to introversion, which is orientation to the internal world.

Family pluralism Recognition of many viable types of family structures.

Feminist theories (of aging) Theory of social gerontology suggesting that, because gender is a central organizing principle in our society, we can only understand aging by taking gender into account.

Fertilization The penetration of an ovum by a spermatozoon, usually occurring in the fallopian tube.

Fertilization age The number of completed weeks of pregnancy counting from 14 days after the beginning of the last menstrual period to the birth of the neonate.

Fetal viability The capability to survive outside the womb, typically requiring at least 25 weeks.

Fetus The developing organism from the 9th week of pregnancy to birth.

Fictive kin Friends who are neither biologically nor romantically related to the family but who are adopted as family and given the same rights and responsibilities as family members.

Fine motor skills Skills based on small muscle movements, particularly in the hands, as well as eye-hand coordination.

Fluid intelligence Abstract reasoning skills.

Formal operations stage The fourth and final stage in Piaget's theory of cognitive development, generally experienced in adolescence. Involves the capacity to apply hypothetical reasoning and to use symbols to solve problems.

Gender dysphoria Feeling one's emotional and psychological identity as male or female to be opposite of one's assigned biological identity.

Gender identity Understanding of oneself as a male or female.

Generalized other A construction that represents how others might view and respond to our behavior.

Generativity The ability to transcend personal interests to provide care and concern for generations to come.

Genes Basic units of heredity, made of DNA and found on chromosomes.

Genetic liability The state of being prone to hereditary disorders.

Genotype The totality of the hereditary information present in an organism.

Germ cell The ova and spermatozoa whose function is to reproduce the organism.

Gestation The length of maturation time from conception to birth. In humans it averages 280 days, with a range of 259 to 287 days.

Gestational age The number of completed weeks of pregnancy counting from the first day of the last normal menstrual cycle to the birth of the neonate.

Global network The social network made up of all social relationships a person has.

Gonads Sex glands—ovaries in females and testes in males.

Grief The normal internal reaction of an individual experiencing a loss, a complex process that is highly individualized.

Grief work A necessary period of working to sever the attachment bond to a lost person or object.

Gross motor skills Skills based on large muscle group movements and most easily observed during whole-body movements, such as hopping, skipping, and running.

Guardianship A stage of psychosocial development proposed by George Vaillant to come between Erik Erikson's stages of generativity and integrity, a stage when older adults take on the task of passing on the traditions of the past to the next generation and extend their concerns to concern for the culture as a whole.

Hospice Program that provides care to the terminally ill. Patients typically receive treatment by a team of doctors, nurses, social workers, and care staff through inpatient or outpatient care.

Hostile aggression Aggression that is an attack meant to hurt another individual.

Human agency The use of personal power to achieve one's goals.

Human capital Individual assets such as talents, skills, intellectual capacity, social development, and emotional regulatory capacity.

Incidental memory Memory that relates to facts a person has learned without the intention to retain and recall.

Indirect bullying Less explicit and less detectable than direct bullying, including more subtle verbal, psychological, and social or "relational" bullying tactics.

Individual education plan (IEP) An individualized, collaboratively developed plan that focuses on facilitating achievement and is designed to respond to the unique needs of a child with a disability in the school setting. Such plans are mandated by the Individuals with Disabilities Education Act of 1990.

Individuation The development of a self and identity that are unique and separate.

Individuative-reflective faith The fourth stage of James Fowler's six-stage model of faith development, a stage when adults no longer rely on outside authority and look for authority within the self.

Infant A young child in the first year of life.

Infant mortality The death of a child before his or her first birthday.

Infertility The inability to create a viable embryo.

Instrumental activities of daily living (IADLs) Activities that are not necessary for fundamental functioning but that do allow an individual to live alone, activities such as doing light housework, doing the laundry, using transportation, handling finances, using the telephone, and taking medications.

Instrumental aggression Aggression that occurs while fighting over toys and space.

Intentional memory Memory that relates to events that a person plans to remember.

Interactive genes Corresponding genes that give separate yet controlling messages.

Interrelational intelligence Based on emotional and social intelligence and similar to Howard Gardner's concept of interpersonal intelligence.

Intersectionality theory A pluralist theory of social identity that recognizes that all of us are simultaneously members of a number of socially constructed identity groups.

Intimacy Characteristic of close interpersonal relationships, includes interdependence, self-disclosure, and affection.

Intimacy versus isolation Erik Erikson's description of the developmental task of young adulthood, a time when individuals move from the identity fragmentation, confusion, and exploration of adolescence into more intimate engagement with significant others or become isolated.

Introversion Orientation to the internal world, in contrast to extroversion, which is orientation to the external world.

Juvenile delinquency Acts that, if committed by an adult, would be considered crimes, plus status offenses such as running away from home, skipping school, violating curfew, and possession of tobacco or alcohol.

Kinkeepers Family members who work at keeping family members across the generations in touch with one another and make sure that both emotional and practical needs of family members are met.

Late preterm birth Birth that occurs at 34 to 36 weeks' gestation.

Lateralization Process in which the two hemispheres of the brain begin to operate slightly differently during early childhood.

Learning play Play that is focused on language and thinking skills.

Life course perspective An approach to human behavior that looks at how biological, psychological, and social factors act independently, cumulatively, and interactively to shape people's lives from conception to death and across generations.

Life event Incident or event that is brief in scope but is influential on human behavior.

Life review A process of evaluating and making sense of one's life. It includes a reinterpretation of past experiences and unresolved conflicts. The process of life review relates to the eighth stage of Erikson's theory of adult development (ego integrity versus ego despair).

Life span theory A theory that begins with the premise that development is lifelong and is based in ongoing transactions between persons and environments; based in psychology, whereas the life course perspective has more multidisciplinary roots.

Life structure In Levinson's seasons of adulthood theory, the patterns and central components of a person's life at a particular point in time.

Living will A document that describes the medical procedures, drugs, and types of treatment that an individual would choose for himself or herself if able to do so in certain situations. It also describes the situations for which this individual would want treatment withheld.

Loss The severing of an attachment an individual has with a loved one, a love object, or an aspect of one's self or identity.

Low birth weight (LBW) A newborn weight of less than 2,500 grams (5 pounds, 8 ounces).

Masturbation Self-stimulation of the genitals for sexual pleasure.

Menarche The onset of menstruation.

Menopause Permanent cessation of menstruation, usually defined as 12 consecutive months with absence of menstruation.

Miscarriage Naturally occurring loss of a fetus prior to 20 weeks' gestation; also known as spontaneous abortion.

Morbidity The incidence of disease and illness in a population group.

Mortality rate The incidence of death in a population group.

Motor skills Control over movements of body parts.

Mourning The external expression of grief, also a process, influenced by the customs of one's culture.

Multifactorial inheritance Genetic traits that are controlled by multiple genes.

Multigravida A pregnant woman who has previously experienced pregnancy.

Multipara A mother who has previously given birth.

Multiple intelligences Howard Gardner's theory that humans have at least eight critical intelligences: verbal/linguistic, logical/mathematical, visual/spatial, musical/rhythmic, bodily kinesthetic, naturalist, interpersonal, and intrapersonal.

Neonate Infant up to 1 month of age.

Neurons Specialized nerve cells that store and transmit information.

Novice phase According to Daniel Levinson, the ages of 17 to 22, in which the transition into young adulthood occurs, including the tasks of leaving adolescence and making preliminary decisions about relationships, career, and belief systems.

Object permanence The ability to understand that objects exist even when they cannot be seen.

Oppression The intentional or unintentional act or process of placing restrictions on an individual, group, or institution; may include observable actions but more typically refers to complex, covert, interconnected processes and practices (such as discriminating, devaluing, and exploiting a group of individuals) reflected in and perpetuating exclusion and inequalities over time.

Palliative care Active care of patients who have received a diagnosis of a serious, life-threatening illness; a form of care focusing on pain and symptom management as opposed to curing disease.

Perimenopause A period of time that begins immediately prior to menopause in women, when there are biological and clinical indicators that a woman's reproductive capacity is reaching exhaustion, and continues through the first year after the last period.

Permissive parenting A parenting style, identified by Baumrind, that involves no limit setting on the part of the parent.

Personal network A subnetwork of the global network that includes the closest social relationships.

Perspective taking The ability to see a situation from another person's point of view.

Phenotype The expression of genetic traits in an individual.

Physical aggression Aggression against another person using physical force.

Population pyramid A chart that depicts the proportion of the population in each age group.

Postconventional moral reasoning Third and final level of Lawrence Kohlberg's stage theory of moral development; morality based on moral principles that transcend societal rules.

Power of attorney (POA) A person appointed by an individual to manage his or her financial and legal affairs. A POA can be limited (in time or scope), general (no restrictions), or durable (begins after reaching a specified level of disability).

Precociousness Early development; most often refers to a rare level of intelligence at an early age but may refer to "premature" ability or development in a number of areas.

Preconventional level of moral reasoning First level of moral reasoning in Lawrence Kohlberg's stage theory of moral reasoning; morality based on what gets rewarded or punished or what benefits either the child or someone the child cares about.

Preoperational stage The second stage in Piaget's theory of cognitive development. Young children (ages 2 to 7) use symbols to represent their earlier sensorimotor experiences. Thinking is not yet logical.

Primary aging Changes that are a normal part of the aging process.

Primary sex characteristics Physical characteristics that are directly related to maturation of the reproductive organs and external genitalia.

Primipara A woman who is giving birth for the first time.

Privilege Unearned advantage that comes from one's position in the social structure.

Productive aging theory A theory that focuses on the positive changes that have occurred in the older adult population over time, including improved health and economic status; focuses on the positive side of aging rather than on the losses of aging.

Programmed aging theories Theories of biological aging that start from the assumption that aging follows a biological timetable.

Prosocial Behaving in a helpful or empathic manner.

Protective factors Personal and societal factors (resources) that decrease the probability of developing and maintaining problem conditions at later points in life.

Pruning Reduction of brain synapses to improve the efficiency of brain functioning; follows a period of blooming of synapses.

Psychological age The capacities that people have and the skills they use to adapt to changing biological and environmental demands, including skills in memory, learning, intelligence, motivation, and emotions; also the age people feel.

Psychological identity Self-definition as a separate and distinct person.

Puberty Stage during which individuals become capable of reproduction.

Recessive genes Genes that express themselves only if present on both chromosomes in a pair.

Reflex An involuntary response to a simple stimulus.

Relational aggression Aggression that involves behaviors that damage relationships without physical force, such as threatening to leave a relationship unless a friend complies with demands or using social exclusion or the silent treatment to get one's way.

Relative poverty A conceptualization of poverty that emphasizes the tendency to define one's poverty status in relation to others within one's social environment.

Reminiscence Recalling and recounting past events. Reminiscing serves several functions: It may be an enjoyable activity, it may be directed at enhancing a person's self-image, it may serve as a way to cope with current or future problems, and it may assist in the life review as a way to achieve ego integrity.

Resilience Healthy development in the face of risk factors. Thought to be the result of protective factors that shield the individual from the consequences of potential hazards.

Risk factors Personal or social factors at one stage of development that increase the probability of developing and maintaining problem conditions at later stages.

Rites of passage Ceremonies that demarcate transition from one role or status to another.

Romantic love An intimate relationship that is sexually oriented.

Secondary aging Changes caused by health-compromising behaviors such as smoking or environmental factors such as pollution.

Secondary sex characteristics Physical characteristics associated with sexual maturation that are not directly related to the reproductive organs and external genitalia.

Self-esteem The way one evaluates the self in relation to others.

Self-theory An organized understanding of the self in relation to others; begins to develop in early childhood.

Sensitive period A time in fetal development that is particularly sensitive to exposure to teratogens. Different organs have different sensitive periods. Also called critical period.

Sensorimotor stage The first stage in Piaget's theory of cognitive development. Infants (newborn to 2 years) learn through sensory awareness and motor activities.

Sensory system The system of senses: hearing, sight, taste, smell, touch; responsiveness to the body's position and sensitivity to pain.

Separation anxiety When an infant becomes anxious at the signs of an impending separation from parents, at about 9 months of age.

Sex chromosomes Chromosome pair number 23, which determines the sex of the individual.

Sex hormones Hormones that affect the development of the gonads, functioning of the gonads, and mating and child-caring behavior; includes androgens, progestins, and estrogens.

Sex-linked trait A trait that is controlled by a gene located on one of the sex chromosomes.

Sex ratio The number of males per 100 females in a population.

Sexual orientation Erotic, romantic, and affectionate attraction to people of the same sex, the opposite sex, or both sexes.

Sexually transmitted infections (STIs) Infectious diseases that are most often contracted through oral, anal, or vaginal sexual contact. Also called sexually transmitted diseases.

Small for gestational age (SGA) Lower than normal birth weight, given the number of weeks of gestation.

Social age Age measured in terms of age-graded roles and behaviors expected by society—the socially constructed meanings of various ages.

Social competence The ability to engage in sustained, positive, and mutually satisfactory peer interactions.

Social construction theory (of aging) A theory that attempts to understand and explain the influence of social definitions, social interactions, and social structures on the aging process.

Social convoy theory A theory that suggests that we each travel through life with a *convoy*, or a network of social relationships that protect, defend, aid, and socialize us, with the closest relationships remaining stable over time and peripheral relationships being less stable.

Social exchange theory (of aging) A theory that attempts to understand the realignments of roles and values in late adulthood in light of the shifting resources that older adults bring to social exchanges.

Social gerontology The social science that studies human aging.

Social identity The part of the self-concept that comes from knowledge of one's membership in a social group and the emotional significance of that membership.

Social support Help rendered by others that benefits an individual.

Sociodramatic play Fantasy play in a group, with the group coordinating fantasies; important type of play in early childhood.

Socioemotional selectivity theory A theory that proposes that social goals change over the adult life course based on shifts in perspectives about how much time one has left to live, and changes in social goals result in changes in one's social network.

Spermarche Onset of the ability to ejaculate mobile sperm.

Spiritual age The position of a person in the ongoing search for meaning and fulfilling relationships.

Spirituality That which gives meaning, purpose, and direction to one's life.

Spontaneous abortion Naturally occurring loss of a fetus prior to 20 weeks' gestation; also known as miscarriage.

Status offenses Behaviors that would not be considered criminal if committed by an adult but are considered delinquent if committed by an adolescent—for example, running away from home, skipping school, violating curfew, and possessing tobacco or alcohol.

Statutory rape A criminal offense that involves an adult engaging in sexual activities with a minor or a mentally incapacitated person.

Stranger anxiety When an infant reacts with fear and withdrawal to unfamiliar persons, at about 9 months of age.

Symbolic functioning The ability to think using symbols to represent what is not present.

Symbolic play Fantasy play, begins around the age of 2.

Synapses Neural connections.

Synaptogenesis The creation of synapses (neural connections).

Synthetic-conventional faith The third stage of James Fowler's six-stage model of faith development; faith that is rooted in external authority.

Temperament A person's disposition and primary behavioral characteristics in infants and young children.

Teratogens Substances present during prenatal life that adversely affect normal cellular development in form or function in the embryo or fetus.

Toddler A young child from about 12 to 36 months of age.

Trait approach A theoretical approach that proposes that personality traits are enduring characteristics rooted in early temperament and influenced by genetic and organic factors.

Trajectories Long-term patterns of stability and change based on unique person-environment configurations over time.

Transductive reasoning Reasoning from one particular event to another particular event rather than in a logical causal manner.

Transitional object Comfort object, such as a favorite blanket or stuffed animal, that toddlers often use to help them cope with separations from parents.

Transitions Changes in roles and statuses that represent a distinct departure from prior roles and statuses.

Trauma A physical or mental injury generally associated with violence, shock, or an unanticipated situation.

Turning point A special event that produces a lasting shift in the life course trajectory.

Universalizing faith The final stage of James Fowler's theory of faith development; a stage in which individuals lead selfless lives based on principles of absolute love and justice.

Very low birth weight (VLBW) A newborn weight of less than 1,500 grams (3 pounds, 3 ounces).

Working model Model for relationships developed in the earliest attachment relationship.

Zone of proximal development According to Vygotsky, the theoretical space between the child's current developmental level (or performance) and the child's potential level (or performance) if given access to appropriate models and developmental experiences in the social environment.

Zygote A fertilized ovum cell.

INDEX

AAMI (age-associated memory impairment), 383

AAP (American Academy of Pediatrics), 52, 105, 121, 123, 126, 159

Abortion, 62–64, 72–73

Abstinence (sexual), 59

The Accordion Family (Newman), 290

ACE (adverse childhood experience), 127

ACL (Americans' Changing Lives) study, 371

ACOG (American College of Obstetricians and Gynecologists), 52

Acquaintance rape, 261

Activities of daily living (ADLs), 422–423, 422 (exhibit), 428

Activity theory, 372–373

AD (Alzheimer's disease), 383–386, 384 (exhibit), 385 (exhibit), 423

Add Health (Longitudinal Study of Adolescent Health), 225

ADHD (attention deficit hyperactivity disorder), 121, 208–210, 209 (exhibit)

ADLs (activities of daily living), 422–423, 422 (exhibit), 428

Adolescence

    biological changes, 227 (exhibit), 228–232

    case studies, 222–225

    challenges, 257–264

    historical and cultural differences, 224–225

    parental conflict, 347

    psychological aspects, 227 (exhibit), 232–241

    puberty, 183–185, 228–229, 233

    sexuality, 251–256, 256 (exhibit)

    social aspects, 227 (exhibit), 241–249

    spirituality/religiosity, 250–251

    stages, 225–228, 227 (exhibit)

    web resources, 267

Adolescence (Hall), 225

Adoption, 69

Adult day care, 406

Adult homes, 406

Advance directives, 432–434

Adverse childhood experience (ACE), 127

Affluence, 32, 144–145

Affordable Care Act, 47, 59, 68, 79, 282, 372, 405

African Americans

    caregiving, 400

    childhood self-esteem, 155

    HIV infection, 256 (exhibit)

    mourning and funeral customs, 441

    parenting styles, 167, 240

    young adult well-being, 305

    See Racial and ethnic variations

Age-associated memory impairment (AAMI), 383

Age norm, 22

Age-segregated groups, 23–24

Age stratification theory, 375

Age structuring, 23–24

Aggression, 150

Aging theories of biological changes, 375–378

Aging Well (Vaillant), 370–371, 417

Ainsworth, M., 117–119

Alegria, M., 284

Allen, P. D., 292

Alzheimer's disease (AD), 383–386, 384 (exhibit), 385 (exhibit), 423

American Academy of Pediatrics (AAP), 52, 105, 121, 123, 126, 159

American College of Obstetricians and Gynecologists (ACOG), 52

Americans' Changing Lives (ACL) study, 371

Amniocentesis, 83

Amyloidal plaques, 385–386

Andropause, 326

Anorexia nervosa, 263, 264 (exhibit)

Anti-aging medicine, 380

Anxiety, 117, 391

Apgar scores, 75

Appalachian emerging adults research, 280

Arnett, Jeffrey Jensen, 277–279

Aroian, Karen, 330

ART (assisted reproductive technology), 65, 67–69

Arthritis, 379

Artificial insemination, 65–66

Asian Americans

    conjoint agency, 28–29

    See Racial and ethnic variations

Assessment, 159, 441

Assimilation, 189

Assisted reproductive technology (ART), 65, 67–69

Astone, N. M., 281

At-risk newborns, 77–80

Attachment, 116–120, 150–151, 159

Attention deficit hyperactivity disorder (ADHD), 121, 208–210, 209 (exhibit)

Character education, 193
Chen, C.-N., 284
Chess, Stella, 114–115
Childbirth
  assisters in, 53–54
  at-risk newborns, 77–80
  case studies, 44–45
  delaying, 76–77
  educational preparation for, 49–51
  genetic anomalies, 80–84, 82 (exhibit), 83 (exhibit)
  labor and delivery, 74–75
  meaning of, 47–48
  newborn intensive care, 79–80
  places for, 51–53
  postpartum depression, 126–127
  practices, 49–54
  premature births, 44–45, 77–79, 94–95, 107, 281
  risk and protective factors, 88–89, 88 (exhibit),
    89 (exhibit)
  special populations of parents, 84–88
  timing of, 342–343
  See also Conception; Families; Infancy and toddlerhood;
    Pregnancy; Reproductive genetics
Childbirth Without Fear (Dick-Read), 50
Child care arrangements, 118, 123–125, 202–203
Childhood. See Early childhood; Infancy and toddlerhood;
    Middle childhood
Child maltreatment
  about, 129–130
  demographics, 207 (exhibit)
  effects, 172, 173 (exhibit), 207–208
  factors contributing to, 206–207
  victims, 206, 207 (exhibit)
Child protective services (CPS) agencies, 206
Children of Immigrants Longitudinal Study (CILS), 303
Children's Defense Fund report, 300
Child Trends study, 291–292, 302
Chinese culture, 369–370, 397
Chinese immigrant study, 284
Chinese oldest old, 22
Chodorow, Nancy, 196
Chromosomes, 55, 82
Chronic illness, 33, 327–328, 328 (exhibit), 329 (exhibit), 378
Chugani, H., 119–120
CI (cumulative inequality) theory, 33
CILS (Children of Immigrants Longitudinal Study), 303
Cisgender, 239
Clark, Kenneth, 155
Clark, Mamie, 155
Clinton, J., 198
Cochrane reviews, 54
Code of Ethics, 7
Cognitive development
  early childhood, 142–143

infancy and toddlerhood, 107–111, 107 (exhibit)
middle childhood, 185–189, 186 photo, 187 (exhibit)
Piaget's stages, 107–110
play and, 157
poverty and, 128–129
prelanguage skills, 110–111
young adulthood, 286–287
See also Brain development
Cognitive developmental approach to moral development,
    146–148, 147 (exhibit)
Cohabitation, 345
Cohen, Patricia, 323, 324
Cohort effects, 20, 419–420
Cohorts
  about, 10–13
  baby boomers, 11, 333, 340, 347–348, 355–356
  historical events and, 31
  millennials, 300
  very late adulthood, 418–420
  young adults, 20–21, 23
Coitus interruptus, 59
Cold cognition, 230, 234
Coleman, B., 198
Coles, Robert, 187–188, 198
Collective agency, 28–29
Collectivist cultures, 28–29, 152, 188
College transition, 245
Colver, A., 231
Communities
  acting as protective factor, 306
  adolescence, 245–249
  assets of, 301
  epidemiology of, 33
  resources provided by, 405, 406–407, 407
  socially toxic environments, 193–194
  very late adulthood, 427
  violence in, 260–261
  young adulthood, 286
Community service, 246
Conception
  case studies, 42–44
  contraception, 58–62
  fertility trends, 279
  fertilization, 70
  infertility treatment/issues, 65–69, 66 (exhibit),
    67 (exhibit), 76–77, 285–286
  reactions to conception, 48–49
  risk and protective factors, 88–89, 88 (exhibit),
    89 (exhibit)
  sterilization, 61–62, 87
  See also Embryonic period; Pregnancy
Concrete operations stage, 108, 185
Condoms, 59–60
Conflict, 37 (exhibit), 158–159, 242

Dick-Read, Grantly, 50
Diet. *See* Nutrition
Dietary Guidelines for Americans, 231
Dillon, M., 339–340
Dimensions of Human Behavior: Person and Environment, 36, 37 (exhibit), 47
Direct bullying, 193
Disabilities, individuals with
  centenarians, 421
  education for, 280–281, 291, 302
  labels, 208
  parents of, 299
  pregnancy and, 86–87
Disability adjusted life year (DALY), 330
Disability insurance, 406
Disaster relief workers, 6–7
Discipline, 116, 165–168, 166 (exhibit)
Disease. *See* Health and illness
Disengaged parenting, 166
Disengagement theory of aging, 372
Disjoint agency, 28–29
Dissonance in cultural diversity, 194–195
Distributive justice, 148
Diversity
  challenges related to, 36
  families, 48
  life course trajectories, 29–31
  marital status at midlife, 345
  middle childhood, 200–201
  recognizing, 31
  See also Cultural context; Racial and ethnic variations
Divorce, 168–169, 213–214, 394
DNA (deoxyribonucleic acid), 55
Doka, K. J., 440
Dokis, D., 240
DOMA (Defense of Marriage Act), 297
Domestic violence, 170–172, 206–208
Dominant genes, 57
Donor eggs, 68–69
Dopamine, 386–387
Dora the Explorer cartoon, 143
Doubt, 113
Doughty, E. A., 440
Doulas, 54
Down syndrome, 46–47, 57, 77, 82
Driskell, J., 394
Drug Abuse Warning Network (DAWN), 283

Early childhood
  about, 138–139
  case studies, 136–138
  cognitive and language development, 142–145
  disruptions in development, 159–160
  education, 160–162

mental and physical challenges, 208–213, 209 (exhibit), 211 (exhibit), 212 (exhibit)
moral development, 145–148, 147 (exhibit)
multigenerational families, 162–163
personality and emotional development, 148–151
physical development, 139–142, 140 photo, 141 (exhibit)
play, 156–159, 156 photo, 157 photo, 158 (exhibit)
protective factors, 172–174
risks, 164–172
social development, 151–156
web resources, 175
Early puberty, 233–234
Early school leavers, 246
Eating behavior
  adolescent eating disorders, 263, 264 (exhibit)
  infants/toddlers, 100–101
  pregnancy and eating disorders, 86
  See also Nutrition
Ecological developmental risk and protection approach, 33
ECP (emergency contraception pills), 62
Ectopic pregnancy, 71–72
Edin, Kathryn, 298
Education
  childbirth preparation, 49–51
  disabilities and, 280–281, 291, 302
  disadvantaged youth and, 291
  early childhood, 160–162
  economic opportunities and, 262–263, 301–303, 371
  middle childhood, 199–202, 200 photo
  midlife reentry, 354
  mothers of very LBW infants needing, 131
  See also Schools
Educational Policy and Accreditation Standards, 7
Education for All Handicapped Children Act, 213
Edward M. Kennedy Serve America Act, 300
Efficacy expectation, 28
Egg donors, 68–69
Ego integrity versus despair, 112, 387, 430
Egocentrism, 143
Elder, Glen, Jr., 10, 19, 20, 24, 26, 28, 31, 36
Embryonic period, 70–72, 70 photo, 71 (exhibit)
Emergency contraception pills (ECP), 62
Emerging adulthood theory, 277–279
Emery, R., 169
Emotional intelligence, 190
Emotions
  contagious nature of, 147
  distress and infertility, 65
  managing with literature, 149–150
  middle childhood behavioral disorders, 210–213, 212 (exhibit)
  self-regulation, 101
  See also Social and emotional development; *specific emotions*

Heterogeneity and individual differences, 36
HG (hyperemesis gravidarum), 72
HGP (Human Genome Project), 55
Hicken, M., 285
Higher education, 26
High school graduation rates, 262–263
High/Scope Perry Preschool Program, 161–162
Hirose, A., 284
Hispanic population. *See* Racial and ethnic variations
Historical time, 20–21
   See also Cohorts
Hitlin, Steven, 28
HIV/AIDS, 87–88, 256, 256 (exhibit), 288
Hoff, Erika, 144–145
Hoge, C. W., 307
Holder, M. D., 198
Holmes, Thomas, 15, 16–17 (exhibit)
Home and school divide, 201
Home births, 51–53
Home health care services, 406
Home-leaving and returning decisions, 26–27,
   279–280
Homelessness, 165
Homicide, 261
Hong, J., 348
Hooyman, N. R., 441
Hormone replacement therapy (HRT), 326, 381
Hospice programs, 406, 434–435, 434 (exhibit)
Hospital childbirth, 51–53
Hospital Insurance Trust Fund, 405
Hostile aggression, 150
Hot cognition, 230
House, J. S., 371
Household resource sharing, 394–395
Housing market influences, 26
Housing options, 428
Howe, M., 121
HRT (hormone replacement therapy), 326
Hser, Y., 14
Hughes, Fergus, 120, 156
Human agency, 28–29, 335–336
Human capital, 301
Human Genome Project (HGP), 55, 381
Humanistic perspective, 37 (exhibit)
Hyde, Janet, 153
Hyde Amendment, 63
Hyperemesis gravidarum (HG), 72

IADLs (instrumental activities of daily living), 422–423,
   422 (exhibit), 428
ICSI (intracytoplasmic sperm injection), 68
ICTs (information and communication technologies),
   248–249, 249 photo
IDEA (Individuals with Disabilities Act), 122–123, 210

Identity
   cultural, racial, ethnic, 155, 189, 240
   developing in young adulthood, 288–290
   gender, 152–153, 196–197, 239
   psychological, 235
   Rosenberg's model of, 236–239, 237 (exhibit),
      238 (exhibit)
   terminology in diversity, 29–30
Identity versus role diffusion, 112, 235 (exhibit)
IEP (individual education plan), 213
Illness. *See* Health and illness
Immigration experiences, 293, 303, 330
Immunological theories, 376
Incarceration, 87, 302
Indirect bullying, 193
Individual education plan (IEP), 213, 291
Individualistic cultures, 28–29, 152
Individuals with Disabilities Act (IDEA), 122–123, 210
Individuation, 241
Individuative-reflective faith, 288, 338
Industry as drive, 192
Industry versus inferiority, 112, 187 (exhibit)
Infancy and toddlerhood
   breastfeeding versus bottle feeding, 126
   case studies, 94–96
   child care arrangements, 123–125
   cognitive development, 107–111, 107 (exhibit)
   components of, 96 photo, 97–99, 98 (exhibit)
   definitions, 97
   development niche, 96 photo, 97–99, 98 (exhibit)
   disruptions in development, 122–123
   emotional control, 114 photo
   Erikson's theory of psychosocial development, 112 (exhibit)
   milestones in, 111 (exhibit)
   mortality and, 77
   multigenerational families and, 125–126
   physical development, 100–107, 104 (exhibit), 105 photo
   protective factors, 130–132
   risk factors, 127–130
   role of play, 120–122, 121 (exhibit)
   socioemotional development, 111 (exhibit), 112–120,
      112 (exhibit), 113 (exhibit), 114 photo
   web resources, 133–134
Infertility treatment, 65–69
Information and communication technologies (ICTs),
   248–249, 249 photo
Initiative versus guilt, 112, 149
Injectable contraception, 60, 62
Innes, A., 423
Insecure disorganized/disoriented attachments, 117–118
Institutional care, 402–403, 427
Instrumental activities of daily living (IADLs), 422–423,
   422 (exhibit), 428
Instrumental aggression, 150

Instrumental evacuation, 64
Integrity, 387
Integumentary system and aging, 380
Intelligence
    crystallized intelligence, 333, 389
    fluid intelligence, 333, 388–389
    interrelational, 188
    late adulthood changes, 387–390
    middle adulthood changes, 332–334
    multiple intelligences, 200
    protective factor of, 174
Interactive genes, 57
Interdependent lives, 24–27
Internet as information source, 253
Interrelational intelligence, 188
Intersectionality theory, 30
Intimacy, 276, 293–294, 426
    See also Friends and friendship; Sexuality
Intimacy versus isolation, 112, 276
Intracytoplasmic sperm injection (ICSI), 68
Intrauterine devices (IUDs), 61
Intrauterine insemination (IUI), 65–66
Intrauterine instillation, 64
Introversion, 321
Intuitive stage, 143
In virto fertilization (IVF), 68, 77
Iron deficiency, 74
Irreversible dementia, 382
IUDs (intrauterine devices), 61
IUI (intrauterine insemination), 65–66
IVF (in virto fertilization), 68, 77

Jacklin, Carol, 153
Japanese young adult transitions, 26–27
Jensen, Lene Arnett, 235
Jin, Kunlin, 375–377
Johnson, S., 230–231
Johnson, Sarah, 120
Joints in middle age, 325
Jones, B., and McAdams, D., 321
Journeys From Childhood to Midlife (Werner and Smith), 355–356
Judice, S., 251
Jung, Carl, 321–322, 335–336, 336 (exhibit)
Juvenile delinquency, 258–259, 302
Juvenile justice system, 225

Karasawa, M., 28–29
Keene, D., 285
Kegan, Robert, 235–236, 235 (exhibit)
Kei-ho Pih, K., 284
Kemp, Candace, 396
Keniston, Kenneth, 276
Kids Count Data Center, 262

Kin, Cecelia, 46–47, 48
Kindergarten readiness, 160
King, Cheryl, 264
Kinkeepers, 344–345
Kitayama, S., 28–29
Kiyak, H. A., 441
Knight, B. G., 293
Knitzer, J., 132
Kohlberg, Lawrence, 146–148, 147 (exhibit), 187–188, 235–236, 235 (exhibit), 286–287
Kosloski, K. D., 400
Kosmitzki, Connie, 98
Kroger, Jane, 225, 233
Krueger, A. K., 232
Krueger, P. M., 232
Kruse, A., 319
Kübler-Ross, E., 431–432, 432 (exhibit)
Kurdek, L., 346

Lacey, H. P., 388
Lachman, M., 332
Lake, Anthony, 203
Lam, V., 240
Lamaze, Fernand, 50
Lamere, T., 253
Lancet Maternal and Child Nutrition series, 100
Langle, A., 388
Language development
    deaf and hard-of-hearing children, 145
    difficulties of foreign-born children, 200–201
    early childhood, 142–143, 143–145
    role of play in, 157
Late adulthood
    biological changes, 379–381
    brain and neurogenerative issues, 381–387, 384 (exhibit), 385 (exhibit)
    caregiving/care receiving, 399–401
    case studies, 360–364, 384 (exhibit)
    cultural influences, 369–371, 371 (exhibit)
    demographics, 365–369, 367 (exhibit), 368 (exhibit), 369 photo
    health and longevity, 378–379
    institutionalization, 402–403
    mental health/disorders, 390–392
    productive aging dimensions, 376 (exhibit)
    psychological changes, 387–392
    psychosocial perspectives, 372–375, 372 (exhibit), 373 photo
    resources for, 404–407
    risk and protective factors, 407–410, 408–409 (exhibit), 410 (exhibit)
    search for personal meaning, 403–404
    theories of biological changes, 375–378
    transitions and life events, 392–399

Punishment, 168
Putney, N. M., 344

Quickening, 73

Racial and ethnic variations
    adolescent pregnancy/childbirth, 254
    bullying, 259
    care of dying, 434, 435
    census information, 368, 368 (exhibit)
    dependency ratios, 366–367
    fathers' role in childbirth, 54
    generativity, 321
    health, 330–331, 378
    juvenile delinquency, 258–259
    living arrangements in late adulthood, 392–393
    maltreatment victims, 206
    marriage, 345, 347
    mental health/disorders, 390–391
    parenting, 167, 349
    poverty, 128–129, 203
    relationships in very late adulthood, 424–425
    school-to-prison pipeline, 259–260, 260 (exhibit)
    social assistance distribution, 305
    spirituality/religiosity, 250–251, 340
    substance abuse, 258–259
    suicide, 264
    See also Cultural context
Racism, 305
Raghavan, R., 307
Rahe, Richard, 15, 16–17 (exhibit)
Rape, 261–262
Rate of living theory, 376
Reactions to conception, 48–49
Recessive genes, 57
Reid, C., 302
Reither, E., 232
Relational aggression, 150
Relationships
    infancy/toddlerhood, 122
    intimacy, 293–294, 294 (exhibit)
    mentoring/volunteering, 299–300
    middle adulthood, 341–342
    parenthood, 297–299
    romantic relationships, 294–297, 295 photo,
        296 (exhibit)
    very late adulthood, 423–426
    See also Families; Friends and friendship; Marriage;
        Multigenerational families
Reminiscence, 403–404
Reproductive genetics
    congenital anomalies, 80–84, 82 (exhibit), 83 (exhibit)
    counseling for, 57–58
    mechanisms in, 54–57, 56 (exhibit)

Reservatol, 380–381
Residential instability/mobility, 278
Resilience, 33, 131–132
Respiratory system and aging, 379
Retirement
    comparison of benefits, 408 (exhibit)
    delays in, 23
    patterns in, 398–399, 399 (exhibit)
    timing of, 353
    trends in, 352–355
Reversible dementia, 382
Rhythm method of contraception, 59
Richmond, Mary, 55, 57
Risk factors throughout life. See specific life stages
Risk taking, 230–231
Rites of passage, 226–227
Rituals, death, 437
Rivas-Drake, D., 240
Roberto, K., 347–348
Robots, 427
Rodriguez, Domenech, 167
Roehlkepartain, E. C., 198
Roe v. Wade, 63
Roggman, L., 159
Role exploration, 238
Romantic relationships, 244, 245 photo
Roof, Wade Clark, 340
Rooting reflex, 102–103, 103 (exhibit)
Roper v. Simmons, 230
Rosenberg, Morris, 236–239, 237 (exhibit),
        238 (exhibit)
Rosenberg's model of identity, 236–239, 237 (exhibit),
        238 (exhibit)
Rosenthal, C., 342
Rothert, K., 281
Rumbaut, Ruben G., 303
Russell, S., 244

Saewyc, Elizabeth, 253–254
Salihu, H. M., 76
Same-sex marriage, 296–297, 346
Sandwich generation, 344
Sapolsky, R., 330
Savin-Williams, R. C., 197
Scales, P. C., 198
Schaie, K. W., 332–333
Schedule of Recent Events, 15, 16–17 (exhibit)
Scherger, Simone, 23–24
Schoen, R., 281
Schooler, C., 378
Schools
    adolescence and, 245–246
    dropping out of, 246
    home support of, 201

ABOUT THE AUTHOR

 **Elizabeth D. Hutchison,** MSW, PhD, received her MSW from the George Warren Brown School of Social Work at Washington University in St. Louis and her PhD from the University at Albany, State University of New York. She was on the faculty in the Social Work Department at Elms College from 1980 to 1987 and served as chair of the department from 1982 to 1987. She was on the faculty in the School of Social Work at Virginia Commonwealth University from 1987 to 2009, where she taught courses in human behavior and the social environment, social work practice, social work and social justice, and child and family policy; she also served as field practicum liaison. She has been a social worker in health, mental health, aging, and child and family welfare settings. She is committed to providing social workers with comprehensive, current, and useful frameworks for thinking about human behavior. Her other research interests focus on child and family welfare. She lives in Rancho Mirage, California, where she is active in environmental justice issues facing farm workers in East Coachella Valley. She finds great joy in time spent with her grandchildren, Auggie, Ruby, and Juliet.

ABOUT THE CONTRIBUTORS

Suzanne M. Baldwin, PhD, LCSW, MSW, BSN, RN, received her PhD in social work from the School of Social Work at Virginia Commonwealth University. She works as a clinical social worker in private practice with families and spent almost 2 decades working as a clinical nurse specialist in newborn intensive care. Her major areas of interest are working with families involved with the court system and military family issues. She has taught human behavior, practice, communications, and research courses and supervised internships at Old Dominion University and at the School of Social Work at Virginia Commonwealth University. She is the mother of three adult children. Her oldest daughter was a patient in the neonatal intensive care unit (NICU), and her daughter's son spent a month in the NICU after his birth in 2009.

Nicole F. Bromfield, MSW, PhD, is assistant professor in the Department of Social Work at United Arab Emirates University. Nicole earned her PhD in public policy from Virginia Commonwealth University with a focus in health policy, and an MSW and BA in anthropology from West Virginia University. Nicole's research interests include issues relating to women's and children's health and empowerment. Her recent publications focus on global surrogacy, the lived experience of divorce for Arabian Gulf women, and child welfare issues such as intercountry adoption and infant and child car restraints, all from a policy perspective.

Leanne Wood Charlesworth, LMSW, PhD, is associate professor in the Department of Social Work at Nazareth College of Rochester. She has practiced within child welfare systems, and her areas of service and research interest include poverty and child and family well-being. She has taught human behavior and research at the undergraduate and graduate levels.

Annemarie Conlon, PhD, MBA, LCSW, is assistant professor in the School of Social Work at Virginia Commonwealth University. Her experience includes individual, family, and group practice in an oncology setting. Her major areas of interest include ageism in health care, end-of-life needs of older adults, and hospice and palliative care. She teaches social work practice and qualitative research and serves as field instructor for students in a health and wellness clinic for low-income older adults.

Marcia P. Harrigan, MSW, PhD, is emeritus associate professor of social work at Virginia Commonwealth University, where she taught human behavior and practice courses. She served as the director of the Master of Social Work Program and the senior associate dean for Student and Academic Affairs. She has practiced in child welfare, juvenile justice, and mental health. Her major areas of interest are nontraditional family structures, family assessment, multigenerational households, and long-distance family caregiving. She is currently involved in the Virginia Great Expectations program, which offers higher education support to young adults aging out of foster care. She is a master gardener and enjoys tennis, snow skiing, reading, bridge, traveling, and, most of all, being a grandparent to Annalee and Charlie.

Kristina Hash, LICSW, PhD, is an associate professor and director of the Gerontology Certificate Program in the School of Social Work at West Virginia University. Her research interests include caregiving, LGBT issues, the use of technology in teaching and research, and geriatric education. Her practice background includes positions in home health care, social work continuing education, and research and program evaluation. Additionally, she has been involved in several volunteer activities with community-based agencies serving older adults. She primarily teaches courses in aging and human behavior in the social environment.

Pamela J. Kovacs, MSW, PhD, is associate professor emerita with the School of Social Work at Virginia Commonwealth University, where for 17 years she taught clinical practice, social work practice and health care, and qualitative research and served as a field liaison. Her earlier clinical practice that influenced her teaching and research included work with individuals, families, and groups in oncology, hospice, and mental health settings. Her major areas of interest were HIV/AIDS, hospice and palliative care, volunteerism, caregiving, and preparing social workers and other health care professionals to work with older adults and their families.

Peter Maramaldi, PhD, MPH, LCSW, is a professor at the Simmons School of Social Work in Boston, where he currently serves as the director of the PhD program. He also serves on the faculty at the Harvard School of Public Health in the Department of Social and Behavioral Sciences, where he teaches social welfare and has developed an opportunity for social work PhD students to earn the MPH degree during their training. Dr. Maramaldi also holds a faculty appointment at the Harvard School of Dental Medicine in Oral Health Policy and Epidemiology, where he mentors postdoctoral trainees and works with interdisciplinary teams on NIH-funded investigations. He is a Hartford Faculty Scholar and National Mentor with expertise in behavioral oncology in older populations. As a social work behavioral scientist, he has had consistent NIH and foundation funding since 2003 for his work across disciplines on research initiatives focused on health promotion. He is currently working on an NIH-funded multi-year study to promote patient safety using

medical informatics. Another current NIDCR-funded study is developing implementation strategies for improved diagnostic coding in electronic health records. Dr. Maramaldi is also working on a foundation-funded national demonstration project using behavioral interventions to reduce childhood caries in high-risk populations of children. Prior to returning to Columbia University to earn his PhD degree and launch an academic career, Dr. Maramaldi was a community organizer and clinical social worker in New York City for more than 25 years.

Holly C. Matto (MSW, University of Michigan; PhD, University of Maryland) is associate professor in the College of Health and Human Services Department of Social Work at George Mason University in Fairfax, Virginia. Prior to that, Dr. Matto was at Virginia Commonwealth University School of Social Work for 10 years, where she taught theories of human behavior, direct practice, and research methods in the master's and doctoral programs. She has more than 15 years of research and practice experience in the field of addiction science and has conducted treatment intervention studies with diverse substance abuse populations. Recently she conducted a clinical trial with Inova Fairfax Hospital and Georgetown University's Center for Functional and Molecular Imaging that used neuroimaging technology to examine functional and structural brain change associated with behavioral health interventions for substance-dependent adults. She is currently engaged in research that examines the effects of an integrated music, imagery, and movement intervention to improve mood and promote cognitive functioning in older adult residents living in a long-term care facility.

Susan Ainsley McCarter, MS, MSW, PhD, is associate professor in the Department of Social Work at the University of North Carolina at Charlotte. She has worked as a juvenile probation officer; mental health counselor for children, adolescents, and families; social policy advocate; and mother. Her major area of interest is risk and protective factors for adolescents—specifically the disproportionate minority contact in the juvenile justice system. She currently teaches research methods and the MSW capstone course and has taught human behavior, social policy, and forensic social work courses at both the undergraduate and graduate levels.

Derek Morch, MSW, is a graduate of the School of Social Work at Virginia Commonwealth University. He has worked in a variety of settings as a clinical mental health clinician for adults with serious mental illness. He has also provided services to children and their families as a home-based counselor and therapeutic mentor. His areas of interest include community-based treatment, mental health and housing issues for those experiencing homelessness, and ongoing practice with multicultural populations.

Matthias J. Naleppa, MSW, PhD, is professor of social work at the University of Applied Sciences in Bern, Switzerland, and a Hartford Geriatric Social Work Scholar. For many years, he held a position in the School of Social Work at the Virginia Commonwealth University. His research focuses on geriatric social work, short-term treatment, and international social work. He regularly conducts workshops on task-centered practice and geriatric social work in the United States, Europe, and Asia. He has an MSW from the Catholic School of Social Work in Munich and a PhD from the University at Albany.

Rosa Schnitzenbaumer is a graduate of the Catholic School of Social Work, Munich, Germany, working as a geriatric social worker and licensed practical nurse for the Caritas Welfare Organization in Miesbach, Germany. She teaches as an adjunct faculty member for the School for Care Management at the University of Applied Sciences Innsbruck, Austria, and is a board member of the Adelheid Stein Institute for Therapeutic Roleplay. Throughout her career, she has been involved in developing and managing programs for older adults, including a regional outpatient gero-psychiatric counseling center, individualized

service systems for older adults, a senior volunteer network, and caregiver training programs. She has also initiated Erzählcafés, volunteer-led groups for persons with dementia.

Meenakshi Venkataraman, PhD, has been assistant professor of social work at West Virginia University and Tuskegee University. She has taught human behavior at the graduate and undergraduate levels. Her research interests include psychological, social, and spiritual aspects of adult severe mental illness.

Cara L. Wallace, LMSW, is a doctoral candidate in the School of Social Work at the University of Texas at Arlington. A recipient of both a Graduate Teaching Assistantship package and the Bob and Anne Utley Fellowship at UTA, Cara teaches both graduate and undergraduate classes. In practice, she worked as a hospice social worker for Community Hospice of Texas. Her research interests are end-of-life care, particularly looking at barriers to care and the impact of family relationships on decision making at the end of life.

David Woody III, PhD, LCSW, is chief program officer for Volunteers of America Texas. After several years in academia at the University of Texas at Arlington and Baylor University, Dr. Woody has returned to work in the local community, focusing on substance abuse treatment for women, community reentry services, and services for those in the community with intellectual and developmental disabilities. In addition to issues related to poverty, Dr. Woody's major areas of interest include research exploring strengths of African American single mothers and initiatives enhancing the significance of fatherhood in the African American community.

Debra J. Woody, PhD, LCSW, is the associate dean for academic affairs in the School of Social Work at the University of Texas at Arlington. She is the director of the Center for Additions and Recovery Studies that provides recovery and parenting services to mothers and their children and school-based substance abuse prevention services to students and their families.

Maria E. Zuniga, MSW, PhD, is professor emeritus from the School of Social Work at San Diego State University, where she taught for 16 years, with an additional 11 years at Sacramento State University. Along with human behavior courses, Dr. Zuniga's areas of focus were direct practice, gerontological practice, and practice with multicultural populations, in particular practice with Latinos. She was also a member of the board of directors of the Council on Social Work Education (CSWE) and helped to develop a CSWE-sponsored conference on cultural competence held at the University of Michigan in 1999. She is a consultant on cultural competence for local, state, and national agencies and publishing houses.

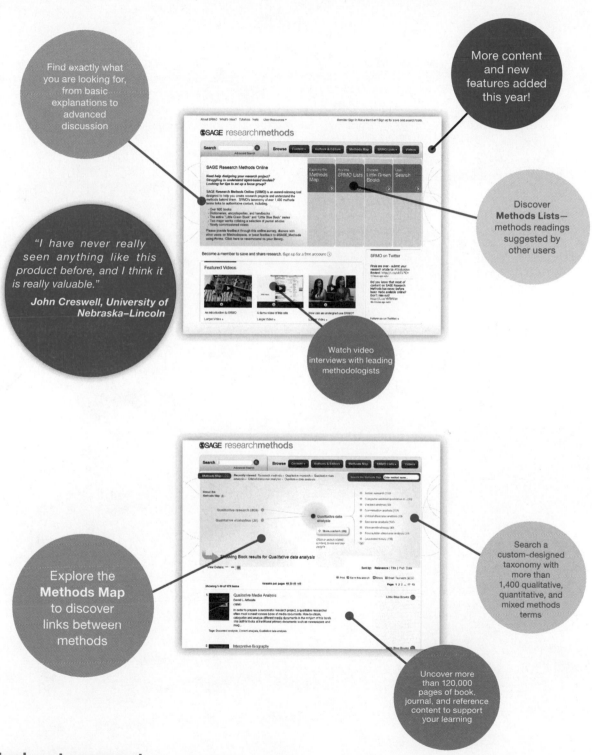

SAGE researchmethods

The essential online tool for researchers from the world's leading methods publisher

More content and new features added this year!

Find exactly what you are looking for, from basic explanations to advanced discussion

Discover **Methods Lists**— methods readings suggested by other users

"*I have never really seen anything like this product before, and I think it is really valuable.*"

John Creswell, University of Nebraska–Lincoln

Watch video interviews with leading methodologists

Search a custom-designed taxonomy with more than 1,400 qualitative, quantitative, and mixed methods terms

Explore the **Methods Map** to discover links between methods

Uncover more than 120,000 pages of book, journal, and reference content to support your learning

Find out more at
www.sageresearchmethods.com